A HISTORY
OF PSYCHOLOGY

IDEAS AND CONTEXT

THIRD EDITION

WAYNE VINEY
Colorado State University

D. BRETT KING
University of Colorado at Boulder

Boston   New York   San Francisco
Mexico City   Montreal   Toronto   London   Madrid   Munich   Paris
Hong Kong   Singapore   Tokyo   Cape Town   Sydney

Executive Editor: Carolyn O. Merrill
Editorial Assistant: Kate Edwards
Marketing Manager: Wendy Gordon
Editorial-Production Service: Omegatype Typography, Inc.
Composition and Prepress Buyer: Linda Cox
Manufacturing Buyer: JoAnne Sweeney
Cover Administrator: Kristina Mose-Libon
Electronic Composition: Omegatype Typography, Inc.

For related titles and support materials, visit our online catalog at www.ablongman.com.

Between the time Website information is gathered and published, some sites may have closed. Also, the transcription of URLs can result in typographical errors. The publishers would appreciate notification where these occur so that they may be corrected in subsequent editions.

Library of Congress Cataloging-in-Publication Data
Viney, Wayne.
    A history of psychology : ideas and context / Wayne Viney, D. Brett King. — 3rd ed.
        p.   cm.
    Includes bibliographical references and indexes.
    ISBN 0-205-33582-9
    1. Psychology—Philosophy—History.   2. Psychology—History.   I. King. D. Brett.   II.
Title.
BF38 .V56   2003
150'.9—dc21   2002276261

Printed in the United States of America
10 9 8 7 6 5 4 3 2 1   07 06 05 04 03 02

Portraits: pp. 50, 56, 68, 72, 96, 109, 150, 371, 378, 396, Lyrl Ahern
Photos: pp. 112, 134, 138, 143,168, 176, 196, 206, 210, 213, 226, 234, 239, 242, 243, 249, 258, 261, 264, 272, 273, 281, 288, 291, 311, 313, 316, 319, 329, 330, 353, 374, 391, 395, 410, Psychology Archives—The University of Akron; p. 355, Clark University Archives.

*To Michael Wertheimer—
a generous friend,
inspiring teacher and scholar,
esteemed colleague*

and

*Noni Viney and Cheri King—
for their
enthusiasm, encouragement, and support*

Contents

PREFACE

A History of Psychology: Ideas and Context, first published by Allyn and Bacon in 1993, was written for students and all who are interested in psychology and its history. The first two editions included numerous distinctive features that are preserved and amplified in this third edition. A number of substantial revisions have been necessary to update the book in accordance with the wealth of historical scholarship that has appeared since the publication of the first two editions. As before, the text strives for comprehensive examples of psychological thought from ancient Eastern and Western cultures, the Roman Empire, the Middle Ages, and the Renaissance. In the modern period, from about 1600, the focus is on intellectual traditions that contributed to the formal founding of psychology as an independent discipline. These traditions include rational and empirical philosophies, advances in physiology, new quantitative techniques, evolutionary theory, naturalistic approaches to emotional problems, and significant humanitarian movements of the nineteenth century. The historical development of psychology from its formal founding is traced in the major systematic treatments of the discipline. An epilogue sketches some late-twentieth-century developments.

The book opens with a brief chapter on historiography that explores selected philosophical issues especially pertinent to disciplinary histories: What are the origins of historical consciousness? Is there a pattern in history? What is history? Can history be objective? We hope that a discussion of such questions will result in a more critical, appreciative, and informed reader who thinks not only about content but also about the complex tasks of the historian.

Chapter 2 focuses on enduring philosophical problems that are encountered repeatedly throughout the history of psychology: Do humans have free will? What are the methods by which we make truth claims? What is science? What is the subject matter of psychology? It is assumed that the history of psychology is much more meaningful to students who have a working knowledge of the classic positions on fundamental philosophical problems. Students with some degree of philosophical sophistication could skip this chapter, but others will find that a careful study of it will help clarify materials encountered in subsequent chapters.

Like many texts, this book presents examples of psychological thought encountered in documents from ancient cultures. Typically, the Greek and Roman periods are covered, but this book adds two important features to the section on ancient thought: First, psychological contributions of important early women such as Theana, Myia, Asera, and Hypatia are included. Second, in addition to reviewing the usual materials from the Greek and Roman periods, this text provides brief overviews of psychological thought as set forth in documents from ancient Chinese, Indian, Babylonian, Persian, Egyptian, and Hebrew cultures. This emphasis on the broad scope of psychological thought is continued in later chapters that include contributions by Arab scholars, Spanish scholars such as Juan Luis Vives and Juan Huarte, and neglected scholars such as Héloise and Oliva Sabuco.

The chapter on the Renaissance includes a consideration of medical, economic, and geographic contexts that contributed to intellectual developments in this remarkable period. The plague, geographical discoveries, new inventions such as the telescope, the breakdown of authority, and the rediscovery of Greek classics had enormous influence on the development of thought. The works of important thinkers such as Galileo, Niccolò Machiavelli, and Michel de Montaigne are highlighted. Montaigne is presented as a pivotal figure because of his powerful influence on subsequent thinkers such as Francis Bacon and René Descartes. The Renaissance period was regressive in some arenas. It was no Renaissance for women! On the contrary, the Inquisition and the witch-hunts amounted to a holocaust for women.

This text devotes extensive space to the intellectual context that contributed to the development of psychology. Most texts show how psychology grew out of developments in empiricism, rationalism, physiology, and evolution. We trace these developments in traditional detail, but we also include an emphasis on the key roles played by the growth of quantitative techniques, particularly those developed by Jacques Quételet and elaborated by Francis Galton. Early applications of statistics by Florence Nightingale and Dorothea Dix are highlighted, as well. We call attention to the fact that psychology, as a formal discipline, was founded in an age of sweeping humanitarian reform movements (e.g., suffrage, abolition of slavery, new prison standards, universal education and education for women, and new treatment conditions for people with mental impairments and emotional disorders). We argue that extensive humanitarian reforms created a context that helped legitimize the new discipline.

The second half of the text outlines the major systems of psychology with an emphasis on the basic and applied contributions of each school. A description of the formal founding of psychology begins with nineteenth-century developments in psychophysics and voluntarism, an early school of psychology founded by the German scientist Wilhelm Wundt. Additional consideration is given to scholars who shaped the new discipline of psychology in Europe and the United States, including Edward Bradford Titchener, Franz Brentano, Carl Stumpf, Oswald Külpe, and Hermann Ebbinghaus.

The seminal work of William James and his American contemporaries figures strongly in the chapter on functionalism. The chapter on behaviorism reviews Russian reflexology, Edward Lee Thorndike's learning theory, and John B. Watson's radical school of behaviorism. The chapter on neobehaviorism describes the work of ten diverse researchers and culminates with an overview of the work of B. F. Skinner. The next chapter focuses on Gestalt psychology, a novel and innovative school that rebelled against conventional approaches to psychology.

The advent of the psychodynamic school is detailed in the evolution of Sigmund Freud's psychoanalytic theory as well as resourceful challenges to his work by Alfred Adler, Carl Jung, and Karen Horney. The intellectual traditions of existential philosophy and phenomenology are traced in the development of the humanistic psychologies of Abraham Maslow, Gordon Allport, Carl Rogers, and Viktor Frankl. Finally, a brief Epilogue outlines major developments in late-twentieth-century psychology.

Disciplinary histories, such as those about art, music, philosophy, or psychology, are commonly *internal* histories that focus on developments within a discipline. Although emphasis on internal developments may be the primary goal in disciplinary histories, these works are nevertheless richer if attention is also directed to *external* history— that is, to contextual political, economic, religious, philosophical, scientific, and social forces that help shape the flow of events within a discipline. In this spirit, we identify several external forces that helped shape psychology. The complex multidimensional characteristics of the task, however, guarantee that it cannot be carried out successfully. Nevertheless, an awareness that the discipline did not develop in a vacuum is itself valuable.

The organization of this book conveys a strong historiographic bias. We believe that nature and history are filled with real discontinuities, disjunctions, and surprises. Events, especially in the intellectual arena, seldom flow with measured, uniform, unvarying regularity. But even if the flow of events had been linear and logical, it would be impossible to present the story in such a fashion. If the historian could function more as a photographer than as an artist, the product would still be based on many arbitrary decisions. In the main, there is an attempt to allow the chronology to dictate the flow of ideas in this text, but at times, it is more reasonable to track an idea forward in time and then to backtrack to follow another idea forward in time. Thus, the interests of coherence sometimes outweigh the dictates of chronology.

Study aids are provided in each chapter to help students focus on the important materials and concepts. A glossary is designed to assist with a review of terms and their definitions as well as of key people and some of their most significant contributions. A phonic pronunciation guide is included for difficult names (e.g., Xenophanes *zeh NAH fuh neez*). Chapter-ending study questions also are provided to assist in the review of materials.

The third edition of *A History of Psychology: Ideas and Context* maintains the basic structure of the first and second editions. We have updated the text with more than two hundred new references, many of which reflect scholarship in the history of psychology since 1998, the date of the second edition. Major substantive additions are included on key figures such as Margaret Floy Washburn, Helen Wooley, Sextus Empiricus, Mary Wollstonecraft, Margaret Sanger, and Franz Anton Mesmer. In preparing this revision, we incorporated new materials on epistemology, rationale for the study of history, perspectives on systems of psychology, as well as expanded coverage on humanitarian reform. An additional feature of the third edition includes new research on the history of curiosity and "forbidden knowledge."

ACKNOWLEDGMENTS

We express sincere appreciation to the literally hundreds of students at the University of Colorado at Boulder and at Colorado State University who read the first two editions of this text. Their enthusiasm, insights, generosity, and suggestions for changes were a major force in shaping the third edition. We are also grateful to Professor Douglas Woody of the University of Northern Colorado who provided numerous substantive suggestions for improvements in the structure and content of this edition.

We express our deepest gratitude to Professor Michael Wertheimer of the University of Colorado at Boulder. We have both engaged in historical studies under his supervision and are in his debt for the generous and detailed support he provided for the first two editions of this text. The third edition continues to reflect his influence.

We also express appreciation to the many scholars who have offered suggestions for this third edition and for previous editions. Specifically, we thank Steve Coleman, Edward Crossman, David Edwards, Laurel Furumoto, Allan M. Hartman, Mary Henle, John Mueller, Robert Presbie, Elizabeth Scarborough, David Schneider, Margaret Thomas, and

William Woodward. We deeply appreciate all the intellectual resources that have been available to us and the helpful and thoughtful suggestions made by our reviewers.

We are grateful for the enthusiasm of Nancy Forsyth, President of Allyn and Bacon, for a third edition of our text. We also thank Carolyn Merrill, Executive Editor of Allyn and Bacon, and her assistant Jonathan Bender for their help on the many administrative details associated with this project. Special thanks to Dona Biederman of Omegatype Typography, Inc., for her excellent editorial work and many thoughtful suggestions. We also express appreciation to Robert Cohen for promoting our book and for his enthusiasm for this edition. We thank David King for his assistance in securing photographs and David Baker, Director of the Archives of the History of Psychology at Akron, Ohio, for his help in providing archival materials. Finally, we express our gratitude to Noni Viney and Alex Sward for their assistance with indexing.

W. V. & D. B. K.

CHAPTER 1

HISTORICAL STUDIES: SOME ISSUES

If we cling to our ignorance of history, error crushed to earth, will rise again, and we will have to go on solving the same old problems again and again.

—Mary Henle (1976)

The story of psychology begins in ancient times. As a self-conscious formal discipline, psychology is little more than a century old, but the subject matter captured the human imagination long before the advent of psychology as a science. We will travel back thousands of years to the epic work of philosophers, theologians, and scientists who wrestled with issues that continue to fascinate modern psychologists. Examining the work of early scholars on such topics as memory, emotions, dreams, perception, brain activity, learning, and mental disorders lends scope and richness to the more recent history of psychology.

Our story will be more compelling if we examine problems associated with the study of history. A number of questions come to mind. What is history? Can the historian offer anything more than opinion? Why study history at all? Developing a sensitivity to such philosophical questions makes for a more stimulating intellectual journey.

WHY STUDY HISTORY?

The study of history can serve numerous purposes. An extensive summary of arguments on why we should study history is available in the literature (e.g., see Wertheimer, 1980a). Let's consider a few arguments supporting the study of history.

History as a Key to Understanding the Future

In his book *The Future of an Illusion,* Sigmund Freud (1927/1961c, p. 5) observed that "the less

[we know] about the past and the present the more insecure must prove [our] judgment of the future." Freud's sentiment is reflected in an earlier statement by Thomas Jefferson (1782/1904, p. 207) who argued that "history, by apprizing [sic] [people] of the past, will enable them to judge of the future; it will avail them of the experience of other times and other nations." There is a pattern in history that, when properly read, may prove consequential to our understanding and possible control of the present and the future. The study of history has utilitarian value. People who appreciate the history of psychology may be in a better position to understand current trends in the discipline and anticipate future directions.

History as a Way to Enrich the Present

We live in a world of spatial, cultural, and temporal dimensions. It is commonly assumed that informed and cosmopolitan perspectives are based on a broad acquaintance with the geophysical world and various social and cultural institutions and organizations. Travel, the study of language and cultures, and the study of geography are ways we overcome our spatial and cultural blindness. Unfortunately, we can be just as narrow and blind with respect to our time frame as we are with our knowledge of the physical world and other cultures. Imagine how contracted, limited, and restricted your life would be if you had no memory for anything but the fading rearward portion of your consciousness. There are, of course, diseases and brain disorders that leave us in such a narrow temporal state. In fact, we can be as "lost" temporally as we are when we cannot find our way in the physical world or when we travel in a culture that is foreign to everything we know.

In a way, history is memory. Just as there is a freedom that goes with a healthy and functional memory, so there is an intellectual freedom that goes with the development of a broad time frame. In a later chapter on humanistic psychology, we will speak of the value of living fully in the present moment, but an extreme emphasis on the present would leave us naive and uninformed in a kind of temporal isolation. We live more fully in the here and now if we have a rich knowledge and memory for the events that have contributed to the present. To neglect the past is to impoverish the present!

History as a Contribution to Liberal Education

The study of history can also contribute to a liberal and informed perspective. Robert I. Watson (1966), a well-known historian of psychology, once remarked that history helps us overcome "narrow provincial, class, and regional prejudices." In his view, psychologists, of all people, should seek to avoid "subjugation to influences of which one is unaware" (p. 64). An advantage of history is that it helps an individual achieve perspective and integration that might not be possible by other means. Knowledge of the history of a discipline accentuates the understanding of influences, developments, and relations and contributes to a more informed and integrated perspective. This achievement alone can be so satisfying that the study of history needs no other justification.

History Teaches Humility

We enjoy an advantage over previous generations because we can build on knowledge and discoveries of the past and avoid unnecessary duplication of earlier mistakes. The perspectives afforded by past knowledge are larger and more informed than perspectives afforded by the present alone. When we study history, we are constantly humbled by the

genius, the effort, and the creative insight of previous thinkers. Helson (1972, p. 116) reminds us that in history "student[s] may meet better minds in the literature than any [they] may have contact with in person." We may also encounter minds that have worked through problems that we assumed to be fresh or original.

History all too often reveals that our discovery is merely a rediscovery of an idea known long ago. The humility that history can teach was experienced by a student who planned a term paper entitled "The New Patriotism." The point of the paper was that twentieth-century patriotism should extend beyond national borders because an interdependent world now makes larger claims on our loyalty—world claims rather than mere national claims. The student was surprised and humbled when his search uncovered an article on "The New Patriotism" published over fifty years before in *Harper's Magazine* (Viscount, 1932). Viscount's paper dealt with the identical theme that was to serve as the theme of the student's term paper.

History Teaches a Healthy Skepticism

Knowledge of history may temper the human tendency to worship methodological or even substantive idols. In every age, masses of people fall prey to grand claims, revolutions that promise more than they deliver, and utopian dreams. Psychology has suffered its share of ideas and methods that were overly promising. Possible candidates include mesmerism, phrenology, craniometry (the assessment of intelligence via the measurement of cranial capacity), and any of a host of modern therapies. History teaches us to be wary of the big claim, the single method to end all methods, and the one and only definition. Helson (1972, p. 116) cautioned against easy acceptance of the belief that our future lies with a solitary panacea— "computer models of brain function, or that there is only one psychophysical law, or that trend analysis is the last answer to statistical treatments." Historical knowledge counsels against the glib acceptance of the latest fad or inflated idea. Jaynes (1973a, p. xi) pointed out that history may help us "to liberate ourselves from the persuasions of fashions." At the very least, we can hope that a knowledge of history will make us less gullible.

History Influences Human Thought Processes

Henle (1976) discussed a seldom appreciated reason for the study of history. She pointed out that most of us find it difficult to see our errors or question our assumptions. She argued that human cognition is usually resistant to criticism and marked by a degree of inertia or self-preservation. Knowledge of history, according to Henle, "gives us distance not only from our immediate objective, but from our own thinking" (p. 16). History heightens awareness of the errors of others, but it also keeps us thinking straight. As Henle warned in the opening epigraph, if we are blind to the lessons of history then we will be doomed to solve the same old problems.

SOME PROBLEMS IN HISTORIOGRAPHY

What makes history? Can history be objective? Is there a discernable pattern or direction in history? Historians are drawn to interesting questions that form the subject matter of historiography. At least three meanings are associated with the term **historiography.** In a narrow and literal sense, the term refers to the writing of history, including research techniques and strategies for investigating specific content areas. The term *historiography* also encompasses philosophical questions about history and historical method (later, we will review some philosophical questions encountered in historical studies). A third meaning of *historiography* refers to the characteristics of a body of historical writings. For example, historical accounts of psychology have sometimes neglected the contributions of women and other cultural minorities. Fortunately, critical awareness of our biases has led to compensatory efforts. Thus, numerous books and articles have addressed previously neglected topics such as the contributions of women (e.g., see Bohan, 1992a, 1992b; Gavin, 1987; O'Connell & Russo, 1983, 1988, 1990; Scarborough & Furumoto, 1987), African Americans (e.g., see Guthrie, 1998; Phillips, 2000; Sawyer, 2000), and Hispanics (e.g., see Martinez & Mendoza, 1984).

On the assumption that history can be more meaningful if certain historiographic questions are addressed at the outset, we will now examine several questions and issues about history and historical method. The position we take on each of these can have a major impact on the way we view the history of psychology, or any other history for that matter.

The Development of Historical Consciousness

Young children seem to live in the spacious present with little thought to the past or future. Gilderhus (1992) suggests that primitive peoples often lacked historical consciousness because they were forced to devote their attention to immediate survival. Even so, survival depends on memory and a temporal awareness of events. This time-based awareness has survival value and contributes to the development of historical consciousness. Both individual and community are served by knowledge of the historical significance of events.

Historical consciousness grows out of strong beliefs in the importance of special events. Regarded as epochal, such events may have profound religious, political, or scientific significance. In Hebrew literature, people are admonished to remember events associated with their delivery from Egyptian bondage. In recent history, phrases such as *never again, lest we forget,* and *united we stand* serve as reminders of the horrors of the Holocaust or the sacrifices of war and terrorism. On certain occasions, historical consciousness is heightened by special political or religious holidays. Christians regard the crucifixion of Jesus as the most central event in history—an event that ushered in a new theological epoch. Indeed, the Christian community measures time itself in terms of this critical event.

Gilderhus (1992) observed that historical consciousness in Greek times grew out of attempts to separate history from mythology. The legendary Greek historian Herodotus (*hi RAH duh tuhs*) (c. 484–c. 425 B.C.) became the first to attempt a comprehensive history of the world. Documenting contemporary episodes as well as past events, he traveled widely, made extensive notes, and gained access to eyewitness testimony whenever possible. Herodotus was one of the first to write history with an emphasis on natural rather than supernatural causes.

The naturalistic approach to history was extended in the work of Thucydides (*thoo SIHD ih deez*) (c. 460–c. 401 B.C.). Remembered for his classic *History of the Peloponnesian War,* Thucydides documented the war between Athens and Sparta from 431 to 404 B.C. Thucydides had a passion for accuracy and for naturalistic explanations stripped of theological overtones. Aware of previous attempts to write history in terms of miracles, mysteries, and divine purposes, Thucydides insisted on discovering positive facts and presenting them in a naturalistic context. Faith in the accuracy of historical writings creates respect for written histories and may foster the growth of historical consciousness. We turn now to one of the most fundamental and challenging issues in historiography—the problem of defining history.

What Is History?

In popular usage, the term **history** sometimes denotes the chronology of events that provide raw material for the historian. The term also refers to stories we tell about our past. Dictionary definitions typically emphasize both meanings (i.e., history as a chronology of previous events and history as a narrative or interpretive study of the past). History has both empirical and explanatory components. The *empirical* component includes data such as unpublished letters; newspaper accounts; audio, video, or digital recordings; and official documents. The *explanatory* component refers to the efforts of historians to make sense of data. Additional perspectives on the nature of history are provided in Table 1.1.

So, how are we to define *history*? Let's begin with the idea that history has an empirical component. That is, real events that took place in the past can enter our present experiences through records. The empirical component can also include eyewitness accounts or personal experiences for more recent events. For instance, where were you on September 11, 2001? If you remember, chances are the episode is vivid in your memory. Events such as the terrorist attack on the World Trade Center resonate, in part, because they provide a way of aligning ourselves with the yardstick of history.

The task of the historian is to become acquainted with as much data as possible. Data collection may include interviews, traveling to archives to examine unpublished letters and documents, reading old newspapers, and the like. After collecting data, the historian must engage in an interpretive study. Such study includes examining contradictions, discriminating between what is relevant and what is not, and assigning weights to different bits of evidence. In a way, the process is a bit like working a complicated jigsaw puzzle when we know in advance that pieces will be missing.

The working definition of *history* suggested here is as follows: History is the interpretive study of the events of the human past. The definition assumes empirical and explanatory components in the work of the historian. The human past is specified because the methods of history per se are not appropriate to analysis of the geological or biological past.

Can History Be Objective?

If we agree that history is the interpretive study of the human past, we nevertheless encounter the problem of the faithfulness or truthfulness of our interpretations. Abraham Lincoln (1856/1950, p. 149) said, "History is not history unless it is the truth." People have a kind of commonsense faith that historical materials—whether they deal with religious, political, scientific, or social topics—are accurate reflections of the landscape of the past. Even the historian embarking on a new project may believe it possible to provide a narrative truer to the chronology of events than did previous works.

The question of objectivity is a critical issue in the philosophy of history. Thousands of pages are devoted to the importance of this problem in historical journals and texts. You might think the case should be closed immediately because, after all, historians do not usually make direct observations. But even if they did, we have no guarantee that they could be objective. Historians must be selective with respect to available data and there may not be well-established criteria for selection. Finally, historians are creatures of the present and, as such, may write history in the light of present personal and cultural perspectives.

TABLE 1.1   *Some Perspectives on the Nature of History*

History as Subjective Study
We read history through our prejudices. —Wendell Phillips
What is history but a fable agreed upon. —Napoleon I (Bonaparte)

History as a Record of the Past
History is not history unless it is the truth. —Abraham Lincoln

History as Cyclical
History repeats itself; that's just one of the things that's wrong with history.
—Clarence Darrow

The Importance of History
Who cannot give an account of three thousand years remains in the darkness of
inexperience. —Goethe
The less we know of the past, the more unreliable our judgment of the present
and future. —Sigmund Freud

The Value of History
If I have seen farther than others, it is because I have stood on the shoulders
of giants. —Issac Newton
History is the witness that testifies to the passing of time; it illumines reality, vitalizes
memory, provides guidance in daily life, and brings us tidings of antiquity. —Cicero

A Presentist View of History
Let the past serve the present. —Mao Tse-tung

A Historicist View of History
We cannot escape history. We . . . will be remembered in spite of ourselves. . . . The
fiery trial through which we pass will light us down, in honor or dishonor, to the last
generation. —Abraham Lincoln

The case against objectivity is not easily closed, however. One reason may be that objectivity is such a desirable ideal. Another reason may be that the complete rejection of objectivity carries the assumption that anyone's opinion is as good as anyone else's. Still another reason may be the hope that historical narratives can rise above the prevailing climate of opinion. Such a quality would make it possible for history to repudiate, disagree with, or tell an unpopular story. Chinese leader Mao Tse-tung (1893–1976) believed that history should serve the Communist revolution (Lifton, 1968, p. 144). Such an extreme position adds fuel to the debate over the merits and possibilities of objectivity, because it is surely reasonable to believe that history is not necessarily bound to serve political, religious, or philosophical ideologies. Is there not some sense in which historians can extricate themselves from a prevailing climate of opinion?

Before proceeding, we should explore possible meanings of **objectivity in history.** The term *objective* could refer to a correspondence between a historical narrative and the events of the past it describes. If objectivity refers to such a correspondence, then the work of the historian would surely be judged as deficient. For one thing, words employed in the historical narrative can never recapture the vibrant fullness of lived experience. Objectivity, as correspondence, is thus suspect. Perhaps historians are more like painters than photographers, but even if they were like photographers, there would always be another angle for a shot, a different way to frame it, a different magnification, or different films with varying sensitivity to color.

Another possible meaning of *objectivity* is represented in the attempt to present all sides of an issue, to portray fairly the perspective with which the writer disagrees. Objectivity, viewed in this way, is an attitude—an attitude we may reasonably expect of a historian. It is an attitude that reminds the historian to be aware of ulterior motives and to hold them in check when recognized. Thus, a northern historian of the American Civil War might agree that a history written by a southerner is an objective history. Objectivity in this instance simply means that northern perspectives are represented.

Before leaving the question of objectivity, let's return to Abraham Lincoln's contention that "history is not history unless it is the truth." Most historians might agree with the quotation if we could add the idea that, for any event, there is more than one possible true history. For example, the Civil War can be regarded not as one war but as many wars. It was a different war for the South than for the North. The two sides could not even agree on the causes of the war. It was also a different war for each of the various states. From this line of reasoning, we could conclude that there can be many true histories of the American Civil War, each of which inevitably disagrees on countless details.

Presentism versus Historicism

The problem of objectivity also manifests itself in the temporal perspective of the historian. Earlier, it was noted that historians are creatures of the present. One of the most important and interesting issues in historiography centers on the nature of the limitations imposed by the ever-shifting present frame of reference. On one extreme, it can be argued that historians, like psychotherapists, must have a well-developed empathic capacity for their subject. If such empathy is possible, then historians may be capable of suspending or neutralizing present biases; that is, they may literally "feel" their way back into the past so that deep and authentic understandings are a real possibility. In such an orientation, the historian attempts to capture the subject of historical inquiry in its own right.

Stocking (1965, p. 212) suggested the term **historicism** for such an orientation and defined it as "the commitment to understanding the past for its own sake." Stocking said that historicism emphasizes the context of a historical figure or event and places emphasis on *understanding* as opposed to *judgment.* Such an orientation seeks to avoid the mistake of using the past as a means of glorifying the present. As noted earlier, an adequate history can tell an unpopular story that is damaging to present interests and perspectives.

An opposite orientation, called **presentism,** emphasizes the funded nature of human experience and the consequent difficulties of separating historical facts from current interests and theories. The presentist raises questions about the extent to which the historian can recapture the objective distribution of things in the past. The presentist argues against the possibility of literalism or the idea that the historian can recapture the past intact. In defense of this position, Buss (1977, p. 254) wrote that "There is no such thing as hard-core, indubitable facts which are invariant across different theoretical explanations." The presentist is deeply tuned to the effects of inevitable selective, judgmental, and contextual forces at work in historical scholarship. The historicist might reply, however, that *because* we can be aware of such forces, we can thereby neutralize their effects.

As with most issues, it is the extremes of historicism and presentism that present difficulties and provoke the most comment. William James (1890/1981), the great American philosopher and psychologist, once referred to absolutism as "the great disease of philosophic thought" (p. 334). Sounding a similar theme, Dewsbury (1990) argued for a moderate and tolerant approach to historiography—an approach that finds room for so-called soft forms of historicism and presentism. Such an approach could be duly sensitive to the role of present beliefs in our understanding of history but also insist that authentic history will shape present beliefs. Dewsbury also raised doubts about the universal superiority of either approach. Perhaps there is room for both orientations with each having its own application depending on such matters as the educational setting and the nature of the problem under investigation.

The issues surrounding historicism and presentism have been the subject of considerable discussion in the historiography of the behavioral sciences (e.g., see Ash & Woodward, 1987, pp. 1–11, 295–309; Dewsbury, 1990; Furumoto, 1989; Harrison, 1987; Henle, 1989; and Young, 1966). The discussions have been fueled partly by differences in the educational backgrounds of those who conduct research in and those who teach the history of the behavioral sciences. Most disciplinary histories (e.g., history of art, music, philosophy, psychology) have been written and taught not by historians but by people educated in their disciplinary areas who happen to have an interest in the history of their disciplines. Such people have been referred to as *house historians* (Woodward, 1987) and typically focus on the historical development of ideas, problems, and issues within their disciplines. They tend to elevate personalities and select and present those features of the past that glorify or justify the present—in short, their approach is presentist. By contrast, there are now historians of science who specialize in the social and behavioral sciences. Such professionally trained individuals have called for greater attention to external and contextual considerations in the writing of history—a deemphasis on presentism.

According to the moderate analysis presented by Dewsbury (1990), there is room for both approaches. Indeed, the field will be strengthened by a diversity of approaches. The historicist approach is more likely to be applicable to specialized and detailed histories written for professionals and advanced students. General introductory histories, in a variety of disciplines, will likely continue to focus on the development of ideas within the discipline and will seek meaningful intellectual links between the past and the present. A deep sensitivity to the issues of presentism and historicism is valuable because such sensitivity provides students with a critical evaluative tool. History is not an easy subject, but if we can operate at a metalevel by thinking not only about history but also about the philosophy of history, then the entire subject becomes more malleable and enjoyable.

Is There a Pattern or Direction in History?

To ask whether history has a pattern or direction is to ask something about the meaning of history. Clearly, there is informational value in patterns,

and the discovery of a pattern can be useful. There have been numerous hypotheses about the direction of history, and each of the major hypotheses is applicable to the history of psychology. We will review the cyclical hypothesis, the linear-progressive hypothesis, and the chaos hypothesis.

Cyclical Hypothesis. According to the **cyclical hypothesis,** history repeats itself. There is ebb and flow and endless repetition. Kingdoms rise and fall, only to rise again; freedom is gained and is lost, only to be gained again. There are cycles of poverty and plenty, war and peace, discovery and intellectual stagnation, innocence and corruption, and revolution and stability. Even our ways of understanding, according to this view, are cyclical. Thus, a rational and scientific era may arise but in time give way to arbitrary political or religious authority, which after a time may be overthrown again by the rational-scientific method.

We can find cycles in any science, and psychology has its share. For example, there has been considerable recent interest in the so-called lateralization of function in the cerebral hemispheres. Do right and left hemispheres mediate different emotional and intellectual processes, or do the hemispheres function in a more integrated fashion? Interest in this question is not new. Over one hundred years ago, C. E. Brown-Sequard (1890) wrote an article entitled "Have We Two Brains or One?" The article is only one of many of that period that struggled with the problem of the lateralization of function. Another example is that, early in the history of psychology, there was strong emphasis on conscious and experiential processes, but with the advent of behaviorism, that orientation was rejected. Now we see the reemergence of a concern with consciousness and experience.

Linear-Progressive Hypothesis. A linear hypothesis can be either progressive or regressive, but let us be optimistic and consider only a linear-progressive view. According to the **linear-progressive hypothesis,** each generation builds on the discoveries of the previous generation; hence, each new generation starts from a stronger base. Accordingly, there is growth and progress in human knowledge and in human institutions. There can, of course, be brief regressions and setbacks, but over-all there is progress and growth. The best-known modern advocate of progress theory was the co-inventor of the calculus, Gottfried Wilhelm Leibniz. Leibniz's theory of history was born in an age of optimism about the potential for scientific discovery. The theory quickly achieved widespread popularity and, according to some historians (e.g., Gawronski, 1975, p. 27), the more enthusiastic adherents of progress theory announced that progress is a law of nature. One of the better-known progress theories is that advanced by Karl Marx.

Those who have studied the living conditions of the past, including the immediate past, may find it easy to be persuaded by progress theory. Bettmann (1974), in a book entitled *The Good Old Days—They Were Terrible,* recounts the hardships of life in the United States from the early 1800s to the end of the Civil War. The filth and pollution in major cities from factories, coal-fired steam engines, vast accumulations of horse manure on city streets, insects, and poor sewers were almost unbearable. Poorly ventilated houses and apartments in an age before air conditioning claimed many lives in summers and winters. Crime in major cities and in the West was often beyond control. "Dominating the record was, of course, the West, where the gun-happy barbarity was damned by observers both foreign and native for producing a 'great dismal swamp of civilization' " (Bettman, 1974, p. 87). Education for women was almost nonexistent, and school conditions for all but the most wealthy men were deplorable. Without refrigeration, food was often spoiled and diets were narrow and inadequate. Epidemics of yellow fever, tuberculosis, smallpox, whooping cough, and measles raged through the country. Child labor laws had not yet been enacted, and unsafe factories took an enormous toll in injuries and death, with almost no possibility of recourse for victims. The problems, of course, were exacerbated for the southern slaves. In sum, few people would really want to return to the "good old days."

By selective sampling, one can argue in favor of the linear-progressive hypothesis. For example, in the field of psychology, there has been a demonstrable growth of knowledge in our understanding of such topics as memory, learning, and sensory

processes. Wetterstein (1975) has argued that histories of psychology are subject to criticism because they fail to present the evolution of the discipline as "a steady development culminating in current theory" (p. 157). The criticism is possibly valid, but there are subdisciplinary areas within psychology, usually those dealing with very complicated topics such as personality or social control issues, that have had turbulent histories not so easily conceived in terms of a linear-progressive hypothesis. This raises the question of whether there is an overall identifiable pattern in the historical development of psychology. Perhaps there are several patterns, some fitting a cyclical hypothesis and some fitting a linear-progressive hypothesis and some also fitting the next hypothesis, the chaos hypothesis.

Chaos Hypothesis.   The coming of the nuclear age dampened earlier optimism about the inevitability of human progress. It became clear that the entire structure of human achievement could be brought to ruin by a chance technological accident or by the design of political systems deficient in world perspective. The Holocaust preceding World War II clearly challenged the hypothesis that progress is inevitable.

According to the **chaos hypothesis,** history itself has no overall identifiable and universal meaning. History is, as noted by Fisher (1936, p. v), simply "the play of the contingent and the unforeseen." The meanings found in history are the meanings we impose, not meanings that inhere in history itself. This idea was captured in a letter from Jean-Paul Sartre to Albert Camus. Sartre (1965) observed, "History, apart from the man who makes it, is only an abstract and static concept, of which it can neither be said that it has an objective, nor that it has not. . . . The problem is not to *know* its objective, but to *give* it one" (p. 103). Chaos theory has perhaps been buttressed by cosmological perspectives such as that expressed in the following passage. Becker (1932) said we must regard human beings as "little more than a chance deposit on the surface of the world, carelessly thrown up between two ice ages by the same forces that rust iron and ripen corn" (p. 14).

The history of psychology can also be seen as a chaotic and incoherent history. In an article entitled "Psychology Cannot Be a Coherent Science," Koch (1969) charged that after one hundred years, psychology has generated a great deal of pseudo-knowledge and unmeaningful thinking. Koch argued that the history of scientific psychology can be seen as "a succession of changing doctrines about what to emulate in the natural sciences—especially physics" (p. 64). But he contended that psychology, to date, has failed to find an adequate methodology for the study of its unique subject matter and is far from demonstrating that it is a cumulative and progressive science.

A major criticism of chaos theory is that it may discourage any attempt we make to take responsibility for our future. If what happens in the future is independent of individual human belief and action, there is little encouragement to work to shape the future.

There are many other theories regarding the direction and meaning of history. We have simply reviewed three of the more dominant theories. A sizable portion of people subscribe to various providential theories, and others embrace particular variations of the theories we have covered. Still others prefer a more pluralistic approach, which suggests that history is no one thing, but rather that there are many histories. Even within a circumscribed field such as psychology, we are not dealing simply with one history. As suggested earlier, it may be possible that parts of history have indeed been chaotic while other parts have been linear and progressive and still others cyclical. A pluralistic approach to history counsels suspicion of any attempt at a sweeping or categorical attempt to characterize all history as fitting any one hypothesis.

What Makes History?

We turn now to another issue that has been a long-standing subject of controversy among historians and one that is especially relevant to students of psychology and its history. The issue centers on whether it is the great person or the "spirit of a time" that makes history. The German terms **Zeitgeist** (spirit of a time) and **Ortgeist** (spirit of a place) are useful in characterizing the position that contrasts with the **great-person theory.**

The great-person theory was illustrated in a section of Ralph Waldo Emerson's optimistic essay entitled *Self Reliance.* History, said Emerson (1841/1981), "resolves itself very easily into the biography of a few stout and earnest persons" (p. 138). Thus, according to Emerson, with Caesar, we have a Roman Empire; with Luther, the Reformation; with Fox, Quakerism; and with Wesley, Methodism. By extension, it is with Wundt that we have the formal discipline of psychology; with Freud, psychoanalysis; with Rorschach, the ink blot test, and so on. Simply, the great-person theory emphasizes the causal role of particular persons in particular circumstances and the ability of the individual to control or to change the direction of events.

Most of us would have to agree that the great-person theory results from a simplistic view of the actual forces at work in the world. Causation in history is extremely complex, so we must be tuned to a multitude of forces that make an idea, event, or institution possible. Even a simple event or invention can hardly be credited to a single individual. As an example, aircraft could never have been developed by any person prior to invention of the internal combustion engine or prior to the development of basic knowledge of aerodynamics. There had to be a relevant background of invention, material, culture, education, and social support. To say that one great person is responsible for anything is to ignore the complexities of life and history. The place (*Ortgeist*) and time (*Zeitgeist*) must be right.

An extreme emphasis, however, on environmental context may result in a historical determinism that overlooks the importance of individual actions in the stream of historical causation. Such a position is illustrated in the work of the English philosopher Herbert Spencer (1873) who believed in the possibility of a "science of history." Likewise, the Canadian naturalist Grant Allen (1878a, 1878b) emphasized the centrality of context by arguing that the great intellectual achievements in ancient Greece were due solely to geography and other external forces and had nothing to do with specific individuals. This philosophy of history is illustrated in Herman Melville's *Moby-Dick* when a crew member advises Captain Ahab to call off the chase for the albino whale. Ahab replies, "This whole act's immutably decreed. Twas rehearsed by thee and me a billion years before this ocean rolled. Fool! I am the fates' lieutenant; I act under orders" (Melville, 1851/1976). Such fatalism may, of course, have its origin in a theological or naturalistic context.

A different approach to the problem of historical causality is encountered in the writings of William James (see James, 1880). James argued for a philosophy in which historical development is viewed broadly in terms of the causal role of the person and the environment. James agreed that environmental circumstances set boundaries, but he also contended that the environment is modified by human effort. Any account of history that neglects the roles played by individuals will be an account that is vague and incoherent (see Viney, 2001). The balance of emphasis in James's approach to this issue is that an individual's idea cannot achieve fruition without social and material support. On the other hand, some ideas might never have become a part of the life of the community had they not been borne in the mind of a unique and creative individual.

We have reviewed here a small sample of issues in historiography. The issues selected are especially relevant to the history of psychology. History studied with these issues in mind is almost certain to be more meaningful. So, we suggest that the history of psychology be studied with such persistent questions in the background: Is there a pattern? What would the discipline be like if it had not been for this or that person and his or her contributions? How has my current perspective changed as a result of my knowledge of history? Awareness of these and other historiographic questions should lend richness to the study of the history of psychology.

THE HISTORY OF THE HISTORY OF PSYCHOLOGY

Interest in the history of psychology is, curiously, as old as the discipline itself. Early writers of textbooks, such as Wilhelm Wundt and William James, were quick to acknowledge earlier contributions by individuals from other disciplines such as physics, physiology, and philosophy. As we noted earlier, people advanced ideas about psychology centuries before it became a formal discipline. So it is understandable that the early psychologists were interested in the history of psychology even as the formal discipline was being established.

In 1913, James Mark Baldwin wrote two small popular volumes entitled *History of Psychology: A Sketch and an Interpretation.* In addition to discussing the works of some of the major psychologists, Baldwin traced psychological thought advanced by some of the early philosophers and physiologists. A classic three-volume work entitled *A History of Psychology,* published between 1912 and 1921, was written by George Sidney Brett. Brett's scholarly work, subsequently abridged and updated by R. S. Peters (1965) and published as *Brett's History of Psychology,* provided an extensive overview of ancient, medieval, and early modern psychological thought. Edwin G. Boring's standard classic text, entitled *A History of Experimental Psychology,* was first published in 1929 and revised in 1950. Following the publication of Boring's first edition, courses in the history of psychology became more commonplace in university curricula. One of the most important early texts was Edna Heidbreder's *Seven Psychologies,* published in 1933. This work still provides an excellent survey of major classic systems of psychology such as behaviorism, structuralism, Gestalt psychology, and psychoanalysis. Another well-known early text, first written by Gardner Murphy in 1949 and currently in its third edition (Murphy & Kovach, 1972), is entitled *Historical Introduction to Modern Psychology.* This text includes more material on the history of applied psychology than is normally included in other texts.

In addition to these major texts, numerous books of readings in the history of psychology have been published (e.g., Benjamin, 1997; Dennis, 1948; Diamond, 1974b; Fancher, 1996; Henle, Jaynes, & Sullivan, 1973; Herrnstein & Boring, 1966; Sahakian, 1968; Sexton & Misiak, 1971; Pickren & Dewsbury, 2002). Some helpful books trace the development of psychology in various countries (e.g., Misiak & Sexton, 1966; Sexton & Misiak, 1976). With the growth of interest in the history of psychology, there is also a growth in the number of guides and sourcebooks that are useful to students writing term papers and to scholars doing research. There are, for example, bibliographies showing how to find biographical information on various psychologists (e.g., Benjamin, 1974; Benjamin & Heider, 1976; Zusne, 1984) and numerous guides and sourcebooks showing how to find other kinds of information on the history of psychology. For example, Viney, Wertheimer, and Wertheimer (1979) produced a large bibliography of sources in English on the history of psychology; Watson (1974/1976, 1978) compiled three volumes that provide lists of the major works of many of the world's great psychologists (Volume 1, 1974), a bibliography of sources about these same psychologists (Volume 2, 1976), and discussions of resources available for the study of the history of psychology (1978). Benjamin and colleagues (1989) prepared a bibliography of sources in the history of psychology compiled from notes and news sections from major journals. Sokal and Rafail (1982) published a guide to manuscript collections in the history of psychology for those interested in sources of archival materials.

Prior to the 1960s, scholarly work on the history of psychology was typically somewhat disjointed and restricted to the isolated efforts of a few interested individuals. There were a few textbooks, a few books of readings, and a small number of journals that would accept historical articles. Informal meetings of interested individuals occurred at the annual conventions of the American Psychological Association.

The decade of the 1960s ushered in a new era in the history of psychology. This remarkable decade witnessed the founding of the *Journal of the History of the Behavioral Sciences,* first published in January of 1965. In November of the same year, the Archives of the History of American Psychology were established at the University of Akron in Akron, Ohio. It was also in 1965 that the American Psychological Association approved the formation of a new division—Division 26, the Division of the History of Psychology. Psychologists who were interested in history quickly established physical, organizational, and social support structures for their scholarly activities. In 1967, the first graduate program offering a Ph.D. in the history of psychology was established at the University of New Hampshire. A year later, another important society was launched—Cheiron, The International Society for the History of the Behavioral and Social Sciences. Cheiron was a centaur in Greek mythology known for wisdom, knowledge, and immortality.

The history of psychology continues as an important topic of study at the outset of the twenty-first century. A survey of over seven hundred psychology departments in American colleges and universities (Fuchs & Viney, 2002) revealed that over 80 percent offer undergraduate courses in the history of psychology. Such courses are typically taught during the junior or senior year and sometimes serve as capstone courses for psychology majors. Further, accredited graduate programs in counseling and clinical psychology include instruction on the history of psychology as a core part of graduate education. Most departments of psychology have made an apparent commitment to offer history as a component of undergraduate and graduate education. Though professional organizations such as Cheiron and Division 26 (History of Psychology) of the American Psychological Association have weathered ups and downs in membership, a substantial body of researchers remains interested in the history of psychology. Because of the growth of scholarly work, the American Psychological Association approved a journal, *History of Psychology,* launched in 1998 under the editorship of Dr. Michael M. Sokal, a prominent historian of science who has served as president of the History of Science Society. The history of psychology may properly be viewed as an important facet of the history of science.

The history of psychology is an intrinsically interesting subject, covering people and their ideas about psychological problems. From the ideas of the earliest Greeks about mental illness, to concepts of childhood in the Middle Ages, to the nineteenth-century vision of a new discipline called psychology—the whole story is an enjoyable and worthwhile adventure. But more important than sheer enjoyment, study of the history of psychology can provide a perspective on the present scene that would be difficult or even impossible to achieve in any other way.

INTERNAL AND EXTERNAL HISTORY

The history explored in this book is different from the usual histories of empires, nations, wars, and political leaders. Disciplinary histories—such as the history of psychology, the history of education, and the history of philosophy—are often viewed as a part of a special kind of history called the *history of ideas.* There are many opinions about the history of ideas and about how this special kind of history should be approached (e.g., see Kelley, 1990). As a field, it typically calls for some degree of expertise in an established discipline and in history. A major criticism of disciplinary histories is that they are often presented from an insular, internalist perspective, as if ideas within a discipline occurred in a social vacuum. Such presentations, focusing on how ideas have been passed from one intellectual hero to the next, often neglect the political, philosophical, and social contexts. **Internal history** refers to accounts of the development of ideas within a discipline, whereas **external history** refers to the context in which ideas developed. Because there is no such thing as an autonomous discipline, it is important to be aware of as much context as possible.

Unfortunately, there are many constraints, even for the professional historian, on the number of external dimensions that can be brought to bear on any given era, person, or problem. For example, someone who has a good working knowledge of Freudian theory may also wish to know as much as possible about Freud's Vienna and his Jewish identity. Ideally, he or she might assemble experts in nineteenth- and early twentieth-century European social, economic, and political history along with other experts in the philosophy, art, music, and religion of the period in an attempt to capture Freud's context in all possible detail. Such an effort will greatly enrich our perspectives on internal history.

However, for those who have practical interests in disciplinary history, it is not always possible to capture all the rich contextual material available for each era or person. Nevertheless, it is hoped that a general history, presented from an internalist perspective, will provoke greater interest in external history and serve as a stimulus for more specialized studies that afford opportunities for deeper understandings that come with a stronger focus on context. In the meantime, a survey of intellectual disciplinary traditions is a proper, practical, and enriching activity that will afford new vantage points for understanding the present state of the field.

REVIEW QUESTIONS _____

1. List and briefly describe five reasons for the study of history.

2. What is historiography? What issues are typically studied in historiography?

3. What is history? Do you agree that history has an empirical component?

4. In what sense can the historian be objective?

5. List and describe three hypotheses regarding the pattern or direction of history.

6. Describe specific developments in the latter part of the twentieth century that contributed to the advance of scholarly work in the history of psychology.

CHAPTER 2

PHILOSOPHICAL ISSUES

But man, proud man, Drest in a little briefe authoritie, Most ignorant of what he's most assur'd, (His glassie Essence) like an angry Ape Plaies such phantastique tricks before high heauen, As makes the Angels weepe.

—William Shakespeare (1604–1605/1964)

As we work our way through the history of psychology, we will find that certain themes and problems recur. We will encounter new discoveries and insights, but we will also see that old problems have a way of coming back to haunt each new generation. The study of the history of psychology is more meaningful if we are attuned at the outset to the perennial problems that have beset the field. This chapter examines some of the philosophical problems that will come up again in other parts of the text. Here, we will attempt to provide definitions of the problems and examine some of the positions that have proved to be durable.

EPISTEMOLOGY

The term **epistemology** is derived from the Greek *episteme,* which means to understand or to know. Epistemology is a branch of philosophy concerned with theories of knowledge. Psychologists have always had a strong interest in epistemological problems, and in recent years that interest has grown. Indeed, with the growth of psychology as a discipline, a wider number of epistemological problems has been investigated. For example, Jean Piaget is well known for his work in what he called **genetic epistemology**— the study of the ways we solve problems as a function of our developmental level. Piaget demon-

strated that our ways of knowing (i.e., our ways of solving problems) change as we mature. Let us turn to a consideration of some of the epistemological issues that have been of special relevance to psychologists.

A Priori and A Posteriori Knowledge

As we read the history of psychology, we are bound to encounter statements to the effect that certain truths are presumed to be known a priori. What does such a statement mean? The term **a priori** means from what is prior, whereas its opposite, **a posteriori,** means from what is posterior. In modern usage, from the time of Immanuel Kant, a posteriori refers to that which is derived from experience, and a priori refers to self-evident truths. For example, consider the following proposition: If *A* is larger than *B* and *B* is larger than *C,* then *A* is larger than *C.* The claim can be made that the truth of the proposition is known a priori. No one would deny that the proposition itself is known through experience. That is, without experience, we would not even know about the proposition. But the claim may still be made that we grasp the truth of the relationships among *A, B,* and *C* through our intellectual insight alone. In other words, we have the capacity to know or to grasp certain relationships without learning or benefit of prior experience. According to the theory of a priori knowledge, it can be argued, for example, that one could immediately grasp the meaning of a statement such as "We cannot both exist and not exist at the same time."

Philosophers and psychologists have long struggled with the role of the a priori in human knowledge. Part of the problem arises from extreme claims. For instance, there are those who argue that knowledge of good and evil is known a priori. On the other extreme, there are those who argue that all knowledge is dependent on experience. Although psychologists have always placed strong emphasis on the centrality of experience as the basis of knowledge, we, like the philosophers, have had to struggle with evidence that there are in fact relationships that are discerned without learning or previous experience.

Nativism versus Empiricism

A close relative to the issue of a priori and a posteriori knowledge is the issue of **nativism** versus **empiricism** in perception. A nativist holds that there are perceptions that are operational from birth, that are built in or a natural outcome of the unique structural and functional properties of the nervous system. An empiricist, by contrast, holds that all perceptions are learned or developed from experience. The dispute between the nativists and empiricists is illustrated in the problem of depth perception. Do we learn to see in depth or is depth perception a natural or unlearned ability? Classic research suggests that newborns, in fact, have perceptual abilities that are difficult to trace to learning. For example, baby goats and chicks only a few hours old will avoid a visual cliff (Gibson & Walk, 1960). It has also been demonstrated that newborn human infants, only minutes old, will turn their heads in the direction of a sound (Wertheimer, 1961). It is difficult to attribute this ability to discriminate correctly the source of a sound to learning or experience. It appears that the empiricist must resort to the possibility of intrauterine learning to explain avoidance of a visual cliff or sound localization. But such a possibility at this point seems rather remote. Later in the text, we will see the empiricist and nativist claims being formulated

by such philosophers as George Berkeley and Immanuel Kant.

Instinct versus Learning

Still another related problem is that of **instinct** versus **learning.** This particular problem has had a turbulent history during the modern era (e.g., see Diamond, 1971, 1974a). Many of the early psychologists placed a strong emphasis on the role of instincts in human as well as animal psychology. William McDougall (1908/1960) was perhaps the best example of an early theorist who believed that instincts play a central role in human life. McDougall believed that curiosity, fighting, escaping (when trapped), and maternal behavior are examples of instincts that are operative in human life. With the advent of behaviorism, such use of the concept of instinct fell into disrepute. The new emphasis was on learning. The assumption of the behaviorist was that we learn to be aggressive, we learn to be curious, and we learn to be good mothers or fathers. Behavioristic research was successful in showing that some behaviors that were assumed to be instinctual were subject to learning. In early studies, Kuo (1921, 1924) demonstrated that rat killing by cats is much more subject to learning than anybody of the time might have believed. Indeed, baby kittens, depending on rearing conditions, may grow up to become rat killers but may also grow up fearful of rats, or may grow up tolerant or even cooperative, living peacefully in the same cages with rats and eating and drinking out of the same dishes with them. Kuo showed that the conditioning history of the individual kitten is the key to understanding that kitten's later interaction with rats. Kuo's enthusiasm led him to entitle one of his articles "A Psychology without Heredity" (1924).

Although behaviorism was successful in demonstrating the importance of learning, it was not successful in promoting a psychology without instincts. There has been a continuing fascination with instinct theory during the twentieth century, and interest in the topic accelerated just after World War II with the work of ethologists such as Konrad Lorenz and N. Tinbergen and sociobiologists such as Edward O. Wilson. Widespread public awareness of instinct theory was also stimulated by popular best-selling books such as *The Naked Ape* by Desmond Morris (1967).

As noted, terms such as *a priori, nativism,* and *instinct* are related in that they all refer to abilities or capacities that are built in or natural parts of living systems. There are also important differences in the capacities denoted by these terms. For example, a priori knowledge is more cognitive than an instinct, which appears to be carried off with a high degree of automaticity. A native ability such as the innate capacity to see in depth also seems less cognitive than a priori knowledge, which refers to real intellectual insight or the capacity to discern certain fundamental relationships. Terms such as *a posteriori, empiricism,* and *learning* are somewhat comparable in that they all refer to the importance of experience to various acquisitions, capacities, or abilities.

What Are the Criteria by Which We Claim to Know Truth?

One of the most interesting epistemological problems is illustrated in the criteria we employ as we go about the practical business of assessing truth claims. Human beings live their lives and make decisions on the basis of epistemological categories that serve as guides to knowledge. These categories have been as controversial and pivotal in human history as the controversies over claims to geographic territory. On what grounds are we to claim that we have knowledge? On the grounds of authority? reason? faith? personal observation? science? The clash of epistemologies is often the essential ingredient in disputes between science and legal systems, science and religion, and even between scientists and other scientists. We will examine some of the common epistemological criteria employed in claims of knowledge.

Authority.   Reference to **authority** is surely the most common method of assessing truth. Authorities exist, in the forms of books, institutions, parents, teachers, and legal codes. In early years, children incorporate values, beliefs, and judgments

of parents—the original authorities in most important matters. Very often we seek no other criterion for verification or substantiation—the word of the authority is sufficient.

In an early book, *Man for Himself,* Erich Fromm (1947) provided a thoughtful treatment of the problem of authority. Fromm pointed out that the great sin in authoritarian epistemology is to become too much like the authority. If we are as knowledgeable as the authority we no longer need to be informed and directed by the authority. Hence, some authorities go to great lengths to discourage questions and to control the flow of information so that followers will not be exposed to contradictory opinions. Authorities may encourage study, but only study that is officially sanctioned and therefore "safe." Any study of the history of ideas uncovers a multitude of examples of the abuse of authority. Such abuse begins when authority teaches that it is the exclusive and sufficient basis of knowledge.

Tragic examples of the abuse of authority are found in the executions of such people as Giordano Bruno (1548–1600) and Michael Servetus (1511–1553). Bruno was condemned to death mainly because of his belief that the sun was the center of our planetary system. Servetus did not conform to accepted scriptural doctrines and was thus regarded as a heretic. The executions of Bruno and Servetus are examples of how extreme commitment to authority can lead to the kind of certitude that makes it possible and even necessary to stifle ideas that challenge or contradict the teachings of authority. The quotation from Shakespeare at the beginning of this chapter was perhaps motivated by outrage at the abuse of authority.

The abuse of authority is unfortunately not a historical relic. There are any number of more recent examples of abusive authoritarian control of art, literature, science, political ideas, and people themselves. The Jonestown Massacre (see *Time,* 1978, pp. 16–22) is a tragic example of abusive authoritarian control. Those who embrace a progress theory of history might hope that civilization, like individuals, will grow from an early reliance on authority to a more democratic, open, and tolerant way of knowing. It is arguable whether such progress is being made. The balance between necessary and abusive authority is one of the critical problems confronting every human group. The irony of abusive authority is that human beings are so easily led to rationalize or even idealize such authority.

The perceived source of authority obviously dictates matters of compliance. We may comply critically and reluctantly with some of our legal codes, recognizing that they must be authoritative for us but are nevertheless pesky human inventions that must be tolerated if we are to enjoy the benefits of civilization. We may comply humorously, patriotically, lovingly, or fearfully with the authority of traditions. Authority perceived as having its origin in religious revelation motivates strict compliance in countless millions of people. Such compliance may be rigidly compulsive, especially in groups that forbid or restrict individual interpretive studies. Science, especially in modern times, also serves as a source of authority. Such authority, however, in the truest spirit of science, has only a provisional and practical quality because experiments sometimes contradict each other. Furthermore, theories are changed or abandoned, and new discoveries constantly challenge our most secure beliefs.

Within the history of psychology, we will encounter the problem of authority over and over again. We will see that traditions, legal systems, scientific systems of thought, and theories can serve as authorities. Other than its potential for abuse, we will see that authority also has utilitarian value. The scientist, for example, may rely on the experiments and words of other scientists. It is not authority per se that presents problems but the way we human beings use it.

Empiricism.   The term **empiricism** is derived from Greek and Latin terms that were close in meaning to our word *experience*. In contemporary usage, there are several shades of meaning associated with empiricism, but in the present context the term refers to a theory of knowledge in which experience plays a central role. Experience of the world depends on information provided by the senses. Knowledge, then, according to empiricism, is based on facts as revealed by observation and as represented in experience. As the story of the history of psychology unfolds, we will see that empiricism is often contrasted with rationalism (discussed below). We will also find advocates of empiricism in most historical periods, but the most famous empiricists were from Great Britain. John Locke (1632–1704) argued that there is nothing in the intellect that was not previously in the senses. An earlier empiricist from Great Britain, Francis Bacon, has sometimes been called the Great Herald of the Empirical Spirit because of his militant campaign to encourage experiment, observation, and data collection. Bacon believed that we should rely less on authority and more on the empirical method.

From an uncritical standpoint, empiricism seems an obvious alternative to authority, tradition, and legalism as a way of obtaining knowledge. But empiricism, as a way of knowing, is filled with problems. First, as we discussed under the topic of a priori and a posteriori knowledge, it may be that we do have certain forms of knowledge that are not dependent on sensory information. We also know that sensory information can be unreliable because of the limitations of the senses. Furthermore, the senses are easily conditioned by emotion, social context, learning, and motivation. Also, we are inevitably concerned about the degree of correspondence between the objects in the world and the objects of our experience. It is little wonder that philosophers and psychologists have raised questions about the adequacy of empiricism as a way of knowing.

Rationalism.   The term **rationalism** comes from the same Latin root as the term *reason*. As a theory of knowledge, rationalism emphasizes the importance of a priori reason or innate ideas. The rationalists argue that the mind has innate organizing principles of its own so that information from the senses is filtered and patterned in ways that are built into the organism. Rationalists believe that sensory information alone is not an adequate basis for knowledge. They emphasize the activity of mind, the capacity to reason, and the ability to discern some meanings on an intuitive basis. Early philosophers and scientists such as Descartes, Galileo, Leibniz, and Kant can be considered adherents of the rational approach.

Early psychologists and philosophers debated whether the new psychology should be based primarily on empiricism or rationalism. Numerous books were written to distinguish the problems and methods of rational psychology and empirical psychology. As early as 1732, Christian von Wolff wrote a book entitled *Empirical Psychology;* two years later he wrote a complementary book entitled *Rational Psychology.* In the United States, Laurens Hickok also wrote separate books under the titles of *Rational Psychology* (1849) and *Empirical Psychology* (1854). These early writers believed that rationalism and empiricism give us different methods and that both methods are useful. The tensions between rational and empirical approaches to psychology are still with us and will be explored in more depth in Chapters 6 and 7.

Aestheticism. **Aestheticism** is a commitment to the belief that the principles of beauty are applicable to other arenas of thought. In this sense, aestheticism is an epistemology or way of knowing. It is well illustrated in the book *The Double Helix* by Watson (1968). After Watson and Crick constructed the DNA model, the comment was made that the model was "too pretty not to be true" (Watson, 1968, p. 134). The aesthetic test has been of historical importance in the humanities—especially art and music—but scientists also seem to take delight in a beautiful model or a "pretty theory." Physicist Paul Dirac, as quoted by Brush (1974b), "stated that a theorist should prefer beautiful equations to uglier ones that yield closer agreement with experimental data" (p. 1167).

Pragmatism. Pragmatic philosophy represents still another approach to the problem of epistemology. The term **pragmatism** is derived from a Greek root, translated as *pragma,* which refers to things accomplished or things done. The beginnings of modern pragmatism are encountered in the works of Francis Bacon who believed we should emphasize theories and propositions that can be tested. Immanuel Kant used the term *pragmatic* to refer to that which is prudent. Pragmatism, in the late nineteenth century, under the leadership of Charles Sanders Pierce (*purse*) and William James, became a major philosophical movement. Pierce and James emphasized the practical consequences of theories, definitions, ideas, and concepts. James, in typical American fashion, talked about the "cash value" of an idea. Does the idea produce real productive work that makes a difference in the world of experience, or does it lead only to dead ends and muddled thinking? James also stressed the importance of the activity level generated by ideas. James believed that ideas that are viable and workable produce sustained intellectual and physical work. For the pragmatist, a good idea or a good definition is not simply committed to memory and followed in a slavish or robotic fashion. James argued that a definition does not close our intellectual quest; on the contrary, a good definition is only a program for more work (see James, 1907/1975b, pp. 31–32).

The pragmatist emphasizes the idea that the world is in flux and thus concepts must be altered and updated so they can be responsive to new discoveries. Also, concepts can outlive their usefulness and may sometimes need to be discarded. Pragmatism judges truth in terms of utility or workability, but this is not the whole story. It is also a philosophy that calls for a deep awareness of the operation of change and a suspicion of big claims that cover too much territory. James (1876b) conveyed a pragmatic sentiment when he defined philosophy as the "habit of always seeing an alternative" (p. 178).

One problem with pragmatism is that ideas or concepts may appear sterile or unworkable in terms of the present intellectual context, and yet such ideas may later harbor important truths. The initial Copernican view of the solar system did not at first seem workable, but it represented a major advance in knowledge of the planetary system. Pragmatism, especially in naive, extreme, or corrupted forms may also discourage theoretical inquiry. William James and other pragmatists, however, would never approve of such a consequence. James had the broadest intellectual appetite and was a staunch supporter of pure and applied science. He was more interested in opening than in closing doors (see James, 1909/1977, p. 19).

Other Epistemologies

There are many additional justifications that human beings have offered in support of their claims of knowledge. Argument from consensus and argument from vividness of experience are often popular. But such arguments are quickly exposed—if millions believed that the earth was flat, millions were deceived. And nothing is more vivid than the argument that the sun moves across the sky, but we now know that the apparent movement of the sun is caused by the turning of the earth. Consensus and vividness are not reliable guides to knowledge. But what is?

René Descartes (1596–1650) was one of the greatest minds ever to tackle the problem of epistemology. In his struggle with the problem of knowledge, Descartes decided to trust only that which he could not doubt; he found that he could doubt almost everything. He could doubt the existence of God and the objective existence of other people (other people and things might be mere projections of his own mind as in a dream); he could even doubt his own material existence. As Descartes searched, he found that the only thing he could not doubt was the fact that he was doubting. But in order to doubt, one must think and in order to think one must exist. His famous dictum "I think, therefore I am" was the result of a tortuous struggle with the problem of knowledge.

Descartes's method provides us with an interesting exercise in logic. He may even convince us that we cannot logically doubt our doubting, but beyond this he does not rescue us from our epistemological problems. Even if there is one undoubtable truth, we still have reason to question the extent to which our beliefs correspond to the way things are. Can we really distinguish knowledge from mere opinion?

The skeptics answer "no" to this question, but the skeptical solution to the problem of knowledge must come to grips with an embarrassing question. How does the skeptic know that we cannot know? This perfectly legitimate question is a challenge to dogmatic skepticism. It is perhaps the anemia of the skeptical solution that makes the position unconvincing and unappealing. We are teased by the possibility of knowledge. The skeptical assertion that we must remain forever in the realm of opinion is itself an opinion—it is not necessarily knowledge.

The Role of Emotions in Knowledge

The problem of human knowledge is complicated by the play of emotions in our belief structures. It is difficult enough to adjudicate among the claims of competing beliefs when we are dispassionate, but when emotions—such as hate, fear, awe, love, and anger—enter the picture, our knowledge problems are compounded. Throughout this text we will visit and revisit tensions between authority and reason prevalent in all historical periods. These tensions are usually shot through with the problem of emotion. Though emotions may be attached to authority *or* to reason, it is likely that strong emotions are more commonly "conditioned to" authority than to reason. The expression *conditioned to* is important because emotions may be attached by any number of means to the claims of reason or to the claims of authority. For example, the dissonance associated with the violation of reason may be a source of emotion.

Let us return, however, to a consideration of emotion and its relation to authority. Authority is a visible presence in our most vulnerable moments such as birth, marriage, illness, tragedy, and death. We sing to authority songs of praise, gratitude, thanksgiving, worship, and allegiance. Though protest music is also used to attack authority, it is rare to encounter music explicitly inspired by the claims of reason, but it is common to encounter music inspired by the claims of authority. We create symbols inspired by authority and then idolize those symbols and pledge our allegiance to them. We set aside special holidays to celebrate authority, and we participate in self-denial and in rituals that underscore our loyalty and commitment. Failure to observe a ritual is often a source of the most intense anxiety and self-criticism. Our very identity as individuals can be tied to reason, as is the case with the *Star Trek* character Mr. Spock, but it is more likely that the personal identities of the overwhelming majority, even in matters such as dress and food choices, are tied to authority. Further, there are legitimate fears of social ostracism for any kind of deviance. Individuals, for example, who have undergone a dramatic conversion from one belief to another are all too often devalued or even disowned by parents or authorities. Though science is valued for its openness, the scientific community, acting as authority, may also ostracize any worker who moves too far afield from standard content or practice.

Emotional problems are compounded further when we believe that authority is absolute and rightfully immune from any kind of reasonable questioning or analysis. Thus, when there is a clash between reason and authority, the problem is not merely intellectual, the problem is emotional. The influence and emotional power of authority is reflected in its pervasive and often comforting presence in memorial processes. Memorization is among the most valued of activities in authority systems, and those who can flawlessly recite the words of authority from memory are held up as role models and examples. Children, especially, are encouraged to commit the words of authority to memory. A purely descriptive and mechanical recitation is often more valued than a truly critical, reflective, and creative analysis.

Few subject areas are as important to human welfare and survival as epistemology, and yet it is a subject that is avoided or neglected because of the vexing questions it raises. There are undoubtedly beliefs with survival value and such beliefs may have their origin in reason or in authority. There are also beliefs that are dangerous and destructive to human welfare and such beliefs have their origin in any number of sources. Unfortunately, emotion along with ignorance and the inevitable blind spots encountered in all belief systems, may undermine the work of critical reflection necessary to an understanding of the consequences of belief structures. The problem of knowledge is by no means a trivial or irrelevant metaphysical issue—it is a practical problem highly relevant to the quality of daily life and should be confronted by wide populations in a vigorous and honest fashion. The quotation from William Shakespeare in the epigraph is a poetic reminder of the certitude that often accompanies ignorance and the outrageous consequences that can follow.

We come full circle now back to our original question. On what grounds can we lay claim to knowledge? We have reviewed some of the epistemological positions that have been important throughout history. We turn now to the relationship of science to epistemology.

Science and Epistemology

Science, conceived as a way of knowing, represents a special kind of epistemology that combines empirical, rational, pragmatic, and aesthetic dimensions. From the beginning of the modern period, philosophers of science have attempted to characterize the unique features of scientific methodology, but such philosophers have been unable to agree on what science is or how it operates. Later in the book, as we explore the beginnings of the modern period, we will observe strong disagreements, particularly between Francis Bacon and René Descartes, about the nature of science. Some of the issues that separated these pioneers are still pertinent today. Because of longstanding disagreements about the nature of science, we must be very cautious about assuming that there is *one* traditional view of science. In what follows, we will briefly examine some of the different views of science that have been dominant in the later part of the twentieth century.

Karl Raimond Popper.   Sir Karl Popper was born July 28, 1902, in Vienna and attended the University of Vienna where he studied mathematics, physics, and philosophy. His book, *The Logic of Scientific Discovery,* first published in 1935, is now considered a classic in the philosophy of science. Popper taught at Canterbury University in New Zealand from 1937 to 1945 and at the University of London from 1945 to 1969. He has held various types of visiting or honorary appointments in a variety of institutions such as Harvard, Stanford, and the University of Vienna.

One of Popper's most original and noteworthy assertions is that scientific theories cannot be verified by observational evidence or by induction.

Thus, regardless of the number of positive instances of an observation, one is still not justified in drawing a universal conclusion. Though every observed swan may have been white, there is no basis for declaring that *all* swans are white. There is thus an inherent limitation in the method of induction so that it cannot serve as a compelling basis for scientific procedure. Indeed, there is nothing in the inductive method per se that serves as an adequate basis for distinguishing between legitimate science and a pseudoscience such as astrology. A pseudoscience may garner many positive observations in support of its theories, but, according to Popper, such observations do not serve as a definitive verification principle.

In place of inductive methods, Popper argues that science should be guided by a hypothetico-deductive system that serves as the basis for the falsification of theories. The task of the scientist is thus to construct theories and deduce testable consequences from them. Such consequences may be consistent with the predictions of the theory or at variance with such predictions. A theory that is falsifiable is a successful scientific theory. A theory that is not falsifiable is not, by Popper's estimate, a scientific theory.

According to Popper, the integrity of the scientific procedure hinges partly on an honest quest for negative instances. One mark of nonscientific or pseudoscientific theories is that they tend to live forever because they are not falsifiable. Survivability is not the first task of a good theory; rather, a good theory possesses the virtues of simplicity and clarity. After scientists construct theories with such virtues, the next task is to search vigorously for empirical materials that are inconsistent with the predictions of the theory.

Popper (1959) argued that there is no such thing as neutral observation; rather, "observation is always *observation in the light of theories. . . .* It is only the inductivist prejudice that leads people to think that there could be a phenomenal language free of theories" (p. 59n). Popper admitted that he is offering a "theory of theories" (p. 59). His larger vision of the scientific enterprise is that it is by no means a basis for certitude. What Popper offers is an evolutionary epistemology that recognizes the crucial but tentative role of theory in human

thought. Popper likens theories to "nets cast to catch what we call 'the world': to rationalize, to explain, and to master it. We endeavour to make the mesh ever finer and finer" (p. 59). Thus, there is the hope of progress, but no grounds for certainty. Popper was deeply concerned with the differentiation between science and pseudoscience. A mark of a genuine scientific theory, according to Popper, is that it is not invulnerable, and a major characteristic of science is that it does evolve.

Popper's philosophy of science has been criticized on the grounds that it ignores the history of science and that it also ignores what scientists actually do (see, e.g., Toulmin, 1972, pp. 478–503). According to the criticism, Popper's theory is not sufficiently empirical. That is, the theory is driven by abstractions of the intellect, by the method of reason, rather than by careful studies of how scientists have actually gone about their work. The result is that we have prescriptions about how scientists ought to work rather than illumination about how they do work.

A stronger criticism comes from those scientists and philosophers who have challenged the doctrine of falsifiability. In his book *Abusing Science,* Kitcher (1982) noted that one problem with falsifiability, at least in its naive applications, is that it may retard or even discourage the quest for legitimate auxiliary hypotheses when a theory is threatened with empirical consequences that it cannot predict. Kitcher gave the example of the failure of Uranus to follow an orbit predicted by Newtonian mechanics. The behavior of Uranus could have been taken as a falsification of Newtonian theory, but astronomers tried a different alternative. They plotted the course of a hypothetical planet whose existence would exert the necessary forces to account for the strange behavior of Uranus. Later, the discovery of Neptune resolved the difficulties because the orbit of Neptune was consistent with the calculations worked out in advance for the hypothetical planet. Many scientists and philosophers would argue that there is a role for falsifiability in scientific procedure, but many would argue that Popper overextends the concept. Its role may be clear enough in some types of scientific activity, but there are other types of activity (e.g., the descriptive mapping of a molecule or the naturalistic observations of the predatory behavior of the cheetah) in which the role of falsifiability is not so clear. A negative consequence of Popper's theory is that it may greatly restrict the range of what counts as legitimate science.

Thomas S. Kuhn.   One of the most influential books in the history and philosophy of science was *The Structure of Scientific Revolutions* (1970) by Thomas S. Kuhn. Kuhn was initially interested in theoretical physics, but after assisting with an elementary science course for nonscientists, he found his interests shifting to the history and philosophy of science. Specifically, he told us that historical scientific studies "radically undermined some of [his] basic conceptions about the nature of science and the reasons for its special success" (p. v).

After extensive and broad-based liberal studies at Harvard and a year at the Center for Advanced Studies in the Behavioral Sciences, Kuhn devoted himself almost exclusively to the development of the ideas later set forth in his book. As we will see, Kuhn's first interest was in the nature or development of scientific advances. He addressed a different central problem than did Popper, but the two theories also cover some common territory, though in different ways.

Kuhn's work emphasized the importance of understanding science in terms of its community structures and its historical development. The scientific community shares an intellectual background, standard reference sources, textbooks, ways of solving problems, and values. The community exerts pressures on the individual, especially during student years and in early scientific-professional years when the young scientist is establishing a reputation. Kuhn did not mean to imply that the scientific community is a closed club. Such an interpretation is an unfortunate "popular caricature of Kuhn's position" (Kitcher, 1982, p. 168). Kuhn fully recognized the important diversities that exist in the scientific community. Nevertheless, at any given time there is much that members of the community share in common.

One particular concern of Kuhn's was the way science develops initially and how it evolves over time. He argued that early prescientific development is marked by competing systems or schools of thought. Such schools argue over basic definitions, methods, and assumptions. He noted that in the early stages of electrical research there were a great number of views about the fundamental nature of electricity. He could as easily have used psychology as an example. The great systems of psychology are marked by fundamental disagreements over subject matter and appropriate methods.

Kuhn (1970) told us that the early search for research consensus is extremely difficult because "all of the facts that could possibly pertain to the development of a given science are likely to seem equally relevant. As a result, early fact-gathering is a far more nearly random activity than the one that subsequent scientific development makes familiar" (p. 15). Nevertheless, in time one of the competing schools prevails over the others. The dominant school has enjoyed sufficient achievement to attract a loyal following and promises to provide a set of problems that are worthy of sustained study. The dominant school is now in charge of the intellectual agenda and we witness the transition to what Kuhn called **normal science.**

Normal science, according to Kuhn, has a record of past achievement; it defines problem areas and provides methods of practice. It is the tradition in which most scientists do their work. Kuhn employs the term **paradigm** as a way to elaborate further the meaning of normal science. In a sociological sense, paradigm refers to "the entire constellation of beliefs, values, techniques, and so on, shared by members of a given community" (Kuhn, 1970, p. 175). The term also refers to conventional ways of approaching and solving problems. There is an obvious economy in having paradigms because they help define the boundaries within which scientists do their work and clarify the legitimate methods of analysis and ways of looking at problems.

Kuhn noted that normal science is comparable to solving puzzles. Individual scientists find selected pieces of the puzzle and fit them into their appropriate places. Kuhn also used the expression *mopping up* to describe the work of most members of the community during the normal science phase. During this phase, there is little focus on novel events. Indeed, mopping up operations aim largely at forcing "nature into the preformed and relatively inflexible box that the paradigm supplies" (Kuhn, 1970, p. 24). According to Kuhn, there are three classes of problems that engage scientists as they proceed with the business of normal science. First, there is a search for facts that the paradigm designates as significant; second, there are attempts to match facts with theory; and third, there are attempts to elaborate and extend the theory further. There are so many rewarding problems driven by the paradigm that there is little inclination to devote energy to the exploration of anomalies, or bits and pieces that do not fit into the large picture.

Nevertheless, in the course of normal science there are serendipitous findings and anomalies that eventually cannot be ignored. Sometimes discoveries occur through accidents and at other times they are theory driven. Kuhn (1970) noted that X-rays are "a classic case of discovery through accident, a type that occurs more frequently than the impersonal standards of scientific reporting allow us easily to realize" (p. 57). He went on to describe the flow of events that led Roentgen to discover X-rays and how even such a notable individual as Lord Kelvin believed they were a hoax. Here, clearly, was a discovery that could not be ignored and that was not predicted by the prevailing paradigm.

In most cases, efforts are made to assimilate new discoveries or anomalies into the prevailing paradigm. Such efforts are understandable because the community has a vested interest in the traditional paradigm. It has commanded loyalties and lifetimes of hard work. However, there may be a succession of anomalous findings that are so compelling that they cannot be ignored. Such a turn of events creates a crisis and slowly causes some members of the community to lose faith. The response of the community is predictable: Some try to find ad hoc hypotheses that will rescue the paradigm, whereas others begin to look for new ways to organize the larger picture.

A scientific revolution, according to Kuhn, is marked by a radically new and more successful organization of the world. There is a paradigm shift and the old way of seeing things is replaced by a new vision. Kuhn (1970) noted that his "book portrays scientific development as a succession of tradition-bound periods punctuated by noncumulative breaks" (p. 208). Following a revolution, the old paradigm is displaced and there is a move back to a normal science that works within the broad outlines provided by the new paradigm.

Both Kuhn and Popper advanced evolutionary epistemologies and both challenged absolutistic approaches to science. Kuhn seems to have a broader interpretation of what counts as legitimate science than does Popper. Thus, mopping up activities, accidental discoveries, and descriptive studies are all part of the work of scientists. Kuhn has been criticized on the ground that he attempts to cover too much with the term *paradigm*. It is a criticism that he has acknowledged and attempted to correct. The definitions offered earlier are representative central meanings of the term in Kuhn's work. The structure Kuhn advanced to characterize the operations and evolution of science can also be subjected to the same criticism leveled against Popper—namely, that it does not do justice to the extreme diversity that we actually encounter in the history of science. We turn now to a third philosophical orientation that is radically different from those of Popper and Kuhn.

Paul K. Feyerabend. In his book *Science in the Making,* Joel Hildebrand, a chemist and former president of the American Chemical Association, challenged the idea that there is *one* scientific method. Hildebrand (1957) argued that "to be successful in unlocking doors concealing nature's secrets, a person must have ingenuity. If [we do] not have the key for the lock, [we] must not hesitate to pick it, to climb in a window, or even kick in a panel" (p. 26). Hildebrand goes on to say that scientific success is more a matter of ingenuity and determination than method.

Hildebrand's statement is by no means esoteric. In *Reflections of a Physicist,* Percy W. Bridgman (1955) said that "there is no scientific method as such" (p. 416). In that same source, he pointed out that scientists do not follow "any prescribed course of action . . . [;] science is what scientists do, and there are as many scientific methods as there are individual scientists" (p. 83). The same sentiment is offered by zoologist P. B. Medawar, who shared the Nobel prize with Sir

Macfarlane Burnet for the discovery of acquired immunological tolerance. In his book *The Limits of Science,* Medawar (1984) declared, "There is indeed no such thing as 'the' scientific method. A scientist uses a very great variety of stratagems . . . [and] no procedure of discovery can be logically scripted" (p. 51).

Medawar is particularly critical of those who think that most breakthroughs follow logically from a calculus of discovery. Perhaps some discoveries do come in such a fashion, but Medawar also emphasized the role of serendipity in science. He illustrated this role with case histories such as the discovery of X-rays. He asked the reader to imagine the derision a scientist would encounter if she or he went to a funding agency just before 1900 with a proposal "to discover a means of making human flesh transparent" (Medawar, 1984, p. 46). The discovery didn't follow any kind of a preplanned logical pathway that was connected to scientific goal setting.

Such disturbing comments by Hildebrand, Bridgman, and Medawar are not from people who wish in any way to undermine respect for science. Quite the contrary, these statements are from people who have given much to science and who have had keen interest in its advancement. What they are saying is that science, at least as they know it, is not as tidy, objective, and coherent as we have been led to believe. A similar theme is sounded by Brush (1974b) in a thoughtful article entitled "Should the History of Science Be Rated X?" Brush shows that what we learn in the history of science may "not be a good model for students" because it may challenge the idealized image so many of us carry.

Extensions and ramifications of some of the ideas we have just reviewed are set forth in a different kind of philosophy of science advocated by Paul K. Feyerabend. Feyerabend's (1975) book, entitled *Against Method,* outlines what he calls an anarchistic theory of knowledge. He is quick to acknowledge the negative implications of anarchism, especially for political science, but finds appropriate and healthy implications for anarchism in epistemology and science.

Feyerabend's analysis of the history of science results in conclusions that are in strong disagreement with those of Popper and Kuhn. Feyerabend (1975) contended,

> The idea of a method that contains firm, unchanging, and absolutely binding principles for conducting the business of science meets considerable difficulty when confronted with the results of historical research—there is not a single rule, however plausible, and however firmly grounded in epistemology, that is not violated at some time or other. It becomes evident that such violations are not accidental events; they are not results of insufficient knowledge or of inattention which might have been avoided. On the contrary, we see that they are necessary for progress. (p. 23)

Feyerabend went on to say that conscious decisions to break away from conventional wisdom and method are not only facts in the history of science but necessary to the progress of science. He believed that successful and creative scientists break or reverse rules, defend ad hoc hypotheses, work inductively then deductively, and work sometimes for unity and sometimes for plurality. The rule, he tells us, is *anything goes.* Feyerabend (1975) argued that "even a law-and-order science will succeed only if anarchistic moves are occasionally allowed to take place" (p. 26). Feyerabend's book is filled with examples from the history of science that are offered as evidence for his major thesis. He contended that "the idea of a fixed method, or of a fixed theory of rationality, rests on too naive a view of [human beings and their] social surroundings" (Feyerabend, 1975, p. 27; Feyerabend, 1988).

The position held by Feyerabend should not be viewed as a debunking of science or as an expression of skepticism regarding the discovery mission of science. His position does, however, call for a closer scrutiny of the history of scientific discovery. It also calls for more detailed empirical analysis of what scientists actually do. For example, is the hands-on method of the wet-lab chemist who manipulates variables in the laboratory the same method as that of the astronomer attempting to calculate the course of a newly discovered comet? Is the method of the abstract algebraist the same as that of the marine biologist attempting to characterize the feeding habits of sharks? Is there one scientific method adapted in slightly different ways in the various fields of science or is there a diversity of methods even within specific disciplines? If there is no *one* scientific method, are there at least features (e.g., the importance of quantification) that all methods share in common?

Relevance of Epistemology to Psychology

A review of epistemology and science is highly relevant to numerous problems we will encounter in the history of psychology. For example, early psychologists had strong disagreements over the appropriate methodology for the new psychology. Should there be one method or many? If there is to be but one, which should it be? The importance of such questions obviously is dictated partly by philosophy of science. Indeed, the very scientific status of psychology hinges, from some points of view, on methodological purity. The status of psychology among the sciences is also dictated by other philosophy-of-science considerations. Thus, within the scheme of things set forth by Kuhn, psychology could be regarded as a preparadigmatic science. It enjoys higher status in Feyerabend's schemes if for no other reason than that the methodological purity of all the sciences is called into question. Further, there is a wider latitude of acceptance in Feyerabend's scheme about what constitutes "normal science."

The issues raised here are of historical interest, but they also command the attention of numerous contemporary scientists and philosophers. As we proceed through the history of psychology, we will repeatedly encounter questions about the nature of science and the scientific status of psychology.

THE PROBLEM OF CAUSALITY

From the time of Aristotle to the present, philosophers and scientists have debated among themselves about the nature and meaning of causation. The problem of causation is one of the richer philosophical problems in psychology. Contributing to the richness of the problem are questions concerning the possible influence of unconscious processes in human life, the role of intention or purpose in determining behavior, and the question of whether the individual can be an agent of change (i.e., a cause). In what follows, we will review some of the classic and modern approaches to the problem of causation.

As we have noted, Aristotle was one of the first to struggle with the meaning of causation, and his original and creative thought on the topic paved the way for centuries of debate and speculation. Aristotle believed that causation is not a simple one-dimensional affair. To know the cause of anything, we must understand several things. First, we must understand the antecedent conditions. Aristotle referred to these conditions as the **efficient cause.** The efficient cause is that which immediately sets a thing in motion. When domino *B* falls after being impacted by *A,* we can say that the movement of *A* is the efficient cause of the fall of *B.* Aristotle also believed that an understanding of the material structure of a thing is necessary to an understanding of causation. When the physician's hammer strikes the patellar tendon (in the kneecap) we normally observe a knee reflex. If the physician's hammer is the efficient cause of the reflex, there must also be a material cause. In this case, we would not observe the reflex if there had been nerve or muscle damage. So, part of the cause of the reflex is the material structure (nerves, tendons, muscles) on which it depends. In other words, the reflex is dependent on a physical substrate, which Aristotle called the **material cause.** Domino *A* (an efficient cause) impacting domino *B* could knock *B* over if both were made of the same material. But if *B* were made of lead and *A* of light wood, then *B* would not fall when impacted by *A.* Thus, the so-called causal sequence is dependent on a material structure as well as antecedent conditions.

Aristotle also taught that the understanding of a sequence of events may depend on having some knowledge of goals and purposes. Let us go back to the example of the knee reflex. We might say that we observe the knee reflex because the physician produced it to fulfill the purpose of completing a neurological examination. Aristotle called this the **final cause,** the end or purpose for which a change was produced. Aristotle might argue that you cannot understand the knee reflex, or rather, the cause of the knee reflex, until you understand the intentions or purposes of the physician.

A fourth kind of cause, according to Aristotle, is the **formal cause.** The formal cause he believed to be the form, shape, or identifying properties of a thing. The same piece of granite may be chiseled and shaped into a bust of Beethoven or Mozart. The material is the same but the form is different and the form carries with it information value. The functional or causal properties of a thing will depend on form. Domino *B* would not fall when impacted by *A* if it were too short or radically different in form than *A*. So form may also be essential to an understanding of a causal sequence. An airplane could be constructed of appropriate material (material cause) and have an excellent propulsion system (efficient cause), but if the wing or some other part were not shaped appropriately (formal cause), the plane would not fly.

For Aristotle, knowledge of causation rests on understanding form, material, antecedent conditions, and the purpose or end for which a thing was intended. Aristotle believed in a balance of emphasis on all these dimensions of causation. His student, Theophrastus, however, believed that science should concern itself primarily with material and efficient causation and not with final causation.

The Aristotelian notion of final causation was consistent with teleological interpretations of the world to be found later in Christian theology. The term **teleology** refers to purpose or design. Technically, *teleology* can be defined as the investigation of evidence that there is design or purpose in nature. The assumption that there is design in nature leads to the next question: What was the origin of the design or purpose? There are two types of teleological answers to that question. **Intrinsic teleology** is the position that design, order, and purpose are immanent in nature—simple manifestations or characteristics of nature. But **extrinsic teleology** makes the claim that any design in nature reflects the work of a designer. Intrinsic teleology presents few problems for most scientists because, by its nature, science seeks to provide a naturalistic account of the world. Hence the scientist, as a scientist, assumes that natural causes alone provide a coherent scientific account of the world.

Intrinsic teleology, close in meaning to Aristotle's concept of final causation, has long since become archaic in physics and chemistry. Teleol-

ogy of the intrinsic variety has not been so easily dismissed by psychologists. Despite attempts by some behaviorists to build a psychological science like physics based on material and efficient causation, teleology has constituted a persistent problem for psychologists. Many psychologists have found it difficult, if not impossible, to resist expressions such as *goal directed, intention, plans, purposive behavior, anticipation,* and *expectancy.* Such terms, unless defined in unusual ways, have a strong flavor of intrinsic teleology or final causation. But can human behavior be explained adequately on the basis of the same material and efficient causation that are invoked to explain the movement of a billiard ball, the trajectory of a comet, or the changes in the metabolism of a cell? Or must we invoke some form of final causation to account for the complexity and quality of human behavior? This is one of the focal problems in the history of psychology. We will see theorists such as Jacques Loeb, John B. Watson, and B. F. Skinner lined up on one side of the issue and theorists such as William McDougall, Edward Chace Tolman, and Gordon Allport lined up on the other side. Arguments for teleological interpretations of psychology have been set forth by Rychlak and Rychlak (1990) and Rychlak (1994).

An entirely different approach to the problem of causation emerged out of the work of the eighteenth-century Scottish philosopher David Hume (1711–1776), who suggested that causation is not a clearly identifiable quality that resides in or inheres in an object. For example, domino *A* impacts domino *B* and *B* falls over. We say that *A* caused *B* to fall. But we would all agree that the reverse could have occurred as easily; *B* could have impacted *A* and *A* could have fallen. Causation is not a quality that resides in *A* or *B;* rather, causation is a construct we invoke to describe the relationship between *A* and *B.* When we say that causation does not reside in *A* or *B,* we simply mean that we cannot find any special feature of *A* or *B* that could be independently labeled as a cause— instead, the term *cause* is descriptive of *A*'s observed relation to *B.* Hume noted that we may infer causation when two events are contiguous in space, when one follows another in time, and when we have observed a constant conjunction between two events. If we observe repeatedly that *B* always falls when impacted by *A,* we form the idea of a necessary connection between *A* and *B*. The fact is, according to Hume, there is no necessary connection between *A* and *B*. The necessary connection is inferred by us and does not reside in the objects "out there."

Hume's approach to the problem of causation had a major influence on scientific metatheory. The claim may now be made that science does not study cause and effect—science simply studies relationships among events in the world. Even those relationships that occur with perfect regularity do not imply causation. Why? Suppose common sense refuses to go along with Hume's skeptical analysis, and that is often the case (e.g., see Taylor, 1967a, p. 66). Still, one might reasonably contend that science is limited to the study of correlations or relationships. Such a contention may be based on the difficulties associated with defining specific causes. For example, let us suppose that *P* is reliably followed by *Q*. The scientist wishes now to study the cause of the underlying relationship, why does *Q* follow *P*? The answer is usually fraught with frustrating ambiguities. First, as noted by the English philosopher John Stuart Mill (1806–1873), there can be a plurality of causes for any event and there can be a plurality of ways to view the cause of an event. For example, consider the difficulties of assessing the cause of a death in an automobile accident. Is a specific death caused by a drunken driver, excessive speed, severe internal bleeding, a mechanical failure, a blow to the head, a failure to yield the right of way, or a failure to wear safety belts? All of these may be involved, so is there one cause? If we narrow the problem to the biological dimension, the cause of death may still be debatable.

We encounter another difficulty when we attempt to specify the cause of an event. That difficulty is associated with the endless chain of causes associated with any given event. A popular example illustrates the point. One might make the claim that there is a causal connection between smoking and lung cancer. But then it would be argued that the real culprit is whatever it is that causes smoking, and so on. Quickly we can begin to imagine an endless chain of causes. Because of

this difficulty, even hardheaded common sense might be brought around to the position that science studies correlations or functional relationships, and not causes. There is, of course, utilitarian value in knowing about strong correlations.

In modern times we are often informed that correlation does not imply causation. But neither does correlation imply that there is not a causal relationship between two events. Correlation is simply neutral with respect to the question of causation. Perhaps causation is not a scientific construct. Maybe it is simply a historical and philosophical curiosity. To be sure, there are those who are content to study correlations or functional relationships. But the idea of causality is so deeply entrenched in common sense that it refuses to become an intellectual relic. Many scientists will still argue that science entails a search for fundamental processes that underlie and explain correlational data.

In psychology, numerous questions associated with the problem of causality will show themselves again and again. Some of the questions are as follows: To what extent are we influenced by events that are not a part of our consciousness? If we are influenced by unconscious processes, then to what extent can we claim to be rational or free? Is it possible to build an adequate science of human experience and behavior on the basis of material and efficient causes? Is there any sense in which we rise above cause–effect relations and exercise freedom of choice? All of these questions will be addressed as we proceed through the book, but this last question is such an important philosophical issue that we must now examine it in more detail.

FREE WILL AND DETERMINISM

This is one of philosophy's oldest problems and one that is highly relevant to psychology. Many of the great psychologists have been explicit about their stance on this issue, and some (e.g., William James, 1884/1979a; B. F. Skinner, 1971) have seen the issue as of sufficient importance to warrant the publication of major position papers. We will see that people such as Freud, Watson, Pavlov, and Skinner are in the determinist camp, whereas people such as James, Jung, Allport, and Rogers are committed to a belief in freedom of choice. The problem of free will and determinism is one of the major sources of controversy between humanistic and behavioristic psychologies. It is an issue that has far-reaching implications for the kind of psychology we embrace. If human beings have some degree of freedom of choice, then a psychological system based on strict determinism cannot do justice to its subject matter. On the other hand, if causality is to be found in all natural processes, including human behavior, then belief in freedom of choice is unwarranted and may even work against our progress in understanding human experience and behavior. We should note that this issue is more alive now than it was at mid-century. It has been the subject of numerous books and articles in psychology (e.g., see Rychlak, 1988; Rychlak & Rychlak, 1990; Viney, 1990).

The doctrine of **free will** is the philosophical position that assumes that human beings make choices that are, to some degree, independent of antecedent conditions. The doctrine assumes that there is some sense in which the integrated personality can rise above genetic, chemical, physical, and social influences. According to this position, people have the capacity to anticipate alternatives, to weigh possible outcomes of various alternatives, and to compensate for past influences that enter into the decision-making processes. Behavior may be predictable to some extent, but there is also an inherent lack of predictability associated with behavior. To the extent that we can rise above causal forces in our lives, we may be viewed as rational or responsible creatures. Most advocates of free will do not attribute this quality to animals.

Most **libertarians** (those who believe in free will) agree that there are limitations imposed by environmental and genetic forces, but they argue nevertheless that there are compelling reasons to believe in freedom of choice. We will soon examine those reasons, but first we must attempt to specify more clearly what is meant by free choice. Imagine a hypothetical situation in which A is chosen over B. Imagine further that following the choice, we can now go back in time to the choice point. The libertarian would argue that it would now be possible for B to be chosen instead of A; a determinist would argue that it would not—

whatever caused A to be chosen would still be the same, so A would have to be chosen again. In our hypothetical example there would, of course, be no memory for the previous choice because we have gone back in time—everything, in every detail, is exactly as it was, yet the opposite choice could, the libertarian claims, be made. In other words, there is true spontaneity, or randomness, in the system. The libertarian is also likely to believe that the person or the self is not simply passive or reactive. Instead, the self acts on the environment with awareness and purpose. Let us consider some of the arguments that have been advanced in support of the libertarian position.

1. *Argument for an adequate explanation of human experience.* It is an empirical fact, about which even the determinist must agree, that we never have been and probably never will be able to achieve perfect predictions of even simple (let alone complex) behavior. For example, we will not write biographies in advance. Failures of prediction are a challenge to the adequacy of strict determinism. There is not a "good fit" between the philosophy of strict determinism and what we all clearly observe—namely, that there is an apparent spontaneity and unpredictable quality in human behavior. A more adequate explanation would result in a better fit between observation and theory. Belief in a moderate degree of freedom of choice is not embarrassed by regularities that we observe, but neither is it embarrassed by irregularities, uncertainties, and novelties.

2. *Logical contradictions in determinism.* Libertarians sometimes argue that, if determinism is true, a determinist cannot logically declare that *he* or *she* believes in determinism. Why? Because the he or she in the previous sentence is not the real believer. Belief is a mere consequence of antecedents. The very words *I believe in determinism* are, according to the theory of determinism, conditioned by more fundamental forces. Therefore, it is not that one believes in determinism but that consequences have come about in such a manner as to result in the statement *I believe in determinism.* The passive nature of the self that is implied in strict determinism is well illustrated by B. F. Skinner's (1983) statement about his autobiography,

"If I am right about human behavior, I have written the autobiography of a nonperson" (p. 32).

3. *Argument from morality.* The libertarian often argues that determinism makes a mess of morality. According to determinism, any immoral behavior can be explained in terms of causes that had no prevision of the ends they were achieving. Thus, individuals are not responsible for their actions. Indeed, the term *responsibility* is a hollow term—it means little more than ability to respond.

4. *Argument from indeterminism.* A final argument often employed by libertarians is that strict determinism is a pre-twentieth-century concept no longer applicable in the physical sciences. With the advent of quantum theory and Heisenberg's uncertainty principle, much of the physical world must now be viewed from a probabilistic rather than a strictly causal framework. The doctrine of **indeterminism** holds that it is not possible to apply strict cause and effect explanations in the world of subatomic particles. This well-known doctrine has led some individuals to argue that the principle of indeterminacy applies to other natural arenas. Thus, it is not unreasonable to assume that there is an inherent uncertainty about behavior.

Consider now the other side of the free will/determinism issue. The doctrine of **determinism** states that there are causes, both known and unknown, for every behavior or experience. We can illustrate the deterministic position by going back to our earlier hypothetical situation in which *A* is chosen over *B*. If we could now go back in time to the choice point, then *A* would once again be chosen over *B*. Taylor (1967b) defined *determinism* as the philosophical doctrine that "states that for everything that ever happens there are conditions such that, given them, nothing else could happen" (p. 359).

The great physicist, Albert Einstein, argued that "God doesn't play dice with the universe" (Michelmore, 1962, p. 128). Einstein was a determinist and to his death believed that the law of cause and effect operates at every level of reality. He once remarked that "God is clever, but . . . not malicious" (Michelmore, 1962, p. 111). Such a statement can be taken to mean that the world, be-

cause of its lawfulness, is knowable. It may be extremely difficult to discover causes and laws, but with persistence we *can* make discoveries—nature is not vicious or inherently unknowable. This is the optimistic side of determinism: Nature is knowable, and problems can be solved when cause–effect relations are discovered.

Belief in freedom of the will may discourage inquiry—indeed, such a belief may be partially responsible for the relatively late development of psychology as a science. The determinist offers a strong rebuttal to the argument from indeterminism. Even if indeterminism is applicable in the world of fundamental particles, it is not applicable in larger physical systems. Thus, a system as complicated, say, as a basketball, remains as a very reliable and determinate system, even if the behavior of the smallest physical units sustaining it are indeterminate. Historically, science has always proceeded on the assumption of the lawfulness or statistical regularity of its subject matter. But now let us turn to a few major arguments in defense of the deterministic position.

1. *Historical argument.* The history of the free will/determinism controversy is a history of victories for determinism and retreats for the theory of free will. With increasing knowledge of brain structure and function, adequate lawful explanations are extended to include an ever-widening spectrum of behaviors. The term *will* once occupied a great amount of space in psychology textbooks, but as knowledge has progressed, there has been less need for the term. As we examine selected topics in the history of neurology, we will see that, time and time again, mechanistic explanations have replaced explanations based on the will.

2. *Argument from morality.* The determinist is likely to counter the libertarian argument from morality by pointing out that belief in free will can also make a mess of morality. Some of the most barbaric and cruel practices have been justified on the grounds that the victim had made a free choice and now deserved a horrible punishment. The late Renaissance and early modern witch-hunts and burnings were often justified on the grounds that the accused had, of her own free will, made a pact with the devil.

3. *Argument from reasonable expectancy.* Without determinism there is no ground for any kind of reasonable expectation. As we think about our world, we find that we do have reasonable expectations based on the assumption that things are, after all, lawful. The world is not capricious—given a specific set of weather conditions, we can have a reasonable expectation that a Chinook wind will hit Boulder, Colorado, within a specified period of time. In a similar manner, we may reasonably expect to find a set of circumstances that have contributed to an emotional breakdown. We need not attribute the breakdown to an act of free choice. Most of us live our lives on the basis of reasonable expectations, and if an expectation is not confirmed, we usually assume that there was some value that we failed to plug into the equation—we seldom assume that nature is capricious.

There are excellent rebuttals that could be made to each of the arguments outlined for free will and for determinism. There are also additional arguments that can be advanced in defense of the two positions. As we examine the various systems of psychological thought, we will be outlining the positions of the various theorists on this issue. On occasion, we will take time to examine some of the arguments used by psychologists in defense of their positions. As we noted earlier, the issue is alive and well in contemporary psychology.

THE MIND–BODY PROBLEM

The mind–body problem is a branch of a subdisciplinary area of philosophy known as *ontology.* Philosophers have not always been consistent in the way they have used the term **ontology,** but for the present, the term may be defined as the study of the nature and relations of being. The question What is real? is an ontological question. Is the mind real? Is there a mind that is somehow independent from the brain? What is the relationship between the mind and the brain? Is there one fundamental reality (monism), two (dualism), or perhaps many (pluralism)? If there is more than one fundamental reality, how do the various types of reality coexist—and do they influence each other? Do psychologists study the mind or do they study

only behavior? All of these are ontological questions because they ask the essential question What is real? Let us examine some of the traditional solutions to the problems encountered in the study of ontology.

Monism

As previously noted, **monism** is the philosophical position that reality, whatever it is, is all of a piece. Everything belongs in some intimate way to everything else. It is, after all, a universe. Monism is appealing because it provides an elegant solution to the problem of ontology. If everything belongs in an intimate way to every other thing, then nothing is really alien or truly foreign because all things are part of one thing. What appears as foreign or alien is only a product of the present gaps in our knowledge. Monism offers the hope that there is potential unity of knowledge because we all study the same thing, but at different levels and from different vantage points. Monism, at least in some of its varieties, can nurture the belief that the field of psychology is ultimately reducible to the field of physics, or vice versa. Monism appeals to a need for simplicity, but a major problem is that monists have been unable to agree with each other about what the one and only reality is. Monism, in fact, comes in deeply opposed forms. Let us consider some of those forms and their implications for the mind–brain problem.

Materialism. **Materialism** is a monistic ontology characterized by the belief that matter is the fundamental constituent of all things. Accordingly, terms such as *mind, spirit,* and *consciousness* are understood exclusively in terms of the material, efficient, and formal operations of brain activity. It follows that there is no mind–brain problem as such because all so-called mental activity is ultimately reducible to physical, chemical, or physiological processes. Many of the key figures in the history of psychology have been materialists. Some of the more notable examples include Democritus, Thomas Hobbes, Julien Offray de la Mettrie, Herman von Helmholtz, Ivan Pavlov, and John B. Watson.

Idealism. A monistic alternative to materialism is encountered in the philosophical doctrine of idealism. **Idealism** emphasizes mind or spirit as the preeminent feature of life and thus represents a radical departure from materialism and a totally different emphasis with respect to the mind–body problem. According to idealism, as the term is employed in philosophy, the mental world of experience is foundational to all science and, for that matter, all knowledge. It would be impossible to know anything apart from consciousness or experience. Thus, the mental world (experience, awareness, consciousness) has priority—it is the only world to which we have immediate access. The material world is regarded as derivative—an intellectual or philosophical product that has its origin in the world of experience. For the idealist, psychology is the science that studies mental processes and experience. Further, an idealist would argue that all science begins with experience and is about experience. Thus, it is the mind or the mental world that has ontological status. The material world is a construction—a mere by-product of a more important reality. Many of the key figures in the history of psychology have identified with idealism. Examples include Plato, Gottfried Wilhelm Leibniz, George Berkeley, and Gustav Theodor Fechner.

Double-Aspect Monism. Another variety of monism displays a deep sensitivity to the legitimate claims of materialism and idealism. **Double-aspect monism** emphasizes the idea that there is a language for mental processes and a language for underlying physical processes but both languages refer to the same reality. We use words such as *mind, experience, consciousness, awareness,* and *thinking.* We also have a rich and growing language that refers to fundamental physical structures and processes such as neurons, neurotransmitters, cell assemblies, and synaptic transmission. According to double-aspect monism, both languages are legitimate but both refer to the same underlying reality approached from two perspectives. Benedict Spinoza, an early advocate of double-aspect theory, argued that human beings may be described in mentalistic terms or in the language of the physical sciences. The two languages

provide two different perspectives just as one may describe a coin from the perspective of the obverse or the reverse. According to double-aspect theory, the mind–body problem is largely a problem of language. The ontological problem, however, remains. What is real? Is reality reduced to words? Despite its problems, double-aspect theory can embrace a tolerant and robust approach to psychology that includes legitimate roles for descriptions that refer to mental and to physical processes.

Epiphenomenalism. A final version of monism known as epiphenomenalism is often classified as a dualistic position, but for reasons that shall soon be apparent, it is more accurately classified as a monistic position. An *epiphenomenon* is an appearance or a kind of "overflow" resulting from the operation of something that is more basic or fundamental.

Epiphenomenalism is a mind–brain position that regards mental processes (e.g., thought, consciousness, cognitions) as a kind of "overflow" or by-product of brain activity. The mental world has no independent status; it is a mere epiphenomenon or appearance. According to epiphenomenalism, causality always runs one way, from the physical to the mental. There is no mental causation because the mind has no independent status apart from its physical substrate. Epiphenomenalism is clearly a variation of materialism, but is sometimes regarded as dualistic because it accords status to the mental world as an appearance. However, because mental events have no causal efficacy and no independent status, this position might better be regarded as a kind of "soft" monistic materialism.

Dualism

In contrast with monism, **dualism** asserts that there are two fundamental orders of reality—mind and body. Each has ontic (i.e., real) status. Naively, most of us experience the reality of mental processes; we also experience the reality of the physical world. According to the dualistic position, we are assured that neither the mental nor the physical world is a mere appearance. For all of its popular appeal, at least to the Westerner, dualism presents a major problem. If there are two orders of reality, how do they get along with each other? Can one influence the other? Or can each influence the other and if so, how? Most of the dualistic mind–body positions address the issue of how mind and body get along with each other. Let us briefly examine the better-known positions.

Interactionism. According to **interactionism,** sometimes called the *commonsense* position, mental events are real—they influence each other and they influence bodily events. Bodily events also influence each other, and they influence mental events. Although interactionism sometimes appeals to common sense, it is not without a number of problems. For example, interactionists typically have difficulty specifying how an immaterial mental system can be causal with respect to a physical system (or, for that matter, how a material system can be causal with respect to an immaterial one). Second, a major problem centers around the locus of interaction. Where do mind and body influence each other? René Descartes, the most famous interactionist, addressed this problem of locus with considerable courage and suggested that the pineal gland, located in the center of the head, is the seat of interaction. Subsequently, we have found that people can function fairly well following a pinealectomy. In this sense, Descartes's theory of the locus of interaction was testable and it proved to be wrong. Descartes also failed to show how a mental event can influence physical events and vice versa. His followers have also been unsuccessful. So, interactionism, for all its commonsense appeal, leaves us with more questions than answers.

Psychophysical Parallelism. According to **psychophysical parallelism,** mental events are real and they may influence other mental events. Bodily events are also real, and they influence other bodily events. Mental events cannot, however, influence bodily events, and bodily events cannot influence mental events. The two orders of reality are nevertheless, by definition, parallel with each other. That is, whatever is happening in one order is, by definition, happening simultaneously in the other order. The philosopher Gottfried Wilhelm

Leibniz, the best-known advocate of this position, argued that mind and body can be viewed as analogous to two clocks that hang on the wall together and always give the same exact time. The two clocks are completely independent in that one has no causal influence over the other, yet they always agree with each other. According to Leibniz, mind and body are by definition parallel, but there is no causal influence between these two independent orders of reality.

Parallelism avoids the problems encountered in the interactionist position, but at a considerable expense—it flies in the face of common sense. Most of us, for example, assume that the experience of pain is causally connected to the chance encounter with the hot stove top and the resulting burn. The burn is mental and physical, and there is surely a causal connection between them. A more difficult problem is that parallelism implies a kind of preestablished harmony between mind and body. Explaining how preestablished harmony works might prove more difficult than explaining an interaction.

Emergentism. The philosophical position known as **emergentism,** in at least one of its variations, argues that mental processes are produced by brain processes, but are qualitatively different. For example, the experience of a toothache emerges out of complex neurological activity that may have been activated by decay or some kind of damage. The experience itself, though emerging out of bodily activity, is not adequately captured by descriptions of bodily activity. The experience seems to have a career of its own and a reality that is qualitatively set apart. An analogy from chemistry helps clarify emergentism. Salt is a product of sodium and chloride, yet the compound salt has properties that are unique and that make it different from predictable summations of sodium and chloride. Sodium alone or chloride alone can be lethal to the living organism, yet their combination in the form of salt is vital to life. The compound seems to have "emergent" properties of its own that are not adequately understood in terms of a simple summation of the separate elements. In a similar manner, mental processes, though produced by brain processes, are radically and qualitatively different. The experience of a sunrise, a poem, or a symphonic passage emerges from brain activity, but the global mental experience with its inspirational, affective, and associative meanings appears to be a reality unto itself quite different qualitatively from the underlying firing of neurons or the neurochemical activities in the synapse.

Emergentism is by no means a unified or consistent philosophical orientation. There are varieties of emergentism such as epiphenomenalism that are more consistent with monism, but other varieties that are more consistent with dualism. Thus, an emergentist might argue that causal forces work from the part to the whole and from the whole to the parts. Such an argument is consistent with a functional or pragmatic dualism if not a metaphysical dualism. Let us turn now to another approach to the problem of ontology.

Pluralism

A final commonsense belief is that we live in a "multiverse" of many separate orders of things. Ontological **pluralism** embraces the reality of mind and body but also insists that these two orders do not exhaust the possibilities. In a discussion of ontological pluralism, MacCormac (1990) pointed out that concepts arise "from physical brain processes . . . but they do not always find their origin solely in brain activity" (p. 417). A concept may have its origin in any of a great number of cultural sources, but because it depends for its expression on the physical system, its causal sources can be highly diverse. An ontological pluralist may believe that there are many separate real things, including fundamentally different types of conscious experience and other orders of reality that do not obey any of the rules that we know. Pluralism raises even more problems than interactionism. For each separate reality we posit, we must now struggle with the problem of the interaction of that reality with others. For example, as the mind–body theorist must struggle with how mind and body influence each other, the classical theist must struggle with the problem of theodicy (the relation of God to the world). It is little wonder that those with a unity-loving nature are repulsed by pluralism—it is a messy philosophy. But the pluralist would insist that the world is not simple. Pluralism has been a topical subject in philosophy throughout the twentieth century (e.g., see Ford, 1990; James, 1909/1977; Reck, 1990).

A major variation on pluralism could be labeled **attributive pluralism.** This position emphasizes the relationship between an object and the words that are used to describe the object. People, as users of words, may attribute any of a number of qualities to an object. For example, to the question What is a sunset? a plurality of descriptive modes is possible. Let us call on a physicist, a physiologist, a psychologist, an artist, a poet, and an astronomer and ask each the question What is a sunset? In studying the answers, we will be confronted with a delightful array of explanatory modes. After all is said and done, we may be invited by a musician, offended at being left out of the group of scholars, to come and listen to a new composition "The Sunset Symphony." For truly sensitive people, the sunset can be best captured in an auditory experience. But, we may ask, what is the real sunset? Is it that of the physicist with all the elegant mathematical formulas, the physiologist with the impressive monitoring of retinal images and occipital activity, the psychologist with the analysis of the perceptual process, or the interesting normative testing on what sunsets mean to different people, or shall we let the poet have the last word? In order to adjudicate the claims of the various participants in our inquiry, we might call in a panel of philosophers consisting of two monists and two pluralists. The monists agree that the true sunset is one thing but disagree on what that one thing is—for one it is physical, for the other, experiential. One of the pluralists argues that there are many objective sunsets. The other contends that there are many legitimate descriptive modes—sunsets are, after all, what we describe them to be. The most fundamental reality is, therefore, our words. But the other pluralist insists that there are realities beyond our words.

Let us now leave the mind–body problem, with the comment that the various schools and systems of psychology we encounter will disagree with each other on this issue. We will encounter materialists, double-aspect theorists, pluralists, interactionists, and others. A major key to understanding a given school or system will be to assess that school's or system's position on the mind–body problem.

Psychogeny

A close relative of the study of mind–body relations is encountered in the problem of psychogeny (*sy KAW gin ee*). The term **psychogeny** is derived from the Greek term **psuche** (*SU kee*), which has been translated as spirit, soul, or mind. Each of these terms has different connotations, but they also share something in common in that they each refer to a principle of existence that embodies mentalistic concepts such as awareness, consciousness, sentience, or experience. Psychogeny may be defined as the study of the origin of psuche or the study of theories of the origin of psuche. Two very broad theories are briefly reviewed in the materials that follow, but more detailed discussion is available (see Viney & Woody, 1995).

Identity Theory. Two key features of **identity theory** are that (1) psuche is instilled in the primitive biological substratum of the organism at a given point in time, and (2) there is continuity or identity between the psychically endowed biological substratum and the later mature, self-reflective, fully conscious adult. Identity theorists have never been able to agree with each other about the time of infusion of psuche into the body. For centuries, theologians argued that an embryo becomes human at forty days if it is male and eighty days if it is female (see De Rosa, 1988, p. 347). In recent years, there has been a strongly held popular belief that psuche is instilled at fertilization. Kuhse and Singer (1993), in their work on embryo experimentation, note that "what this claim amounts to is that the newly fertilized egg, the early embryo, and I are in some sense of the term, the same individual" (p. 66). Because of its emphasis on the independence of psuche, identity theory is consistent with idealism and some forms of dualism. Although identity theory has popular appeal, it is not without a host of problems, many of which have surfaced from recent work in embryo experimentation.

An example of a major problem with identity theory is encountered in research on microsurgical sectioning of fertilized eggs. According to some forms of identity theory, conception (the fertilization of an egg) marks the entry point of psuche into its material substrate. A colony of cells (a morula or blastocyst) develops following conception and results, according to identity theory, in one body and one psuche. But we now know that following conception the morula can be surgically divided resulting in two, three, four, or more individuals. Each piece can be transplanted into a host and we can artificially create twins, triplets, or quadruplets. Such procedures are used in the production of dairy cattle (see Seidel & Elsden, 1989) and are in theory, if not practice, available to humans (see Elmer-DeWitt, 1993). At conception, according to identity theory, there was one psuche and one body. But assume now that the developing blastocyst or morula is cut in half and there are now two bodies. If both bodies possess a psuche, the second psuche must have been instilled *after* conception. Thus, the theory of the entry of psuche exclusively at the time of conception is severely compromised.

There are other problems for identity theory. For example, in the early days of pregnancy, two separate colonies of cells (twins) developing in the uterus may float together and now form one individual—a chimera (see Austin, 1989). If both bodies possessed a psuche prior to floating together, what happened to the second psuche after the two came together? Clearly, for all of its popular appeal, identity theory is not without serious problems. We turn now to a consideration of a second theory of psychogeny.

Emergentism Revisited. **Emergentism,** as a mind–body position, contains an implicit theory of the origin of psuche. Psuche, according to this position, has no independent origin of its own, but rather develops with the developing body. Further, the complexity and the functional properties of the mental arena are dependent on the health and well-being of the organism. Emergentism avoids some of the problems of identity theory, but comes with a set of problems of its own.

One of the major problems associated with emergentism has to do with the arbitrary time of emergence. According to the theory, psuche is associated with some arbitrary level of neural complexity, but how much complexity is required? Is there some remote sense in which a single cell is conscious? Is a colony of cells, without a nervous system and without a circulatory system, conscious? At the other end of the scale, one might insist that consciousness is not consciousness until it is aware of itself. But how do we know when an organism has the capacity for reflective self-awareness? Emergentism suffers the same problem as identity theory. Neither theory provides a satisfactory scientific answer regarding the time of infusion or emergence of psuche into a material substrate.

Another problem for emergentism has to do with the experienced continuity of consciousness. It is the same *I* or *me* today as it was many years ago. Although my world may have been unstable resulting in experiences I could never have imagined, and though I may not believe the same things I once did, it is nevertheless the same me that has done the changing. The persistent and obstinate nature of experienced continuity challenges emergentism. We live in a constantly changing world that should result in major personality shifts, yet most of us experience ourselves to be remarkably consistent over time.

The emergentist might argue that there are pathological discontinuities and disassociations in personality, and these often result from environmental changes or neurological damage just as an emergentist might predict. Such a rebuttal appears appropriate. Discontinuities in personality may well present a challenge to identity theory with its emphasis on a somewhat autonomous psuche. But it is also true that continuity of personality, especially in the face of change or even crisis, presents a challenge to emergentism with its emphasis on a more fragile and dependent psuche. There are many other problems and issues, including some interesting moral issues, associated with both theories (see Viney & Woody, 1995).

The relationship of mind and brain, like the problem of free will and determinism, is neither a relic of the past nor exclusively a philosophical problem. Indeed, there may be a greater outpouring of scholarly work on this problem at the dawn of the twenty-first century then at any other time in history. Contemporary philosophers, biologists, neuroscientists, computer scientists, and psychologists have produced a wealth of thoughtful approaches to the problem (see, for example, Buncombe, 1995; Crick, 1994; Dennett, 1991; Edelman, 1992; Searle, 1992, 1995a, 1995b; and Tye, 1995). The mystery of the mental arena remains as elusive as ever, but contemporary advances in the neurosciences, the computing sciences, biology, psychology, and philosophy may provide additional pieces for a puzzle that is of unparalleled complexity.

In this chapter, we have attempted to sample some of the major philosophical problems that have been of special interest to psychologists. There are additional important problems. Do human beings have an essential built-in moral nature (i.e., Are we morally good, evil, or simply neutral at birth?). What constitutes an adequate explanation? Can we explain best with names, numbers, analogies, or models? What is the appropriate unit of study in psychology? Should we focus mainly on part processes such as reflex activity or should we focus on the whole organism in its natural environment? These and other issues will surface as we consider the various systems of psychology. Detailed treatments of philosophical issues in psychology (e.g., Wertheimer, 1972; Eacker, 1972, 1975; Rubenstein & Slife, 1988) are recommended for those with special interests in this area.

REVIEW QUESTIONS _____

1. Define the term *epistemology.*

2. Distinguish between a priori and a posteriori knowledge.

3. Differentiate between nativist and empiricist accounts of depth perception.

4. Briefly explain at least five different ways of assessing truth.

5. According to Karl Popper, what is the key distinguishing feature between a legitimate science and pseudoscience?

6. Trace Kuhn's view on the development of science. What does Kuhn mean by terms such as *normal science* and *paradigm*?

7. If you were arguing for Feyerabend's philosophy of science, what evidence would you employ?

8. List and briefly describe Aristotle's four kinds of causation.

9. Distinguish between intrinsic and extrinsic teleology.

10. Advance three arguments in support of determinism and three arguments in defense of free will.

11. Outline two monistic and two dualistic approaches to mind and brain.

12. Which of the various mind–brain positions seems most adequate to you? What are some of the problems with this position?

13. Outline two major problems for identity theory encountered in recent research on embryo experimentation.

CHAPTER 3

ANCIENT PSYCHOLOGICAL THOUGHT

We must not be too sure of the ignorance of our ancestors.
—Will Durant (1954)

The story of psychology begins with early curiosity about such problems as the nature of memory, sensation, feeling, motivation, and adjustment. The story is told in ancient manuscripts and documents such as the Vedas of the Hindus, the Talmud of the Hebrews, the Avesta of the Zoroastrians, and the early Greek epic narratives and poems such as *The Iliad*. These and other ancient writings are rich in speculative as well as practical psychology. The ancients were interested both in the nature of psychological processes and in the treatment for psychological disturbances. Though there is a common theme of interest in psychological topics in all ancient cultures, such cultures often existed in relative physical and intellectual isolation. Accordingly, historical development in early times is not as coherent or linear as it is in later periods of history. Nevertheless, even if the story is a bit disjointed, it is worth telling, so let us briefly review some selected examples of psychological thought from several ancient civilizations and then turn our attention to early Greece.

EARLY CHINESE PSYCHOLOGIES

In a survey of the social history of Chinese psychology, Petzold (1987) called attention to "the special sensitivity of psychology to political and ideological influences" (p. 213). Early psychological thought in China was clearly tied to a larger worldview organized around the number 5. The Chinese believed there were five basic elements: wood, fire, metal, earth, and water. They also believed there were five basic sense organs,

including the ear, the eye, the nose, the mouth, and the body, and five corresponding sensations of hearing, vision, smell, taste, and touch. Colors, smells, sounds, and tastes were also organized around the number 5; for example, the five tastes were sweet, sour, salt, bitter, and acid. Basic colors were thought to consist of green, red, yellow, black, and white, whereas basic smells were identified as burning, fragrant, goatish, rank, and rotten. In later developments there were attempts to identify the basic emotions, parts of the body, and virtues. In one early classification the basic emotions or impulses were identified as anger, joy, desire, sorrow, and fear (Fernberger, 1935, p. 547).

The number 5 also served as a guide to the types of human relations. Confucius (551–479 B.C.), easily the most well-known Chinese philosopher, held that the types of human relations include "ruler and minister, father and son, elder brother and younger brother, husband and wife, and one friend and another" (Chan, 1967, p. 189). The five, in this case, illustrate the paternal emphasis in Chinese culture. Confucius was interested largely in the moral life and harmony among human beings. Although he was a great humanist, his teachings were counterproductive for the development of some of the sciences. For example, his belief that the body is sacred was used for centuries as an argument against dissection.

One of the greatest Chinese philosophers, Hsün Tzu (c. 298–c. 212 B.C.), is sometimes compared with Aristotle. The comparison is appropriate because Hsün Tzu, like Aristotle, was a naturalist who emphasized the regularity and orderliness of nature. He argued for rational and empirical methods and against superstition. He believed that nature goes its own way and we cannot count on divine intervention. Accordingly, he said that it was inappropriate to seek to control natural phenomena such as rain by praying. Hsün Tzu was a strong advocate of the importance of learning in human life. He believed basic human nature is evil, but we can attain goodness through education.

Ancient Chinese philosophy, and hence its psychology, was dominated by the concepts of **yin** and **yang**. Yin and yang were viewed initially as opposite cosmic forces, but later were seen as both opposite and complementary. Yang is associated with such qualities as force, hardness, masculinity, heat, and dryness, whereas yin is associated with such qualities as weakness, softness, femininity, hearing, coldness, and moistness. Equilibrium between yin and yang was viewed as essential to physical and psychological well-being and to social balance. Much of Chinese medical and psychological practice was aimed at restoring and maintaining balance or equilibrium. For example, acupuncture, dating from the third millenium B.C., was designed either to stimulate or to drain hypothetical secretions necessary to the maintenance of balance. Other therapies were also aimed at the restoration or balance of yin and yang forces. Castiglioni (1941), for example, noted the importance of organ therapy by pointing out that warriors "drank blood or ate the liver of tiger" (p. 103). Such a practice was thought to increase yang, and with increased yang came greater courage.

The early Chinese emphasized the importance of mental processes. Indeed, in Chinese thought, the mind can play a dominant role, whereas the body can be viewed as a servant. This does not necessarily imply a radical separation of mind and body because it was recognized that mental processes are nurtured in the physical substrate of the body. Chinese thought opened the door to a truly physiological psychology whereby psychological processes are as important as physiology.

BABYLONIA

Babylonia, one of the greatest ancient civilizations, had an extensive and lasting influence on other nations in the Mediterranean basin. Many of the intellectual traditions of the Greeks, Egyptians, Jews, and Arabs can be traced to the Babylonians. The ruins of Babylon, the key city in the Babylonian empire, are situated about sixty miles south of the present city of Baghdad. The ruins are close to the old riverbeds of the Tigris and Euphrates.

The Babylonians had a keen interest in mathematics, geography, astronomy, law, medicine, and language. Writing was an important art among the elite and skilled Babylonians. Many of their cuneiform writings on clay tablets have been deciphered by scholars during the past one hundred years. Two of the most famous Babylonian works include the Epic of Gilgamesh and the Code of Hammurabi.

The world for the Babylonians was populated by thousands of major and minor gods associated with everything from astronomical events to taxation. The gods of Babylon were limited only by the human imagination. They were anthropomorphic, interested in the affairs of human beings, sometimes friendly and sometimes hostile. Help from the gods was invoked through magic rites, prayers, incantations, and the special powers and methods of priests and physicians.

The power of the gods was challenged by a universe of demons who, like the gods, were specialized. Alexander and Selesnick (1966) pointed out that "each disease had its specific demon. Insanity was caused by the demon Idta" (p. 20). Demons were exorcised through special medicines (selected plants were thought to have the power to kill demons), confessions, magic rites, and other procedures designed to bring the individual back into harmony with beneficent transcendent forces. The Babylonians emphasized prevention as well as treatment. Devils could be warded off with charms, religious symbols, and virtuous behavior. It was also wise to avoid women who were thought to have the power to entice devils into inhabiting an individual.

The Babylonians represent a curious blend of empirical and magical-religious approaches to science. They left surprisingly accurate descriptions of certain diseases and their astronomy was sufficiently advanced to permit predictions of eclipses. They were interested in human and animal anatomy and they showed considerable mathematical sophistication. However, there was a constant tension between empirical–rational and superstitious and magical explanations; in that tension they were not unique.

EGYPT

As in many early civilizations, Egyptian science, to say nothing of psychology, cannot be easily separated from prevailing religious perspectives. There were few things the polytheistic Egyptians could not find to worship. A great variety of plants and animals, the sun, the moon, the stars, rivers, mountains, and people all served as objects of worship. It is well known that Egyptian religion placed an unusual emphasis on immortality. This emphasis served as part of the motivation for the art of mummification and elaborate Egyptian burial customs. The Egyptians believed that the ability of the soul to survive after death and to make the transition to immortality is related to the quality of the preservation of the body.

There is considerable evidence that many of the Egyptians viewed the heart as the seat of mental activity (see, e.g., Laver, 1972). When we consider the relation between strong emotions and heart activity, it should come as no surprise that some of the ancients viewed the heart, rather than the brain, as the source of mental life. Though the ancients observed correlations between head injuries and disorders of speech, memory, and movement, they could still argue that the brain is subservient to the heart. Although most Egyptian source material points to the heart as the seat of mental life, the Egyptians were apparently the first to provide a description of the brain. In his classic book, *A History of Medicine*, Castiglioni (1941) pointed out that many Egyptians recognized the brain as the source of mental activity (p. 57).

Laver (1972) noted that the Egyptians placed great emphasis on the importance of names. There was a close identity of name and thing so that the cursing of a name or the destruction of a name could have great psychological importance. The Egyptian emphasis on the importance of names may have carried over later into Jewish culture.

It is of interest that the women of Egypt achieved higher social status than their counterparts in most ancient and modern cultures. Women held political offices, took the initiative in courtship if they wished, owned property, made formal proposals for marriage, and, in general, held positions of considerable power in their homes. It is true that the pharaohs and some of the wealthy had harems and that there were captive women as well as men. Nevertheless, in the majority of common monogamous families, women enjoyed unusual status and power.

One of the well-known hallmarks of Egyptian civilization was its superior engineering. The construction of great canals and the pyramids required engineering skills that are a marvel even in the twentieth century. Egyptian science, with the possible exception of geometry, was less impressive. The Egyptians' medicine was a blend of superstition and empirical observation. They believed that insects, filth, and devils were responsible for disease. They treated disease with rituals, incantations, rest, surgery, enemas, and medications designed for ingestion or external applications. The medications were made from plants, honey, animal dung, oil, blood, and animal organs. The Egyptians placed considerable emphasis on hygiene and regularly practiced circumcision and fumigation of the vagina. Alexander and Selesnick (1966) noted that the Egyptians "recognized the emotional disorder that the Greeks later called 'hysteria.'" It was assumed that an emotional disorder was caused by a uterus that had wandered from its normal resting location, and the vagina was fumigated in attempt to bring the uterus back to its normal resting location. This explanation for hysteria (named after the Greek word for uterus, *hysteron*) remained for centuries—even into the late Middle Ages.

OTHER ANCIENT EASTERN PSYCHOLOGIES

Some of the oldest of civilizations, dating from the fourth millennium B.C., are known to have existed in what is now India and Pakistan. Some of these civilizations enjoyed well-constructed houses connected to sewers, streets, shops, and baths. Bronze and copper utensils and pottery have been discovered, along with jewelry and copper weapons.

Some of the earliest psychological thought from the area that is now India and Pakistan comes out of the ancient **Vedas**. The Vedas are the oldest sacred books of India, dating according to orthodox Hindus from the beginning of time, and according to historical scholars from earlier than 1000 B.C. The term *Veda* means knowledge. Philosophic knowledge is typically contained in Vedic treatises called **Upanishads.**

Examination of verses from the Vedas and Upanishads affords a sense of early Indian beliefs on selected psychological topics. A major theme centers on the problems of knowledge and desire. Knowledge via rational *or* empirical methods is deemphasized. As we will see, the Greeks debated the relative merits of the senses versus the intellect. In ancient Indian philosophy, neither is to be trusted. The emphasis was on the development of the deepest respect for the mystery of life. Intuition and the development of spiritual sensitivities were encouraged. The Indians believed that a false consciousness, inordinate desire, and an undisciplined nature are the inevitable by-products of too much involvement with the particulars of the world. The emphasis was on austerity, self-denial, and cleansing of the excessive desires of the senses by fasting and by meditation.

Perhaps because the senses were not to be trusted, they were not the subjects of intensive study; neither were there significant advances in anatomy. The Indians were, however, careful observers of pregnancy and believed that personality traits of the infant were traceable to characteristics of the mother during pregnancy. An ill-tempered mother might give birth to an epileptic, an alcoholic mother might have a child with a weak memory, and an immoral mother could give birth to an effeminate son. Women thus had the potential for extensive influence and, possibly for this reason, were subjected to stringent controls. The following texts from the Code of Manu illustrate the point. "No act is to be done according to her own will by a young girl, a young woman, or even by an old woman. . . . The good wife of a husband . . . must never do anything disagreeable to him" (see Welles, 1957, p. 33). Women were always to be subjected to the will of their father, husband, or sons.

Indians believed that diseases result from devils, filth, or imbalance of humors. Mental disorders could result from excessive emotional expression. To combat disease, the Indians used charms, incantations, meditation, and exorcism. They emphasized personal hygiene and, following Siddhartha Gautama's (The Buddha or Enlighted One) teachings, they engaged in psychotherapeutic exercises designed to induce a quiescent spirit and resignation.

THE HEBREWS

Jewish philosophy and psychology must be understood in the context of radical monotheism—a religious faith that stood in marked contrast with the polytheisms of the Babylonians, Egyptians, and Greeks. Jewish life and thought were conditioned by one of the most famous religious expressions in history, "Hear, O Israel, the Lord our God, the Lord is One." The task of every Jew was to know the one God by properly understanding the word of God as set forth in the Torah. Hence, scholarly activity was held in high regard and has remained so through the centuries.

The Hebrews viewed God as an all-powerful source of reward and punishment. At the same time, there was a strong emphasis on human responsibility and freedom of choice. Human beings were also viewed as victims of a natural duplicity. On the one hand, they are creatures of the flesh, manifesting self-serving biological drives, but they are also spiritual creatures with a spark of the divine and capable of self-renunciation for community benefit. On occasion, the Hebrews embraced a kind of fatalism, but the stronger tradition might be characterized in terms of an if–then belief system. *If* the people would obey God's commandments, *then* beneficial consequences would follow, but failure to obey results in punishment. The future is open and rewards or punishments are contingent on human behavior—this basic orientation has pervaded much of Western thought.

It is clear that the Hebrews had some rather well-developed notions of mental disorders. Rotenberg and Diamond (1971) provided evidence that the Hebrews had a concept of moral insanity or psychopathy. The Hebrews also had a concept of disorganized behavior, illustrated in the description in Daniel 4:33 of Nebuchadnezzar's isolation from people and his apparent delusion that he was an animal. According to the Hebrews, madness or mental illness might be brought about by the anger of God (Deut. 28:28), but such anger was thought to be initiated by human disobedience. Demonological approaches to mental and physical ailments are also encountered in Hebrew thought and later in Christianity, but such approaches have always been in tension with Hebrew concepts of the absolute oneness of God. This tension will be illustrated later in the philosophy of Spinoza (discussed in Chapter 7).

The Hebrews gave the leading role to the man in marriage but the Talmud admonished men to honor their wives above themselves. The Hebrew people were unique in their regard for children. The "fruit of the womb" was viewed as a gift from God (Ps. 127:3) and children's children as "the crown of old men" (Prov. 17:6). At the same time, the duties imposed on children were extensive. "Honor thy father and thy mother: that thy days may be long upon the land" was literally true, because wayward or rebellious children could be put to death.

It should be noted that infanticide was widely practiced in most ancient cultures and may, in certain periods, have been practiced in a limited fashion by some of the Hebrews who were influenced by Egyptian or Babylonian beliefs. In most of the countries of the Mediterranean basin, there is impressive evidence that unwanted children were exposed on hillsides, sacrificed to the gods, thrown into rivers, or sold to strangers (see DeMause, 1974, ch. 1). Children were often destroyed because of real or imagined defects and child sacrifice was sometimes demanded by religious belief. Girls were victims of infanticide far more frequently than boys.

PERSIA

The great Persian empire, once as large as the continental United States, included the countries surrounding the eastern Mediterranean and extended east to the Indus River in India. It included much of what is now Iran and Afghanistan. The Persian empire had its beginnings about 900 B.C. and thrived from about 600 B.C. It ended with Alexander the Great's conquest in 331 B.C. For about 200 years the Persians were contemporaries and rivals with the Greeks.

Persia was the birthplace of the Zoroastrian religion, which had its origin in the teachings of a prophet named Zarathustra. The teachings of the God Ahura-Mazda were said to have been revealed to Zarathustra and the holy book of the Zoroastrians was called the **Avesta** (sometimes the **Zend-Avesta**). Although Zarathustra taught that there is one God, his followers saw the world in terms of a struggle between Angro-Mainyus, the prince of devils, and Ahura-Mazda. This theological dualism had considerable influence on the belief systems of the Persians. Diseases and emotional disorders were viewed as the work of the devil and the treatments were predictable: exorcism, incantations, and magical and religious rites. Human beings were viewed as the testing ground for the forces of good and evil. Human beings, according to Zarathustra, have free will, so they can choose to follow Ahura-Mazda or Angro-Mainyus.

Crimes were viewed as crimes against Ahura-Mazda and punishments could be severe—public whippings, crucifixion, mutilations, and stonings were common. The intellectual climate was not friendly to the growth of philosophy or science.

GREECE

MacLeod (1975) is one of many historians who suggested that the period from 600 to 300 B.C. in Greece was one of the great creative periods in human history. That the Greeks were influenced by the Egyptians and other earlier peoples of the Mediterranean and that ideas sometimes attributed to the Greeks had earlier origins in other cultures is clear. Nevertheless, many of the intellectual traditions of the Western world can be traced back to the Greeks.

The earliest barbaric Greeks evidently occupied the isle of Crete and other smaller islands off the coast of the mainland as early as 3000 B.C. As with other cultures, the distinction between legend and history is often blurred. For example, Agamemnon was once viewed as a legendary figure and Troy was viewed as a legendary place that existed only in Homer's tales. But the view that Troy was only a legend was shattered in 1871 when Heinrich Schliemann made the greatest archaeological discovery of the nineteenth century: The ruins of Troy were uncovered (see Schliemann, 1875/1968; Schuchhardt, 1891/1971). Schliemann's discovery underscores the difficulties of assessing the stories that came down from the past. Our incredulity can be unwarranted as often as our credulity.

The reasons for the growth of intellectual curiosity in Greece are not understood. Geographically it was far from the best, but not the worst of locations for the support of life. Only about 25 percent of the land on the rocky peninsula was fit for growing crops, but fishing and hunting provided food and forests provided fuel. The climate was variable but well suited much of the time to outdoor activity. The institution of slavery also provided leisure time for upper classes. For whatever reasons, the Greeks were able to turn their attention to intellectual activities that produced remarkable accomplishments in science, literature, philosophy, political theory, and the arts. Some of the earliest naturalistic approaches to psychological topics are products of the Greek mind.

The Cosmologists

The earliest Greek philosophers were interested in the nature of the universe (cosmology) and the origin of the universe (cosmogony). The cosmologists introduced concepts such as evolution and atomic theory that are important today. The cosmologists also speculated about topics of a psychological nature.

Thales. Thales (*THAY luhs*) of Miletus was probably born a few years before 625 B.C. What little we know of him comes from the writings of Aristotle, Plato, and the historian Herodotus. Thales may be viewed as one of the pivotal figures who ushered in a scientific era that replaced earlier mystical and religious interpretations of the world. He is best known for his position that water is the primal substance of the world from which other things derive. We do not know Thales's rea-

sons for the selection of water as a natural substrate, nor does he tell us how things are derived from water. It is, of course, readily observable that life is supported by water, which, in its three forms (solid, liquid, and vapor or steam), seems to imitate or characterize the world as we know it. Thales, possibly under the influence of Egyptian cosmology, believed that the earth was somewhat like a flat-rimmed saucer that floated on the sea.

Thales's interest in the primal substance of the world was complemented by his interest in the problem of movement. What makes it possible for a thing to move or what is responsible for movement? That is one of the enduring philosophical problems and the focus of a centuries-old tension between mechanistic and animistic explanations of the world. Thales's interest in the problem of movement was manifested by his curiosity about the forces at work in magnets. There is some evidence from the writings of Aristotle (Kirk & Raven, 1957, pp. 93–95) that Thales believed that magnetic stone possesses soul. Apparently, Thales believed that soul has kinetic and motive force that makes movement possible. So far as we know, Thales did not speculate about how the primal physical substrate of the world (water) interacts with soul.

Anaximander. Thales's successor and pupil was Anaximander of Miletus (610–c. 547 B.C.). Like Thales, Anaximander (*uh NAHK suh man der*) was interested in the basic element from which other things derive, but he could not agree that water was the appropriate substance. How could water be the basic substrate of fire? If water could not serve as the basic substance, neither could any other single thing that we observe. The matter we see (water, wood, rocks, etc.) is, however, a manifestation of something more basic, but that something is not apparent to the senses. Anaximander believed the basic stuff of the universe was infinite and formless. He named it *apeiron,* meaning "without boundary."

Anaximander believed in a succession of worlds, each of which goes through a cyclical process of beginning, development, and decay. In the beginning, some of the waters dry up and form the land—a crust on which land creatures can develop. Life develops out of the interaction of opposites—moisture and fire, coolness and heat. Anaximander believed that the first creatures were encased in a protective hard surface. As such creatures aged, they moved out of the waters onto the dry land, and their protective body surface gradually changed. Often viewed as the first recorded evolutionary theorist, Anaximander advanced the position that humans came from other species. He pointed out that, unlike many other creatures, humans have a long period of dependency, so the first human infants must have been nurtured by some other creature. Originally, humans came from creatures that were somewhat like fish (see Kirk & Raven, 1957, p. 141). Because of the dependency resulting from a long infancy, Anaximander believed that the first humans could not have survived by themselves.

Anaximander is often credited with constructing the first world map; he may also have been the first Greek to construct a sundial. His interests ranged over all the sciences, from astronomy to biology.

Anaximenes.   Anaximenes (c. 588–c. 524 B.C.) was also a member of the Milesian school of Thales and Anaximander. Like Thales and Anaximander, Anaximenes (*uh NAHK suh meh neez*) was interested in cosmological problems. He taught that air is the primal substance of the universe and that it becomes other things through rarefaction and condensation. Through condensation, air becomes clouds; through further condensation, clouds become rain; rain becomes hail. With further condensation, water becomes land and condensed land is rocks. Through rarefaction, heavy, windy air becomes lighter air, and very light air becomes fire. Condensation is associated with coldness and rarefaction with heat. Earthquakes could result from disturbances of air—too much moisture or extensive drought.

Anaximenes taught that the soul is rarefied air and that air is the principle of living things. He taught that the soul holds the body together. The basis for such a belief might be found in the idea that the body decomposes when the breath of life or soul leaves the body, but this interpretation may represent a departure from the historical Anaximenes. He also believed that the world is held together by cosmic air and that the air is a god. The difficulties of interpreting Anaximenes's theory of the soul are discussed by Kirk and Raven (1957, pp. 158–162).

Pythagoras.   Pythagoras (c. 580–c. 500 B.C.) exemplifies a different kind of philosophical orientation. Born on the island of Samos, he is one of the enduring figures in Western intellectual history. The term **philosophy,** constructed from *philo* (meaning love) and *sophia* (meaning knowledge or wisdom), was likely coined by Pythagoras, who called himself a philosopher—one who loves wisdom. Pythagoras represented a colorful mixture of pure and applied interests. He had a deep love for the search for abstract and universal principles, but as the founder of a religious society, he was also interested in the application of philosophy and science to ethical conduct and the good life.

With Pythagoras, we encounter a shift of emphasis from explanations based on primordial substances to explanations based on the formal mathematical properties of things. The Pythagoreans believed that all things have number—the heavens, the earth, and objects on the earth. With the Pythagoreans, we encounter another shift of emphasis. Interest in cosmology was now complemented by an interest in human problems. The Pythagoreans viewed the brain as the seat of mental life; they were also among the first Westerners to use music as therapy.

Their religious emphasis resulted in prescriptions that had psychological significance. The Pythagoreans believed in immortality and the transmigration of souls. For this reason, they advised against eating animals—by killing an animal one might be invading the habitat of the soul of an ancestor. They emphasized discipline and balance and an avoidance of the expression of too much laughter. Presumably, the expression of strong emotion could undermine dignity and character. The Pythagoreans valued study, especially before speaking on matters pertaining to Pythagorean belief. Their beliefs led to many prohibitions and injunctions that must have resulted in compulsive behavior. Examples abound: There were prohibitions against putting the left shoe on first, wearing rings, looking in mirrors beside lamps, eating beans, or allowing swallows to nest under your roof.

It is of interest that women played important roles in the school established by Pythagoras. Indeed, his wife **Theana** was apparently an accomplished philosopher who played a key role in educational activities of the society. Waithe (1987b) listed the names of numerous women associated with Pythagorean societies over a period from the sixth to the second centuries B.C. Later, several women were associated with neo-Pythagorean schools as late as the third century A.D. One of the earliest Pythagoreans was **Myia,** a daughter of Pythagoras and Theana. Myia provided some of the earliest advice on the care of infants. She emphasized the importance of milk and bland foods, moderation in temperature, good ventilation, and soft clothing. Her emphasis was always on moderation and balance (see Waithe, 1987b, pp. 15–16). The same emphasis on balance is found in a fragment on human nature written by one of the later Pythagorean women named **Aesara.** She argued that physical and mental health result from harmony. She was one of the first to emphasize a kind of homeostatic or balance theory of health.

Xenophanes. Another group of pre-Socratic philosophers is sometimes called the Eleatics because their school was located in Elea, a town in southern Italy. The Eleatics turned to a different set of problems. Their major concern was with epistemology. The first of the Eleatics was Xenophanes (*zeh NAH fuh neez*) born about 560 B.C. in Colophon. Xenophanes is known primarily for his epistemological skepticism and his attack on the anthropomorphic gods of Homer. He distinguished between knowledge and opinion and declared that human beings do not have certain knowledge—only opinion. Xenophanes argued for a strict monotheism and against Homeric polytheism with its emphasis on gods that could be guilty of jealousy, deceit, adultery, and other human actions and emotions. In an early psychological approach to religion, he noted that Ethiopians view their gods as Ethiopian and that Thracians view their gods as Thracian. He thought it strange that people view their gods as wearing clothes. He argued that if animals could draw, they would draw their gods to look like themselves. The one god, above all gods, according to Xenophanes, is in no way (physically or mentally) similar to mortals.

Xenophanes taught that a new sun, made of ignited clouds, arises each morning and goes on in a straight line forever. The idea that there are many suns may have been motivated by Xenophanes's antipolytheistic views. Xenophanes was interested in other meteorological and astronomical problems, but his major importance was to epistemology. He was one of the first to make an explicit distinction between knowledge and opinion.

Parmenides. Parmenides (*pahr MEHN ih deez*) of Elea, born around 515 B.C., is another pivotal figure in pre-Socratic philosophy. He is pivotal because his work focused attention on the problem of rationalism versus empiricism and the related problem of being versus becoming. Parmenides also had some interest in the mechanisms of perception. His influence on later philosophers, especially Plato, was extensive.

Parmenides speaks through a poem that was thought to have been entitled "On Nature." The poem relays a message from a goddess on "the way of truth" and "the way of seeming." The way of seeming is the way mortals view the world; the way of truth is the way an immortal might see the world. There is controversy surrounding the appropriate interpretation of various parts of Parmenides's poem, but it is clear that he taught that reason and the senses provide us with contrasting information about the world. Through the senses, we are aware of plurality, division, and change. But reason can show that "every attribute of reality can be deduced from every other" (Kirk & Raven, 1957, p. 268). Parmenides believed that there is unity and permanence in the real world. His emphasis on reason as the means by which we get beyond the realm of appearance marks him as one of the first rationalists. He was also one of the first philosophers to emphasize a philosophy of being as opposed to a philosophy of becoming. This last statement calls for further elaboration.

A philosophy of becoming emphasizes process, change, variety, and transition. Few things are more *apparent* than the inevitability of change. But the word *apparent* is well chosen, especially to those who embrace a philosophy of being. For such a philosophy, the change that we observe with the senses may be illusory. A philosophy of being emphasizes unity, permanence, and a larger reality that forms the backdrop of transient things. Philosophies of being and becoming have strikingly different implications for psychology. The following modern implications, as stated by Maslow (1962, p. iv), could almost have been written by one of the early Greeks. Being-psychology, as opposed to becoming-psychology, contrasts "the perfect with the imperfect, the ideal with the actual . . . the timeless with the temporal, end-psychology with means-psychology."

As noted earlier, Parmenides was also interested in the mechanisms of perception. He apparently believed that "like" perceives "like" whereas some of the other early philosophers taught that we perceive by virtue of opposites. For example, the theory of opposites holds that we experience the heat of hot water by virtue of the contrast between the temperature of the water and the temperature of the skin. But Parmenides argued that we perceive light because we have fire or light within us. The light in the pupil of the eye responds to "its own kind." A corpse could not perceive light because the light or fire is deficient in the corpse. But the corpse could know coldness, silence, and so on (see Kirk & Raven, 1957, p. 283).

Zeno. Zeno of Elea and Melissus of Samos were students and followers of Parmenides. They both devoted themselves to a defense of Parmenides's philosophy of being. Melissus, also known for defeating an Athenian fleet in a sea battle, wrote a book entitled *On Nature or What Exists.* In his book, Melissus argued that what exists is infinite and homogeneous. He noted that most theories of becoming or change imply that something can come from nothing. Melissus believed that there is a true reality that is one in nature and that undergirds the plurality of things we know with our senses. In this assertion, he is a forerunner of the Greek atomists (to follow).

Zeno is best known for his paradoxes of motion. None of the extant fragments of Zeno's teachings contains all of his arguments about motion, but the essential idea is illustrated as follows.

Suppose an archer releases an arrow at point A and the arrow is aimed at a target at point B. The arrow must first traverse half the distance. Once it has gone halfway, it must traverse half of the remaining distance, and so forth. Because we can continue dividing the remaining distance by 2 indefinitely, there is a logical problem about whether the arrow can ever reach its goal. Now, how does such a paradox relate to Parmenides?

A plausible interpretation is as follows. Sense and reason result in two different analyses of the situation. But in Zeno's paradox, common sense is offended more by reason than by the senses. So, how could the paradox support Parmenides? An interpretation offered by Vlastos (1967) is that Zeno's paradox shows us "that commonplaces may conceal absurdities and hence [we have] the need of reexamining even the best entrenched and most plausible assumptions" (p. 378).

Heraclitus. Whereas Parmenides was the best-known early philosopher of being, Heraclitus (*hehr uh KLY tuhs*) was the best-known philosopher of becoming. There is little available biographical information about Heraclitus that is not suspect. His dates are unknown, but he was probably active about 480 B.C. He apparently lived his life in Ephesus. He was an elitist who had little respect or liking for other philosophers; this feeling was apparently mutual, because philosophers who followed him often disparaged his work. Heraclitus was unpopular with other philosophers because of his arrogance, his attacks on them and their works, and his philosophy that ran counter to much of prevailing opinion. Although his immediate successors such as Plato and Aristotle depreciated his work, he has been treated with much greater respect over the succeeding centuries. Heraclitus is most famous for his statement, "Upon those that step into the same rivers different and different waters flow" (Kirk & Raven, 1957, p. 146). For Heraclitus, constancy is illusory; change is real. Even the most immutable element is subject to change over long periods of time. Heraclitus believed that fire is symbolic of nature because fire is ever changing and through fire one thing is exchanged or transmuted to another. Heraclitus, like Xenophanes, believed that the sun is new each day.

Heraclitus was also interested in psychological matters. He believed that the soul could be wet or dry and that wetness is deleterious—complete wetness is death. Partial wetness interferes with normal functioning. For example, drunkenness wets the soul and thus interferes with judgment. A dry soul is wise. Heraclitus seems to be arguing against excess emotions in one of his fragments that asserted, "It is hard to fight with anger; for what it wants it buys at the price of soul" (Kirk & Raven, 1957, p. 211). Heraclitus trusted the senses more than his contemporaries or successors, but some senses he thought to be more trustworthy than others. For example, he believed vision to be more accurate than audition. Heraclitus believed that the senses become clogged in sleep and memory is lost. Memory, however, returns with the reactivation of the senses in wakefulness.

Heraclitus had little respect for the knowledge and opinions of most people. He accused people of being deaf to what they hear and, in an ancient anticipation of some well-known modern popular books and films, he saw humans as apes when compared with a god. The moralistic Heraclitus had contempt for the masses who lack discipline as evidenced by overeating. Although he was disliked in his times, his influence in later science, philosophy, and even theology has been extensive.

Heraclitus mocked conventional religion. He was particularly offended by blood sacrifices and prayers to idols, a practice he thought little different than talking with houses! It is little wonder that Heraclitus lived his life in semi-isolation and, according to one story, ended his life at age sixty (Kirk & Raven, 1957, p. 182).

Leucippus and Democritus. The story of early Greek philosophy, science, and psychology takes on a strikingly modern flavor as we turn to a consideration of the work of the early atomists Leucippus (*loo KIHP uhs*) and Democritus (*duh MAHK rih tuhs*). Leucippus, who lived around 500 B.C., was the founder of atomic theory, but Democritus (c. 460–c. 370 B.C.) developed and refined the theory. Although little is known about the life of Leucippus, we do know that Democritus was a citizen of Abdera in Thrace. He apparently traveled around much of the Mediterranean

world and had interest in a great range of subjects including science, religion, and ethics.

According to Leucippus and Democritus, reality is composed of both atoms and the void. The void is empty space, and Leucippus noted that movement would be impossible without the void. Atoms were thought to be so small as to elude human perception. If any tangible object could be divided again and again one would, in the final division, reach a unit that could not be divided— the atom. Leucippus and Democritus taught that atoms vary in arrangement, position, and shape. There were hooked atoms, rough atoms, smooth atoms, and so on. The sensible qualities one experiences result from the arrangement and shapes of atoms. Thus, a dense and heavy object is more compact, possibly consisting of many atoms hooked together. Fire consists of smooth atoms, and the soul, according to Democritus, consists of smooth atoms that disperse at death.

The atomists taught that all things come into existence out of a great whirl of atoms. Atoms in the whirl begin to separate, like being attracted to like, and in time worlds are generated. They believed in many worlds, some moist, some dry, some supporting plants and animals, and others devoid of life.

Democritus argued for a strict determinism. He believed that randomness was an appearance. Behind the appearance of randomness was reason and a strict necessity. When he spoke on psychological topics, he employed the language of causation. For example, bitter taste is caused by small spherical atoms, whereas salt taste is caused by large jagged atoms. In one of the earliest psychological theories of religious belief, Democritus argued that belief in popular Greek gods was motivated primarily by fear.

Democritus believed that all objects give off images of themselves, consisting of thin layers of atoms shaped like the object. As these thin layers move through the void and impact our senses, we develop a perception of the object, provided we have like atoms that can respond to the layer of projected atoms—like responds to like. Democritus's ethical system consisted of a sophisticated pleasure theory. Pleasure is desirable but may be attained through discipline rather than through indulgence and through austerity rather than through possession of things.

Early Greek Concepts of Illness

In early Greek thought, human strengths and weaknesses were often attributed to the gods. Thus, following encouragement from the goddess Athene, Diomedes could fight the Trojans with almost unbelievable strength and courage, but madness befell Ajax when Achilles's armor was awarded to Ulysses. Both mental and physical calamities could be brought upon those who, for whatever reason, were on the wrong side of a god. There was a constant quest to appease the gods and to invoke their pleasure and assistance through prayer.

There is disagreement among scholars regarding the autonomy of the individual in Homeric thought. Simon and Weiner (1966) represent traditional views when they pointed out that in Homeric thought "the tendency is to ascribe origins of mental states to forces or agencies outside the person. . . . If Achilles forbears and does not slay Agamemnon on the spot, it is because Athena comes down, pulls Achilles by his hair, and says 'wait'" (p. 307). Smith (1974), however, argued that "Homeric man was not a puppet of the gods as has often been charged" (p. 315). In defense of his contention, Smith quoted lines from *The Odyssey* in which Zeus declares that humans blame the gods too readily and that they bring sorrows on themselves in addition to ordained sorrows.

Even if there was some room for individual initiative, it is hardly arguable that fate and divine ordination played a major role in human problems. Indeed, early Greek concepts of health and illness were comparable in many respects to Babylonian concepts. The transition to more naturalistic approaches was slow.

Aesculapius. The earliest mythic figure in Greek medicine was Aesculapius (*EHS kuh lop ee uhs*) (or Asclepius), the son of Apollo, the god of Greek medicine. Aesculapius was mentioned by Homer as the father of Machaon and Podaleirius, two surgeons who served with the Achaean forces in their war with the Trojans. Aesculapius is also reputed to be the father of Hygieia, commonly re-

garded by the Greeks and Romans as the goddess of health.

Over three hundred temples were built in Greece and Rome to carry on the healing traditions associated with Aesculapian mythology. The temples, always located in places of beauty, were designed to fill the people with expectations of imminent recovery from their ills. Therapy consisted of sleep, suggestion, diet control, drugs, massage, and baths. Apparently suggestion played a major role and remission of symptoms was common. The Aesculapian physicians suggested that their patient have dreams of Aesculapius and that such dreams would be prophetic of actual cures.

The snake, as a symbol of mystery, power, and knowledge, was employed by many of the ancients in their healing rites; it was also used by the Aesculapians. An antique statue in the Vatican museum shows Aesculapius with a serpent wrapped around a rod—a symbol of medicine that has persisted into modern times. The Aesculapians represented a mixture of rational and mystical techniques, but the greater emphasis appeared to have been on mystical techniques somewhat comparable to the techniques of contemporary faith healers.

Alcmaeon. One of the major milestones in Greek medicine is encountered in the work of Alcmaeon (*ALK mee on*) of Crotona. Alcmaeon's exact dates are uncertain, but his work is generally believed to date from about 500 B.C. He was one of the first to advance an empirical approach to anatomy and physiology by practicing dissection. The fragments that are available on his work suggest that he attempted to trace sensory channels to the brain. He also understood that the brain is the organ of thought. He believed that sleep occurs when blood is carried away from the brain to the large blood vessels. Juhasz (1971) noted that this is the first known theory of sleep. Alcmaeon also believed that many sensory defects result when the channels to the brain become clogged.

In addition to his anatomical work, Alcmaeon advanced a homeostatic-equilibrium theory of health. He believed that health prevails so long as there is balance between coldness and warmth, wetness and dryness, and sweetness and bitterness. Such an emphasis has credibility and empirical appeal because we all observe the roles of dehydration or excessive moisture in common illness. We also observe the roles of fever or shivering in illness, and bitterness or a bad taste in the mouth is commonly associated with illness. According to Alcmaeon, death results when any of the paired opposites is too strong. Alcmaeon also emphasized the lack of moderation (e.g., eating too much or too little) as a cause of disease.

Empedocles. Empedocles (*ehm PEHD uh kleez*) (c. 490–c. 430 B.C.) was another early homeostatic theorist strongly influenced by Parmenides and Pythagoras. Empedocles taught that four basic elements (fire, earth, air, and water) are born out of two first principles (love and strife). The idea of four basic elements may have been borrowed from earlier Mediterranean cultures, but the principles of love and strife are original with Empedocles. According to Empedocles, the principles of love and strife act as forces of attraction and repulsion that interact with the four basic elements. If all things are composed of fire, earth, air, and water, we still must have principles to account for the organizations and combinations. Love, or the force of attraction, accounts for organic unity, whereas strife or repulsion accounts for disintegration and the breakdown of objects or events. Empedocles believed that thought and reason have their substrate in the blood because, according to this theory, the four elements are perfectly blended in blood. Blood represents a near equal mix of fire, earth, air, and water. This position opens the possibility that a thought disorder can be viewed as the result of an imbalance of the elements in the blood.

Because he believed in the transmigration of the soul, Empedocles was a vegetarian. He taught that there is a "greatest god" that is not anthropormorphic. He believed that the principles of love and strife operate in the cosmos as well as within the individual life. Thus, principles of attraction and harmony are responsible for the birth and organization of the world.

Empedocles, like Anaximander, also believed in a form of evolutionary theory. He argued that those creatures survive that are "accidentally compounded in a suitable way; but where this did not happen, the creatures perished and are perishing

still" (Kirk & Raven, 1957, p. 337). Empedocles believed that nature had experimented with grotesque creatures without necks, partly male and partly female, with eyes "strayed alone," and with animal-like features. These creatures, the result of strife and improper mixtures of the elements, perished. But when like chanced to meet like, appropriately, and when there was harmony in the process of organization, then creatures were produced that survived.

Empedocles spoke against animal and human sacrifice as the primal sin. The following condemnation is but one of several expressing Empedocles's outrage: "Father lifts up his own dear son, his form changed, and, praying, slays him— witless fool; and the people are distracted as they sacrifice the imploring victim" (Kirk & Raven, 1957, p. 350).

Hippocrates. Hippocrates (*hih PAHK ruh teez*) (c. 460–c. 377 B.C.) was the most famous of the Greek physicians. He was born on the island of Cos and practiced medicine there as well as in Athens. He helped establish an empirical approach to medicine in the medical school of Cos. The body of writings attributed to Hippocrates (*Corpus Hippocraticum*) contains material on a great range of medical subjects and varies considerably in style. Accordingly, it is sometimes difficult to know what to attribute to Hippocrates and what to attribute to his colleagues. What follows is attributed to Hippocrates as the representative leader of the school of Cos. Much of the material probably came from other physicians.

Sometimes called the founder of medicine, Hippocrates advanced a naturalistic account of all disease, both physical and mental. Like Empedocles, Hippocrates taught that disease results from a disturbance of balance—and the goal of treatment is the restoration of balance. For example, intelligence results from a proper blend of the elements of fire and water but if there is an excess of water, stupidity is the result. Visible symptoms include slowness, weeping without reason, and suggestibility. An excess of fire could result in an impulsive person, one who rushes from one thing to another without being able to focus or concentrate. Hippocrates believed that such a condition could turn to madness unless treated properly. Treatment for an excess of fire included eating fish in place of meat, moderate (natural) exercise, induction of vomiting after surfeits, eating barley bread rather than wheat, and reduction of the frequency of sexual intercourse.

Hippocrates saw dreams as indicators of illness. The greater the contrast between the dream and reality, the greater the illness. Dreams represent the activity of the soul. "When the body is awake the soul is its servant . . . but when the body is at rest, the soul, being set in motion and awake, administers her own household" (Goshen, 1967, p. 12).

The Cos school accepted the four-element theory (fire, earth, air, water) advanced by Empedocles. The manifestations of these elements in the body were thought to be found in four humors: black bile, yellow bile, blood, and phlegm. The four elements and humors were thought to be associated with the four qualities of cold, hot, dry, and wet. There were apparently differences of opinion about how the humors were associated with the various qualities. According to one classification (Castiglioni, 1941, p. 162), blood is associated with heat, phlegm with coldness, yellow bile with dryness, and black bile with wetness. At any rate, health was thought to result from an organic balance of the four humors and disease from an imbalance. The empirical basis for Hippocratic thought is evident. High body temperatures, sweating, jaundiced conditions, pallor, discoloration of urine, and excess of phlegm—conditions associated with illness—can be easily related to the four-humor theory. Treatment was designed to restore balance to the humors.

Hippocrates employed a great variety of treatments to restore balance. He was a strong believer in diet control, honey being a favorite prescription. He advocated therapies such as exercises, fresh air, rest, laughter, baths, and bleeding. Hippocrates also employed a variety of surgical techniques, including trephining to relieve pressure from brain tumors. He taught that the brain is the seat of intellectual activities and he was the first to classify emotional disorders. His classification included mania, melancholia, paranoia, and epilepsy. Paranoia referred to disorganized behaviors

and epilepsy was viewed as a natural disease of the brain.

As mentioned, Hippocrates believed that dreams are indicators of health or illness. The sleeping soul can, through dreams, reveal a host of important messages about the body. For example, dreams of abnormal rivers may signify blood disorders, trees barren of fruit may foretell reproductive problems, and troubled seas may indicate disorders of the stomach.

Hippocrates and the school at Cos had arrived at a medicine without gods and demons and devoid of the mystical and superstitious medicine of earlier times. Psychological problems were also treated within the framework of a thorough naturalism. Hippocrates argued that if physicians could do no good, they should do no harm. Accordingly, many of the treatment techniques undoubtedly had beneficial and pleasant consequences. The Hippocratic period was a brief era of enlightenment.

Relativism

Before leaving the pre-Socratic philosophers, we must consider another issue in epistemology that occupied a central role in Greek thought. The issue centers on questions regarding the status of truth. Is truth relative or are there independent and enduring truths that reason can discern? In this section we will discuss the relativistic doctrine of Protagoras, and in the materials that follow, we will consider the arguments against **relativism** offered by Socrates.

Protagoras.   Protagoras (c. 485–c. 410 B.C.) was born in Abdera and lived most of his adult life in Athens. He was a famous sophist (teacher) remembered for a relativistic doctrine summarized in the belief that the human being is the measure of all things. What is the meaning of such a statement? Does it describe the way things are or does it represent an unjustified deification of the individual—an anthropocentric view of the world?

Let us examine arguments for Protagoras's relativistic doctrine. These arguments are related to the problem of subjectivism and objectivism discussed in Chapter 2. Protagoras argued that the world is conditioned by our senses. For example, if a food item tastes good to one person but not to another, then it is true that the food item is good and it is also true that it is bad. Truth is relative. If a picture is ugly to one person and beautiful to another, then it is true that the picture is ugly and it is equally true that the picture is beautiful. Protagorean relativism, extended to groups, contributed to democratic notions of majority rule. If a group votes for a given kind of legislation, then that legislation has truth value for that group.

However we judge the philosophical basis of Protagorean relativism, there is little question that it had major implications for psychology. Psychologists have always had an interest in how people construe their worlds. Techniques such as projective tests, free association, introspection, and phenomenological descriptions are but some of the ways in which we have attempted to understand the world of the individual—a world that has a face value and legitimacy all its own.

The Golden Age of Greece

The work of the early cosmologists and physicians was followed by a much more comprehensive approach to philosophy, especially in the work of Plato and Aristotle. The range of their interests covered topics in the physical and biological sciences, psychology, political science, sociology, and such traditional topics in philosophy as logic, metaphysics, and ethics. During the Golden Age of Greece, contributions to psychology were extensive.

Socrates. The varieties of legends and stories about Socrates have a unique capacity to stir the imagination of the history student. Saint, martyr, grotesque, degenerate, brilliant, independent, ugly, courageous, dignified, and deranged are but a few of the descriptors that have been used to portray a figure so pivotal in Greek thought that philosophy before him is often called pre-Socratic. Little is known of the historical Socrates, however. What is known comes from several sources that often contradict each other. Plato, who was Socrates's student, is appropriately regarded as the most reliable source of information, but Plato may pre-

sent a picture that is shaded by his own philosophical position.

Socrates was born about 470 B.C. in Athens and died in 399 B.C. in the same city. His mother was a midwife and his father was possibly a sculptor. Socrates was apparently deeply influenced by a young woman philosopher named Aspasia. She appears in his dialogues and he refers to her as his teacher in his memoirs. In an early work on women in science, Mozans (1913) suggested that Aspasia's emphasis on equality and the rights of women may have influenced both Socrates and Plato. Socrates served time in the Athenian army during the Peloponnesian War and won distinction for his courage. The same courage would show itself later in civilian life when he faced imprisonment and execution. Socrates was almost a victim of philosophy; he loved it more than family, material comfort, or social success. The picture that emerges is of a human being so completely dedicated to ideas that he devoted little thought to ordinary needs such as food and clothing. He was disciplined, independent, simple in his tastes, and an engaging conversationalist. One gains the impression of a human being with excellent social presence complemented by an ability to listen carefully to the viewpoints of other people.

Socrates enticed people into conversation on topics such as the nature of justice, virtue, or prudence. He asked simple questions about how the person defined terms, then listened carefully. After the person completed a definition, Socrates asked questions about how the definition covered this or that situation. Often the questions proved embarrassing, revealing that the individual really did not have an adequate grasp of the concept. But the nature of the dialogue was so captivating that Socrates often found himself surrounded by curious listeners. Apparently he had many disciples among young people, who in any society are attracted to ideals, integrity, intellectual excitement, and inspiration.

If Socrates was an inspiration to many of the young people of Athens, he was a nuisance and a threat to the political and religious establishment. Most conservative Athenians preferred answers to questions, and the constant probing into established or conventional wisdom became an unbearable

Socrates

irritation. As a consequence, Socrates was brought to trial on three trumped-up charges: (1) corrupting youth, (2) denying Greek gods, and (3) attempting to establish new gods. Historians have often argued that the charges were simply not defensible and that the real reason for Socrates's trial is that he had made too many personal enemies by criticizing powerful Athenian political and military leaders and exposing their incompetence.

Socrates turned his trial into a condemnation of his judges and accusers. He refused to compromise on any point as he steadfastly maintained his innocence. It is generally agreed that had Socrates made any gesture of appeasement, he would have been given a light sentence and the whole affair would have been forgotten, but he was a man of uncompromising integrity and could find no grounds for yielding on any point, even at the expense of his life. So he was sentenced to die. There were many opportunities to escape during the thirty days that elapsed between his sentence and his execution, but he refused to break the law in any manner. Plato, in his *Phaedo,* provided a moving account of the execution. Several of Socrates's disciples who were present wept bitterly, but were reprimanded by Socrates for their weakness. So, at seventy years of age, Socrates calmly drank the hemlock poison and walked briefly around the room making observations about the poison's effect before he died.

The work of Socrates has to be understood partly as a reaction to the teachings of the sophists. It will be recalled that the sophists were teachers who received money in exchange for their instruction. There have been disagreements about the range of topics taught by the sophists, but their teachings undoubtedly included rhetoric and argument. The range of their activities may have been considerably greater. In an article on the beginnings of psychotherapy, Pivnicki (1969) pointed out that Antiphon, a **sophist,** had a doorplate advertising his qualifications to heal grief and melancholia by means of words. Guthrie (1960) noted that "the Sophists were not a particular philosophical school, but rather a profession. They were itinerant teachers, who made a living out of the new hunger for guidance in practical affairs" (p. 66). Socrates undoubtedly accepted the good things accomplished by the sophists, but believed their practical concerns overshadowed their love of wisdom. He also took issue with their emphasis on sensation and relativism. This point deserves elaboration.

As we saw in the previous section, the sophist Protagoras argued that individual perception is the source of knowledge. Socrates claimed that we obtain knowledge through analysis of concepts. For example, we may ask someone to define a triangle. Individual triangles may be small or large, and they may come in a variety of colors or materials. Although color or size may be qualities associated with a particular triangle, they are not associated with triangles in general. In forming an appropriate concept of triangles, we must abstract only those qualities that all triangles have in common. For Socrates, there are objective and universal qualities that participate in a correctly framed concept, and following the appropriate conceptual work we can assess whether a specific shape is or is not a triangle. As noted by Stace (1962), "It is no longer open to anyone to declare that whatever he chooses to call a triangle is a triangle. . . . The Sophist can no longer say 'whatever seems to me right, is right for me'" (p. 145). Thus, Socrates emphasized the power of reason; he believed that through the rational process we can discern objective truths. This orientation exerted an enormous influence on Plato and Aristotle and on subsequent thought.

Socrates had little interest in physics, astronomy, or the biological sciences. For this reason, he is sometimes regarded as having had a detrimental effect on these disciplines. His major object of inquiry was psychological rather than physical or biological. While it is true that most of Socrates's thought was directed inward, his quest for truth was in the scientific spirit.

Socrates believed that self-knowledge is vital to virtue. He believed that human beings do not knowingly engage in evil but rather that evil results from ignorance. It follows that the role of the good teacher is crucial. The teacher assists the student in the quest for knowledge, and as knowledge increases, virtue increases. Because virtue includes a host of socially desirable behaviors, knowledge is the means by which the individual and society may advance. But true knowledge is elusive. Socrates believed himself to be ignorant but at the same time wiser than those who were not even aware of their ignorance. The tensions between Socrates's personal admission of ignorance and any claims he might have made to be a virtuous man are still topical in philosophy (e.g., Brickhouse & Smith, 1990). He believed that most people are informed by half-truths, misinformation, and false concepts.

Smith (1974) argues that Socrates was among the first to formulate a scientific approach to psychology that emphasized multiple (moral, social, anatomical, and physiological) causes of behavior. In explaining his reasons for choosing death by poison, Socrates argued that his decision was not based on any one simple set of factors. In other words, the cause was not simply mental, physical, or social but rather a combination of all these factors. Smith argues that Socrates would have opposed twentieth-century reductionism.

One of the students present at Socrates's death was Aristippus, head of a school of philosophy at Cyrene. Following the death of Aristippus, the school was headed by his daughter Arete. Waithe (1987a, p. 198) noted that we know nothing about Arete's personal views, but we do know something about the teachings of her school at Cyrene. It was one of the first to advance a systematic treatment of the roles of pleasure and pain in human life. The Cyrenaics advanced a sophisticated approach to

pleasure, arguing that discipline, knowledge, and virtuous actions are more likely to result in pleasure, whereas negative emotions such as anger, fear, and remorse should be avoided because they multiply pain. In her thirty-five years as a teacher, Arete was thought to have "written forty books, and to have counted among her pupils one hundred and ten philosophers" (Waithe, 1987a, p. 198). The school at Cyrene provided one of the first approaches to psychological hedonism—a doctrine that would surface again as a systematic philosophical position in the eighteenth and nineteenth centuries under the leadership of Jeremy Bentham. Richardson (1990) notes that, "Towards the end of the *Protagoras* Socrates suggests that the 'salvation of our life' depends upon applying to pleasures and pains a science of measurement" (p. 7). The meaning of hedonism (or the pursuit of pleasure) in the works of Socrates and Plato is a subject of lively discussion (e.g., see Richardson, 1990; Weiss, 1989).

Plato. As we have noted earlier, there are few extant writings of the philosophers we have covered thus far; by contrast, there is a sizable collection of Plato's writings. Plato (c. 428–c. 347 B.C.) typically presented his ideas in the literary form of the *dialogue*. Participants in the dialogue argued the various facets of concepts such as justice or virtue. Some of the dialogues turned into monologues as one participant held forth on a topic for a lengthy period. The collected works of Plato include a few letters as well as the numerous dialogues, including such well-known works as *The Apology, The Laws, The Meno, The Phaedo, The Republic, The Sophist, The Symposium, The Theaetetus,* and *The Timaeus.* In addition to his recognition as a philosopher and teacher, Plato is often regarded as one of the great literary masters of the Western world.

Plato was born to a wealthy family in Athens between 429 and 427 B.C. The Peloponnesian War between Athens and Sparta had started in 431 B.C. and would not end until 404 B.C. Accordingly, Plato lived his youth in a turbulent period marked by the hardships of war. Plague was also rampant in Greece at this time. Though few details are known of Plato's youth, it is generally agreed that, as a member of an aristocratic family, he received an excellent early education. As a young man, he participated in the war effort against Sparta, but little is known about the extent of his military activities. The most pivotal association in his younger years was with Socrates. He was with Socrates in the last years of the great teacher's life and, as noted earlier, was one of those present at Socrates's death in 399 B.C. Plato was embittered at Socrates's death and was disillusioned with politics. Members of his own family had been part of a corrupt ruling party following the war. Though Plato's family power almost guaranteed a political future, Plato withdrew, traveled to numerous Mediterranean countries, and finally returned to Athens, where he founded an **Academy.** The exact date of the founding of the Academy is in dispute, but it was in the Academy that Plato spent the rest of his life—a period of approximately forty years. It was here that Plato did his important philosophical work. He taught his students and disciples and, like Socrates, charged no fee. Plato died at age eighty-one, probably in 347 B.C. His nephew, Speusippus, succeeded him as head of the Academy, but the successor who was destined for fame was Plato's student, Aristotle.

The early dialogues show the strong influence of Socrates, but in later works Plato's originality begins to assert itself. In his mature philosophy, we encounter a comprehensive system that includes topics in ethics, politics, law, art, religion, epistemology, and psychology. He is important to the history of psychology, among many other reasons, because he was one of the first to introduce a conflict model of human psychological disorders. Let us turn now to a consideration of some of his psychological views.

Method.   The claim is often made that Plato rejected empirical knowledge or knowledge that is based on sensory information. Such a claim is not a misrepresentation of Plato, yet the claim is too strong unless it is qualified. In fact, descriptive sciences were taught in the Academy. The *Timaeus* included materials on astronomy based on observation and materials on anatomy based on dissection. Thus, Plato accorded a more important role to the senses in practice than he did in theory. Never-

theless, his position was that rational processes provide true knowledge, whereas sensory information alone provides only appearance and opinion. But appearance and opinion are not, according to Plato, without value. For example, a person may have a correct opinion about tomorrow's weather or the stock market. The correct opinion, though not certain knowledge, may still be of considerable practical value.

Theory of Forms.   According to Plato, sense objects always have a particular or individual quality. Furthermore, objects of sense are always changing. They are in the process of becoming— either growing or decaying. In contrast with the world of sense is the world of forms, known through intuition or rational processes. The **theory of forms,** according to Plato, is the true world, a world of absolute being, independent of individuals and particulars. If there were no individual triangles available to the world of sense, that would not undermine the principles of triangularity or the form of the triangle, which, for Plato, has absolute being. Sense objects (e.g., particular triangles) may participate in or partially represent the real world of forms, but individual objects of sense are always incomplete, temporal, spatial, and changeable. The form is timeless, immutable, and unextended. Even if the world as we know it ceased to exist, the principles of triangularity and the formal nature of the triangle would continue as part of the very fiber of the absolute world of forms. If the world of forms is not known through the senses, how is it known?

While it is the body, via the senses, that reveals the changing, illusory, temporal world, it is the soul that reveals the world of forms. Plato believed that the soul of human beings is immortal. Plato also believed that the soul may be reincarnated into another body. In its new incarnation, the soul may have dim recollections of the real world of forms that it once knew. Now, chained to the body and the senses, it is a difficult task for the soul to comprehend true forms. Juhasz (1971) noted that "the metaphor 'eye of the soul' was originated by Plato in the *Republic*" (p. 51). The **eye of the soul** perceives the real world of forms through memories, images, and higher cognitive functions. The soul's vision of true reality is diminished when it concentrates on the welter of sensory information.

Nature of the Soul. Plato's thoughts on the nature of the soul are complex and often appear contradictory. Reasons for the apparent contradictions are readily identified. First, Plato's writings cover several decades, and his thought on the nature of the soul did not remain static. Because scholars cannot always agree on the chronological order of Plato's writings, we are not certain how his thought developed. Another reason for apparent contradictions is that Plato was fond of speaking in metaphors, and, in different periods, different metaphors were used. Thus, at one time the soul was compared to a scribe, and at another time it was compared to a charioteer (reason) trying to control two powerful horses (appetite and spirit) that often work against each other. Let us first consider the problem of the definition of *soul* in Plato, then turn to a consideration of the functional and structural properties of the soul.

Plato's term **psyche,** or more accurately **psuche,** is typically translated as soul. But there is disagreement among scholars as to the exact meaning of *psuche.* Soul is a reasonable translation in the sense that Plato believed that psuche was immortal. But Plato also ascribed mental properties to psuche so that the term *mind* could serve as a reasonable translation. Unfortunately, Plato did not provide us with an unambiguous definition, so analysts typically proceed by attempting to understand the functional and structural properties of psuche.

We encounter many functional qualities of the soul in platonic literature. The soul is active; it compares, discriminates, organizes, exercises control, and masters. In a helpful article on the Platonic model of the mind and mental illness, Simon (1972) enumerated some of the mental activities carried on by the soul or mind. These are characterized in terms of higher and lower activities. Thus, sleeping is lower, whereas waking is higher. Similarly, childishness, conflict, and appetite are lower, whereas adulthood, harmony, and rational processes are higher activities. Plato's views on the soul's activities included most of the things that

come under the heading of psychological activities. Hence, memory, ideation, knowing, feeling, and willing were all viewed as activities of the soul.

The structure of the soul in Platonic thought can be viewed in several ways. The soul is unitary in the sense that parts can be in harmony and in the sense that higher rational functions can be in control. As we will see shortly, the emphasis on the unity of the soul had implications for new understandings of mental health and illness. Plato also believed that the soul is marked by duplicity. Such duplicity is manifested in the conflict between rational (reasonable) and irrational (animal-like) forces at work in all of us. Plato also advanced a structural theory in which *psuche* is divided in terms of three major functions. The rational soul is highest among the three and the appetitive soul is lowest. Intermediate between the other two is the affective soul. In this structural arrangement, the rational soul is located in the head, whereas appetite is located in the gut; the affective soul is located in the chest. The tripartite division was illustrated with the famous example of the charioteer and the two horses mentioned earlier. On the matter of the structure of the soul, Plato was also fond of metaphors that emphasize the entrapment of the soul in the body. Thus, we have the famous allegory of the cave. We are all chained in a cave in such a manner as to prevent our seeing the real world. With the senses tied to the body, we see only the shadows on the walls of the cave. But even if we are thus trapped and chained, the soul can overcome its handicap and, through reason, know the real world outside the cave.

Memory. Several conceptions of memory are set forth in Plato's writings. There is a capacity of the rational soul to recollect material it knew in the real world of forms prior to the present incarnation. Of more interest to the psychologist is Plato's metaphor of the soul as a wax slate. Juhasz (1971) pointed out that "in different persons the quality of the wax as well as the quality of the pattern varies" (p. 52). We remember according to the quality of the wax and the pattern. The metaphor of the scribe in Plato's *Philebus* implies processes of storage and retrieval, as well as comparison. Clearly, memory is an important concept in Platonic philosophy, but its chief importance is the bridge it provides between the world of sense and the world of forms.

Learning and Education. Plato's life was devoted to learning and education, and he has been credited with the founding of the first European university—the Academy. He saw the acquisition of knowledge as central to good political leadership. Indeed, in the ideal Platonic state, leaders would be selected only from among those who had attained great achievements in learning. Plato also saw learning as important to the attainment of individual virtue. He accepted the Socratic notion that ignorance is the major culprit in wrongdoing. For Plato, learning and education are important in their own right but they also serve utilitarian ends. Virtue, harmony in society, harmony within the individual, and knowledge of universal forms are all products of learning.

Perception. As we have already noted, perception provides, at best, an approximation to reality and, at worst, outright illusion. Plato did little work on the mechanisms of sensation and perception, but the *Timaeus* does contain some passages that are devoted to how the senses operate. Vision takes place, for example, when fire in the eye communicates with fire in the world. In other words, we see by virtue of the correspondence of like elements. In vision, fire from the eye proceeds outward, but in audition, shock propagated by the air impacts the ear. Plato believed that small passages from the tongue to the heart are responsible for tastes. He believed that we see through the eyes but not with them. The eyes, as the other senses, provide only a chaos of sights, sounds, tastes, and so on. But seeing also involves comparisons, organization, memory and other activities of the rational soul.

Motivation. Plato recognized the roles of pleasure and pain in human life (e.g., see Weiss, 1989), and although these belonged to the lower appetitive realm, he nevertheless believed that pleasure in moderation is likely to represent harmony and balance, whereas pain represents discord. A particular motive was understood in terms of a complex interaction of appetite, spirit, and reason. For example, fear might be present in the appetitive dimension, but depending upon spirit and reason, might or might not manifest itself in behavior.

Spirit and reason might complement fear with courage and with a rationale to stand one's ground. But if there is a deficiency of courage in the affective division of the soul, then cowardly behavior might be associated with fear. Plato believed that human beings seek pleasure, but the source of pleasure may change with growth. Thus, with maturity, the greatest pleasure results from the highest activities of philosophy—the comprehension of the ideal world of forms.

Mental Disorders. From the time of Homer to the time of Plato, there was a marked evolution from theological to naturalistic concepts of mental disorders—a development that would occur again in the transition from the Middle Ages to the modern era. In early Greek thought, mental disorder was conceived in terms of acts of supernatural forces. Later, it was conceived in terms of an imbalance of the humors, and still later, Hippocrates emphasized the role of the brain. Socrates and Plato, as well as other scholars of the day, focused on psychological forces involved in the development of mental disorder. Simon (1972) outlined several important contributions of Plato's work: (1) the recognition that there are powerful irrational and asocial forces that may erupt and dominate the psychological apparatus; (2) the view that mental disorder results from discord among the rational, appetitive, and affective components of the psuche; and (3) the belief that mental problems result from ignorance. Let us elaborate further on each of these three contributions.

Plato believed that irrational and beast-like forces are present in all human beings. He argued that evidence for these forces is found in dreams that reveal the most bizarre instincts such as incest with a parent or unnatural unions with gods or beasts. As an aside, the Greeks had sexual fantasies about their beautiful and sometimes anthropomorphic gods, and they, as well as other ancients, were also sexually attracted to statues—an attraction called *agalmatophilia* (see Scobie & Taylor, 1975).

In the *Timaeus,* Plato spoke of mental disease as a lack of intellectual function. Madness results when the appetitive psuche dominates a weak rational psuche. The impulsive and unbridled appetitive psuche was viewed as asocial. It is of a lower order, being tied to the selfish aims of the body. It is the rational soul, capable of participating in the real world of forms, that can bring sanity into the system. Plato spoke of justice in the soul, apparently referring to the importance of an appropriate relationship between the divisions of the soul. Lack of justice results in madness for the individual just as lack of justice produces a troubled social order.

Simon (1972) outlined two kinds of ignorance that, for Plato, play a role in mental disorder. The first is the ignorance associated with deficiencies in self-knowledge. This is the same type of ignorance of which Socrates spoke. But another kind of ignorance is ignorance of the ideal and of the world of forms. Reliance on the sensual, the temporary, the illusory world of the senses is a form of ignorance and may ultimately lead to the ascendance of the appetitive soul—an unfortunate consequence for emotional health.

Plato saw philosophy, especially dialectics, as an ideal basis for changing cognitions about the world. Thus, philosophy becomes a kind of therapy, or talking cure, for faulty cognitions. Plato also recognized the role of learning in mental disturbance, arguing that many children's stories and fairy tales have bad effects; he also believed that other aspects of family life may have negative effects on children. In *The Republic,* Plato saw a role for the professional in the care and rearing of children. He was not impressed with the qualifications of the typical parent.

Love. The Platonic vision of love and its significance has been a dominant theme in Western thought. Plato's approach to love may be characterized by the same kind of hierarchical arrangement that we encounter throughout his entire philosophical system. There are higher and lower forms of love. Eros, or erotic love, is bound to the body or the senses, but the soul can progress in its capacity to love. Stace (1962) pointed out that in all love, Plato believed we are searching for beauty. We may find beauty first in eros, but then in people, then in knowledge, and finally in philosophy.

Plato's impact on Western thought has been extensive. His dualism of body and soul and his division of the soul's activities were particularly compatible with later Christian thought. Plato's

emphasis on the conflict between rational and irrational forces of the mind foreshadowed some of the work of Sigmund Freud. Plato's lasting influence on Western thought is illustrated by the terms *Platonism* and *neo-Platonisnim*—terms that often refer to the philosophies of individuals or groups who emulate Plato.

Aristotle. Aristotle was born in Stagirus in 384 B.C. His father, a physician, died when Aristotle was a small boy, so he was reared by a guardian. At age seventeen, Aristotle joined Plato's Academy in Athens; he remained in the Academy until he was thirty-seven years old. With the death of Plato in 347 B.C., Aristotle left the Academy and resided for brief periods in Atarneus in Asia Minor, and in Mytilene, located on the island of Lesbos in the eastern Aegean Sea. Then, at the invitation of Philip of Macedonia, Aristotle became tutor of Alexander, later to be known as Alexander the Great. Following a five-year period as Alexander's tutor, Aristotle returned to Athens and founded a school that came to be known as the Lyceum. Aristotle taught at the Lyceum for thirteen years but was forced to leave Athens following an abrupt change in the political climate. As Alexander's tutor, Aristotle had been viewed by the Athenians as pro-Macedonian. With the death of Alexander in 323 B.C., the pro-Macedonian party was overthrown and replaced by a party that was hostile to Macedonia. In order to escape persecution and the possible fate of his intellectual grandfather, Aristotle left Athens and took up residence in Chalcis, but died shortly thereafter, in 322 B.C., at sixty-three years of age.

Aristotle achieved distinction and acclaim as the teacher of a prince. This capacity afforded many benefits and opportunities, including an abundance of supplies. His most productive years were in the **Lyceum,** where he established a library and scientific laboratories. Many of his four hundred books (most of which were quite brief) were produced in this period.

Several general features of Aristotle's thought stand out. First, he was much more a creature of this world than Plato. Aristotle was interested in particulars and facts as experienced via the senses. Although he remained sympathetic to certain features of Platonic rationalism, he was much more of an empiricist. As such, his attention was focused more on the immediate and available world than on the abstract world of forms. A second feature of Aristotelian thought is its comprehensive quality. He was acquainted with the mathematics, astronomy, and physics of his day and made many original contributions in the physical sciences. But he can also be counted as the Father of Zoology, as he was the first known collector and classifier of zoological specimens. He developed a careful deductive logic, and the logic typically taught today in the first course is Aristotelian logic. He was creative in political philosophy, metaphysics, and axiology, and he was acquainted with much of the medicine of his day and advanced some important views on a number of psychological problems. Aristotle's intellectual activities and achievements span the range of available topics of his day. Such achievement, which may be impossible in an age of specialization such as our own, is highly impressive. He is among the leading scholars of all time.

Another feature of Aristotelian thought is his emphasis on the importance of understanding causes. Earlier, in Chapter 2, we discussed Aristotle's notions of material, efficient, formal, and final causation. The concept of final causation,

Aristotle

for which Aristotle has been severely criticized, attempted to establish reasons, purposes, or ends for which things in the world exist. Aristotle rejected the idea that the universe is irrational or chaotic. Development is also a key feature in Aristotle's thinking. He emphasized the idea that there is direction in nature and that this direction is toward reason. Let us turn now to a consideration of some of Aristotle's more specifically psychological concepts.

Soul and Body.   In his work entitled *Aristotle's Psychology,* Robinson (1989) noted, "It is a mark of Aristotle's intellectual independence that, after no less than twenty years of instruction in the Academy, he would arrive at a conception of soul so radically different from the Socratic one passed down in Plato's dialogues" (p. 44). Guthrie (1960) pointed out that for Aristotle "we cannot understand the soul if we neglect the body . . . so, with a particular sense; we cannot understand sight unless we examine the structure and workings of the eye" (p. 147). Aristotle advocated a thoroughgoing physiological psychology. Soul and body are as interdependent as matter and form. Jager and VanHoorn (1972) noted that in the natural philosophy of Aristotle there is material and form and "in the phenomenal world there can be no real separation between the two; no shape without some solid material; no solid material without some shape" (p. 321). Jager and VanHoorn stated that Aristotle's views are sometimes called **hylomorphism,** a term from *hule* meaning matter and *morphe* meaning form. The matter–form interdependence is applied by Aristotle to the soul–body question. In *De Anima,* Aristotle affirmed that "we can wholly dismiss as unnecessary the question whether the soul and the body are one: it is as meaningless as to ask whether the wax and the shape given to it by the stamp are one" (Aristotle, *De Anima,* 412b, 5). So "seeing" (or that which is mental) is not separable from its physical substrate. Aristotle's hylomorphism, applied to the mind–body problem, establishes the legitimacy of both domains but at the same time sounds a cautionary note to those who are tempted to go to the extremes of materialism or idealism. Either extreme can result only in a strained and fragmentary psychology. Whereas mind, according to Aristotle, is closely tied to the body, it is more than a set of organizational properties operating in a physical substrate (see Green, 1998). Indeed, mental processes are more than a mere addition of their physical elements. Formal processes depend on a physical structure, but also enjoy some degree of independence and causal efficacy.

Let us turn attention now to Aristotle's views on the functions of the soul. First, all life forms have a nutritive function. Here, Aristotle is referring to the processes of growth and reproduction. Beyond the nutritive function, animals have sensitive functions (sensing or perception) and movement (locomotion) functions; over and above these there is the function of reason, which is divided into passive and active components. Passive reason is closely associated with the senses and with the function of common sense, which ties one sense to another through the ability to compare or make judgments. Aristotle argued that the passive mind is "related to what is thinkable, as sense is to what is sensible" (Aristotle, *De Anima,* 429a, 15). But now we must come to grips with some ambiguities in Aristotle's writings that we alluded to earlier. These ambiguities pertain to the relationship of soul to body. There are numerous passages in *De Anima* that present Aristotle's hylomorphic or unified approach to soul and body. But some of Aristotle's writings introduce an apparent qualitative split between soul and body. One attempt to resolve the contradiction is to claim that it is the early Aristotle, still under the influence of Plato, who embraces the qualitative split and that the later Aristotle believed in hylomorphism. Another way to resolve the conflict is to claim that the active mind is qualitatively "other than" the body and immortal, whereas the passive mind is the mind that is correlative with the body. Within the extant writings, however, there is not a sharp enough distinction between the active and passive mind to warrant such a conclusion. It is little wonder that there have been centuries of debate over the appropriate interpretation of Aristotle's passive and active minds and his views on the soul–body relationship. For the present, we may regard Aristotle's hylomorphism as an extremely useful approach to the mind–body problem—an approach

with important implications for the science of psychology. We leave unanswered the nature of those dimensions of soul that for Aristotle appear to be transcendent and immortal.

Memory. In his work *On Memory and Reminiscence,* Aristotle began by reminding his audience that the object of memory is the past, whereas the object of perception is the present and the object of expectation is the future (in this connection, Aristotle noted that it might be possible to have a science of expectation). Aristotle argued that memory must be based on something within us like an impression or a picture. If the receiving surface is too soft, too hard, frayed, or decaying, memory will be defective. Similarly, impressions are not received efficiently by those who are too quick or too slow. Aristotle believed that the old have poor memories because of decay and the very young have poor memories because of their rapid growth. Aristotle pointed to defects of memory as one of the symptoms of mental derangement. A common symptom is the inability to discriminate a mere phantasm or picture in the head from a real memory. Aristotle argued that memory is a faculty of sense perception—a faculty that perceives time.

Aristotle distinguished between memory and recollection. He said that recollection is a "searching for an 'image' in a corporeal substrate" (Aristotle, *On Memory and Reminiscence,* 453a, 15–16). Recollection involves effort and an active process of searching. Aristotle pointed out that memory can occur without recollection (i.e., there can be a spontaneous quality about memory). Recollection, however, cannot take place without memory; Aristotle probably meant that recollection is successful only when the so-called imprint, or picture, is found. He pointed out that failures of recollection imply a need for relearning.

In his discussion of the pragmatics of recollection, Aristotle outlined some of the important laws of association that are still with us today. How are we to proceed most efficiently with the task of recollection? He noted that an ordered event is easy to remember, but "badly arranged subjects are remembered with difficulty" (Aristotle, *On Memory and Reminiscence,* 452a, 3). Recollection is facilitated by similarity, contrast, contiguity

(Aristotle, *On Memory and Reminiscence,* 451b, 15) and frequency (Aristotle, *On Memory and Reminiscence,* 452a, 30). Aristotle also pointed out that recollection is more efficient if we begin with the first item in a series, but failing that, we may be successful if we recover a middle item. Mistakes in memory result from the numbers of associations that can be made for any event. In the recollection of a name, for example, the mind can be deflected from the right direction so we may mispronounce or even make a mistake.

Sensing. Aristotle noted that sensation depends partly on sense objects. Some sense objects, such as color or timbre, are of such a nature that they can be detected by only one sense. Aristotle said that "such objects are what we propose to call the special objects of this or that sense" (Aristotle, *De Anima,* 418a, 15). In addition to special objects, Aristotle argued that there are "common sensibles" or movements that are common to all the senses. Robinson (1989) pointed out that common sense "is not a separate and distinct sense in itself but a mode of perceptual integration" (p. 75). The "common sensibles" were thought to be figure, number, magnitude, movement, and rest. If the term *figure* refers to a sensory pattern, then one could well imagine that patterns of various sorts could be detected within any sensory domain. Aristotle was not specific about how each "common sensible" operates in each sensory domain.

In Aristotle's general theory of sensing, sense objects serve as actualizing stimuli. But such stimuli must interact with the organism through a medium. Jager and VanHoorn (1972) pointed out that Aristotle's general theory of sensing must be understood in terms of his theory of actuality and potentiality. Potential sensing is present, for example, when one is listening for the chime of the clock and actual when hearing and chiming occur together. Smith (1971) stated that Aristotle's theory "requires an object-organism interaction through a medium of contact" (p. 375). Aristotle was not always clear about what that medium is. For sound, the medium was the air; for smell, he said, the medium had no name (Aristotle, *De Anima,* 419a, 30). He found evidence for a medium in the fact that the object of sense "sets in movement only what lies between, and this in turn sets the organ

in movement: if what sounds or smells is brought into immediate contact with the organ, no sensation will be produced" (Aristotle, *De Anima,* 419a, 28–30). But if there is a medium for sight, smell, and sound, what are the mediums for taste and touch? Aristotle argued that these latter two do have mediums, "for we do perceive everything through a medium" (Aristotle, *De Anima,* 423b, 5).

He argued that the skin and the tongue are merely related to the real organs of touch and taste. Thus, the skin is the medium of touch and not the organ of touch. Presumably the same is true for the tongue—it is simply a medium. Aristotle found evidence for this conclusion in the fact that direct contact with the skin produces a sensation of touch. The skin must therefore be the medium rather than the organ of touch. Recall that Aristotle believed that direct contact with the sense organ itself results in no sensation. It is noteworthy that Aristotle was troubled over whether touch is a single sense or a group of senses (Aristotle, *De Anima,* 422b, 15). As for gustation, he believed that there are two contrary simple tastes, sweet and bitter. Secondary tastes include saline on the side of bitter and succulent on the side of sweet. Between the extremes are other secondary tastes such as harsh, pungent, astringent, and acid. He believed that smells follow the same patterns as tastes: sweet, bitter, pungent, and so on.

Aristotle was one of the first to write about perceptual illusions. Johannsen (1971) provided examples of illusions discussed in Aristotle's writings. The first, possibly discovered by Aristotle, is obtained by crossing the second finger over the first. With the eyes closed, the adjacent sides of the fingers are then stimulated by a common object, creating a tactile illusion of two objects. Aristotle believed that the illusion possibly results from the fact that, in natural finger position, the same object seldom stimulates the two outer sides of the fingers simultaneously. Another illusion reported by Aristotle was one of movement, described in his work on dreams. It is illustrated when we turn away from a moving object and fix our eyes on something steady, we may continue to perceive motion.

Imagination and Thought. Juhasz (1971) observed that the term *phantasia* in Aristotle's writings has been translated as imagination. Phantasia can be taken as a synonym for mental image. Aristotle drew a sharp distinction between imagination and perception or sensation (these latter two terms are equivalent for Aristotle). Aristotle argued that "perception of the special objects of sense is always free from error" (Aristotle, *De Anima,* 427b, 10). But imagination, which we can call up any time, can lead to falsehoods. Juhasz (1971) pointed out that imagination in Aristotle's theory "is pure appearance without the subject of the perception. As such it is at once highly susceptible to error" (p. 54). Perception, according to Aristotle, cannot be called up any time because it is dependent on the correspondence between the sense object and the sense organ.

Because thinking often (typically) takes place in the absence of the objects of perception and because it is impossible to think without mental images, thinking is also susceptible to error. Thus, perceiving, as a correspondence between external and internal movements, is accurate, but imagination does not have the corrective influence of the external world; so additions, deletions, and distortions are possible. Thinking that is dependent on images or imagination can easily go astray.

The relationship among sensing, imagination, and thinking helps clarify Aristotle's empiricism. It is important to remain close to empirical observables because in so doing we minimize the risk of error. But we must now point to a difficulty in the interpretation of Aristotle's theory of thought. It appears that Aristotle also believed in the existence of a form of thought that is independent of sensing and that is active in nature, a form that is perhaps a manifestation of a higher order of the soul. Thus, for Aristotle one kind of thinking may be conditioned by imagination, but he seems also to have believed in a higher reason closer in nature to platonic beliefs about reason.

Dreams.   In many ancient cultures, dreams were explained as messages or signs from God, but Aristotle argued that dreams are not sent from God. He believed that lower animals also dream and that persons of the most inferior type claim to foresee the future in dreams sent by God. Such persons, he said, are "garrulous and excitable" and given to so many prophetic experiences that they, like gam-

blers, have occasional luck. But it is only chance when a vision predicts some event in the world.

In advancing a naturalistic account of dreams, Aristotle called attention to the persistence of movement that we so often observe in nature. Waves from a pebble thrown into a pond persist across the pond; something heated by a fire loses its heat only gradually. Aristotle believed that the same principle holds for the senses. Thus, if we look at a bright light, and "we close the eyes, then, if we watch carefully, it appears in a right line with the direction of vision (whatever this may be), at first in its own colour; then it changes to crimson, next to purple, until it becomes black and disappears" (Aristotle, *On Dreams,* 459b, 10). Aristotle also called attention to the persistence of the perception of movement and strong odors. He proceeded to the conclusion that "the dream proper is a presentation based on the movement of sense impressions, when such presentation occurs during sleep" (Aristotle, *On Dreams,* 462a, 25).

But do dreams have any significance beyond the fact that they represent complicated afterimages? The answer is yes. If they fail to convey divine messages in a theological sense, they nevertheless have a biological significance of their own. The dream may be a message of the development of pathology. When large movements of the body (e.g., walking) have subsided, we have in sleep and in the dream a special sensitivity to small movements. Thus, Aristotle noted, the smallest residual light image may register in the dream as lightning or the smallest sound as thunder. By extension, small changes in the body may be represented in the dream—so he agrees with the popular medical thought of his day that physicians as well as speculative philosophers "should pay diligent attention to dreams" (Aristotle, *On Prophesying by Dreams,* 463a, 5).

Motivation and Values.   Aristotle believed that human beings seek pleasure and happiness, but in so doing they should also seek the good. Stace (1962) observed, "For Aristotle an action is not good because it yields enjoyment. On the contrary, it yields enjoyment because it is good" (p. 315). But what is the good? Some of Aristotle's views on motivation can be inferred from his discussion of the good. Because human beings, unlike other animals, have a unique capacity for reason, one manifestation of the good is the development of that capacity. Goodness and virtue also consist partly of subordinating the appetites and passions to rational control. Aristotle believed that many failures to achieve goodness are associated with our excess or lack of moderation. We should seek a golden mean between extremes. Thus, as noted by Guthrie (1960), "Courage is a mean between cowardice and foolhardiness, temperance a mean between abstinence and self-indulgence, generosity between meanness and extravagance, proper pride between abjectness and arrogance" (p. 155).

Aristotle recognized the importance of at least four sets of contributing factors in achieving the good: individual differences, habit, social supports, and freedom of choice. His recognition of individual differences is manifested in his idea that the mean between extremes may vary from person to person. Thus, what is courage for one person would be foolhardiness for another. Aristotle placed strong emphasis on the centrality of learning and habit as keys to good or ethical behavior. Numerous times in his discussion of ethics he refers to the importance of habit (Aristotle, *Nicontachean Ethics*, 1095b, 1–9) and to the close correspondence between happiness in people and virtuous actions (Aristotle, *Nicomachean Ethics*, 1100b, 10). Aristotle believed that social supports and good fortune (e.g., friends, riches, power, good children, beauty, good family) are helpful instruments in the attainment of happiness; those who are childless, solitary, or physically unattractive will have greater difficulty attaining happiness. But even in the face of misfortune, there is redemption in effortful and habitual virtuous activity. Aristotle believed we can attain a certain amount of durable happiness in spite of circumstance and "bear the chances of life most nobly and altogether decorously if [we are] 'truly good' and 'foursquare beyond reproach' " (Aristotle, *Nicomachean Ethics*, 1100b, 20). It is of interest that emphasis on the importance of habit in human life would be echoed over 2,000 years later by the American psychologist William James.

The subject of motivation concerns why people do what they do. As we work our way through the history of ideas on motivation, we will see a great variety of approaches, including grand monistic schemes in which all human motivation is conceived as derivative from one wish that is presumed to be all-pervasive. The wish may be for power, sex, economic justice, self-preservation, or union with some mystical force. Contrasting with the monistic theories are pluralistic approaches that acknowledge the complexity and the diversity of the causes of human behavior. Aristotle was in this latter camp. We do what we do because of appetite, but we are also capable of reason. Habit plays a central role in human life, but many events occur by sheer chance. We are capable of making some real choices, but we are also subject to the various kinds of causality. Clearly, Aristotle saw the complexity of causation in human life.

Psychological Thought Following Aristotle

With the departure of Aristotle from Athens, his student Theophrastus (c. 372–c. 287 B.C.) assumed leadership of the Lyceum. Theophrastus, like his teacher, had great breadth of interest, so many of the scientific and philosophical traditions of the Lyceum were continued. For example, in philosophy, he extended some of Aristotle's work on logic. In biological science, he is remembered for two major botanical works that contained the first system for classifying plants. He is sometimes called the Father of Botany. Some of his psychological interests are included in a book titled *Characters,* which provides descriptions of negative character traits such as boorishness and tactlessness. Theophrastus also extended Aristotle's work on the senses and argued for the central role of the brain in sensation. He was more of an empiricist than Aristotle, believing that science should emphasize material and efficient causation rather than final causation.

If the Aristotelian tradition was carried on for a brief period under the capable leadership of Theophrastus, it did not survive long as a dominant force in Greek thought. What happened after the death of Aristotle was well summarized by Stace (1962) who argued that "the rest of the story of Greek philosophy is soon told, for it is the story of decay" (p. 339). The decay was illustrated by a new emphasis on narrow practical concerns such as how to be happy and how to maximize personal gains. There was a loss of interest in the pursuit of wisdom for its own sake and a growing demand for knowledge that results in immediate gratification. Investigation of great questions in science and metaphysics was replaced by self-centered concerns and there was a consequent decline in the generation of new ideas. For a long period after the Golden Age of Greece, philosophy was largely derivative.

The major schools or systems of philosophy following Aristotle were stoicism, epicureanism, and skepticism. These schools, along with neo-Platonism, a later school, will be considered in the next chapter. As Stace (1962, p. 340) noted, all of these schools have something in common in that they focus on individuals and their concerns. To be sure, some of the representatives of these philosophies may sometimes address great issues, but the great issues were secondary concerns for them.

REVIEW QUESTIONS

1. Discuss psychological thought as it is encountered in documents and manuscripts from ancient cultures such as China, Egypt, and India.

2. Many of the early Greeks were interested in the primal substance of the world. Contrast Thales, Democritus, Anaximander, and Anaximenes with respect to their views on the primal substance.

3. Myia, of the Pythagorean school, provided some of the earliest advice on the care of infants. Briefly summarize her advice.

4. Contrast the philosophy of becoming as advanced by Heraclitus with the philosophy of being as advanced by Parmenides.

5. Trace the development of Greek medical thought from Aesculapius to Hippocrates.

6. How did Socrates argue against the relativism of Protagoras?

7. Briefly outline the contributions of Socrates to psychology.

8. Outline Plato's conflict model of mental disorders.

9. Discuss Plato's methodology. Include in your discussion a statement about Plato's theory of forms and explain the meaning of his metaphor "eye of the soul."

10. Briefly state Plato's position on memory, perception, and motivation.

11. Contrast Plato with Aristotle with respect to their approaches to knowledge.

12. What was Aristotle's approach to the soul–body question?

13. Outline Aristotle's positions on memory, sensing, and motivation.

14. Briefly discuss Aristotle's approach to dreaming.

15. What are the essential features of psychological and philosophical thought following Aristotle?

CHAPTER 4

THE ROMAN PERIOD
AND THE MIDDLE AGES

But soul is not in the universe, on the contrary the universe is in the soul.
—Plotinus, *Enneads,* V, p. 411

What historians call the Roman period spans over ten centuries, from its obscure beginnings in the seventh century B.C. to 476 A.D., when the last of the Roman emperors was deposed. The beginnings of a formally organized Roman republic date from the fifth century B.C., and by 100 A.D. Rome had become a mighty empire that appeared all but invincible. At the height of its power, the Roman Empire included all of the countries of the Mediterranean Sea. It extended to the western shores of Spain and as far east as the Persian Gulf. On the north, it included much of what is present-day England and its southern command included the countries of northern Africa, extending well into southern Egypt. This huge expanse was the result of the well-known military successes of Rome, but, as with all military success, there was a price. The acquisition of so much territory placed a heavy drain on material, economic, and human resources. Thus, Rome's successes contributed to the ultimate collapse of the empire.

As early as the second century B.C., the population of the city of Rome was approximately one million, but the greater Empire contained fifty to one hundred million people. The people of Rome changed markedly over the centuries. In the early development of the Empire, its citizens were superstitious, polytheistic, patriotic, practical, disciplined, and oriented toward the family. The society was paternalistic; legal power was vested in the father. An unfaithful woman could be put to death and a disobedient child could be severely punished or even sold into slavery. Conformity, duty, obedience, order, loyalty, and perseverance were among the qualities expected of the good citizen. Valued activities included legal, economic, military, business, and industrial endeavors. The Romans loved technology but had little use for science.

In later periods, the Roman character changed, partly as a result of the great influx of Christians, Jews, northern barbarians, Greeks, and Ethiopians. Roman polytheism, already in decline, was challenged by Jewish monotheism. Greek educators provided breadth of perspective to Roman students and Greek physicians were viewed with a mixture of admiration and paranoia. We shall soon return to this mixed reaction to Greek physicians. By the first century A.D., the Romans had developed a great love for the material comforts and pleasures provided by years of conquest. Baths and swimming and exercise facilities abounded. Soaps, cosmetics, exotic clothes, jewelry, and music imported from Greece became part of the Roman way of life. A proliferation of holidays afforded opportunities to attend games and circuses that soon degenerated into the spectacles for which the later Empire is so well remembered. Wild animals imported from Africa and the North, and slaves, captives, and professional gladiators were pitted against each other in varieties of combinations designed to shock, surprise, and delight the bloodthirsty populace. A few civilized Romans spoke against the slaughter of animals and people, but such dissidents were greatly outnumbered.

The fertile intellectual climate necessary to the nourishment of the scientific spirit was not to be found among the masses who were addicted to the games. But neither was it to be found among more serious leaders whose concerns were focused in the military, economic, and legal arenas. There was little reward or support for a disinterested search for basic natural processes in a society obsessed with immediate practical results. Thus, Rome produced few scientific achievements; Roman science borrowed from Greek thought. The Romans did have some interest in geology, probably because Italy is prone to earthquakes and volcanic eruptions. The Romans used geometry ingeniously in their architecture, but did little to advance the discipline itself. An interest in the stars was motivated mainly by astrology. Medicine flourished because of the practical needs for keeping a large military machine in good repair. Let us briefly examine some aspects of Roman medicine, because in that context we encounter some psychological speculation.

ROMAN MEDICINE

Early Roman medicine was riddled with superstition, and psychological cures or miracle cures abounded. An Aesculapian temple erected in the third century B.C. proved popular with the Romans, who basked in the gentle and relaxed atmosphere. Early surgery in Rome was practiced by barbers, captives from other countries, and quacks. The relationship between Greek and Roman medicine was apparently turbulent. In general, the Greeks were better trained, but when their surgery or medicine failed, the Romans became suspicious or even paranoid. A Greek physician named Asclepiades (c. 124 B.C.), practicing in Rome, was one of the earliest of the period to devote attention to mental disorders. Asclepiades distinguished between delusions and hallucinations and argued that therapy for mental disorders should be pleasant and administered promptly. Like Hippocrates, he relied heavily on diet control, music, massage, baths, and exercise. During his life he apparently attracted many patients and students.

Galen

Second in importance only to Hippocrates in the history of medicine is Claudius Galenus (A.D. 129–c. 199), by far the best-known Roman physi-

cian. Galen studied philosophy in Pergamum and anatomy in Alexandria, Egypt. In his time, dissection of human cadavers had been outlawed in Rome, so Galen conducted his anatomical studies on pigs and apes. As physician and surgeon for gladiators, he also had opportunities for limited studies of human anatomy. Galen was the author of approximately four hundred medical treatises covering a great range of topics, but today only eighty-three of his works are extant. He devoted considerable attention to psychological topics, including emotional disorders.

Galen subscribed to the four-humor theory (black bile, blood, phlegm, and yellow bile), advanced by the Greeks. In addition to the humors, he argued that four qualities (cold, warm, dry, and moist) play a role in sickness and health. Galen believed that humors and qualities are somewhat seasonal. Thus, for example, blood, warmth, and moistness are more likely to be prevalent in the spring whereas phlegm, coldness, and moistness are associated with the winter. Galen believed that various foods and treatment procedures could increase or decrease the humors and qualities. Additionally, he noted that geography, occupation, and age influence the humors and qualities. Galen believed also in a constitutional basis for the distribution of the humors and qualities. He used the terms *sanguine* (cheerful, optimistic), *choleric* (quick tempered), *melancholic* (tendency toward depression), and *phlegmatic* (lethargic, inactive) to refer to temperaments possessing mild natural excesses of certain humors and qualities. When one is in good health, he believed, there is a balance among humors and qualities.

According to Jackson (1969), Galen believed in a physiological basis for mental disorders, but also believed that functional or psychological causes have consequences for physiology. As an example, Jackson related Galen's account of the discovery of some physiological manifestations of the emotional state of a woman in love. The woman in question was being examined by Galen for insomnia. During the course of the examination, Galen was about to conclude that the woman had an excess of black bile, resulting from melancholia. But then some other person in the examining room talked of having gone to the theater to see the popular dancer Pylades. Immediately, the patient's expression changed and Galen observed that her heart rate became very irregular. In subsequent examinations he found that reference to other dancers had no impact on her heart rate, but the mere mention of Pylades caused a reliable physiological reaction. Galen concluded that the woman was in love and went on to point out that mental states may have important physiological consequences.

Galen believed that most mental disorders are the result of an imbalance in the various humors and qualities. Thus, as noted above, black bile may be implicated in melancholia. Mania (excessive excitement) was thought to be a "hot disease" related to excesses of yellow bile and heat. Treatments often consisted of applying opposites to counteract excesses. Thus a "cold wet disease" might be treated with warm and dry remedies, and vice versa.

Galen was one of the first to emphasize the importance of education, advice, or counsel in the control and alleviation of emotional problems. His book *On the Diagnosis and Cure of the Soul's Passions* contains advice on the importance of seeking the counsel of another person for emotional problems. The other person, as noted by Jackson (1969), should be "an older man—mature, respected, free from passions—who would point out the other person's faults in regard to his passions." This is a clear example of an ancient concept of psychotherapy. To be sure, such therapy must have been authoritarian and directive, but it stressed education and confrontation of passions (e.g., greed, anger, jealousy, etc.) thought to be responsible for psychological problems.

Galen was a vitalist. He embraced the concept of the **pneuma,** which he used in several ways. On the one hand, *pneuma* referred to air that is drawn in as we breathe and distributed to the various tissues. On the other hand, *pneuma* was also thought to be manifested in three kinds of vital principles. The first was **natural spirit,** involved in simple vegetative (maintenance) life processes. Natural spirit, largely unconscious, is found in all life, plant and animal; in animals it was thought to come to the blood from the liver. A second manifestation of pneuma was called **vital spirit;** its seat was in the heart and it was thought to be involved in the regulation of the heat of the body. Galen also spoke

of the *psychic pneuma,* which is usually translated as **animal spirit.** The animal spirit, according to Galen, had its seat in the brain and was involved in higher cognitive function.

Galen's concept of the pneuma related to some of his views on motion. He believed that passive motion characterized nonliving things. They move by virtue of the operation of physical laws such as gravity. Living things are also subject to passive motion but, in addition, living things manifest vital actions or active motions. Active motion is autonomous or self-generated movement, made possible by the pneuma in its various manifestations.

The central role of the pneuma (especially in its manifestation as *animal spirit*) in human life was viewed by early Christian religious leaders as entirely consistent with church doctrine; the body is subservient to the soul. As a consequence, Galen's medical doctrines were assimilated into Christian theological doctrines. This development, coupled with laws against empirical medicine (e.g., dissection), served to create the basis for centuries of medical dogmatism based largely on the teachings of Galen. Galen's legitimate discoveries were perpetuated, but in the absence of experimentation, so were his errors. For 1,500 years, until the seventeenth century, major psychological topics (e.g., movement, thought, perception, etc.) were explained largely in terms of vital principles or animal spirits. Pneuma theory remained unchallenged until the discoveries of the seventeenth- and eighteenth-century physiologists.

It is unfortunate that so much of Galenic medicine became rigid dogma because Galen himself was motivated by empirical studies on animals and extensive travel to search for medications and ideas. Galen could respect authority but he supplemented such respect with research. As the substantive aspects of Galen's medicine became dogmatized, those empirical components of his system that might have had salutary consequences not only for medicine but also for related disciplines such as physiology and psychology were lost.

ROMAN PHILOSOPHY

The major schools or systems of philosophy in the Roman period were stoicism, Epicureanism, skepticism, and neo-Platonism. All of these schools were largely derivative. They are not known for original contributions or for concern about great world questions. The primary focus was on the individual and how to escape the ills of the world and how to live the good life.

Stoicism

The school of **stoicism,** founded by Zeno of Cyprus (c. 335–c. 263 B.C.), thrived for over five hundred years. Although a few of the early leaders of the stoic school were interested in the physical sciences, the major thrust of the school was on discipline, self-control, reason, and the absolute lawfulness of nature. Psychologically, the stoics advocated suppression of self-will and appetite. Virtue was to be found in an ascetic existence based on duty, reason, principle, and extinction of the passions. Pleasure was not to be sought in its own right, but such happiness as can be achieved was to be found as one of the benefits of the life of discipline.

The stoics argued that states (nations) are completely arbitrary geographic divisions that are absurd. They believed that human beings should be identified with each other in such a manner as to expose the irrationality of nations. They thought that true wisdom precludes identity with a state, but they also noted that, pitiable as it is for the world, the number of the wise is a mere trifle. Most human beings, according to the stoics, are fools.

Epictetus. A slave by birth, Epictetus (*EHP ihk TEE tuhs*) was a stoic whose teachings had widespread appeal to poor Romans and possibly to early Christians who could identify with the plight of slaves. His birth is estimated to have been approximately between the years 50 and 55 and he died about 130. He was lame, possibly from mistreatment as a slave, and apparently freed in his late teen years. He attended lectures and devoted himself to philosophy, which he viewed as a cure for the soul. According to Meredith (1986), Epictetus saw the lecture room of the philosopher as a kind of hospital, a place where restoration and healing could take place.

A central theme in the teachings of Epictetus is the importance of distinguishing between the things that are within our control and the things that are beyond our control. As a slave, Epictetus had undoubtedly developed deep sensitivities to things that are beyond human influence and control. He believed there is a wisdom in resignation to those things we cannot possibly remedy by our own actions. All we can do in such cases is trust there are larger forces we may not understand and that these forces are somehow unfolding as they should. Contentment and happiness are undermined by raging against inexorable forces. It could be argued that there is a strong stoic element encountered in Paul's prison epistles, such as Philippians 4:11 that states, "I have learned in whatever state I am, *in this* to be content." Though there are parallels between stoicism and the early Christian teachings of Paul, there are also major differences (see Wilson, 1997). Later Christians, though largely hostile to all pagan thought, were nevertheless, in practice if not theory, remarkably stoic. Yet, below the surface, the differences here may also be far greater than the similarities (see James, 1902/1985, p. 45).

Epictetus loved simplicity, order, moral courage, self-control, discipline, and forebearance. Hallie (1967) noted that Epictetus demanded daily self-examination as a means of promoting self-knowledge. He demanded that human beings take responsibility for the things they can control. Though we often find ourselves in circumstances we cannot control, nevertheless, we can control our attitude toward such circumstances and avoid complaining. Epictetus was known to have had a strong influence on the Roman emperor Marcus Aurelius (A.D. 121–180), who was one of the most eminent of the stoic philosophers. Marcus Aurelius argued that things beyond our control that seem disagreeable should nevertheless be accepted because such things are undoubtedly a significant part of the whole. If we could but see the whole picture, we would discover that a whining and critical attitude is selfish. In any critical appraisal, we must admit that stoic philosophy, conscientiously followed, may foster an admirable tranquility in the face of difficulties. On the other hand, could stoicism lead to passivity and an underestimate of our abilities to effect changes that might benefit ourselves and others? Could stoicism have provided an adequate philosophical base for later scientists and humanitarian reformers, outraged at suffering and injustice and eager to understand and control natural forces?

Epicureanism

Named after Epicurus of Samos (341–270 B.C.), **Epicureanism** was founded at about the same time as stoicism, approximately three hundred years prior to the advent of Christianity. The Epicureans believed that pleasure is a positive good and that pain is an evil to be avoided. They noted that the world is structured in such a fashion as to preclude the possibility of sustained pleasure. They counseled against excesses such as gluttony that may produce temporary pleasure but long-term discomfort. Examples of other things that interfere with pleasure include false opinions, fear of death, or excessive fear of the gods. The Epicureans advised against excessively heavy social responsibility. Instead, one should strive for a simple uncomplicated existence. Psychologically, expression is to be preferred to suppression so long as such expression is judicious. The school of Epicureanism survived until at least A.D. 200.

Lucretius.   The philosophy of Lucretius (c. 96–c. 55 B.C.) is expressed poetically in his work *De Rerum Natura* ("On the Nature of Things" or "On the Nature of the Universe"). The work is composed of six books, on matter and space, movements and shapes of atoms, life and mind, sensation and sex, cosmology and sociology, and meteorology and geology. Many of the ideas are clearly derived from earlier Greek thought, but there are those (e.g., Latham, 1967, p. 99) who suggest that the originality of Lucretius may be underestimated. Consider briefly some of his psychological concepts.

Lucretius argued strongly for the unity of body and mind. He insisted that mind cannot exist apart from body: "Mind and body as a living force derive their vigour and vitality from their conjunction" (Lucretius, *On the Nature of the Universe,* p. 113). He supported his position in several ways. Mind and body grow together—if they were independent, why do they parallel each other so closely? He argued that the mind is not birthless—it comes into existence with the birth of the body

and grows with the body. In further defense, he asks us to suppose that spirits are just slipped into the body from outside and then argues that "it is surely ludicrous to suppose that spirits are standing by at the mating and birth of animals—a numberless number of immortals on the look-out for mortal frames, jostling and squabbling to get in first . . . or is there perhaps an established compact that first come shall be first served?" (Lucretius, *On the Nature of the Universe,* p. 119).

Like Leucippus and Democritus of old, Lucretius believed that all things are composed of atoms and that the qualities we encounter are based on the different sizes and shapes of these atoms. However, he argued that atoms, as they fall through space, are known to swerve ever so slightly from their path; the swerve interferes with a completely determinist order of things and serves as a theoretical basis for human free will. Latham (1967) noted that Lucretius wanted to demonstrate "that voluntary action arises from within and ultimately from the unpredictable movement of a single atom" (p. 101).

As we noted, Lucretius followed the early teachings of the Epicureans regarding knowledge. The senses provide information about the material world, so the senses and their functions are keys to understanding the mind. Latham (1959) noted that Lucretius argued that "psychologists are wrong in thinking that the mind is anything other than an assemblage of very mobile particles that easily group themselves into patterns or images in conformity with other images that impinge upon them from outside objects" (p. 11).

Because sensation was the basis of knowledge, Lucretius was interested in the workings of the sense organs. He embraced an atomic film theory to account for sensation. Vision, an extension of the sense of touch, is activated by thin atomic films emanating from objects. Taste results in the mouth "when we squeeze it out by chewing food, just as if someone were to grasp a sponge full of water in his hand and begin to squeeze it dry. Next, all that we squeeze out is diffused through the pores of the palate and the winding channels of the spongy tongue" (Lucretius, *On the Nature of the Universe,* p. 149). Different tastes result from the commingled food atoms and the interatomic atoms of the channels. Thus, what tastes good to one person may not taste good to another.

Lucretius taught that fear of death and fear of Hell are great evils to overcome. As an Epicurean, he was interested primarily in ethics and in that way of life that maximizes pleasure and minimizes pain. He argued against immediate gratification and for the value of discipline. He valued true piety, which for him was the capacity to philosophize with an undisturbed mind. Lucretius lamented the superstition that parades as piety, the "oftrepeated show of bowing a veiled head before a graven image; this bustling to every altar; this kowtowing and prostration on the ground with palms outspread before the shrines of the gods; this deluging of altars with the blood of beasts; this heaping of vow on vow" (Lucretius, *On the Nature of the Universe*, p. 208).

In his book on cosmology and sociology, Lucretius proposed a theory of the evolution of social groups, religion, and language. He believed that early human groups evolved because of a contract to protect the weak. Such a contract may have been motivated partly by the necessity of first protecting defenseless offspring and then others who were also weak. Groups who broke the contract failed to survive. As for religious beliefs, Lucretius argued that many of them are born in fear of the forces of nature. He proposed that language evolved gradually; we first imitated the sounds of animals and gradually recognized the practical convenience of communication via verbal symbols.

Lucretius, the empiricist, the materialist, the Epicurean, was a creature of this world, and his philosophy conveys his love of nature and his preference for parsimonious explanations. We turn our attention now to a school of philosophy that contrasts sharply with the naturalistic tradition embraced by Lucretius.

Neo-Platonism

In terms of lasting influence, **neo-Platonism** was the most important school of philosophy following Aristotle. It was important partly because it called attention to some of the affinities between earlier Greek traditions and Jewish and Christian mysticism. For good or ill, it was a participant in the wedding of philosophy and religion that was to be a dominant feature of the Middle Ages. Generations of theologians, beginning with Augustine, were deeply influenced by neo-Platonism. The corruption and transience of the material world, the problem of evil, and the illusory nature of sense perception were emphasized along with the importance of intellectual principles and the activities of the soul.

Plotinus. Plotinus (A.D. 205–270) was among the last of the great Roman philosophers and is often viewed as the founder of neo-Platonism. He was probably born an Egyptian, but received a Greek education in Alexandria. He traveled extensively and apparently developed considerable knowledge of Indian and Persian philosophies. About 245, he settled in Rome and made friends with the emperor Gallienus. Plotinus enjoyed over twenty productive years in Rome. He attracted numerous students and, with the editing skills of his student Porphyry, produced six volumes entitled *Enneads*. Plotinus probably left Rome following the assassination of Gallienus in 268.

The Platonic character of Plotinus's thought is immediately evident. He argued that the "Soul is not in the universe, on the contrary the universe is in the Soul; bodily substance is not a place to the Soul; Soul is contained in Intellectual-Principle and is the container of the body" (Plotinus, *Enneads*, V, p. 411). Moore (1946) pointed out that Plotinus is arguing that "knowables cannot be external to mind." Mental processes, or activities of the soul, therefore have a certain primacy; they are not to be regarded as derivative.

Plotinus believed that the world of matter is a world of multiplicity and divisibility. He noted that there were three unextended or nonmaterial things that are above matter. The first of these was an abstract notion of the one that may be regarded as God, or the highest order of reality. The second was an abstract notion of intellectual principle. This order of reality was comparable to Plato's realm of forms containing principles, such as the principle of triangularity, that rise above particulars. The third order of incorporal things was that of the soul. Souls were instantiated in bodies that were temporary carriers. The body could be a burden to the soul and weigh it down or alienate it, but the soul transcended the body and would be reincarnated in a new body later. Plotinus also believed in direct communication of one soul with another via extrasensory means.

Moore (1946) pointed out that Plotinus recognized an active quality in perception. She called attention to the fact that "for Plotinus, the perceiving mind has and is a unity. It is not a subordinate of the external object, nor of any physical reality" (p. 48). She quoted Plotinus on this topic; he said, "There can be no perception without a unitary percipient whose identity enables it to grasp an object as an entirety" (Plotinus, *Enneads,* IV, p. 346). Thus, for Plotinus, perception is not just a matter of imprints or impressions; there must be something more, something that provides organization and unity. Plotinus argued for a similar active principle in memory. "Sensation and memory, then, are not passivity, but power" (Plotinus, *Enneads,* IV, p. 341).

Plotinus also addressed the problem of self-understanding and happiness. Happiness is attained in knowing the "true-self" through the process of self-knowledge. Merlan (1967) notes that "the concept of the unconscious plays a decisive role in the system of Plotinus" (p. 358). Self-knowledge is elusive; it is attained through contemplation and in the consistency of action and thought. We do not have self-knowledge when we are torn by multiplicity or when we fail to be guided by intelligence.

Plotinus speculated on numerous other psychological topics. In a brief essay, for example, he treated the topic "how distant objects appear small" (Plotinus, *Enneads,* II, 8). He reviewed existing theories but seemed to prefer the Aristotelian idea that we perceive both color and size. As an object recedes, its color or brightness fades and its details become fuzzy. We lose perspective on individual parts and begin to respond to the thing as a whole. Plotinus believed that when details are seen, then perception is more accurate. Plotinus argued for freedom of choice and against the then popular notions of astrology. He was willing to admit small influences from the stars but believed that astrology, in strong forms, is not rational. Further, his belief in the primacy of the soul was inconsistent with astrological views.

Hypatia of Alexandria. The most important leader of the neo-Platonic school in the fourth century was undoubtedly the celebrated philosopher-mathematician Hypatia (c. 370–415). She was the daughter of Theon, a mathematician-astronomer who worked at the library at Alexandria. Though little is known about Hypatia's education, there is evidence that she benefited from the instruction of her father and the cultural opportunities afforded by the library. By her late twenties, Hypatia was the leader of the neo-Platonic school at Alexandria. She lectured to students who came from all parts of the known world and was the teacher of several prominent philosophers of her era.

Hypatia is remembered primarily for her expertise in geometry and astronomy, but she probably accepted most of the teachings of the neo-Platonic tradition. Indeed, Hypatia's use of music therapy in the treatment of mental disorders may have been one of several heresies that led to her murder (see Richeson, 1940). Music therapy was apparently associated with various forms of paganism, and Hypatia lived in a time when there were tremendous tensions between the Christian church and various pagan religions. For a complicated set of reasons, some ideological and some political, Hypatia somehow came under the suspicion of Cyril, the Bishop of Alexandria. During Lent in

Hypatia

415, she was attacked by a group of monks who dragged her into a church, dismembered her, and burned her remains. Her tragic story has been the subject of considerable comment (Viney, 1989; Waithe, 1987a) and is another reminder of an all too human reluctance to allow philosophy to be free.

We turn now to another dominant school in post-Aristotelian and -Roman philosophy that challenged dogmatic beliefs in immutable truths.

Skepticism

The historical roots of **skepticism** are found in the works of such pre-Socratic philosophers as Anaximander, Xenophanes, and Heraclitus, all of whom emphasized the changing nature of things. It was Pyrrho (c. 360–c. 270 B.C.), however, who introduced a systematic philosophy of skepticism that attacked philosophical dogmatism. Pyrrho believed we must live our lives on the basis of opinion, appearance, and probability. The skeptics noted that for every argument there seems to be a counterargument. Authorities disagree with each other and, furthermore, our sensory impressions are not consistent. Skeptics also called attention to the fact that different animals have different sensory systems. How do we know that our sensory system is superior to all others? If we cannot trust our senses, neither can we trust reason, because reason is always based on initial propositions that are plain assumptions. The skeptics also called attention to the fact that circumstances condition the way we react to our world.

Sextus Empiricus.   The leader of the skeptical school in the late second and early third centuries was the Greek physician Sextus Empiricus. His birth and death dates are uncertain; neither are historians certain about where he did his work. Sextus argued that human beings should suspend judgment on most matters and live on the basis of probable truths. Skepticism does not have to deny altogether that there is immutable truth, but even if there is, how do we know with certainty that we possess it? Dogmatic certainty could lead to the greatest anxiety, frustration, unhappiness, and disillusionment if it is confronted with overwhelming contrary evidence. On the other hand, the openness

that goes with suspended judgment can lead to a modicum of contentment, happiness, and tranquillity. Further, according to Sextus, the skeptic is free to consider all sides of an argument and to weigh everything as equally probable in an open and honest fashion. One can even make a commitment and live life on the basis of a probability, always aware, however, that one may be wrong.

The skeptics sought to avoid the pretension, presumption, and rash personal qualities they found in dogmatists. They admired the humility associated with the admission of our human frailties in matters of knowledge. Indeed, in later historical periods, skeptics argued that pretension is the original human malady, and it is pretension that leads to all kinds of personal and social strife including war. Skepticism as a recognized school of thought, died out as Christianity became more and more dominant. As we will see later, however, it will be a Christian outraged at Protestant-Catholic wars in the sixteenth century who will resurrect a very powerful form of Pyrrhonian skepticism designed to challenge religious certitude.

THE FALL OF ROME

It is understandable that historians have been so interested in the fall of Rome. When we consider the preeminence of Rome at the height of its power, we can hardly help wondering about the reasons for the demise of such an awesome political, economic, and military experiment. Ironically, Rome's success contributed to its downfall. The borders of the empire extended to great distances and defense became an unbearable economic burden. When economic growth was needed there was a great decline in the population and consequently in the tax base. As early as the second century, masses of people were enjoying the luxury of smaller families. In the third century, the plague decimated the Roman population. It is also likely that infanticide checked population growth; female infants especially were killed in large numbers. Extensive military campaigns and emasculation of slaves also reduced the population. The downfall of Rome must be understood as the result of a complex pattern of the demise of economic, moral, social, and political institutions. The tensions between Rome and the Christian church also contributed—it was, after all, the church that would become preeminent during the Middle Ages.

THE EARLY CHRISTIAN FAITH

It is an oversimplification to think of the early Christian faith as a single system. As early as the first, second, and third centuries in Rome, the faith was beset with internal strife. Heresies such as Gnosticism, Marcionism, and Montanism vied for disciples, and well-known leaders such as Irenaeus, Tertullian, and Origen did not always agree on matters of doctrine. During the fourth and fifth centuries, early church councils did make some progress toward a more unified approach to the faith. The chief problem for the early church, however, was its conflict with the secular powers in Rome. Widespread persecutions began with the burning of Rome in 64 A.D. These persecutions had far-reaching implications for the development of doctrine. It is unknown whether the doctrines that became ascendant in the face of injustice and persecution would also have prevailed in a more hospitable environment. In any case, what developed was an emphasis on other-worldliness. The immediate material world and physical existence were viewed as without value. Life was but a temporary testing ground for human souls on their journeys to other worlds that would compensate for the injustice of this world. Thus, it was thought that peace and happiness await the righteous in heaven, and torment awaits the wicked in hell. The only important knowledge was provided by revelation and authority. With the value of this life and this world called into question, science was viewed as trivial. One was better advised to attend to the affairs of the soul than to engage in such frivolities.

It is of interest that church doctrine in the Roman era undoubtedly departed significantly from the teachings of Jesus. Indeed, there is considerable modern scholarship on this topic. One example will illustrate the point. Several scholars (e.g., Christen, 1984; Daly, 1968; Southard, 1927) have called attention to profound discrepancies between attitudes toward women in the patristic church and the attitudes displayed by Jesus. For example, Jesus spoke to women, even foreign women, in public, in clear violation of the customs of the day that forbade looking at women, let alone speaking to them (see Jeremias, 1975, p. 363). Jesus accepted women as travel companions and included them in instructional activities. Both of these practices were radical violations of existing gender barriers. He also struck at existing divorce standards that greatly favored males. His parables sometimes accorded greater moral status to women than to the conventionally religious and powerful. In the patristic church there was an obsession with blaming woman for the "fall" but in no instance does Jesus do this. The original teachings and practices of Jesus regarding women are not remotely recognizable in the later male-dominated church. There were undoubtedly departures from original Christian doctrine in many other areas and many such departures are understandable in view of the social context of early Christianity.

In the fourth century, the Roman Emperor Constantine converted to Christianity; there was a declaration of religious freedom and restoration of property to the church. At the same time, "barbarians" were pushing against the borders and the Roman Empire was essentially in ruins. Authority shifted from state to church, and gradually it was the church that defined the legitimate boundaries of the intellectual arena. It was church leaders such as Augustine and Aquinas in the Christian faith, Maimonides in the Jewish faith, and Avicenna in the Islamic faith who established the intellectual agenda. Before turning to the teachings of these leaders, we will consider some of the general characteristics of what has been called the **Medieval period.**

THE MEDIEVAL PERIOD

The term *medieval* is derived from the Latin terms *medius* (middle) and *aevium* (age). The Middle Ages is that lengthy period of history in Europe between the fall of Rome and the Renaissance. The starting date of the Middle Ages is arbitrary. There is no one discrete event in history that marks the fall of Rome or that ushers in the Middle Ages. Similarly, the ending date is arbitrary because the transition from the Middle Ages to the Renaissance was gradual. For our purposes, we may regard the

Middle Ages as a period that extends from about A.D. 400 to about A.D. 1300.

The Middle Ages were marked by many curious and contradicting trends. It is an accommodating period for historians when they wish to find evidence in support of their preconceptions. If they look for the stagnation of thought, they can find it. If they look for the regression of thought, they can find it. If they wish to point to mischievous and corrupt influences of the church, examples will abound in every century, and if a person of a different persuasion wishes to highlight the growth and influence of religious compassion and charity, another set of examples can be found. As with all historical periods, we can also point to isolated islands of enlightenment somehow surviving in a sea of ignorance. There are also examples aplenty of real discovery and real progress. Thus, in the Middle Ages, we witness the beginnings of the modern university and the modern hospital. We witness the creation of eyeglasses and the invention of the clock. Gunpowder and magnetized needles for the compass were rediscovered, having first been put to use by the Chinese. There were many advances in practical chemistry leading to improved glues, dyes, inks, cosmetics, and enamels. The Medieval period also witnessed some impressive architectural achievements. Neither was there a complete absence of highly imaginative and speculative thought. For example, in the thirteenth century, Roger Bacon (c. 1220–1292) announced the theoretical feasibility of submarines and airplanes. Two centuries earlier, Oliver of Malmesbury died when he launched a flying contraption from a high place (Mumford, 1934, p. 22).

Alongside the progress and discovery, we can find evidence of the regression of thought in some intellectual arenas. For example, in many places there was a return to primitive magical and superstitious thinking. This regression often had an influence on psychological and medical thought, resulting in belief systems that were primitive compared to the naturalistic approaches advocated earlier by Hippocrates and Galen. The beliefs in a world occupied by mysterious occult powers and mischievous demons led to outrageous superstitious practices designed to ward off potential malevolent influence. There is no shortage of examples.

White (1896/1910) gave an example of a medical treatment: "If an elf or a goblin come, smear his forehead with salve, put it in his eyes, cense him with insense, and sign him frequently with the sign of the cross" (p. 102). Medications were often chosen for their presumed ability to offend and drive out an indwelling demon. Thus, in the combat with the forces of evil, one might call on priestly saliva, wolf dung, or any of a number of bitter or offensive materials.

In much of the Middle Ages there were beliefs in signs, omens, prophecies, soothsaying, astrology, and palmistry. A sign or omen could be found in almost anything—a fly that lands on one's forehead, a sneeze, the prolonged stare of a dog, a change in the weather, the spilling of food, or any kind of accidental encounter with presumed unlucky numbers such as 666 or 13. The effects of signs and symbols could often be warded off with quick action. The sign of the cross, a quick prayer, the wearing of a cross, the rubbing of a stone, the repetition of a verse or formula, any of these and countless other superstitious actions were viewed as defenses against the myriad mischievous forces or as placations of the demands of benevolent forces.

Let us turn now briefly to the problem of knowledge as we encounter that branch of philosophy in Medieval thought. It is sometimes assumed that most of the knowledge claims of the period were based on the method of authority or on mystical revelations of divine wisdom. One can find numerous examples that support the assumption and some of the examples now strike us as outrageous.

For example, trial by ordeal and trial by combat were often used as tests of truth. Trial by combat, different in intent than a duel, was often based on the assumption that God would not permit an injustice to occur; therefore, truth and God's way would be revealed by who wins the combat. A given party in a dispute also had the right to hire a champion, a professional, to fight on his or her behalf. Insults, challenges, disputes, or sometimes political decisions were adjudicated on the basis of "God's will," as revealed by the outcome of trial by combat. The church opposed this practice, but often to no avail. Trial by ordeal, a practice that was common during witch-hunts, typically involved the infliction of some injury such as a burn on an accused individual. If the individual still showed evidence of the injury after a specified time, say three days, he or she was guilty. If there were no evidence of the injury, it was taken as a sign of God's intervention and the individual might be judged as not guilty.

While these rather bizarre methods of knowing were employed in the Middle Ages and while there was heavy reliance on authority, we should also remember that there was some serious epistemological work accomplished in this period. Later we will review Thomas Aquinas's struggle with the reconciliation of faith and reason.

Before proceeding, we should remind ourselves that what we call the Middle Ages covers a vast expanse of time and space—over a thousand years of history, a geographic region extending from the western shores of Spain to kingdoms in the Northern and Baltic Seas, to Islamic territories (after the seventh century) in the south and east, to what some people regard as "holy land." Three major religious traditions (Christian, Islamic, and Jewish) as well as variations in the economic, social, physical, and political dimensions of cultures contributed to a seldom appreciated diversity among peoples. Accordingly, it is advisable to be cautious about easy generalizations or sweeping epitaphs such as the Dark Ages, though one can point to specific times and places for which that term appears to be applicable. In the psychological arena we must also resist easy generalities because there was no one all-prevailing viewpoint on psychological topics such as learning, mental illness, motivation, and so on. But that will become clear as we examine selected leading thinkers.

Aurelius Augustine

More commonly known as St. Augustine (*AW guh steen* or *aw GUHS tihn*), Aurelius Augustine (354–430) was a pivotal figure in the transition from the Roman period to the Middle Ages. In St. Augustine, we encounter a combination of Greek and Christian thought. He was particularly influenced by the works of the Platonists and by the similarities between Christian and Platonic thought. He also saw differences in Christian and Platonic

St. Augustine

thought, but the workable combinations of the two systems are clearly reflected in St. Augustine's major works. His work became a powerful intellectual force throughout the Middle Ages.

Augustine was born in the town of Tagaste in northern Africa. His father and mother were a study in contrasts. His mother, Monica, was a devout Christian and his father was a man of the world with only a compromised dedication to wife and family. In his early years, Augustine followed the path of his father, but it was Monica who had the long-term telling influences on the direction of her son's life.

At no small financial expense to his parents, Augustine attended school in Madura and later in Carthage, both in northern Africa. In his famous retrospective autobiography *Confessions,* he told of his waywardness as a youth. He spoke with candor of his sexual exploits and his love of praise by his rowdy friends. Following his schooling at Carthage, Augustine taught grammar and rhetoric and lived with a concubine, a legal arrangement under Roman law. He fathered a son whom he named Adeodatus (meaning "given of God"). Augustine's great loyalty to his son represents one of the few loyalties in his early life. His experiences, both with women and philosophies, were transient and all the while his dissatisfaction increased. He separated from his concubine and procured another mistress during an engagement to still another girl. He described himself as "a slave of lust" and as "in bondage to a lasting habit" (Augustine, *Confessions,* p. 132). Augustine read Aristotle, studied astrology, and, for a time, embraced Manichaeism, a religion that rivaled Christianity. Augustine also flirted with skepticism, but was finally converted to the teaching of neo-Platonism and Plotinus. Still, he was unhappy.

The story of Augustine's conversion is partly a story of his own intellectual and spiritual journey, but it is also a story of the persistent impact of Monica on his life. Prior to his conversion, Augustine described himself as sick and tormented. Total dedication to the faith meant giving up what the sensuous Augustine loved most: "My old mistresses, trifles of trifles and vanities of vanities . . . still enthralled me. They tugged at my fleshly garments and softly whispered: 'Are you going to part with us?' " (Augustine, *Confessions,* p. 174). Then, in a moment of tearful crisis, Augustine heard the voice of a child say, "Pick it up, read it" (*Sume, lege*). He took this to be a divine command to open the Bible and read the first passage he saw. The random selection of a biblical passage (*sortes sanctorum*) was, for centuries, justified as the basis for an authentic communication from God. Augustine picked up a Bible and opened it to a scripture that condemned the very activities he loved the most. He was immediately converted and was baptized in 387 by the well-known church father Ambrose. As an aside, it is of interest that psychologists interested in religious experience have viewed Augustine's conversion as classic—it has often been the subject of psychological discussion (e.g., see Coe, 1900, p. 210).

Augustine returned to Africa, where he lived out his life in poverty and celibacy as preacher, writer, bishop, and defender of the faith. Augustine, perhaps more than any other, set the tone of Western thought for centuries to come. Coe (1900) observed that "Augustine, always intemperate where feeling was concerned, was now intemperately temperate" (p. 212). As an example, Coe, quoting from the *Confessions,* cites materials from Book 10, Chapter 33, noting that Augustine now felt guilt any time he was moved by the aesthetics of church music rather than its message. Augustine founded the first

monastic order and worked faithfully for the church until his death in A.D. 430.

Augustine discussed a great number of psychological topics, including infant motivation, the origin of speech, memory, grief, and unconscious motivation in dreams. We examine here some selected psychological topics found in his writings.

Infant Motivation. Psychologists have long been divided over questions of infant motivation. Augustine emphasized the self-seeking, asocial, and even brutish nature of the infant. Speaking of his infancy, he recalled his selfishness, jealousy of other children, desire to win at any cost, and temper tantrums. He also observed the self-serving nature of children's prayers, noting that he "prayed with no slight earnestness that [he] might not be beaten at school" (Augustine, *Confessions,* p. 39). This was apparently a prayer that was not answered in the affirmative very often.

Though punishment was commonplace in the schools of Augustine's day, he did not view it or its accompanying fear as a sound basis for learning. Augustine argued that fear of punishment interferes with curiosity and a general frame of mind conducive to learning. He speculated that threats and cruel punishments in school had interfered with his learning of Greek, but his learning of Latin had been facilitated by a supportive environment free from the pressure of punishment.

Grief. Augustine plumbed the extremes of more than one kind of emotion. His descriptions of grief show unusual sensitivity and understanding. He describes his bitter grief upon the death of a beloved friend. The description (see Augustine, *Confessions,* pp. 81–83) shows the pervasiveness of grief and the religious turmoil that often accompanies grief. During his period of grief, he experienced a severe episode of death anxiety or fear that he might die. He observed that his own fear of death, during the grief period, might have been caused by the fear that his death would mean a more complete death for his friend. At least his friend lived on in his consciousness. If he now died, his friend would be all the more dead. Augustine observed that the consolation of his friends and new associations and ideas that came in the course of time contributed to the dissipation of his grief.

Habit Breaking.   Consistent with a psychology that emphasized the will, Augustine saw rebuke as a key factor in habit breaking. He told the story of a young man (Augustine, *Confessions,* p. 123) who was addicted to and wasted much time observing the gladiatorial games. The young man, by chance, heard part of one of Augustine's speeches rebuking those who were addicted to the madness of the games. The young man accepted the rebuke and stopped attending the games. Augustine recognized that rebuke can also have an opposite effect, but nevertheless saw a place for its judicious use.

Memory.   Augustine's interest in memory is evident in the considerable space he devoted to the topic in book 10 of the *Confessions.* He referred to memory as a storehouse and drew a clear distinction between recognition and recall. He argued that in sensory memory we do not remember things themselves but only the images of things, but he believed that the nature of the image is obscure in affective memory. What, for example, is the image involved in a memory of joy or sadness? Augustine was also troubled by the mechanism that makes it possible to remember a previous joyful state when we are in a state of sadness or vice versa. Although most memories are mediated by images, Augustine nevertheless also believed that there are things that we "intuit within ourselves without images and as they actually are" (Augustine, *Confessions,* p. 212). Mathematical relations and certain moral truths are included in such intuitions, but memory even for these things must be exercised. Otherwise, they become dispersed or submerged and are called out again only with great effort. It should be noted that Augustine believed in a priori knowledge but rejected Plato's idea that the soul recalls knowledge of the forms that it knew in a previous existence. This latter idea was inconsistent with Augustine's Christian theology.

Dreams.   With typical honesty, Augustine visited with his readers about the dreams he had after his conversion. He continued to dream of former pleasures that were now forbidden. He noted that thoughts of fornication were subdued when he was awake, but such thoughts had great power in sleep. Indeed, some of his dreams of fornication were as real as the act itself. Augustine pointed out that peace of conscience need not be disturbed by forbidden dreams, though one may regret that such dreams are carried on in us. His own analysis was that such dreams are obviously not possible without memory, and in his discussion of memory he alluded several times to deeply buried or hidden memories. He doubted that such hidden memories could be controlled by reason during sleep. Augustine was a keen observer of the deceptive qualities in some psychological processes. For example, he pointed out that the soul often prepares an excuse as a defense; thus we may say that we need a certain portion of food for our health when that portion is really only for pleasure (see Augustine, *Confessions,* p. 227).

All of Augustine's psychological thought must be understood in the context of his theocentric view of the world. His larger theocentric vision is set forth in his classic work, *City of God,* written partly as a rebuttal to the simplistic popular idea that Rome was the city of God. Augustine saw human beings and history itself as caught between the tensions of the earthly city and the city of God. The earthly city is temporary and corrupt. Within it, we are caught up in lust, greed, selfishness, hatred, ambition, and petty concerns. The city of God, by contrast, is permanent and is ruled by love, order, and beauty. We can participate in the city of God, even as residents of this temporary, corrupt earthly abode, but we may also choose to be ruled by the earthly city and participate enthusiastically in its folly and its hatred for God. The key to our loyalty to the earthly city or to the city of God is our love and our will. The love of self and carnal pleasure that Augustine knew so well might move the will to assent to the demands of the earthly city. But a purer love may also incline the will to embrace those eternal values that reside in the city of God.

Though Augustine's works are rich in psychological insights and though he has been celebrated as one of the great psychologists (see Brett, 1912–1921/1965, p. 225); he nevertheless promoted ideas that took root in Medieval thought and that worked against the development of scientific ways of knowing. Harrison (2001) points out that Augustine viewed worldly curiosity as a spiritually dangerous intellectual vice that dates back to the sin of Adam and Eve. Harrison notes further that curiosity, in subsequent Medieval thought, was often associated with the sins of pride, vanity, conceit, and lust. Humility, submission, meekness, and self-abasement were virtues that, for centuries, were widely valued and fostered. There were a few thinkers who embraced the moral and intellectual values of doubt and curiosity, but a wider acceptance of such values so necessary to the scientific spirit would lie in the distant future.

Boethius

Along with Augustine, a Roman statesman and philosopher, Anicius Manlius Severinus Boethius (*bo EE thee uhs*) (c. 480–524), helped set the direction of Western thought. Knowles (1967) contended that "Boethius may rightly be called an eminent founder of the Middle Ages" (p. 329). Boethius attempted to use the reason that he had learned from reading the Greeks to support and defend Christian doctrine. In his attempts to combine reason, authority, and revelation, Boethius was a precursor of those scholastics of the later Middle Ages who employed reason to defend the faith.

Boethius wrote numerous treatises on philosophy, science, and theology, but his most influential book was *On the Consolation of Philosophy*. The *Consolation* was written while Boethius was in prison awaiting execution for treason. The grounds for his conviction are obscure, but execution by strangulation and bludgeoning was carried out in 524. The *Consolation* dealt with some of the problems that would occupy Medieval philosophy—the nature of evil, the attempted reconciliation of divine foreknowledge with human free will, and the nature of God. In the difficult struggle with his own death sentence, Boethius pondered the source of true happiness and found it in oneness with God. His writings on his encounter with adversity served as a source of comfort to others for centuries.

Islam

The seventh century witnessed the beginning of the powerful new Islamic religious tradition on the Arabian peninsula—a tradition that united the Arab peoples (at least until the death of Mohammed in

632) and that quickly constituted a serious challenge to the Jewish and Christian traditions. Within a century of the birth of Mohammed in 570, the Islamic faith had a holy book (the Koran), three holy places (Mecca, Jerusalem, and Madinat an-Nabi), and hundreds of military victories that resulted in the acquisition of a vast expanse of territory, including the entire Arabian peninsula, Syria, the northern coast of Africa, most of Spain, part of southern France, and the Persian Empire (including what is now Iran, Afghanistan, and Pakistan). The northern military momentum of Islam was finally checked near Tours, France, in 732 in one of the most pivotal battles in history. Had the Islamic armies won the battle of Tours and conquered France, the distribution of Muslims, Jews, and Christians in Europe would probably have changed dramatically. We will examine here some representative Islamic contributions in science and philosophy.

Rhazes. A physician whose full name was Abu Bakr al-Razi, Rhazes (*RAH zees*) (c. 854–c. 925) was a writer of medical textbooks with wide-ranging interests in psychology, philosophy, and religion. In a predominantly religious culture in tenth-century Baghdad, Rhazes spoke out against demonological concepts of disease and the arbitrary use of authority in science. Ronan (1982) noted that Rhazes "was quite prepared to criticize ancient authorities, whoever they were, and even wrote a book with the title *Doubts Concerning Galen* (p. 236). Rhazes attacked superstitious religious beliefs and the concept of miracles. He argued strongly for scientific rationalism and against fanaticism and arbitrary authority.

Philosophically, Rhazes stood in the tradition of Democritus, Empedocles, and Hippocrates. He subscribed to atomic theory, the four-element (fire, earth, air, and water) theory, and the humoral theory. He was an empiricist, but religious restraints on freedom of inquiry placed severe limitations on his investigations. Dissection was forbidden and religious conservatives believed that all questions worth asking were answered by the Koran. Even so, Rhazes, working in such an authority-ridden situation, was as empirical as he could be under the circumstances. For example, he was particularly well known for his accurate descriptions of many diseases. He was also an astute observer of the relationship between hygiene and disease. According to Gordon (1959, p. 163) he was the first person to apply the science of chemistry to medicine. Gordon also pointed out that Rhazes's chemical writings and experiments led to personal difficulties. He apparently gave one of his books on chemical experiments to Prince Al-Mansur. The Prince was delighted with the book, but when Rhazes was unable to demonstrate one of the experiments successfully, the Prince became enraged and bludgeoned Rhazes over the head. The beating produced blindness from which Rhazes did not recover. He died in poverty in about 925.

Rhazes had considerable interest in psychological topics. He wrote on social influences on therapy and offered explanations for why some people place faith in quacks rather than in legitimate healers. He acknowledged that quacks sometimes produce highly visible results with a particular kind of complaint. As a result, some people then overgeneralize and credit the quack with having medical knowledge that could come only with years of study. Rhazes noted that legitimate healing is often slow and the public cannot see immediate visible results. He stressed the importance of distractions, music, diet, bathing, and chemical remedies in treating illnesses. Gordon (1959, p. 158) noted that Rhazes advocated games such as chess playing and music as diversions for melancholia.

Avicenna. The most influential philosopher and physician of the Islamic world was Avicenna (*AH vuh SEEN uh*) (980–1037), a mercifully shortened Western version of Abu 'Ali al-Husayn ibn 'Abd-Allah ibn Sina. Avicenna's interests ranged over medicine, metaphysics, cosmology, logic, political and religious philosophy, and psychology. Ronan (1982) pointed out that Avicenna has been called "the 'Galen of Islam' partly because of his encyclopedic book entitled *Canon* of medicine" (p. 236). According to Gordon (1959, p. 178) the *Canon* became the medical textbook of choice in the European universities and, until the year 1650, was used in the schools of Louvain and Montpelier. Avicenna is remembered less for his originality than for his ability to integrate and systematize the knowledge of the past.

Avicenna, the son of a tax collector, was born near Bokhara. He was apparently a child prodigy who had an unusual memory and a great desire to learn. By the age of ten he had memorized the Koran and displayed considerable skill in literature and the sciences. In his late teens he had learned much of the medical art of his day and was already practicing medicine. He was also an avid reader of Greek and Roman literature and philosophy. Avicenna's life was complicated by the political strife of tenth- and eleventh-century Persia. For a brief time he lived close to the Caspian Sea near the now famous city of Teheran, but political turmoil interfered with his work as he moved to Hamadan. Because of political changes in Hamadan, Avicenna was forced to move to Isfahan, but a shift in the political climate later made it possible to return to Hamadan. In spite of the turmoil in which he lived, Avicenna was able to practice medicine and write. He is credited with the authorship of about one hundred books on a great range of topics in science, medicine, and philosophy. He is undoubtedly the most famous Arabian philosopher, scientist, and physician of the Middle Ages. He died at the age of fifty-seven in about 1037.

It can be argued that Avicenna's greatest intellectual contribution was his attempt to reconcile faith and reason. Avicenna's work on this problem in the Islamic world is paralleled by the work of Maimonides in Jewish intellectual history and by St. Thomas Aquinas in Christian intellectual history. Afnan (1958) stated that "nowhere in Islamic philosophy are the problems of reason and revelation better contrasted, and an agreement in essentials more consistently attempted, than in the system of Avicenna. . . . He was deeply animated by the desire to see both disciplines (philosophy and theology) brought into harmony" (p. 168). Temperamentally, Avicenna was both a rationalist and a mystic. The rationalist was interested in a subject for its own sake and believed that human beings should be guided by reason. The mystic had a love of mystery and often resorted to symbolism and allegory. Avicenna believed that human beings may apprehend truth through the use of reason and through intuitive or mystical processes. He believed that the two are not necessarily contradictory.

Avicenna's psychological interests ranged over theoretical and applied topics. As a physician, he naturally encountered many psychological problems. Like Galen, he observed the relationship between emotions and physiological states such as heart rate. He also accepted humoral explanations of psychic states. For example, Gordon (1959) pointed out that Avicenna believed that "unconsumed bile and black bile will cause melancholia; . . . abundance of yellow bile leads to irritability, confusion and violence. An increase of putrefied phlegm causes a morose and serious mood" (p. 175). Though his knowledge of anatomy was limited, Avicenna speculated on the relations between psychological disturbances and the brain. For instance, he believed that intellectual dysfunctions (e.g., feeblemindedness) result from disturbances in the middle ventricles. He argued that perception and common sense are mediated by the frontal parts of the brain and that memory is handled by the posterior parts of the brain.

Avicenna employed the usual range of medical treatments for physical and mental disturbances. He also employed psychological techniques. For example, Gordon (1959, p. 176) observed that Avicenna believed that one could cheer melancholic patients by reading to them or employing music as therapy. He was also known to use a form of shock (fear) as a treatment for more severe disturbances. Alexander and Selesnick (1966, pp. 63–64) related the story of Avicenna's treatment of a patient suffering from a psychotic delusion that he was a cow. Apparently, the patient was bound and then informed that a butcher was on the way to slaughter him. At the last minute, it was declared that he was too thin and therefore unfit for the slaughter. After his release, the patient gave up his delusion and gradually recovered.

Avicenna's view of the soul is clearly in the tradition of an Aristotelian faculty psychology. Afnan (1958, p. 136) pointed out that Avicenna believed in soul as a single genus divided into three species. Within each species there are faculties or functions. The *vegetative soul* is illustrated in the functions of nourishment, growth, and reproduction; the *animal soul* is illustrated in the receptive and motor functions of perception and movement; and the *human soul* is illustrated in powers presumed to be

unique to human beings—intellectual processes, rational powers, and the ability to apprehend universals. Avicenna believed that faculties exist in a hierarchical arrangement and that they serve and sustain each other. For example, nutrition serves growth and reproduction, and perception serves imagination. The hierarchical arrangement of faculties in Avicenna's system shows the influence of Plato, but Avicenna rejected Plato's notion of the transmigration of the soul.

To summarize, Avicenna preserved elements of Aristotelian and Platonic thought on the soul and integrated these with Islamic thought. He believed in the oneness of the soul, but that even in its oneness, there are many faculties. Consistent with Islamic thought, he argued for the separation of soul and body at death and the immortality of the soul.

Alhazen. One of the most important historical figures in the study of optics and vision is the Islamic scientist and physician Ibn Al Haitam (965–1039), known in the West simply as Alhazen (*AL haze uhn*). Few details of Alhazen's life are known. He was apparently born in Basra (located in what is now eastern Iraq) but lived most of his life in Egypt. Alhazen's *Book of Optics* marks him as one of the greatest Islamic scientists. He is important because of his originality and his influence on later science. Let us briefly address both topics.

Crombie (1961, p. 102) noted that Alhazen rejected the idea that the transmission of light is instantaneous and also rejected the Platonic theory of extramission (i.e., that light rays are emitted from the eye). Gordon (1959, p. 179) credited Alhazen with being the first to show that light comes to the eye from external objects. Alhazen conducted original experiments on angles of refraction and was aware of the effects of the density of the atmosphere on the perception of objects. For example, he believed that objects appear larger on the horizon than at the zenith because of differences in the density of the atmosphere.

Alhazen's *Book of Optics* was a major source of inspiration to later European scientists who studied optics. For example, Roger Bacon's work on optics (e.g., see his *Opus Majus*) clearly built on the foundations established by Alhazen. Time and time again, Bacon quoted Alhazen on such topics as binocular vision, apparent size, double vision, and color perception. Alhazen is, unfortunately, a neglected figure in the history of visual perception.

Averroës.   The last Arabian philosopher-physician of the Middle Ages we will consider is ibn Rushd (1126–1198), known in the West as Averroës (*uh VEHR oh eez*). Tsanoff (1964) called Averroës "the greatest Arabian philosopher" (p. 186). In terms of his enormous influence on Western thought, he may indeed be the greatest among a number of important Arab philosophers.

Averroës was born in Cordoba, Spain. Little is known of his personal life, but apparently he spent most of his years in Spain and in Marrakesh, Morocco. It is known that he served as chief justice in Seville and that he also served as court physician for the calif of Marrakesh.

Averroës was known as a philosopher in his own right, but was perhaps even more famous for his extensive commentaries on the works of Aristotle. His commentaries, translated into Latin, became a major intellectual force in Europe. His substantive scientific and philosophical contributions were also extensive. Crombie (1961) credited him with being the first to discover "that the retina rather than the lens is the sensitive organ of the eye" (p. 102). He wrote a major treatise on medicine that was translated into Latin and used in European universities. He was also one of the first to observe that patients become immune to smallpox if they survive an attack of the disease. Philosophically, Averroës was clearly in the Aristotelian tradition; he is known for his attempts to reconcile faith and reason. He emphasized the power of reason and argued that many of the tenets of faith must be taken metaphorically or symbolically.

Toward the end of Averroës's life, hardheaded fundamentalist "know-so" religious authority was beginning to prevail over reason. Those with a philosophical bent, including Averroës, were persecuted and their books were burned. The intellectual traditions of the Greeks, preserved for a time in the Arab world, were rediscovered in Europe even as they were being discarded in the Muslim world. The age-old cycle between authority and reason was being repeated with predictable consequences for both Arab and European cultures.

Judaism in the Middle Ages

Jerusalem, in the Middle Ages, as in the modern period, was the battleground for the conflicting religious claims of Christians, Jews, and Moslems. Deprived of a peaceful home of their own, Jews settled in the other countries of the Mediterranean basin. By the seventh century there were Jewish settlements in the major cities of northern and southern Europe.

There were brief times in isolated locations in Christian and Moslem countries when Jews lived in peaceful, friendly surroundings. Unfortunately, such times were the exception rather than the rule. More often than not, Jews existed in the midst of social, political, and religious hostilities. They typically paid more than their fair share of taxes, and they were often blamed for natural disasters and social ills. During periods of tension they were sometimes given the choice between converting to the socially dominant religion (Islam or Christian) or moving to a new location. Converted Jews remained under constant suspicion and were rarely treated well. Outright pogroms against Jews were a commonplace in the Middle Ages. In spite of all the hardship, Jewish culture was rich in its depth and variety. There was always a powerful emphasis on education, the family, cleanliness, and faith.

Like Christians and Moslems, the Jewish community was often torn between the rival claims of faith and reason. As noted by Durant (1950),

> The medieval Jews, like the Moslems and the Christians, covered reality with a thousand superstitions, dramatized history with miracles and portents, crowded the air with angels and demons, practiced magical incantations and charms, frightened their children and themselves with talk of witches and ghouls, lightened the mystery of sleep with interpretations of dreams, and read esoteric secrets into ancient tomes. (Durant, 1950, p. 416)

The needed correctives that could have been provided by science and philosophy were to be found only in the isolated work of a few scholars. We turn now to the work of one of the greatest philosophers of the Middle Ages.

Maimonides.   The greatest philosopher-physician among the Jews of the Middle Ages was Rabbi

Moses ben Maimuni (1135–1204), known in Europe as Moses Maimonides (*my MAHN ih deez*). Maimonides was one of several scholars in the late Middle Ages known for their attempts to reconcile faith and reason. Born in Cordoba, Spain, Maimonides early distinguished himself as a student of the secular education provided by Arab teachers. He was also well versed in Hebrew literature and tradition.

When Maimonides was thirteen years old, a moderate political climate in Cordoba was overthrown and fanatic Islamic leaders gave heretics their choice of conversion to Islam or exile. For many years, first in Spain, then in Morocco, and later in Egypt, Maimonides felt the sting of religious bigotry. For a time during an exile in Morocco, Maimonides pretended to be a convert to Islam. It was probably during this period (early 1160s) that Maimonides studied medicine. He became well known as a scholar during his exile in Morocco, but it was extremely dangerous and unsatisfactory to make a pretense of being Islamic, so Maimonides moved first to Palestine, then to Alexandria, and finally to Cairo. It was in Cairo that Maimonides distinguished himself as a writer. He wrote numerous medical texts, a commentary on Jewish laws and traditions, and a systematic treatise on Jewish religious beliefs. But by far his best-known book was *Guide of the Perplexed,* a book destined to create storms of protest in Christian, Jewish, and Moslem cultures.

The *Guide* was written for knowledgeable Jews who were caught in the intellectual tensions between Greek rationalism and religious traditions based on authority and revelation. Although the book was written for Jews, it was also relevant to informed Moslems and Christians who were similarly torn between the claims of rival epistemologies. The *Guide* was read widely; it was used as a text in many European universities, where it was often praised or burned, depending on local circumstances.

In the *Guide,* Maimonides argued that ancient scriptural texts were written in such a manner as to be meaningful to simple and unlearned human beings. As a result, many truths were presented in the form of stories and parables. God was even presented in anthropomorphic terms, and many symbolic or fictional stories were told in order to convey spiritual messages to uneducated and primitive peoples. Maimonides argued that reason and truth cannot be separated from God. If truth is discovered through reason, such truth is from God. Maimonides believed that conflict between reason and faith results when people attempt to take all the scriptures literally. But a marriage of faith and reason is possible for individuals who enjoy a certain level of cognitive complexity and who can discern the essential spiritual truths behind the concrete, picture-like representations in many scriptures.

Maimonides was an intellectual elitist who believed that many people had no need of his book and little need of reason. Indeed, it was best for such people to live their lives under the authority of a simple, childlike faith. The perplexed were those who had experienced the dissonance between faith and reason and needed some kind of workable resolution. An important aspect of Maimonides's work was that it helped legitimize reason and thus made a contribution to the development of the new mentality that would later emerge in the scientific revolution.

The Rise of the European Universities

The tenth and eleventh centuries witnessed the beginnings of European universities that are the precursors of the modern university. The term *university* was derived from the latin *universitas,* referring to a whole or a group organized around a common goal. Some of the earliest universities made use of the physical facilities of the great European cathedrals such as Notre Dame. In other cases, groups of students simply gathered around self-appointed masters who taught in marketplaces or rented rooms. Initially, there were no diplomas, no entrance requirements, and no set curriculum. Often, the major attraction was the reputation of, the eloquence of, and the intellectual ferment created by a teacher. By the twelfth century, the university movement had gained great momentum throughout Europe. Formal curricula were established, degrees were conferred, guilds were formed to protect both teachers and students, and physical plants were built. There was a growing attraction to learning and an emerging admiration for inspired teachers. Indeed, students often traveled great distances to hear a debate or to hear a renowned teacher. Teachers such as William of Champeaux, Peter Abelard, and Robert Grosseteste became legends in their own times.

The rise of the European university, an interesting story in its own right, was one of the most important intellectual developments of the time. Theology, law, and medicine, practical professions of the time, were soon complemented by the liberal arts. Learning became important in its own right and, at least in isolated quarters, the fragile but persistent voice of reason was again heard by eager students. Let us examine the contributions of some of the central figures associated with the early European universities.

Peter Abelard.   Born at Pallet in France, Peter Abelard (*AB uh lahrd*) (1079–1142) was undoubtedly the most renowned teacher and scholar of the early twelfth century. He is remembered for his original work in the fields of ethics, logic, and theology; for his lectures given in well-known centers such as St. Geneviève and Notre Dame in Paris; and as the founder of an important convent for women. Abelard is also remembered for his tragic love affair with Héloise, a woman with unusual intellectual gifts and an insatiable love of learning. The story of Abelard and Héloise is often regarded as one of the great love stories of all time. A novel *Stealing Heaven* (Meade, 1979) was inspired by the affair between Abelard and Héloise. Subsequently, a motion picture based on Meade's novel was also released under the title *Stealing Heaven* (see George & Donner, 1988).

Abelard's academic career, his affair with Héloise, and his subsequent difficulties are set forth in a brief autobiography entitled *Historia Calamitatum* (History of My Calamities), translated under the title *The Story of Abelard's Adversities* (see Muckle, 1992). Abelard was a renowned though controversial teacher, known for his eloquence and his polemic style. For example, after studying briefly with Anselm, Abelard offered the opinion that Anselm's name "rested on long practice rather than on ability or learning . . . [and that Anselm] was a wonder in the minds of his listeners, but a nobody in the estimate of his questioners" (Muckle, 1992, p. 21). Abelard used the same polemic style to at-

tack "the shortcomings of the clergy, the immorality of priests and monks, the sale of indulgences, [and] the invention of bogus miracles" (Durant, 1950, p. 946). In an ultraconservative age, it would be a wonder if such a fierce and searching intellectual analysis did not lead to calamity.

The greatest calamity in Abelard's life can be traced to the day he was hired by Héloise's uncle Fulbert to tutor her in philosophy and theology. Fulbert was a canon of the church who was delighted with the prospect that his niece might be tutored by the most renowned teacher in the land. Abelard, keenly aware of the beauty of his student, worked out an arrangement in which he could live in Fulbert's home. Abelard was almost two decades older than his student and, as a teacher of sacred theology, he had taken the vow of celibacy. Thus, from the viewpoint of Fulbert, the arrangement was apparently appropriate and safe. Soon, however, the tutoring sessions were accompanied by intense, frequent, and prolonged romantic interludes. To this point in his life Abelard had been devoted exclusively to the life of the mind, but now he compared himself to a ravenous wolf consumed by love.

Soon the effects of the affair were all too obvious as Héloise's pregnancy became apparent. There were complicated disputes and deceptions among the key players (Fulbert, Abelard, and Héloise) about Héloise's pregnancy, living accommodations, and marriage. Abelard preferred marriage, but Héloise placed Abelard's career above her own interests and needs knowing that an official marriage would interfere with his career. In time, Héloise gave birth to a son whom they named Astralabe (after an instrument used for charting the heavens). Subsequently, Abelard and Héloise were married, but Fulbert's anger against Abelard was unrequited. He had been deceived and, as the legal guardian of Héloise, he could have profited if he had arranged a marriage to a wealthy candidate. For a variety of reasons, Uncle Fulbert hired a gang of thugs who took a terrible revenge on Abelard at the very source of his sin. Castrated and humiliated, Abelard blamed himself for his calamity and withdrew into the monastic life. He prevailed on Héloise, against her wishes, to become a nun. Their son, Astralabe, was raised by Abelard's sister.

Abelard's work as a monk was no less controversial than his work as a teacher. He alienated church authorities by challenging church dogmas and traditional ways of thinking. He was accused of treating God as an object that could be torn apart and analyzed by the methods of cold reason. Though such an accusation was not entirely true, Abelard's methods must have seemed harsh to those who preferred a purely uncritical, faith-based approach to theological questions. Pope Innocent II ordered that Abelard's books be burned and that he be placed under house arrest and forced to accept the imposition of perpetual silence. Although he had been castrated, his enemies accused him of continuing to lust after Héloise. Though Abelard was condemned as a heretic and enemy of the faith, and though his books were burned, his reputation as a theologian and his works survived. The story of Abelard and Héloise also survives as one of the great love stories of all time. The remains of Abelard and Héloise are buried side by side in a cemetery in Paris, a site still visited by thousands each year.

Abelard's Work.   The battle between faith and reason reached a new level of intensity in the work of Abelard and his followers. Abelard believed that reason was no less a gift from God than were the scriptures. We know truth through reason, and we know truth through the scriptures. Both truths are from God, and God cannot be self-contradictory. Nor can truth contradict itself. What are we to do when scripture and reason contradict each other? Abelard took the position that revelation and scripture must be interpreted by reason, and that an adequate faith will always be undergirded by reason. His work helps establish a declaration of independence for logic and philosophy. Through much of the Middle Ages these products of the Greek mind were forced to serve as the handmaidens of theology, but Abelard insisted that scripture and revelation must be subjected to the light of reason.

If reason is a gift of God and if reason is conveyed through Greek thinkers such as Socrates, Plato, and Aristotle, then it follows that God's light is not the exclusive property of the Hebrews or the Christians. Abelard's message was that the God of conventional or orthodox theology was too small.

Such liberal thoughts guaranteed retaliation from those who placed scripture and revelation in higher priority than reason.

Abelard approached some of the theological problems of his day through an early variation of the dialectical method. One of his best known works, entitled *Sic et Non (Yes and No)* employed the method of opposition to explore theological and philosophical questions. A given question, scripture, or issue was stated in a simple way. Then, contrasting and supporting positions were set forth. Abelard pitted scripture against scripture and authority against authority. Thus, famous leaders of the church were contrasted in terms of the strongly opposed positions they had taken on various issues. Abelard made little attempt at synthesis; that was the task of the reader. The effect of the work was to create doubt and uncertainty. The church had taken the position that doubt, especially in theological matters, was a sin, but Abelard saw doubt in positive terms because it was a motive for inquiry. He believed that doubt followed by inquiry and reason leads to a more informed and intelligent faith. Abelard argued that we should not believe a thing because we think God said it. Rather our beliefs should be based on the solid rock of reason, which was also a gift of God.

According to Clanchy (1997) "Abelard was the first modern 'theologian' in the sense that he was the first teacher to promote the word 'theology' and to use it to mean the reconciliation of human reason with Christian revelation" (p. 5). Abelard had an intellectual thirst for a deep understanding of religious and philosophical issues. He criticized blind memory work so common in the chants, prayers, and rituals of his day as little more than mindless parrot-like repetition of phrases for which there was little or no comprehension. Abelard also raised embarrassing questions that were troublesome to those who placed authority and revelation in higher priority than reason. Why would those who had never had a chance to hear the Christian message be condemned to hell? How could the sin of Adam and Eve be inherited by subsequent generations? If God knows everything there is to know in advance, what is the meaning of confession? His detractors believed that Abelard raised too many questions—questions that had best remain buried.

Vain curiosity had been the original sin of Adam and Eve. Ignorance and humility were to be preferred to the pompous faith in human reason manifested in the works of Abelard.

Abelard was one of the first to imbue his listeners with a spirit of independence and a courage to employ reason as the major tool in the quest for knowledge. He paid dearly for his epistemological sins and his earlier affair with Héloise, but he is remembered today as a bold spirit who attempted an integration of Greek and Christian ways.

Héloise.   Héloise (*EL uh weese*) is typically discussed only in terms of her relation to Abelard, but she, too, was a gifted scholar with knowledge of Latin, Greek, and Hebrew. She had extensive knowledge of Greek and Roman philosophy and Christian theology. In his brief autobiography, Abelard notes that in terms of literary excellence, Héloise was "the most renowned woman in the whole kingdom" (Muckle, 1992, p. 26). There have been disputes about the authenticity of the extant writings of Héloise, but recent scholarship strongly suggests that she did, in fact, write the works attributed to her (Waithe, 1989, pp. 68–72). She may also have made some substantive contributions to some of the writings attributed exclusively to Abelard.

Some of Héloise's intellectual concerns grew out of the social and personal complexities associated with her love affair with Abelard. These concerns touched on social, psychological, and ethical issues. She may be properly regarded as an intellectual precursor of modern psychologists who have studied the meaning of loving relationships. In letters to Abelard, Héloise explores tensions between love that is a means to an end (e.g., satisfaction of sexual appetites) and what she called *indifferent love.* This latter term refers to love in its own right or love for the sake of love and not for mere physical satisfaction. Indifferent love also seems to refer to a love that transcends limitations imposed by the rules and regulations of society. For example, in the Middle Ages a formal social contract (a marriage certificate) gave the man legal conjugal rights, and a woman was expected to "perform her wifely duties." Héloise understood the necessity of contracts and social conventions, but she also understood that they may impose limitations

and distortions in our understandings of a difficult subject such as love.

Héloise's psychology and philosophy of love played out in an interesting, practical way. Under pressure from Abelard she acquiesced to marriage, but she did not approve of the marriage. Héloise understood that marriage would interfere with Abelard's desire to conform to the religious constraints of the time. For her part, as noted by Waithe (1989), "she prefers prostitution, as she calls it, to marriage because marriage would not be for Abelard's good" (p. 79). Abelard preferred a secret marriage that would permit him to continue his work as a teacher, but would also sustain legitimate physical access to Héloise.

Like Abelard and other scholars of the period, Héloise embraced a strong teleological psychology. She believed that the morality of human action must be understood in terms of intention. Abelard had argued that any number of actions, even those that tragically result in the death of another person, are not necessarily immoral. Immoral actions, according to Héloise, are those that result from a purposeful violation of conscience. According to such a view, a psychology based on material, efficient, and formal causes would be a psychology that is inadequate as a means of adjudicating moral issues. The issue is as alive today as it was in the Middle Ages (see Rychlak & Rychlak, 1990).

A final word on Héloise. Unlike Abelard, who saw the "hand of God" in his calamities, Héloise could find no such resolution. If the castration of Abelard was a chastisement from God, then this was not a God she wished to know or serve. She could no longer accept the God of Abelard and the Church. Nevertheless, she became a nun as a means of pleasing Abelard and played the part to perfection. Under the facade, however, she regarded herself as a hypocrite because it was not God she loved, but Abelard.

Roger Bacon.   We have only fragments of information about the life of Roger Bacon (c. 1220– c. 1292), but it is clear that he was an important, original, and controversial figure in the thirteenth century. Bacon was born in England, but evidence is inconclusive about the exact location of his birth or his family background. He studied at Oxford and at the University of Paris. Until he was forty, he was an independent scholar and then, for unknown reasons, joined the Franciscan order. Unfortunately, he was not to enjoy an untroubled relationship with the order. For his part, he was indiscreet in his condemnations of the educational background of other members of the order. He stressed the importance of mathematics and the sciences as keys to the understanding of theology and God. His superiors were also offended by his beliefs in astrology, his experiments in alchemy, and his wild speculations. As a result of his tensions with the Franciscans, Bacon's freedoms were greatly restricted. Indeed, as late as 1278, Bacon was summoned by the General of the Franciscan order and imprisoned because of "certain suspected novelties." Bridges (1976, p. 32) suggested that some of the suspected novelties may have been Bacon's beliefs that the Greeks as well as the Jews had experienced providential guidance, that the personal morality of the stoics is superior to that of many Christians, that ethical values are manifested in Islamic literature, and that changes in religious faith accompany conjunctions of Jupiter and Mercury.

Bacon is remembered for his *Opus Majus* (completed about 1267), which contains chapters on topics such as optics, philology, mathematics, experimental science, and moral philosophy. Bridges (1976) pointed out that Bacon understood the magnifying powers of convex lenses, and "he imagined, and was within measurable distance of effecting, the combination of lenses which was to bring far things near, but which was not to be realized til the time of Galileo" (p. 39). Bridges also noted that Columbus was probably inspired to make his voyage partly because of a passage from the *Opus Majus* that had been quoted in Pierre d'Ailly's *Imago Mundi*. One of Bacon's chief contributions was in epistemology. Let us briefly examine this contribution.

In Part I of the *Opus Majus* (see Burke, 1962, pp. 3–35), Bacon discussed four general causes of human ignorance and error: unjustified reliance on authority; the human tendency to remain a slave to habit, tradition, and custom; popular prejudices that blind us; and conceit about our own knowledge or wisdom. On this latter topic, Bacon championed breadth of experience and advocated the importance of learning from common people, the importance of technology, and a broad curriculum including languages, mathematics, science, and philosophy.

Bacon represents a kind of intellectual bridge between the Middle Ages and modern thought. Like other important thinkers in the late Middle Ages, he hoped to reconcile faith and reason. In his time, the church vacillated between tolerating and condemning the psychology, science, and philosophy of Aristotle. Bacon hoped to reform the church and teach it not only that there is nothing to fear from the Greeks but also that their works could only strengthen a worthy theology. Some church authorities were prepared to give audience to Bacon's radical thought, but, by and large, he was a misfit in his time. Like so many other historical figures, he would be heard—but not until later.

Thomas Aquinas. Another star product of the University of Paris, the greatest church doctor since St. Augustine, was Thomas Aquinas (*uh KWY nuhs*) (1225–1274). Thomas, born of an influential family, received an excellent early education in a Benedictine abbey, then studied the liberal arts at the University of Naples. At the age of twenty, Thomas decided to join the Dominican habit, a decision that implied that he would lead the life of a scholar, teach, and serve God in absolute poverty. His bitterly disappointed family kidnapped Thomas and imprisoned him for a year in order to persuade him against what they considered an unacceptable vocational choice. Unsuccessful in their "deprogramming" efforts, the family finally released their captive son and he proceeded to the University of Paris, from which he received a doctorate in theology in 1256. The bulk of Thomas's teaching and writing career was at Paris and in several Italian monasteries. Though he lived only fifty years, his writings are extensive; the work for which he is most remembered is the *Summa Theologica*. In 1323, approximately one hundred years from the date of his birth, Thomas was canonized as a saint of the Catholic church by Pope John XXII.

Thomas, like Bacon, Maimonides, and Avicenna, was deeply committed to a reconciliation of faith and reason. He believed that there are revealed truths that are not discernible from a rational stand-point, but on the other hand he also urged that the voice of reason be given an open and sympathetic audience. Thomas was the foremost Aristotelian of his time, but can also be characterized philosophically as a moderate in that he attempted to construct a system of thought that accommodates reason and faith and that encourages an open consideration of rival positions on intellectual issues. Like Aristotle, Thomas was keenly interested in psychological problems.

Thomas's interest in psychology ranged over a wide array of topics, including emotions, intelligence, the senses, motivation, social influences on human beings, consciousness, and habit. His frequent comparisons between humans and animals also demonstrate his interest in comparative psychology. He had strong interests in topics that today would come under headings such as philosophical psychology and philosophy of science. In many respects, his psychology follows that of Aristotle, but he made many original contributions, and his reflective philosophical work is a continuing source of inspiration (see McCool, 1990). So far as the history of psychology is concerned, his major contributions lie in his efforts to reconcile faith and reason. He helped reestablish the scientific empirical approach to nature propounded earlier by Aristotle.

Body and Soul.   Copleston (1962, p. 94) claimed that Thomas Aquinas accepted the soul–body hylomorphism advanced by Aristotle. Recall from Chapter 3 that *hylomorphism* refers to the complete interdependence of form and matter. Copleston pointed out that, in Thomas's thought, "The name 'man' applies neither to the soul alone nor to the body alone, but to soul and body together, to the composite substance" (p. 94). Thomas rejected the Platonic idea that the soul is imprisoned in the body. Instead, he viewed the union of body and soul as natural and desirable. The completeness of the union of soul and body is illustrated in Thomas's views on various psychological topics. Thus, emotion must be understood in terms of its physiological and psychological qualities—the two are not separable. Likewise, sensation, as noted by Copleston (1962), "is an act not of the soul using a body, but of the *compositum;* we have no innate ideas, but

the mind is dependent on sense-experience for its knowledge" (p. 102). Thomas's emphasis on the unity of body and soul informed the rest of his psychology. Although he did not advance a psychological system in the modern sense, his psychology nevertheless bears the mark of his fundamental assumption about soul and body. It is a psychology that emphasizes the material substrate in relation to experience or mental activity. There is also an emphasis on wholeness or completeness. For Thomas, personality meant wholeness or completeness.

Thomas's emphasis on the unity of body and soul has long raised a question as to how he could take such a position and, at the same time, believe in the survival of the soul at death. It is debatable whether Thomas provided a satisfactory answer to the question, but he did argue that the soul is immortal and that its mode of knowing is conditioned by the state in which it finds itself. Thus, in the body, it knows via the senses, but in another state it has other modes of cognition. Therefore, the soul, when separated from the body, could still have a cognitive capacity, though while it is united with the body, cognition results from the interdependence of physiological and psychological processes.

Theory of Knowledge.   Gerard (1966, p. 318) noted that Thomistic psychology is based much more on empiricism than on authority. For Thomas, the sensory image was a key building block in the development of knowledge, but he also emphasized the role of intellectual activity in organizing sensory information. McInerny (1990) argued that "Thomism is solidly based on the assumption that we know the world first through our senses and then via concepts formed on the basis of our sense experience" (p. ix). Thomas thus sought a middle road between the extremes of empiricism and rationalism.

For Thomas, scientific activity begins with simple sensory components, and these are organized by practical conceptual processes. He accepted a moderate form of realism, contending that it is reasonable to believe in a certain degree of conformity between the mental and physical worlds. He understood, however, that human accounts of the world are highly variable and that claims may disagree with each other. But disagreements, in his view, are a major stimulus for further study. In matters of science, Thomas believed that each serious viewpoint should receive a fair hearing and that there should be a continuing search for new data pertinent to disagreements. As a leading theologian, it is especially important that he took the position that an adequate theology has little to fear from science and reason. He was persuasive on this point and thus made major contributions to the reconciliation of faith and reason.

There are disagreements about the work and influence of Thomas Aquinas. Russell (1959, pp. 156–160) offered both an appreciative and a critical analysis of Thomas's work and influence. He agreed that Thomas's version of Aristotle dominated thought until the Renaissance, but that Thomas, unlike his predecessors, was at least a "thorough and intelligent student" of Aristotle. Russell contended that the conclusions in Thomas's philosophy "are inexorably imposed beforehand by Christian dogma. We do not find the disinterested detachment of Socrates and Plato, where the argument is allowed to take us whither it will. On the other hand . . . opposing points of view are always stated clearly and fairly" (p. 156).

In any analysis of the impact of Thomas Aquinas, we must recall that prior to his work, Aristotle was quite often forbidden. For example, there were papal edicts that forbade the teaching of Aristotle even in relatively cosmopolitan centers such as the University of Paris. In this historical context, Thomas's work is noteworthy because, as pointed out by Ronan (1982), "Almost alone he was able to make the theological faculty [at the University of Paris] change course and come to terms with Aristotelian teaching" (p. 260). Thomas elevated the role of reason and broadened the conception of the sources of revelation. God could be revealed in nature and through reason. If Thomas's teachings did indeed become dogma after his death, he should not be held accountable.

Gerard (1966) offered a largely appreciative appraisal of Thomas. He noted that Thomas "reveals an approach to behavior which would seem to be described more accurately as an observational empiricism than as a blind Aristotelianism or a religious dogmatism" (p. 327). Thomas was surprisingly empirical for his times and represents a challenge to those who treat the Medieval period as a time that was void of psychological contributions in the modern sense.

William of Ockham.   Before we conclude our review of the Medieval period, we should make at least brief mention of the work of William of Ockham (c. 1285–1349), another Franciscan, who was strongly influenced by Thomas Aquinas. William was born near London around 1285 and studied at Oxford University. Like Roger Bacon before him, William was suspected of embracing heretical ideas. Indeed, he was finally excommunicated because of his repeated conflicts with the church over questions of papal authority and succession.

William carried on the empirical tradition that was set forth in the works of Thomas Aquinas. However, he is best remembered today for what has come to be called the principle of parsimony or "Ockham's Razor." William argued that explanations containing fewer assumptions are to be preferred to those containing more assumptions. He believed that complexity is not to be assumed without necessity. Indeed, other things being equal, simplicity and economy are preferable to complexity. Ockham's Razor, or the law of parsimony, has guided scientific methodological thinking and is especially pertinent to a discipline such as psychology. Psychologists have too often been tempted to attribute human qualities to animals, and we often violate the law of parsimony in human psychology. We shall have reason to come back to this methodological issue several times throughout this book.

Closing Comment

Gerard (1966) noted that the Medieval period was once written off by historians as a period dominated by otherworldly theological preoccupation, blind allegiance to authority, and superstition and ignorance. It is true that if the historian is looking for such qualities in Medieval thought they are easily found. For example, the great poet and author Dante (1265–1321), sometimes regarded as a representative Medieval thinker, was preoccupied with heaven and hell and earth as the temporary abode of human beings. Dante's *Divine Comedy,* perhaps the greatest Medieval literary masterpiece, paints the picture of an earth-centered universe with heavenly spheres above dominated by a highest heaven, the abode of God, and with an awesome hell, located beneath the earth, divided into geographic regions especially designed to punish its inhabitants for their specific earthly sins. In Dante's famous work, we can find confirmation for our preconceptions of Medieval thought processes. There is a preoccupation with theological matters, an emphasis on revealed truth, and a strong emphasis on teleology.

But over and against such Medieval thought patterns, there were also important intellectual contributions such as those outlined in this chapter. In recent years, we have come to view the Middle Ages as an important period that witnessed many scientific achievements that prepared the way for the modern period. No longer can we legitimately write off this period of history—its full and proper rediscovery is an important modern task.

REVIEW QUESTIONS

1. List and briefly define (in a word or two) Galen's constitutional types.
2. Explain Galen's pneuma concept of the soul.
3. Describe the basic teachings of Epicurus, Zeno, and Pyrrho. In what sense are their teachings comparable?
4. What did Plotinus mean when he argued that the "soul is not in the world, rather the world is in the soul"?
5. What is the significance of Augustine's *Confessions* for psychology? Explain Augustine's thought on infant motivation, grief, dreams, and habit breaking.
6. Why, according to Rhazes, do people trust quacks rather than legitimate healers?
7. List and describe major substantive contributions coming out of the works of Avicenna, Averroës, and Alhazen.
8. What is the essential message contained in Maimonides's book *Guide of the Perplexed*?
9. Outline Abelard's position with respect to the roles of faith and reason.
10. What did Héloise mean by indifferent love?
11. According to Roger Bacon, there are four causes for human ignorance and error. What are they?
12. Briefly outline the views of Thomas Aquinas on methodology.
13. Outline some of the general intellectual characteristics of the Middle Ages period and the Roman period.

CHAPTER 5

THE RENAISSANCE

No truth [is] so sublime but it may be trivial tomorrow in the light of new thoughts.

—Ralph Waldo Emerson (1841/1969)

The transition from the Medieval to the modern period is often called the **Renaissance,** meaning "the rebirth." MacLeod (1975) noted that "the metaphor of the Rebirth suggests that freedom had been born and had flourished during the time of the Greeks, that it had subsequently died, and that it was now being reborn" (p. 87). Whether the period in question deserves such an extravagant title is debatable. Nevertheless, it is clear that the Renaissance, a period that in our treatment will include the fourteenth, fifteenth, and sixteenth centuries, witnessed an almost unprecedented growth and change of perspective. There was a kind of intellectual rebirth. However, as we will see, the period was stagnant or regressive in some areas.

Any sketch of the major intellectual trends in the Renaissance would have to include the new trend in art to depict the concrete and natural characteristics of the individual. In literature, the new emphasis was on human beings and their lives in this world rather than on God and the afterlife. Music, almost universally adored throughout Europe, was increasingly secularized so that folk music, art songs, court music, and street music were enjoyed in addition to the religious music that had long been part of church life. There were new developments in music theory, a growth in the number of schools of music, and an increasing demand for musical instruments. Intellectual boundaries were expanded by new geographic discoveries and by the rediscovery of the Greek classics. The broadening of new intellectual vistas was enhanced by the increased availability of infor-

mation made possible by the growing use of the printing press. Another major development during the Renaissance was the powerful revolt against authority as a way of discerning truth.

EFFECT OF THE PLAGUE

It is of interest that the Renaissance was ushered in by one of the greatest and most destructive calamities in human history. The plague (sometimes called the Black Death) has struck with devastating consequences throughout history, but the brief period from 1347 to 1350 in Europe witnessed a biological and medical holocaust that decimated the population. The toll in human numbers is difficult to calculate because population statistics prior to and after the epidemic are not well established. Further, the fairly accurate counts of the dead in some localities may not provide a basis for estimating mortality statistics in other localities. It is known that hundreds of communities were completely destroyed or deserted, and that the dead across Europe in this tragic period numbered in the millions. It is not unlikely that as much as one-third of the European population was destroyed between 1347 and 1350, but for some communities the death rate was far higher.

The economic and social consequences of the plague left a permanent mark on the European intellectual landscape (see Herlihy, 1997). With the loss of one-third of the population, workers were in short supply, the equilibrium between supply and demand was disrupted. With the loss of entire families, wealth was sometimes redistributed. Community services were often pushed completely beyond capacity by the high death rate. In many communities, the problem of sanitation, severe enough under the best of circumstances, was exacerbated by inadequate burial services and the resulting grotesque accumulation of corpses. As with many disasters such as earthquakes and floods, there was often a breakdown in law and order manifested by dramatic increases in theft and violent crime.

The human reaction to the plague is of particular interest to historians and to those who study the psychology of disaster. One encounters examples of stoic resignation, self-sacrificing heroism, opportunism, and reckless abandon to short-term pleasure in the face of inevitable death. Flight from cities and communities and isolation in remote areas were sometimes adaptive strategies, more often open to the wealthy than to the poor. There was also the inevitable tragic search for scapegoats, with Jews as the target of choice. According to Ziegler (1969/1991), "the massacre [of Jews] was exceptional in its extent and its ferocity; in both, indeed, it probably had no equal until the twentieth century set new standards for man's inhumanity to man" (p. 80). Jews were scapegoats partly because they had been denigrated in Christian theological teachings, but they were also resented because of their financial success. For centuries, the church followed a strict literal approach to scriptures that opposed loans of interest (e.g., Deut. 23:1; Luke 6:35). Church leaders viewed it as a sin to make money on money. St. Ambrose even argued that money lending for interest is as much a crime as murder (see White, 1910, p. 266). Those Jews, however, who were not biblical literalists, were free to lend money for interest and this contributed to their financial success, which in turn fostered resentment and jealousy. For a variety of theological, social, and economic reasons, Jews were blamed for the plague. They were tortured, imprisoned, and massacred sometimes at "the mere news that the plague was approaching" (Ziegler, 1969/1991, p. 77).

When hostility was not directed at others such as the Jews, it was sometimes turned inward. The most common theological explanation for the plague was that it was sent by God as a just punishment for the sins of the people. If such were the case, perhaps God's wrath could be appeased by sincere self-inflicted punishment. Such a response to catastrophe has not been uncommon in the past, but during the plague years it achieved new levels of organization and zealotry among the brotherhood of the flagellants. Large numbers of flagellants marched through towns beating themselves with sharpened pieces of metal attached to leather thongs. In the words of Ziegler (1969/1991), "Each man tried to outdo his neighbor in pious suffering, literally whipping himself into a frenzy in which pain had no reality. Around them the townsfolk quaked, sobbed and groaned in sympathy, encouraging the brethren to still greater excesses" (p. 66). Flagellation, at best, may have sometimes salved a guilty conscience, but if anything, the open wounds and the crowds of people served only to aggravate conditions favorable to the spread of the Black Death. Tragically, the knowledge structures necessary to an understanding of the plague were not yet in place. Later, it would be understood that this epidemic disease was caused by *yersina pestis*, a germ transmitted via the flea from infected rats (see Biddle, 1995, pp. 165–170).

The most interesting result of the plague is that it contributed to doubts about the adequacy of authorities and institutions. The people were told that the plague was God's punishment for sin, but they could not help but observe that the most godly in their midst, including priests and other church officials, were stricken with the same ferocity as the population in general. Trusted institutions (particularly the church) were powerless to protect the people against a nightmare of hideous proportions. The resulting doubts and the resentment directed at existing authorities are clearly part of the intellectual backdrop of the Renaissance. We will now consider some of the other characteristics of the period that were of significance to the growth of science in general and psychology in particular.

EXPANDING GEOGRAPHIC KNOWLEDGE

Imagine an individual living in the early sixteenth century who strongly believed that the earth is the center of the universe, that the earth is immovable as proclaimed in pontifical decrees, and that the sun is red in the evening because it reflects the fires of hell (see White, 1896/1978, p. 97). Imagine further the emotional and intellectual dislocation experienced by such a person when confronted in 1522 with the news that a remnant of Magellan's crew had returned home after sailing around the world. Magellan's voyage, completed under the leadership of Juan Sebastian del Cano following Magellan's death, as well as other fifteenth- and sixteenth-century geographic discoveries, had scientific and commercial ramifications, but they also had an unprecedented impact on human thought processes. If it became necessary to expand geographic boundaries, perhaps it was also necessary to expand intellectual boundaries. Some people may have had the capacity to expand one without expanding the other, but in many cases geographic discoveries contributed to the growth of curiosity and a new openness to other ideas.

INFLUENCE OF THE GREEK CLASSICS

By the fifteenth century, there were numerous collections of Greek manuscripts in European centers of learning and in private libraries. Some of the manuscripts were brought to Europe by traders who profited from the expeditions of the crusaders. Delaunay (1958, p. 5) pointed out that many of the manuscripts were also brought to Italy by Byzantine scientists who were forced to leave Constantinople when it fell in 1453. There were also a few wealthy bibliophiles who went to great trouble and expense to acquire private collections of old manuscripts.

The influence of the Greek manuscripts on Renaissance thought is difficult to assess. At a minimum, the presence of the classics appears to have stimulated an interest in the Greek language and in editing and translation. A case can also be made that the classics had a substantive impact on ways of thinking. It was refreshing to witness the Greek courage to allow speculation to run its course without having to affirm conclusions dogmatically imposed beforehand. The classics may have been of particular importance to the reemergence of a naturalistic approach to topics of a psychological nature. Delaunay (1958, p. 5) offered the opinion that the birth of Renaissance humanism occurred with

the return of Hellenic values. Whatever their precise role, it is clear that the rediscovery of the classics was closely accompanied by a growth of interest in human problems and a reduction of interest in theological matters.

DIFFUSION OF AUTHORITY

During the Medieval period, the Roman Catholic church was the central force in the political, intellectual, and religious life of Europe. The power and authority of the church, however, were severely diluted during the Renaissance. The reasons for such dilution are to be found in forces at work within the church itself and in external cultural developments. Perhaps the single most important challenge to church authority came from emerging nation-states. The leaders of the new nation-states were typically jealous to protect their territory and thus viewed the church as a foreign competitor. There was widespread resentment over the flow of money to support a church with a physical location and a base of power in a distant foreign land.

Another cultural development that constituted a challenge to existing authority was a larger reading public and the ready availability of new translations of the Bible. Though new translations, such as that provided by Martin Luther, were sometimes condemned and placed on the **Index of Forbidden Books** (see Haight, 1978, p. 4), they nevertheless found their way to an ever larger reading public. The increased availability of the Bible may have contributed to the belief that human beings have direct access to God and therefore no need of a church-based intermediary. The concept of the individual priesthood of the believer carried with it the assumption that all persons could read and interpret the scriptures for themselves. Even so, Protestants who were free to read the scriptures were often not free to read Catholic literature. Indeed, censorship was rampant in both Protestant and Catholic countries (see Grendler, 1988, pp. 45–44).

As noted, there were also forces at work within the church that contributed to the demise of its power and influence. As a large institution, the church had enormous financial needs. In order to meet those needs, it turned to money-raising tactics that offended the spiritual sensitivities of many of the faithful. Examples of tactics considered offensive were the sale of political or religious offices and the abuse of indulgences. An **indulgence** involved an exchange of money for a spiritual favor. Thus, one might pay for forgiveness for a personal sin or for intercession for a change of status in the conditions of the afterlife for a deceased relative. During the fourteenth and fifteenth centuries, there were also debilitating power struggles among church leaders. These struggles centered on whether authority should be vested in a single leader or in church councils. It was the difficulties within the church itself that provided the fertile soil for the major rupture that produced the Reformation.

Martin Luther (1483–1546), an Augustinian monk and theologian, was the key figure in the initiation of the **Reformation.** Prior to Luther, however, there had been a succession of would-be reformers and dissidents who had attempted to call attention to the problems within the church. In 1517, Luther nailed ninety-five theses on the door of a church in Wittenberg, Germany, and thereby initiated the reform movement that was to be successful. Luther's goal was not to start a new church but to reform Catholic doctrine and practice. However, his actions were interpreted by authorities within the church as anti-Catholic. His continuing conflicts with the church finally resulted in his excommunication and his exile to Saxony. From the time of his excommunication in 1521 until his death, he spearheaded the Protestant movement.

There are legitimate differences of opinion about the influence of the Reformation on the development of science. Watson and Evans (1991, p. 151) concluded that Renaissance science and philosophy gained nothing from the Reformation. They pointed to the Protestant John Calvin and his well-known justification for burning Michael Servetus at the stake. Servetus had "described the Holy Land as a barren wilderness (which it was), thus contradicting the scriptural description of it as a land of 'milk and honey' " (Watson & Evans 1991, p. 151). Many of the leaders of the Reformation were as intoxicated with authority as those against whom they rebelled. MacLeod (1975) argued, however, that "just as Luther . . . could exhort his followers to read the Bible and draw their own conclusions, so could other Protestants exhort

their followers to look at nature (as Aristotle had done) and draw their own conclusions" (p. 91). The role of the Reformation in Renaissance science remains subject to interpretation and debate.

GROWTH OF EMPIRICAL STUDIES

The Renaissance period is particularly noteworthy for a host of new discoveries that resulted from empirical study. Consider a few examples. During the Renaissance, mapmaking was reestablished as a scientific activity. Fairly accurate descriptions and drawings of coastlines, harbors, and peninsulas were based on careful observations of explorers. Late in the Renaissance period, in the year 1543, Andreas Vesalius published his classic *The Fabric of the Human Body,* an anatomy text that was based on actual dissections of the human body. Other anatomists such as Gabriello Fallopio (1523–1562), Bartolommeo Eustachio (1520–1574), and Michael Servetus (1511–1553) were also making significant contributions to anatomical knowledge. The studies of the anatomists were, of course, complemented by the anatomical interests of artists such as Leonardo da Vinci (1452–1519). We shall return later to a detailed consideration of da Vinci's many contributions. During the high Renaissance period, there were also advances based on empirical observation in botany and zoology. More detailed and more accurate descriptions of plants and many animal species were being published during the 1500s. The empirical spirit earlier articulated by the Greeks and by scholars of the Middle Ages such as Roger Bacon and Moses Maimonides was now being realized on a large scale.

QUANTIFICATION

Commenting on the debate about whether there was indeed a Renaissance, Bochner (1973) stated that there needs to be no such debate about a Renaissance of interest in mathematics. He declared that "there was indeed a mathematics of the Renaissance that was original and distinctive in its drives and characteristics" (p. 178). Interest in mathematics during the Renaissance was fueled partly by the practical demands of navigation, and by business, banking, and commercial activities. At the same time, there was a strong interest in mathematics for its own sake and there were numerous original contributions, especially in algebra and geometry.

Ronan (1982) illustrated the popular interest in mathematics during the Renaissance when he pointed out that "between the years 1472 and 1500 no less than 214 mathematical books had been published to feed the increasing demand for mathematics by banking houses, merchants, workshops, public administrators, astrologers and scholars" (p. 322). Another sign of popular interest noted by Ronan was public contests in which participants vied with each other to solve mathematical problems. It is clear that there were many needs for the applications of mathematics, but there were also major schools in Germany, Italy, and France at which mathematics was valued in its own right, independent of practical application. The Renaissance witnessed the development of new mathematical symbols and the solution of numerous equations. The rediscovery of Pythagoras and Euclid, along with the original mathematical discoveries of the Renaissance, helped set the stage for the scientific revolution and for the growth of a new optimism about the applicability of quantitative techniques. Such optimism later served as a decisive force in the development of psychology.

CHANGING VISIONS OF THE WORLD

The late Renaissance and early modern period witnessed revolutionary changes in cosmology. The term **cosmology** refers to theories of the nature of the universe, including the relation of the earth to the rest of the solar system. The prevailing view for many centuries was that the earth is located in the very center of the universe and that a stationary earth is circled regularly by the sun, moon, and planets. The technical details of the old **geocentric** (earth-centered) cosmology and the new **heliocentric** (sun-centered) cosmology belong properly to the histories of astronomy and physics. However, changing beliefs about the solar system constitute an important intellectual and philosophical backdrop for the history of the social sciences and life sciences because our world visions have far-reaching consequences for how we view ourselves and the status we accord to a science of human nature (see Berenda, 1965).

The geocentric astronomy that dominated thought throughout the Middle Ages and much of the Renaissance was a curious combination of theology wedded to the work of the Egyptian astronomer, geographer, and mathematician **Ptolemy** (c. 100–c. 165). Ptolemy (*TAHL eh mee*), working in Alexandria in the second century, argued that the earth sits motionless in the center of the cosmos. He believed in a spherical earth circled regularly by the moon, sun, and planets. The stars beyond the immediate planetary system were regarded as fixed points of light. The observed motions of the sun, moon, and planets cannot be predicted from the assumption that such bodies follow strict circular pathways around the earth. Accordingly, Ptolemy, following the thinking of earlier Greeks, constructed an elaborate, if somewhat awkward theoretical explanation to account for locations, movements, and transits of moving bodies (see Thurston, 1994).

One of Ptolemy's proofs for the immovability of the earth is that if the earth moves, then an object tossed up vertically should fall in a location different from the point from which it was tossed. If the earth is moving while the object is in the air, the object should fall in a location somewhat removed from the point of the toss. Ptolemy's proof fails to take account of the fact that, if the earth is moving, the object that is tossed up vertically is moving at the same speed as the earth at the time of the toss. Hence, even with a moving earth, the object tossed up vertically should fall in the same relative location from which it was tossed. Ptolemy's arguments for a stationary earth located in the center of the universe squared beautifully with many of the theological beliefs of the Middle Ages. Such beliefs were thought to be grounded in scripture and church tradition. Though there were questions about the shape of the earth (e.g., was it flat, disc-like, or spherical?) there was general agreement that it was stationary and central in the scheme of things. By the later Middle Ages, the prevailing belief was in a central, stationary, and spherical earth.

Although geocentric cosmology was widely accepted, its scriptural basis was not without nagging biblical perplexities (e.g., Does the earth hang upon nothing as mentioned in Job 26:7, or does it rest on foundations as implied in Job 38:4, Ps. 102:25, and Ps. 104:5? Does the earth rest on foundations as implied in the previous sacred texts or is it founded upon the seas as implied in Ps. 24:2?). Would the earth abide forever as proclaimed in Ecclesiastes 1:4, or would it some day be burned up as proclaimed in II Peter 3:10? Clearly, the sacred theory was not without interpretive difficulties. If some biblical texts were to be taken literally, others must be taken metaphorically.

The geocentric worldview was integral to the larger philosophical and theological picture of the world and, thus, an abiding source of emotional and intellectual support. A stationary earth was the very center of the entire universe and Jerusalem was the central point on earth. Human beings were at home and confident in the belief that they were the key players in an orderly and meaningful universe designed explicitly for them. The heavens, literally *up there* (not *out there*), radiated the perfection of a God who had designed a specific kind of abode and a purpose for human beings. The negative counterpart of heaven was to be found below the earth in a hell that was presumed to have a complicated architecture of its own. A typical Medieval view of hell is set forth by the great poet and author Dante (1265–1321). Dante's *Divine Comedy,* perhaps the greatest Medieval literary masterpiece, paints a graphic picture of heavenly spheres dominated by a highest heaven, the abode of God. Dante provides an even more graphic and detailed picture of a hell located beneath the earth and divided into distinct geographic regions especially designed to punish inhabitants for their specific earthly sins. It is important to realize that questions about the structure of the universe were not just questions about astronomy or physics, but questions about human destiny, theology, philosophy, and the very purpose of life on earth. The task of disentangling science from theology in this period was not just vexing and difficult from an intellectual standpoint, it was fraught with danger to the well-being and life of those who dared raise questions.

The Heliocentric Theory

Some of the early Greeks had argued for a moving earth, but their work was not taken seriously on a wide scale until the sixteenth century. Nicolaus Copernicus (1473–1543), a Polish astronomer and

canon of the Church, is sometimes regarded as the founder of modern astronomy. His book *On the Revolution of the Celestial Spheres,* published just days before his death in 1543, regarded the earth as a planet turning once daily on its own axis and moving in a yearly circle about the sun. In terms of calendar predictions, the theory advanced by Copernicus represented little improvement over Ptolemy's geocentric theory. Like Ptolemy, Copernicus believed that the circle is the most perfect of geometric figures. Thus, it was inconceivable that movement in the heavens should be based on anything other than perfect circular motion. The assumption of perfect circular movements was a major stumbling block in the old geocentric and the early heliocentric theories. Johannes Kepler (1571–1630), a German astronomer and mathematician, later discovered that the planets move in elliptical or oval-shaped motions around the sun. Kepler's calculations were instrumental in delivering a death blow to the old geocentric theory, but advocates of the old theory would not be quick to yield. We turn now to a brief consideration of the work of one of the most central figures in the battle between the dominant theological perspective and the new sciences.

Galileo Galilei

The Italian astronomer and physicist, Galileo (*Gal uh LAY oh*) (1564–1642) is one of the most celebrated figures in the history of science. He is remembered for improving the telescope and for employing telescopic observations as a new tool in the debate over the nature of the solar system. He is also remembered for his pioneering work on motion and for the rigorous application of mathematics to physical phenomena. Galileo's empirical observations coupled with his powerful arguments for the Copernican system brought him into direct conflict with the Roman Catholic church and with Protestant reformers. Late in his life he was tried before the Roman Inquisition and forced to recant doctrines such as the movement of the earth that were regarded as contrary to the faith. He was under house arrest the last eight years of his life.

Galileo was born in Pisa, but received his early education in a school near Florence. Later, he returned to the University of Pisa, where he studied medicine from 1581 to 1585. Because of shifting interests and shortage of funds Galileo withdrew from medical training prior to receiving a degree. After 1585, he studied mathematics and physics. In 1586, he achieved widespread recognition for his work on a hydrostatic balance, an instrument that could be employed to determine the specific gravity of objects. Galileo held a professorial position in mathematics at Pisa from 1589 to 1592. In 1592, he was awarded a chair in mathematics at the University of Padua.

Early in his career Galileo was convinced of the truth of Copernican theory, but he was fearful of the consequences of going public with his convictions. By 1609, he had built an excellent 32 power telescope and was the first to systematically employ this instrument in the study of astronomy. Galileo's telescopic observations proved increasingly contradictory to the old geocentric theory and added to his confidence in Copernican theory. Contrary to the predictions of the old geocentric theory, Galileo discovered that the surface of the moon is not perfect. Instead, as we know, it is pocketed with craters, rocks, mountains, and all sorts of irregularities. He also discovered the moons of Jupiter, the phases of Venus, the rings of Saturn, and sun spots. In contrast with prevailing theories, he demonstrated that there are objects in the heavens not visible to the naked eye. His observations were a daunting challenge, not just to geocentric theory, but to the prevailing worldview and to a treasured way of knowing. In 1610, Galileo returned to Florence as philosopher and mathematician in the employment of the Grand Duke of Tuscany.

Galileo's observations received widespread acclaim, and in 1611, he visited the pontifical court in Rome where he demonstrated the telescope. The friendly atmosphere in Rome emboldened Galileo to take a stronger stand in favor of Copernican theory. His new bolder arguments, however, were met by fierce criticism and personal attacks by his ecclesiastical and academic enemies. Thus, five years after his successful demonstration of the telescope in the pontifical court, he was summoned back to Rome in 1616 for an official assessment of possible heresy. Although he was not found guilty of heresy, he was ordered to refrain from *holding* or

defending Copernican doctrine. It should be noted that there were members of the church hierarchy who defended Galileo, but a much larger and more influential conservative group was in control.

In 1624, Pope Urban VIII denied Galileo's request to reverse the prohibition of 1616, but granted Galileo the right to publish a work comparing geocentric and heliocentric theories. It was understood that Galileo was to treat the heliocentric view as a mere hypothesis and that conclusions were to be consistent with the theological truths that were already known. With the pope's permission in hand Galileo devoted many years to the research and writing of what turned out to be a classic masterpiece in cosmology. His book *Dialogue Concerning the Two Chief World Systems—Ptolemaic and Copernican* was first published in 1632. The story of how the book survived church censors and how it was actually published is a lengthy and somewhat contradictory tale of intrigue interesting in its own right (see Shea, 1986).

The more interesting story, however, is the storm of controversy created by the *Dialogue*. It was recognized immediately as a major literary and scientific achievement, but within a year, Galileo was forced to travel to Rome to stand trial before the Inquisition. There can be little question that Galileo used the *Dialogue* as a basis for advocating Copernican cosmology. Accordingly, he was found guilty of believing and teaching the hated doctrine and ordered to recant. He was forced to kneel before the holy cardinals, lay his hands on the Bible, abjure and curse his errors, and swear that he would never again do anything to cause suspicion regarding his orthodoxy. Because of his advanced age of seventy, he avoided imprisonment and was instead confined, away from family and friends, in his country estate where he resided until his death in 1642. Galileo's *Dialogue* and Copernicus's *Revolutions* were placed on the *Index of Forbidden Books*.

The storm of controversy over competing cosmologies was not just about the structure and nature of the universe. To miss the importance of the roles of competing epistemologies in the dispute is to miss a central feature with long-term implications for the development of all the sciences. As noted by White (1896/1978) the dominant theological position was "that the divinely appointed way of arriving at the truth in astronomy was by theological reasoning on texts of scripture" (p. 131). Further, as noted by White, many Protestant and Catholic authorities believed "that the church alone is empowered to promulgate scientific truth" (p. 133). Methodologically, the controversy was over the authority of scripture taken literally versus the authority of the new observational sciences. It is important to note, however, that at least some of the devout were opposed to biblical literalism and favored Galileo's beliefs.

There were many arguments against Galileo and the Copernican system but a few examples illustrate the complexity of the debate. Clerics argued from scriptures such as Psalms 93:1 and 96:10 that declare that the earth is established so that it cannot be moved. One of the claims of the new heliocentric view was that the moon merely reflects light from the sun. This claim was challenged with Genesis 1:16 that refers to a lesser light that rules by night. The standard interpretation was that the moon was a real light, not merely a body that reflects light. Galileo's discovery of the moons of Jupiter was denounced as an illusion caused by the telescope or by the devil. Some of the authorities refused to look through the telescope convinced that they, like Galileo, would succumb to illusions or delusions. Pope Paul V declared that "the doctrine of the double motion of the earth about its axis and about the sun is false, and entirely contrary to Holy Scripture" (White, 1896/1910, p. 138). The Protestant reaction to heliocentrism was somewhat mixed and less well-organized than the Catholic reaction (see Westman, 1986). Martin Luther complained that "whoever wants to be clever must agree with nothing that others esteem. . . . This is what the fellow does who wishes to turn the whole of astronomy upside down. . . . I believe the holy scripture, for Joshua commanded the sun to stand still and not the earth" (Luther, 1539/1967, pp. 358–359). However, there were some liberal Protestant reformers as well as Catholics who saw no incompatibility between the new cosmology and the essential Christian message.

The Larger Meaning of the Copernican Revolution

Prior to the Copernican revolution there was little appreciation for the possibility of natural causes.

Deason (1986) calls attention to the beliefs of Reformation theologians Luther and Calvin that nothing in nature happens through inherent forces. Thus, Luther, as quoted by Deason, "chided physicians and philosophers for ascribing procreation to 'a matching mixture of qualities, which are active in predisposed matter' " (Deason, 1986, p. 176). According to Catholic and Protestant theology of the period, active causal power resides in God alone and is not inherent in natural forces. With Copernican cosmology, however, there was a new emphasis on inherent, lawful, predictable, and quantifiable natural forces that exist independently and are thus understandable without reference to any extrinsic causal force. Geographic discoveries and now the new astronomy fed a growing belief that the dominant theology had been wrong about cosmology. Was it not also possible that it had been wrong about the philosophy that was so closely connected to that cosmology? Such questions and doubts provided fertile intellectual soil for the growth of new openness, first to the physical sciences and later to the life sciences. The Copernican revolution was one of the defining forces of what came to be known as the modern period.

PSYCHOLOGICAL THOUGHT IN THE RENAISSANCE

Let us turn now from a description of the general characteristics of the Renaissance to an examination of representative psychological thought of the period. We will find that along with the geographical discoveries and the new emphasis on humanistic studies and quantification there was an isolated but significant interest in a more naturalistic approach to psychological topics. We will find that some of the key figures in Renaissance psychological thought prepared the intellectual groundwork for an understanding of the roles of learning and social influence in human life. The period also witnessed the publication of the first treatise on individual differences. This period saw the beginnings of a slow and gradual trend to deemphasize what was called the "will" and to recognize other influences such as intelligence, aptitude, temperament, and learning. In what follows, we will find that the period produced some highly original and influential thought that contributed meaningfully to the later optimism that there could indeed be a science of human nature.

Petrarch

Francesco Petrarch (1304–1374) was an Italian poet, scholar, moralist, and visionary who is properly regarded as the founder of **Renaissance humanism.** From his earliest years as a student, Petrarch (*PEH trark*) was obsessed with the recovery, transcription, and study of ancient Roman and Greek manuscripts. Although his ability with the Greek language was limited, he enjoyed Latin translations of Greek works. Petrarch was educated as a Christian, but he was deeply aware of the epistemological limitations and sterility of intellectual Christianity in the form of Medieval scholasticism, with its emphasis on hairsplitting logic applied to remote theological problems. By contrast, he found something refreshing in Roman and Greek approaches to philosophy, science, literature, and poetry. Roman and Greek concerns with this world and with the immediate and practical problems of life appealed to Petrarch's emotional and intellectual nature. Although he remained loyal to the Christian tradition, he hoped to widen the horizons of the faithful, to focus their attention on the importance of the present, and to emphasize the compatibilities between Christian thought and classic thought.

Petrarch is also remembered for advocating a broader approach to Greek classics. Aristotle had been elevated in the works of Aquinas and in Catholic theology, but Petrarch preferred Plato to Aristotle. Following the work of Petrarch there were heated debates between those who preferred Plato and those who preferred Aristotle. The debates encouraged deeper studies of a broad range of the classics and thus widened Greek influence in the Renaissance. Kristeller (1967) points out that "Petrarch assigned second place to Aristotle, but he was far from holding him in contempt. . . . He repeatedly suggested that the original Aristotle may be superior to his medieval translators and commentators" (p. 127). Petrarch's counsel was to study Aristotle and other Greeks in the original rather than through the filters of scholastic writers.

Petrarch set the stage for the expansion of humanistic studies in the Renaissance. Human beings were to be understood not just in the context of theology, but also in the context of their natural setting. Petrarch found great joy in nature, society, secular studies, and travel. In his work we encounter the strong claim that we have the right to be creatures of this world. Such a claim is foundational to the ultimate development of a science of human nature.

Niccolò Machiavelli

The Italian civil servant Niccolò Machiavelli (*MAK ee uh VEHL ee*) (1469–1527) is often regarded as the founder of modern political science. He can also be regarded as one of the founders of modern military science. His importance in the history of the social and behavioral sciences is established by his descriptive and objective methodology that rejected moralistic approaches to human behavior. Machiavelli's substantive views on the malleability of human behavior suggested new possibilities for understanding and control—key elements in any science. He was one of the first to recognize the powerful role of social influence in human life and can thus be properly regarded as one of the important intellectual ancestors of modern social psychology.

Machiavelli was born to a poor family in Florence, Italy. Little is known about his early years, but he apparently acquired considerable education, especially in the humanities. When he was twenty-nine years old, he was selected for a minor bureaucratic government position in Florence. An effective administrator, he was soon given more authority and responsibility and sent on diplomatic missions. As he traveled broadly and came into contact with powerful political figures, Machiavelli developed a fascination with the social psychology of power, leadership, and authority. His fascination was later to result in major treatises on these topics.

The political climate during Machiavelli's life was highly unstable. In Italy, a host of city-states were vying with each other for power. At the same time, France, Germany, and Spain were attempting to influence political developments in Italy. Various city-states within Italy were often allied with foreign powers, while others were separate or allied with the papacy. In the early sixteenth century,

Florence was allied with France, but forces loyal to the papacy were seeking to drive the French from Italy. Machiavelli trained and led a small Florentine army that sought to defend Florence, but his army was defeated by the superior forces devoted to the papacy. The French were driven from Italy and a new political order was established in Florence. Machiavelli was imprisoned and tortured but managed to avoid the stake. After being released, he moved to a rural estate near Florence where he lived in poverty. During a fourteen-year exile, he wrote extensively and at the same time worked to regain a civil service position in Florence. During his exile, Machiavelli produced the books that would give him a permanent place in history. His best-known books, *The Prince* and *The Discourses,* were written in 1513. Other works included Machiavelli's *History of Florence* and *Art of War.* He also wrote comedies, plays, biographies, and short stories. Machiavelli enjoyed a brief return to public service in 1525, but an unstable political situation prevented him from regaining his former position of power. He died in 1527.

Machiavelli's works aroused more than a small amount of indignation and controversy. Thorne (1969, p. 828) pointed out that Pope Clement VIII condemned *The Prince.* Gilbert (1967) noted that Machiavelli's works were placed on the *Index of*

Niccolò Machiavelli

Forbidden Books in 1559 and that "Cardinal Reginald Pole said that Machiavelli 'wrote with the finger of the devil' " (p. 121). The indignation against Machiavelli's works may lie partly in their objectivity. For example, Machiavelli observed that religion may be used effectively to invoke obedience and control. He pointed out that the effective leader will use religion to call people back to their roots or back to their founding principles. Such action serves to unite or solidify and to weed out corruption. Religious values in such a scheme are subordinate to political values, and religious people are used by the clever leader to achieve desired ends. Leaders who publicly condemn Machiavelli nevertheless have employed his principles without hesitation.

Earlier we noted that Machiavelli was important because of his emphasis on the malleability of human nature. If he held a somewhat cynical view about basic human nature, he was nevertheless optimistic about the possibility of attaining a good social order. The suggestibility of the masses and the proper use of political and social influence could work for the good of humankind. Machiavelli was keenly interested in the larger social good and helped create the optimistic belief that an ideal society is attainable.

Wood (1968, p. 507), addressing a common misconception, pointed out that Machiavelli did not advocate immoral acts. Rather, such acts are sometimes excused if a larger good is attained. For example, deception in Machiavelli's treatment is never an end in itself, but its use is acceptable if a larger good can be achieved. In some degree, most of us are probably Machiavellian when we employ mild deception and avoid a "hard truth" because we believe the former will do no harm whereas the latter may result in unnecessary pain. In psychological literature, the term **Machiavellianism** is sometimes used to refer to "an amoral, manipulative attitude toward other individuals" (Gutterman, 1970, p. 3), but when used in such a manner, the term is a corruption, because Machiavelli was not, strictly speaking, amoral. At one level, Machiavelli simply advanced a descriptive science of human social and political behavior without regard to whether such behavior is moral or immoral. He attempted to describe what people actually do.

Thus, he worked much as today's social scientists who describe what people do. Machiavelli went a step further to show what we *can* do. In this regard, he was also like those social scientists who see control of human behavior as a goal. For Machiavelli, efficiency, practicality, and the common good take precedence over all moral principles as ends in themselves.

As noted earlier, Machiavelli was one of the first to contribute to the belief that human behavior can be understood in a naturalistic-scientific context. His views on human nature contained an interesting blend of pessimism and hope. On the pessimistic side, basic human nature was regarded as brutish, selfish, shortsighted, vain, and imitative. Machiavelli believed that self-preservation is the strongest motive and that it could induce violence and destruction or, under proper leadership, great industry and accomplishment. He taught that the human tendency to imitate is inconsistent with a high degree of creative thought, but the imitative capacity also makes the masses malleable for shaping. Thus, virtue and constructive social effort can be enhanced by astute leaders and institutions. Machiavelli placed strong emphasis on development, socialization, and suggestibility. These were the processes that could be exploited to mold character to desirable ends and to ward off the evils that could result from the unbridled expression of basic human nature. His emphasis on the importance of socialization would be echoed in the later works of philosophers, educators, and psychologists who turned increasing attention to the systematic investigations of socialization and the consequences of different socialization procedures. Let us now turn from Machiavelli's social psychological thought to an investigation of a Renaissance philosopher-psychologist with a broader range of psychological interests.

Juan Luis Vives

Watson (1915) has argued that, in terms of the methods employed and the problems investigated, the Spanish humanist Juan Luis Vives (1492–1540) should be viewed as the true originator of modern psychology. As we will see, Vives, almost one hundred years before Francis Bacon, was an advocate of the empirical-inductive method. He also believed that of all worldly knowledge, knowledge of the soul is most important. Such knowledge is to be attained through the method of direct observation.

Vives was born in Valencia, Spain, in 1492, the same year Columbus launched his fateful voyage and also the year in which Jews were expelled from several Spanish cities. Vives, of Jewish ancestry, was given a Christian education, a result possibly of the fact that his mother had been converted to Christianity a year before his birth. Vives attended school in Valencia where he studied Latin grammar, rhetoric, poetry, and the Greek classics. At seventeen years of age, he left Valencia to continue his studies at the University of Paris. Tragically, his parents were later victims of the Spanish Inquisition, which unfortunately was still guided by the unusually oppressive and cruel tactics installed earlier by the Dominican monk, Tomas de Torquemada (1420–1498). Though the records are not complete, Vives's father was very likely burned at the stake. Years after her death, his mother's body was removed from a Christian cemetery and burned. Doubt had been cast on the authenticity of her earlier conversion when witnesses testified in a typical posthumous inquisition trial that they had seen her enter a Jewish synagogue after her conversion (Norena, 1970, p. 20). So far as we know, Juan Luis Vives never returned to Valencia.

Vives's stay in Paris was brief. His education at the University of Paris was a disappointment to him; he completed only the three-year arts course. At the time, the secular and religious forces were fighting for control of the university and the quality of the institution and its instructional programs had been undermined. Vives had few pleasant memories of his years in Paris. The year 1512 found him leaving Paris for the Netherlands.

From 1512 to 1523, Vives worked in the Netherlands, first as a student and later as a teacher. In 1520, he was granted a license to give public lectures at the University of Louvain. The intellectual climate in the Netherlands was a haven of freedom compared with much of the rest of Europe. During this period of his life, Vives met and established a friendship with Desiderius Erasmus (1466–1536), who was undoubtedly the most respected scholar of his day. Vives also developed a reputation as a highly respected and sought-after teacher and scholar.

In 1523, Vives moved to England where he received an appointment at Oxford University. He hoped to settle comfortably into teaching and scholarly activities, but political events were to interfere with that possibility. He established a close friendship with Henry VIII and Catherine of Aragon. He also became the close friend of the English scholar Sir Thomas More. More opposed the divorce of Henry and Catherine and was later executed when he took the position that Henry could not legally become head of the Church of England. No such misfortune befell Vives, but he lost the friendship of both Henry and Catherine during their divorce proceedings. Catherine had asked Vives to be one of her advocates, but the Queen was disappointed, even enraged, with Vives's counsel that she forego any defense. In 1528, Vives left England to return to the Netherlands. His final years were spent in relative seclusion. They were, however, highly productive, resulting in the publication, among other works, of *De Anima et Vita,* the book that, according to Norena (1970), "inaugurated in European thought the study of man based on reflection and observation without any metaphysical scheme" (p. 117). Vives died in 1540, just two years after the publication of *De Anima.*

Most scholars agree that the title of Vives's work *De Anima et Vita* is misleading. Vives had little interest in the nature of the soul per se; rather, his interest was in the operation of the soul. Brett (1912–1921/1965) argued that with Vives "the high *a priori* road is abandoned and the variety of the soul's manifestations begins to take rank above the formal deduction of its powers" (p. 326).

In an overview of the physiological-psychological thought of Vives, Clements (1967) pointed out that sometimes Vives's "writings seem to show brief but almost brilliant flashes of physiological and psychological insights, e.g., his insistence that medication first be tried on rats and guinea pigs, and his casual observations of the conditioned responses of animals" (p. 234). Clements noted, however, that at other times Vives's writings seem unfocused because of his tendency to pursue moral, religious, or poetic tangents. Let us now turn to a consideration of some of Vives's psychological thought.

Emotions.   Vives had a strong interest in the effects of emotions on human beings. He believed that there are inherent temperamental differences that influence emotions, but he also emphasized the effects of environmental or social influences on emotions. For example, he believed that emotions are influenced by climate, material culture (including our houses and belongings), and our relationships with other people. Vives believed that emotional processes may influence the state of the body and the state of the body may influence emotions. For example, Norena (1970) pointed out that Vives thought that "sadness causes black bile and black bile increases sadness" (p. 273). Vives believed that the control of emotions is important because unbridled emotions interfere with perception, judgment, and reason. Clements (1967, p. 231) stated that Vives was also sensitive to the beneficial consequences of emotions. Thus, even emotions such as pride, which are often judged negatively, have their origin in a quest for the good. Clements also argued that Vives's attempt to describe emotions objectively and his strong physiological emphasis were to have a substantial impact on Descartes.

Memory.   Vives's work on association, memory, and forgetting is a largely neglected chapter in the history of psychology. Zilboorg (1941) pointed out that Vives "cites example after example of associations through similarity, contiguity, and opposites. The first in the history of psychology, he recognizes the emotional origin of certain associations" (p. 192). On this latter topic, Vives once recalled that as a youth he had eaten cherries while ill with a fever. Years later, the taste of cherries resulted in such vivid recall of the fever that it was almost as if he experienced it again (see Zilboorg, 1941, p. 192). Vives is clearly among those philosophers dating back to Aristotle who emphasized the centrality of association in human intellectual processes.

Vives's work on memory was characterized less by an interest in what memory is than in how it works. He believed that anything that disturbs the spirits of the brain may have an impact on memory. Illness, alcohol, age, and intelligence are but a few of the factors associated with our ability to remember. Vives believed that a memory image can be completely erased, in which case relearning is necessary for a reinstatement of the image. In most cases, memory images are not completely lost but are simply weakened. In these cases, recollection is facilitated when we recover any image that is strongly associated with the to-be-recalled image.

Learning.   In addition to his interest in psychological problems, Vives was one of the pioneers in pedagogy and education. Unique in his time, Vives was an advocate of education for women and for the poor. He believed in secular education and emphasized the importance of individual instruction. Vives's thoughts on education were products of his conviction that knowledge and education are necessary to desirable social reforms.

Vives's significance in the history of psychology should not be underestimated. He influenced a large number of later scholars, including René Descartes and the British associationists. His book remained unusually popular even one hundred years after his death.

Leonardo da Vinci

One of the legendary figures of the Renaissance is remembered primarily for such world-famous paintings as *The Mona Lisa* and *The Last Supper.* But Leonardo da Vinci (1452–1519) was also a mechanic, architect, engineer, inventor, and man of science. His extensive notes (see Richter, 1970) testify to Leonardo's originality and to the great breadth of his scientific and engineering interests. In his notes, for example, we encounter sketches of flying machines, including an anticipation of the helicopter; extensive and highly detailed anatomical drawings based on over thirty dissections that Leonardo personally conducted; sketches of irrigation systems and various military weapons; numerous drawings representing Leonardo's interest in physical geography (it is noteworthy that da Vinci advised Columbus to plan a trip around the world); and many architectural drawings that included plans for towns, canals, streets, churches,

and palaces. Leonardo's place in the history of psychology centers on his contributions to knowledge of the senses with particular reference to vision, the sense that he viewed as sovereign among the senses.

Leonardo was born in the vicinity of Vinci, between Florence and Pisa. He was the illegitimate son of Pietro da Vinci, a notary. Leonardo was raised by his father and members of his father's family; little is known of his natural mother. He showed early signs of artistic talent and was apprenticed to a well-known Florentine artist, Andrea de Verrocchio. It was from Verrocchio that da Vinci received most of his education.

In 1483, Leonardo moved to Milan where he was to enjoy a sixteen-year period of creative activity. Following his years in Milan, he moved back to Florence for six years. During this period, he was employed to make military maps and to offer suggestions for the military defense of Florence. He also continued his anatomical studies by conducting autopsies at the Hospital of Santa Maria Nuova. Leonardo's six-year stay in Florence was followed by a second Milan period from 1506 to 1513. He then moved to Rome for three years. It was during this time that he painted *The Mona Lisa.* Da Vinci's last years were spent in France where he enjoyed status as a recognized artist in the court of Francis I. Leonardo worked with enthusiasm and energy to the date of his death, May 2, 1519.

For all of his accomplishments, da Vinci did not leave the world with a major published book; we have only his extensive notes, which were subsequently published. His achievements were obviously vast but he also suffered many failures. He started artistic and engineering projects that were never finished because of the slow pace of his work and his tendency to depart from his initial plans. The very breadth of his interests and skills, coupled with his compulsivities, perhaps undermined the magnitude of accomplishment that would have been obtained with greater focus. Leonardo the artist was undoubtedly compromised by Leonardo the scientist and vice versa. Leonardo regretted the encroachment of one interest on another, but with his characteristic breadth of appetite was helpless to do anything about it. Let us turn now to da Vinci's psychological contributions.

Leonardo viewed the eye as the premier instrument of human knowledge. As such, and in the interest of "seeing," he approached visual perception from several vantage points. He was interested in the anatomical-physiological, psychological, physical, and geometric properties of vision. He struggled with the ancient notion that "vision is power" or that the eye emits rays, but rejected this in favor of the idea that the eye is simply responsive to light energy. He left many anatomical drawings of the visual system (e.g., see Calder, 1970, pp. 58–69), including cross sections of the human eye and illustrations of the optic chiasma. Leonardo believed that images are inverted prior to reaching the lens and reinverted by the lens so they are right side up on the retina. We now know that images on the retina are inverted. Da Vinci was interested in comparative vision and was known to have dissected the eyes of many animals (including a lion, dogs, and an owl) in an attempt to understand their visual capacities.

In his classic book *Sensation and Perception in the History of Experimental Psychology,* Boring (1942) pointed out that Leonardo da Vinci made many contributions to our understanding of visual perception. As an example, Leonardo illustrated contrast effects by showing that white can appear whiter when contrasted with a darker color. Interestingly, Leonardo also argued that "beauty and ugliness seem more effective through one another" (Zubov, 1968, p. 137). Boring (1942, p. 266) stated that Leonardo also contributed to our understanding of *aerial perspective,* the effects of atmosphere on distance perception. Leonardo understood that colors fade with distance. He also noted that objects lose clarity with distance. There are disputes (see Boring, 1942, p. 284) about whether da Vinci understood the possible role of retinal disparity in space perception. He wrote down many rules for painters pertaining to contrast effects and aerial perspective, but while he was interested in the practical applications of his rules, his interests were deeper, more scientific. He was interested in perception in its own right as a guide to understanding nature.

Leonardo had many other psychological interests. He wrote about the other senses and had a strong interest in emotional expression. This latter interest was also motivated by artistic interest in portraying human emotion. In his work *Leonardo da Vinci and a Memory of His Childhood,* Freud (1910/1957b) pointed out that Leonardo sometimes accompanied "condemned criminals on their way to execution in order to study their features distorted by fear and to sketch them in his notebook" (p. 69).

Some of da Vinci's other psychological interests are represented in scattered maxims. For example, he pointed out that "the part always has a tendency to reunite with its whole in order to escape from its imperfection" (Richter, 1970, vol. 2, p. 238). He emphasized the unity of body and spirit by pointing out that "the spirit desires to remain with its body, because, without the organic instruments of that body, it can neither act nor feel anything" (Richter, 1970, vol. 2, p. 238).

It is seldom appreciated that Leonardo was an important forerunner of Francis Bacon and René Descartes. These two philosophers were later to struggle with the problem of human knowledge and the nature of the scientific method. In a set of maxims, Leonardo also outlined a method that was closer to that advocated later by Bacon than to that advocated by Descartes. Leonardo argued that we should first consult experience and then reason. He believed that reason and judgment are more likely to err than experience. At the same time, more in line with Cartesian thought, he argued that without the application of mathematics, there can be no certainty. He also maintained that practice without science is like a sailor without a compass (see Richter, 1970, pp. 239–241).

Leonardo da Vinci was an artist and a man of science, and in both capacities his interests inevitably turned to matters that would later occupy the thoughts of psychologists. His influence in psychological matters may not have been extensive, because many of his contributions were discovered long after his death in his unpublished notes. He does, however, illustrate that there were some important psychological discoveries during the Renaissance period.

Paracelsus

One of the most enigmatic figures of the Renaissance was the physician-alchemist-astrologer-scientist Philippus Aureolus Theophrastus Bombastus von Hohenheim, who went by the nickname Paracelsus (1493–1541). Paracelsus was born in Switzerland. His father, a physician, took responsibility for Paracelsus's early education. There are only minimal records regarding his later education, but it appears likely that he studied at several European universities and completed a doctorate in medicine.

Paracelsus's greatest contributions were his medical innovations and particularly his applications of chemistry to medicine. As an alchemist, he learned the simple herbal remedies for illness employed by common people. He believed that common remedies are often effective. He worked to simplify many of the medicinal applications of his day and emphasized the importance of empirical studies of the effects of simple medicines on specific ailments. Simplification of chemical remedies was an important contribution in his day because chemical remedies of the time often consisted of complicated mixtures known primarily for their rank smell or bitter taste.

On psychological matters, Paracelsus argued against demonology but accepted the possibility that the stars may influence personality. He believed that mental processes may have an impact on the health of the body and vice versa. He taught that harmony with the order of nature is the key to human happiness. Thus, "if nature takes its proper course, we are happy [but] if nature follows the wrong course we are unhappy" (Jacobi, 1958, p. 203). Paracelsus had a strong belief in the important role of external physical forces in human health. This part of his theory, and his astrology, were to have an impact later on Franz Anton Mesmer.

Paracelsus is also known for his radical or even fanatic comments on epistemology. He presented the strongest polemics against the ancients and appealed for a new science based on experience rather than on the rational schemes of older authorities. The term *bombastic* is possibly derived from Paracelsus's name Bombastus. The term accurately characterizes the style he employed. He held forth in a near rage as he denounced older authorities and on one occasion he publicly burned the books of Avicenna. Ronan (1982, p. 310) pointed out that Paracelsus was persuaded "that knowledge comes

not from books in the old scholastic sense but from a study of nature."

Paracelsus's major contribution may have resided in his agitation for mastery over nature. Such mastery was to be achieved through wisdom based on observation. But he also believed that the mastery of nature would come about through astrology and alchemy. Rogers (1912) stated, "Paracelsus is the type of a host of men who sprang up all over Europe—men of enthusiasm for nature, and to some extent of original and high ideal, but men whose undisciplined imaginations led them beyond the bounds of sober thinking" (p. 231). People such as Paracelsus represent an important bridge from Medieval scholasticism to modern science.

Julius Caesar Scaliger

The contemporary expression *Renaissance person* is used to describe a versatile individual with knowledge in several areas. In an age of specialization such persons are rare, but during the Renaissance, as in earlier times dating back to Greece, it was possible for an individual to possess up-to-date information in several disciplines. The expression *Renaissance person* could have been inspired by the intellectual breadth of Leonardo da Vinci and many of the people discussed in this chapter. Another candidate for the title would be Julius Caesar Scaliger (1484–1558). According to one of his biographers, Scaliger was "a soldier, doctor, philosopher, grammarian, textual critic, physicist, botanist, poet, and the author of a poetics" (Hall, 1950, p. 152).

Scaliger was born in Verona and was tutored in his early years by a famous architect and scholar, Giovanni Giocondo. Scaliger was known during his youth for his great strength and vitality and for an enormous capacity for work. For many years he was in military service, but evenings found him with books. Though the details of Scaliger's formal education are sketchy, he is known to have attended the University of Bologna. It is also known that he read very broadly but was increasingly attracted to medical studies. It was medicine that Scaliger would turn to as a source of livelihood.

In Scaliger's day, one did not have to hold a degree to practice medicine, and it is not clear whether Scaliger ever took a formal medical degree. He did, however, become a highly respected doctor. In 1529, at age forty-five, he married a sixteen-year-old girl (an age difference not uncommon in that period) who was to bear him fifteen children. Scaliger's practice in Agen, France, attracted many students, including François Rabelais, another well-known Renaissance physician and literary scholar, and Michel de Nostredame (Nostradamus), later to become known for his claims to be able to predict the future. Scaliger attracted students because he was recognized as one of the leading authorities on ancient writers such as Hippocrates and Aristotle.

Among other things, Scaliger is remembered for his original work on kinesthetic and muscle senses. Brett (1912–1921/1965) stated that Scaliger may have been the first who believed in a muscle sense. Scaliger's interest in a possible muscle sense led him also to speculate that the muscles play an important role in what we today would call cognitive-affective processes. For example, he noted that "brave men feel the force of an insult in those muscles which serve for striking" (Peters, 1965, p. 328). Scaliger believed that muscles play a key role in the support of habit—a position that would be emphasized in twentieth-century behavioral psychologies.

Michel de Montaigne

Earlier in this chapter we observed that one of the characteristics of the Renaissance was a new emphasis on human beings in this world rather than on God and the afterlife. This new emphasis is well illustrated in the writings of the French skeptical philosopher Michel Eyquem de Montaigne (*mahn TAYN*) (1533–1592). According to Bloom (1987), "Montaigne, until the advent of Shakespeare, is the great figure of the European Renaissance, comparable in cognitive power and in influence to Freud in our century" (p. 1). Groethuysen (1963) pointed out that Montaigne attempted to "comprehend life in its own immediate terms without recourse to religious or metaphysical postulates" (p. 634). Montaigne expressed his views in the form of *Essais (Essays),* a new literary form that he originated. His essays have long been recognized as masterful introspective studies that project a self-portrait and a spontaneous and informed opinion on a variety

of topics, many of a psychological nature. Montaigne's most important philosophical essay was entitled "Apology for Raimond Sebond." This essay resurrected earlier Greek and Roman skepticism about the possibility of attaining genuine knowledge. Popkin (1967, pp. 366–368) characterized the "Apology" as a pivotal work that structured the intellectual issues of seventeenth-century thought by serving as a foil for the efforts of such men as René Descartes and Francis Bacon who, disturbed by skepticism, sought to reestablish faith in the possibilities of knowledge.

Montaigne was born near Bordeaux in the southwest part of France. He received his formal education at the Collège de Guyenne and then at the University of Toulouse. Following his formal education, he practiced law in Bordeaux, but by 1571 decided to retire from public life. After his retirement, he initiated work on the *Essays* that would secure for him a place of prominence in intellectual history.

Montaigne was deeply troubled by the intense religious rivalry between Protestants and Catholics. He lived at the time of the St. Bartholomew Massacre and undoubtedly witnessed firsthand many other atrocities carried out in the name of religion. He was Catholic but friendly to some Protestant ideas. His moderate theology aroused suspicion in the extremists on both sides. He maintained a keen intellectual interest in all religions. Many of the world's scholars, including Shakespeare, Burton, Byron, Emerson, and Aldous Huxley, have expressed their debt to Montaigne. We will now examine some of his specific contributions and beliefs.

Montaigne's Skepticism. As noted, Montaigne's skepticism, as set forth in his longest and most influential essay "Apology for Raimond Sebond," served as a powerful stimulus to focus the thought of subsequent generations of scholars on the problem of knowledge. The *Apology* was apparently motivated by attacks on Raimond Sebond's *Theologia Naturalis,* a work that Montaigne had earlier translated from Latin. The *Apology* was also undoubtedly motivated by Montaigne's attempts to work through his own bitterness over the religious wars between Protestants and Catholics. Sebond, like many of the theologians of the time, argued in his *Natural Theology* that reason can be employed in the support of the major contentions of the Christian faith. His specific examples, however, were subject to criticism and arguments that his reasoning was unsound. Montaigne, who grounded his religion in faith alone, strongly disagreed with Sebond's contention that reason could be employed in support of faith. Nevertheless, he believed that Sebond's arguments were as good as those of his critics. The *Apology,* as noted by Frame (1960, vol. 2, p. 113), is misnamed because it defends Sebond only in the sense that it points out that his errors are no greater than the errors of his critics. The *Apology* itself turns into a trenchant attack on the arrogance of human beings who claim knowledge when such knowledge is based on experience or reason.

Before reviewing the specific skeptical arguments that were to have such impact on subsequent thinkers, we should note that Montaigne was apparently fearful of those who believed that their faith was buttressed by reason. He found too many people who, out of religious zeal, are willing to march in armies. He lamented that "there is no hostility that excels Christian hostility" and contended that "our religion is made to extirpate vices; [but] it covers them, fosters them, incites them" (Montaigne, *Apology,* p. 120). Montaigne believed that virtue is the real product of truth. Given his beliefs, we may view the *Apology* as an attack both on the arrogance of reason and on the impotence of reason.

Montaigne opened his skeptical attack by pointing to presumption as the original human malady. He argued that humans are arrogant and filled with unjustified vanity. He then devoted over thirty pages to anecdotes and demonstrations of the many arenas in which animal virtue and intelligence are superior to such qualities in humans. He finally concluded that there are no grounds for our claims that we are superior to the animals. Indeed, humans, according to Montaigne, are, in many respects, not as good or as knowledgeable as animals. Following his comparison of humans with animals, Montaigne moved to arguments that were directly relevant to his skeptical thesis.

Montaigne proposed to examine those excellent and select human beings who are recognized for having achieved the most and who are studied most extensively. He then proceeded to list the most blatant contradictions in the thought of over two dozen of the most famous scholars and philosophers. Next he mentioned the contradictions in philosophies of government, the variability of customs, and the defects of language that render it difficult to convey clearly a single thought to another person. Indeed, Montaigne argued that most of the troubles of the world are grammatical; lawsuits, wars, and interpersonal difficulties stem from doubts about meanings. Montaigne pointed out that it is with the "mad arrogance of speech [that humans seek] to bring God down to their measure" (Montaigne, *Apology,* p. 217), and asked the reader to consider the sheer nonsense of many early religious beliefs and practices. Montaigne quoted with approval St. Paul's contention that those who profess to be wise become fools (Romans 1, 22).

Montaigne pointed to the effects of emotions and motives on beliefs. Pay a lawyer a bit more, contended Montaigne, and that lawyer will find new interest in your case and declare that your case has become more believable. Preachers who preach with emotion become more convinced of their doctrines, and a proposition defended in anger may thereby be made more memorable and convincing. Montaigne found that the cognitive-rational apparatus is weakened by wishful thinking.

Even science changes, declared Montaigne, and what is taken to be true in one era is replaced in another. How can we then be sure that what is now taken for scientific truth will not be replaced tomorrow? Montaigne also launched powerful attacks against the claims made for the accuracy of sensory information: There may be realities for which we have no sense, we are subject to illusions, we do not always recognize illusions as such, bodily conditions and emotions color sensory information, and our upbringing affects our senses. The argument is advanced that we are always changing and that our metamorphosis governs the way we see our world.

Montaigne's attack on human knowledge was influential. Indeed, according to Durant and Durant (1961) Montaigne's "influence pervaded three centuries and four continents" (p. 413). According to Winter (1976), the essays were especially well received "in Holland and in England, where at the time a less restrictive political and religious climate prevailed" (p. 106). Popkin (1967) pointed out that Montaigne "succeeded in intensifying the doubts already produced by the religious crisis of the Reformation, the humanistic crisis of the Renaissance, and the philosophical-scientific crisis of revived Pyrrhonism. . . . Bacon, Herbert of Cherbury, and Descartes were to seek new philosophical systems to provide for human knowledge a basis impervious to Montaigne's doubts" (p. 368).

Montaigne's Psychology. As we have seen, Montaigne's skepticism played an important role in the scientific revolution. Montaigne's essays also explored pyschological topics such as thought, emotion, motivation, and conflict in their own right. Montaigne approached such topics in his essays through a fresh introspective analysis that is remarkable in its contrast with the earlier introspective technique of St. Augustine. Augustine's introspections took the reader to the innermost parts of the troubled soul. By contrast, Montaigne's lighter approach, though introspective, was not morbidly introverted. The reader does not just observe, but actively participates with Montaigne in the psychological analysis of topics such as anger, fear, happiness, and folly. Though Montaigne did not pretend to develop a coherent psychology, he did introduce a useful method to study a number of topics of psychological interest. We will briefly examine Montaigne's views on selected topics, including child rearing and education, the impossibility of pure experience, and the inconsistency of human action.

Child Rearing and Education. Montaigne lamented the cruel child-rearing practices he witnessed in his day and openly questioned why the courts ignored all the children who were physically abused. He believed that many parents use punishment not for correction but for revenge. He also condemned the schools of his day for their strict discipline. The schools, he argued, were like jails and the inmates were tortured by wrathful teachers. Montaigne believed that children should find pleasure in learning, but with punishment, he argued, the children are turned into dullards. He be-

lieved that the beginnings of cruelty are nurtured by parents who laugh when their children torment a pet or bully a peer. DeMause (1974), after surveying the lives of seventy children living prior to the eighteenth century, pointed out that "all were beaten except one: Montaigne's daughter" (p. 40).

Experience Is Never Pure. Several of Montaigne's essays bring up an issue about human experience that was to be a focus of concern for many of the early psychologists. The issue is whether there are pure experiences of simple or elementary things, or whether experience is always composed of a compound or mixture of elementary things. For example, is there a pure feeling of joy or is there a pure sense of sweetness? Are there elements in our experience that are not mixed with other elements or that present themselves in an undiluted form? Montaigne's answer, based on his self-observations, is an unqualified no.

In his essay, "We Taste Nothing Pure," he compared human experience to metals such as gold, that serve best when they are debased or combined with other materials. Similarly, of our experiences, Montaigne declared that upon close examination, they always reveal an admixture or a combination. Thus, "our utmost sensual pleasure has an air of groaning and lament about it" (see Frame, 1960, vol. 2, p. 381). Indeed, we are so constituted, according to Montaigne, that we cannot endure intense or sustained pleasure; we escape to more neutral, safe ground. He quoted, with approval, Socrates's contention that some god must have become confused during the creation of pain and pleasure, and, after botching the job, tied the two together by the tail. As we cannot sustain intense pleasure, pain also has its accompanying satisfactions. Over three hundred years later, Sigmund Freud was also to point to the tensions and confusions between pleasure and pain. Both men would have been keenly interested in late twentieth-century research demonstrating the release of endorphins (opiate-like neurotransmitters) that apparently stimulate feelings of well-being or even pleasure following hard work or painful experiences.

The thoroughness with which Montaigne rejected pure experience is illustrated by his confession that his "best goodness . . . has some tincture of vice" (Frame, 1960, vol. 2, p. 383). Throughout his essays, we find evidence of Montaigne's suspicion that a manifest behavior or experience serves as a cover for its opposite counterpart. He was close to an awareness of what would later be called a *reaction formation*. Though such awareness was evident in his writings, Montaigne did not bring himself to the bold investigation and analysis of the human psyche that Freud would later undertake.

Inconsistencies of Human Actions. As a close observer of human behavior, Montaigne found that consistency of actions within individuals is rare, whereas inconsistency is almost a rule of action. He declared that few of us demonstrate stability of conduct or opinion and that irresolution is "the most common and apparent defect of our nature" (Frame, 1960, vol. 2, p. 1). Montaigne finds several reasons for human inconsistency; the first is the result of the variations and vicissitudes of appetite. We follow our appetites, but our appetites are constantly changing.

Inconsistency is also brought about by changes in context or circumstance. Montaigne observed that the same individual may be bold and adventurous in one context, but fearful or even cowardly in another. According to Montaigne, context and circumstance play powerful roles in courage, fear, valor, and many other human virtues and vices. The emphasis on the importance of context and circumstance would later be verified by a host of social psychological experiments.

Though Montaigne saw conduct as a product of circumstance, he also argued that our inconsistencies result from the different roles we play and the different masks we wear. Montaigne's work on inconsistency went beyond earlier work in that he identified some of the sources (e.g., variability of appetite, context, role playing, influence of authority, etc.) that contribute to the problem. Growth toward consistency and integrity was, in his view, one of the greatest challenges confronting human beings. He believed that most of us are unable to bridle appetite, or resist flattery, or avoid prostituting ourselves in the marketplace to whatever advantages might be offered. Montaigne valued the integrity associated with self-directedness.

It is apparent that Montaigne introduced some important psychological insights in the late Renaissance period. However, his major contribution consisted of the attitudes he conveyed. As we noted, his skepticism stimulated other scholars to give serious consideration to the problem of human knowledge. His ability to describe human experience and behavior as he found them also helped open the door to more naturalistic studies of human beings. He is a key figure in the history of the cognitive and behavioral sciences.

Oliva Sabuco

Work attributed to Oliva Sabuco (*SUH bu ko*) de Nantes Barrera (1562–?) has been the subject of a long-standing and difficult historiographical problem. An influential book dedicated to Phillip II and entitled *New Philosophy on the Nature of Man* was first published in 1587 in Madrid under her authorship. Shortly after the original publication, Oliva's father Miguel Sabuco issued a legal statement claiming that he was the sole author of the work, and that he had allowed the book to be published under his daughter's name as a way of honoring her. Miguel's subsequent attempts to gain recognition as author, including an attempt to publish an edition of the book in Portugal, met with no success. In fact, the book went through four editions including one that was edited extensively (with deletions and interpretive commentary) by the Spanish Inquisition. All editions were published under the authorship of Oliva Sabuco. The question of authorship is still subject to debate, and there are scholars who believe that Miguel Sabuco is the author (see Norena, 1975). There are, however, good reasons (see Waithe, 1989) to believe that the book was indeed authored by Oliva Sabuco. In the context of the times, with existing gender differentiations, it seems unlikely that the legitimate claims of a man would have been ignored.

Little is known about the personal lives or the educational backgrounds of Miguel or Oliva Sabuco. Most of Oliva's education may have been of an informal nature. She was apparently one of the eight children of Miguel Sabuco and Francisca de Cozar. Oliva was married when she was eighteen, and *New Philosophy on the Nature of Man* was published when she was twenty-five.

Oliva Sabuco was one of the first to write deeply on the subject of the passions and their effects. She appears to have had a deep sensitivity to the physical and psychological consequences of emotions such as anger, fear, jealousy, hatred, and depression. She pointed out that such emotions, unchecked, lead to physical and emotional imbalance and even death. She also addressed the salutary consequences of love, hope, happiness, and moderation. Sabuco understood the importance of balance and harmony and the wisdom of avoiding the extremes of emotional expression. She also understood the importance of environmental context as a means of maintaining harmony and balance. She believed that extremes in sounds, colors, tastes, and odors can contribute to illness, whereas moderate and harmonious surroundings promote health.

Oliva Sabuco understood the close connection between physiology and psychology. According to Waithe (1989), Sabuco also viewed "human nature as a microcosm of nature itself" (p. 268). It follows that psychology must be based on a broad epistemological foundation. Sabuco stressed introspection as a way of knowing, but she also emphasized close observation of the physical causes of psychological states. She underscored the importance of intellectual processes and the imagination, but she placed equal, if not greater, emphasis on the central role of emotions in human life. Above all, she emphasized the wisdom of moderation in all things and a broad-based approach to knowledge.

Juan Huarte

One of the most significant breakthroughs in the psychological thought of the late Renaissance period came from the pen of one of Montaigne's contemporaries, Juan Huarte (c. 1530–c. 1592). Huarte (*WAHR tae*) can properly be regarded as one of the important pioneers in the study of aptitude, temperament, and individual differences. His book *Examen de Ingenios para las Sciencias (The Examination of Men's Wits)* stands as one of the great classics in differential psychology.

Unfortunately, little is known of Huarte's personal life. He was apparently born in San Juan de Pie del Puerto in Navarre, but spent most of his life in Baeza, Spain. He earned a medical degree at the University of Alcala and enjoyed a successful practice. Throughout his medical career, he was interested in the psychological topics that he set forth in the *Eramen*. The book itself was translated into many languages and went through dozens of printings. Some of the printings were placed on local indexes of forbidden books during the Inquisition because they were offensive to prevailing religious doctrine. An example, as noted by Rogers (1959, p. vii), was Huarte's contention that poetic skill has a natural rather than a divine origin.

The essential thesis of the *Examen* regarding aptitudes is set forth in the first chapter. Huarte claimed that it is undeniable that children may be found who are capable of one kind of knowledge or activity but not another. Given such different abilities, children should be studied early in order to discover the nature of their abilities and to determine what studies would correspond most closely with their natural capacities. Huarte was also sensitive to the importance of introducing subjects at appropriate developmental levels. Thus, language (largely a memory task) may be introduced early because small children have excellent memories. Logic, which requires the development of understanding, should be introduced later in the curriculum.

Huarte based his theory of individual differences on the operation of humoral temperaments. Heat, cold, moistness, and dryness were thought to be responsible for all individual differences. Humoral temperaments were also used to account for age differences, racial differences, and intellectual differences. For example, Huarte's theory may be illustrated as applied to differences in memory and understanding as a function of age. He regarded memory as dependent on moistness, and understanding as dependent on dryness. He believed that the brain of an old person is dry and filled with understanding, but such a brain is poor when it comes to memory. By contrast, children whose brains are endowed with moisture have excellent memory, but very poor understanding. Huarte argued also that for all of us, memory is superior in the morning because moisture accrues during sleep. Through the day, the brain dries and hardens and, as a result, memory becomes less facile.

Diamond (1974b) pointed out that Huarte emphasized "somatic determinants of behavior" (p. 368). Specifically, the determinants have their origin in the condition of the brain. Although Huarte quoted Galen, Aristotle, and Hippocrates, he also had the courage to refute these early scholars. His final product represented a curious blend of Greek philosophy with emphasis on the natural determinants of behavior and Christian theology that emphasized occasional miraculous enlightenment. The strong orientation of Huarte to the natural determinants of behavior marks him as an important pioneer in the study of differential psychology.

Huarte, as a product of the sixteenth century, perpetuated the prevailing views on sex differences. Huarte counseled that women are not to be blamed for their dullness, for they can do nothing about the coldness and moistness that are characteristic of their sex. Huarte's efforts in the understanding of individual differences, coupled with his paternalistic biases, underscore the importance of raising gender-differentiated questions as one reads history.

Huarte's views on women and men were consistent with the contention of Kelly-Gadol (1977) that there was no Renaissance for women. If anything, their social status declined during the three hundred years that are so often viewed as a period of intellectual rebirth. We thus come back to the question about whether the period deserves the extravagant title of *Renaissance*. The reasoned response must surely be yes and no. There was a Renaissance in some areas, but in others human beings remained in darkness.

On the positive side, the Renaissance ushered in new geographic and technical discoveries that contributed to an expansion of intellectual boundaries. The era also witnessed a rediscovery of the Greek classics and a strong rebellion against existing authority. Such rebellion may have reinforced the growth of empirical studies and a new confidence in individual judgment. The resurrection of Greek skepticism, particularly as set forth in Montaigne's widely distributed essay "Apology for Raimond Sebond," served to stimulate interest in the problem of human knowledge. Pioneers in both empirical (e.g., Francis Bacon) and rational (e.g., René Descartes) traditions sought to secure a basis for knowledge that could withstand the criticisms of the skeptic. Thus, indirectly, Renaissance skepticism made an important contribution to the epistemological foundations of modern science.

The Renaissance produced some noteworthy contributions to psychological thought, though such thought occurred as but a few rather isolated islands in a sea of ignorance. As we move to the modern period (from 1600), we will discover more clearly discernible threads of thought marked by ideas building on each other. Such threads of thought will be clearly evident in the chapters that follow on empiricism, rationalism, and the growth of the mechanistic perspective. Returning to the discussion on patterns in history in Chapter 1, history may indeed be sometimes chaotic and sometimes linear.

REVIEW QUESTIONS

1. Describe five general characteristics of the Renaissance period.

2. How did the plague contribute to the changing climate of opinion in the Renaissance?

3. Contrast geocentric and heliocentric world views and their implications for a science of human nature.

4. Discuss Machiavelli's importance to the history of the social and behavioral sciences.

5. Outline at least three of Vives's contributions to psychological thought.

6. Discuss Leonardo da Vinci's contributions to perception. What are some specific ways in which Leonardo contributed to the growth of empirical studies?

7. In what way does the thought of Paracelsus serve as a bridge from scholasticism to modern science?

8. Outline some of Montaigne's skeptical arguments. Why was Montaigne's skepticism important to the development of modern science?

9. Briefly describe Montaigne's position on child rearing.

10. In what way does Juan Huarte serve as an important pioneer in the study of individual differences?

CHAPTER 6

EMPIRICISM, ASSOCIATIONISM, AND UTILITARIANISM

I admit nothing but on the faith of eyes.
—Francis Bacon (in Anderson, 1960, p. 26)

In his book *The History of Skepticism from Erasmus to Spinoza,* Richard Popkin (1979, p. 43) argued that "Renaissance skepticism became crucial in the formation of modern philosophy." As we noted in the previous chapter, it was Michel de Montaigne who was the leading force in the resurrection of skepticism. According to Popkin, Montaigne's attack on human knowledge, as set forth in his "Apology for Raimond Sebond," was so successful and influential that it contributed to an intellectual crisis in the early seventeenth century. As a result of the crisis, one of the tasks of philosophy was to respond to the criticisms raised by Montaigne and to restore faith in human knowledge. Popkin pointed out that both Francis Bacon (1561–1626) and René Descartes (1596–1650) attempted to refute Montaigne's skepticism. The refutations of these two original philosophers established them as leaders of two intellectual traditions: empiricism and rationalism. These traditions helped shape modern thought and contributed to the development of modern science.

In this chapter we will examine the empirical-inductive philosophy, beginning with Francis Bacon and culminating with the radical empiricism of David Hume. We will then examine associationism and utilitarianism, two intellectual traditions inspired by empiricism.

In the following chapter we will explore rationalism, beginning with Descartes and culminating with Immanuel Kant. We will also examine those commonsense philosophies that are close intellectual relatives of rationalism. We will find that both the empirical and the rational traditions made unique and major contributions to the development of psychology.

EMPIRICISM

The English term *experience* is roughly equivalent to the term **empiricism,** which was derived from the Greek *empeirikos* and its Latin equivalent *empiricus.* Empirical philosophy elevates the roles of observation and experience and diminishes the role of reason in human knowledge. Empiricists also reject the idea that the mind at birth is already furnished with knowledge. Modern empiricism, beginning with Francis Bacon, was conceived largely as a promising method for the new inductive sciences.

Francis Bacon

Few figures in intellectual history have evoked as much controversy among scholars as Francis Bacon (1561–1626). Mathews (1996) has provided an extensive historical overview of the disagreements over Bacon's contributions. On the appreciative side, Bacon has been regarded as the Great Herald of the Empirical Spirit, the first to emphasize the methodological unity of the sciences, the first to advocate the importance of massive social support for scientific education, and the first to appreciate the human benefits to be derived from

Francis Bacon

scientific discovery. Bacon is also credited as a source of inspiration for scientific academies that came into being after his death. Philosophers and scientists such as Charles Darwin, René Descartes, John Locke, and Sir Isaac Newton specifically acknowledged their debt to Bacon. It is remarkable, in view of their vast philosophical differences, that Immanuel Kant dedicated his book *Critique of Pure Reason* to Francis Bacon.

Bacon has also been the subject of considerable criticism. It has been noted correctly that he was not a scientist and that he had little appreciation for the mathematical foundations of science. He also failed to appreciate or acknowledge some of the major scientific breakthroughs of his day, such as John Napier's logarithms or William Harvey's discovery of the circulation of the blood. Bacon also refused to accept Copernican theory and failed to appreciate the significance of Galileo's scientific contributions. At the same time, Bacon's emphasis on induction represents a charting of an intellectual procedure that was to be paramount in the development of the experimental sciences.

Francis Bacon was born on January 22, 1561, in London. Following two years of study at Cambridge University, Bacon worked in Paris on the staff of Sir Amias Paulet, ambassador to France. By 1582, Bacon was back in England and practicing law with a firm in London. In 1584, he was

elected to Parliament. Bacon's best-known work, *Novum Organum,* meaning new instrument of the mind, was published in 1620. The triumph of the publication of the *Novum Organum* was followed, however, by a major reversal. Bacon was convicted of participating in bribery and was forced to resign his office, pay a heavy fine, and serve a brief prison sentence. At age sixty, Bacon turned his attention from legal and legislative matters to science and philosophy. In his remaining years he published three major works, including *History of the Winds* (1622), *History of Life and Death* (1623), and a Latin translation of his earlier book *The Advancement of Learning,* first published in 1605. Bacon's death in 1626 was precipitated by a chill and a resulting cold that he caught after stuffing a chicken with snow to assess the preservative effects of such a procedure.

Bacon's major intellectual concerns focused on the problem of human knowledge. He was dismayed that centuries of intellectual activity had produced such a paucity of useful knowledge. The problem, according to Bacon, was that prevailing methods of inquiry were radically flawed. The human intellect was tragically held bondage by authority, and the methods employed within the scholastic and philosophical traditions were insufficiently wedded to the facts of experience. Bacon had a keen appreciation for the legitimate claims of skepticism and even joined ranks with the skeptics as he called attention to the sources of error that fostered and reinforced ignorance. At the same time, Bacon believed that skeptics overextended their claims. He believed that with the employment of proper methods, there was room for optimism regarding human knowledge.

Bacon is often remembered for his list of **Idols,** or phantoms of the human mind. The Idols are common sources of error that lead us astray in our quest for knowledge. Some of the Idols reflect weaknesses in the human intellect itself, whereas others illustrate the unfortunate consequences of social forces. On this latter topic, Bacon was one of the first to give explicit recognition to the idea that for science to flourish, a special supportive social and economic structure is required. But let us now turn to an examination of the Idols.

Bacon believed there were inherent limitations in the human intellectual apparatus; he called these the **Idols of the Tribe.** An example is the idea that external objects may be distorted by the sensory processes that transport such objects to the brain. Another Idol of the Tribe is illustrated by intellectual inertia, which manifests itself when human beings are satisfied with limited information or when we construct simplicity when such simplicity is not to be found in the nature of things. Bacon argued that one of the most unfortunate sources of error results from the common practice of lumping too much together into one category. He felt that people were too quick to embrace the "all" and too lazy to respond to the "each."

A second type of error that interferes with human knowledge was called the **Idols of the Cave.** These are the prejudices, the strongly preferred hypotheses or theories, or preferred explanatory modes, that blind us to alternative interpretations. Bacon believed that the first concern of the investigator should be with data. Individuals should be more interested in truth and less interested in confirming a favored hypothesis or theory. Bacon argued that generalizations should be developed only after masses of specific instances have been cataloged. He also argued for flexibility and for the development of a capacity to examine alternative interpretations of data.

Still another set of errors that interfere with human knowledge was labeled the **Idols of the Marketplace.** Bacon was concerned here with several aspects of the so-called nominal fallacy: the temptation to take words too seriously or to believe that the mere naming of a thing explains it. Bacon was concerned that we take our terminology too seriously and that we are misled by common usage of terms and definitions that are part of a prevailing climate of opinion. Bacon would approve the constant reexamination of definitions and classification systems. He recommended vigilance with respect to the ways we use words and the ways we allow ourselves to be used by words.

The final set of errors addressed by Bacon was called the **Idols of the Theatre.** Bacon was referring to "the mischievous authorities of systems, which are founded either on common notions, or on a few experiments, or on superstition" (Bacon, 1620/1960, p. 63). Bacon appeared to be cautioning against the easy acceptance of widely held systems or paradigms that come and go. He cared little whether such paradigms had rational or empirical basis (pp. 60–61) or whether they had been corrupted "by superstition and an admixture of theology" (p. 62). Bacon's Idols of the Theatre challenged the individual to avoid the easy acceptance of authority.

Bacon (1620/1960) found it understandable that in the quest for true knowledge the human mind at "first distrusts and then despises itself" (p. 103). There are, however, many grounds for hope and for transcending the despair and skepticism that can hinder us in our quest for knowledge. Thus, despite all the forces that work against human knowledge and despite the lack of progress and the inadequate methods of the past, Bacon was an optimist. He envisioned a world in possession of a positive science that would inevitably yield fruits that benefit virtually all dimensions of human life. Bacon realized that his personal work was not, properly speaking, in the mainstream of such a science; he was merely a prophet who had a vision of the possibilities of science.

Bacon believed that skepticism was fatally flawed and that the skeptic was subject to some of the same intellectual errors that others make. For example, skeptics were fond of demonstrating the illusory nature of certain types of sensory information. Bacon granted that there are indeed illusions, but the demonstrated illusions are made possible by careful selection of materials. He argued that the demonstration that there are illusions does not justify an attack on *all* sensory information. Bacon was correct in pointing out that skeptics were guilty of overgeneralization, but his defense of sensory information represented little more than a kind of practical commonsense faith in the validity of sensory data. In defense of the validation of sensory data, Bacon pointed out that instruments can serve as aids to the senses and can correct information revealed to the unaided senses. Furthermore, he pointed out that one type of sensory information can be used to cross-check another type. He might have added that even the skeptic must place faith in some form of sensory information in order to call attention to the truth of an illusion.

Bacon did not formulate an explicit and coherent statement of scientific methodology, but devoted sufficient comment to the topic to make it possible to construct an outline of his beliefs. It is noteworthy that Bacon realized he was making a provisional statement regarding scientific method. His anticipation of the further evolution of methodology is illustrated in his statement that "the art of discovery may advance as discoveries advance" (Bacon, 1620/1960, p. 120).

Bacon's positive approach to science is illustrated in a metaphor he employed to characterize the work of researchers. Some, he said, are like ants who only collect and use materials. Others are like spiders, busy spinning webs out of their own substance. Between the extremes of mere collection and the spinning of designs out of one's own substance is a middle road characterized by the bee, who gathers materials from a great variety of sources and transforms and digests these materials in community activity (Bacon, 1620/1960, p. 93). It is this middle road that Bacon advocated. He clearly understood the limitations of mere collection, and repeatedly cautioned that empirical philosophy can give rise to as much misinformation as rational philosophy, especially when empirical philosophers leap to hasty generalizations based on inadequate experiments (p. 61). But Bacon reserved his most vigorous attacks for the rationalists, who were divorced by their methods from the data of experience. Bacon's middle road is best described as a new inductivism that rejects the big leap, the temptation to entertain, or the temptation to place excessive trust in the intellect. The new inductivism demands the "reform of human understanding by grounding it solidly in experience" (Stephens, 1975, p. 60). Bacon was often accused of advancing a kind of naive empirical inductivism that entails mere collection of facts. Such an accusation, however, is inaccurate. Bacon emphasized the importance of assimilation and generalization, but cautioned that such activities should not be premature; they should follow the collection of masses of data from many sources.

Bacon warned that the great danger is that we shall be overly hasty in our claims to have attained knowledge. Thus, Bacon's optimism regarding the possibilities of knowledge was tempered somewhat by his conservatism regarding scientific claims. He recommended that all investigators bind themselves

to two rules at the outset of any inquiry: "first, to lay aside received opinions and notions; and second, to refrain the mind for a time from the highest generalizations" (Bacon, 1620/1960, p. 119). Bacon's emphasis was first and foremost on the extensive collection of particulars. A massive number of observations should be collected and, if possible, organized for presentation in tabular form. Due attention should also be given to negative instances. The second step in Bacon's method was the search for generalizations or higher principles, but, again, the researcher should enter into this step with great caution.

Bacon was also keenly interested in the manner of communication of scientific results. With a long-standing interest in rhetoric, he cautioned against the "grand style" and argued for a subdued and modest style that emphasizes objective data based on observation. He recognized that human beings can be seduced by style. Accordingly, the researcher should deemphasize style and focus on substance.

The Baconian inductive method, with its strong emphasis on observation, occupies a significant niche in the evolution of modern science. The deficiencies of the method—the failure to appreciate the roles of hypotheses and mathematics—are by now well understood, but the new emphasis on observation was a crucial prescription in a time marked by a tendency to rush to first principles. Bacon also helped restore confidence in human knowledge and his optimism shaped the thought of several succeeding generations of philosophers and scientists.

Francis Bacon found his way into the history of psychology via another route as well. In his classification of the sciences, he included most of the topical areas treated by contemporary psychology. He believed that society should support empirical studies of such topics as sleep and dreaming; development from infancy to old age; the senses; affections such as anger, love, and fear; and cognitive abilities such as imagination, thinking, and memory. Bacon called for the construction of complete natural histories of each of these areas and for all other scientific areas. He believed that an understanding of the natural history of an area provides the foundation for scientists to erect new knowledge structures. Bacon did not believe that his great plan for the restoration or renewal of the sciences could be properly initiated without the background provided by well-researched and well-written natural histories. At the same time, natural history without the new empirical instruments would be sterile.

The legacy of Bacon's extreme emphasis on observation can be debated. His emphasis was, at least, an understandable rebellion against opposite rationalistic intellectual extremes. Bacon's vision for a natural history and an empirical science that studies psychological topics is less debatable. Brett (1912–1921/1965) points out that "the ideas which he expressed ruled the progress of inductive or experimental psychology all through its development." We shall witness the strong stamp of his influence as we proceed with our examination of the development of empiricism. Let us turn now to a consideration of the life and work of one of Bacon's successors, a man who is easily the equal of Bacon in terms of his influence on Western intellectual history.

John Locke

The possibilities and limitations of empiricism as a way of knowing emerged out of the work of a succession of seventeenth- and eighteenth-century philosophers, most of whom were British. Those who followed Bacon, who were properly regarded as empiricists, deemphasized the methodological focus of Bacon's work. Instead, they explored the larger metaphysical dimensions of empiricism. Bacon's most important immediate successor, John Locke (1632–1704), has been described as "the most widely influential philosopher of English speech" (Tsanoff, 1964, p. 329). If Bacon can be viewed as the Great Herald of the Empirical Spirit, it is Locke who launched a serious inquiry into the nature of an empirical theory of knowledge.

John Locke was born in Wrinton, Somerset, on August 29, 1632. He was the eldest of the two sons of John Locke (1606–c. 1660) and Agnes Keene (1597–1654). At age fourteen, Locke entered Westminster School, where he pursued classical studies. In 1652, at twenty years of age, he entered

John Locke

Oxford University, where his interests shifted from classical studies to the natural sciences. His bachelor's degree was awarded in 1656 and his master's degree was conferred in 1658. With the death of Locke's father (c. 1660) and his younger brother Thomas (1663), most of the family estate went to Locke. This left him with a small inheritance that provided a degree of independence.

After completing his master's degree, Locke devoted his time to the study of the natural sciences and medicine. Though he never practiced medicine on an extensive basis, he was qualified to practice and accepted a few patients. His best-known patient and close friend and associate was Lord Ashley, Earl of Shaftesbury. In addition to serving as Shaftesbury's personal physician, Locke accepted some administrative and political responsibilities and served as tutor for Shaftesbury's grandson. Locke also served as an adviser to the government on coinage and as Commissioner of Appeal. These positions left time for Locke to devote himself to philosophy, and it is in the period from 1689 to 1704 that we witness an outpouring of the works for which he is so well remembered. His best-known psychological works include *An Essay Concerning Human Understanding* (1690/1959) and *Some Thoughts Concerning Education* (1693/1989).

Most of Locke's philosophical interests were related in one way or another to the problem of epistemology. Soles (1985) pointed out that Locke saw himself as an early "philosopher of science with the self-appointed task of providing epistemological foundations for the emerging empirical sciences" (p. 339). Locke's work on education may also be viewed as an extension of his epistemological interests. Though he never married, he had a deep interest in children and was especially interested in how children acquire knowledge and how the teaching–learning process may be improved. Politically and religiously, Locke was a liberal who advocated public education for all people, majority rule, and the right of all individuals to study religious questions for themselves and hold opinions that are not dogmatically imposed by religious or political authority.

One of the most celebrated and controversial ideas in Locke's work centers on his strong supposition that the mind, at birth, is as "white paper, void of all characters, without any ideas" (Locke, 1690/1959, p. 121). Fraser (1959, p. 121) suggested that the metaphor was not intended to mean that the intellectual apparatus is without latent capacities; it simply meant that the mind of the newborn is not furnished with knowledge or ideas of any kind. Locke's position, though not new, was set forth in a persuasive way, and the *Zeitgeist* of the seventeenth century was such that the "white paper" hypothesis and its implications could be seriously entertained. If the hypothesis is true, the role of experience in human knowledge becomes preeminent and thus we have a radical alternative to earlier theories that stress the role of innate ideas or a priori principles in human knowledge. Recall from Chapter 4 that the great poet Dante had even made the claim that we have innate knowledge of good and evil. It was precisely this kind of claim that inspired John Locke to launch such a vigorous attack on belief in innate ideas. Let us turn to a consideration of this attack.

In his *Essay,* Locke devoted three chapters to criticisms of belief in innate ideas. He argued that there is no evidence for innate moral ideas, no innate ideas of God (though he believed that the wise of all nations have come to a belief in God), no innate speculative principles, and no innate practical principles. Locke pointed out that we cannot find universal agreement on any topic, but even if

we could, such agreement would not necessarily prove innate ideas. Universal agreement, if it did exist, might indicate little more than common experience with some regular feature of the world. Locke's attack on innate ideas included arguments of a practical nature. Thus, the belief in innate ideas leads to the most unfortunate intellectual laziness by discouraging inquiry and research into possible exterior sources of ideas.

If ideas are not innate, what is their origin? Locke contended that some ideas come to the mind via one sense only. Two events in the same sensory domain in close temporal or spatial conjunction may be associated and result in what Locke called an idea. Other ideas result from the operation of two or more senses. Locke also believed that some ideas result from reflection, which is based on extrapolations from previous sensory information. A given idea may also have its origin in a complicated combination of sensation and reflection.

Locke's strong empirical position on the origin of knowledge called attention to the importance of learning and education and to the social and environmental context in which these activities take place. If all of this seemed obvious to subsequent generations, it was by no means obvious in a time when children were often held accountable for misdeeds and subjected to the harshest punishments, including capital punishment. Under Locke's treatment, the individual does not shoulder the full responsibility for deficits in knowledge—the requisite information may never have been provided. If individual responsibility is somewhat diminished in Locke's system, social responsibility for others (especially children) is enhanced.

Locke's search for the origin of ideas led him to a consideration of the relationship between ideas and those stimulus objects in the world that produce ideas. The relationship between the physical world and the psychological world (the world of ideas) was a necessary step for Locke, who was concerned about the validity of human knowledge. *Validity,* here, refers to the correspondence between ideas and objects. Locke hoped to demonstrate that ideas can correspond to real things in the physical world; otherwise, in his words, "The visions of an enthusiast and the reasonings of a sober man will be equally certain" (1690/1959, p. 227). Locke believed that our brains are often filled with imaginations, dreams, chimeras, and illusions, but we may also possess real knowledge. Otherwise, Locke argued, "Our most serious thoughts will be of little more use than the reveries of a crazy brain" (1690/1959, p. 228). What then are the grounds for believing in a correspondence between ideas and stimulus objects?

Locke believed that certain simple ideas furnished by the senses accurately reflect the external nature of things. For example, we have a simple idea of solidity and Locke said, "If anyone asks me *what this solidity is,* I send him to his senses to inform him" (1690/1959, p. 156). Solid objects are known by the sense of touch, and the idea of solidity is not a fiction or a fancy but the inevitable result of a conformity between psychological and physical realities. Two solid objects struck together produce a real effect and we are so constituted as to be able to have knowledge of that effect. Locke also argued that our knowledge of mathematical truths represents real knowledge.

It is of interest that Locke, though he may be regarded as the first to present a formal empirical philosophy, found it impossible to be a consistent empiricist. Just as he took a commonsense approach to the existence of certain qualities of physical objects, he took an intuitive approach to the certainty of his own existence. Like Descartes, he believed that to think, we must exist. Locke was also friendly to the rationalist camp on the question of God's existence. Although we have no innate idea of God, we can nevertheless demonstrate God's existence through reason (Locke, 1690/1959, Book 4, Ch. 10). Though Locke was not a through and through empiricist, some of his followers would make more concerted efforts along this path.

Locke's intense interest in the problem of knowledge led him to agree with earlier scientists such as Galileo and Boyle that there are two kinds of qualities that seem to characterize stimulus objects in the physical world. **Primary qualities** are those qualities that reside or inhere in an object and are independent of perception. Although there were disagreements about what counts as primary qualities, some examples include extension, fig-

ure, mobility, and solidity. **Secondary qualities** are hidden powers of an object that result in specific sensations. Thus, color, sound, warmth, and taste are examples of secondary qualities. If we examine a red cube, its shape and solidity may be taken as primary qualities, but the redness is a secondary quality. The redness does not reside in the cube in the same manner as does figure and solidity. To illustrate, if we lower the lights in a room, the color of the object seems to change, but the solidity and shape of the object do not change. Color, as a secondary quality, seems to emerge as a result of the interaction among light conditions, the object, and the perceiving subject. The characteristics of the perceiver contribute in a substantial way to the perception of secondary qualities, but such is not the case for primary qualities. For example, back to our red cube: Certain color-blind animals would not see the color red; they would see only shades of gray. Thus, the redness resides in the perceiver and not as an inherent quality of an object, though the object has the power to evoke the perception of redness in some perceptual systems.

The foregoing example from comparative psychology can be extended to clarify further the nature of secondary qualities. Thus, most humans may delight in the taste of vine-ripened tomatoes or fresh cucumbers or radishes, but we would find it surprising to encounter a dog who relishes such objects. By the same token, odors that appear to be of consuming interest to a dog are avoided by humans. To summarize, secondary qualities seem to be separable from an object; they result from the interactions of sensory systems and external objects. Primary qualities, by contrast, reside or inhere in an object and are independent of the perceiver.

In other words, it would be difficult to separate a primary quality from an object without destroying the object. Indeed, Galileo suggested a subtraction test as a means of distinguishing between primary and secondary qualities. If a quality can be subtracted from an object without destroying the identity of the object, then that quality is secondary. We could subtract the color orange from a triangle and the triangle would retain its identity as a triangle. The subtraction of figure, however, a primary quality, cannot be accomplished without destroying the identity of the object. The distinction between primary and secondary qualities raises all kinds of problems and, as we will see, this distinction will capture the attention of Locke's successors.

Sahakian and Sahakian (1975) claimed that Locke's book *Some Thoughts Concerning Education* (1693) "was destined to have a profound influence during the course of two centuries upon the education of children in all classes of society throughout the western world" (p. 86). The major ideas for the book had originally been set forth in letters that Locke had written to his friend, Edward Clarke, who had asked for the philosopher's advice on how to rear his eight-year-old son. Garforth (1964) pointed out that we know little about the sources of inspiration for Locke's thoughts on education, but we can be certain that he drew heavily from his own experiences at Oxford. Locke was also undoubtedly influenced by such writers as François Rabelais, John Milton, and John Drury, and he may have been influenced by the educational ideas of the Spanish humanist Juan Luis Vives. Locke's actual educational writings covered a great range of subjects, including relations between parents and children, methods of training, the role of reward and punishment in maintaining discipline, the personality characteristics of the tutor, and curriculum. Let us briefly turn to a consideration of selected educational views set forth in Locke's writings.

Locke's ideas on education were generally consistent with his empirical philosophy. Thus he argued that, for the great majority of human beings, education contributes more to character than does nature. Locke recognized that there are natural abilities and biases and that these are sometimes difficult to overcome. Nevertheless, it is the environment that largely determines what we will become. For this reason, it is important to attend to a range of environmental influences from the food we eat, to parental influences, to pedagogical technique.

According to Locke, children should have plenty of sleep, fresh air, and exercise. The educator should give close scrutiny to the child's diet: There should be no eating between meals and care should be taken to keep the child from consuming too much sugar. Locke clearly understood the relationship between learning and good health. At the same time, he adopted older notions of **hardening,** a concept that emphasizes rigorous conditioning so that the child might endure pain, hardship, and fatigue. Thus, a bed should be hard because feathers may contribute to physical weakness. Hardening could also be accomplished by forcing the child to endure reasonable amounts of coldness or wetness. Consistent with his views on hardening, Locke believed that crying is a fault that should not be tolerated. If crying cannot be abated with harsh or disapproving looks, then blows are acceptable. Persuasion, however, is preferable to physical punishment.

Although Locke believed in the judicious use of physical punishment, his emphasis was on reward and on a positive, affectionate relationship between children and adults. He believed that punishment, especially excessive punishment, works against learning and against the development of good character. Locke argued that excessive physical punishment may undermine confidence and interfere with vigor and industry. Punishment in learning situations may result in an aversion to learning. Locke also counseled against reward that is not genuine, but he viewed credit for real accomplishment as a cardinal rule of education. Locke recognized that excessive work and overly rigorous assignments will result in avoidance of the very topics we teach. Thus, the good teacher will be sensitive to the pace of the assignments and will seek ways to make learning an enjoyable experience.

While many of Locke's educational views, especially his views on hardening, were subsequently discounted, he nevertheless represented an important turning point in the history of educational psychology. In *Letters Concerning the English Nation* (1733/1980), Voltaire extolled Locke's systematic approach to the study of education. Voltaire credited Locke for advocating the study of step-by-step progress in the development of a child's understanding. He also praised Locke for attempting to examine what humans have in common with animals and how we differ. Clearly, in Locke's work we have an emphasis on topical areas that will later form an important part of the new discipline of psychology. We also encounter an unusual early emphasis on the idea that personality and behavior are shaped by the environment.

George Berkeley

It is evident from the materials presented thus far that Francis Bacon and John Locke were key figures in the founding of modern empirical philosophy. As we have seen, Bacon and Locke emphasized observation, the collection of data, and the role of the environment and experience as the central means by which human beings attain knowledge. It remained for Locke's successor, George Berkeley (1685–1753), to extend the empirical philosophy set forth by Locke. With Berkeley, we encounter a radical emphasis on the primacy of experience in human knowledge and we gain a vision of the larger implications of an untrammeled empiricism. We will see that Berkeley's radical empirical philosophy, and the still more radical steps taken by his successor, David Hume, produced shock waves in the philosophical world. Indeed, the empiricism that emerged in the work of Berkeley and Hume served as a foil against which subsequent philosophies reacted. The compelling task of philosophy, following Berkeley and Hume, was to elevate faith in common sense and reason.

Though George Berkeley is commonly regarded as an Irish philosopher, he apparently identified with his British ancestry. He was born in Kilkenny, Ireland, in 1685. Berkeley enrolled in Trinity College, Dublin, in 1700. He earned his B.A. in 1704 and M.A. in 1707. By 1709, Berkeley had written the book that now is regarded as a classic psychological treatise: *Essay Towards a New Theory of Vision.* In his essay, Berkeley argued against Descartes's contention that there are geometric principles known innately that contribute to depth perception. We will return later to a consideration of Berkeley's alternative view that emphasizes the role of experience in depth perception. Within a year, Berkeley had written another more important work, *Treatise Concerning the Principles of Human Knowledge.* This book set forth the empirical philosophy for which Berkeley was later to become so well known.

Berkeley's philosophy created unusual frustration for its author. On the one hand, his contemporaries either could not refute it or did not bother to try to refute it. On the other hand, they did not believe it or could not find it in themselves to take it seriously. As a consequence, Berkeley wrote what may now be regarded as one of the great philosophical classics, *Three Dialogues Between Hylas and Philonous,* in which he argued his case through Philonous (meaning love of the mind) and the materialist philosophy through Hylas (meaning matter).

Berkeley held several university posts following his formal schooling at Trinity College; however, he had long had interests in the New World. His interests, largely religious, centered on conversion of the slaves and so-called savages, the spread of the Protestant faith, and the education of the colonists. Finally, in the year 1728, Berkeley set sail for America, where he hoped to pursue some of his missionary-religious interests. He was particularly interested in founding a college in the New World. One month prior to the voyage to America, Berkeley married Anne Forster, the daughter of an Irish magistrate.

Berkeley and his wife resided in America for three years. During that time, he lived on a farm he purchased in Rhode Island. He preached sermons in the Episcopal Church and helped organize a philosophical society. Berkeley's stay in America was brief partly because money from a grant approved by Parliament to help found a college was not forthcoming. So, in 1731, Berkeley and his wife and their infant son Henry, born in 1729, set sail for London. Another child, a daughter born in America, died shortly after birth. Berkeley donated his farm to Yale University and contributed books to the Yale and Harvard libraries. A major city and university in California would later carry Berkeley's name. Berkeley died in January of 1753. Biographers describe Berkeley in very positive terms as a vigorous and handsome man who possessed the sometimes unlikely combination of humility and genius.

Berkeley's major battle was with the materialistic and skeptical dimensions of the so-called new philosophy. His major mission was to restore faith in spiritual interpretations of the world. Interestingly, it was in Locke's empirical philosophy that Berkeley discovered an opening for an attack on the prevailing materialistic interpretations of the world. Recall that Locke's primary qualities supposedly reside in objects and are independent of the observer. To be sure, primary qualities are observed by the senses, but Locke's assumption was that such qualities reside in an object whether we discover them or not. With Berkeley, this distinction between primary and secondary qualities became untenable. He confronted his readers with the idea that it is absurd to ask what the world is like, independent of experience. The shape of the triangle must be experienced just as the color must be experienced. Furthermore, a figure or shape changes, depending on the angle of perspective, just as color changes, depending on illumination. In his book *Three Dialogues Between Hylas and Philonous,* Berkeley placed in the mouth of Hylas, his adversary, the idea that real things "have a fixed and real nature, which remains the same notwithstanding any change in our senses, or in the posture and motion of our bodies" (Berkeley, 1713/1935, pp. 55–56). Such, of course, was the materialistic assumption about primary qualities; they were assumed to reside in a material substance that is independent of the perceiver. But in the *Three Dialogues,* we find Philonous responding to Hylas by declaring that *all* sensible qualities, including size, shape, color, and so on, are continually changing and are conditioned by the context or the medium through which we make our observations. So-called primary qualities vary as much as secondary qualities.

With Berkeley, it is not just the distinction between primary and secondary qualities that is challenged, but the status of primary qualities independent of experience is called into question. Extension, figure, and motion, the so-called primary qualities, exist in experience, just as do color, taste, sound, or temperature. In an earlier, more innocent time, human beings could take refuge and find comfort in a host of absolutes. Primary qualities were among the absolutes. But the absolutes, one by one, were challenged. At one time, people could believe that Jerusalem was the absolute center of the universe, but following the Copernican revolution, there was no absolute location; loca-

tion was relative and changing as the earth spins on its axis and follows its orbit around the sun. How many miles do you suppose you have traveled since you started reading this chapter, or, for that matter, how far have you traveled just in the past five minutes? If there were no absolute location, we could still hold on to the idea of absolutes that exist in objects around us. But with Berkeley, these absolutes were challenged. An object viewed one way is a square, but viewed another way, it is a trapezoid. Another object viewed one way is a circle, but viewed from another perspective is an ellipse. From one perspective an object is large, but from another it is quite small. Berkeley thus contributed to the demise of absolutes, but it is the absolutes of materialism that he attacked. He left his readers with some spiritual absolutes, which remained for Hume to attack.

Let us return to the thread of thought that bears more directly on Berkeley's empiricism. Berkeley argued that there are no legitimate grounds for assuming that some ideas represent real properties of an object. How can an idea (that which is mental) in any way represent the property of an object (that which is physical)? Thus, for Berkeley, there was no world-in-itself that is separate and distinct from the lived world of experience! In fact, the *only* real world *is* the world of experience or the world of the mind. Berkeley is remembered for his famous dictum *esse est percipi:* to be is to be perceived. Such was the case even for Locke regarding secondary qualities such as color, taste, and odor, which had no absolute being in themselves. Rather, they depend for their existence on a perceiver. But for Berkeley, the expression "to be is to be perceived" applied also to the rest of the world.

By following the conclusions of Berkelean empiricism, we now encounter a new kind of skepticism regarding the claims for the materialist interpretation of the world. In his dialogues between Hylas and Philonous, Berkeley, speaking through Philonous, declared that he was convinced "that there is no such thing as what philosophers call *material substance*" (Berkeley, 1713/1935, p. 11) and later he declared that "all that we know or conceive are our own ideas" (p. 61). Subjective experience thus becomes the centerpiece of empiricism pushed to this extreme position. The real world is not a nonperceptible world of material substance; rather, the real world is the world just as we know it in our own experience. There is an elegant simplicity in this philosophy, just as there is in materialism or any other monistic orientation. But simplicity, desirable as it is to some (perhaps most) human beings, always comes with a price. A philosophy that meets our needs for simplicity sometimes falls short of meeting our equally valid demands for adequacy.

A major problem we encounter in Berkelean empiricism centers on the consistency and coherence of experience. There is no principle in experience per se that explains the orderliness of our subjective world. Yet, the world of experience does hold together in a remarkably orderly way. When I finish this cup of coffee, I will leave this restaurant, get in my automobile, drive one mile south, turn right into the faculty parking lot, find a parking space (if I'm lucky), get out of the car, walk to the office, and meet my 9 A.M. appointment. I do not now perceive the automobile or any of its parts, the street, the stoplights, the parking lot, my office, or desk, but I am convinced all these things exist and the world of my immediate future experience will be reasonably coherent and orderly. How can I account for such order and coherence if my experiences are not driven by the orderly world as such, out there, that makes its step-by-step contributions to the content of my subjective experience? Surely, the orderly content of the mental realm must be tied to the world of objects and such objects contribute to the coherent succession of experiences that will attend my getting from the restaurant to my first appointment.

Berkeley anticipated this criticism, but before we consider his reply, it is important to caution against acceptance of the popular misconception that Berkeley was altogether denying the existence of the real world. What Berkeley was denying was the objective and independent status of primary qualities. If secondary qualities are known only in experience, so also are primary qualities known only in experience. In taking such a step, Berkeley was also denying that primary qualities represent a material substance that has objective and independent status. John Locke believed that material substance forms the world of objects. The

qualities of objects to which we respond (i.e., the attributes, manifestations, or properties) are either primary or secondary. A secondary quality resides in subjective experience, but a primary quality is supported by a material substance that is not directly perceived. What is perceived is an attribute (e.g., a figure, solidity, etc., of an underlying material substance). Asked what this material substance is, Locke declared that it is "something, he knew not what."

Berkeley denied the existence of any mysterious metaphysical material substance that has objective or independent status. Berkeley did not deny the existence of the real world; rather, he gave us a new vision of what the real world is. It is the materialist account of the world that is rejected, an account that paradoxically uses experience to declare that experience is derivative, and that accords primacy to a mysterious metaphysical material substance that is not directly perceived. The real world for Berkeley was the intimate world of ideas and experience, whereas the material world is derivative.

How did Berkeley respond to the criticism that we mentioned earlier concerning orderliness of experience? First, Berkeley did not discount the existence of other minds that are perceiving, and, as a religious man, Berkeley believed in an omnipotent and omniscient God whose apprehension of the world extends throughout space and time. The world in its entirety is thus held together and operates in an intelligible and orderly way through the extensity of God's awareness. So, all of the things that exist are being perceived at all times. The glue for Berkeley's empiricism is thus found in his theism, which is itself supported on rational rather than empirical grounds. It will remain for David Hume to provide us with an empirical philosophy that is stripped of theistic and rational support.

The accusation is sometimes made that Berkelean empiricism leads inevitably to solipsism. **Solipsism** refers to the philosophical position of extreme subjectivism, which holds that only self-knowledge is possible. It is understandable that Berkelean empiricism should be associated with solipsism because few of us can resist the temptation to view ourselves as *the perceivers* when we are confronted with the dictum "to be is to be perceived." But Berkeley recognized other minds or other perceivers and was quite explicit in his recognition of the permanent perceiver, God. Thus, we participate in a wider reality and are not necessarily consigned to solipsism. The problem, however, is how we participate in a wider reality. The reader who can take the leap of faith with Berkeley that we live in a wider reality that is tied to God's apprehension is thus rescued from solipsism. Others may find it difficult to reject the contention that Berkelean empiricism leads to solipsism.

Earlier we referred to Berkeley's theory of space or depth perception and we must now return briefly to that topic. Space, like all else according to Berkeley, is reduced to the status of a secondary quality. If space is not a primary quality, why is it such a compelling feature in perception? Furthermore, how can we learn to see in depth, given that all objects in the visual field are represented on the relatively flat surface of the retina?

Berkeley's empirical approach to depth perception as set forth in his book *An Essay Towards a New Theory of Vision* is now counted as a classic psychological treatise. Berkeley argued that there is a close relationship between sight and touch (see Pastore, 1965) and that a vivid visual sensation will be associated with a tactile sensation of closeness, while a less vivid visual sensation may be associated with a sensation of reaching. We thus learn to interpret sensations of nearness or distance through the medium of touch. The implication of Berkeley's theory is that distance in and of itself cannot be seen. Berkeley believed that one who was born blind and who later gained sight suddenly would not be able to perceive depth. Berkeley also believed that associations between visual and auditory sensations provide clues to depth perception.

Berkeley's detailed work on depth perception was to become a precursor of later psychological investigations of all the senses. Though most psychologists, as well as philosophers, rejected Berkeley's metaphysical scheme, they were nevertheless stimulated by many of the questions he raised. Like other empiricists, he also contributed to a growing emphasis on the importance of learning and association in human life. As we noted earlier, his extreme emphasis on empiricism also

served as a stimulus for further work on the problem of knowledge.

David Hume

In the works of David Hume (1711–1776) we encounter one of the most complete, most radical statements of empirical philosophy. Hume, more than any other, provided a picture of the implications of untempered empiricism. We also find in Hume an extensive concern with psychological topics, and this marks him as a key figure in this particular intellectual history.

Born near Edinburgh, Scotland, in 1711, David Hume was the second of the three children of Joseph Hume and Catherine Falconer. When David was three years old, his father died, but the resolute and devoted Catherine rose to the occasion of rearing and educating the children. David matriculated in the University of Edinburgh when he was twelve years old. Though there was family pressure to pursue legal studies, Hume, early in his academic career, displayed an unusual interest in literary and philosophical studies. Shortly after leaving the university, at about fifteen years of age, Hume suffered a nervous breakdown. The most informed treatment of the day included plenty of fresh air and exercise and close attention to a balanced diet. Within two years, Hume regained his health and was deeply involved in reading literature and philosophy. In 1734, he went to France, where he wrote his first philosophical work, *A Treatise of Human Nature.* The *Treatise* was divided into three parts, with Part I devoted to the problem of human knowledge, Part 2 to the passions, and Part 3 to morals. The first two parts were published in 1739; their reception was a disaster. Reviews were hostile, the book did not sell, and Hume was later to say the book fell deadborn from the press. If the book was a failure in the beginning, it was nevertheless rescued by history and is now viewed as a classic in philosophy. In 1740, Hume published Part 3 of the *Treatise,* dealing with such moral subjects as justice, virtue, and objects of allegiance.

Although Hume's first publication was a disappointment, his later works enjoyed success. In 1748, he published a revision of Part 1 of the *Treatise* under the title *Philosophical Essays Concerning Human Understanding* and in the same year published *Three Essays, Moral and Political.* Hume died in 1776, the year of the American Declaration of Independence, a cause he supported.

David Hume stood for many unpopular causes and was often reviled for his unorthodox religious views. All of his books were placed on the *Index of Forbidden Books.* Though he was the victim of harsh and unfair criticism and though he was prevented from obtaining university positions because of his religious beliefs, he was nevertheless described in most glowing terms by his friends as energetic, enthusiastic, cheerful, good natured, generous, and amiable. His sense of humor is illustrated in his reply to a colleague who was complaining about the spitefulness of the world. Hume jokingly insisted that things were not so bad, for he had written on all sorts of subjects—moral, political, religious—that could excite hostility, and yet he "had not made a single enemy; unless, indeed, all the Whigs, and all the Tories, and all the Christians" (Burton, 1846/1967, p. 443). Hume's self-appraisal is illustrated in the following passage from a letter sent to a friend in London. Hume was apparently asking his friend to find him some lodging for a forthcoming visit to London and pointed out that "a room in a sober discreet family, who would not be averse to admit a sober, discreet, virtuous, regular, quiet, goodnatured man of a bad character—such a room, I say, would suit me extremely" (Huxley, 1898, p. 40).

Following Berkeley's lead, Hume agreed that the events of experience constitute the primary subject matter of philosophy. But the events of experience, according to Hume, are not held together by any "necessary connection" that can be established through reason. Neither can it be established that a meaningful sequence of events in experience is driven by an external succession of events that reflect cause–effect relations. Thus causality, in Hume's treatment, reduces to a psychological problem. Causality cannot be viewed as a primary quality. If domino *A* impacts domino *B,* and domino *B* falls, Hume finds nothing in *A* per se that could be labeled as a cause. Causality does not inhere in an object; rather, causality is more like one of Berkeley's secondary qualities.

Causality is what *we* see and what *we* attribute to things, but it does not reside in objects as a substantial quality. Thus, there are no necessary connections "out there," but only our ways of making sense of succession or sequence. All we really know is that when *A* is activated and impacts *B, B* falls. What we take to be objective causality reduces to our habitual ways of seeing things. Hume noted that our notions of causal connections are based on temporal priority (*A* precedes *B*), spatial contiguity (*A* and *B* are close together), and constant conjunction (*B* regularly falls when impacted by *A*). We form the idea of objective necessary connection only from the regularity of our impressions. Hume's treatment of causality had implications for some of his psychological concepts, so it will be necessary for us to return to the topic of causality as we explore other dimensions of Hume's thought.

Mental life for Hume could not be based on any kind of mental substance that can be verified through reason. Following the lead of his radical empirical approach to knowledge, Hume found only impressions and ideas. *Impressions* present themselves directly with considerable force. They include sensations, passions (motives), and emotions. Thus, a taste, a color, a hunger pang, a sound, a startling stimulus resulting in fear, or an odor would each constitute an impression. *Ideas* are fainter images of impressions. The recollection of a taste thirty minutes after eating would constitute an idea, which in this case is a weaker recollection of the original impression. Hume pointed out that impressions or ideas may be simple, such as a single clear tone, or compound, such as we might encounter as we respond simultaneously to the color, taste, odor, and feel of a food object such as an apple.

Hume's views on causality, coupled with his position on the sources of knowledge, led to a particularly interesting psychological question. What, according to Hume, is the nature of the self? Most of us experience a strong continuing sense of personal identity and a sense of a causal connection between one idea and another and between our ideas and our actions. According to Hume, this sense of personal identity cannot be based on any mysterious mental substance; neither can it be based on objective causality. How, then, is personal identity to be explained?

First, Hume believed that the sense of personal identity may be exaggerated. Tsanoff (1964) summarized Hume's position nicely as follows: "All that we find in inspecting our so-called 'selves' is a bundle of sensations, a collection of different perceptions. As in a kind of theatre, they pass, repass, glide away, and mingle in boundless variety" (p. 361). What Hume was describing was not a stream of consciousness but a kind of disjointed parade of impressions and ideas that present themselves in no necessarily logical order. The parade is simply ongoing with now an entertaining entry, now a sad entry, now a vivid entry, now a dull entry of which we are hardly conscious, now an intense emotional and ecstatic entry, only to be followed by a sobering entry that we attend with resentment. In some entries we may perceive ourselves as active, as if we were in the parade being observed by others, whereas in other entries, we may perceive ourselves as passive observers. There is no necessary or logical connection between one entry and another. The parade comes from we know not where and proceeds to we know not where. Neither do we know when it will stop. Happily, some seem to enjoy the whole nonsensical succession but others are not so blessed.

Most of us, if we try, can muster the intellectual empathy to feel our way into this radical empirical Humean world. If you reflect on your day, it may be that you recall only the major, rather punctuated entries—entries that simply succeeded each other without meaningful connections. As I reflect back on this day, I must confess that in retrospect it could be described rather accurately by Hume. There I was, eating breakfast with my wife. Quite illogically, the next major awareness seems to be of a pleasant drive to another closeby town. Abruptly we are in an art gallery, admiring a watercolor with the captivating title *Awareness*. In retrospect, time was rather empty until we are suddenly caught up in conversation with a friend about the advantages and problems of achieving a balanced federal budget. I recall that during the course of the conversations there were unexplainable intrusions pertaining to my need to get to the library to check out a book on Thomas Reid. And just now,

here I am, writing about David Hume. Who knows what the next focal point will be in this parade? It would surely be a mere accident if the next entry had even the appearance of being causally related to the current entry, but if a causal connection were perceived, that would reflect merely our way of attending to the transitions in our experiences.

But we must now return to Hume's attempt to account for self-identity. Hume, as we have already noted, rejected any notion of a substantial self and failed to find a single impression or idea that can account for our strong sense of continuity or identity. In Hume's system, we most accurately encounter a succession of selves. But in normal experience, these selves are one and the same. It is the same me that now enjoys breakfast and later enjoys the drive to a nearby town, even if I concede that there are gaps between the two experiences and that the two experiences are not necessarily related to each other. In the final analysis, continuity or personal identity is, according to Hume, a product of the imagination, and one cannot make an objective claim in behalf of such an imagination. We perceive causal connections among the entries in our parade of impressions and ideas when the entries appear to be similar, when one entry regularly follows another, or when entries are close together in space or time. Thus, the sense of personal identity is a product of the peculiar way we attend to the succession of ideas. In the end, personal identity is a construction that grows out of the ways we organize the entries and gaps in our experiences.

The second volume of Hume's *Treatise* is devoted to a study of what was commonly called the passions. The topic includes discussions of such emotions as pride, humility, love, hate, respect, and contempt. Several general features of Hume's treatment of the emotions deserve mention because they were incorporated into later studies on the topic.

An important feature of Hume's approach to emotional life is his continuing emphasis on comparative studies. He notes that studies of animals have been useful to anatomists and physiologists and that comparisons of the "anatomy of the mind" may also be useful (see Hume, 1739/1978, Book 11, Section 12). Hume argued that some emotions in animals have the same origins as comparable emotions in humans (see Hume, 1739/ 1978, pp. 326, 363, 398, and 448). He recognized that generalizations from one species to another may not always be permissible, but was ahead of his time in recommending comparative psychological studies.

Another important feature of Hume's approach to the emotions was his assumption that all emotions "are founded on pain and pleasure" (Hume, 1739/1978, p. 438). Hume believed that emotions such as joy, desire, and hope are derivative from pleasure, whereas sorrow, aversion, and fear are derivative from pain. Still another general feature of Hume's approach to the emotions was his attempt to provide what he called experimental demonstrations of his propositions. In a subtitle to his treatise, Hume declared that the book is "an attempt to introduce the experimental method of reasoning into moral subjects." Hume's so-called experiments typically consist of what might be called anecdotes or demonstrations. Even so, he attempted to provide a means of tying his propositions to observable events. For example, in a section in which Hume discussed the transfer of an emotion from one object to a contiguous object, he proposed that we observe the frequency with which a quarrel with one family member may lead to hatred for other family members even though the other family members have done nothing to deserve hatred.

Hume's greatness as a philosopher derives from his originality, intellectual courage, and integrity. His work on the problem of causation was the most original work on that topic since Aristotle. Hume's courage and integrity were manifested in his uncompromising efforts to construct a thoroughgoing philosophy of experience.

Hume is a central figure in the history of psychology for several reasons. He, more than the other empiricists since Bacon, focused attention on the emotions with the hope of establishing a nomenclature of emotions, of understanding their origins and the role they play in human intellectual life. The problem of the self and the related problem of self-identity may have been elevated in importance partly because many subsequent scholars considered Hume's treatment of these topics a disaster. Hume's emphasis on habit and

association also marked him as a key contributor to topics of lasting psychological interest. Finally, Hume's seminal work on the problem of causation left a lasting mark on scientific metatheory. Following Hume, the debate over what scientists study would never be the same.

Any estimate of Hume's legacy would be incomplete without pointing out that the products of his philosophical labors created an intellectual crisis in the eighteenth and early nineteenth centuries, comparable to the one that Montaigne's skepticism had created in the seventeenth century. Bozeman (1977) pointed out that Hume demonstrated "with an awful cogency, that 'the common Lockean philosophy,' when driven to an ultimate conclusion, supplied a sandy foundation for such crucial premises of inductive science as the actual 'existence' of an external world of objects or the operation of causes in that world" (p. 9). The compelling task of philosophy was thus to reconstruct the conceptual foundations of the experimental sciences. The next chapter will examine some of the reactions to Hume's thought.

EMPIRICISM ON THE CONTINENT

The British are typically credited as the founders of modern empirical philosophy, but important contributions to empiricism were also made on the continent. The French philosopher Voltaire (1694–1778), particularly vocal in his praise of British philosophy, was instrumental in importing that philosophy to the continent. In the works of Bacon and Newton, Voltaire found an approach to knowledge that held special promise as a means of challenging oppression and dogmatic philosophies that had so long prevailed on European soil. Voltaire's literary works, as well as his philosophical treatises, conveyed his suspicion of untestable theories and theological dogma and his support for a philosophy established on observation and experiment. As is well known, his enthusiasm for British thought, as manifested in his singular praise for John Locke, resulted in a warrant for his arrest and a lengthy exile from Paris. Voltaire's enthusiasm for the new empirical philosophy had a direct influence on two important French empiricists, Étienne Bonnot de Condillac (1715–1780) and Claude-Adrien Helvétius (1715–1771).

Etienne Bonnot de Condillac

Condillac (*Kohn de YAHK*), active in the fields of psychology, philosophy, education, and economics, was born in Grenoble, France, on September 30, 1715. Condillac studied philosophy, science, and some theology at a Catholic seminary at Saint-Sulpice and at the Sorbonne. For a time, he was in the regular company of Rousseau and Diderot, and enjoyed acquaintance with many other philosophers and scientists of note, including Voltaire, d'Alembert, Condorcet, Helvétius, d'Holbach, and Cabanis. Condillac enjoyed great prominence in his time, being appointed both to the French Academy and to the Royal Academy of Berlin. Condillac's comments on education were in constant demand and his services as tutor for the children of royalty were highly regarded. The philosopher's later years were devoted almost exclusively to writing. He died in 1780, just after completing a major treatise on logic.

Condillac rode the crest of a growing criticism of the rational philosophies of Descartes and his followers. The task of philosophy, according to Condillac, is not to discover the nature of the mind but to find out specifically how the mind works. In this emphasis, Condillac can be viewed as a forerunner of functional psychologies. There can be little question that Condillac, like John Locke and René Descartes (see Leary, 1980), was attempting to establish a moral basis for the new psychology. He wished to establish a mental science that could make a difference in people's lives.

Condillac's practical psychological interests dominated his thought—he avoided lengthy consideration of those metaphysical problems of causality and the nature of the real world that had so captivated Berkeley and Hume. Instead, Condillac focused intensively on the genetic basis of knowledge. With a thoroughness unequaled even by Locke, Condillac sought to analyze the origins of knowledge.

Condillac asked us to imagine a marble statue organized internally as human beings and with an intellect that includes no innate ideas. Condillac proposed that we imagine intellectual growth by hypothetically opening one sensory channel at a time. He began with the sense of smell and presented one stimulus event (the smell of a rose) to his statue. Condillac argued that with one stimulus alone, his statue will now display such intellectual functions as attention and a sense of existence. When the smell of a rose is followed by the smell of a sweet pea, the statue is now capable of such intellectual functions as discrimination and a sense of contrast. Condillac proceeded by opening the other sensory channels one at a time and hoping to demonstrate the emergence of all intellectual functions. If a given stimulus is too intense (painful) or of optimal intensity and quality to yield pleasure, the statue quickly acquires motivation to minimize pain and maximize pleasure. Condillac argued that we derive a powerful sense of the external world through the sense of touch, which produces compelling sensitivities to resistance, solidity, motion, hardness, softness, and so on. As noted earlier, Condillac did not focus extensively on whether these awarenesses are to be regarded as subjective or objective. As a practical philosopher, he was largely interested in the implications of his sensationist philosophy for learning and education.

Condillac is also remembered for his original and intense studies on the origin and meaning of language in human life. He argued that language provides symbols that represent sensations, needs, or desired actions. Through language, intellectual operations such as discrimination, memory, and thought may be employed to communicate experiences and secure advantages. Condillac argued that the excellence of science will be based partly on the excellence of scientific language. Accordingly, scientists must work to avoid common language with its many errors and to ground scientific concepts in the precise language of mathematics. Condillac also emphasized the importance of accurate classification systems and taxonomies in science.

Condillac's focus on the importance of the language of science was highly influential in the late eighteenth and early nineteenth centuries. It pointed in the direction of positivism, which was to develop later in the nineteenth century. His greatest legacy, so far as the history of psychology is concerned, is that, under his treatment, empiricism became at once more practical and more psychological. Condillac demonstrated the more practical uses of empiricism in the investigation of such problems as the development of language and the learning process.

Claude-Adrien Helvétius

In the work of Helvétius (*ehl VA shus*) we encounter an early version of a radical behaviorism that emphasized the Lockean white paper hypothesis carried to the extreme of denying all inborn capacities or aptitudes. In his essays on the history of materialism, Plekhanov (1967) pointed out that Helvétius was so consistent and thoroughgoing in his materialist philosophy that he "horrified other materialists" (p. 92). The reaction of other materialists might have been stimulated by the candid manner in which Helvétius approached the moral implications of his psychology. Under his treatment, the virtues we most treasure are results of education. Human vice and corruption often result from poor legislation and a failure to provide for the education of the masses. Helvétius gives us one of the earliest visions of an extreme environmental psychology that challenges freedom of choice and autonomy. Such a vision is rarely popular.

The father of Claude-Adrien Helvétius, Jean Claude Adrien (1685–1755), was a physician who was highly favored by Queen Marie Leszczynska. Possibly through family connections, Claude-Adrien Helvétius secured a government post, which permitted him to amass sufficient wealth within the ten-year period from 1738 to 1748 to purchase an estate and retire. Following his retirement, he turned to philosophy, and by 1757, completed the book *De l'esprit* (on the mind). The book was immediately condemned by religious authorities and Helvétius was forced to recant some of his opinions. Nevertheless, the book was widely read and became a major influence on the continent and in the British Isles.

Helvétius placed major emphasis on the motivating effects of pleasure and pain. He argued that human beings are controlled largely by the system of rewards and punishments that society employs. At the root of all behaviors are self-interest, the pursuit of pleasure, and the avoidance or the threat of pain.

Helvétius, as we noted earlier, denied hereditary influence. Even genius was thought to result from environmental influence. Thus, either we learn to learn or we develop a negative attitude toward learning and remain ignorant. How, then, is it possible that two people given excellent educations should turn out differently, with one being brilliant and productive and the other being mediocre? Helvétius argued that chance (encounter with just the right teacher or just the right experience) plays a role in accounting for such differences. Under his treatment, we all have the potential to be geniuses.

Helvétius was not an original thinker but was influential. His environmentalism and hedonism had a profound effect on the development of utilitarianism (to be discussed later) and his emphasis on the malleability of human beings elevated the importance of learning and education.

ASSOCIATIONISM AND UTILITARIANISM

The associationists and utilitarians of the eighteenth and nineteenth centuries were inspired by the practical implications growing out of the thought of empiricists such as Locke, Berkeley, and Hume. If knowledge is acquired through experience, then the means of its acquisition is elevated as a topic of study. Knowledge can no longer be taken for granted as a mere given, a gratuity bestowed by deity or the benevolent forces of nature. The specifics of how knowledge is acquired now becomes a focus of inquiry and a central task in any science of human nature.

David Hartley

David Hartley (1705–1757) is commonly regarded as the founder of modern **associationism.** He was also concerned with problems of motivation and the structural and functional characteristics of the nervous system.

Hartley was born in Armley, Yorkshire, England, and was educated at Cambridge. Originally, he planned for a career in the ministry, but doctrinal questions ultimately led him away from the ministry and into medicine. His most noteworthy treatise, published in 1749, was entitled *Observations on Man, His Frame, His Duty and His Expectations.* This work was inspired by Locke's earlier emphasis on the importance of sensation. Hartley further elaborated on the doctrine of association and speculated in some detail about how it worked. He also set forth an early classification system of pleasures and pains. He practiced medicine, but had strong interests in history, music, philosophy, poetry, and religion. Hartley's son, also named David (1732–1813), described his father as a gentle, caring physician who treated both mind and body. Hartley was a liberal who argued in favor of inoculation at a time when such a medical practice was regarded with deep suspicion. His liberal perspectives were adopted by his son, who opposed the slave trade and England's war with America. Hartley died in Bath, England, in 1757.

Hartley was one of the first to classify the varieties of pleasure and pain. He identified seven sources of pain and pleasure from (1) the external senses, (2) imagination, (3) opinions of us held by other people, (4) our possessions of the means of happiness, (5) sympathy or empathy with the status (joy or suffering) of other people, (6) the sense of our relationship with deity, and (7) our moral sensitivities toward goodness and beauty or evil and deformity. Hartley thought the greatest pleasures derive from the latter three categories. As a religious man, he deemphasized the pleasures associated with the first four categories and emphasized the cultivation of the so-called higher pleasures.

Hartley's approach to association was influenced by Isaac Newton, John Locke, and John Gay. Gay was a minister who argued for the "possibility of deducing all our intellectual pleasures and pains from association" (Stephen & Lee, 1960, p. 67). Thus, what we enjoy or avoid intellectually is subject to the laws of learning or association. Hartley was quick to see the moral or religious implications in such a position. Values themselves are understandable in terms of scientific psychology and a psychology of morality and religion is possible.

Hartley's associationism was complemented by a neurophysiology inspired by Newtonian physics.

Newton had argued that information from the senses is transmitted to the brain by vibrations set up in the nerve fibers. Hartley extended the idea by contending that vibrations from the senses may set off miniature vibrations, or *vibratiuncles,* that persist for brief periods of time following the initial stimulus. As noted by Smith (1987), Hartley thought that "the vibrations set up by external energies gradually die away leaving only miniature vibrations or vibratiuncles" (p. 127). Memory itself, according to Hartley, is based on vibrations and will quickly fade unless it is reactivated by the appropriate conditions. Sources of reactivation are extensive because vibrations in one region may be associated with vibrations in another region. There are thus a multitude of sources of support for learned connections and for memories. Smith (1987) pointed out that Hartley's associationism is similar to many of the concepts that Pavlov later set forth in his *Conditioned Reflexes,* though there is no evidence that Pavlov was directly influenced by Hartley. Hartley did, however, have a major influence on later utilitarians and empiricists such as Jeremy Bentham, James Mill, and John Stuart Mill.

Jeremy Bentham

The suspicion of the early British empiricists regarding innate knowledge was echoed in the practical work of the associationists and utilitarians. A specific example of the suspicion is found in the work of Jeremy Bentham (1748–1832), who called for massive reform in jurisprudence and legal philosophy. Lawmakers and court officials in Bentham's day prided themselves on their intuitive grasp of absolute moral principles. Bentham challenged this belief with the same zeal that John Locke displayed earlier when he attacked the concept of innate ideas.

Bentham called attention to the fact that punishments in his day bore little relationship to the real social consequences associated with specific crimes. Instead, punishments were based on revulsion at the particular crime that was the subject of litigation. Thus, a sex crime without any known widespread consequences might be punished with great severity, whereas a crime with major social consequences might receive but a mild reprimand. Bentham advocated a more empirical, more objective basis for legal decision making. Thus, punishment would be based on the measured social consequences of behavior.

Jeremy Bentham was born in Houndsditch, in London, on February 15, 1748. He was a precocious child who was already learning Greek and Latin by age four. He entered Queens College at Oxford in 1760 and graduated with a B.A. degree when he was sixteen. In 1766, he was awarded the M.A. degree from Oxford and went into legal practice in 1767. Bentham quickly discovered a distaste for practical law, partly because of his belief that, with a minimum of effort, most cases could be settled out of court. Though Bentham had little interest in practical law, he had great interest in the more abstract problems of law and jurisprudence. As a consequence, he devoted his life to problems in the philosophy of law. In 1789, he published a major theoretical work entitled *Introduction to the Principles of Morals and Legislation.* Most of his work was published by his friends after his death. Some of Bentham's most thoughtful and influential work focused on his utilitarian approach to reward and punishment. Bentham exemplified the philosophy he taught. Even in old age, he exuded a buoyant, optimistic, and happy spirit. He died June 6, 1832. In characteristic altruism, he had requested that his body be donated to the study of science for the benefit of the living.

Bentham argued that the intuitive approach to jurisprudence results in a system riddled with subjectivity and inequality. He contended that there are objective grounds for political, social, and legal theory. These objective grounds are summed up in a single principle of **utilitarianism** sometimes called the *hedonic calculus.* The basic idea is that any action should be judged in terms of its total social consequences for pleasure and pain. We should maximize pleasure and minimize pain and seek the greatest pleasure for the greatest number of people. Punishment should also be meted out in terms of utilitarian principles. For example, a leader who is caught dealing illegally with an enemy is deserving of more punishment than another leader who, for instance, is caught having an affair. A wealthy person caught embezzling a large sum of money from a financial institution should be punished more than a person who steals to provide food for her children.

Bentham's utilitarian approach to punishment was in direct conflict with intuitionalism and retribution theory. Though there are varieties of retribution (e.g., see Cottingham, 1979), the purpose of retribution is generally to inflict a penalty on the individual. The emphasis in Bentham's theory is to protect society or even to reform the offender. The relative merits of the two theories are still open to debate (e.g., see Benn, 1967), but Bentham provided a new way to think about punishment, and his theory served as a corrective for the extremes of retribution. Following the work of Bentham, there was a growing sensitivity to the necessity of curbing cruel and unusual punishments. There were also growing sensitivities to the importance of applying different standards of punishment to children and adults.

Bentham also believed in **psychological hedonism,** the idea that human beings personally seek to gain pleasure and avoid pain. Indeed, this was the central psychological principle in Bentham's system. It is a principle that many psychologists would later embrace. No psychologist ever stated the principle more eloquently than Sigmund Freud (1930/1961a), who noted that "the purpose of life is simply the programme of the pleasure principle. This principle dominates the operation of the mental apparatus from the start" (p. 76).

Bentham and his followers debated such issues as whether one could quantify pleasures and pains and whether justice could actually be based on a theoretical and practical balancing of pleasures and pains. Most theorists were not optimistic. Such theoretical debates are of less historical significance than Bentham's powerful attack on intuitionalism. Following the work of Bentham, it was possible to think that social systems could profit from closer scrutiny and that a more objective set of punishment standards could be established. With his work, a psychological analysis of human motivation is also elevated in importance.

Mary Wollstonecraft

The empirical vision of a world that can be improved through proper education served as a challenge and an inspiration to Mary Wollstonecraft (1759–1797), the most visible early pioneer in the battle for the emancipation of women. Though Wollstonecraft is not easily associated with any single philosophical system, she can be viewed as one who grasped some of the important implications of empiricism. If the mind at birth is as "white paper," as Locke contended, then the role of education in shaping the content of character is paramount. Further, the white paper hypothesis suggests the possibility that differences between men and women may be attributable to differences in educational opportunities.

Differences between men and women had long been explained in terms of **essentialism.** The term *essence* refers to "the intrinsic nature or character of something; that which makes it what it is" (Brown, 1993, p. 852). As noted by Braaten and Viney (2000), "An essentialist philosophy applied to gender emphasizes natural differences neatly boxed and separated by clear boundaries" (p. 576). Thus, women were regarded as naturally or essentially more emotional than men, deficient in judgment and in scientific and mathematical skills, and largely unconcerned about politics and affairs of state. Such beliefs, based on an essentialist philosophy, were used to argue against educational opportunities for women and against the right of women to vote or to own property. Empirical philosophy provided a plausible alternative explanation for observed gender differences. Perhaps the differences could be explained in terms of the paucity of opportunities available to women. Wollstonecraft, in her classic book, *A Vindication of the Rights of Women,* seized on this alternative explanation.

Mary Wollstonecraft was the second of the seven children of Edward John Wollstonecraft and Elizabeth Dixon. Edward, a weaver, inherited a large sum of money from his father, but squandered it on gambling, poorly planned business ventures, and alcohol. Some of Mary Wollstonecraft's earliest memories, in the words of Jacobs (2001), were of "her parents as unequal warriors, her mother weak and pretty, her father a sentimental tyrant who fawned over his family one moment, then beat them the next because he was drunk or out of sorts" (p. 18). She resented the tyranny of her father and

the martyrdom of her mother and the favoritism they displayed toward her oldest brother, who had inherited money from his grandfather and who would be the sole heir of any money remaining in the estate. Mary Wollstonecraft developed an early awareness that women, under English law, did not enjoy property rights and that educational opportunities for women were extremely limited and in most cases nonexistent. She sensed her intellectual superiority to her older brother and was offended that education for her brothers included the classic scholarly subjects while she and her sisters learned merely to cook and sew.

Despite all the social barriers of her day, Mary Wollstonecraft acquired an informal education by extensive reading and by cultivating the company of progressive thinkers. She accepted such employments as were available to women within the constraints of the social system. She served for a time as a teacher and gradually worked her way into a career as a writer. It was a career that seldom provided sufficient funds for her debts or for her efforts to provide financial help for her younger sisters. Her writing, however, afforded an outlet for her rage over the presumptions, ignorance, and injustices of her day.

A Vindication of the Rights of Women was written over a period of only six weeks. According to one biographer, "it is ill arranged and full of repetitions, yet its directness, its sincerity and the terse militant strength of some passages make it one of the creative books of its age" (Brailsford, 1963). In her introduction, Wollstonecraft (1792/1929) points to her "wish to persuade women to endeavor to acquire strength, both of mind and body, and to convince them that the soft phrases [of the day such as], susceptibility of heart, delicacy of sentiment, and refinement of taste, are almost synonymous with epithets of weakness, and that those beings who are only the objects of pity . . . will soon become objects of contempt" (p. 5). Her book is a trenchant condemnation of those who would keep women in a state of ignorance, stupid acquiescence, and "childhood" as a means of preserving their innocence. According to Wollstonecraft (1792/1929, p. 69), "Ignorance is a frail base for virtue!" She argued that passive women who are mere toys, who have been taught to please their husbands, will have a short honeymoon and soon find their charms have evaporated. Wollstonecraft was outraged that women had been trained to be deceitful, coquettish, delicate, and docile like trained pets.

Her book cries out for nothing less than fierce honesty on the part of men and women to come to terms with the silly but ruinous social conventions that robbed women of genuine personhood and that robbed men of the richer and more meaningful companionship that could result from a just and equitable system. For all of its technical faults, this hastily written book is a truly original work with remarkable insights rolling off every page. In the words of Jacobs (2001), it is the first "feminist manifesto in the history of human rights" (p. 99). Wollstonecraft demanded equality of education in coeducational systems and economic independence for women brought about by wider employment opportunities. She observed that beyond domestic duties, women of her day had little to do in society, but to loiter in a graceful fashion. The anecdote was to train women in such fields as medicine, business, government, and politics. She believed that good men would find rational fellowship with competent women to be far more satisfying than blind obedience.

Wollstonecraft also spoke with power and passion about parent–child relations. She observed that "Meek wives are, in general, foolish mothers; wanting their children to love them best, and take their part, in secret, against the father, who is held up as a scarecrow" (Wollstonecraft, 1792/1929, p. 166). She notes that, in such cases, the wife typically did not discipline the child in a responsible way, but left that to the husband. She lamented the fact that parental affection in all too many cases "is but a pretext to tyrannize." Children, who are rational creatures in their own right, must not be subjected to selfish and demanding authority in perpetuity, but such too often is the case, and is more likely to afflict girls than boys. She argued that the subjection of a person who is of age to "the mere will of another . . . is a most cruel and undue stretch of power, and perhaps as injurious to morality as those religious systems which do not allow right and wrong to have any existence, but in the Divine will" (Wollstonecraft, 1792/1929, p. 168).

Mary Wollstonecraft believed that love should be merited, not coerced!

A Vindication of the Rights of Women has been severely criticized as has its author. Wollstonecraft was criticized for being overly sentimental, impulsive, and indelicate in her love affairs (Stephen, 1993). Most of the criticisms have amounted to *ad hominem* attacks on her troubled life and style, rather than on the substance of her work. She was, for a time, the common-law wife of Gilbert Imlay, an American traveler and merchant. Her first child, Fanny, resulted from this relationship, but when Imlay deserted her Wollstonecraft attempted suicide. After recovering from her despondency over Imlay, she married the philosopher William Godwin. Their short-lived but happy relationship resulted in the birth of a daughter, who was also named Mary. Tragically, Mary Wollstonecraft died at the age of thirty-eight from infection caused by medical attempts to recover the undescended placenta following the birth of her second daughter. Her first daughter Fanny died by her own hand. Her second daughter, later to become Mary Shelley, was celebrated as the author of the well-known novel *Frankenstein* (Seymore, 2001).

James Mill

James Mill (1773–1836), a close disciple, trusted colleague, and friend of Jeremy Bentham, played a key role in popularizing and expanding the implications of Hartley's associationism and Bentham's utilitarianism. Mill was born April 6, 1773, the eldest son of James Mill, a cobbler, and Isabel Fenton. Though Mill studied for the ministry and was licensed to preach, he was not enthusiastic about or successful in this work. In 1802, Mill moved to London, where he embarked on a career as an editor and a writer. In 1805, he married Harriet Burrow and the first of their nine children, John Stuart Mill, was born in 1806.

James Mill's income was meager, coming largely from his writing. His best-known literary work was *History of India,* published in 1818. Because of his extensive knowledge of India, Mill received an appointment as an official in the India House. Mill educated his own children in a stern, businesslike atmosphere marked by an exclusive emphasis on cognitive acquisitions and a repression of feeling. Though Mill was largely a disciple, extending and amplifying the work of others, his work was important because it added to the visibility of the new philosophy with its emphasis on education. Mill died June 23, 1836.

James Mill's best known psychological work, *Analysis of the Phenomena of the Human Mind* (1829), presents an uncompromising mechanistic approach to mental processes. Beliefs, memories, and expectancies—even purposes and aesthetic preferences—are all grounded in association or conditioning. Character and cognitive ability are the products of proper educational procedures. In his autobiography, John Stuart Mill (1873/1969) credited his father for adding "greater length and depth" to David Hartley's associationism (p. 43). Inspired by the implications of associationism, Mill became a staunch advocate for education for the masses and education of the whole person.

John Stuart Mill

According to Robinson (1982), John Stuart Mill (1806–1873) "contributed directly and indirectly to any number of turns psychology would take toward the end of the nineteenth century. His philosophy of science put the older empiricism of Bacon and Locke on modern footing and lent plausibility to the claim that an *experimental* science of mind was within reach" (p. 75). Mill was also one of the great liberal thinkers of the nineteenth century. He argued powerfully for freedom of expression, representative government, the importance of the individual, and, contrary to popular opinion of his day, the emancipation of women. Mill's interests ranged broadly from epistemology and logic to history, political theory, literature, and psychology. He ranks as one of the great British philosophers.

John Stuart Mill was born May 20, 1806. The story of young Mill's early life is well known. He was a precocious child, who, in the words of Bertrand Russell (1959), "had his father's educational doctrines ruthlessly inflicted on him. 'I never was a boy,' he complained later in life" (p. 266). Mill, educated by his father, started Greek at age three and Latin at age eight. At age eight, he

was already reading the Greek classics. The pace of learning was strained, even for a precocious child. "I was continually incurring his displeasure by my inability to solve difficult problems for which he did not see that I had not the necessary previous knowledge" (J. S. Mill, 1873/1969, p. 9). The educational program to which young Mill was subjected, harsh by twentieth-century standards, was nevertheless marked by the benefit of individual instruction and an extremely knowledgeable teacher. Mill's appraisal of his education was a mixture of praise and criticism. He lamented the absence of holidays, the neglect of manual arts and skills, and the failure to recognize the crucial role of feeling in human life. At the same time, he appreciated his father's interest, diligence, and knowledge.

As a young man, Mill was employed by the Examiners Office of the India House, where he was, again, under his father's supervision. He wrote for the press, commenting that "the writings by which one can live, are not the writings which themselves live" (J. S. Mill, 1873/1969, p. 51). He was nevertheless able to earn a living and to find ample time for philosophical inquiry. Some of his first serious articles were on freedom of speech. Together with his father, Mill was a member of a small group of influential people who came to be known as Benthamites. Later, John Stuart Mill used the term *utilitarian* and it gradually became the popular term for nineteenth-century liberal thought that stood for Hartleian metaphysics, complete freedom of discussion, representative government, universal education, full employment, and voluntary birth control. John Stuart Mill was once jailed overnight for distributing birth control information.

In the autumn of 1826, Mill suffered a severe depression, declaring later that "the whole foundation on which my life was constructed fell down ... for some months the cloud seemed to grow thicker and thicker" (J. S. Mill, 1873/1969, p. 81). He lamented having no one to talk with, no one who would understand, least of all his father. In the midst of his depression, he came to the conclusion that the cultivation of feeling had been lacking in his education. He then explored his feelings by turning to art, poetry, and music. One day, in a moment, he experienced an epiphany. He was reading a passage from Marmontel's *Memoirs* describing his father's death and the subsequent inspiration of a son to replace the father. Mill said, "A vivid conception of the scene and its feelings came over me, and I was moved to tears. From this moment my burden grew lighter" (J. S. Mill, 1873/1969, p. 85).

In 1830, Mill met Harriet Taylor, a woman unhappily married but unable in that day to divorce. The friendship developed and deepened over a twenty-year period. Mill and Taylor were married in 1851 after the death of her first husband in 1849. In his autobiography, Mill claimed that his relationship with Harriet Taylor was most beneficial to his intellectual and emotional development. He regarded her as a genius, "a woman of deep and strong feeling, of penetrating and intuitive intelligence, and of an eminently meditative and poetic nature" (J. S. Mill, 1873/1969, pp. 111–112). She served as a sounding board and often as a foil for Mill's intellectual work. He spoke in the most glowing and appreciative terms regarding his personal and intellectual companionship with Harriet Taylor. Tragically, Harriet Taylor lived only about seven years after her marriage to Mill. Devastated, but somehow still productive, Mill lived another fifteen years in a house he built to overlook Harriet Taylor's grave. In his final years, he was attended by one of Taylor's children by her first husband. Mill died on May 8, 1873.

Robinson (1982) argued that "Mill anticipated and encouraged the sort of research ordinarily identified as 'behavioristic' . . . he avoided the temptation to rush psychology into scientific status by biologizing it" (p. 75). Instead, the central organizing themes in Mill's conception of psychology are association and the pleasure principle. Mill accepted the principles of association advanced by his father and by Hartley. Thus, elementary laws of the mind were easily demonstrated by the usual experimental methods of inquiry. But Mill raised doubts about whether the mechanical approach to association could do justice to the more complex phenomena of the mind. He pointed out that "the phenomena of mind are sometimes analogous to mechanical, but sometimes also to chemical laws" (J. S. Mill, 1843/ 1974, p. 853). By this, he intended to convey the idea that elements are not necessar-

ily identifiable in complex ideas. He noted, for example, that we may see white when prismatic colors are properly mixed. We do not see each of the elements. According to Mill, this is an example of "mental chemistry: in which it is proper to say that the simple ideas generate, rather than that they compose, the complex ones" (J. S. Mill, 1843/1974, p. 854). Mill warned, however, that psychological chemistry does not relieve us of the responsibility of identifying the basic properties of complex ideas any more than the chemist is relieved of the responsibility of identifying the elements of a chemical compound.

Mill's optimism about the possibility of a science of human nature was illustrated in his strong belief that we are governed by many laws about which we have little or no knowledge. He compared human nature with the phenomena of meteorology. The weather is surely governed by the laws of such things as heat, pressure, and electricity, and when these laws are understood we will thereby have a better understanding of the weather. By the same token, human nature is governed by basic biological and sociological laws. According to Mill, it is no disparagement against certain sciences such as meteorology or a science of human nature that predictions will be couched in terms of probabilities or approximations.

Mill asked if there is a science of psychology. He answered, "All states of mind are immediately caused either by other states of mind, or by states of body" (J. S. Mill, 1843/1975, p. 849). There is not only a science of psychology that studies successive states of mind or bodily influences on mind but there is also a science of character formation, which Mill called *etholog*. Ethology, like psychology, can be studied by observational and experimental methods. Mill thus embraced the concept of an applied psychology (ethology) and a basic psychology.

As noted earlier, Mill was deeply concerned about Victorian attitudes toward women. His book *The Subjection of Women* (Mill, 1869/1988) was received with predictable hostility by men who wished to conserve the status quo. Mill called for nothing less than radical change. He argued that "the principle which regulates the existing social relations between the two sexes—the legal subordination of one sex to the other—is wrong in itself, and now one of the chief hindrances to human improvement; and that it ought to be replaced by a principle of perfect equality, admitting no power or privilege on the one side, nor disability on the other" (Mill, 1869/1988, p. 1). Mill believed that male chauvinism often parades in the sciences as natural law or in religion as true theology based on an ordinance of God. He had faith, however, that sexism would ultimately yield "before a sound psychology, laying bare the real root of much that is bowed down to as the intention of Nature and the ordinance of God" (p. 2).

The origin of Mill's feminist perspective is grounded partly in his empiricism and utilitarianism. It was common in Mill's day to justify inequality by referring to presumed deficiencies in the nature of women. As a good empiricist, Mill argued that we cannot claim adequate knowledge about the nature of women so long as they live in political and social circumstances that undermine the development of their natural abilities. Speculating on the origin of Mill's feminism, Okin (1988) pointed out that "it is certain that, from the time they met, Harriet Taylor was a major influence on the development of Mill's feminism" (p. ix). Mill also credited Taylor for sharpening his sensitivities to the practical, day-to-day consequences of sexism.

Mill's philosophical work and his interest in sexism are highly suggestive for a science of human nature. His comments on the subjection of women clearly suggest the possibility of applied social psychological studies that could shed light on the benefits of equality of the sexes. His philosophical work and his social interests are powerful intellectual forerunners of basic and applied psychology. Like many of the philosophers included in this chapter, Mill was interested in a new science of human nature that would "understand in order to improve human behavior" (Leary, 1980, p. 292).

It is of interest that Mill had a direct influence on Alexander Bain (1818–1903), who founded the journal *Mind* in 1876. This journal, initially edited by George Croom Robertson (1842–1892), was the first psychological journal (King, 2000). It served as an important publication outlet for many of the early scholars in psychology. Bain not only founded the first psychological journal but also wrote some of the early psychology texts. His books *The Senses and the Intellect* (1855) and *The Emotions and the Will* (1859) had an enormous influence on the early generation of psychologists.

Empiricism, under Bacon, started, at least partly, as a reaction to the skepticism of the French philosopher Montaigne. The emphasis of empiricism on the importance of personal experience and observation had a direct influence on all the sciences including psychology. A summary of the influences of empiricism will, at a minimum, include the following:

1. Empiricism provided a new methodology (in Bacon's words, *Novum Organum*) that served as a corrective to years of intellectual stagnation and that challenged scholasticism, authority, revelation, and tradition.

2. With empiricism, there was a new emphasis on the importance of learning and universal education. If the mind at birth is as "white paper" as John Locke contended then mental content is dependent upon the environment and social structures friendly to education.

3. John Locke's philosophy also helped open the door to the study of children and their learning processes.

4. The work of empiricists such as Berkeley and Condillac emphasized the importance of the scientific study of the senses. If knowledge comes via the senses, we had best understand the limits and capacities of these "windows to the mind."

5. Early empiricists were important pioneers in the study of motivation and emotion. David Hartley provided a classification of pleasures, and Jeremy Bentham was one of the most important pioneers in the study of punishment. David Hume was a pioneer in the study of the emotions.

6. John Stuart Mill and Harriet Taylor, following in the tradition of Mary Wollstonecraft, helped challenge old stereotypes about the abilities of women. Empiricism helped establish an intellectual context friendly to the liberation of women.

7. Hume's work on causality might properly be regarded as the most creative work on that subject since Aristotle.

Clearly, many of the intellectual components necessary to the development of a formal science of psychology were in place following the work of the early empiricists and utilitarians.

REVIEW QUESTIONS _____

1. Briefly list and describe Bacon's four Idols. What are some of the Idols in our day?

2. What is the Baconian approach to scientific methodology?

3. Distinguish between Locke's primary qualities and secondary qualities. Give examples of each.

4. Discuss some of the implications of Locke's contention that there is nothing in the intellect that was not previously in the senses.

5. What was Berkeley's objection to primary qualities? Briefly argue in defense of Berkeley's position.

6. Outline Hume's general approach to the problem of causality.

7. Show how empiricism evolved from a method (epistemology) under Bacon's treatment to a position on the nature of being (ontology) in the work of Berkeley and Hume.

8. Outline contributions to empiricism made by continental philosophers Condillac and Helvétius.

9. Briefly discuss the nature of the legal problems that contributed to the development of utilitarianism. What were the implications of utilitarianism for a science of human nature?

10. Review Hartley's seven varieties of pleasure.

11. Briefly outline Hartley's contributions to associationism.

12. Distinguish between the concepts of mental mechanics (James Mill) and mental chemistry (John Stuart Mill).

13. In what ways did John Stuart Mill contribute to the development of applied psychology?

14. Outline some of the ways empiricism contributed to an intellectual climate friendly to the development of psychology as a discipline.

CHAPTER 7

RATIONALISM

A desire which springs from reason can never be in excess.
—Benedict Spinoza (in Gutmann, 1949, p. 233)

As noted in the previous chapter, seventeenth-century philosophy was confronted with the task of combating skepticism and restoring faith in human knowledge. Empirical philosophy, under the leadership of Francis Bacon and John Locke, placed emphasis on experience and the association of sensory data as the vehicles through which knowledge is attained. By contrast, rational philosophy, the subject of this chapter, turns to axiomatic first principles and reason as the guides to knowledge. The term **rationalism** was derived from the Latin *ratio*, which means to reason, to think, or to reckon. Rational philosophy may be contrasted with empirical philosophy in many ways. First, rational philosophy places emphasis on a priori knowledge, whereas empiricism emphasizes the idea that knowledge is derived from experience. Second, in rational philosophy the mind is regarded as active in the sense of its capacity to select, organize, and discriminate, whereas in empirical philosophy the mind is regarded as passive, like a blank slate. Finally, deductive reasoning is emphasized in rationalism, whereas inductive reasoning is emphasized in empiricism. A more detailed consideration of each of these contrasting perspectives is presented in the following materials.

EMPHASIS ON A PRIORI KNOWLEDGE

According to rationalism, certain essential truths are apprehended in an a priori manner. For example, statements such as *All bachelors are unmarried* or *A line cannot be perpendicular to itself* are grasped as necessarily true once the terms are fully understood. Granted, we have had experience with language and with specific terms such as *bachelor* and *unmarried* or *line* and *perpendicular* but, according to rationalism, the self-evident nature of the proposition itself is grasped on an a priori basis. In the first example about bachelors, we understand that the predicate completely unpacks the subject. In a similar manner, we may grasp more complex relationships. Thus, if it is given that *A* is larger than *B* and *B* is larger than *C,* we know also that *A* is larger than *C*. Rationalists also emphasize certain innate capacities and preferences such as the capacity to see in depth or the preference for sweet, rather than bitter, tastes.

THEORY OF THE ACTIVE MIND

According to empiricism, the mind receives information via the senses. Knowledge about the world is gradually built up through associations based on such external influences as contiguity, similarity, contrast, and reinforcement. According to rationalism, the mind is not a mere passive repository of sensory information. The mind actively organizes, selects, rejects, discriminates, and acts on sensory data. The theory of an **active mind** is intimately connected to the emphasis of rationalism on a priori truths. Such truths would be of little significance if they did not translate into action.

DEDUCTION VERSUS INDUCTION

It is incorrect to argue that rationalism relies on reason but empiricism relies on experience. Both reason and experience play a role in both philosophies. Nevertheless, in rationalism the emphasis is on deductive reason, whereas empiricism is more concerned with the rules of induction. A **deductive argument** is one in which the premises are claimed to provide definitive grounds for the conclusion. If a deductive argument is valid, then it is impossible for the premises to be true while the conclusion is false. An **inductive argument,** by contrast, is one in which one intends to show that the conclusion is more likely than not, given the premises. If an inductive argument is strong, then the conclusion is shown to be more probable than not, given the premises. It is characteristic of induction to reason from samples to populations. Conclusions are given in the language of probability in induction, whereas conclusions can be offered as *"proved,"* in a strict sense, in deductive reasoning.

Clearly, rationalism and empiricism result in contrasting views of human beings and in different philosophies of science. This chapter will examine the thoughts of some of the leading rationalists of the seventeenth, eighteenth, and nineteenth centuries. The implications of rational philosophy for psychology will be explored as we proceed.

RENÉ DESCARTES

René Descartes, born March 31, 1596, was the fourth child of Joachim Descartes and Jeanne Brochard. The rearing of the young philosopher was to fall to his maternal grandmother and a nurse, as Descartes's mother died in May of 1597 while giving birth to a fifth child. Descartes's father, a practicing lawyer and judge, enjoyed social prestige and advantage, which made it possible for him to provide the family with a comfortable level of independence and financial security.

Little is known of Descartes's early years, but it is clear that as a child he did not enjoy good health. At the same time, his father recognized that Descartes possessed unusual curiosity and intellectual power. Because of his frail condition, he was pampered and his formal education was delayed. In 1604, when Descartes was eight years old, his father arranged for his enrollment in a Jesuit School at La Flèche, north of Touraine. In the

René Descartes

first five years, the curriculum consisted largely of composition, literature, Latin, Greek, music, and French. In the final three years, the focus of the curriculum was on philosophy, astronomy, physics, and mathematics. Descartes was recognized as a cooperative and brilliant student with unusual skills in mathematics. He found his greatest satisfaction in mathematics because it offered greater certainty than other areas of inquiry.

The period from 1612 to 1628 represents a curious mixture of activity that is not obviously predictive of the work that would later secure Descartes's fame as the Father of Modern Philosophy. In 1616, he took a law degree from the University of Poiters, but he was disinterested in the practice of law. Filled with doubts about what he knew with certainty, he turned from academic life to the "book of the world" and to careful introspection into his own life. During this period he experimented extensively with military life, volunteering for duty first in Holland under Maurice of Nassan, Prince of Orange. Later, he served in the Bavarian Army and, still later, as an officer in the Imperial Army of Hungary. Descartes traveled extensively throughout Western Europe, all the while occupied with the problems of human knowledge. During this period he established a friendship with Isaac Beeckman, a Dutch professor who recognized Descartes's mathematical skills.

Partly through Beeckman's influence, Descartes's long interest in mathematics was kindled to new intensity. By the latter part of the decade of the 1620s, Descartes's skills in mathematics were being recognized and he was encouraged by the well-known Catholic Cardinal Pierre de Berulle to commit himself unreservedly to intellectual activity. In 1628, Descartes left France to take up residence in the Netherlands. The period from 1628 to 1649 witnessed an outpouring of the major works that secured Descartes's prominent place in history.

Shortly after arriving in Holland, Descartes began work on his book *The World.* He worked from 1629 to 1633 and produced a treatise that in many essentials was in agreement with the conclusions of Galileo's *Dialogue on the Two Chief Systems.* He agreed with Galileo and Copernicus that the earth is not immovable and that it is not the center of the universe. But in 1633, he received disturbing news that Galileo had been imprisoned by the Inquisition and that his book had been burned. Descartes was caught between his loyalty to the authority of the Catholic faith and his passion for truth. Vrooman (1970) pointed out that it was unlikely that Descartes would have suffered his "Italian contemporary's fate, which was first strict confinement and later, while still under surveillance, weekly recitation of the seven penitential psalms for a period of three years" (p. 84). Nevertheless, for the time being, authority ruled. In a letter to his friend Marin Mersenne, Descartes declared that he thought his arguments for the movement of the earth were based on clear proofs. Nevertheless, he said, "I would not wish, for anything in the world, to maintain them against the authority of the church" (see Kenny, 1970, p. 26). Accordingly, Descartes decided to suppress his treatise and thus four years of work. Fortunately, the treatise was not suppressed forever. It was finally published in 1664, fourteen years after his death. Other important works produced in the period from 1628 to 1649 include *Rules for the Direction of the Mind* probably completed around 1628, but published posthumously in 1684; *Discourse on the Method of Rightly Conducting One's Reason and Seeking the Truth in the Sciences, and in Addition the Optics, the Meteorology and the*

Geometry, Which Are Essays in This Method, first published anonymously in 1637; *Principles of Philosophy,* 1644; *Description of the Human Body,* published posthumously in 1664; *The Passions of the Soul,* 1649; and Descartes's most celebrated work, *Meditations on First Philosophy,* 1641. These and other works are published in a two-volume collection entitled *The Philosophical Writings of Descartes* (Cottingham, Stoothoff, & Murdoch, 1984–1985).

The final phase of Descartes's life is well known. By the late 1640s, Queen Christina of Sweden had developed interest in the philosophical work of Descartes. In 1649, she invited him to Stockholm to become her personal tutor. Descartes was filled with reservations about the northern climate, the voyage itself, and the demands of courtly life. As a Catholic, he was also concerned about living in a Protestant country. His greatest and most justifiable concern centered on his need for privacy and solitude and whether this need would be compromised in the Queen's court. Despite his concerns, he accepted the invitation and landed in Stockholm on October 1, 1649. Tragically, he had less than five months to live. An unusually severe winter and an inconvenient and demanding schedule that included tutoring sessions for the Queen at 5 A.M. took their toll. In early February, Descartes developed pneumonia and died on February 11, 1650.

Descartes was uniquely qualified to initiate the integrated system of thought that helped shape the modern scientific and philosophical outlook. From his earliest years, he was keenly interested in the problem of knowledge. Furthermore, he was concerned about the threat posed to science and philosophy by the skeptical leanings of such writers as Charron and Montaigne. As noted by Popkin (1979a) Descartes hoped to establish an "intellectual fortress capable of withstanding the assaults of the skeptics" (p. 173). Not the least of his qualifications for the erection of such a fortress were his unusual mathematical gifts. Unlike Bacon, he appreciated the unique role that mathematics must play in the sciences. Descartes was also well versed in the discoveries of the empirical sciences of his day. In terms of both interest and intellectual qualifications, he was remarkably qualified to construct a philosophy that was adequate for the new sciences.

Descartes's Method

Descartes is traditionally regarded as a rationalist because of his emphasis on the primacy of reason as the appropriate means of attaining scientific knowledge. As we will see, however, some scholars (e.g., see Clarke, 1982) have demonstrated that Descartes, the scientist, reserved a crucial role for experience in his scientific work. Nevertheless, we encounter in his major works an emphasis on innate ideas, a priori truths, and a preference for deduction. As we proceed, we will demonstrate that the role of experience is not compromised in Descartes's philosophy of science.

Descartes's search for an intellectual edifice that could withstand the assaults of skepticism began with the method of skepticism as an instrument of analysis. He agreed with Montaigne that it is possible, as an intellectual exercise, to doubt many things—the existence of God, the past, the world, one's own body, and the existence of other people. Descartes's real goal was to push doubt to the limits, to engage in a kind of hyperbolic doubt to see if he could discover something that was immune to doubt. In the course of his work, he found something he could not doubt—namely, the fact that he was doubting. But in order to doubt, one must think and in order to think, one must exist. Hence, we encounter the basis of Descartes's celebrated axiom "I think, therefore I am." For Descartes, this was a clear and distinct idea and it constitutes a central illustration of a key feature in the Cartesian method. Let us turn now to a consideration of the steps in that method.

Like Bacon, Descartes believed we should lay aside old prejudices and received opinions. He was, however, quick to separate science and faith. As noted by Mahaffy (1969); "In the first he is a sweeping reformer; in the second a strict conservative" (p. 24). Our concern here is with Descartes the reformer who, in his *Discourse on Method,* established procedural rules for the intellect and a "strong and unswerving resolution never to fail to observe them" (Cottingham, Stoothoff, & Murdoch, 1985, vol. 1, p. 120). The four rules are as follows:

1. Never accept anything as true unless it is so clear and distinct as to be immune from doubt.
2. Divide all difficulties into as many parts as possible.
3. Start with the easiest and best-known elements and proceed step by step to knowledge of the more complex.
4. Make complete enumerations and comprehensive reviews so as to assure that nothing is left out.

Descartes declared that his method was modeled after that of the mathematicians who alone provided "certain and evident reasonings" (Cottingham, Stoothoff, & Murdoch, 1985, p. 120). Descartes believed that his mathematical–deductive method could be extended to a great range of problems and usher in a new era of discovery of certain knowledge.

Although Descartes's system betrays a preference for deduction from self-evident truths, he nevertheless reserves a role for experience in scientific procedure. To be sure, he was conservative in his views of experiments because he realized that an experiment is only a special form of observation that can be poorly conceived and thus result in misinformation. Clarke (1982, p. 18) pointed out that Descartes is quick to reject the results of experiments that run counter to reason. At the same time, Clarke called attention to the fact that Descartes "commends the appropriateness of ordinary experience as a foundation for physical science" (p. 23). An illustration is provided by Mahaffy (1969), who calls attention to one of Descartes's letters to his friend Marin Mersenne, where he expresses the wish "that some patient person would write down an exact description of the actual state of the heavens, without hypotheses or conjecture, after the manner of Bacon. This would be the greatest help to the theorist" (p. 55; see also Kenny, 1970, p. 24).

The method of Descartes, then, includes a place for ordinary experience and simple day-to-day observation. Indeed, Descartes trusted ordinary experience more than experiments and believed that simple observation of natural events followed by critical reflection provides the foundation for science. In Part VI of his *Discourse,* Descartes noted that at the beginning of an investigation "it is better to resort only to those [observations] which, presenting themselves spontaneously to our senses, cannot be unknown to us if we reflect even a little. The reason for this is that the more unusual observations are apt to mislead us" (Cottingham, Stoothoff, & Murdoch, 1985, vol. 1, p. 143). Clarke called attention to Descartes's simple anatomical observations on beasts killed in butcher houses and to his claim that in unambiguous situations "reasoning is useless without experience" (Clarke, 1982, p. 205). The role of experience, then, in Descartes's method, is to provide material for reflection. It is reflection based on sensory information that is the source of scientific procedure. Sensory information alone cannot be trusted; it leads only to superficial and existential appearances (see Green, 1985, pp. 53–87).

Descartes did not deny that discoveries may result from chance observations or blind trial and error, but such discoveries are not, in a formal sense, a part of the scientific method. For Descartes, scientific knowledge presupposes a conceptual or theoretical framework. Clarke (1982) called attention to Descartes's dismay that "the telescope was discovered by experimental manipulation of lenses without a theory to explain the result: 'To the shame of our sciences, this discovery, which is so useful and admirable, was initially made only by experimenting and by chance'" (p. 37).

To summarize, Descartes's emphasis on deduction, mathematical proofs, and self-evident truths betrays a rationalist approach to the philosophy of science. Nevertheless, for Descartes, simple common experiences play a key role in the initial stages of inquiry. If one wants to initiate geographic inquiry, Descartes would undoubtedly counsel that one should begin by making observations of coastlines, mountain ranges, the courses of rivers, and so on. Just as a map of the heavens would be helpful to the science of astronomy, so would a well-constructed map be useful to a science of geography. Descartes reserves a role for simple experience; what he opposes is premature, poorly conceived, or unmeaningful experiments that lack an adequate conceptual base. With his emphasis on the role of common experience,

Descartes does not quite fit the role of the "rationalist spider" in Bacon's metaphor that spins webs out of its own substance.

Descartes had a continuing influence on those philosophers who followed him in the rationalist tradition. References to Descartes's pioneering studies abound in the works of seventeenth-, eighteenth-, and nineteenth-century philosophers who were interested in the problem of knowledge and the new sciences. Descartes's immediate successor, Benedict Spinoza, was especially influenced by Descartes's philosophy of science. As we will see, Spinoza extended Descartes's method in an uncompromising way and thus forged an important conceptual basis for a science of human nature.

BARUCH SPINOZA

Intense religious persecution prompted a mass exodus of Jews from Spain and Portugal in the late sixteenth century. The Jewish family of one of the greatest philosophers of the seventeenth century was among those who fled the cruelty of the Inquisition to take up residence in Holland, known at the time as a haven of religious freedom. Baruch Spinoza was born in Amsterdam, Holland, on November 24, 1632. He later changed his given Jewish name, Baruch, to its Latin equivalent, Benedict.

The young Spinoza was recognized early as an outstanding student in his Jewish school in Amsterdam. His brilliance was at first a source of admiration, but later it became a source of consternation to the orthodox Jewish community. The young Spinoza raised penetrating questions about fundamental beliefs and was critical of answers based on authority and tradition. In desperation, the rabbis offered Spinoza a sizable scholarship to assist him with his education on the condition that he abandon his unorthodox religious views. But Spinoza, as much as any figure we have encountered thus far, was caught in the grip of an irresistible urge to take ideas seriously. The life of the mind could not be compromised, so the scholarship was refused. The personal result for Spinoza was most painful. He was subjected to public ridicule and on one occasion assaulted by a knife-wielding religious fanatic. In 1656, he was excommunicated from the synagogue. Excommunication

Baruch (Benedict) Spinoza

came with the stipulation that the community of the faithful refrain from speaking with Spinoza or reading his works.

Spinoza's uncompromising dedication to the search for truth was put to the test on numerous other occasions by offers of financial support. But most sources of support come with conditions and Spinoza was unwilling to accept conditions that could compromise his intellectual integrity. As a consequence, he earned a meager living with his manual skill as a lens grinder. He worked on philosophy in the remaining available time. By 1663, he had published his *Principles of the Philosophy of René Descartes* (see Curley, 1985, pp. 221–346). He also started work on two controversial works that would be published only after his death, *Treatise on the Emendation of the Intellect* (see Curley, 1985, pp. 3–45) and his best-known work, *Ethics* (see Curley, 1985, pp. 401–617). A central theme in the philosophy of Spinoza is the denial that an epistemology based on revelation has any special status as a means of attaining truth. For Spinoza, rigorous rational inquiry was the special method that held promise as a way of ascertaining truth and a way of coming to know God. Few of his contemporaries could appreciate his arguments, so it is little wonder his works were widely banned.

By the 1660s, Spinoza's fame had spread and he was in correspondence with numerous important intellectual figures, including philosopher Gottfried Wilhelm Leibniz. In 1673, Spinoza was offered a chair in philosophy at Heidelberg University with a promise of academic freedom. The offer was accompanied, however, with an expression of trust that Spinoza would refrain from doing anything to upset the religious establishment. Spinoza refused the offer. One of the greatest testimonies to the integrity of the philosopher came in 1673. A representative from the court of Louis XIV promised a pension if Spinoza would dedicate a new work to the king. Spinoza refused.

In 1675, Spinoza had completed his greatest work, *Ethics*. However, his efforts to publish the work resulted in such a storm of protest from the clergy that he abandoned the project. *Ethics* was published posthumously and was promptly banned. Spinoza's life was undoubtedly shortened by his occupation as a lens grinder. He contracted a disease of the lungs and died at the age of 44 on February 21, 1677. During his life and for a century thereafter, Spinoza's name was anathema to orthodox Catholics, Protestants, and Jews. Though he was not a resident of Spain, his name was on the "wanted list" in the Spanish Inquisition. He was accused of atheism and of denying revelation. Strictly speaking, neither charge was true; Spinoza simply left the world with a new vision of God and of revelation.

In Descartes's philosophy, we encounter a dualism of soul and body, at least where humans are concerned. Such a radical separation of soul and body leaves room for free will in humans, but animals may be viewed as automata. Such a split between humans and animals contributes to a polarization of the free will/determinism issue. There was still another split between the sacred realm that includes a transcendent God and the secular world. What is most evident in Spinoza is an unrelenting quest for unity—a quest that results in a denial of the legitimacy of distinctions between sacred and secular, mind and body, and free will and determinism. Let us begin with Spinoza's vision of the union of the sacred and the secular.

By denying the metaphysical basis of demonology, Spinoza figured in the humanitarian reform of the treatment of the mentally ill. He specifically denied that there are devils and hence that the mentally ill are possessed. Spinoza argued that there is only one ultimate reality and that reality is God. There are not separate spiritual powers that control natural events such as the weather, earthquakes, or mental illness. Rather, God is the only spiritual power and God is imminent in nature and inseparable from truth. What is true is of God, indeed *is* God. When we discover a natural truth, we are thereby discovering something about the infinite substance that is God. With Spinoza, it is not God *or* nature; rather, it is God *in* nature. Spinoza believed that the common view that God is separate from nature was a product not of rational reason but of imagination. It was also imagination that projected the popular anthropormorphic God with human needs and a human form, including a sexual identity. Spinoza's view is essentially pantheistic; it argues that God is in all things. Thus, any distinction between sacred and secular is false. The scientist or the rationalist is discovering as much or more about God as is the theologian.

We have already pointed out that in his time Spinoza was reviled and even excommunicated. Delahunty (1985) noted, "To his immediate successors, his 'hideous hypothesis' seemed a ruseful version of atheistic materialism, honeyed words coating poisoned messages" (p. 125). But Spinoza was neither an atheist nor a materialist, and within a century of his death he was viewed as a "God-intoxicated man, the last magnificent blaze of the Hebrew religious imagination" (Delahunty, 1985, p. 125).

Spinoza also challenged the Cartesian notions that there are separate substances, mind and body, and that these separate substances interact in the pineal gland. How, he asked, can a nonphysical mind be causal with respect to a physical substance and how does causal interaction take place in the pineal gland? According to Spinoza, mind and body are not radically separate; rather, they are two aspects of the same fundamental reality. Thus, psychological and neurophysiological processes coexist, and the world of experience (the psychological world) and the world of behavior (the physiological world) are but two expressions of the same thing. Such a position assigns a role to psychology as a scientific discipline. Mental processes are a part of

the natural order—the human mind is a part of nature and is subject to nature's laws.

If the human mind is subject to nature's laws, there is no absolute or unconditioned free will. There is, however, a kind of freedom associated with knowledge of the laws of nature. For example, knowledge of the cause of a disease greatly enhances our freedom to deal with the disease, so we need no longer be victimized by it. Spinoza also believed that we are freer when we are not dominated by our passions. Spinoza's book, *Ethics,* deals extensively with ways in which freedom has meaning within a deterministic context. We will encounter this approach to freedom and determinism again in the thought of Sigmund Freud who, like Spinoza, believed in the lawfulness of the psychic apparatus, but also embraced the possibility of a hard-won but weak form of freedom that emerges when the ego is not dominated by irrational forces.

It can be argued that Spinoza contributed more to the philosophical and intellectual spadework necessary for the development of modern psychology than any thinker we have encountered so far. His philosophy challenges the special and separate status of mental processes implied in earlier dualistic theories. Though Spinoza was reviled in his own day, his thought served as an inspiration to many of the leading thinkers of the eighteenth and nineteenth centuries. His influence on the history of scientific psychology is documented by Bernard (1972), who showed direct ties between Spinoza and such early pioneers as Johannes Müller and Gustav Theodor Fechner. His influence on Helmholtz and Wundt was also extensive. Alexander and Selesnick (1966, pp. 98–100) pointed out that Spinoza understood many ideas such as repression, overcompensation, reaction formation, and the role of pleasure that later formed such key parts of Freudian psychology.

Spinoza's psychological thought as set forth in his *Ethics* is rich in insight and worthy of detailed study. For example, he claimed that "anything may be accidentally the cause of either hope or fear" (Gutmann, 1949, p. 163). He connected this proposition with the development of superstition. Spinoza contended that the strength of an emotion is a function of the number of simultaneous causes

(Gutmann, 1949, p. 259). In a discussion of the origin and nature of emotions, he noted that if we begin to develop a hatred for a thing that was once loved, we will hate with greater intensity than we would if we had never loved the thing in the first place. He argued that the greater hatred is fueled by sorrow over the loss of love (Gutmann, 1949, p. 156).

Spinoza's rationalism is evident in his use of the geometric method. His ideas were often set forth in terms of axioms, numbered propositions, and demonstrations. Like Descartes, he emphasized the capacity to grasp intuitively certain essential truths. Spinoza also insisted on careful examination of definitions and a procedure that begins with what is self-evident or clearly grasped. He was as suspicious of unexamined sense data as he was of authority or tradition. Spinoza romanticized rationalism, claiming that human beings who are governed by reason wish no advantage for themselves that they do not wish for others and that reason produces "just, faithful and honorable" people (Gutmann, 1949, p. 203). Also he declared that "a desire which springs from reason can never be in excess" (Gutmann, 1949, p. 233).

Spinoza's radical monism and his attacks on traditional theology served as a foil for one of his most important successors, Gottfried Wilhelm Leibniz. Though the two men shared a belief in the importance of reason, Leibniz strongly disagreed with the contention of Spinoza that all things are simply modes of one fundamental substance. The rational philosophy of Leibniz also rejected the determinism of Spinoza and the idea that plurality is nothing but appearance.

GOTTFRIED WILHELM LEIBNIZ

A contemporary of John Locke and Sir Isaac Newton, Gottfried Wilhelm Leibniz was an unusually gifted genius of the late seventeenth and early eighteenth century who played a major role in shaping European thought in such diverse areas as mathematics, law, history, politics, religion, philosophy, and psychology. Leibniz and Newton are remembered as independent inventors of the differential calculus. Leibniz is also remembered as one of the first to develop a calculating machine.

Leibniz's work as a philosopher can be characterized as a quest for the world's unity, but, unlike Spinoza, Leibniz's philosophical perspective allows for a stronger role for plurality or diversity within unity.

Leibniz's concern for unity also extended to practical political problems. For example, he sought ways to unite Protestants and Catholics and to bring medicine and science into closer harmony. He also had a vision of a universal language and of a world united and ruled by reason, science, and an essentially Christian ethic. His practical quests for unity were, of course, severely frustrated and his metaphysical quest for unity, anchored as it was in theology, fared no better.

Leibniz was born in Leipzig, Germany, in 1646. His father, a professor of moral philosophy at the University of Leipzig, died when his son was six years old. By the time Gottfried was eight, he was given regular access to his father's library. The library brought the young Leibniz into direct contact with the work and values of his father and he made excellent use of its resources. Leibniz was a precocious student with a broad appetite for studies in language, mathematics, history, religion, and philosophy. At age fifteen, he enrolled in the University of Leipzig, where he completed in five years a course of study for a doctorate of law. For reasons that are not entirely clear, the authorities were reluctant to award the degree to a man who was only twenty years old. Consequently, Leibniz immediately withdrew and enrolled at the University of Altdorf. Within a few months of his enrollment, he presented a dissertation and successfully defended it. His doctorate was awarded on February 22, 1667, when he was only twenty-one years of age.

Leibniz refused university positions, believing he could accomplish more of his goals if he worked in the service of ruling princes and political authorities. Though his intellectual interests were often compromised by courtly routine, he was nevertheless able to enjoy a remarkably productive career. He worked four years in Mainz, Germany, under Johann Philipp von Schonborn, but most of his work was in Hanover where he served under a succession of three rulers, Johann Friedrich, Ernst August, and Georg Ludwig.

Leibniz enjoyed many honors in his lifetime. To name a few, he was elected to the Royal Society, the Paris Academy of Sciences, and the Accademia Fisico-Matematica in Rome, and he was nominated president of the Paris Academy of Sciences, the Society of Sciences in Vienna, and the Berlin Society. On one occasion he was offered the position of custodian of the Vatican library (Aiton, 1985, p. 159). Leibniz died in 1716 at the age of seventy. Later, the town of Hanover, where he labored for forty years, erected a marble bust to his memory.

Monadology

As we noted in the previous section on Spinoza, the major difficulties in Descartes's interactionist approach to mind and brain were quick to surface. Spinoza's solution to the mind–brain problem avoided the difficulties of interactionism but introduced a new set of difficulties of its own. In Spinoza's system, diversity was never an equal partner with unity; the former was mere appearance, the latter was reality. Thus, the only possible differences between mind and brain were of an attributional nature. Leibniz was also critical of Cartesian interactionism, but neither could he accept the singular vision of Spinoza. He sought to give equal status to the claims of the mental and physical realms and at the same time preserve the world's unity—no small task.

Leibniz's approach to mind and brain must be understood in the context of his emphasis on the concept of the monad. The term **monad** (*monas*) was probably adopted by Leibniz from the philosophers Lady Anne Conway and F. M. Von Helmont (see Merchant, 1979). Anne Conway, an influential philosopher in her day, worked for a middle road between the extreme dualism of Descartes and the extreme monism of Spinoza. She most likely had a strong influence on Leibniz. The term *monad* itself refers to a principle of existence, or an ultimate unit of being. The monad is a unity or an entity harmonious with the entire universe. Leibniz believed that the universe was created with a **preestablished harmony** of its individual parts. The analogy by which Leibniz's preestablished harmony is understood is that of independent synchronized clocks. Each of many synchronized

clocks are truly individual and independent, yet the individuals are in accord about the time. Following the analogy, the mental realm is a principle of existence, as is the physical realm. Both are accorded a place in the scheme of things and the two orders are perfectly synchronized. The mental is truly individual, yet it corresponds perfectly with the physical, thus the cry of pain is parallel with the physical burn and the burn is parallel with the cry of pain. Every individual monad carries the rest of the universe along with it. The cry of pain carries the burn and the burn carries the cry of pain.

It is immediately obvious that Leibniz's system avoids the problems of interactionism and leaves us with real diversity or individuality within unity. But we now encounter a violence to causality as it is commonly understood. In Leibniz's system, no monad is causal with respect to any other monad—they are all simply in harmonious accord by virtue of the assumption of preestablished harmony, but how are we to account for preestablished harmony? Leibniz's answer is found in his theology. The marvelous synchronicity of the monads reflects the perfect order of God's creative activity. It is testimony to the influence of Leibniz that some of the early psychologists who could not accept preestablished harmony nevertheless embraced psychophysical parallelism. It was a practical solution to the mind–brain problem that avoids the difficulties of interactionism yet enfranchises both the mental and the physical realms.

Highly relevant to later psychological thought, Leibniz advanced the position that monads vary with respect to degrees of consciousness. Although all monads were viewed as having purposive or goal-directed qualities, some were viewed as being more aware than others. Leibniz believed that some monads are conscious while others possess higher self-conscious qualities and some are unconscious. Aiton (1985) pointed out that Leibniz "distinguishes between perception, which consists in being conscious of something, and apperception, which consists in being aware of a distinct perception" (p. 283). On the other end of the scale, Leibniz believed that there are **petites perceptions,** or small perceptions, of which we are not aware. But many small perceptions in concert form the basis of perception. We may not hear a single drop of water or even a few drops of water at a waterfall, but thousands of drops in chorus form a mighty roar. The idea of *petites perceptions* suggests the importance of unconscious processes, absolute thresholds, and difference thresholds—all concepts that would serve important roles in the early development of psychology.

One of Leibniz's major quarrels was with the Aristotelian and Lockean emphasis on the role of the senses in knowledge. To Locke's famous dictum "Nothing is in the intellect that was not previously in the senses," Leibniz quipped, "Nothing save the intellect itself." Leibniz's emphasis on the activity of the intellect was driven partly by the importance he gave to energy. All monads were viewed as being invested with energy. Accordingly, the mind could not be a passive receptacle; rather, it is active and it is its nature to be involved in thinking activities. One cannot pour knowledge into the mind through the senses as one pours water into a bowl. Thinking activity has its own career, it is not dependent on something external. This is not to argue that sensory activity is unimportant, but it is not *all* important. The active thinking process itself is not the result of something poured in from outside; rather, it is an inherent part of the mental monad. In Leibniz's view, sensory input is not causal (recall that he denied interactionism); instead, it is parallel with thinking processes. Leibniz would find no accident in the fact that sensory enrichment is correlated with certain mental advantages and that sensory deprivation is correlated with certain mental deficits. But neither the sensory nor the mental side must bear the whole brunt of causal explanation. Rather, sensory enrichment and sensory deprivation simply illustrate the harmony or the parallelism of the monads.

There is still another dimension of Leibniz's thought that had important implications for the sciences and for psychology in particular. Leibniz argued that "nature never takes leaps" (see Aiton, 1985, p. 283); rather, natural processes are characterized by a law of continuity. This same principle later guided Sir Charles Lyell in his classic *Principles of Geology* as he struggled with the tensions between **uniformitarianism** (the concept that change is gradual and occurs over long periods of time) and special creation with its emphasis on

abrupt change or radical discontinuity. In psychology, Leibniz's view emphasized lawful and gradual gradations from unconscious processes to conscious processes. It also underscored the importance of growth and development, but emphasized the maintenance of identity in change. It is the same individual today as yesterday as last week and last year. There is continuity of identity within an evolution that emphasizes the importance of the past to the present and the present to the future. Needless to say, there was a deemphasis on miracles in a system that emphasized preestablished harmony and continuity. At the same time, such a system provides a rich intellectual framework that preserves the uniqueness of psychological processes and yet brings such processes clearly within the province of science. Such a view undoubtedly nourished the development of a science of psychology.

Christian von Wolff

The work of Leibniz was extended by Christian von Wolff (1679–1754), a thoroughgoing rationalist who drew much of his inspiration from Leibniz. Wolff was a graduate of Leipzig University and later taught mathematics and philosophy at Halle. In 1723, he was exiled because he embraced beliefs offensive to the theological faculty and King Frederick I. He was in exile in Marburg, where he taught mathematics and philosophy for seventeen years, and was allowed to return to Halle in 1740. He taught and held administrative posts until his death in 1754.

Wolff was one of the first to use the term *psychology* in a major publication. In 1732, he published a book entitled *Empirical Psychology*. This book was complemented by another entitled *Rational Psychology,* published in 1734. According to Wolff, empirical psychology, as the name implies, studies the facts associated with the powers of the soul. It includes events in the senses, feelings of pain and pleasure and so forth. Rational psychology, clearly superior to empirical psychology, according to Wolff, involves the use of reason in the metaphysical study of the soul. Through rational psychology, one might hope to discover principles and laws. Wolff accepted the Leibnizian concept of preestablished harmony. He also advanced an early faculty psychology that influenced many subsequent thinkers such as Immanuel Kant and Franz Joseph Gall.

IMMANUEL KANT

Immanuel Kant

Based on criteria such as originality and lasting influence, Immanuel Kant (1724–1804) takes his place among the great philosophers of all time. Like René Descartes and David Hume, Kant had enormous influence on subsequent intellectual developments. Though we include him here as a rationalist, his work may be characterized as a quest for a middle road between the extremes of empiricism and rationalism. He rejected the radical empiricism of David Hume, recognizing that such an empiricism leaves us with nothing but an incoherent succession of sensations. At the same time, in his *Critique of Pure Reason,* he accepts the idea that "all our knowledge begins with experience" (Kant, 1781/1965, p. 41). Even so, Kant believed that sensory information is not pure; rather, it is shaped or filtered by a priori considerations. Kant's major work is of an epistemological nature, but like those of Descartes, his contributions extended to many fields of inquiry including psychology. We will examine several of his contributions, but first let us turn to his biography.

The story of Kant's life can be reviewed rather quickly because, in most ways, it was an uncomplicated life. He did not marry and he traveled infrequently and then only for short distances. He lived his life in Königsberg, where he was born on April 22, 1724. He attended the University of Königsberg and graduated with a doctorate from that institution in 1755. As a student, he lived in poverty, often interrupting his studies to engage in tutoring as a means of generating a meager income. After taking the doctorate, Kant taught a variety of subjects as a private instructor. Only in later years did he secure a professorial position with a decent income.

Kant's early years were marked by rigorous routine, privation, and an absence of individual freedom. Religious instruction was extensive and aversive as it dwelt on heaven and hell rather than the value of life. In a biographical sketch, Cassirer (1981), quoting from Kant, pointed out that "the

sum of pleasure is 'less than nothing' and the goal of life is not 'happiness' but self sufficiency and independence of will" (pp. 15–16). Though his youth was somber, the young Kant as a teacher, if we may believe his student Johann Gottfried Herder, had overcome many of the limitations of the past. Herder, as quoted by Durant, described Kant as follows: "He had at his service, jest, witticism, and humorous fancy, and his lectures were at once instructive and most entertaining" (Durant & Durant, 1967, p. 532). Kant, perhaps reacting to the religious dogmatism of his past, was also described by Herder as remarkably open. "No cabal or sect, no prejudice or reverence for a name, had the slightest influence with him in opposition to the extension and promotion of truth. He encouraged and gently compelled his hearers to think for themselves; despotism was foreign to his nature" (Durant & Durant, 1967, p. 532).

As noted earlier, Kant worked as a private instructor for many years after taking his doctorate in 1755. Finally, in 1770, he was offered a professorship and the following decades witnessed the outpouring of his major works. Among the most important are *Critique of Pure Reason,* 1781; *Critique of Practical Reason,* 1788; *Critique of Judgment,* 1790; and *Religion Within the Limits of Reason Alone,* 1793. This latter work aroused the ire of King Frederick William II, who accused Kant of undercutting the authority of scripture. The king threatened Kant and received a reply of assurance from the then seventy-year-old philosopher that he would from that time on refrain from talking or writing about religion.

Immanuel Kant died February 12, 1804. Cassirer (1981) illustrated the fame of the philosopher by pointing out, "His funeral turned into a great public ceremony, in which the whole city and the inhabitants of all quarters of it took part. . . . Amid the tolling of every bell in Königsberg, young students came to Kant's house to take up his body, from whence the innumerable procession, accompanied by thousands, wound to the university cathedral" (pp. 414–415). An inscription at his grave reads "The starry heavens above me, the moral law within me."

Sense Experience and Reason

The goal of Kant's epistemological work can be understood partly on the basis of a distinction between analytic a priori knowledge and synthetic a priori knowledge. **Analytic a priori** knowledge refers to formal truths in which a predicate completely unpacks a subject. An example might include a statement such as *All bachelors are unmarried.* Such purely formal statements play important roles in deductive logic, but taken by themselves they can be trivial or tautological. A *tautology* is an expression that contains a redundancy or pleonasm—that is, a word and its synonym are placed in close conjunction. Examples include statements such as *She was a sophomore in her second year* or *It is a true fact.*

Kant hoped to establish **synthetic a priori** truths that are not trivial but informative. Descartes's statement "I think therefore I am" may be regarded as an example of a synthetic a priori truth in that it is informative. It is not tautological in the same sense as a statement such as *If A is larger than B, then B is smaller than A.* Kant believed that many basic propositions in mathematics are informative about the world. An example might include a statement such as *A line is the shortest distance between two points.*

Kant believed that knowledge begins with sensory experience, but sensory experience by itself would not be intelligible apart from certain a priori considerations. For example, we grasp in an a

priori way that one object succeeds another in time or that there are spatial differences between objects. Kant also believed that there is an intuitive or a priori sense of causality so that the mind itself imposes an if–then judgment. There are thus ordinary principles of the mind that are yoked with sense experience and the two together, sense experience and ordering principles, contribute to knowledge. Kant referred to ordering principles such as the intuition of time, space, and causality as **categories of understanding.**

In marked contrast with John Locke, Kant regarded the mind as an active agency as opposed to a passive receptacle. In Kant's view, the mind as an active agency transforms sensory materials into meaningful configurations, connections, and structures. For Kant, reason alone and experience alone are equally suspect as sources of knowledge; rather, knowledge results from the interaction and complementary activity of reason and experience.

Social Psychology

Kant kept a watchful eye on both the American and the French Revolutions. He was particularly fascinated with the formation in America of a federation of states. It is well known, of course, that the American experiment proceeded over the protests of those who demanded sovereignty for the individual states. The fear was that diversity would be impossible within unity and that the federation would undermine basic freedoms by setting up a remote and insensitive central governing agency. Kant was interested because America represented a microcosm of what he envisioned for Europe and the world. If the American experiment could work, then perhaps the same thing could take place on a larger scale (see, for example, his short essay written in 1795 and entitled "To Perpetual Peace: A Philosophical Sketch" [in Humphrey, 1983, p. 341]). Kant's vision called for a world order that could intervene when there was a threat of war between states but that would nevertheless be so constituted as to permit sovereignty for states to pursue nonhostile activities.

Kant looked with disdain on the kind of nationalism that undermines humane values. He believed that human beings should work for educational, historical, and humane perspectives that rise above local biases. He was optimistic that, through good education, human beings could widen their context and enjoy the benefits of moral progress that would result from a broader identity.

Kant was one of the first to advance a theory of moral development. He believed that human beings are caught in tensions between heteronomy and autonomy. **Heteronomy,** or government from the outside, is manifested by goodness based on authority, rules or threats, or rewards and punishments. The task of the individual is to grow into moral autonomy manifested in sensitivity to moral maxims or moral imperatives. **Autonomy** refers to self-government and the ability to act in a moral manner, not just to please an authority or not just because such action is rewarding but because of an intrinsic moral requiredness in a given situation. Kant's theory of moral action is intimately related to his belief in the possibility of individual freedom. Kant also believed that truly moral actions will be based on our regard of other human beings as ends rather than as means. To regard someone as a means carries the risk that we will use them for our own purposes, whether economic, sexual, political, or whatever. When we view another human being as an end, we place emphasis on the intrinsic worth of the person.

Kant is remembered as one of the great philosophers of all time, but he is also important in the history of science. He, along with Descartes and Laplace, believed in the evolution of the solar system. It is also clear that Kant believed in geological and biological evolution, though he failed to pursue these topics. He was also interested in meteorology, earthquakes, and geography, and made contributions in each of these areas. His most important legacy, however, is that he pointed to a middle road between the extremes of empiricism and pure reason. The middle road he delineated influenced generations of psychologists and philosophers and formed the intellectual groundwork for contemporary philosophies of science.

JOHANN FRIEDRICH HERBART

Kant's successor at Königsberg, Johann Friedrich Herbart (1776–1841), was a mathematician, philosopher, and psychologist. Herbart's interests in psychology ranged from its applications to clinical and educational problems to the quantification of a great variety of mental functions. He was also interested in the role of unconscious processes in human life. Herbart was born in Oldenburg on May 4, 1776. He studied at the University of Jena and later earned his Ph.D. in philosophy at the University of Göttingen. The bulk of Herbart's academic career (1809–1832) was at the University of Königsberg, but his final appointment was at Göttingen. He died there in 1841.

Herbart can be properly regarded as one of the important pioneers in educational psychology and in mathematical psychology. His educational psychology is set forth in a book entitled *The Science of Education* (Herbart, 1902/1977), first published in English in 1902. Herbart outlined pedagogical techniques designed to facilitate learning and retention. He believed that good teachers should always help students review familiar material and then relate new materials to older more familiar material. He also advocated the importance of demonstrating practical applications whenever possible.

One of the goals of education, according to Herbart, was to build what he called the **apperceptive mass.** The term **apperception** was used extensively throughout the nineteenth and early twentieth centuries. Though there were differences in the way different individuals used the term, it typically referred to mental operations more complex than those involved in perception. According to Herbart, apperception sets humans apart from the rest of the animal kingdom. He regarded apperception as more than passive awareness and more than a mere set of complex associations. It implies an active capacity to assimilate ideas from one arena and apply them to another. It also involves the ability to apply lessons learned from old problem situations to new problems. Mental illness or a head injury might interfere with apperception because the individual would be capable only of operating effectively in concrete problem situations. Apperception implies a capacity to operate at higher levels of abstraction or at a metalevel.

Herbart also saw moral development as the central goal of education. By this he meant that education should instill a capacity for effort, the ability to forego present pleasure for future gain, the development of sensitivities to moral issues, the capability to see things from a variety of vantage points, and the evolution of goodwill. The latter involves the capacity for empathy and a willingness to abide by laws for the larger good.

Herbart's mathematical psychology attempted to account for the fusion and blending of concepts. The actual mathematical formulas that Herbart set forth are of little interest today, but the problems that occupied his thought were very important in the early development of psychology. For example, he believed that concepts or components of concepts can be below the surface of awareness or in the unconscious. He believed that concepts strive to get into consciousness and that there are barriers more or less permeable between unconscious and conscious processes. In his work, we encounter concepts of suppression, repression, threshold, and the unconscious. All of these were, of course, part of the stock and trade of later psychological thought. Herbart did not have a clear grasp of the possibility of a truly experimental psychology that manipulates variables. However, his work served as an inspiration for those who founded the formal discipline of psychology.

THOMAS REID AND COMMONSENSE PHILOSOPHY

Still another attempt to bridge the extremes of empiricism and rationalism is encountered in the **commonsense philosophy** of Thomas Reid and his followers. The expression *common sense* has many meanings, and it is likely that most philosophers and scientists have believed that their systems appeal, in one way or another, to common sense. The expression sometimes refers to the unreflective or naive opinions of ordinary people or to collective opinion. These meanings are not, however, what philosophers typically mean by common sense. In philosophy, the expression is more likely to refer to a deeply felt opposition to beliefs that are counterintuitive or that do violence to our experience of the world. Robinson (1982) used the term *necessity* to refer to Thomas Reid's concept of common sense. According to Robinson, "When Reid spoke of the principles of common sense he was referring neither to opinion nor [even] to judgment. Rather, he was proposing those very activities of mind and laws of conduct by

which life becomes possible" (p. 48). For example, belief in an external world, in causation, and in the self as an active manipulator are among the things that make life possible and that contribute to adaptation. According to Reid and his followers, the radical empiricism of Berkeley and Hume had left us with a world that was unnatural and that violates common sense at every turn.

Thomas Reid (1710–1796) grew up in a small town in rural Scotland and enrolled at age twelve in Marischal College in Aberdeen. After graduating at age sixteen, he turned his attention to theological studies. For a number of years, Reid had a pastorate in New Machar, but in 1751 he accepted a position at King's College in Aberdeen. In 1758, he helped form the Aberdeen Philosophical Society, a group of scholars that met regularly over a period of fifteen years. In 1764, Reid succeeded Adam Smith in the chair of moral philosophy at Glasgow. He remained at Glasgow until his death in 1796. Reid's best-known works include *An Inquiry into the Human Mind* (1764/1970), *Essays on the Intellectual Powers of Man* (1786), and *Essays on the Active Powers of Man* (1790).

According to Reid, an adequate empiricism would not lead to the skeptical crisis created by Hume. Indeed, an adequate empiricism, in Reid's view, will discover some important truths in experience that Hume failed to see. Such truths uncover a very different picture of the world than that provided by Hume. What Reid discovered in experience, according to Lehrer (1989), "are innate principles of our constitution yielding conceptions and convictions of the operations of our own minds, of the minds of others, of the qualities of external objects, and of the laws of nature" (p. 8). Thus, according to Reid, there are innate principles of the mind leading to convictions that we find as a natural part of experience and common sense. In other words, there are natural necessities. Robinson (1982) pointed out that "even skeptical Hume took for granted that he had sensations and this not out of choice or opinion but because of a natural *necessity*. He could not think otherwise" (p. 48).

Reid believed that a truly empirical philosophy, one that resonates appropriately to what is commonly found in human experience, will find natural necessities that are more complicated than mere sensations. For example, it is experience it-self that contributes to belief in the external world. Reid (1764/1970, p. 24) asked why the smell of a rose is more vivid in the presence of the rose than it is in memory. He pointed out that the same question can be asked of any sensation. Why is the taste of an apple more vivid during the act of eating than in memory a few hours later? Experience itself contributes to the belief that we are not the causes of those vivid sensations that occur when we are, for example, smelling or tasting. Reid (1764/1970) argued, "I could as easily doubt of my own existence, as of the existence of my sensations" (p. 24). He went on to say that sensation compels "our belief of the present existence of the thing, [and] memory a belief of its past existence" (p. 25).

Reid argued for a number of propositions that he referred to as "first principles." Examples (see Lehrer, 1989, pp. 160–161) are as follows:

1. "The thoughts of which I am conscious, are the thoughts of a being which I call MYSELF, my MIND, my PERSON."
2. "Those things do really exist which we distinctly perceive by our senses."
3. "We have some degree of power over our actions."

Thus, through experience itself and common sense, Reid attempted to restore faith in the external world, a self with real continuity, and a belief in causality.

Reid's influence was extensive in Europe and America. His admirer, Dugald Stewart, believed that Reid had restored the Baconian vision and had cleared the way for an intelligible science of human nature. Stewart's influential book *Elements of the Philosophy of the Human Mind* (1792/1802) extended Reid's thought and applied it to such psychological topics as attention, memory, association, and imagination. Reid and Stewart believed that the mind can be divided into faculties or powers. This concept was developed further by Franz Joseph Gall (1758–1828), who attempted to associate each faculty with a specific area of the brain.

Enfranchising Curiosity

In earlier chapters we explored the issues of curiosity and forbidden knowledge. For centuries, curiosity about the natural world had been regarded as an intellectual vice, a mark of foolish pride, and an affront to God. Numerous scriptures were taken as warnings against those who attempted to probe into the secrets and mysteries of the world. Paul had warned in I Corinthians 1:20 that "The wisdom of this world is foolishness with God." Such an assertion, at the proper level of abstraction, would not necessarily serve as an impediment to curiosity, but such scriptures were taken in a very literal and concrete fashion. Such a literal approach foreclosed on any possibility of discovering deeper and richer meanings that might surface in alternative interpretive modes.

The empiricists and rationalists disagreed on many things, but they shared in common a radically new interpretation of the role of curiosity in human life. To be sure, the climate of opinion was already shifting and the public was ready for a fresh approach to old questions. The empiricists and the rationalists were eager to outline such an approach. Harrison (2001) pointed out that Francis Bacon linked curiosity to charity and thus softened attitudes regarding worldly wisdom. Bacon opened his defense of curiosity by agreeing with those who had spoken against it. Curiosity could indeed motivate investigations and produce knowledge that results in pride, conceit, and arrogance, but that is only half the story. God, after all, had made the world. Further, the benefits from studying the world could be used for charitable purposes to aid the poor, the sick, and the disadvantaged. Surely charity was among the most valued of religious virtues. There were those who doubted the sincerity of Bacon's theological justification of curiosity. It seems highly probable that in his private thought, Bacon would have valued curiosity in its own right. For whatever reasons, he did resort to theological justifications and these undoubtedly had appeal in many quarters.

Other philosophers such as John Locke, David Hume, René Descartes, and Benedict Spinoza added to a growing literature in defense of curiosity as a natural human quality that should be nurtured and disciplined. In time, the virtues of curiosity and wonder were celebrated as a hallmark of modern thought (see Keen, 1973). Relentless curiosity seems now firmly and legitimately attached to all categories of human thought. Indeed, the reversal in attitudes toward curiosity is so complete, that it now seems possible that older attitudes could eventually slip from the grasp of our comprehension.

The rationalists, like the empiricists, reacted to the late Renaissance skeptical crisis initiated by Montaigne. They hoped to restore faith in human knowledge and construct an adequate philosophical base for the new sciences. In the process, they helped construct the intellectual foundations that would ultimately support the new discipline of psychology. Though the rationalists were interested largely in the problem of knowledge, they also wrote many thoughtful works dealing with theoretical and practical psychological questions. Their pervasive influence was illustrated in extensive references to their work by early pioneers in psychology such as William James and Wilhem Wundt. At a minimum, the specific contributions of the rationalists to an intellectual atmosphere friendly to the development of the human sciences should include the following:

1. René Descartes, like Francis Bacon, sought to overcome the extreme skepticism of Montaigne by advancing a new method designed to restore faith in human knowledge. Thus, modern rationalism, like empiricism, begins as a new methodology supportive of a scientific approach to the world.

2. Philosophers such as Leibniz and Herbart were among the first to investigate concepts of the threshold, a topic later to become a preoccupation of some of the early psychologists.

3. The concept of thresholds also supported the idea that there is real mental activity not currently in consciousness. The investigation of subconscious and unconscious processes were later topical in some of the systems of psychology.

4. By emphasizing the lawfulness of psychological processes, Spinoza helped lay the conceptual groundwork for a science of psychology. His attacks on demonology also contributed to naturalistic approaches to the study of emotional disorders.

5. Some of the earliest treatises with specific psychological content came from the pens of the rationalists. For example, Christian von Wolff's *Empirical Psychology* (1732) and *Rational Psychology* (1734) were among the early modern attempts to elevate the study of mental powers as a foundational part of philosophy.

6. Some of the rationalists were pioneers in educational and mathematical psychology. Herbart's book *The Science of Education* was an early attempt to explore pedagogical techniques designed to foster learning and improve memory.

7. Rationalists provided a broad vision of the world of experience. They did not deny that observation and association are important in the acquisition of knowledge, but argued that some connections are grasped intuitively or in an a priori fashion.

Like the empiricists, the rationalists contributed enormously to the intellectual and cultural context from which psychology as a formal discipline was born.

REVIEW QUESTIONS

1. Identify three ways in which rationalism differs from empiricism.

2. Briefly list four procedural rules for the intellect set forth by Descartes in his *Discourse on Method*.

3. Outline Spinoza's contributions to the intellectual spadework necessary to the development of psychology.

4. What do you see as the advantages and disadvantages of Leibniz's approach to the mind–body problem?

5. Outline Kant's distinction between analytic a priori and synthetic a priori knowledge. What is the significance of the distinction?

6. Briefly describe Kant's theory of moral development.

7. Distinguish between the terms *apperception* and *perception*.

8. Explain what Thomas Reid meant by common sense and explain how Reid argued against Hume's skepticism.

CHAPTER 8

MECHANIZATION
AND QUANTIFICATION

*There is no bodily or mental attribute . . . which cannot be gripped
and consolidated into an ogive with a smooth outline.*

—Francis Galton (1883/1907)

From earliest times, human beings have been interested in the practice and theory of measurement. Such interest was motivated by simple practical questions such as How many days? How far? How much of this product in exchange for that product? How many pieces of wood of what sizes and shapes will I need to build a house? How fast? How many of our soldiers compared with their soldiers? How much pressure? These and other questions are answered only by the practices of measurement. Because errors can be devastating to economic, social, and physical well-being, measurement has always been of great importance.

Breakthroughs in measurement have had a profound influence on science, on technology, and even on how we view ourselves. For example, in the nineteenth century, the great German scientist, Hermann von Helmholtz, was able to measure the speed of conduction of a nervous impulse. Commenting on the importance of the accomplishment, Boring (1950) pointed out that it laid the groundwork "for all later work of experimental psychology on the chronometry of mental acts and reaction times. . . . It brought the soul to time, as it were, measured what had been ineffable, actually captured the essential agent of mind in the toils of natural science" (p. 42).

This chapter focuses on developments in the measurement of some of those physiological and behavioral events that were regarded for centuries as ineffable and, hence, resistant to quantitative studies. The conceptual groundwork for the devel-

opment of new quantitive studies in physiology and behavior was reinforced, at least in part, by the growth of the mechanistic perspective. Hence, our story begins with early modern mechanistic philosophy. One of the most visible and influential representatives of the mechanistic perspective was the British philosopher, Thomas Hobbes.

THOMAS HOBBES

Thomas Hobbes (1588–1679) argued that the subject matter of philosophy is simply bodies in motion and that the goal of philosophy should be to employ the method of numerical comparison to assess magnitudes, distances, motions, and proportions. As noted by Peach (1982), Hobbes made extensive use of the mechanical model. Thus, "The heart is a spring, the nerves are strings, the joints are wheels giving motion to the whole body" (p. 840). Such a mechanical model opens the possibilities for the development of psychology as a science that promises to discover material and efficient causes.

Hobbes was born on April 5, 1588, a time when the English people were greatly troubled by rumors of the approach of the Spanish Armada. Rogow (1986) called attention to the fact that Hobbes's mother may also have been troubled about the predictions of certain biblical numerologists who had come to the conclusion that there would be great earth-shattering catastrophes exactly 1,588 years after the virgin birth. The young Hobbes was deeply

Thomas Hobbes

sensitive to the anxieties of his times and, as noted by Mintz (1962, p. 1), was plagued by fear of the dark, fear of death, and fear of persecution by his enemies. Yet for all his fear, Hobbes was such a fearless intellectual adventurer that he has been called the "Great Columbus of the Golden Lands of New Philosophies" (see Reik, 1977).

Hobbes was educated at Oxford, but had little interest in the scholastic curriculum. He earned his bachelor's degree when he was twenty years old and immediately accepted a position as tutor to Baron Hardwick, son of William Cavendish. As a tutor in a well-to-do family, Hobbes enjoyed good pay, access to libraries, travel, and considerable leisure. Aside from brief positions as Francis Bacon's secretary and tutor in the family of Sir Gervase Clinton, Hobbes was associated with the Cavendish family throughout his life. His masterpiece and one of his most important works from a psychological standpoint was *Leviathan,* published in 1651.

Hobbes was a contemporary of some of the greatest minds of the seventeenth century. Around 1635, he visited with Galileo, who may have been a major source of inspiration to extend the concept of motion to all aspects of natural philosophy. Hobbes corresponded with Descartes and quarreled with him about which of the two first

conceived of color as a secondary quality. Actually, Galileo had set forth the subjective nature of color prior to Descartes or Hobbes. Hobbes was also acquainted with such notable figures as Marin Mersenne, physicist and mathematician; John Bramhall, Bishop of Derry; and William Harvey, who discovered the circulation of the blood.

During his life and after his death, Hobbes was a highly controversial figure. He was regarded as a corrupter of morals partly because he spoke against biblical literalism, the authority of the pope, and all excessive reliance on authority. Despite the charges against him, those who knew Thomas Hobbes held him in high regard and defended him even when they disagreed with his philosophy. Hobbes died in 1679 at the age of ninety-one.

Like others of his day, Hobbes was deeply interested in the problem of human knowledge. He argued that knowledge has its origin in sensory impressions. Such impressions result from external physical movements that activate the sense organs. The sense organs in turn activate the brain via the nerves. Thus, bodies in motion in the external world set off motions in the sensory channels, and these set off motions in the brain. Ideas, or what Hobbes called phantasms, result from motions in the brain. Superficially, the emphasis on the sensorial origins of knowledge places Hobbes in the empirical tradition, but Hobbes defies easy classification as an empiricist because he argued that experience by itself is incapable of establishing anything universally (Hobbes, 1650/1962a, p. 18). Through experience we can have knowledge only of specific events, and such knowledge can hardly serve as an adequate basis for a science.

Tsanoff (1964) called attention to the fact that "Hobbes, like Bacon, demanded the fullest survey of the facts in order to apprehend their basic characteristics, but he sought demonstrative conclusions by strict deductions from evident principles" (p. 264). As noted by Matson (1982), the Hobbesian view of science is that it "is a body of organized knowledge, for which geometry provides both the model and the starting point" (p. 852). Hobbes's deep admiration for the method of geometry with its emphasis on axioms and deduction places him in the rationalist tradition. But Mintz

(1962, pp. 23–24) contended that Hobbes also represents a nominalist approach to knowledge. According to Hobbes, we begin with knowledge from the senses which provide information about many singular things such as houses, animals, vehicles, and the like. Through reason, we establish all-inclusive names and classification systems that provide order for specific experiences. According to Mintz (1962), "The truth which reason yields for Hobbes is the truth about words, not things; it is a hard truth to find because words are such notorious snares" (p. 25). Epistemologically, Hobbes represents a complicated combination of rationalism, nominalism, and empiricism. Fortunately, his ontology is more straightforward than his views on knowledge.

As noted at the outset, Hobbes was a thoroughgoing materialist. Whatever exists must have a material nature, and that includes God. A material God could, of course, serve as a first or efficient cause for the rest of material reality. But after serving as first cause, we find that Hobbes's mechanistic and materialist philosophy finds few remaining duties for a deity. There may be a place within such a philosophy for humans to honor God, but there is little real work left for God. Those who believe in a continuously active God have often raised questions about the seriousness of Hobbes's theism.

If the seriousness of Hobbes's theism could be called into question, there could be no question about the seriousness of his views on human nature. His views, set forth with unusual vigor and clarity, sent shock waves through the intellectual world. It is hardly surprising that Hobbes's major works were under constant attacks by Cambridge Platonists and by Catholics and Protestants. Zagorin (1968) noted, "In 1683 the University of Oxford condemned a number of his works to the flames" (p. 485).

Hobbes's views of human nature were derived from his materialist metaphysics and buttressed by the work of his friend William Harvey on the circulation of the blood. The centrality of motion in the physics of Galileo and Kepler and the physiology of Harvey were extended by Hobbes to psychology. As noted earlier, sensations and thoughts are to be understood in terms of motions in the sense organs and brain. But other psychological processes were also assumed to be based on movements that, in theory, are quantifiable. For example, "Feelings of pleasure and pain result from alterations in the vital motion of the body" (Watkins, 1965, p. 115). For Hobbes, psychological processes are completely dependent on a physical substrate; thus, the behavior of human beings can be understood on the basis of the same kind of quantitative science that Galileo had applied to the physical world.

Hobbes also assumed that basic human nature is governed by powerful drives toward self-interest and self-preservation. It is largely fear and awe of collective power that restrains us from inflicting our selfish interests on others. In *Leviathan*, Hobbes called attention to the idea that without a civil state there is always the danger of war of every one against every one (Hobbes, 1651/1962b, p. 113). But with a powerful state that holds us in awe, egoism is held in check. Because of the civil state, we can have invention, industry, culture, navigation, the arts, and knowledge. But without the civil state, we have, in Hobbes's words, "continual fear, and danger of violent death; and the life of man [is] solitary, poor, nasty, brutish, and short" (Hobbes, 1651/1962b, p. 113). Hobbes chides those readers who are shocked by his pessimism and asks them to consider whether they lock their doors when they sleep. He also reminds them that they probably secure their valuables and protect their children. He then argues that such actions betray the same accusations against humankind as do the words in his manuscript.

Hobbes's reduction of philosophy to the study of bodies in motion marks him as an important early figure in the history of psychology. Matson (1982) pointed out that "philosophy to Hobbes, is simply science" (p. 851). With such a view of philosophy, we encounter the possibility of a psychology uncompromised by dualistic or theological considerations. Hobbes is an especially key figure in the intellectual genealogy of behavioral psychologies and classic psychoanalytic psychology. In a broader sense, his views of human beings suggest the importance of physiological and social influences studied by the same quantitative methods that were proving so successful in the physical sciences.

RENÉ DESCARTES REVISITED

Like his contemporary Thomas Hobbes, René Descartes was obsessed with the problem of movement. But unlike Hobbes, Descartes was not content to restrict himself to philosophic inquiry. He wanted to understand the specific mechanisms responsible for movements in the living organism. Hence, he moved from the books to the laboratory and to the study of anatomy and physiology. Based on his observations, Descartes advanced provocative and testable theories about specific mechanisms of action. As we will see, most of his theories were wrong, but they stimulated other researchers and thus contributed to the advancement of physiological knowledge that was directly relevant to psychological questions.

In the previous chapter, we covered some of the details of Descartes's life and his epistemological work. We turn now to his physiological work with specific reference to the problem of movement. Descartes was well acquainted with pneuma concepts of movement dating back to Galen, but was not satisfied that such concepts provided an adequate account of the way things actually work. Perhaps the source of Descartes's dissatisfaction can be traced to the fact that, in his day, there were many mechanical inventions (toys, clocks, windmills, etc.) that were capable of intricate movements, all understandable quite simply in terms of material and efficient causation. An example of the intricate movements to which we refer was provided by Strandh (1979), who describes a fourteenth-century clock that was once on the Cathedral at Lund in Sweden: "Two medieval knights on the dome of the clock hourly exchange blows to the number of the hour. At twelve o'clock, after the twelfth blow, a hymn resounds from a mechanical trombone, a little door beside an image of the madonna opens, and the three kings from the East come out, followed by servants, and file, bowing, past the virgin Mary" (p. 51). If such an elaborate and intricate movement could be accomplished on a mechanical basis, could it be that animal and human movements might also be approached from a more natural or mechanistic rather than a vitalistic perspective? Perhaps the pneuma concepts of movement were wrong and we should now look to simpler explanations.

In his *Treatise on Man,* Descartes refers to moving statues that one might observe in grottoes and fountains erected in royal gardens in the seventeenth century. The statues, powered primarily by hydraulic force, served as a kind of model for Descartes's theory of bodily movement. The details of the model are difficult to decipher (see Popplestone, 1995), but at a minimum, it is clear that Descartes drew specific comparisons between nervous action and the water pipes that were involved in the movements of the statues. In an article entitled "The Problem of Animate Motion in the Seventeenth Century," Jaynes (1973) speculates about some of the possible details of the hydraulic model.

The discovery of the nerve cell would not come until the nineteenth century, but large nerve fibers (consisting of bundles of axons in a kind of conduit) were visible to the naked eye and had been identified from early times. Descartes believed that the nerve fibers, like the water pipes in the statues, were filled with fluids that served to activate muscles and tendons, the basic machinery of movement. In the case of the nerves, however, the fluids were highly refined and distilled from the finest elements of the blood. The blood also had been distilled from the finest elements of the digestive juices. Descartes referred to the fluids in the nerves as spirits or animal spirits. He argued that the spirits were composed of very small or fast-moving particles, which were likened to fine wind or a very pure and lively flame (Descartes, 1637/1985a, p. 138).

As noted by Jaynes (1973), Descartes believed "the nerve pipe fed into the muscle, and when the fluid came down, it billowed the muscle out like a balloon, and so made the limb move" (p. 171). In addition to the fluids in the nerves, Descartes believed there were extremely small threads running through the length of the nerves. The threads, when activated by a stimulus, triggered valves in the endings of the nerves in the ventricles of the brain. With the opening of the valves, the spirits stored in the ventricles were released to move through the nerves to the muscles. The belief in the threads and animal spirits may have been encouraged by the statues at St. Germaine, which moved by both mechanical and hydraulic action.

In his *Treatise on Man,* Descartes provided a specific example of how the machinery of the body functions in response to a simple stimulus. The sequence of events is illustrated in Figure 8.1. A fire (A) touching the skin (B) activates the tiny fiber or string (cd). The string simultaneously opens a valve in the ventricle of the brain. Animal spirits stored in (F) rush back to the foot, providing the force for its removal from the fire. Simultaneously, other animal spirits travel other routes to the eyes, hands, and trunk to contribute to the total response pattern away from the flame. All of this happens with near instantaneous speed. Indeed, the mechanical action of the thread is instantaneous. Descartes likened it to the pulling of a rope that rings a bell (Descartes, 1664/1985c, p. 101).

Descartes believed that many movements in humans and all movements in animals are of a purely mechanical or nonreflective nature. Thus, many movements have their origin in the senses that activate the so-called spirits in the ventricles of the brain and these in turn result in purely automatic actions. The automatic actions may include sighing, yawning, startle patterns, or more complex activities such as walking or eating. All of these activities are shared in common with the beasts and follow naturally from the actions of nerves, muscles, and senses "in the same way as the movement of a watch is produced merely by the strength of its spring and the configuration of its wheels" (Descartes, 1649/1985b, p. 335).

Descartes repeatedly referred to the body as a machine and to body parts, such as nerves, ventricles, muscles, and tendons, as analogous to pipes, storage tanks, springs, and wheels. He applied the mechanical-hydraulic explanation to all animal movement and to involuntary human movement. In his view, there was only a quantitative difference between animals and the moving statues. To be sure, animals, as God's creation, were better machines than those machines made by humans, and the superiority of animals to moving statues was manifested in the smoothness and complexity of

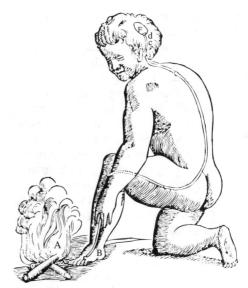

FIGURE 8.1 *Descartes's Model of the Reflex*

movements. But there were not qualitative differences between machines and animals. As noted by Jaynes (1973) "Animals were mere water statues, not conscious, not really living—machines without will or purpose or any feeling whatever. He dissected them alive (anesthetics were far off in the nineteenth century), amused at their cries and yelps since these were nothing but the hydraulic hisses and vibrations of machines" (p. 170). But if animal motion could be adequately explained by a mechanical-hydraulic model, why couldn't the same model be applied to human motion? That was a step Descartes was unable to take.

Descartes argued that, in the case of humans, God had united a rational soul to the physical machine (Descartes, 1664/1985c, p. 102). With characteristic intellectual courage, and trapped in the irresistible grip of curiosity about the mechanics of soul–body interaction, Descartes declared that "there is a little gland (the pineal gland) in the brain where the soul exercises its functions more particularly than in other parts of the body" (Descartes, 1649/1985b, p. 340). Descartes believed that the soul is joined to the whole body, but specific soul–body interactions take place in the pineal gland, which is single while so many other parts of the body are double. It was convenient that the pineal gland is located in the very center of the head. Descartes also believed, erroneously, that animals do not have pineal glands.

Descartes argued that the pineal gland is richly supplied with nerves that provide the basis for it to be influenced by the body and to influence the body. He pointed out, for example, "When the soul wants to remember something, this volition makes the gland lean first to one side and then to another, thus driving the spirits toward different regions of the brain until they come upon the one containing traces left by the object we want to remember" (Descartes, 1649/1985b, p. 344). When the spirits find the traces, the gland is informed and recognizes the stored information. The soul can also exercise will via the gland, but cannot in all cases have full control over the passions. The reason is that strong passions affect the heart and blood and animal spirits in such a violent way that the soul cannot prevent some movements. The soul is tied to the body and cannot exercise complete autonomy.

Thus, one may exercise will power to divert attention from a mild pain, but a strong pain so arouses the body that no amount of will power can divert attention from it. Only when the body returns to quiescence can the will again gain control. It follows that in some instances self-control is best assured by finding a circumstance that permits time for recovery from excess arousal. Thus the soul can exercise will, but the power of will is limited. In his treatise *The Passions of the Soul*, Descartes applied his model to an analysis of conflict situations and to the control of the passions.

Descartes's legacy in the quantification and mechanization of physiological and behavioral processes was set forth in provocative and testable theories about the mechanics of movement. He thus influenced the course of neurology and physiology long after his death. What were some of the testable theories? First, he argued that muscles are literally inflated by animal spirits; second, he tied the muscular system to the ventricles of the brain via the tiny threads or strings that he thought he observed in nerves; third, he ascribed both sensory and motor functions to the same nerve; fourth,

he spoke of some nervous transmission as being instantaneous or extremely fast; and fifth, an early concept of the reflex is clearly evident in his work. Finally, his speculations about the beast-machine, in the words of Rosenfield (1968), "became a fountainhead of inspiration for many years" (p. 64). Rosenfield's book *From Beast-Machine to Man-Machine* documents the war of ideas about animals and animal rights in the years following Descartes's death. The deep division between humans and animals envisioned by Descartes was an unwitting but intense stimulus for a range of intellectual activity from poetic celebration of animals to scientific investigations in comparative anatomy, physiology, and psychology (see King & Viney, 1992). Many of the studies and experiments to which we now turn were directly inspired by Descartes's provocative theories. His fame as Father of Modern Philosophy is secured as much by the empirical studies he inspired as by his original work on epistemology.

JAN SWAMMERDAM

One of the first tests of Descartes's theory of movement was conducted by Jan Swammerdam (1637–1680), a Dutch physician who is remembered largely for his expertise in entomology and respiration. Swammerdam devised a set of brilliant demonstrations that proved embarrassing to Descartes's notion that muscles are inflated by a flow of animal spirits from the brain. In his classic work *The Book of Nature* (1758), Swammerdam showed that a muscle with an attached nerve from a frog's leg will continue to contract even when separated from the body. This demonstration alone rules out the ventricles of the brain as a source of animal spirits. Swammerdam also demonstrated that the muscle continues to contract even after small cuts are introduced that separate some of the fibers. Swammerdam (1758) comments as follows: "Tho' the muscle be cut, and its moving fibers separated from each other, all these parts move again, as it were naturally, as soon as the nerve which belongs to them is irritated" (p. 124). Surely animal spirits should escape through the cuts and thus fail to inflate the muscle, if Descartes's theory were correct.

The most conclusive evidence against the idea that animal spirits literally inflate a muscle comes from a more complicated demonstration. Swammerdam prepared a cylinder that opened at the top into a narrow pipette, as illustrated in Figure 8.2. A piston with an attached brass wire with an eye hook was prepared so that it could be inserted into the bottom of the cylinder. A silver wire, also with an eye hook, was then passed through the eye of the brass wire. A frog's muscle with attached nerve was placed in the cylinder and the nerve was carefully passed through the eye of the silver wire. The other end of the silver wire passed along the side of the piston and out through the bottom of the cylinder. A drop of water is placed in the pipette and the silver wire is pulled to activate the nerve and the muscle. If the muscle grows in size when contracted, as predicted by Descartes's theory, the drop of water should be forced upward. The

water did not move upward; indeed, if anything, it dropped a bit. These results were clearly inconsistent with Descartes's prediction that a muscle is inflated by animal spirits.

Swammerdam (1758) concluded that at least no "sensible or comprehensive bulk flows through the nerves to the muscles. . . . From these experiments therefore, it may, I think be fairly concluded, that a simple and natural motion or irritation of the nerve alone is necessary to produce muscular motion whether it has origin in the brain, or in the marrow, or elsewhere" (p. 125).

Pubols (1959, p. 134) pointed out that Swammerdam anticipated the importance of the distinction between sensory and motor nerves and challenged the necessity of the distinction between voluntary and involuntary activity. A strong distinction between voluntary and involuntary activity had been central to Descartes's theory. In fairness, Descartes may also have realized the importance of a distinction between sensory and motor nerves, but also believed that individual nerves have both sensory and motor functions. Pubols pointed out that Swammerdam was far ahead of his time, both conceptually and methodologically. His work clearly demonstrated the importance of well-conceived experiments, and it paved the way for increased numbers of naturalistic studies on the measurement and mechanics of physiological and behavioral events.

NEILS STENSEN

Further critical comment on Descartes's speculations about the pineal gland came from Jan Swammerdam's friend Neils Stensen (1638–1680), sometimes called Nicolas Steno. Though Stensen had the greatest respect for Descartes's general philosophical method, he was nevertheless obliged to expose the anatomical errors of the great philosopher. Recall that Descartes had said that the pineal gland leans from one side to another and by such action drives the spirits toward various parts of the brain. Stensen argued that the pineal gland could not possibly lean from side to side. He also understood that the pineal gland is not richly supplied with nerves and, therefore, could not be implicated

FIGURE 8.2 *Swammerdam's nerve-muscle preparation demonstrating that a contracted muscle does not occupy more space than a relaxed muscle*

in complex cognitive functions. Finally, Stensen was aware of the fact that animals have pineal glands. With such a searching anatomical critique, another major building block in the Cartesian system was destroyed.

It is of interest that Stensen took no delight in attacking Descartes and, even in his criticisms, was careful to protect the memory of the philosopher. In a lecture delivered in Paris and published eighteen years after the death of Descartes, Stensen pointed out that all anatomists had made mistakes and that Descartes, though he had made mistakes, had gone beyond all his predecessors in attempting to give a complete account of all human and animal actions (see Fearing, 1970, p. 40). Yet the anatomical errors of Descartes and others had a profoundly disturbing effect on Stensen's beliefs. Scherez (1976) quoted from correspondence from Stensen to Leibniz: "If these gentlemen have been so mistaken with material things which are accessible to the senses, what warranty can they offer that they are not mistaken when they talk about God and the Soul?" (p. 33). That very question was undoubtedly on the lips of many people following the host of geographic and scientific discoveries that ushered in the modern era.

Because of the errors of the past, Stensen called for a new program of anatomical studies that would include less extravagant terminology (terms such as *animal spirits* were unacceptably vague), a more careful and detailed cataloging of anatomical parts, and greater conservatism with respect to assigning functions to anatomical structures. Though Stensen was friendly to the geometric method and to the rationalism of Descartes and Spinoza, he called for a more empirical science of anatomy that looked for structures and efficient causes.

STEPHEN HALES

McHenry (1969) pointed out that it was Stephen Hales (1677–1761) who first clearly demonstrated a spinal reflex. Unfortunately, Hales did not publish his experiment, but, according to McHenry, "Hales decapitated a frog and found that reflex movements of the hind leg could still be obtained by pricking the skin, and that the frog would hop about" (p. 112). Such a finding would hardly surprise anybody who has observed decapitation. Reflex activity remains for varying periods of time, depending on the ambient temperature and the species of animal (spinal reflexes remain for many hours or even days in some animals such as snakes or turtles). But Hales took another step and found that such activity disappears immediately if the spinal cord is destroyed. Hales's research demonstrated that some reflexes could be carried on without the brain but not without the spinal cord.

ROBERT WHYTT

Hales's experiment was replicated and subjected to closer scrutiny by Robert Whytt (1714–1766), who was probably the most accomplished neurophysiologist of his day. Whytt (*white*) received an M.A. in the arts from St. Andrews University in 1730. He studied medicine at Edinburgh, London, Paris, and Leiden and earned medical degrees from Rheims and St. Andrews. He practiced and taught medicine in Edinburgh and was named fellow of the college in 1737.

When Whytt repeated Hales's experiment, he ran a red-hot wire lengthwise through the spine of a decapitated frog. He noted that following this procedure "there is no sympathy between the different muscles or other parts of the body as was observed when the spinal marrow was entire" (McHenry, 1969, p. 114). Whytt also observed that some reflex actions remain if small segments of the spinal cord are left intact. Thus, many motions persist after removal of the brain, some motions still persist if small segments of the spinal cord are left intact following decapitation, but all motion stops when the entire spinal cord is destroyed. Based on his research, Whytt emphasized the idea that movement has its origin in the action of a stimulus that excites nervous activity. Herrnstein and Boring (1966), commenting on Whytt's work, remarked, "One can now perceive the essentials of the chain of events that ultimately established the reflex as a fundamental concept: a stimulus acts on nervous tissue, leading to a muscle movement whose magnitude is in some way proportional to the strength of the stimulus" (p. 283). Watson and Evans (1991) credited Whytt with introducing "the terms 'stimulus' and 'response'" (p. 248).

Whytt drew distinctions between voluntary and involuntary actions and actions based on habits, which he viewed as being somewhere between voluntary and involuntary actions. Among involuntary actions, he included digestive processes, coughing and sneezing, blushing, salivation, heart action, respiration, and pupillary reactions to changes in light. Because of his extensive research on pupillary dilation and contraction, the pupillary reflex is called *Whytt's reflex* (McHenry, 1969, p. 116). He emphasized the protective or adaptive nature of reflexes and anticipated the empirical findings that formed the foundation of nineteenth-century work on classical conditioning. Whytt, as quoted by Fearing (1970), noted that "the sight or even the recalled idea of grateful food, causes an uncommon flow of spittle into the mouth of a hungry person; and the seeing of a lemon cut produces the same effect in many people" (p. 80).

JOHANN AUGUST UNZER

Though Whytt did most of the intellectual spadework necessary for the development of the concept of the reflex, it was Johann August Unzer (1727–1799) who popularized the concept. Though Unzer's work was not highly original, it was systematic. According to Fearing (1970), "The concept of reflection seems firmly established in Unzer, and implies an element of necessity. The conversion of an afferent impulse into an efferent impulse by a mechanism of reflexion gives us a concept of reflex action which is adequate even in the modern sense" (p. 92). McHenry (1969) credited Unzer as "the first to employ the word *reflex* in connection with sensory-motor reactions" (p. 119). Clarke and O'Malley (1968) also noted that it was Unzer who introduced the terms **afferent,** meaning to move inward toward the central nervous system, and **efferent,** meaning to move outward toward the muscles or glands.

Unzer earned his M.D. degree from the University of Halle in 1748. He practiced medicine and conducted research, but is best remembered for his book *Principles of Physiology,* published in 1771. Unzer's interests in medicine were supplemented by philosophical interests, particularly on the nature of mind and consciousness. His work

on reflex action led him to a consideration of the relationship between consciousness and nervous activity. Was consciousness involved in all nervous activity or was consciousness a product only of high-level, integrated activities mediated by the brain?

Such questions were all the more salient in view of social circumstances that had aroused popular interest in the humanitarian considerations associated with various forms of capital punishment. In 1792, in France, the unfortunate thief Nicholas-Jacques Pelletier became the first victim of the famous new beheading machine named after its advocate, Dr. Joseph Ignace Guillotin (1738–1814). The public took a morbid interest in the new machine that was put to such widespread use, but there were questions about whether death by guillotine was really painless. Such questions were based partly on the idea that movement, regardless of its location, may represent some degree of consciousness. The violent thrashing following decapitation struck fear into curious spectators who speculated about whether such thrashing revealed consciousness of pain. Walker (1973) noted that "there were suggestions that the victims' heads responded after severance—Charlotte Corday's face was slapped [following decapitation] and [reportedly] showed annoyance" (p. 103). Popular curiosity about the locus of consciousness and sensitivity to pain undoubtedly stimulated scientific inquiry and Unzer was one of the first to address the issue.

Unzer pointed out that reflexes may be identical in decapitated and intact animals. He reasoned that if an impression moving toward the brain cannot reach its destination because of decapitation, it may nevertheless get turned around and follow an efferent path and produce the same motion that it would have produced had the animal been intact. But he argued that such reflexes in decapitated animals are unconscious and, therefore, there is no pain. Unzer believed that the conscious experience of pain is dependent on brain activity. Thus, the movements following decapitation are purely mechanical.

The pioneering work of Hales, Whytt, Unzer, and others paved the way for the development of the modern concept of the reflex. It was a concept that would play a major role in early psychological research and in various systematic psychologies, including the psychology of Pavlov and American behaviorism. The concept of the reflex was a central building block in the mechanistic viewpoint because it sharpened the distinction between voluntary and involuntary action. Many of the early physiologists denied that the soul plays any role in involuntary actions. We now turn to a philosophy in which we encounter an eighteenth-century mechanistic view that completes the picture initiated by Descartes.

JULIEN OFFRAY DE LA METTRIE

The French physician and philosopher Julien Offray de La Mettrie (*lah MEH tree*) (1709–1751) was one of the most important and thorough materialists of the eighteenth century. His book *Man a Machine* included human beings in the mechanistic program that had its beginnings in the work of Descartes.

La Mettrie was born in St. Malo, Brittany. He studied anatomy and medicine at the University of Paris and took his medical degree at Reims. He also studied under the great Dutch anatomist and physiologist Hermann Boerhaave (1668–1738). La Mettrie's most important book, *Man a Machine* (1747/1912), set forth such a deterministic, evolutionary, and mechanistic viewpoint that it created an outrage even in normally liberal Holland. As a result, La Mettrie moved to Berlin, where he attained some security through Frederick the Great and where he was honored by being named to the Royal Academy of Sciences. La Mettrie died at the age of forty-two of a violent fever apparently brought on by severe indigestion. Though his name was vilified by his enemies, his radical mechanistic thesis lived on as a continuing source both of inspiration and outrage.

La Mettrie argued that those things we regard as mental are completely dependent on the body. While he was in the French army, he once observed during a period of illness that the clarity of his thought corresponded to his body temperature. He also called attention to the close correspondence between brain injuries and mental capabil-

ities. He noted that we are more likely to be mentally healthy when we are physically healthy and that mental outlook suffers with physical debilitation. According to Vartanian (1967), La Mettrie saw the brain in terms of "the model of a 'thinking machine' into which sense perceptions feed ideas in the form of coded symbols that are, in turn, stored, classed, compared, and combined by the cerebral apparatus in order to engender all the known varieties of thought" (p. 381). With the work of La Mettrie the journey from beast machine to human machine is completed.

La Mettrie failed to find a qualitative gap between humans and animals. He believed that the possession of language marks us as human, but even here he was not convinced of our uniqueness. As noted by Rosenfield (1968), "Could they [the apes] but be taught language, he [La Mettrie] suggested—and the task would not be too difficult—they would be identical with primitive man" (p. 146).

La Mettrie, was, of course, a thoroughgoing determinist. Judges who pass sentences on human beings should be replaced by intelligent doctors who look for causal connections and ways to heal. Society must be protected from those who are ill or not well socialized, but punishment as retribution makes little sense. La Mettrie believed that happiness and health are the supreme goals of medicine and philosophy. Old notions of sin and evil, vice and virtue, must be replaced with more scientific concepts. La Mettrie was a major figure in the intellectual genealogy of behaviorism, reflexology, cybernetics, and information processing approaches to human behavior. As noted, his work represents the logical extension of Descartes's animal-machine model. The move toward a quantitative-mechanical approach to life finds its boldest and most complete expression in the work of La Mettrie.

PIERRE JEAN GEORGES CABANIS

La Mettrie's mechanistic vision was echoed in the thought of the influential French physician Pierre Jean Georges Cabanis (*Kah bah NEEZ*) (1757–1808). Physician to Comte de Mirabeau, Cabanis was a friend of many of the important intellectuals of his day, including Condillac, Condorcet, and deTracy. He was also acquainted with Benjamin Franklin and Thomas Jefferson. Like La Mettrie, Cabanis emphasized the close connections between psychological processes and organismic and environmental influences. According to Cabanis, psychology must be understood in a naturalistic context because psychological processes such as memory, intelligence, and sensation are products of neurological activity. Cabanis also emphasized the connections between external environmental events and behavior. Following the philosophic work of La Mettrie and Cabanis, there was a growing interest in the exploration of the nervous system for its own sake and as a key to understanding psychological processes.

MAPPING THE CENTRAL AND PERIPHERAL NERVOUS SYSTEMS

In the early nineteenth century, there was growing optimism about the possibility of discovering the neurophysiological basis of mental and physical functions. Such optimism was an important precursor to the founding of a formal science of psychology. The methodological tools of science were now to be employed in the search for the soul or the mind. As in the case of most scientific discoveries, there were many false starts, but, as is also often the case, some of the false starts proved to be productive.

Localization of Function

A major breakthrough in the mapping of the nervous system came with the discovery of the sensory and motor tracts in the spinal column. In a series of independent experiments, Sir Charles Bell (1774–1842) of England and François Magendie (1783–1855) of France demonstrated that the ventral or anterior roots of the spinal column influence muscular contraction. Though Bell was first to make the discovery, a fact acknowledged by Magendie, Bell's initial experiment established only the motor function of the ventral root. Magendie's experiments clearly established the sensory functions of the dorsal or posterior root and

the motor functions of the ventral or anterior roots. Though there were bitter controversies over priority, the discovery, one of the most important in physiology, is now appropriately called the *Bell-Magendie Law.*

Sir Charles Bell. Sir Charles Bell attended school in Edinburgh and studied anatomy with an older brother who was a surgeon. In 1804, Bell established residence in London where he served as principal lecturer at the Great Windmill Street School of Anatomy. Bell worked in London until 1836, when he returned to Edinburgh University as professor of surgery. His best-known book is *Idea of a New Anatomy of the Brain,* published in 1811. In addition to his work on sensory and motor tracts, Bell is remembered for his unusual gifts as an anatomical artist; his discovery of the thoracic nerve, which goes by his name; and his analysis of facial paralysis (Bell's palsy) resulting from injury to the seventh cranial nerve.

Sensory and motor functions of the nervous system had been appreciated from the days of Aristotle, but the first experimental work on the topic was outlined by Bell in a letter to his brother. An excerpt from the letter, as quoted by McHenry (1969, p. 183), is as follows:

> *Experiment 1.* I opened the spine and pricked and injured the posterior filaments of the nerve—no motion of the muscles followed. I then touched the anterior division—immediately the parts were convulsed.

> *Experiment 2.* I now destroyed the posterior part of the spinal marrow by the point of a needle—no convulsive movements followed. I injured the anterior part and the animal was convulsed.

François Magendie. François Magendie (*muh zhon DEE*), the son of a surgeon, was born in Bordeaux, France. He was reared according to the liberal precepts outlined by Rousseau in his famous book *Emile.* Though he did not start school until age ten, he progressed so rapidly that by age sixteen he was hired as an assistant in a Paris hospital to conduct anatomical dissections. When he was twenty years old, he was accepted as a medical student and he received his medical degree at age twenty-five. Magendie worked briefly on the medical faculty of Paris, but because of interpersonal difficulties he set up a private practice. He also provided private instruction in anatomy and physiology. In 1821, he was honored with elections to the Royal Academy of Medicine and the Academy of Sciences.

Magendie must be considered one of the major pioneers of modern experimental physiology. He founded a publication outlet called *Journal of Experimental Physiology* and argued persistently for empirical studies that place emphasis on facts derived from well-controlled experiments. In addition to his neurological contributions, Magendie made extensive contributions to the understanding of the physiology of digestion. Grmek (1974) also pointed out that "Magendie introduced into medical practice a series of recently discovered alkaloids: strychnine, morphine, brucine, codeine, quinine, and veratrine. He also generalized the therapeutic use of iodine and bromine salts" (p. 9).

Magendie, less hampered by animal rights activists in France than Bell was in England, was able to conduct vivisection experiments that more definitely established the motor and sensory roots of the spinal column. Magendie developed techniques that permitted him to sever the anterior roots without disturbing the posterior roots. Using several species of animals he systematically severed anterior and posterior roots one at a time and in combination. The results clearly revealed that severing the anterior roots interferes with movement and severing the posterior roots interferes with sensation. Severing both results in loss of sensation and movement.

The discovery of the separation of the sensory and motor functions of the spinal roots undoubtedly contributed to the idea that other nerve channels are highly specialized. Indeed, an early statement on specific energies of nerves was set forth by Sir Charles Bell in 1811, but the doctrine of specific energies, implying radical qualitative separation of the various senses, was most clearly elaborated by the great German physiologist Johannes Müller.

Johannes Müller.   Along with Sir Charles Bell and François Magendie, Johannes Müller (1801–1858)

is one of the great pioneers in modern experimental physiology. Müller, born on July 14, 1801, in Coblenz, Germany, was a gifted student with excellent work habits combined with unusual curiosity and ambition. In 1818, he enrolled as a student at the University of Bonn and earned his medical degree in 1822. Following further studies in anatomy in Berlin, Müller returned to Bonn where he taught comparative anatomy, physiology, and pathology. By 1830, Müller was full professor with a comfortable salary. In 1833, he moved to Berlin University as professor of anatomy and physiology. He was married to Nanny Zeiller and they had two children, Maria and Max. Müller is best remembered for his massive *Handbuch der Physiologie des Menschen* (1833–1840), which, according to MacLeod (1968a), became "The standard reference work for physiologists throughout Europe" (p. 525). Though Müller was highly productive and acclaimed, he nevertheless suffered recurring, lengthy, and incapacitating bouts of depression, clearly aggravated by his work pace and the excessive and exacting demands he made of himself. The magnitude of Müller's influence is illustrated by Steudel (1974), who stated, "Almost all German scientists who achieved fame after the middle of the nineteenth century considered themselves his students" (p. 568).

Müller's interests in anatomy and physiology were very broad, but our focus here will be on his work on the neurophysiology of the senses. Strongly influenced by Sir Charles Bell, Müller elaborated on the doctrine of **specific energies of nerves** in his *Handbuch,* where he argued that, for each of the five senses, there is a "specific nerve energy" such that the nerve itself imposes the quality of sensation on mental processes. According to Müller, a nerve is capable of transmitting one and only one kind of sensation. Thus, no matter how the nerve is stimulated it will transmit *only* its quality of sensation. For example, pressure on the eye will result in a visual sensation, whereas pressure or a blow to the ear will result in auditory sensations such as ringing. It follows that one nerve could not substitute for another. Indeed, Boring (1950) noted that Emil du Bois-Reymond, one of Müller's students, "went so far as to say that, were it possible to cross-connect the auditory and optic nerves, we ought to see sounds with out ears and hear light with our eyes" (p. 93).

The influence of the doctrine of specific energies was not limited to physiology. The philosophical implication was that knowledge itself is conditioned by the sense organs. Elaborating on the point, Boring (1950), pointed out, "The central and fundamental principle of the doctrine is that we are directly aware, not of objects, but of our nerves themselves; that is to say, the nerves are intermediates between perceived objects and the mind and thus impose their own characteristics upon the mind" (p. 82). Such a doctrine represents another important step in the transition from vitalism to mechanism because it ties the mind to the machinery of the body.

Müller's doctrine was one of the most widely accepted physiological doctrines of the early nineteenth century and, as such, shaped the direction of many later physiological and psychological theories. The doctrine was quickly extended to the idea that there are specific nerve fiber energies corresponding to various psychological qualities. Thus, Thomas Young and Hermann von Helmholtz suggested that there are three different optical fibers for the primary colors (see Herrnstein & Boring, 1966, pp. 40–44). Helmholtz also suggested that there are thousands of specific auditory energies corresponding to each discriminable tone. Other investigators extended the idea of specific energies to other sensory modalities, resulting in the belief that each elementary sense quality was associated with specific nerve fibers. By 1896, the youthful Edward Bradford Titchener calculated a kind of psychological table of elements that included thousands of visual and auditory qualities. Titchener found far fewer qualities associated with the other senses (e.g., four taste qualities and four skin qualities), but his total number of elementary qualities for all senses was formidable.

The doctrine of specific energies shaped early psychological thought in many other ways. For example, it suggested a radical isolation of the senses from each other. According to Helmholtz, the sense qualities were so heterogeneous that there were no meaningful transitions from one to another. Thus, questions such as whether "sweet is more like blue or red, can simply not be asked"

(Helmholtz, 1896, p. 584). Though there were later challenges to the concept that the sense qualities have nothing in common with each other (e.g., see Hartshorne, 1934; Köhler, 1947; Viney, 1991), such a view prevailed in mainstream psychology for a long time. The doctrine of specific energies was also consistent with nineteenth-century faculty psychologies, including phrenology.

Gall and Spurzheim: A Productive False Start. A German anatomist, physiologist, and physician, Franz Joseph Gall (1758–1828), developed the conviction that mental functions and personality characteristics are located in specific areas of the brain. Further, he assumed that the surface of the skull conforms to the relative development of regions of the brain associated with intellectual and personal abilities or deficiencies as shown in Figure 8.3 (Sizer & Drayton, 1892). Thus, a given indentation or protrusion in a specific location on the surface of the head was considered evidence for the relative development of the corresponding part of the brain that lies immediately beneath that location. Gall and his student Johann Kaspar Spurzheim (1776–1832), worked out elaborate charts designed as guides to the assessment of intellectual abilities and personality characteristics based on the shape of the head. Originally, Gall referred to his techniques for measuring the skull as cranioscopy. Later, however, under the leadership of Spurzheim, the theory and measurement techniques were called **phrenology,** meaning science of the mind.

From the outset, phrenology was highly controversial among scientists and professionals. It was also offensive to many religious and political leaders. Indeed, Gall was forced out of Vienna and his works were banned shortly after the turn of the nineteenth century. Scientists were justifiably suspicious of Gall's methodology while religious and political leaders were concerned with the moral implications of a theory that emphasized the role of natural causes in human experience and behavior. Although phrenology was controversial in some circles, it nevertheless enjoyed great popularity in much of Western Europe and the United States. There were phrenology societies, popular lectures, journals, and practitioners

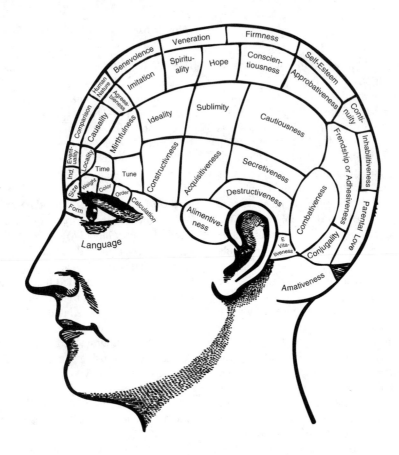

1. AMATIVENESS.—Connubial love, affection.
A. CONJUGAL LOVE.—Union for life, pairing instinct.
2. PARENTAL LOVE.—Care of offspring, and all young.
3. FRIENDSHIP.—Sociability, union of friends.
4. INHABITIVENESS.—Love of home and country.
5. CONTINUITY.—Application, consecutiveness.
E. VITATIVENESS.—Clinging to life, tenacity, endurance.
6. COMBATIVENESS.—Defence, courage, criticism.
7. DESTRUCTIVENESS.—Executiveness, push, propelling power.
8. ALIMENTIVENESS.—Appetite for food, etc.
9. ACQUISITIVENESS.—Frugality, economy, to get.
10. SECRETIVENESS.—Self-control, policy, reticence.
11. CAUTIOUSNESS.—Guardedness, care-taking, safety.
12. APPROBATIVENESS.—Love of applause and display.
13. SELF-ESTEEM.—Self-respect, dignity, authority.
14. FIRMNESS.—Stability, perseverance, steadfastness.
15. CONSCIENTIOUSNESS.—Sense of right, justice.
16. HOPE.—Expectation, anticipation, perfect trust.
17. SPIRITUALITY.—Intuition, presence, faith.
18. VENERATION.—Worship, adoration, deference.
19. BENEVOLENCE.—Sympathy, kindness, mercy.

20. CONSTRUCTIVENESS.—Ingenuity, invention, tools.
21. IDEALITY.—*Taste,* love of beauty, poetry and art.
B. SUBLIMITY.—Love of the grand, vast, magnificent.
22. IMITATION.—Copying, aptitude for mimicry.
23. MIRTH.—Fun, wit, ridicule, facetiousness.
24. INDIVIDUALITY.—Observation, curiosity to see.
25. FORM.—Memory of *shape,* looks, persons, things.
26. SIZE.—Measurement of quantity by the eye.
27. WEIGHT.—Control of motion, balancing.
28. COLOR.—Discernment, and love of colors, hues, tints.
29. ORDER.—*Method,* system, going by *rule,* arrangement.
30. CALCULATION.—Mental arithmetic, numbers.
31. LOCALITY.—Memory of place, position, travels.
32. EVENTUALITY.—Memory of facts, events, history.
33. TIME.—Telling *when,* time of day, dates, punctuality.
34. TUNE.—Love of music, sense of harmony, singing.
35. LANGUAGE.—*Expression* by words, signs or acts.
36. CAUSALITY.—*Planning,* thinking, philosophy.
37. COMPARISON.—Analysis, inferring, illustration.
C. HUMAN NATURE.—Sagacity, perception of motives.
D. SUAVITY.—*Pleasantness,* blandness, politeness.

FIGURE 8.3 *Phrenological Chart*

who provided diagnostic services and advice on personal growth and development. Many physicians interested in psychiatric problems employed the methods of phrenology.

Phrenology is an example of a productive false start in the modern quest for an understanding of the nature of the relationship between the mental and physical worlds. There can be little question that the work of Gall and Spurzheim mobilized other scientists to investigate the problem of the localization of function. Further, and equally important, phrenology helped shape public opinion regarding the central role of the brain in intellectual and personal arenas. Although flawed methodologically and substantively, phrenology contributed to the growing climate of opinion that there could be a science of human nature (Sokal, 2001).

Pierre Flourens. Some of the earliest and most credible scientific evidence against phrenology grew out of the experimental work of the French physiologist Pierre Jean Marie Flourens (*flew RAHNS*) (1794–1867). Although trained in medicine, Flourens decided to devote himself to research in neurophysiology. His highly distinguished scientific career resulted in many honors, including election to the French Academy of Sciences.

Flourens studied brain function by employing the method of ablation, which consists of surgical removal or isolation of specific structures in order to assess functions. He found that respiratory functions are located in the medulla oblongata, that muscular coordination is mediated by the cerebellum, and that perceptual and intellectual functions are located in the cerebrum. Although he recognized some degree of localization of function, Flourens argued that the various parts of the brain such as the cerebrum function as a whole. He found no evidence in favor of the contention of the phrenologists that there are highly specific regions of the brain and corresponding cranial protrusions associated with specific intellectual or personal attributes. On the contrary, his work suggested that the brain is more like a large interconnected network of activity. His work implied that there is considerable plasticity in the brain and that, within limits, some parts

of the brain might be able to take over for other injured parts.

Flourens is remembered for many other achievements in science. He discovered the anesthetic properties of chloroform shortly after such properties had been demonstrated for ether and for nitrous oxide. His research led to an understanding of the role of the semicircular canals in equilibrium. He was also well known as a biographer of well-known scientists. His studies with the method of ablation had a lasting influence on the development of neurophysiology.

Paul Broca. Flourens successfully challenged the claim of the phrenologists that intellectual and personal abilities are located in specific localized regions of the brain. Now it remained for another French physician to demonstrate the possibility that some functions are localized within specific regions of the brain. Paul Broca (1824–1880), like Flourens, was a highly versatile and eminent physician-scientist with broad-ranged interests. Indeed, he is often considered one of the founders of modern physical anthropology. He was also elected to the French Senate as a representative for science. Broca published in many fields of medicine, including anatomy, pathology, and surgery.

Broca is best known for his discovery that the anatomical location for articulate, or spoken, speech is in a small region of the left frontal lobe—the inferior frontal gyrus. Broca performed an autopsy on a patient who had been unable to speak. The patient had been intelligent and had communicated by other means. Further, the patient had shown no evidence of motor impairment that might be responsible for the speech deficiency. Broca's autopsy revealed lesions in the left frontal convolution—an area subsequently known as *Broca's area.* Broca correctly concluded that this region of the brain played a vital role in the production of speech. By 1874, the German neurologist and psychiatrist Carl Wernicke (1848–1905) showed that damage to the posterior third of the superior left temporal gyrus interferes with speech comprehension. This region was later named *Wernicke's area.* Although Broca's clinical method was not rigorous by scientific standards, it was far more credible than methods employed by the phrenologists. Broca's discovery was embarrassing to phrenology on two counts—the methodology was superior and the speech area was not located in the front of the head as proclaimed by the phrenologists. Broca's discovery also weakened the claims of Flourens by demonstrating that some functions within specific regions of the brain are localized.

Extending the Powers of Observation

Progress in understanding nature inevitably follows the development of new ways of seeing the world. For example, new instruments such as the telescope, X-rays, and microscope contributed immeasurably to human powers of observation and to the evolution of scientific methodology. Much of our progress in mapping the nervous system has depended on the development of new observational techniques.

Fritsch and Hitzig.   In 1870, German physicians and physiologists Gustav Theodor Fritsch (1838–1927) and Julius Eduard Hitzig (1838–1907) collaborated on a classic paper on the electrical stimulation of the cortex. Their paper helped establish the field of electrophysiology and their research findings provided a major breakthrough in our understanding of the problem of the localization of function. Fritsch and Hitzig demonstrated that small electrical currents applied to specific regions of the cortex of a dog produced highly reliable movements on the side of the body that is opposite of the source of stimulation. It is now well understood that damage to specific regions on the right side of the brain results in the loss of motor functions on the left side of the body, and vice versa. The work of Fritsch and Hitzig provided additional evidence in favor of localization of function though their substantive findings did not support the specific claims of the phrenologists. More importantly, electrical stimulation of the brain, pioneered by Fritsch and Hitzig, has been refined and remains as a powerful methodological tool in the neurosciences. According to Clark (1972), Hitzig influenced psychology in another way. He was a powerful advocate of a more scientific approach to the study of emotional prob-

lems, and he was influential in calling for more humane treatment for psychiatric patients.

Camillo Golgi and Santiago Ramón y Cajal.   Another example of the importance of new observational techniques in the study of nature is provided by the work of the Italian pathologist and histologist Camillo Golgi (*GOHL gee*) (1843–1926). Because of their fine structure and embeddedness in other tissue, nerve elements are extremely difficult to observe, even with a microscope. Golgi provided a highly original approach to the problem by developing a staining procedure that still bears his name and that enhances the features of nerve elements. The Golgi stain clearly revealed for the first time some of the central features of the fine anatomy of nerve cells.

Santiago Ramón y Cajal (1852–1934), a Spanish physician, histologist, and anatomist, was one of the first to employ and refine Golgi's staining methods in the study of the fine structure of the nervous system. Ramón y Cajal (*ro MOHN ee ka HALL*) discovered the anatomical gap between nerve cells, and he understood that transmission proceeds from the synapse to the axon. His extensive productive research and his prolific publication record establish him as the central figure in the discovery of the modern theory of the neuron. In 1906, the Nobel prize was shared by Golgi and Ramón y Cajal for their extensive contributions to our understanding of the anatomy of the nervous system.

Sir Charles Sherrington.   The work of pioneers such as Flourens, Fritsch, Hitzig, Golgi, and Ramón y Cajal had provided important new study methods and substantive knowledge about the nervous system, but the knowledge was highly fragmented and disjointed. The most comprehensive and integrative work on the structural and functional properties of the nervous system came from the research of the English neurophysiologist Sir Charles Sherrington (1857–1952). In 1906, Sherrington published a monumental work entitled *The Integrative Action of the Nervous System*. This book, more than any other, laid the foundations for modern neurophysiology. Sherrington's work did for neurophysiology what Newton's *Principia* did for classical physics. Indeed, Sherrington's book has been called the *Principia of Physiology,* because it defined the field and set the stage for future work. Sherrington is remembered, among other things, for coining many of the common terms employed in the neurosciences (e.g., *synapse, prorioceptive, neuron pool, neuron threshold, nociceptive*), for mapping a variety of neural pathways, and for his extensive investigations on the integrative work of the reflexes.

It is seldom appreciated that a simple task such as standing upright involves an extremely complicated network of reflex activities carried on without conscious awareness. Thus, reflexes are not necessarily isolated or discreet events, but are integrated in an adaptive fashion with ongoing routine activities. Sherrington identified what was then a new type of receptor that detects information in the interior of the muscles and the joints. He referred to information from such receptors as *proprioception.* He showed that the role of proprioception in complex motor activities often involves a kind of reciprocity. Thus, when one set of muscles is stimulated, another antagonistic set may be automatically inhibited. Following the work of Sherrington there was a much greater appreciation for the complexity and the integrative activity of reflexes. There was also a deeper appreciation for the role of reflexes in "higher nervous functions" though, as noted by Swazey (1975), Sherrington resisted reductionism. Thus, "the physical is never anything but physical, or the psychical anything but psychical" (Swazey, 1975, p. 401). Nevertheless, Sherrington believed that the two domains are complementary and integrative, and he received many honors throughout his long and productive career. In 1932, he was awarded the Nobel prize in recognition of his pioneering work on the nervous system.

Speed of a Nervous Impulse

We noted earlier that Descartes believed that the pulling of the thread running the length of the nerve resulted in the instantaneous release of animal spirits. Following Descartes, it was commonly assumed

that the rate of nervous transmission was instantaneous, or at least comparable to the speed of light. Johannes Müller believed that nervous transmission was so fast as to be unmeasurable, but Müller's student, Hermann von Helmholtz, initiated a laboratory investigation that laid to rest still another Cartesian doctrine. Helmholtz's method was fairly simple. A myograph, invented by Helmholtz, consisted essentially of a rolling chart recorder. The recorder, moving at a known rate, registered the action of a stimulus and a response. With the myograph, Helmholtz was able to record the time lag between stimulation of a nerve and muscle contraction. Next Helmholtz stimulated the nerve at a point far from the muscle and then at a point near the muscle. The difference in contraction time between the far and near points divided by the distance between points yielded a measure of velocity. The rate of transmission calculated by this method was surprisingly slow. Times ranged from 50 to 100 meters per second, so the velocity that was supposed to have been close to the speed of light was not even as fast as the speed of sound. What is important about Helmholtz's work is not the speed of the nervous impulse per se but that another important physiological process had been captured by scientific technique and quantified.

By mid-nineteenth century, there was a heady optimism in many scientific circles about the ascendance of materialistic philosophy and the appropriateness of that philosophy to a science of human nature. The new optimistic spirit was captured dramatically by several of Johannes Müller's students, who apparently took an oath on the proposition that there are no forces in the living organism except those of a physical-chemical nature (see Wertheimer, 1987, pp. 46–47).

Thus, faith in the quantitative methods of science was complete, at least in the minds of such key nineteenth-century luminaries as Hermann von Helmholtz, Emil DuBois-Reymond, Karl Ludwig, and Ernst Brücke. All that remained was to apply quantitative methods systematically to the entire range of the life sciences. We were on the threshold of a science of psychology. Specific quantitative methods, so successful in physiology, were now needed in the larger realm of behavior. Such methods were already surfacing in the work of scientists devoted to the study of probability theory.

Measuring Behavior

What has sometimes been labeled the *origin myth* is nowhere better illustrated than in probability theory and statistics. What was the origin of the science of statistics? Some of the activities described by the term **statistics** date to early times. The term itself comes from a Latin root meaning "state." Political facts and figures, including population and census data, have always been associated with the term statistics, but political facts and figures per se fall short of the mark concerning statistical theory and method. Hence, it is erroneous to view statistics as having originated in early census activities.

Strong origin claims might come from the pioneers of dicing and gaming. Games of chance date to early times, and those who worked on the laws of chance provided an important step in the direction of the development of modern statistics. Among the best known early modern pioneers in probability theory were Blaise Pascal (1623–1662), a French scientist-philosopher; and Galileo Galilei (1564–1642), a famous Italian astronomer-physicist. Galileo worked on the probabilities of obtaining given numbers associated with throws of dice. For example, we all know that in the throw of two dice, the number 12 is less likely than, say, the number 8. The reason is that there is only one way to obtain 12; both dice must fall so as to display the number 6. But the number 8 can come about in a number of ways; 4 and 4, 3 and 5, and 2 and 6. Galileo was one of the first to calculate probabilities in games involving dice.

Pascal also made many contributions to the formalization of probability theory. His work, along with the work of other early probability theorists, provided a means for making educated predictions within arenas characterized by uncertainty. Such thinking makes it possible to discover that there are lawlike principles behind irregularities and uncertainties.

The derivation of the well-known symmetrical bell-shaped curve is surely one of the most important developments in the science of statistics. The original derivations were set forth in 1733 by the French mathematician Abraham DeMoivre (1667–1754). The other names associated with the development of the curve are Pierre Simon de Laplace (1749–1827) and Carl Friedrich Gauss (1777–1855). The curve is typically called the *Gaussian curve,* or sometimes the *normal curve.*

Jacques Quételet.   The original work of Gauss and Laplace on the Gaussian curve was on human errors of observation, but it remained for a Belgian mathematician and astronomer to see the wider applications of the so-called normal curve, Lambert Adolphe Jacques Quételet (*kat LUH*) (1796–1874) is one of the most underestimated figures in the history of psychology. Tylor (1872) claimed that two broad contributions to "physiological and mental science" can be attributed to Quételet. First, according to Tylor (1872, p. 45), Quételet

> has been for many years the prime mover in introducing the doctrine that human actions, even those usually considered most arbitrary, are in fact subordinate to general laws of human nature. . . ; second, he has succeeded in bringing the idea of a biological type or specific form, whether in bodily structure or mental faculty, to a distinct calculable conception, which is likely to impress on future arguments a definiteness not previously approached.

If individual behavior appears at times to be arbitrary or even capricious, such behavior could nevertheless be shown to participate in overall patterns that display amazing regularity. What impressed Quételet was the remarkable orderliness between variables such as age and criminal activity. Quételet found far more thefts committed by those in the twenty-one to twenty-five age group than by those between ages thirty-five and forty. Such a relationship between biological and ethical dimensions of behavior suggested important hidden causal links. Quételet also showed that there are lawlike relationships between literacy level and crime, age of offender and type of crime, time of day and frequency of suicide attempts, and type of crime and sex of offender. On the issue of literacy level and crime, Quételet showed in one of his studies that 61 percent of those accused of various crimes in France in 1828–1829 could not read or write, 27 percent could read or write imperfectly, and 12 percent could read or write well or had superior education (Quételet, 1842/1968, p. 85). Quételet believed that such a finding implicates society at large and suggested the possibility of a causal link between illiteracy and criminal activity.

Quételet did extensive studies on the physical characteristics of human beings. Chest measurements, height, weight, grip strength (measured with a hand dynamometer), heart rate (relative to age peers), respiration, and length of leap were among the physical characteristics he studied. He also investigated mortality statistics and medical epidemiology. He found not only that many physical qualities are distributed in terms of the familiar bell-shaped curve but also that moral or psychological qualities are often distributed in exactly the same way. Hence, there are regularities in nature that were heretofore unsuspected—regularities that suggested the possibility of a new science. Tylor (1872) pointed out that with Quételet's work we have "the introduction of scientific evidence into problems over which theologians and moralists have long claimed jurisdiction" (p. 49).

One of Quételet's more celebrated concepts is that of the *homme moyen,* which is typically translated as the "average man." The important point is that there is a central type in every population and that variation around that central type is lawful. Most people tend to cluster close to the average, and departures on either side of the average occur with decreasing frequency. The practical benefits of Quételet's quantitative work are immediately obvious. For example, accurate mortality statistics are useful to the insurance industry, and extensive knowledge of the physical characteristics of a population makes feasible the mass production of clothes.

The practical consequences of Quételet's work were important, but the theoretical consequences were even more so. Quételet (1842/1968) spoke of the importance of determining "the period at which memory, imagination, and judgments commence, and the stages through which they successively pass in their progress to maturity; then, having established the maximum point, we may extend our inquiries to the law of their decline" (p. 74). Quételet suggested experiments that could

be done on memory, and asserted his belief in its lawfulness and its relationship to age. He also believed that reason and imagination could be approached scientifically and cautioned that "we can only appreciate faculties by their effects; in other words, by the actions or works which they produce" (Quételet, 1842/1968, pp. 74–75). Quételet provided the intellectual foundation for a scientific developmental psychology and a scientific psychology of individual differences. His importance in the development of statistics is undisputed, but he occupies an equally important position in the intellectual ancestry of psychology. As much as any other, he advanced the idea that behavior can be measured and thus added to the scientific domain.

Sir Francis Galton. Gould (1981, p. 75) remarked, "No man expressed his era's fascination with numbers so well as Darwin's celebrated cousin, Francis Galton." Galton's fascination might even be viewed as an obsession that was fueled by the belief that "there is no bodily or mental attribute . . . which cannot be gripped and consolidated into an ogive with a smooth outline" (Galton, 1883/ 1907, p. 36). As we will see, Galton's enthusiasm for measurement sometimes ran ahead of his better judgment. For example, his interpretations of racial and gender attributes were based on inadequate data and reflected prevailing prejudices. He nevertheless made significant contributions to the theory and practice of measurement and to the psychological study of individual differences. His contributions had important implications for the development of a science of psychology.

Sir Francis Galton (1822–1911) was born in England, in the vicinity of Birmingham. He came from a family of great wealth and, because of a sizable inheritance, was able to pursue any interest of his choice. For a time, he studied medicine, but he interrupted his medical training in favor of a more general liberal arts degree. While in his third year at Cambridge University, he suffered an emotional breakdown. His health problems contributed to his failure to take an honors degree in mathematics, but he did eventually complete a degree at Cambridge. Though Galton returned to medical school in London following his work at Cambridge, he never

Sir Francis Galton

completed his medical training. His enthusiasm for medicine had always been mixed. Except for his unusual intellectual appetite, Galton might have lived a quiet life of leisure, enjoying his wealth. But he had been stimulated by his medical training and his liberal education, and was thus incapable of resisting intellectual exploration.

Following his formal schooling, Galton traveled extensively in Africa and the Middle East. He led an exploration into the interior of Africa and produced some of the first accurate maps of parts of central southwest Africa. Because of his contribution to geography, the Royal Geographical Society awarded him a gold medal and later made him a Fellow.

In 1853, Galton married Louisa Butler, who was from a family distinguished for its academic and intellectual achievements. Galton enjoyed new family ties with scholarly inlaws and he maintained contacts in London with the leading scientists of his day. He enjoyed correspondence with his cousin Charles Darwin and often visited with Admiral Fitzroy, who had been captain of the *H.M.S. Beagle* on Darwin's voyage. Galton settled into an enthusiastic work routine that was to result in a remarkably productive career. His bibliography of popular and scholarly publications has well over three hundred entries on a wide range of topics.

Partly because of his travels, Galton developed a keen interest in the weather and became one of the pioneers of meteorology. He drew some of the first weather maps and discovered the importance of low- and high-pressure gradients in weather prediction. He had strong interests in scientific instrumentation as well as skill as an inventor of instruments. For example, he developed an improved heliostat for flashing signals on sunny days, proposed a printing telegraph, and improved several meteorological instruments (see Forrest, 1974, p. 294). Galton was also a pioneer in the use of fingerprinting as a means of identification. Galton is best known, however, for the development of new statistical techniques with wide application to psychological topics. Before turning to some of Galton's specific contributions to measurement theory and practice, let us briefly characterize what has often been called his obsession with counting.

Examples abound, but consider just two typical ones. Galton recorded the number of fidgets in scientific meetings as a measure of boredom and found that fidgets were markedly reduced when attention ran high and increased with increasing boredom. His almost unlimited interest in measurement is illustrated in one of his most controversial papers entitled "Statistical Inquiries into the Efficacy of Prayer" (Galton, 1872). Galton observed that length of life does not appear to be related to the amount of prayer offered in a person's behalf. He noted that missionaries often die early, even though they are almost certainly the objects of considerable prayer. He also found no differences in the life spans of clergy, lawyers, and physicians and argued that public prayers for state leaders are ineffective, because such leaders had shorter than average life spans.

Galton's paper was part of a larger debate in the early 1870s that raged over experiments (see Brush, 1974a) proposed by well-known scientists such as the physicist John Tyndall. The proposed experiments, designed to test scientifically the efficacy of prayer, triggered an emotional debate among some scientists and the clergy. The clergy were quick to point out that all outcomes of the proposed experiments would be subject to a hopeless array of interpretations. The most interesting part of the debate is that it illustrated an unbounded Victorian optimism in the possibility of a near limitless application of measurement techniques to human problems. Such optimism would, of course, be quick to accommodate or even mandate a science of psychology. Galton was one of the chief representatives of that optimism.

Galton's specific contributions to measurement theory and practice had important implications for experimental design and for the kinds of problems that could be investigated by psychologists. Diamond (1977) stated that without Galton's contributions, "it would have been a far more difficult task to give psychology its new directions, that is, to change it from a normative science, which had been conceived as the propaedeutic basis for philosophy, into a functional science of behavior, independent of philosophy" (p. 47). Galton's most important discoveries were in the areas of regression and correlation, but he was also a pioneer in the development and use of other statistical concepts such as the median and the percentile.

Galton's original contributions to the concepts of regression and correlation grew out of his interests in heredity. He used scattergrams to characterize the relationship between the heights of parents and the heights of the adult children. In a scattergram values of one variable (height of a parent) could be laid out along an *x* axis and values of another variable (height of an adult child) could be laid out on the *y* axis. Points in the field of the scattergram could show simultaneously both values for a large number of parents and their children. Galton was the first to use the term *corelation* (later changed to *correlation*) and he contributed extensively to the technical mathematical characterization of correlations. In his early work, he was interested primarily in correlations of physical traits (e.g., height, weight, circumference of head, etc.), but later he realized that the technique of correlation had much wider significance, with implications for the study of a host of sociological and psychological problems. In addition to his contributions to the development of correlation techniques, Galton was also the first to use the term *median,* an important contemporary measure of central tendency. Galton also made extensive use of percentiles, and

indeed introduced the term *percentile,* although the concept itself was not new with him.

Applications of the New Measurement Techniques

Psychology was deeply influenced by the emerging nineteenth-century faith in new measurement techniques and new methods of analysis. Furthermore, early discoveries of the lawful distribution of physical and behavioral measures of human beings contributed to optimism about the possibility of the extension of science into the human arena. But the benefits associated with unprecedented advances in the techniques and theory of measurement were somewhat offset by occasional unfortunate abuses. In his book, *The Mismeasure of Man,* Gould (1981) outlined some of them. Specifically, he documented the unfortunate results of early craniometry, which typically assumed that intelligence is related to the size of the brain. Gould showed that carelessness and poor sampling techniques resulted in beliefs that whites have larger brains than blacks. Thus, craniometry was used in the service of racial prejudice. It was also used to support sexual prejudices. Gould further traced some of the unfortunate abuses of psychological measures of intelligence.

Although measurement techniques were occasionally abused, they did provide important new scientific research tools. Simple descriptive social statistics also paved the way to a public awareness that many events, when seen in numerical context, are best conceived in terms of the operation of natural law. This point can be illustrated by referring to some early examples of the use of social statistics.

One of Quételet's admirers was the famous nurse Florence Nightingale (1820–1910), who is remembered primarily for her efforts to improve sanitary conditions in hospitals and in battlefield emergency hospitals designed to care for sick and wounded soldiers. Florence Nightingale was fascinated with Quételet's efforts to quantify human behavior and immediately saw an application of statistical techniques in the field of nursing. Nightingale had deplored the failure of hospitals to keep uniform statistical records on births, deaths, number of days for convalescence, and the like. As a consequence of her concerns, she agitated for major reforms in the keeping of medical records. She demonstrated that, during war, disease and poor sanitary conditions resulted in more deaths among British soldiers than did the enemy! She was among the first to use graphs to illustrate her arguments. Because of Florence Nightingale's contributions to descriptive social statistics, she was elected to fellowship in the Royal Statistical Society and as an honorary member of the American Statistical Association. Nightingale saw a role for statistics in moral and political reform efforts. She also saw that many questions of social and psychological significance could be explored statistically.

It is of interest that the American reformer of mental institutions, Dorothea Lynde Dix, an admirer of Florence Nightingale, also made use of descriptive social statistics in her campaigns to improve the treatment environment for mental patients. In her memorials to state legislatures, Dix presented tabular information on admissions, mortality, cure rates, age of onset of illness, and hospital costs. In her reports to legislative bodies, Dix sometimes included frequency data from hospitals on presumed causes of mental illness, including such factors as loss of property, domestic difficulties, grief, unemployment, head injuries, and extravagant religious excitement.

The increasing use of social statistics in the nineteenth century was an important development. Events that had been viewed previously as capricious, or as acts of the will, or as acts of God, could now be seen in a naturalistic context. Discovery of such regularities in human behavior undoubtedly contributed to the acceptance of the possibility of a science of psychology.

REVIEW QUESTIONS _____

1. Briefly discuss Hobbes's position on epistemology.

2. In what way did Hobbes's work encourage naturalistic and quantitive studies?

3. Briefly describe Hobbes's beliefs about basic human nature.

4. Outline Descartes's views on reflex activity.

5. List and describe four testable hypotheses found in Descartes's views on the physical basis of movement.

6. Briefly describe why Swammerdam's experiment on the nerve muscle preparation was embarrassing to Descartes's theory.

7. List three arguments advanced by Neils Stensen against Descartes's views on the role of the pineal gland.

8. Briefly characterize Hales's and Whytt's contributions to reflex theory.

9. According to Unzer, the guillotine provided a painless death. What was Unzer's rationale?

10. Why is the work of La Mettrie and Cabanis important to the development of scientific psychology?

11. Briefly describe the Bell-Magendie Law and how it was discovered.

12. What is the doctrine of specific energies and who was its chief advocate?

13. Briefly outline Helmholtz's technique for measuring the speed of conduction of a nervous impulse. Approximately what was the speed?

14. Why is the work of Jacques Quételet so important in the history of psychology?

15. Briefly outline Francis Galton's contributions to the development of quantitative techniques.

CHAPTER 9

NATURALISM AND HUMANITARIAN REFORM

In no case may we interpret an action as the outcome of the exercise of a higher psychical faculty, if it can be interpreted as the outcome of the exercise of one which stands lower in the psychological scale.

—Conwy Lloyd Morgan (1894/1977)

Naturalism, as a philosophical perspective, is the doctrine that scientific procedures and laws are applicable to all phenomena. Naturalism also includes the assumption that all events in the world have a history that is understandable in terms of identifiable forces. One of the defining features of the modern period is the contrast between naturalistic approaches to the world and older approaches with their emphasis on supernatural interpretations (see White, 1910; Lindberg & Numbers, 1986). The early modern period and late Renaissance witnessed new naturalistic accounts of the history of the solar system and the earth. Later in the modern period, the naturalistic perspective was extended to account for the origin of life, the origin of physical diseases, and the causes of emotional disorders. This chapter explores the extension of naturalism in evolutionary theory and in modern accounts of emotional disorders. As we will see, evolutionary theory and naturalistic accounts of mental disorders play a crucial role in the background of psychology.

EVOLUTIONARY THEORY

As we have already seen, evolutionary thinking has been with us from the time of the Greeks. Anaximander, as early as the fifth century B.C., had advanced a protoevolutionary theory that, in many respects, anticipated modern ideas. Goudge (1973,

pp. 174–175) pointed out that protoevolution can also be found in early Buddhism, Taoism, and the teachings of Confucius. Our concern here, however, is with the emergence and influence of evolutionary theory in modern times.

In a sense, evolution is a part of the broader discipline of **cosmogony**—the study of the origin of the cosmos or the universe. Formal theories about an evolving solar system followed quickly in the wake of the new Copernican cosmology. The idea of an evolving earth with a natural history also found fertile intellectual soil in the new cosmology. Although we encountered the idea of organic evolution in earlier cultures, modern theories of organic evolution were a relatively late development. Let us briefly examine selected modern theories of the evolution of the solar system, geological evolution, and organic evolution.

Evolution of the Solar System

By the midseventeenth century, the Aristotelian view of the immutability and permanence of the sun and stars was under attack. The new Copernican cosmology was quickly accompanied by bold and imaginative new cosmogonies. Most notable were theories proposed by René Descartes (1596–1650), Immanuel Kant (1724–1804), and Pierre Simon de Laplace (1749–1827). Each of these theorists advanced the idea that our solar system had a natural history, though Descartes, perhaps fearful of the Inquisition and knowing what had happened to Galileo, disclaimed any intention of contradicting the biblical account of creation in the book of Genesis.

The names of Kant and Laplace are associated with the so-called **nebular hypothesis.** According to this cosmogony, matter in the form of gaseous clouds was once distributed extensively through the solar system. In conformity with known laws of motion, attraction, and repulsion, it was assumed that denser regions attract lighter ones and that at some point a series of concentric rings became well elaborated. Forces of attraction within each ring gradually formed spheres corresponding to our planets. The material in the center of the field formed the sun. It was assumed that all planets should exist more or less on the same plane and that denser planets should be closer to the sun. The same laws responsible for our solar system were assumed to operate in other systems as well. The idea that the solar system evolved according to natural laws was an important first step in modern evolutionary thought. The next step was a natural evolutionary account of the history of the earth itself.

Geological Evolution

One of the most interesting figures in the history of evolutionary thought is the Frenchman George-Louis Leclerc, who is best known by the title Comte de Buffon (1707–1788). Buffon enjoyed unusual wealth and eminence during his life and is generally considered, along with such figures as Diderot, Voltaire, and Rousseau, as one of the great Frenchmen of the eighteenth century. Among other things, Buffon is remembered for his massive *Histoire Naturelle,* a forty-four-volume encyclopedic effort that covered the author's thought on a great range of topics in zoology, botany, geology, meteorology, theology, philosophy, and psychology (see Buffon, 1780–1785/1977).

Buffon advanced the view that the earth has gone through epochs in its natural history. It existed once in a molten stage; later there was a universal sea; a volcanic stage came still later; then the formation of continents was followed by the emergence of land animals and finally human beings. Buffon realized that cooling of such a large mass from a molten stage would require much time. In order to estimate the cooling time, he heated several spheres made of different materials and calculated their cooling time. By extrapolation from the results, he came to the conclusion that the cooling time for the earth from the molten stage had been just under 43,000 years, and that the total age of the earth was almost 75,000 years, far older than the 4,004 years calculated by Archbishop Ussher from biblical chronology.

Buffon's geological heresies resulted in more than one investigation by ecclesiastical authorities. Early concerns expressed by the faculty of theology at the University of Paris were temporarily satisfied when Buffon published in Volume IV of his *Histoire Naturelle* a retraction which, in part, read as follows: "I abandon whatever in my book concerns the formation of the earth, and in general all that might be contrary to the narration of Moses" (see Fellows & Milliken, 1972, p. 82). But the faculty did not appreciate Buffon's efforts. It was very likely the king who saved Buffon from extended harassment. Fellows and Milliken (1972) pointed out that when Buffon's *Époques* had been denounced before the theology faculty, the king urged a special investigative "committee to proceed with circumspection, an admonition that so impressed the assembled doctors that their committee never reported, some few taking covert revenge in dropping hints that the work had been judged the harmless product of senility" (p. 83).

Buffon was one of the first to advance an evolutionary perspective. He clearly embraced cosmological and geographic evolution and was among the first moderns to entertain ideas of organic evolution. Buffon demonstrated the anatomical similarities among animals and speculated about common ancestries. Yet, Goudge (1973) pointed out that Buffon "publicly denied that species are mutable" (p. 177). So organic evolution remained, for him, in the realm of a weak hypothesis. A stronger statement at this time would undoubtedly have had undesirable repercussions with ecclesiastic authorities. Clodd (1897/1972) stated that one must read between the lines to understand

Buffon, who was conveying many modern ideas before the world was ready to receive them. He also argued that Buffon was "the most stimulating and suggestive naturalist of the eighteenth century" (p. 111).

As we have seen, the idea of geological evolution was taking hold, but the great landmark in the history of that idea was the publication of the classic *Principles of Geology* (1830–1833) by Sir Charles Lyell (1797–1875). Lyell's work is so pivotal that he is often regarded as the founder of modern geology. He argued for **uniformitarianism**— the view that changes on earth occur at a very slow pace over vast stretches of time. This view contrasted with **catastrophe theory** advanced by the French biologist Georges Léopold Chrétien Frédéric Dagobert Cuvier (1769–1832), who had argued that there had been great earth-wrenching catastrophes that had annihilated entire species and changed the features of the terrain suddenly. With Lyell, uniformitarianism replaced catastrophe theory; for well over one hundred years it became the orthodox position. It was a position that played a central role in Darwin's thought.

Evolution in Other Arenas of Intellectual Discourse

Before discussing organic evolution, it may be helpful to recall that evolutionary thinking was applied to many other areas of discourse. We too readily forget that there were fierce intellectual battles over natural developmental (evolutionary) explanations of these other areas. For example, consider long-standing explanations of the origin of language. White (1910) pointed out that "each people naturally held that language was given it directly or indirectly by some special or national deity of its own; thus, to the Chaldeans by Oannes, to the Egyptians by Thoth, to the Hebrews by Jahveh" (pp. 168–169).

Western thought was dominated for centuries by the idea that Hebrew was a divine language used by God and Adam in the Garden of Eden, and that all other languages derived from Hebrew. But with the advent of scientific philology in the seventeenth and eighteenth centuries and with the classification of languages and studies of comparative grammars, doubt was cast on the divine origin of language. Languages were viewed naturalistically, or from an evolutionary perspective. It is noteworthy that belief in the evolution of language may come easier than belief in organic evolution. One can easily see that words are derived from earlier languages. Ongoing changes are also clearly evident as new words are coined and new meanings get attached to old words. The natural evolutionary approach to language becomes very clear to anyone who attempts to read old manuscripts or documents.

Evolutionary thought was also evident in accounts of the history of ideas. Consider, for example, the evolution of ideas about such topics as slavery, air flight, the origin of disease, the role of women in society, the nature of mental illness, and the role that capital punishment should play in society. On this latter topic, we do not have to go back very far in history to encounter the practice of executing ten- and eleven-year-old children for minor crimes. Drawing and quartering and burning at the stake were not uncommon practices. By contrast, in recent times, many countries have outlawed capital punishment altogether. Where it is practiced, its efficacy and morality are subjects of intense debate.

It is clear that evolution conceived as a process of natural change is applicable to many intellectual arenas and that, as early as the Renaissance, the stage was set for the development of theories of organic evolution.

Organic Evolution

Modern theories of organic evolution developed within the context of the new naturalistic approaches to cosmology and geology. Modern theories also developed within the context of a history of raging theological debate about sacred theories of origins. Indeed, it is a mistake to assume that there was only one sacred theory of origins. Even within the Christian community there were serious quarrels about the details of creation theory. A brief examination of some of the divergent views is informative to those who wish to gain a better understanding of the intellectual context of evolution.

We can enumerate only a few of the many questions about creation theory that were debated for centuries by theologians. It is important to note that the debates were not necessarily between scientists and theologians, but more often between theologians and theologians. For example, what was the mode of creation? Did God speak things into existence as implied in the first chapter of Genesis, or work like a sculptor as implied in the second chapter of Genesis? Were the fowl brought forth out of the waters (Gen. 1:20) or out of the ground (Gen. 2:19)? What was the order of creation of life forms? In the first chapter of Genesis the order is: plants, fish, birds, cattle, wild beasts, and human beings. In the second chapter the order is given as: plants, the male of the human species, beasts, birds, and a female. One of the early tasks of theologians was to attempt to reconcile these differences.

It was often argued that there were no thorns, stingers, or poisonous fangs until after Adam and Eve were expelled from the Garden of Eden. The fossil record, however, reveals the existence of such lethal weapons and abundant evidence of animals that had devoured other animals long before humans show up. Many theologians had argued that no species could ever become extinct because God does not make mistakes. Further, it was argued that no new species had appeared since creation. The sexual nature of plants was strongly resisted for a time, but was gradually crushed by overwhelming evidence. The unique distributions of animals in remote regions such as South America and Australia were also problematic. Why were the fossil remains of the ancestors of all animals not to be found in the vicinity of the mountains of Ararat, the presumed resting place of Noah's Ark? All animals should have fanned out from that point, but there is no evidence for such a presumption. Clearly, the existing sacred theory of origins, like the sacred theory of the structure of the universe, was beset with problems that divided biblical scholars. There was an obvious need for alternative explanations and, as noted earlier, the Comte de Buffon was one of the first to advance a more naturalistic approach to the question of origins.

Buffon did not publicly endorse a full-blown doctrine of organic evolution. He even denied the mutability of species. Yet, as a pure hypothesis, he was willing to ponder whether humans and apes might have common ancestors. He was also one of the first moderns to be fascinated with the developmental history of individuals. Such interest has always been part and parcel of evolutionary thought modes. Buffon wrote on intrauterine development, infancy, puberty, and old age. He was particularly interested in mortality statistics of infants, noting that Simpson's mortality tables, published in London in 1742, showed that "a fourth of [infants] died in the first year, more than a third in two years, and at least one half in the first three years" (Buffon, 1780–1785/1977, p. 393). Buffon pointed out that those who survive should consider themselves favored by the Creator, but then went on to point out that infant survival in France was better than in England. This hint of a geographic or natural determinant of survival rate on the heels of a statement regarding the providential determinant of survival rate is characteristic of the duplicity of Buffon, who repeatedly pulled his reader into the tensions between naturalistic and supernaturalistic worldviews. Buffon provided growth data in his discussion of infants and spoke of the importance of good nutrition. He believed there is a relationship between length of time it takes an organism to develop and the length of that organism's life. He wrote in detail on the changes in physiology associated with aging.

Erasmus Darwin (1731–1802), an English physician and biologist, and grandfather of Charles Darwin, also made important contributions to the theory of organic evolution. Ronan (1982, p. 420) pointed out that Erasmus Darwin was a member of Lichfield, England's Lunar Society, a society named after the habit of its members to meet as close as possible to the time of the full moon in order better to see their way home from their meetings. The society included about a dozen eminent members such as James Watt, developer of the steam engine; astronomer Sir William Herschel; and Joseph Priestley, known for the isolation of oxygen, ammonia, and carbon dioxide. Some of the members were known not only for their scientific achievements but also for their modern political and theological thought. Erasmus Darwin was a deist who believed that natural processes evolved from the time of creation without divine intervention. Priestley, sympathetic to the American and French revolutions, was, despite his fame as a scientist, viewed by many as a traitor and anti-Christ. His home was burned by a mob and he finally emigrated to the United States. Discussions in the Lunar Society were carried on in an atmosphere of honesty and intellectual freedom, but many of the ideas that were of absorbing interest in the society were anathema to the larger society. For this reason, Darwin, possibly fearful of repercussions, did not present his views on organic evolution until the latter part of the eighteenth century—just a few years before his death.

Darwin believed that plant life preceded animal life and that all animals evolved from the same basic organic material. He rejected the idea that there had been many separate creations for various species. He believed that human beings were not far removed from a former existence as quadrupeds. The mechanism for evolution, according to Erasmus Darwin, was **inheritance of acquired characteristics.** Thus, a given trait is developed from a need (for example, a long coat develops from a need for warmth in a cold climate) and that trait is passed on to offspring. Darwin saw evidence for evolution in changes observed in domestic breeding, in climatic effects on animals, and in breeding anomalies. Darwin's view on the mechanism of evolution—namely, the inheritance of acquired characteristics—was destined to become a major source of controversy, but it was a view that would prevail for a considerable period of time and reached its apogee in the work of our next pioneer in evolutionary history, Jean-Baptiste Pierre Antoine de Monet Lamarck.

The famous French biologist Jean-Baptiste Lamarck (1744–1829) is remembered mainly for an early theory of organic evolution and as one of the pioneers in invertebrate paleontology. Lamarck's personal life was riddled with tragedy, and his scientific contributions, though of immense importance in the history of nineteenth-century evolutionary thought, were the subject of continuous

ridicule. On the matter of his personal life, Ronan (1982, p. 421) pointed out that Lamarck "married three or (possibly) four times, but death overtook each wife—Lamarck lived on the poverty line; his personal effects, books and biological collections had to be auctioned to pay for his funeral and he left his large family unprovided for. It included one son who was deaf and another who was insane. Added to all this, he went blind eleven years before his death" (p. 421).

Lamarck's name is sometimes associated with *progressionism,* the idea that there is a steady linear advance in nature from simple to more complex forms of life. Taylor (1983) wrote that, in later developments of his thought, Lamarck believed in a "branching evolution and the vanishing of many forms" (p. 39). (This was a bolder claim than it looks; the orthodox claimed that God could not have made mistakes and therefore there could be no vanishing forms.) No writer before Lamarck so well appreciated the importance of the concepts of extinction of species and adaptation.

Lamarck argued that species are human constructions based partly on our need for convenient classificatory schemes; individual plants or animals in nature are simply steps in an ongoing process. Each individual may be different from its ancestors, and its offspring may acquire still different characteristics that will fit them the better to their environment.

The most controversial aspect of Lamarck's theory was the proposed mechanism of evolution. Lamarck, like Erasmus Darwin, believed that environmental changes (e.g., climate changes, food supply changes, changes in predator populations, etc.) had obvious and profound impact on the needs of living organisms. Once a need is created, such as a behavior pattern to avoid a new predator, adaptive mechanisms are set in motion. The adaptations that are thus acquired are transmitted genetically to the offspring. Thus, the development of features such as a rough skin or armor, a longer coat for warmth, or avoidance behaviors are passed on to offspring. The sequence, then, according to Lamarck, is that changes in the environment impact the animal's needs. Changing needs alter the animal's behavior and new behaviors impact biological organization and structure. The new organizations and structures are then passed along.

Taylor (1983, pp. 39–40) pointed out that Lamarck did *not* say that environmental conditions per se affect heredity. Nevertheless, Lamarck's proposed mechanism was not and is not accepted by mainstream biologists, though the idea of the inheritance of acquired characteristics has been, for some reason, quite compelling and thus slow to die. We will encounter it again and again. It appeared later in the work of William McDougall and for many years it had strong appeal in Soviet science because of its consistency with Marxist-Leninist thought. It survives today in unorthodox fringes of biology, but supporting and compelling experimental evidence has not been forthcoming (see the discussion in Taylor, 1983, pp. 48–54).

Charles Darwin

Charles Darwin

We have seen that theories of cosmological, geological, and organic evolution were well entrenched in scientific literature prior to Darwin. What was missing was an adequate account of the theoretical mechanism of evolution and adequate supporting evidence. Darwin provided supporting biological evidence and, simultaneously with Alfred Russel Wallace (1823–1913), advanced a mechanism for evolution that was acceptable to the scientific community.

Charles Darwin (1809–1882) was the fifth of the six children of Robert Waring Darwin and Susannah Wedgwood. Charles's mother was from a family that established an international reputation for the excellence of their work in pottery, fine china, and ceramics. Her role in Charles's life was cut short by her early death in 1817 when Charles was only eight years old. Robert Waring Darwin was the third son of Erasmus Darwin and his first wife Mary Howard. Robert was a highly successful physician who was known for his ability to treat his patients with great sympathy and understanding. Indeed, Wichler (1961) pointed out that "his greatest success was a new method of treatment that is today called psychotherapy" (p. 153). Robert Darwin had a forceful personality and he played a strong role in his son's life.

There is little in Charles Darwin's formal educational accomplishments to suggest that he would later achieve eminence in the scientific world. He had no love for primary school and most of his work there was of a perfunctory nature. At age sixteen, he entered Edinburgh University to pursue a medical degree, but was bored with the classroom experiences and developed a profound aversion for the observation of surgical procedures. After two years of mediocre work, Charles abandoned his studies at Edinburgh and enrolled as a theological student at Cambridge University. His enthusiasm for theological studies was no greater than for medicine. He did complete a degree in 1831 but never put it to use.

From his early years, Darwin had a keen interest in natural science and a special fondness for organization and collection. He developed unusual expertise in the classification and identification of beetles. His knowledge of birds, plant life, and sea fauna was also extensive. During his years at Cambridge, Darwin attended scientific lectures, took every opportunity to retreat to natural settings, and worked long hours collecting beetles—unusual activities for a theological student! He soon commanded the respect of important professors in the natural sciences. Indeed, when Captain Robert Fitzroy wrote to the botanist professor Henslow for a recommendation for a naturalist to accompany him on his forthcoming South American voyage, it was Charles Darwin who got the recommendation. In the opening lines of his account of the voyage of the *Beagle,* Darwin (1897) described the difficult beginning and the purpose of the expedition:

> After having been twice driven back by heavy southwestern gales, her Majesty's ship *Beagle,* a ten-gun brig, under the command of Captain Fitz-Roy, R.N., sailed from Devonport on the 27th of December, 1831. The object of the expedition was to complete the survey of Patagonia and Tierra del Fuego, commenced under Captain King in 1826 to 1830—to survey the shores of Chile, Peru, and of some islands in the Pacific—and to carry a chain of chronometrical measurements around the world. (p. 1)

The voyage of the *Beagle* did not end until October 2, 1836. The *Beagle* sailed southwest past the Canary Islands, to the coasts of Brazil and Argentina and further south to the Falkland Islands and Tierra del Fuego, the southern tip of South America. The voyage proceeded up the west coast of South America to the Galapagos Islands—the most important natural laboratory for Darwin's theory. Then the *Beagle* sailed westward, visiting many of the islands of the Pacific before reaching New Zealand and Australia. By early May of 1836, the Cape of Good Hope was in sight, but unfavorable winds carried the *Beagle* back to the coast of Brazil instead of to the more northern goal of the Cape de Verd Islands. On the last day of August, the *Beagle* made port in the Cape de Verd archipelago and on October 2, the shores of England were in sight. Throughout much of the journey Darwin suffered seasickness, but the rewards of his excursions on land more than compensated for the miseries he experienced at sea.

Darwin's account of the voyage of the *Beagle* is recommended reading for those who wish to gain an appreciation for the development of his evolutionary theory, the keenness of his ability to observe, and his geological, botanical, and zoological knowledge. Darwin's anthropological interests are also punctuated in many passages that reflect a combination of scientific and humane interests. For example, in Tierra del Fuego he noted that the Fuegians devoured their old women before they devoured their dogs during the winter months of short food supply. Darwin dwelled on the miserable life of the Fuegians, whom he regarded as the most wretched of savages. He was interested in how they got to Tierra del Fuego in the first place, how they survived, and what they could know of pleasure. Commenting on the Fuegians, Darwin (1897) observed,

> The different tribes have no government or chief, yet each is surrounded by other hostile tribes, speaking different dialects, and separated from each other only by a deserted border or neutral territory: the cause of their warfare appears to be the means of subsistence. Their country is a broken mass of wild rocks, lofty hills, and useless forests: and these are viewed through mists and endless storms. The habitable land is reduced to the stones on the beach; in search of food they are compelled unceasingly to wander from spot to spot, and so steep is the coast, that they can only move about in their wretched canoes. They cannot know the feeling of having a home, and still less that of domestic affection; for the husband is to the wife a brutal master to a laborious slave. Was a more horrid deed ever perpetrated, than that witnessed on the west coast by Byron, who saw a wretched mother pick up her bleeding dying infant-boy, whom her husband had mercilessly dashed on the stones for dropping a basket of sea-eggs! (pp. 215–216)

Darwin goes on to compare the skills of the Fuegians to the instincts of animals. One can see the evolutionary approach taking shape in Darwin's recorded thoughts as he accumulated experiences with the peoples of strange lands, with plant and animal life, and with the terrain. It is important to emphasize the fact that the evolutionary approach to life was based on the interpretation of extensive field experience and masses of geological, botanical, zoological, and anthropological data. At every turn, the importance of the environment in shaping life's forms forced itself upon Darwin's thinking. But how does evolution work? What is the mechanism? In Tierra del Fuego, Darwin (1897) speculated, "Nature by making habit omnipotent, and its effects hereditary, has fitted the

Fuegian to the climate and the productions of his miserable country" (p. 216). The conclusion that the effects of habit are hereditary would have to be modified later.

It was in the Galapagos Islands that Darwin encountered one of the world's finest natural laboratories for the study of species variation. The Galapagos are located about five hundred miles west of Ecuador. The equator cuts through the northern part of the largest island, but most of the archipelago is just south of the equator. There are ten major islands, with neighboring islands often no more than ten miles away and clearly visible from a given island. Climate, altitude, and soil conditions are comparable throughout the archipelago, yet Darwin found surprising and unexplained differences in plant and animal life from island to island. For example, finches on one island had developed a heavy parrotlike beak, whereas their near relatives on another island had developed a long and graceful beak. Darwin found plant and animal species that were unique to given islands or groups of islands and other species that were common to all the islands, but that varied from one island to the next. Strong currents between the islands probably prevented most animals from traveling from island to island. Darwin (1897) stated, "Most of the organic productions are aboriginal creations, found nowhere else" (p. 377). He went on to speculate that with these islands, "We seem to be brought somewhat near to that great fact—that mystery of mysteries—the first appearance of new beings on this earth" (p. 378). Nevertheless, for the time, the mechanisms of change and adaptation eluded Darwin.

A reading of Darwin's account of his voyage sensitizes us to the central emphasis he placed on environmental setting, adaptation, and the sheer indifference and brutality of nature and people. On this latter topic, Darwin, the detached observer-naturalist, was often dominated by Darwin, the empathic and caring human being. For example, after witnessing numerous instances of the beating of slaves and the separation of slave families at auctions, Darwin (1897) bitterly remarked, "I thank God, I shall never again visit a slave country. . . . These deeds [atrocities against slaves] are

done and palliated by men who profess to love their neighbours as themselves, who believe in God, and pray that his will be done on earth!" (p. 499).

Upon his return to England, Darwin proceeded with the preparation and classification of the many plant and animal collections he brought back from the voyage. During this time he also set forth the results of his voyage in many scientific papers and books. His early works, published years before his *Origin of Species,* were highly regarded in scientific circles and established Darwin as a leading scientist of his day.

In 1839, Darwin married his cousin Emma Wedgwood. The pace of his life for the next forty-three years, until his death in 1882, was dictated largely by the condition of his health. Plagued by such symptoms as nausea, headaches, sleeplessness, and dizziness, Darwin retreated more and more from conventional social activities into the structure of routine scientific work. The couple settled into a house in Down, south of London, located on a small acreage that provided room for greenhouses for botanical studies and facilities for other biological studies. Darwin lived a work-oriented life of unusual routine. The strict schedule was undoubtedly a source of therapy, but it was also the basis for an unusually productive career.

The story of the publication of Darwin's *Origin of Species* is often repeated and the subject of continuing scholarly investigation. At the time of Darwin's return to England, many pieces of the puzzle of evolution did not fit together. A breakthrough of sorts came in 1838, when Darwin read *An Essay on the Principle of Population* by Thomas Robert Malthus (1766–1834). Malthus, an English economist, argued that population increases geometrically while the means of subsistence tends to increase (in the best of situations) in a slower arithmetic progression. Thus, without proper checks, populations outgrow their food supplies and there is an inevitable struggle for existence and possible catastrophe. Although Malthus saw as clearly as anyone the catastrophic implications of unlimited population growth, he nevertheless rejected birth control—viewing it as a mortal sin. Darwin, long an observer of the struggle for existence in all kinds of plant and animal populations, felt an immediate debt to Malthus. deBeer (1964) pointed out that "Darwin had already grasped the importance both of variation and of selection; the effect [of Malthus's work] was to suggest to him the inexorable pressure exerted by selection in favour of the better adapted and against the less well adapted" (p. 99).

Even with the impetus provided by Malthus's essay, Darwin proceeded very slowly with his work. Then, in 1858, Alfred Russel Wallace (1823–1913), an English biologist, sent Darwin a manuscript in the hope of receiving helpful critical comment before forwarding the manuscript to a publisher. The manuscript spelled out the theory of evolution through natural selection. The ideas, in remarkable detail, were the same as Darwin's ideas. Wallace, like Darwin, had also been inspired by Malthus's essay on population. Eiseley (1957, p. 206) claimed that Darwin, though shaken, was tempted to let the credit for the theory go to Wallace. But Darwin's friends, Charles Lyell and Joseph Hooker, insisted that the equitable solution to the problem would be for Darwin and Wallace to present a joint paper announcing the new approach to evolution. The joint paper was published in the *Journal of Proceedings* of the Linnean Society of London on August 20, 1858. The joint publication attracted little attention, but Darwin, now under great pressure, quickly summarized his extensive work in the now famous *Origin of Species,* which was published in 1859. There are continuing questions about priority in the discovery of evolutionary theory and equally important questions about the treatment of Alfred Russel Wallace (see, for example, Brackman, 1980). Perhaps it would be more appropriate to think in terms of the Darwin-Wallace or even the Wallace-Darwin theory.

The essential technical features of the theory are as follows. First, all species populations tend to produce more individuals than can possibly survive. Second, there is variation in all populations. Third, there is a struggle for survival, but in specific environmental niches some variations are, by chance, better adapted to survive than others. Fourth, those variants that are better adapted will tend to endow their offspring with genetic advantages. Thus, there is a **natural selection** both for survival and for extinction.

Taylor (1983) pointed out that Darwin said "(1) that *all* changes which become fixed did so in this way, (2) that all changes occurred by *imperceptible gradations,* and (3) that all changes arose in the first instance by *chance*" (p. 17). Darwin assumed that species are always in more or less tension with their environments and thus evolution is always an ongoing affair. There was much evidence in support of the theory—the extinction of entire species, the fact that offspring are similar to their parents but also depart from their parents, and the production of variations through selective breeding. Given sufficient time, it was assumed that such variations may result in new species. Some of the original technical features of the theory have been called to question, most notably the assumption that all change is gradual. Nevertheless, the broader outlines of the theory have been an integral part of biology since the publication of the *Origin.* Further, the implications of the heritage of Darwin in a great variety of intellectual contexts (e.g., philosophy, religion, history, science, morals, etc.) is a topic of continuing interest (e.g., see Kohn, 1985; Richards, 1987).

SIGNIFICANCE OF EVOLUTIONARY THEORY FOR PSYCHOLOGY

In an early paper entitled "The Influence of Darwin on Psychology," James Rowland Angell (1909) pointed out that in Darwin's time there was already "a disposition to view mental life as intimately connected with physiological processes, as capable of investigation along experimental and physiological lines, and finally as susceptible of explanation in an evolutionary manner" (p. 152). Angell went on to state that with Darwinian thought, new emphasis was given to functional, developmental, and comparative processes, as opposed to the simple analysis of the normal adult mind that had interested some of the early psychologists.

A similar conclusion regarding the effect of evolutionism on psychology was set forth by the well-known German zoologist Ernst Heinrich Haeckel (1834–1919), who was one of the first to embrace and promote Darwin's theory. Haeckel (1905) noted,

> The greatest progress which psychology has made, with the assistance of evolution, in the latter half of the century culminates in the recognition of *the psychological unity of the organic world.* Comparative psychology, in co-operation with the ontogeny and phylogeny of the *psyche,* has enforced the conviction that organic life in all its stages, from the simplest unicellular protozoon up to man, springs from the same elementary forces of nature, from the physiological functions of sensation and movement. The future task of scientific psychology, therefore, is not, as it once was, the exclusively subjective and introspective analysis of the highly developed mind of a philosopher, but the objective, comparative study of the long gradation by which man has slowly arisen through a vast series of lower animal conditions. (p. 108)

Haeckel's name is often associated with the idea that **ontogeny** (the origin and history of the individual) **recapitulates phylogeny** (the origin and history of the species). Volume 1 of Haeckel's book, *The Evolution of Man* (1905), demonstrated the difficulty of differentiating between human embryos at various stages of development and the embryos of other animals. Although Haeckel's idea that ontogeny recapitulates phylogeny is not completely true, it nevertheless contributed to the growing awareness of the importance of developmental studies of the individual.

Darwin, of course, was also a pioneer in the study of individual development. His article, "A Biographical Sketch of an Infant," first published in the journal *Mind* (July 1877), was based on his careful observations of his infant son's sensory acuity, reflexes, and associations. This classic in developmental psychology helped set the stage for studies that have provided normative data on the physical and psychological development of children.

Haeckel also argued that the difference in the consciousness of human beings and the consciousness of animals is a matter not of quality but only of degree. Such a position, derived from evolutionary thinking, carries with it a justification for comparative studies as a way of building a science of the mind. Haeckel argued strongly for a scientific psy-

chology based on physiology and the assumed lawfulness of mental processes and evolution.

Comparative Psychology

There is little question that Darwin's work encouraged the development of comparative psychology. Shortly after the appearance of Darwin's *Origin,* there was an explosion of interest in comparisons between animals and humans. The interest had widespread popular appeal and was the subject of a great many articles published in popular or cultural magazines, often written by well-known psychologists. The articles investigated an impressive range of subjects: the mental capacity of the elephant (Horndav, 1883), the intelligence of ants (Romanes, 1881), queen ants and queen bees (Wheeler, 1906), the formation of habits in the turtle (Yerkes, 1900), babies and monkeys (Buckman, 1895), and morality in animals (Leuba, 1928). Important theoretical issues quickly surfaced in the early literature of comparative psychology. Much of the early work was anecdotal; that is, interesting stories were told perhaps by an animal's owner or a hunter or naturalist about an individual animal. The stories included how an animal found its way home or how it "solved" some other kind of problem. Based on the anecdote, enthusiastic observers often hastened to make inferences about the animal's impressive psychological capacity.

There were a large number of pioneers devoted to the study of comparative psychology (e.g., see Dewsbury, 1989), but arguably the most visible of the early pioneers was George John Romanes (1848–1894), an English biologist who was inspired by Darwin's *Origin.* Romanes's books *Animal Intelligence* (1882) and *Mental Evolution in Man* (1888) were enthusiastic but anecdotal attempts to found a science of animal behavior and to show continuity in the phylogenetic scale with respect to psychological capacities such as reason. Romanes's work helped call attention to the possibility of a comparative psychology, but was subject to the criticism that it focused excessively on individual stories or incidents of remarkable animal feats. Romanes was keenly aware of a need to establish definite general principles and to avoid anecdotes, but was unable to avoid the charge that his work reflected an excess of anecdotalism and anthropomorphism, if not sensationalism. Some of the strongest criticisms came from the American psychologist Joseph Jastrow (see Cadwallader, 1987) and from Wilhelm Wundt (1894/1977).

Important methodological and substantive contributions to comparative psychology come out of the work of the English biologist, philosopher, and psychologist Conwy Lloyd Morgan (1852–1936). Wishing to counter the anthropomorphism in much of the early comparative psychology, Morgan argued for a special application of Ockham's Razor, or the **principle of parsimony.** Recall from Chapter 4 that the fourteenth-century philosopher William of Ockham (c. 1285–1349) had argued that "entities are not to be multiplied without necessity" (see Moody, 1967, p. 307). In an extension of that idea to the field of comparative psychology, Morgan (1894/1977) contended, "In no case may we interpret an action as the outcome of the exercise of a higher Psychical faculty, if it can be interpreted as the outcome of the exercise of one which stands lower in the psychological scale" (p. 53). This statement came to be called Lloyd Morgan's canon and was accepted by the majority of animal researchers and comparative psychologists. As a result, interpretations of animal data gradually became more cautious and, interestingly, the more conservative and scientific approach to animal behavior was also communicated in popular publications (see, for example, Thorndike, 1899).

Some might argue that by following Morgan's canon we shifted to another extreme—the extreme of preferring precise explanations that may meet the test of simplicity but fail to do justice to the richness and complexity of the living organism. We will later encounter this criticism applied to the work of animal researchers such as Jacques Loeb, John B. Watson, and, in more modern times, B. F. Skinner. The tensions between what Wertheimer (1972, pp. 173–214) discussed as richness versus precision have been salient from the earliest days of comparative psychology. In the *precision orientation,* we run the risk of oversimplification and

of thus doing violence to our subject matter. In the *richness orientation,* we run the risk of reverting to constructs that have no scientific basis.

Developmental Psychology

Another contribution of Darwinian theory was its major impact on developmental psychology. The study of the development and care of children was an occasional topic of interest prior to Darwin. Such philosophers as Rousseau and Locke are well known as pioneers in this area. But following the publication of Darwin's *Origin,* we witnessed a self-conscious child study movement with leaders often acknowledging their debt to evolutionary theory.

We have already pointed out that Darwin's publication "A Biographical Sketch of an Infant" marks him as one of the pioneers in the systematic observation of infancy. The classic textbook in developmental psychology was written by the German physiologist William Thierry Preyer (1841–1897). Preyer's studies, set forth in his book *Die Seele des Kindes* (1882), were translated into English as *The Mind of the Child.* Preyer reported on his observations of the mental growth of his son over a four-year period. Zusne (1975) contended that "Preyer's book provided the greatest single impetus to the development of modern ontogenetic psychology" (p. 161).

The study of infant and child development, like the study of the new comparative psychology, understandably had unusual popular appeal. Accordingly, the works of psychologists on infancy and childhood found their way into popular and cultural magazines. The range of subjects is illustrated in just a few titles of articles put out for public consumption. For example, see Preyer (1888), "The Imitative Faculty of Infants"; Taine (1876), "Lingual Development in Babyhood"; Gale and Gale (1902), "Children's Vocabularies"; Baldwin (1894), "The Origin of Right-Handedness"; Jastrow (1903), "Helen Keller: A Psychological Autobiography"; and Sully (1886), "Development of the Moral Faculty." In addition to popular articles such as these, other psychologists were writing to provide general information to the public on the child-development movement. For example, writing for *Harper's Magazine,* G. Stanley Hall (1910) outlined the history of the systematic study of development and discussed specific content areas such as growth norms, language development, and moral development. Sully (1894, 1895, 1896), in a series of articles in *Popular Science Monthly,* conveyed the need for scientific studies of childhood and also discussed specific areas that were being studied, including imagination, play, childhood art, and childhood fears. Clearly, following Darwin's work, the child became a major focus of interest. The causal link between Darwin's work and the study of childhood is suggested by the acknowledged debt that pioneers such as G. Stanley Hall and William Preyer paid to Darwin.

Emphasis on Adaptation

Darwin's emphasis on survival, adaptation, and the shaping forces of the environment played a major role in defining the directions of the new psychology. Following Darwin, the frontiers of psychology were expanded. The detailed study of sensory processes that occupied much of the attention of the earliest psychologists was complemented by a more worldly psychology interested in education, the workplace, the home, and all those institutions and circumstances that impact adaptation. The leaders of American schools of psychology were especially influenced by Darwin. Later, in our discussions of the work of such leaders as William James, John Dewey, James McKeen Cattell, and G. Stanley Hall, it will become clear that each acknowledges a debt to Darwin.

Individual Differences

The acknowledged pioneer in the study of individual differences is Sir Francis Galton (1822–1911), the well-known half-cousin of Charles Darwin. We have already discussed Galton's life and his contributions to measurement theory in Chapter 8. Now we will turn to his pioneering work in individual differences—a work clearly inspired by his cousin's *Origin.*

It is of interest that, prior to the publication of Darwin's *Origin,* differences among individuals were often attributed to differences in the will. Older psychologies had stressed the importance of training the will, and expressions such as *diseases of the will* and *defects of the will* were common. Even Darwin, prior to reading Galton's work, had emphasized zeal and hard work as the major determinants of individual differences. But after reading Galton's classic *Hereditary Genius,* Darwin wrote to his cousin, "You have made a convert of an opponent in one sense, for I have always maintained that excepting fools, men did not differ much in intellect, only in zeal and hard work" (quoted in Pearson, 1914, p. 6).

Galton believed that differences among individuals are enormous and that many of the differences are innate. In his classic *Hereditary Genius,* a work he later wished he had called *Hereditary Talent* (see Forrest, 1974, p. 88), he attempted to show that exceptional accomplishment runs in families to such an extent as to suggest the operation of a powerful hereditary component. Galton did demonstrate that musicians tend to come from families of musicians, judges from families of judges, poets from poets, commanders from commanders, and so on. He did not, however, effectively control for the possible effects of environmental influence. Nevertheless, following Galton, differences in memory, mathematical ability, musical ability, literary ability, and the like were regarded less as matters of willpower and individual responsibility and more as matters amenable to scientific investigation. Thus Galton opened the door to an important arena of psychological inquiry. His radical emphasis on the hereditary basis of individual differences would later be replaced by an equally radical emphasis on the role of environment in shaping the individual.

It should be noted that Galton's work, a product of the late nineteenth century, had a strong sexist and racist bias that is offensive to contemporary sensitivities. Galton's biases were also quickly assimilated into the public attitude where there was an all-too-ready willingness to believe that white male accomplishments are attributable to innate superiority rather than to the educational opportunities that white males had long enjoyed.

Though Galton's biases left some unfortunate legacies that would later have to be challenged and corrected, he also did much to open the door to the very methods that were of value in challenging his biases. As noted in Chapter 8, he introduced correlation methods and, following Quételet, sensitized us to the importance of statistical measures of variability as scientific tools. He also pioneered in the study of identical twins as a method for the investigation of the differential effects of heredity and environment.

Herbert Spencer

Any discussion of the impact of evolutionary theory on psychology would be incomplete without mentioning the contributions of the influential English philosopher Herbert Spencer (1820–1903). Spencer may have been the most enthusiastic advocate of evolution—he advanced his own theory based partly on Lamarckian thought, prior to the publication of Darwin's *Origin.* However, his theory created little public interest, partly because it was largely speculative. The publication of Darwin's *Origin* in 1859 sharpened Spencer's evolutionary enthusiasm, and he embarked on the task of applying the theory to all branches of human knowledge. Thus, evolution became the foundation or unifying principle upon which Spencer sought to build philosophy, psychology, and science. He wrote on psychology, sociology, biology, ethics, and other topics, always stressing growth from simplicity to complexity. As with Darwin, the themes of adaptation, survival of the fittest, and continuity ran through his writings.

Spencer, often regarded as a forerunner of functionalism, was clearly in the British utilitarian tradition. He believed that goodness is that which gives long-term pleasure. And he believed that we tend to repeat those activities that result in pleasurable circumstances—an idea that would be often rediscovered in the later learning literature. Like Darwin, Spencer believed that many evolutionary changes occur by chance mutations. Part of Spencer's importance lies in his influence on other early psychologists; for example, William James repeatedly quoted Spencer, whose two-volume *Principles of Psychology,* first published in 1855, was standard reading for most of the early pioneers.

Goudge (1973) pointed out that "evolutionism is a family of conceptions having great vitality and viability" (p. 188). One part of that family of conceptions is the technical biological theory advanced by Darwin. But evolutionism is more than a technical theory; it is an attitude, an intellectual paradigm. As we have seen, it opened doors to the study of developmental psychology, comparative psychology, individual differences, and adaptation. Its contribution to the biological sciences and to psychology has been enormous. The work of Darwin specifically placed human experience and behavior in an uncompromisingly thoroughgoing naturalistic context. Very likely, it is no accident that the first laboratory in psychology was functioning within twenty years of the publication of the *Origin of Species.*

The full implications of Darwin's theory for the study of mind and behavior have yet to be explored. Though Darwinism places mind and behavior in a naturalistic context, the resulting image of human beings need not be pessimistic. Indeed, numerous scholars (e.g., Richards, 1987; Teilhard de Chardin, 1961) have argued that evolutionary theory need not result in moral and ethical nihilism (see especially, Richards, 1987, pp. 595–627).

NATURALISTIC APPROACHES TO EMOTIONAL DISORDERS

The naturalistic perspective in modern history invaded virtually every intellectual arena, including the fields of astronomy, geology, meteorology, and biology. Though naturalism met resistance in each of these areas, it soon prevailed as it challenged and dislodged older explanations based on the presumed operation of mysterious vital, paranormal, or supernatural forces. We turn now to a consideration of modern naturalistic accounts of emotional disorders. Understandably, naturalistic explanations applied to emotional disorders encountered unusual resistance. There were long-held, deeply entrenched beliefs in the idea that spirit forces were responsible for the origin of both physical and emotional problems. Such beliefs were reinforced by literal interpretations of sacred books and by institutional authority. In order to appreciate the naturalistic accounts of emotional disorders, it is necessary to review older approaches based on beliefs in demons and various spirit forces.

Demonology

Explanations of mental illness based on beliefs in demon possession are often associated with early times and the Middle Ages, but Kirsch (1978) contended that such explanations were more widespread during the Renaissance than in the Middle Ages. He argued that demonology reached its apogee in the mid-seventeenth century. There can be little doubt that **demonology** has been with us from early times, and that it was practiced during the Middle Ages. But it is important to be reminded that it has been prevalent or even widespread in more recent history.

Kirsch (1978, p. 155) pointed out that in 1609, the year Kepler published his accounts of the elliptical motion of planets, *pricking* was announced as a method of diagnosing demon possession. The method of pricking consisted of sticking victims with a pin until a spot was found that was insensitive to pain or did not bleed. Such a spot was regarded as the point through which a devil had gained access to the body. Such a method was added to an arsenal of diagnostic techniques that had been set forth earlier in a highly influential "bible" on demonology.

The Witches' Hammer

In 1484, Pope Innocent VIII authorized Heinrich Kramer and James Sprenger, Dominican friars and professors of theology, to serve as inquisitors in northern Germany where, according to the pope, many men and women had "abandoned themselves to devils" (see Summers, 1971, p. xiii). During the course of their work as inquisitors, Kramer and Sprenger wrote the classic ***Malleus Maleficarum,*** meaning *The Witches' Hammer,* or *The Hammer against Witches.* The *Malleus,* first published in 1486, was one of the most influential books of the fifteenth and sixteenth centuries. It had gone through fourteen editions by 1520 and was translated into several European languages. The *Malleus* was a response to individuals and groups that were

viewed as revolutionary and corrupt. It was also motivated by fear of anarchy and of the techniques used by those who were viewed as conspirators against civilization. Summers (1971, p. xix), in an introduction to the *Malleus,* cited examples of the techniques that were the source of so much fear. One technique was the age-old method of making an image of that which one wished to destroy and then thrusting pins in the image or melting the image.

That the techniques of witchcraft "worked" should come as no surprise in view of widespread belief in the efficacy of magical and supernatural techniques. Evidence for the strength of belief in witchcraft is found in the fact that almost all European countries passed laws against its practice. Laws were necessary partly because common people could be moved to panic at the mere thought that a witch might in some way be influencing their lives. The credulity and fear of the people made it possible to use witchcraft as a form of blackmail. It is little wonder that strong actions were taken to combat the so-called black arts.

The *Malleus* itself was divided into three parts, devoted to (1) a classification of devils and witches and how their influence in the world can be reconciled with God's omnipotence; (2) methods by which devils and witches accomplish their work, along with defenses and remedies against these methods; and (3) judicial and ecclesiastical procedures for trying witches and bringing them to justice. In Part II of the *Malleus,* Kramer and Sprenger argued that devils may actually enter the heads of human beings and manipulate mental images. Such entry may come about at the request of a witch. Entry may also result from the light or heavy sin of another person. For example, an individual's child may be possessed by a devil because that individual has engaged in a sin. Possession may also take place as a result of one's own light sins or heavy sins. Some possessions, according to the *Malleus,* are for an individual's greater advantage. For example, Kramer and Sprenger told the story of one priest who was particularly gifted in expelling devils. Because of his ability, he became famous and fell victim to the vice of vanity. Overcome with guilt, he prayed that, as a punishment for his sin, he might be possessed by a devil for a period of five months. According to the *Malleus,* "He was at once possessed and had to be put in chains, and everything had to be applied to him which is customary in the case of demoniacs. But at the end of the fifth month he was immediately delivered both from all vainglory and from the devil" (Kramer & Sprenger, 1486/1971, p. 130).

Whatever the reason for possession, it could result in virtually any physical or mental symptom. Some of the more common symptoms discussed in the *Malleus* included sterility, impotence, loss of sensory functions, loss of motor functions, mental disorganization, pain, somnambulism, epilepsy, mania, and death. The means by which witches worked their mischief were many and varied. It was thought that many witches could accomplish their purpose by a mere look or glance. They also used charms, incantations, and poison. In individuals with sufficient credulity, the verbal threat of a witch was sufficient to create the most intense anxiety and stress. The gradual or speedy death of the victim of a threat is reported in numerous early records.

A common view of emotional disorders was that they were the end result of the voluntary collaboration of an individual with a devil. They might also result from a hex or the action of a witch. In any case, prescribed treatments were designed to cast out the demons that caused the illness. Such treatments included exorcisms with sacred words, confessions, prayers, visits to holy shrines, repetitions of approved scriptures, and reverent participation in church ceremonies. It is of interest that the pages of the *Malleus* are filled with admonitions against the use of superstitious practices in combating devils and witchcraft. In general, one could be assured that a practice was not superstitious if it was in good accord with church doctrine. Not surprisingly, some of the same techniques used to combat the so-called possession of an individual by a demon, were also employed to combat hailstorms, illness in animals, tempests, and so on, that were perceived as works of witches or devils. The sprinkling of holy water, the ringing of church bells at an approaching storm, the making of the sign of the cross, or the utter-

ance of prescribed prayers were among the available interventions.

Not all physical and psychological disturbances were viewed as the works of demons or witches. The *Malleus* includes passages that recommend treatments for disorders that are not due to witchcraft. For example, a man made sick by inordinate love for a woman may be treated in any of several ways. "He may be married to her, and so be cured by yielding to nature. . . [;] his love [may be directed] to a more worthy object. . . . He may be directed to someone who . . . will vilify the body and disposition of his love, and so blacken her character that she may appear to him altogether base and deformed. Or, finally, he is to be set to arduous duties which may distract his thoughts" (Kramer & Sprenger, 1486/1971, p. 171).

Before examining the intellectual transition from demonology and witchcraft to more naturalistic approaches to mental illness, consider one of the more unfortunate by-products of beliefs in witches and devils. The witch was viewed as the enemy of civilization and as the source of natural calamities and great suffering. Accordingly, there was an urgent need to identify witches, expose their work, and bring them to justice. Thus, witch-hunts and trials for witchcraft were widespread in Europe, especially in the sixteenth and seventeenth centuries. Virtually all the European countries were caught up in a nearly hysterical effort to stamp out the threat of witchcraft.

Historians have tried to estimate the number of people who were executed after being accused of or convicted for witchcraft. The numbers are elusive, however. One reason is that many of the court records are incomplete. Kieckhefer (1976, pp. 106–147) listed over 500 European witch trials that took place during the relatively inactive period between 1300 and 1500. Many of these trials included multiple defendants but the records are often incomplete, failing to specify the exact charge or the outcome of a case.

Summers (1965) pointed to another reason that the numbers are elusive: "The people, frantic with superstitious fears, may often have taken the law into their own hands" (p. 359). There is, however, enough evidence to suggest that the witch-hunts in Europe, especially at their height during the sixteenth and seventeenth centuries, amounted to a holocaust that resulted in tens of thousands, or perhaps more accurately, hundreds of thousands of executions. Many towns throughout Europe were decimated. Summers (1965), quoting the commissary Claude de Musici of Treves, pointed out that "from 18 January, 1587, to the 18 November, 1593, there were executed for witchcraft in the diocese of Treves three hundred and sixty-eight persons of both sexes; this does not include the number of sorcerers who were burned at Treves itself" (pp. 486–487). Bromberg (1954) tells of a French judge who "boasted that he had burned eight hundred women in 16 years on the bench" (p. 52). Documentary evidence of large numbers of executions can be found in the legal records of town after town throughout Europe. Apparently no country was immune.

Unfortunately, legal codes were written with little thought of protecting innocent people. Such protection was hardly necessary in view of the prevailing theological view that God would protect the innocent. Such a comforting belief undoubtedly contributed to procedures of judicial inquisition that later generations would uniformly condemn. Let us briefly examine some of those procedures.

In Part III of the *Malleus,* it was pointed out that the usual procedure for initiating a trial was that one party accused another and then offered evidence in court that supported the accusation. If the accusing party was irresponsible or if that party initiated a frivolous charge, it was liable to a countersuit. But in the search for witches, the *Malleus* pointed out that the usual procedure was dangerous, because the individual who accused a witch and served as witness might be vulnerable to the witch's retaliatory powers. It is of interest that Pope Boniface VIII decreed that in heresy trials (which included witch trials) the inquisitor may withhold the names of accusers or witnesses if there was reason to believe that such witnesses or accusers were in danger. A second procedure, often used in witch trials, was for an individual simply to serve as an informer. Such an individual provided evidence to the court but did not serve as a witness, thereby being protected from the suspected

witch. The third procedure, most common in witch trials, was to initiate a process without an accuser or an informer. This procedure began when there was a suspicion that witches were active in a given locality. Given such a suspicion, a judge could bring charges and proceed with a trial. The citizens were simply given warnings that an inquisition was beginning when a general citation was posted on parish churches or town halls. Any person, under any kind of suspicion, could be placed on trial. For example, if an individual touched or held a baby, and if that baby later became ill, then the individual could be suspected and tried for witchcraft.

Deceptive techniques were openly advocated in the questioning of suspected witches. For example, in a section on examination techniques Kramer and Sprenger (1486/1971) suggested, "Let her [a suspected witch] be asked why she persists in a state of adultery or concubinage; for although this is beside the point [in a particular trial], yet such questions engender more suspicion than would be the case with a chaste and honest woman who stood accused" (p. 213). Inquisitors placed great weight on an individual's reactions to questions. Denials were often interpreted as cover-ups, but an overly emotional reaction could also be taken as a sign of guilt.

In addition to reactions to questioning procedures, certain signs or tests were taken as evidence of demonic possession and/or witchcraft. For instance, suspected witches were sometimes thrown into water. Floating was taken as evidence of guilt or possession, whereas sinking was taken as evidence of innocence. Another test was to determine whether a suspect could weep. It was commonly believed that witches had an inability to shed real tears. The judge nevertheless had to use the weeping test with caution and with close supervision of attendants, because it was thought that witches were capable of false tears or of assuming a weeping posture and cleverly smearing spittle on their faces. Still other signs of possession or witchcraft included birthmarks, unusual growths, scars, or moles.

It was desirable to inquisitors that witches make confessions before being sentenced for their crimes. To this end, torture was sometimes employed and with such efficiency that most of the accused confessed to the point of giving the inquisitors exactly what they wanted to hear. Russell (1980) suggested that, in Lorraine, "only 10% persisted in denying their guilt to the moment of death" (pp. 79–80). Thumb screws, toe screws, leg vices, racks, whippings, and sustained imprisonment were among the torture techniques employed. Confessions that were extracted often went into lurid detailed descriptions of how the victim had sworn allegiance to the devil, attended witches' sabbats and other diabolical assemblies, engaged in intercourse with Satan, or eaten the flesh of infants. Such confessions were often made with the expectation that they would sway the court to impose a more humane death sentence. In most cases, confessions served only to reinforce popular stereotypes about the power of witches. Many confessions included lists of accomplices, often enemies of the defendant. Such accomplices were then, of course, also subject to trial. Russell (1980, p. 80) told of one defendant who named all the court officials as being secretly involved in witchcraft.

Fear of the power of witches was so extensive that unusual precautions surrounded most legal proceedings. Jailers were cautioned against letting a witch touch them or stare at them. If they were touched with the witches' bare hands, they were immediately to apply a remedy such as salt that had been consecrated on Palm Sunday or a "Blessed Disc of Wax" stamped with a lamb and blessed by a Holy Father. Witches were led into the courtroom backwards so that their eyes might not fall on the judge before his eyes fell on them. Otherwise, the judge might succumb to the witches' power and offer a lighter sentence. Witches were sometimes carried in a basket, under the assumption that their power was diminished so long as their feet were not on the ground. Many suspects were stripped of all their clothes and all hair was shaved from their bodies. This was done because of the assumption that devils or evil spirits might hide or lurk in hair, especially pubic hair.

Most of those convicted of witchcraft were executed, although the sentence might be lighter for those accused of the use of magic or witchcraft in an attempt to accomplish a good purpose, such as healing. Executions were often by burning, although many other techniques were also employed. By the end of the eighteenth century, most of the witch-hunts and the executions had ceased.

The vast literature on witchcraft includes much discussion on the causes of such a belief system. Harris (1974) suggested that "the best way to understand the witch mania is to examine its earthly results rather than its heavenly intentions" (p. 237). It is true there was a theological backdrop that supported demonological views, but in addition, any problem—a death, a natural calamity, a financial failure, a physical or emotional illness—could be blamed on demons. Harris also noted that there was an economic basis for the witch-hunts. Property was confiscated and sold and profits were made from the legal proceedings. Whatever the causes, the ideological basis of witchcraft was stubborn—it died a slow death.

The Demise of Witchcraft

Russell (1980, p. 84) wrote that as early as 1563 Johann Weyer (1515–1588), a physician, wrote a treatise *On Magic* that argued that witches were really harmless old women suffering from mental disorders and that most alleged cases of witchcraft were really susceptible to natural explanations. Because of such a bold claim, Weyer was himself accused of being a witch.

A stronger challenge to witchcraft came in the thought of philosophers such as Baruch Spinoza and René Descartes. Lea (1957, p. 1361) pointed out that Spinoza denied altogether that there could be any intermediate forces between human beings and God. Spinoza viewed belief in demons as nonsense and attempted to undermine biblical authority for demonology by suggesting that Jesus acquiesced to popular superstitions when he made references to demons.

Spinoza transformed the radical monotheism of his Jewish heritage into a monistic naturalism. There was a unity between God and nature and an emphasis on natural causality. Spinoza wished to understand all things, including human actions, in terms of natural forces. There were no other forces with which to contend. In his emphasis on causality and on the unity of nature, Spinoza constituted a challenge to the kind of dualism, animism, and vitalism inherent in demonological views of the world. His thought was markedly similar to the scientific thought that would prevail later.

Still another major challenge to demonological viewpoints came with the work of René Descartes. Lea (1957, p. 1357) wrote that Descartes's strong emphasis on the relationship between brain activity and psychological processes (e.g., dreams, images, memory, etc.) left no room for other agencies such as demons. Descartes's emphasis was on the relationship between the activities of the soul, presumably seated in the pineal gland, and the soul's interactions with other parts of the body. The significance of Descartes's work is that it emphasized the role of the brain in human and animal life.

HUMANITARIAN REFORM

Numerous intellectual traditions provided a friendly context for the birth of psychology in the late nineteenth century. Empiricism, rationalism, advances in physiology, the development of new quantitative tools (especially statistics), evolutionary theory, and the naturalistic approach to mental and emotional disturbances all contributed, sometimes directly and sometimes indirectly, to an intellectual climate supportive of a new science and profession. Aside from these intellectual developments, it should not be forgotten that psychology arose in an age of social agitation for radical reforms on such issues as slavery, universal education, improved sanitation, equality for women, birth control, animal rights, prison reform, work conditions in factories, the treatment of the mentally ill, and child protection.

Each of the reform movements raised questions that called for the development of new knowledge and for scientific investigation into new kinds of problems. For example, labor movements were a response to deplorable eighteenth- and nineteenth-century factory conditions, but there were legitimate concerns on the part of both management and labor about how to balance their respective interests. Clearly there was a growing need for studies on such topics of work environment, work behavior, work motivation, efficient organizational structures, and equitable distribution of profits.

The naturalistic approach to mental and emotional problems opened the door to studies on etiology and the effects of various treatment environments. The reformers themselves realized the need for controlled studies and sometimes collected informal data pertinent to their reform agendas. For example, Dorothea Dix observed that loss of employment and unusual religious excitement were often precursors to emotional breakdowns.

It is no accident that psychology was born in an age of humanitarian reform. Once established, though, concerns arose about whether the new discipline was prepared to assist with practical problems. It will be noted in subsequent chapters that some psychologists believed that the first step should be to build a fund of basic knowledge. Others were impatient to apply psychology to problems in education, mental disorders, industry, and the law. The United States provided fertile soil for attempts by the new discipline to answer the problems of daily life. In particular, a reform agenda built around the humane treatment of mental disorders played a critical role in the social and cultural background of the new psychology.

Reform in the Treatment of Emotional Disorders

The metaphysical challenge to witchcraft and demonology paralleled a challenge of a different sort in a reform movement designed to provide humane care for people with mental illness. Revolutionary in its scope, the idea was to treat insane patients not as witches or demons or animals, but as human beings. Although beliefs and practices varied, the work of humanitarian reformers brought sweeping changes both in psychiatric treatment and in the public perception of mental disorders. As we will see, Europe and the United States played host to some of the more dramatic advances in humanitarian care. Such treatment grew partly out of a naturalistic approach to emotional disorders, as illustrated in the work of Franz Anton Mesmer.

Franz Anton Mesmer. The son of a forester, Franz Anton Mesmer (*MEZ mur*) was born on May 23, 1734, in Iznang in the German province of Swabia. His mother, Maria Mesmer, encouraged several of her nine children to enter the priesthood and one son, Johann, fulfilled her dream. Franz Anton began preparing for the ministry at age nine, but found himself occupied by music and other interests. Mesmer journeyed in 1759 to Vienna, where he earned a medical degree in 1766. At age thirty-two, Mesmer had earned an M.D. as well as a Ph.D. with his doctoral dissertation on "The Influence of the Planets on the Human Body" (Buranelli, 1975). In the tradition of the Renaissance alchemist Paracelsus, Mesmer proposed a theory of "animal gravitation" in which celestial bodies affect the health of our minds and bodies.

Brimming with charisma, Mesmer enjoyed friendships with the most celebrated figures in European society. In 1768, he married a rich widow named Anna Maria von Bosch and they made their home in a mansion in the affluent suburb of Landstrasse. The lavish garden at his Vienna home featured a theater where Mesmer's friend Wolfgang Amadeus Mozart gave the first performance of his short opera, *Bastien and Bastienne* (Landon, 1990). A patron of the arts, Mesmer was an amateur musician who excelled at the piano, cello, and glass armonica—an instrument of musical glasses designed by Benjamin Franklin in 1761 (Gallo & Finger, 2000).

Like many scholars of his day, Mesmer had a long-standing interest in electricity and magnetism. In the 1770s, he consulted a professor of astronomy named Maximillian Hell (an ironic last name given that Hell was also a Jesuit priest). Mesmer was entranced as Hell described his use of magnets in healing the sick. Curious, the young physician conducted his own investigations on eliminating sickness by restoring the magnetic balance inside the body. Mesmer's magnetic therapy would soon bring fame beyond his wildest dreams. Hell protested that Mesmer unfairly borrowed the idea from him, but to no avail.

Mesmer believed that the magnetism of iron, like the planetary bodies, affected a magnetic fluid in the body that controlled health and disease. He passed magnets across the bodies of his patients and found that some drifted into a trance. Bolstered by his findings on "animal magnetism," he treated patients with a variety of physiological symptoms including deafness, paralysis, blind-

ness, rheumatism, headaches, and chronic pain. He even claimed he could cure epilepsy and hysteria.

Although popular with Viennese society, the scientific community greeted Mesmer's animal magnetism with skepticism and scorn. In a celebrated case, he treated a blind concert pianist named Maria Theresia von Paradis, who happened to be a friend of Mozart's. After Mesmer claimed he had restored her sight, several eminent physicians challenged his results and branded him a charlatan. In 1777, he was expelled from the medical faculty of the University of Vienna and barred from the practice of medicine. With his gift for controversy, it would not be the last time Mesmer would clash with medical authority.

Abandoning his family in 1778, Mesmer took exile in Paris where he caused an immediate sensation. In many ways, his flair for grandiosity seemed perfectly suited to the extravagance of pre-Revolutionary Parisian society (Hoffeld, 1980). Nestled in a suite at the Place Vendôme and later at the fashionable Hôtel Bullion, his clinic introduced the idea of psychotherapy as theater. In a dimly lit salon, patients gathered around a *baquet,* a large wooden tub filled with mystical chemicals that Mesmer described with a Cartesian flourish as "animal spirits" (the tub contained nothing more than water and bits of metal, stone, and ground glass).

In one of the earliest attempts at group therapy, patients were instructed to take an afflicted part of their body, a paralyzed arm, say, and press it against iron rods rising from the sides of the *baquet.* As music from a glass armonica soothed in the background, Mesmer made his grand entrance dressed in a lilac robe and brandishing a long iron wand, looking more like a sorcerer than a physician. He wandered from person to person, touching them with the wand and staring deep into their eyes. When he gave the command "*Dormez*" ("sleep"), his patients would slip into a trance. In the spell of this "crisis," some would tremble or twitch as if in the throes of a seizure. Others would groan or laugh or scream. A few would spin in a frenzied dance or collapse in a cold faint. But after the crisis had passed, most appeared to be free of their affliction.

Before long, Mesmer and his celebrated therapy were known to both rich and poor. Among the wealthy and titled, Marie Antoinette and the Marquis de Lafayette joined the thousands who flocked to the clinic for the privilege of being mesmerized. As Mesmer's popularity soared, Mozart made mesmerism the stuff of friendly satire in his comic opera, *Così Fan Tutte* (Landon, 1990).

As in Vienna, however, the French medical community came to detest the practice of animal magnetism. Armed with a keen wit and the sort of bombast that might have impressed Paracelsus, Mesmer did not back down from his critics. With characteristic audacity, he issued a challenge to the French Academy of Medicine to select twenty patients at random; ten would be given to him for treatment and the remaining half would be assigned to the care of academy members. Confident in his healing powers, Mesmer believed the clinical results would demonstrate the potency of his therapy. Unimpressed, the academy declined to participate in the contest. For Mesmer, the academy's reluctance must have seemed a small victory in itself.

In its day, Mesmer's controversial magnetic theory was debated with the same intensity and passion that would later surround the work of Sigmund Freud. Like Freud, Mesmer recognized the advantage of spreading his message to an American audience. With support from the Marquis de Lafayette, Mesmer corresponded with George Washington about the possibility of introducing mesmerism to the United States (Buranelli, 1975). Out of respect for Lafayette's distinguished service during the Revolutionary War, Washington was polite but noncommittal.

By 1784, the rift between Mesmer and his medical colleagues swelled into a heated confrontation that would travel all the way to the court of King Louis XVI. Sympathetic to Mesmer's cause, a group calling itself the "Society of Harmony" called on the monarchy to investigate. In our world of congressional hearings, it is not uncommon to have government investigate a medical practice, but it was a rarity in Mesmer's time. The king convened a panel of experts to determine if mesmerism was a legitimate medical practice or little more than a dangerous magic trick. The blue-ribbon panel boasted such intellectuals as the American states-

man and scientist Benjamin Franklin (an ambassador to France at the time), the chemist Antoine-Laurent Lavoisier, the astronomer Jean-Sylvain Bailly, and Joseph Guillotin, a physician and proponent of the beheading machine (both Lavoisier and Bailly would be guillotined during the French Revolution). After examining the evidence, a verdict was issued on August 11, 1784:

> The commissioners have ascertained that the animal magnetic fluid is not perceptible by any of the senses; that it has no action, either on themselves or on the patients subjected to it. . . . Finally, [the commissioners] have demonstrated by decisive experiments that imagination apart from magnetism produces convulsions, and that magnetism without imagination produces nothing. (Binet & Féré, 1887/1891, pp. 16–17)

Unable to find support for mesmerism, the commission insisted that any positive effects of the treatment were the product of deception or the power of suggestion (Bromberg, 1959).

The commission's decision shattered Mesmer's reputation and career. Denounced as an impostor, Mesmer closed his notorious practice and left Paris in disgrace. After a move to London and later Germany, he practiced animal magnetism, but never regained the fame and fortune he had enjoyed in Paris. Mesmer died in obscurity in 1815, but his legacy is well preserved in the modern use of hypnotherapy.

Did Mesmer practice hypnosis? In the formal sense, no. But the practice of mesmerism relied on methods of suggestion that would be refined and investigated by a number of later hypnotherapists including the Marquis de Puységur (1751–1825), James Braid (1795–1860), and Jean-Martin Charcot (1825–1893). Outside of psychology, Mesmer's ideas remained a source of fascination for the public and notable intellectuals of the nineteenth century. The novelist Charles Dickens (1812–1870) dabbled with mesmerical experiments as did Ada Lovelace (1815–1852), a British mathematician and daughter of Lord Byron (Woolley, 1999).

Philippe Pinel.   After Mesmer, the face of humanitarian reform shifted to the work of a bold physician named Philippe Pinel (*pe NEL*), who spearheaded widespread reform in French asylums. A scientist more than a showman, Pinel enjoyed a medical respectability that forever eluded Mesmer.

Born near Castres, France, in 1745, Pinel was the first of seven children and the product of a rich medical heritage—Pinel's father was a surgeon and his mother's family included several physicians. Following an early literary education, Pinel studied theology at Toulouse in 1767, then switched to medical studies and earned his medical degree in 1773. Condillac's analytic method had a profound impact on Pinel's thinking (Riese, 1951), as did the ideas of Locke, Hippocrates, Rousseau, and Voltaire. A new way of thinking was taking shape with an emphasis on equality, freedom, education, and the improvement of all societal institutions. Disadvantaged people were no longer regarded as possessed or evil, but rather as sick or as victims of cruel and uncaring social institutions.

In this climate of optimism about human perfectibility, Pinel introduced legendary reforms at the hospital of the Bicêtre and later at the Salpêtrière. Prior to his arrival in 1792, inmates at the Bicêtre hospital were confined in cramped, poorly ventilated, foul-smelling quarters where they lived in accumulations of filth. Disturbed by the horrible conditions, Pinel petitioned the French government about a plan to experiment with new methods of treatment. At last, an official visited the Bicêtre hospital and witnessed firsthand the spectacle of patients chained in cells and shouting obscenities. The government official granted the freedom to experiment, but warned that Pinel would likely become the victim of his own show of mercy.

The time had come for dramatic reform. Slowly and cautiously, Pinel liberated fifty patients. The poignant release of one man is illustrated in a memoir from Pinel's son as translated and abridged by Dix (1845/1971):

> The experiments commenced with an English captain, whose history was unknown; he had been in chains forty years! As he was thought to be one of the most dangerous, having killed, at one time, an attendant with a blow from his manacles, the keepers approached him with caution; but first Pinel entered his cell unattended. "Ah, well captain, I will

> cause your chains to be taken off; you shall have liberty to walk in the court, if you will promise to behave like a gentleman, and offer no assault to those you will meet." "I would promise,' said the maniac; "but you deride me, you are amusing yourself at my expense; you all fear me, once free." "I have six men," replied Pinel, "ready to obey my orders; believe me, therefore, I will set you free from this duress, if you will put on this jacket." The captain assented; the chains were removed, and the jacket laced;—the keepers withdrew, without closing the door. He raised himself, but fell: this effort was repeated again and again; the use of his limbs, so long constrained, nearly failed: at length, trembling, and with tottering steps, he emerged from his dark dungeon. His first look was the sky! "Ah," cried he, "how beautiful!" The remainder of the day he was constantly moving to and fro, uttering continually exclamations of pleasure;—he heeded no one: the flowers, the trees, above all the sky, engrossed him. At night he voluntarily returned to his cell, which had been cleansed, and furnished with a better bed: his sleep was tranquil and profound. For the two remaining years which he spent in the hospital, he had no recurrence of violent paroxysms, and often rendered good service to the keepers, in conducting the affairs of the establishment. (pp. 30–31)

In dealing with patients, Pinel placed emphasis on logical consequences. For example, on being released from confinement or chains, patients were informed that continued freedom would depend on their behavior. Patient after patient responded to his humane treatment. In time, the fame of the reformer was assured and his techniques were sometimes revered as an original discovery. In truth, Pinel's methods signaled a return to the psychological medicine of the ancient Greeks.

Based on clinical observation, Pinel's classic book, *A Treatise on Insanity* (1806/1977), outlined a simplified and improved classification of mental disorders. Influential in its time, his classification system distinguished five major clinical categories which he called "species." The first was *melancholia,* a disorder that includes depression and/or delusions, especially delusions of persecution or involving suspicion. The second species was *mania without delirium,* a disorder characterized by poor impulse control or acts of fury. Pinel's third species involved *mania with delirium,* characterized by continuous or intermittent nervous excitement and intellectual deterioration. He called the fourth species *dementia* and described it as "marked by ideas unconnected amongst themselves and without relation to external objects" (Pinel, 1806/1977, p. 161). The final category, *idiotisme,* involved a general reduction of intellectual capacity.

With regard to etiology, Pinel rejected the popular belief of his day that all mental disorders have an anatomical or physiological basis. Although he believed that some disorders are associated with malformed skulls, his own research revealed that many mental patients have no identifiable physiological or anatomical abnormality. An individual's environment and lifestyle, Pinel argued, play powerful roles in the creation of mental illness.

Because the home environment might contribute to mental disorders, he encouraged the admission of patients to mental hospitals. In a 1794 address before the Society for Natural History, Pinel appealed to the Revolutionary French government to construct asylums designed for humane care (Weiner, 1992), a cause later taken up by the American reformer Dorothea Dix. Pinel concluded that hospitals should group patients according to the nature and severity of their disorders. Hospital management and treatment should be interrelated so that patients live in clean and uncrowded quarters with a chance to enjoy fresh air and sunlight as well as opportunities to engage in work. Physical restraint should be used only when necessary.

As one of the founders of *moral therapy* (a precursor to psychotherapy), Pinel dedicated a major section of his *Treatise* to "The Moral Treatment of Insanity." Moral therapy consisted of *talk treatment* in a generally supportive atmosphere in which the therapist had a healthy respect for the dignity and responsibility of the patient. In several respects, Pinel's therapeutic philosophy foreshadowed the modern school of humanistic psychology discussed in Chapter 17.

Benjamin Rush. Robinson (1977) has noted some striking parallels in the lives of Philippe Pinel and Benjamin Rush. Both were born in 1745 and raised during periods of violent revolution. They each developed an interest in the work of William Cullen, a famous Scottish physiologist. Both men considered the ministry before deciding on medical careers and each served in post-Revolutionary positions in their respective governments. Of course, both are remembered as great reformers.

Benjamin Rush was born on the outskirts of Philadelphia, the fourth of seven children. His father, John Rush, died when Benjamin was only five. During the next three years, he lived with his mother, Susanna Hall Harvey Rush, before joining a boarding school run by his uncle, Samuel Finley.

After boarding school, Rush entered the College of New Jersey (now Princeton), where he earned his bachelor's degree in 1760. He served in a medical apprenticeship from 1761 to 1766 and took courses at the College of Philadelphia. In the fall of 1766, he enrolled at the University of Edinburgh, where he received his medical degree in 1768. In 1776, Rush returned to Philadelphia and practiced medicine, primarily among the poor. That same year, he married Julia Stockton (1759–1848). He was appointed chair of chemistry at the College of Pennsylvania, where he established a national reputation as a medical educator (one of his students, Nathaniel Chapman [1780–1853], became the first president of the American Medical Association in 1848). Rush briefly served as surgeon general of the army under George Washington. Disagreements with Washington over the quality of medical service, however, led to Rush's resignation.

As a member of the Continental Congress, Rush was one of the original signers of the Declaration of Independence. He enjoyed friendships with key figures of the day including Thomas Jefferson and John Adams. In fact, Rush was instrumental in reconciling the former American presidents after bitter political quarrels in the 1790s led them to stop speaking (McCullough, 2001). Rush had a long-standing interest in dreams (Binger, 1969) and he shared a prophetic one with Adams that involved a reunion with Jefferson. With subtle manipulation, Rush edited disparaging comments in a letter from Jefferson and sent Adams the more laudatory remarks (Ellis, 1993).

After further prodding by Rush, Adams and Jefferson resumed their friendship in 1812, and a remarkable correspondence followed that now stands as one of the greatest literary exchanges in the English language. Both men died on the same day, July 4, 1826, the fiftieth anniversary of the signing of the Declaration of Independence.

During his lifetime, Rush pursued many social causes and wrote articles for the popular press in support of his reform interests. While Jefferson remained silent on the slavery issue, Rush was active in the abolition movement (Plummer, 1970). He also advocated improved education for women, a national university system, and greater flexibility in school curricula with a stronger emphasis on practical subjects. He questioned the utility of Greek and Latin and placed emphasis on the importance of modern languages.

Rush (1806) protested the use of punishment as a means of controlling behavior. He called for reform of inhumane prison conditions and opposed public and capital punishment. He also disliked corporal punishment in schools because it interfered with learning and seemed contrary to the best ideals of a free people. Disruptive classroom behavior, Rush thought, would be better handled by private conversation with the student or by a period of detention after school.

He was strongly influenced by the British empiricists, especially the physiological psychology of David Hartley. At the same time, he embraced traditional Christianity though he was not formally affiliated with any church (theologically, he may have been most comfortable in the community of Christian Unitarians). He emphasized universal salvation with its strong emphasis on social reforms and once remarked, "It is possible to convert men into republican machines. This must be done, if we expect them to perform their parts properly, in the great machine of the government of the state. . . . The wills of the people . . . must be fitted to each other by means of education before they can be made to produce regularity and unison in government" (Rush, 1806, pp. 14–15).

Benjamin Rush remained active in government, medicine, and social activism until his death in 1813. He was buried at Christ Church in Philadelphia. Upon hearing of his death, Adams wrote to Jefferson, "I know of no character living or dead who has done more real good for his country" (McCullough, 2001, p. 612). Rush's wife mourned his death for more than thirty years and, as a side note, Julia Rush's diary entries have been analyzed as a case study in the psychology of coping with loss (Thielman & Melges, 1986). Two of Benjamin and Julia Rush's thirteen children became prominent professionals: James Rush (1786–1869) was a physician-psychologist and Richard Rush (1780–1859) was a lawyer and diplomat.

As with his dedication to political and social issues, Rush was a visible leader in the care and treatment of mental patients. In 1812, he wrote *Medical Inquiries and Observations Upon the Diseases of the Mind,* the first psychopathology textbook in America. He is recognized as the first American psychiatrist, and his image is immortalized in the official logo of the American Psychiatric Association.

In contrast with Pinel, Rush's approach to mental disorders is a curious blend of conservative Christianity and scientific materialism. On one hand, he believed in a theocentric universe and in a doctrine of original sin (see Carlson & Simpson, 1964, pp. 290–214; Carlson, 1977, pp. 74–104). On the other hand, Rush (1812/1818) claimed that all psychopathology was the product of physiological processes. As suggested in the title of his classic 1812 book, Rush viewed psychopathology as the study of "diseases of the mind." Mental disorders were thought to have their origin primarily in the blood vessels of the brain. In his opinion, disturbances of circulation were the cause of all disease including mental disorders. As evidence for his theory, he pointed to the common symptomatology between mental disorders and disorders such as strokes that have a known blood vessel pathology. When Rush observed abnormalities of pulse in mental patients, he took it as further proof for his circulation theory.

Rush sometimes departed from his circulation model when studying certain types of mental disease, although he seldom strayed from organic explanations. He was also a pioneer in the study of multiple personality disorder, today called "dissociative identity disorde." (DID). The 1811 diagnosis of an American woman named Mary Reynolds (1793–1854) is often regarded as the first DID case study. In fact, Rush had described three earlier cases of dissociation in which he accounted for this "doubling" as the product of an abnormal brain (Carlson, 1981).

He also conducted the first medical studies on alcohol, which he described in a treatise called "An Inquiry into the Effects of Ardent Spirits upon the Human Body and Mind" (Keller, 1943). At a time when physicians believed that drunkenness was neither a disease nor a compulsive condition, Rush became the first to claim that alcoholism was both an addiction and a progressive disease (Levine, 1978).

Given his theoretical differences with Pinel about the etiology of mental disorders, it is not surprising that Rush advocated treatments that differed from moral therapy. He was open to a variety of treatments and even considered ones discredited by his colleagues. Years after his friend Benjamin Franklin had failed to find compelling value in Mesmer's work, Rush researched animal magnetism in 1789 and 1812 (Schneck, 1978). Although he rejected Mesmer's theory, he believed in the validity of suggestion and imagination and incorporated them into his clinical practice.

Like many physicians of his day, Rush practiced bloodletting, a method dating back to Hippocrates. An excess of blood was thought to be responsible for both mental and physical disease. When George Washington developed what was likely a throat infection, his physicians drained almost two-thirds of his blood and he died hours later at Mount Vernon (Morens, 1999). Ironically, Rush was on trial in Philadelphia at the time for malpractice charges relating to his use of bleeding.

Some of Rush's more notorious and unorthodox treatments were inspired by his circulation theory. He invented a device known as the *gyrator,* a machine that whirled the patient rapidly in a circle to stimulate blood flow in the brain. Not surprisingly, many patients passed out after taking a spin in the gyrator. Rush also designed a *tranquilizing chair,* a large wooden chair into which maniacal patients were strapped until they regained

composure. He believed this technique was more humane than binding people in straitjackets.

If Rush's methods appear inhumane, they were nevertheless motivated by sincere humanitarian concern. Mackler and Hamilton (1967) point out that Rush had a genuine regard for the dignity of his patients and regularly demanded adequate heating, baths, and employment for them. They also note that his treatments were not always physical; Rush recognized the importance of a supportive social and psychological environment.

Despite the attention given to his views on mental disease, Rush's work on psychology has been unduly neglected. His lectures on the mind reveal far-reaching psychological interests (Carlson, Wollock, & Noel, 1981). His syllabus for a course on "physiology, pathology, hygiene, and the practice of medicine" covered such topics as the history of the nature of mind, instinct, memory, imagination, perception, association, hunger, thirst, dreams, sleep, somnambulism, reason, and volition.

Although not generally recognized, Rush coined the word *phrenology* (Noel & Carlson, 1970). He believed that phrenology need not refer to spirits or to an abstract philosophy of being; instead, he saw it as an intelligible and useful science of the mind (Carlson, Wollock, & Noel, 1981). It was intelligible in that a close connection between mind and body paved the way for understanding the operations of the mind via physical events. Rush argued that phrenology was useful to the physician because disorders of the mind influence diseases of the body (Noel & Carlson, 1973).

As with his circulation theory, Rush's ideas about phrenology and psychology were grounded in physiology. He observed that physiological states have a direct influence on moods. For example, a person may be irritable prior to breakfast, but afterward the same individual may be affable. Diet was important to mental outlook and Rush claimed that vegetables (as opposed to meat) had particular beneficial consequences for the passions. Climate also plays a role in human emotional life, with fog and rainy seasons producing negative affect and sunshine producing happiness. Rush believed that human emotions may be further influenced by light and darkness, music, cleanliness, pain, and idleness (which he took to be the parent of all vice).

Like Philippe Pinel, Benjamin Rush's work was critical in the development of psychiatry and humanitarian reform. Despite their influence, the reforms proposed by Pinel and Rush did not translate into a social movement. Indeed, for a time, reform remained a local affair. Often, humane treatments were discovered independently in other localities.

Reform in Other Places

In 1796, the famous York Retreat was opened by the British Quaker William Tuke (1732–1822) and the Society of Friends. Tuke, a philanthropist and merchant, had become distraught over the maltreatment and subsequent death of a friend who had been confined in the York Asylum. Without benefit of a medical background, Tuke founded the York Retreat based upon principles of humane treatment that resembled the methods employed by Pinel (at the time, Tuke was unfamiliar with the French reformer's work).

In contrast with most of Europe's inhumane and squalid asylums, the York Retreat resided on a sprawling, picturesque country estate where patients enjoyed fresh air, rest, and the tranquility of nature. Tuke opposed the use of manacles and chains and he did away with the widespread practice of bloodletting. Gentle supportive treatment and meaningful occupations were encouraged, along with education programs for attendants.

Later, the York Retreat was run by Tuke's great-grandson, Daniel Hack Tuke (1827–1895), who took a medical degree from Heidelberg University in 1853. Daniel Hack Tuke distinguished himself as a leading authority on mental disorders and served as an editor of the *Journal of Mental Science*. He wrote numerous papers and wrote or edited several classic books, including *A Dictionary of Psychological Medicine* (1892), *Illustrations of the Influence of the Mind Upon the Body in Health and Disease* (1872), and *Insanity in Ancient and Modern Life with Chapters on Prevention* (1878).

In Italy, Vincenzo Chiarugi (1759–c. 1820) instituted humanitarian reform while working at

Bonifazio Hospital and was one of the first to employ psychodrama as a clinical tool. Chiarugi's classification system and studies on etiology and treatment were remarkably similar to (and in many cases more advanced than) Pinel's work. Because Chiarugi's views were published prior to Pinel's, we are left to wonder why history has not given greater recognition to this Italian pioneer. One possibility is that Pinel, who was the subject of much public and scientific recognition, was harsh in his judgment of Chiarugi's work (see Harms, 1967, pp. 75–85). As a result of Pinel's criticism, which was perhaps unjustified, Chiarugi's work lost prestige and fell into obscurity.

At about the same time, Germany played host to several reform movements as well as a few important theoretical works. Some of the most influential ideas flowed from the pen of Johann Christian Reil (1759–1813), who is often considered one of the founders of modern psychotherapy. Harms (1967, p. 86) described Reil as a "psychological phenomenologist for whom the modern concepts of *Ganzheit*, totality, unity, centricity are basic elements of scientific interpretation."

Reil viewed mental illness in terms of a failure of the basic unity of psychological processes. The failure of unity or centricity may result from either physical or social-psychological disturbances. Reil's approach to therapeutic intervention included psychodrama, occupational therapy, music therapy, and the encouragement of socially acceptable means of expressing emotion.

Although it would not arrive until a half century later, Reil anticipated the day when worthwhile experiments would be conducted on the senses. He felt that such research (see Harms, 1967, p. 91) would aid in understanding mental processes and psychopathology. Clearly, he saw a practical role for scientific psychology in the study of mental disorder.

Reform Becomes a Social Movement: Dorothea Dix

Reform in the care and treatment of mental disorders was, for a time, restricted to local settings. But by the midnineteenth century, humanitarian reform

Dorothea Dix

strated an unusual love of learning. She had an insatiable appetite for knowledge.

In 1816, Dix went to Worcester to live with an aunt. In Worcester, at age fourteen, she was allowed to start a private school for small children. She attempted to hide her youth with adult dress and mannerisms. As a teacher, she adopted the stern techniques of her time, demanding strict obedience, punctuality, respect, extensive drills, and memory work. Discipline was enforced with a birch rod. After three years of successful work as a teacher in Worcester, Dorothea Dix returned to her grandmother in Boston, continuing her studies and availing herself of every possible educational opportunity. She took private instruction and enrolled in public lecture courses given by professors from Harvard University. She made extensive use of public libraries and enjoyed the intellectual and spiritual stimulation provided by the preaching of the well-known Unitarian preacher William Ellery Charming. Dix developed a special fondness for history, science, and literature and established considerable expertise in botany and astronomy.

By 1821, Dix had opened a "dame" school at her grandmother's home in Orange Court. This school was one of many of the day that served to prepare students for public grammar schools. Students were expected to be able to read prior to entering the public schools, hence there was a large demand for private preparatory schools. In addition to her regular "dame" school, Dix opened a free evening school for poor children who could not afford the usual private schools. Dix was an unusually devoted teacher who continuously sought to expand her knowledge so that she might be more effective in the classroom. In spare hours she worked on a book designed to provide parents and teachers with useful, well-researched information on how to answer children's questions on common natural topics. Questions such as What causes a rainbow? What are clouds? or Where do diamonds come from? were difficult for many parents and teachers of the day. Dix's book, dealing with over three hundred questions of this kind, first published under the title *Conversations on Common Things,* went through sixty editions.

spread rapidly throughout the United States and Europe. The key figure in the reform movement was an American woman named Dorothea Lynde Dix (1802–1887). She, more than any other, was the catalyst in a humanitarian attempt to make the enlightened techniques of Pinel and Tuke available on a large scale. Such techniques had been available to the upper classes who could afford the best treatment, but not to the poor.

Dorothea Dix was born in Hampden, Maine, on April 4, 1802. A childhood filled early with adult responsibilities prepared her for the rigors of her later work as a reformer. As a child, she cared for two younger brothers, cooked, cleaned house, and cared for her invalid mother. She also stitched and pasted her father's sermons, which were printed on loose sheets and sold as religious tracts. Her father, an itinerant Methodist preacher, was away from home much of the time.

For reasons that are not entirely clear, at age twelve Dorothea Dix left home to live with her Grandmother Dix in Boston. In the new setting, Dorothea was exposed to a demanding discipline that required long hours of rigorous work. Whatever the task (stitching a quilt, cleaning a room), the demand was for compulsive attention to detail, and perfection was always the goal. The young Dix attended school in Boston and quickly demon-

By 1841, it appeared that Dorothea Dix's career as a teacher was over. A chronic pulmonary disorder had forced her on numerous occasions to take leave of teaching activities for enforced periods of bed rest. In March of 1841, she was recovering from an extended illness but had nevertheless made a decision to help a young Unitarian ministerial student by substituting as a teacher in a Sunday School class to be held in the East Cambridge jail. What Dix observed at the jail on a cold March morning in 1841 changed her life.

Typically at that time, one might find hardened criminals, mentally disadvantaged individuals, alcoholics, and the mentally ill housed together in unheated jail cells filled with filth. Shocked by the stench and the misery she witnessed, Dix pleaded with the jailer at least to provide some heat for the prisoners who were huddled together and shivering from cold. The jailer refused, declaring that insane people cannot feel heat and cold. The inhumane conditions prevailing in the jail prompted Dix to seek court action to clean up the jail and to provide heat. Her appeal to the court was victorious and soon the conditions in the East Cambridge jail were improved.

Dix then proceeded to investigate the conditions of mental patients and prisoners in other parts of Massachusetts. At the same time, the scholarly former schoolteacher started to read the available literature on mental illness and to consult with authorities so that she might be in touch with the most advanced views on the topic. Dix was particularly impressed with the views of the Tukes in England and Pinel in France. Their enlightened techniques stood in marked contrast with the prevailing custodialism in most almshouses and jails.

In extensive travel throughout the state of Massachusetts, Dix found that the conditions she had encountered in the East Cambridge jail were typical. Quarters in almshouses and jails were unfurnished, sanitation was neglected, heat was seldom provided, and diets were inadequate. Many of the mentally ill and feebleminded simply roamed the countryside. The latter may have been more fortunate than those who were confined.

Conducting some of the earliest social research in America, Dix armed herself with the facts of her extensive investigation and prepared a memorial for the lawmakers of Massachusetts. With the help of powerful political figures such as Horace Mann, Senator Charles Sumner, and Dr. Samuel Gridley Howe, she was able to convince the legislators that additional facilities and personnel were needed to provide for the care and treatment of the mentally ill. As a result of Dix's research and her memorial, funds were set aside for an expansion of the state hospital at Worcester. Instead of the one hospital at Worcester, Dix would have preferred the erection of an additional smaller hospital in a different location. Nevertheless, her memorial was successful and her career as a reformer was launched.

After the victory in Massachusetts, Dix proceeded to other states. Her reform activities followed a pattern that became familiar: extensive research into existing conditions, contact with key political figures, preparation of a memorial describing existing conditions, and requests for new or additional modern facilities. While she made no public speeches, she was typically able to persuade key political figures to read her memorials to legislative bodies. Her accomplishments in forty years of reform work were extensive. She played a key role in the founding of thirty-two mental hospitals, several schools for the feebleminded, training facilities for nurses, and improvements in prisons and mental institutions.

Her success may be attributed partly to her efforts occurring during an era that was particularly receptive to humanitarian reform. She was also well organized, energetic, and persuasive. Her success was also enhanced by her extensive knowledge of mental disorders. Indeed, Dain (1964, p. 171) contended that her knowledge compared favorably with that of the leading authorities of her day. Research into her memorials (see Viney, 1996b; Viney & Bartsch, 1984) showed that she had a grasp of the history of concepts of insanity and was well acquainted with the legal aspects of the subject. Her views on etiology recognized physiological, psychological, and social contributions. The brain was the organ of the mind but insanity was also *the offspring of civilization*. She was particularly impressed with the role of unemployment, loss of family or possessions, and abnormal religious excitement in the etiology of mental disorder. She believed that treatment should include good diet, exercise, amusement (including music, games, and reading), and meaningful occupation. Dix was strongly opposed to custodialism, except for hopelessly incurable cases. The emphasis in her memorials was on treatment and curability. Accordingly, she raised money, not only for buildings but also for libraries, musical instruments, museums, and, in one case, a bowling alley. She had a keen interest in anything that would facilitate therapeutic intervention.

Stevens and Gardner (1982, p. 62) pointed out that Dorothea Dix represented the conscience of early psychology. They also argued that without Dix and other humanitarian reformers, psychology might have been restricted to laboratory investigations or might have stagnated. It is clear that popular and practical concern may help create a friendly atmosphere for the development of a new discipline. Because of her great ability to mobilize public opinion about problems that were psychological in nature, Dix's contributions may be greater than has generally been recognized.

During the Civil War, Dix's work as a reformer was interrupted while she served as Superintendent of Union Army Nurses. Following the war, she returned to her work as a reformer, but was no longer as effective as she had been in earlier years. By the time of her death in 1887, attention was less focused on the needs of the mentally ill. During the next decade and the early part of the twentieth century, conditions in mental hospitals deteriorated. Unfortunately, many of the hospitals became almost as custodial as the jails and almshouses they replaced.

Reform in the Care and Treatment of Mental Deficiency

Prior to the modern era, physical and mental disabilities were often regarded as the work of demons or as evidence of the sins of the parents. Having intercourse during menstruation is an example of a sin that was viewed as a major cause of defective children. Ranke-Heinemann (1990, pp. 22–23) documented the teachings of numerous thirteenth-century theologians who attributed a great variety of defects to the poisonous effects of menstrual blood on the male seed. Children born with disabilities might also be regarded as *changelings,* a term that refers to the belief that a defective child could be substituted by an evil force for a legitimate, beautiful, and normal child. Needless to say, children regarded as changelings were often neglected, abused, abandoned, or sacrificed.

More naturalistic approaches to mental deficiency, along with reforms in care and treatment of the mentally deficient, occurred alongside the reforms in the care and treatment of the mentally ill. A key pioneer in the study and training of mental deficiency was Jean Itard (1775–1838), a French teacher of the deaf. Itard's work with mental deficiency was initiated by the accidental discovery by some hunters of a wild boy near Aveyron in France. The boy, about ten years of age, had apparently been abandoned by his parents, but had somehow managed to survive in the wild. When he was first captured, he displayed many of the characteristics of a wild animal, appearing to be all but unmanageable. Itard worked with the "wild boy of Aveyron" for approximately two years. Although he failed to teach the boy to speak, he was nevertheless able to produce many desirable changes. The boy became affectionate and responsive. He was clearly able to understand many words and was able to engage in useful tasks. Among later commentators there is a general consensus that the boy probably was retarded and that this was the reason for his inability to acquire language skills. Itard's work was suggestive of what might be accomplished on a larger scale with other retarded children.

Another Frenchman, Edouard Seguin (1812–1880), developed a systematic approach to the training of mentally deficient individuals. Seguin sought ways to assist individuals in developing their innate sensory and motor capacities so that they might engage in useful skills. He worked first in France and later in the United States; his methods and results caught the attention of the public. Soon fund-raising efforts made by reformers such as Dorothea Dix resulted in training facilities for those with mental deficiency. There was a greater need for the systematic study of learning processes and the development of training techniques. Thus, another reform movement created a need for the systematic study of topics such as learning, sensory and motor processes, and motivation that were later to become standard content areas of psychology.

Women's Reform Movements

In Chapter 6 we discussed Mary Wollstonecraft's classic work, *A Vindication of the Rights of Women* and John Stuart Mill's work, *The Subjection of Women.* These visionary writers were reacting to the long history of the subordination of women. Women, compared with men, were commonly regarded as less intelligent, less creative, more emotional, and relatively disinterested in commercial, political, economic, and philosophical questions. Sex stereotypes were used to justify restrictions on property rights, educational opportunities, voting privileges, and work opportunities for women. It was further argued that women were incapacitated once each month because of the menstrual cycle.

By the mid- to late-nineteenth century there was growing agitation for women's rights and a corresponding public interest in the abilities of women. Public interest was stimulated by an outpouring of popular magazine articles on such topics as the education of women, the intelligence of women, sex differences in emotional expression, and voting privileges for women. Many of these articles were written in defense of old stereotypes, but many challenged the older ways of thinking. Such challenges, along with the demands of reformers in the women's movement, helped create a climate friendly to impartial studies of sex differences. In fact, many of the sex stereotypes lent themselves to experimental investigation and some of the early psychological research delivered a death blow to many of the old attitudes about women. For example, Leta Stetter Hollingworth (see Chapter 12) conducted research demonstrating that women were not mentally or physically incapacitated by the menstrual cycle.

The women's reform movements grew out of a long and painful history with deeply entrenched

ideas that were sometimes grounded in traditions regarded by many as sacred. Following the American Civil War, there were continuing disputes in religious magazines about whether women should be allowed to speak in church services (see Knowlton, 1867; Torrey, 1867). Such disputes undoubtedly grew out of the interpretive difficulties of scriptures such as I Corinthians 14:34–35, which was used as a source of authority for those who forbid women to speak in church. If women could not speak in church, there was little possibility for them to assume positions of spiritual leadership. The undercutting of leadership roles for women in the religious arena was common in Western as well as Middle Eastern and Islamic traditions (Lippman, 1995, p. 96). It may be argued that the subordination of women in some religious traditions did not reflect true interpretations of those traditions, but as a practical fact, such subordination took place and continues to take place in some traditions. In many religious and cultural traditions, women were required to lower their eyes, cover their heads, veil their faces, avoid adorning themselves with jewelry, and to cultivate habits of humility, obedience, submission, domesticity, and chastity. Leadership roles could be filled only by men.

The late nineteenth century witnessed an unprecedented battle for a whole new orientation toward women and a new and informed appraisal of their intellectual abilities and personal and spiritual gifts. Such an appraisal, of course, would become grist for the work of psychologists. The battle itself was waged on many fronts (e.g., access to university education, new employment opportunities, property rights), but the most visible facet of the battle was in the arena of suffrage or the right of women to vote. The intensity of the battle, spearheaded in the United States by such reformers as Susan B. Anthony and Elizabeth Cady Stanton, is illustrated by the fact that legislation was introduced in Congress each year for more than forty years before the Nineteenth Amendment to the constitution was finally passed in 1920. The depth of feelings and the fervor of the battle were also illustrated in the radical claims set forth by those who opposed the legislation. An example is provided by then former president Grover Cleveland who argued from the pages of *The Ladies Home Journal* that good conservative women had no desire to vote and that they understood their divinely appointed roles (Cleveland, 1905).

Margaret Sanger and Family Limitation. Another facet of the women's movement was every bit as intense and controversial as suffrage and, in some quarters, remains controversial to the present day. The dynamics of family life and the effects of family structures on individual personality development would later become important topical areas for social and developmental psychologists, but some of the early sensitivities to these topical areas are found in the work of reformers in the women's movement.

Margaret Sanger (1883–1966) was the sixth of the eleven children of Ann (Purcell) Higgins and Michael Hennessey Higgins. Even as a child, Sanger was deeply aware of the enormous demands of eleven children, all weighing more than ten pounds at birth, on the health of her mother. She was convinced that the birthing and rearing demands of such a large family contributed to her mother's premature death at age forty-nine. Sanger observed many other families, large and small, in her New York neighborhood and came to the conclusion that there were many differences in the two, one of the chief being economic. Large families were generally poor; smaller families were not. In her early years, she developed a concern with issues pertaining to the quality of life for children and for women. Her mother remained a devout Catholic to her death while her father is best described as an intellectual, an impractical artist, a fiercely independent thinker, and an atheist. Margaret identified with the plight of her mother and with the intellectual independence of her father. Her life at home prepared her well for her subsequent career as a reformer with its demands to fight for a cause while standing firm against the relentless attacks of her critics.

Sanger was educated as a nurse and through her work became deeply moved by the plight of poor women. Once again, she developed an awareness of the poverty commonly associated with large families, but she also faced continuing inquiries

from poor women about how to control conception. Women sometimes begged for the secrets of birth control, but Sanger had no satisfactory answers. Doctors often advised women simply to avoid sex, but the effectiveness of such advice assumed the cooperation of husbands. A turning point in Sanger's career came with the death of one Sadie Sachs. Sanger had been called to the apartment of Sachs who was desperately ill from the effects of a self-induced abortion. Following her recovery, Sachs pleaded with the attending physician to provide information on how to avoid another pregnancy. The physician gave the usual unsatisfactory answer. A few months later, Sanger was called back to the apartment, but this time Sachs slipped into a coma and died from yet another self-induced abortion. Tragic events of this kind continued, as in earlier periods of history, to be common in the late nineteenth and early twentieth centuries. But this particular death was pivotal in Sanger's life. She would now devote herself to women's health issues with a particular focus on acquiring and publishing information on safe and effective means of gaining control over reproductive functions.

Margaret Sanger believed deeply that women's health and their ability to function on a more equal footing in modern society depended, at least partly, on birth control. She started her campaign to improve public knowledge of reproductive functions by publishing pamphlets that described the varieties of safe birth control methods known in her day. Later she formed organizations such as the National Birth Control League, the Voluntary Parenthood League, and the American Birth Control League, subsequently to become the Planned Parenthood Federation of America. As there had been strong resistance to suffrage, so also there was strong and highly vocal resistance to the work of Margaret Sanger. In Sanger's day there was a law known as the Comstock Law, named after the conservative reformer Anthony Comstock (1844–1915), who had led a crusade against literature that he had deemed as obscene. Birth control literature was included under the Comstock Law. This law forbid the U.S. Postal Service to deliver obscene materials. Sanger's pamphlets on birth control, containing explicit descriptions of birth control devices, were deemed obscene by the Postal Service and confiscated. In 1916 Sanger opened the first birth control clinic in the United States for the purpose of offering information and distributing contraceptive materials. Crowds of desperate women were lined up to take advantage of clinic services, but within nine days of the opening of the clinic Sanger was arrested and jailed on charges of creating a "public nuisance."

The trial aroused public interest because it dealt with important moral issues of the day. For example, should a physician be allowed to prescribe condoms for a husband with venereal disease or should a woman simply risk her health and well-being to satisfy her husband? The issue, of course, cuts both ways because the health of either sex is threatened by sex partners with venereal disease. Should a woman already incapacitated by tuberculosis or some other common disease of the day, be forbidden access to potential lifesaving information about birth control? These were examples of the kinds of problems that Sanger encountered in the women who had visited her clinic.

The final outcome of Sanger's trial was a small but significant victory. Though the Comstock Law itself was not thrown out, it was ruled that physicians could provide contraceptive advice as a means of preventing disease. In 1937 the American Medical Association endorsed the teaching of contraception in medical schools. Shortly after Sanger's trial, birth control information could be sent through the mails, but it was not until 1967 that the Supreme Court of the United States officially extended the right of birth control to married couples (Garraty & Carnes, 1999). Health psychology and human sexuality would later become important content areas in a maturing discipline of psychology. Margaret Sanger must be counted as an important part of the early intellectual context for these topical areas.

Sanger and her work, nevertheless, remain highly controversial at the outset of the twenty-first century. Like Mary Wollstonecraft before her, Sanger's detractors call attention to what they regard as disagreeable features in her character and personal life. She was a strong advocate of birth control for minority groups and is thus accused by some of her critics of racism. The basis of such an accusation is highly questionable, because minority groups were often poor, and it was poverty and its effects that were the real focus of Sanger's efforts. Sanger was known to be a socialist, she had affairs, her first marriage ended in divorce, and she was as vocal in her criticism of her detractors as they were of her. Hostility to Sanger was based partly on the fact that her work challenged doctrines regarded by many as sacred though leaders in numerous religious traditions supported her work. Sanger deepened public sensitivities to issues pertinent to human health and particularly to the health of women. Her reform program opened the door to increased reproductive freedom by challenging and modifying the restrictive legal structures of her day. Her work also had a direct effect on scientific work. Indeed, she provided the funding that led directly to the development of the birth control pill.

The naturalistic perspective, extended to topical areas such as the origin of life and the nature and origin of emotional problems, helped create an intellectual climate friendly to the development of psychology. It is particularly noteworthy that psychology was born as a formal discipline in an age of unprecedented humanitarian reform and on the heels of Darwin's revolutionary work. The formal birth of psychology cannot be understood apart from the intellectual context created by the radical extension of naturalism and by humanitarian reform.

REVIEW QUESTIONS

1. Outline the development of evolutionary thought regarding the solar system and geology.

2. Trace key developments in the theory of organic evolution prior to Darwin.

3. List and describe four technical features of Darwin's theory of evolution.

4. Discuss the significance of evolutionary theory to psychology and show specific influences of evolutionary theory on the development of psychology.

5. List at least six major social reform movements that took place in the nineteenth century.

6. Briefly describe the three major subdivisions of the *Malleus Maleficarum.*

7. How did Spinoza and Descartes challenge beliefs in witchcraft?

8. Outline the contributions of Benjamin Rush and Phillipe Pinel to reforms in the understanding of mental illness.

9. Dorothea Dix was a great social reformer but also had substantive views on mental illness. What were her views on the origin and treatment of mental illness?

10. Briefly, how did Jean Itard and Edouard Seguin advance our understanding of mental deficiencies?

CHAPTER 10

PSYCHOPHYSICS AND THE FORMAL FOUNDING OF PSYCHOLOGY

I have proceeded on the conviction that law and order even if they are not fundamentally sound are better than contradictions and lawlessness.

—Hermann von Helmholtz (1896)

As we have seen in the previous chapters, many important intellectual forces contributed to a climate friendly to the birth and nourishment of the discipline of psychology. The most direct influences, however, came from developments in physiology, pointing to the possibility that mental processes could be measured (Evans, 2000). This chapter examines selected scientific projects in physiology that led almost inexorably to the founding of the new discipline of psychology. The chapter then examines the formal founding of psychology and the first systematic approach to the discipline.

PSYCHOPHYSICS

The term **psychophysics** refers to the study of the relationships between the properties of stimuli as measured by a physical scale and the psychological or subjective impressions of those stimuli. The informal beginnings of psychophysics are encountered in speculation and wonder about the nature of the relationship between objects in the world and our perceptions of those objects. In Chapter 2, we reviewed various theoretical positions regarding what we can claim to know about objects in the world. One extreme position is encountered in the solipsistic claim that we are isolated in our subjective worlds. According to this position, we can know only our own private ex-

perience. Another extreme position, naive realism, contends that we see external things as they are. In a limited and modest way, early studies in psychophysics challenged both extreme positions.

As noted, psychophysics involves the study of the properties of stimuli as measured by a physical scale and psychological impressions of those stimuli. For example, a series of tones can be measured in terms of vibrations or frequencies. The term *hertz (Hz)* is used as the international unit equal to one cycle per second. With proper equipment, a graded series can be presented with known physical characteristics. One of the most obvious discoveries about any graded series is that there are values on the lower and upper extremes that do not register in experience. For tones, the average young person hears values from approximately 20 Hz to 20,000 Hz. In other words, there are lower and upper thresholds. The measurement of thresholds provides a small quantitative opening into the world of private experience. Part of the early work in psychophysics was directed at investigating *lower* and *upper thresholds* for varieties of stimuli in all sensory modalities. Such **thresholds** were typically defined operationally as that minimal or maximal (for upper thresholds) stimulus intensity that is detected 50 percent of the time.

Another type of threshold that was investigated was called the **difference threshold**—that minimal stimulus difference that is detectable 50 percent of the time. For example, an experimenter may stimulate the surface of the skin of a subject with two points of an adjustable compass known as an **aesthesiometer.** The subject, under certain conditions, may report the presence of only a single sensation, even though both points of the aesthesiometer clearly make contact with the skin. The task of the experimenter is to assess the two-point threshold (that distance where two points are experienced as two points instead of one point). It has been found that there are relatively insensitive areas (e.g., the back and thigh) where the two-point threshold may be well over 40 mm (over 1.5 inches). At the other extreme, the two-point threshold may be as small as 1 mm in a sensitive area (e.g., the tip of the tongue or the tips of the fingers).

An important contribution of psychophysics is that methods were forged that permitted a quantitative assessment of certain mental processes. The limits of possible experiences within a single dimension could be established for each of the senses by assessing absolute thresholds. Early psychophysics represented an interesting challenge to naive realism because it demonstrated measurable stimulus values that were below or above the threshold of awareness. As illustrated with the example of the aesthesiometer, there are also stimulus differences that cannot be experienced by the unaided senses. In fact, some stimulus differences must be surprisingly large to be experienced. Studies in psychophysics also uncovered lawful relationships between stimulus differences according to a physical scale and experienced differences. Such lawful relationships opened the possibility of finding a scientific handle for mental processes. A science of the mind was no longer an unattainable goal. The discovery of lawful relationships between physical values of stimuli and experience also challenged extreme solipsistic views. Such discoveries suggested that our experiences are tied to the physical world in lawful ways and that comparisons between individuals are meaningful.

The formal and systematic beginnings of psychophysics are found in the work of the German physiologist Ernst Heinrich Weber (1795–1878)

and physicist-philosopher Gustav T. Fechner (1801–1878).

Ernst Heinrich Weber

Little is known about the early life of Ernst Heinrich Weber, but it is known that he was born June 24, 1795, the third of thirteen children. His father was a professor of theology at the University of Wittenberg. At age sixteen, Ernst enrolled at the University of Wittenberg but later transferred to the University of Leipzig, where he completed a thesis on the anatomy of the sympathetic nerves. Weber was so highly regarded at Leipzig that the university officials offered him a position. He accepted the offer and stayed at Leipzig for the remainder of his career.

Weber worked in the fields of anatomy, physiology, physics, and biology. One of his most notable contributions was carried out in collaboration with his brother, Eduard. They discovered the inhibition of heart action following stimulation of the peripheral end of the vagus nerve. Kruta (1976) noted that this discovery, together with subsequent research, "showed that inhibition is a common phenomenon in the central nervous system and that an adequate balance between excitation and inhibition is indispensable for its normal function" (p. 200). In 1826, Weber turned his attention to the skin and muscle senses. His pioneering work in this area resulted in one of the classics in experimental psychology entitled *The Sense of Touch.* Weber retained his chair in anatomy at Leipzig until 1871, just eight years before Wilhelm Wundt launched his laboratory in psychology. Weber died January 26, 1878.

Weber's Work on the Sense of Touch

Weber (1834/1978) employed the two-point threshold technique to systematically map the cutaneous sensitivity of the human body. As noted earlier, sensitivity varies widely depending on which part of the body is stimulated. In the process of his investigations, Weber observed that we are less sensitive if the two points of the compass are applied longitudinally along the length of a limb than if they are laid transversely or in a crosswise direction to the axis of the limb. He noted that our sensitivity is greater when the two points of the compass come in contact with contiguous body parts, such as the inside or red part of the lip and the outside skin just adjacent to the inside lip. Weber showed that the two points of the compass appear to spread apart when moved over the surface of relatively insensitive areas. By contrast, subjects may experience a converging of the two points when they are moved over relatively sensitive areas. The experience of the divergence of the two points when moved over insensitive areas and the convergence of the two points when moved over sensitive areas is known as **Weber's Illusion.**

Weber also found that sensitivity is less when the two points of the compass are presented simultaneously and greater when they are presented successively (one just preceding the other). Similarly, perceived differences in the weights of objects are greater when such weights are presented successively. The same holds for perceived temperature differences.

Weber's work on two-point thresholds clearly demonstrated that the world as experienced by the subject does not directly correspond to the physical characteristics of the stimuli presented by the experimenter. In further explorations of the relationship between the physical and psychological worlds, Weber investigated just noticeable differences of weights of small containers filled with lead.

Assume that a measurable level of stimulation is presented to a subject, such as a small jar weighing 50 gm. The subject lifts the jar and has a sense of its weight. How much weight must now be added in order for the subject to detect a difference between the original (standard) weight and the new (comparison) weight? The smallest detectable difference between the standard and the comparison is called the **just noticeable difference, or jnd.**

After conducting many experiments with many stimulus values, Weber observed a law-like relationship between standard and comparison stimuli. The amount that must be added in order to produce a jnd was a function of the amount of existing stimulation. Thus, a subject might reliably detect a difference between a standard jar weigh-

ing 50 gm and a comparison jar weighing 51 gm. The subject is then asked to heft a jar weighing 100 gm. How much would the comparison jar have to weigh before the subject could consistently detect a difference? The comparison jar would have to weigh about 102 gm. Again, the jnd is a function of the amount of existing stimulation. Weber was then in a position to write the first formula that attempted to bridge the physical and psychological worlds. The formula is as follows:

$$\frac{\Delta R}{R} = K$$

Where R = the amount of existing stimulation
ΔR = the amount of stimulation that must be added to produce a jnd
K = a constant

Presumably, one could establish a fraction and then predict the jnd for any new stimulus value. As an example, for lifted weights, the fraction is about 1/50 (.02). Thus, for a 300 gm standard weight, the comparison should be about 306 gm.

Weber had forged an opening into a hitherto inaccessible world. We cannot directly measure a psychological event, but we can quantify perceived differences in relation to scaled physical stimulus values. Psychological events, or jnds, can be studied in conjunction with measurable physical stimulus values. There was now justifiable optimism that psychological processes could be quantified—something that Immanuel Kant had declared an impossibility.

Weber's work was the inspiration for hundreds of early research projects investigating jnds in each of the sensory modalities. His work also served as an inspiration for the development of new and more rigorous methodologies for the study of thresholds. The individual who was most inspired by Weber's work was Gustav Theodor Fechner. We will now turn to a consideration of Fechner's contributions to psychophysics.

Gustav Theodor Fechner

Few human beings have been so captivated by the relationship of mind and body as Gustav Theodor Fechner (1801–1887). The two realms, mind and body, suggest a fundamental duality in nature, but

Gustav Theodor Fechner

Fechner, as noted by Ward (1876), was "a thoroughgoing monist, regarding body and soul as but a double manifestation of one and the same real thing" (p. 452). Fechner devoted much of his scientific career to the study of the relationships between the mental and the physical realms. His systematic research program in psychophysics represents a vital building block for the new discipline of experimental psychology.

Fechner's father was Samuel Fechner, a Lutheran pastor, and his mother was Johanna Dorothea Fischer Fechner. After completing his gymnasium studies, Fechner enrolled at the University of Leipzig. He completed an M.D. degree in 1822, but his early scientific interests were in physics. Indeed, by 1831 he had established his reputation in physics and in 1834 he was appointed professor of physics at Leipzig.

The year 1839 was an unfortunate turning point in Fechner's life. It marked the beginning of a severe emotional disturbance that forced Fechner to resign his university position. His emotional maladies may have been initiated by a temporary partial blindness caused by his study of afterimages. He gazed at the sun through inadequately shielded lenses, resulting in debilitating visual problems. His visual problems were aggravated by loss of appetite, severe anxiety, and hallucinations. His

doctors tried treatments ranging from animal magnetism and homeopathy to moxibustion (the burning of herbs on the skin) and a "magnetized" therapy that involved a high-tension electric current (Adler, 1996). He was convinced that he would never have normal vision again, but by 1843 he was regaining his sight and emotional health.

Fechner finally resumed work at the University of Leipzig in 1848, but as professor of philosophy. His new position afforded unique opportunities to pursue both philosophical and scientific interests. On the philosophical side, Fechner called attention to two deeply opposed ways of viewing the universe. The basic stuff of the universe, including mental phenomena, was viewed by Fechner as inert matter. He referred to such an extreme materialistic position as the *night view.* By contrast, Fechner noted that one might start with the assumption that all things have a psychic component. Fechner argued that plants have a psychic life and that any organic whole has psychic qualities. He referred to his panpsychism as the *day view.* He created a pseudonym, *Dr. Mises,* to give expression to his mystical belief in the day view. For more than fifty years, the writings of Dr. Mises provided an outlet for Fechner's humanistic and aesthetic interests in art, music, dance, and poetry as well as more satirical topics (e.g., the comparative anatomy of humans and angels). Indeed, in 1851, Fechner first outlined his psychophysics program in a book on human immortality, the *Zend-Avesta, or Concerning Matters of Heaven and the Hereafter* (see Boring, 1963). He hoped to accumulate evidence for the day view in his experimental work in psychophysics.

In 1860, Fechner published his *Elements of Psychophysics,* a book destined to become a classic in psychology. In 1876, he published *Vorschule der Aesthetic,* a seminal work in the experimental approach to aesthetic judgments. Fechner is remembered for his substantive contributions and for the development of methods that were to become fundamental in the new psychology. He continued to work diligently on problems in psychophysics and experimental aesthetics until his death in November of 1887. Angell (1913) called attention to Wundt's memorable words in his funeral oration for Fechner: "We shall not look upon his like again" (p. 49).

Fechner marked October 22, 1850, as the date when it occurred to him that there must be a discernible quantitative relationship between sensations and stimuli. Without knowing about Weber's work, Fechner believed there was not a one-to-one relationship between perceived increases in stimulus intensity and increases in stimulus values as measured on a physical scale. Indeed, Fechner concluded that perceived increases on the mental side were in all probability related to the amount of existing stimulation on the physical side. His conclusion is consistent with Weber's discovery.

Following this insight, Fechner discovered Weber's work and launched a vigorous experimental program. Fechner, as quoted by Angell (1913), reported that "for several years I considered it a daily task to experiment about an hour for the purpose of testing Weber's Law and for elaborating new methods of research" (p. 47).

Weber's formula provided the intellectual spadework for Fechner to develop a more ambitious formula for the measurement of sensation. By integrating Weber's formula, Fechner generated the new formula:

$$S = k \log R$$

where S is the mental sensation and R is the *Reiz* or stimulus magnitude. The formula specified that the strength of a mental sensation is a constant logarithmic function of the stimulus. It further specified that as a mental series increases arithmetically, the stimulus series must increase geometrically. Fechner's formula also correctly predicted the observation that is well known to anyone who has advanced a three-way light through a series from 100 to 300 watts. Equal increments in a physical scale are experienced in terms of a diminishing series called **response compression.** Thus, the difference between 100 and 200 watts appears much greater than the difference between 200 and 300 watts. Fechner, deferring to Weber's pioneering work, called his formula **Weber's Law.** Today, we think of it as **Fechner's Law** and the earlier simpler formula that inspired it as *Weber's Law.*

The testing of the Weber and Fechner Laws occupied a prominent if not central place in early psychology laboratories. One benefit was that research on these laws contributed to the construction of sensory scales, such as the decibel scale for dealing with the intensity of auditory stimuli. Another benefit was a greater understanding of the capacities of the sensory systems. Research confirmed that the Weber and Fechner Laws were accurate primarily for the middle ranges of sensory information. Predictions are generally not as accurate for the lower and upper extremes of physical intensity.

Fechner's Methods. Fechner's substantive contributions were complemented by important methodological contributions that he developed in his investigation of thresholds. Fechner's methods became an integral part of experimental psychology. The importance of the psychophysical methods stems partly from their applicability to a variety of problems. Let us briefly examine Fechner's methods.

The Method of Limits. Fechner referred to this method as the method of *just noticeable differences.* He noted its early use by Delezenne in tests of tonal intervals and by Weber in research on weights, touch, and vision (see Fechner, 1860/ 1966, p. 62). The **method of limits** consists of presenting a standard stimulus along with variable or comparison stimuli of greater and lesser value than the standard. The comparison stimuli are presented in ascending and descending series. For example, a standard weight of, say, 100 gm may be presented along with a comparison weight of 105 gm. The difference will easily be detected. In a descending series, subsequent comparison weights of 104, 103, 102, and 101 gm may be presented alternately with the standard weight. Then an ascending series may include comparisons of 100, 101, 102, 103, 104 gm, and so forth. In each series, the experimenter can assess the point at which a difference is no longer detected or the point at which the difference is first noticed. The average for several ascending and descending series defines the jnd.

This method is also applicable to absolute thresholds. In this case, single stimulus values are presented in ascending and descending series. For example, tones of 17, 18, 19, 20, and 21 Hz may be presented in an ascending series and a subject's task is to report when the tone is first detected. In a descending series, starting above threshold (e.g., 25, 24, 23, 22 Hz, and so forth), the subject must specify the frequency at which the tone is no longer heard.

Fechner believed that the method of limits is the method of choice for preliminary studies but that other methods are superior for more rigorous studies (see Fechner, 1860/1966, p. 63).

The Method of Constant Stimuli. Fechner referred to this method as the *method of right and wrong cases.* In this method, comparison stimuli are coupled with the standard stimulus in a random fashion, and the subject's task is to report whether the comparison stimulus is equal to, greater than, or weaker than the standard, or alternatively, detected or not detected. For absolute thresholds, single stimulus values above and below threshold are presented randomly. The subject simply reports whether the stimulus is detected. The **method of constant stimuli** avoids certain errors commonly associated with the method of limits. For example, errors of habituation (i.e., falling into the habit of saying that one stimulus is of greater or lesser value than the other) are easily established in a graded series. Such errors are eliminated when comparison values are randomized.

The Method of Average Error. Sometimes called the *method of adjustment,* the **method of average error** permits the subject to manipulate a comparison stimulus until it appears to match a standard. Following the adjustment, the difference between the standard and the comparison stimuli can be measured. For example, a standard might consist of a light of a given brightness. The comparison could be a light source activated by a variable switch that permits the subject to adjust brightness. The subject could then adjust the brightness of the comparison stimulus until it appears to match the brightness of the standard. Normally,

several ascending and descending series are employed and a mean is determined. Thus, in one series, the comparison starts as a higher or brighter value and is adjusted downward, and in a subsequent series the comparison starts at a lower or dimmer value and is adjusted upward.

Although Fechner's methods generated criticism (Adler, 1998; Michell, 1999), his work had wide applicability and became a standard part of the training programs for experimental psychologists. Several issues that Fechner raised more than a century ago are still evident in contemporary psychophysics research and signal detection theory (Adler, 1998; Link, 1994; Murray, 1993). Variations of Fechner's methods are employed today by psychologists investigating problems as divergent as perception of air quality to the capacity of a particular species to discriminate among stimulus patterns. Fechner's dream of solving the mind–brain problem may have been overly ambitious, but he did provide the foundations for an experimental approach to psychological processes. In the history of science, there are many instances in which the major goal of a research effort is unrealized, but in its place other fortunate benefits accrue by productive accident.

Rudolph Hermann Lotze

Weber and Fechner had a profound influence on Rudolph Hermann Lotze (1817–1881), the author of the first book on physiological psychology. Lotze was born in Bautzen, Germany, on May 21, 1817. After completing school in Zittan, Lotze enrolled at the University of Leipzig. He studied anatomy and physiology under Weber and physics under Fechner. After completing Ph.D. and M.D. degrees, he attempted a brief medical practice. Within a year he was back at Leipzig where he accepted a faculty position from 1839 to 1844. In 1844, he joined the faculty at Göttingen and held that position until 1881. He then accepted the chair of philosophy at the University of Berlin, but died within weeks after his move.

Despite Lotze's broad interest in psychology, he set forth no systematic approach to the field. An examination of his *Outlines of Psychology,* first published in 1881, reveals interests in such topics as memory, unconscious processes, psychopathology and treatment, and sensory processes. His theory of space perception had a direct influence on his successors.

E. G. Boring (1950) identified three reasons for Lotze's prominent place in the history of psychology. As noted earlier, he wrote the first book claiming to be about physiological psychology, his *Medizinische Psychologie oder Physiologie der Seele,* first published in 1852. The second reason was Lotze's theory of space perception (a theory we shall presently consider). The third reason for Lotze's prominence was his influence on others. He was enthusiastic about the new discipline of psychology and regularly taught courses on it at Göttingen.

Lotze accepted the Kantian notion that the mind can discern spatial relations in an a priori fashion. At the same time, he argued that the perception of spatial relations develops as a function of experience. Specifically, a nonspatial stimulus such as a particular light intensity may create a "local sign" or stimulated point in the eye. In the **theory of local signs,** an external object may consist of several colors, contours, surfaces, and projections, each resulting in a corresponding brightness intensity or local sign on the surface of the retina. The relationships between brightness intensity points from the object and corresponding points on the two-dimensional surface of the retina do not in themselves provide unambiguous cues to depth perception because slight movements of the eye or head result in a whole new distribution of points on the retina. But in time, relational discriminations are established such that the local sign in the retina for a given point on the object is discerned from the local sign for a different point on the object. Relational discriminations based on local signs become cues for the perception of depth.

Lotze also emphasized the role of the muscle sense in depth perception. Local signs for an outstretched arm are distinct from those for an unextended arm. Lotze (1881/1973) noted that people who are born blind construct an image of space by means of touch, but he doubted "whether the concept of space which the sense of touch affords

a person born blind, is at all similar to that of one who sees" (p. 50). The assumption of such radical discontinuity between information from two sensory realms was challenged later by others (e.g., see summary in Viney, 1991).

Gotesky (1967) pointed out that "Lotze's influence in Germany, France and England was considerable during his lifetime. Philosophers became more empirical-minded, less dogmatic" (p. 89). Though Lotze left no formal system of psychology, he had a strong influence on key figures involved in the founding of the new discipline, such as Hermann von Helmholtz, Wilhelm Wundt, Franz Brentano, Carl Stumpf, Georg Elias Müller, and George Trumbull Ladd.

Hermann von Helmholtz

Psychology owes an immense intellectual debt to Hermann Ludwig Ferdinand von Helmholtz (1821–1894), one of the most celebrated scientists and inventors of the nineteenth century. His original contributions in physics, physiology, and psychology mark him as one of the last geniuses who could remain on the forefront of multiple scientific fields.

Born August 31, 1821, Helmholtz was the first of four children of August Ferdinand Julius Helmholtz and Caroline Penne. Boring (1950) reported that Helmholtz was an ordinary student, but his academic mediocrity might have been attributable to his intellectual independence. At age seventeen, Helmholtz enrolled in a medical institute in Berlin. He obtained a government stipend that covered the costs of his medical education in exchange for eight years of military service following graduation. Helmholtz completed his dissertation under Johannes Müller and established close friendships with Müller's other students. A group of Müller's students, including Ernst Brücke, Emil DuBois-Reymond, Karl Ludwig, and Helmholtz, were strongly dedicated to a natural physicochemical approach to the study of life processes.

Helmholtz completed the M.D. in 1842 and served until 1848 as an army surgeon. He was released early from military duty to accept a faculty position in physiology at Königsberg. In 1855, he

Hermann von Helmholtz

accepted a position in anatomy and physiology at the University of Bonn. One year after arriving at Bonn, he published Volume I of his classic *Handbook of Physiological Optics.* Kahl (1967) pointed out that this seminal work is "frequently called the *principia* in its field" (p. 469). The handbook established Helmholtz as one of Europe's most promising young scientists. By 1858, he accepted an appointment to the chair of physiology at the University of Heidelberg. He remained in that position for thirteen productive years before accepting a position in 1871 as professor of physics at the University of Berlin. Turner (1972) stated, "By 1885 Helmholtz had become the patriarch of German science and the state's foremost advisor on scientific affairs" (p. 243). Helmholtz died on July 12, 1894.

Helmholtz's Contributions.   Helmholtz rejected the idea that vital forces or mysterious energies influence physiological or psychological processes. He believed that all movements within the organism are, in principle, understandable in terms of physical laws (Turner, 1977). He demonstrated that a simple muscle contraction generates a slight increase in temperature. The total energy expended in a given unit of time is related to the way the organism metabolizes food. Helmholtz believed that

the conservation of energy applies to living organisms just as it applies to physical phenomena. Furthermore, there are no mysterious forces or unknowable energies that activate the organism. The psychology that Helmholtz envisioned was to be firmly grounded in physiology. Physiology, in turn, was to be firmly grounded in physics and chemistry. Helmholtz's vision of the unity of the sciences was such that, according to Wertheimer (1991), "he hardly knew when he was doing psychology, physiology, or physics."

Visual Perception.   Although accomplished in many provinces of science, Helmholtz's most enduring contribution may have been in the study of sense perception (Wade, 1994). His masterpiece, the *Handbook of Physiological Optics,* is a case study of the breadth of his interests in psychological, physiological, and physical problems. The physics and physiology of vision are covered in chapters on such topics as the physical characteristics of light, the crystalline lens, the cornea, refraction in the eye, mechanisms of accommodation, and the retina. The discussion of the retina includes detailed descriptions of the rods and cones along with an analysis of their distributions. On psychological matters, the handbook contains chapters covering such topics as illusions, the perception of depth, and color vision.

The handbook also covers methodological topics in optics. Helmholtz made one of the greatest methodological breakthroughs when he invented the **ophthalmoscope,** an instrument for viewing the retina. Helmholtz's genius is beautifully illustrated in the handbook as he discussed the theory of the ophthalmoscope (see Southall, 1962, pp. 226–228). Helmholtz called attention to the fact that light that reaches the retina is partly absorbed and partly reflected. His ophthalmoscope was an ingenious instrument that made it possible to intercept rays that are reflected. Thus, an observer could, for the first time, see images and anatomical details of the retina of another person's eye. If the senses are the windows of the mind, then Helmholtz's contributions made it possible to peer into those windows and to entertain the hope that science could forge ahead into another frontier.

Helmholtz's empirical approach to the study of perception was set forth in an 1894 article entitled "The Origin and Correct Interpretation of Our Sense Impressions" (see Kahl, 1971; Stromberg, 1989). A child repeatedly hears sounds in the form of common names associated with objects in the world. After many repetitions, there are strong connections between sounds (words) and objects in the world. Subtleties are slowly developed through connection of descriptive adjectives with nouns. Thus, finer and finer discriminations are possible. Helmholtz (1894/1971) pointed out that, in time, "we are able to follow the subtlest, most varied shadings of thought and feeling. If, however, we tried to say how we acquired this knowledge, we could explain it only in the form of a general proposition: we always found certain words used in certain ways" (p. 502).

Helmholtz argued that something similar takes place with respect to sense impressions. For example, a baby's hand provides reliably different information when grasping a sphere rather than a cube. At the same time, reaching and grasping are reliably associated with visual cues. When the connections are invariant, the baby gains a sense impression of a sphere and a cube. "I conclude from these facts that the meaning of some of the simplest, most important visual images for a human infant must be learned" (Helmholtz, 1894/1971, p. 506). Even if the baby were articulate, it could not specify how it gained its sense impressions. Thus, Helmholtz emphasized "unconscious inferences" in perception. Such inferences, according to Helmholtz, are built up through countless repetitions of stimulus and response events.

Helmholtz employed this same line of reasoning to explain depth perception. For example, we learn that object A is more distant than object B because of invariant connections between A and the feeling of the outstretched arm versus B and the feeling of the arm when it is closer to the body. There are, of course, many other connections (visual, proprioceptive, and perhaps verbal) that occur together and that gradually contribute to sense perceptions. It would be nearly impossible to specify all the cues that contribute to a given perception, but we do draw unconscious inferences that are exquisitely conditioned by our interaction with objects in the environment.

Helmholtz was particularly interested in depth perception including the study of monocular cues such as size, contours, shadows, and aerial perspective. He also discussed binocular cues, some of which could be amply demonstrated with the **stereoscope,** an instrument that produces a compelling three-dimensional effect by simultaneously presenting slightly different views of a visual scene to the left and right eyes. Much of Helmholtz's discussion of depth perception is still relevant today and is commonly included in introductory psychology texts.

Color Vision.   Interest in the nature of color and color vision was undoubtedly stimulated in ancient people by such phenomena as color blindness and the appearance of the rainbow and by questions about whether animals see in color. One of the first naturalistic theories of color was attributed to Aristotle, who apparently believed that all colors result from admixtures of lightness and darkness (see Barnes, 1984, pp. 1217–1228). Modern theories of color date from the work of Isaac Newton (1642–1727), whose classic work in optics described the properties of light. Newton demonstrated that a beam of sunlight passing through a prism is dispersed into a spectrum of colors. He also demonstrated that white light is attained again when the dispersed colors are recombined with a converging lens. Newton's demonstration was particularly damaging to the then popular belief that white light was pure and devoid of color.

In time, it was understood that colors are reliably associated with specific wavelengths. But how do we see in color? Do we have a specific structure for each discriminable wavelength? If so, the physiology of color vision would have to be very complex because it is possible to split the visible spectrum into hundreds of different hues. A much simpler solution was proposed in 1802 by the physiologist Thomas Young (1773–1829), who argued that all colors can be produced with various combinations of red, green, and blue (violet). It followed, for Young, that there must be three types of specialized retinal structures, each sensitive to a specific primary color. Color primaries for additive mixtures with light sources are different, though, the latter primaries are generally considered to be red, yellow, and blue. Boring (1942) pointed out that by positing specialized nerves for color primaries, Young's theory "anticipated Johannes Müller's theory of specific nerve energies" (p. 112).

Interestingly, little experimental work was conducted on color vision in the two-hundred-year period from Newton to Helmholtz. Indeed, Young's work on color vision, provocative as it was, was primarily speculative. By the middle of the nineteenth century, Helmholtz was conducting experiments on color mixtures. As in other research on visual perception, Helmholtz held to the empiricist position and found himself in conflict with the German physiologist Ewald Hering (1834–1918), who defended nativism in the study of color vision. In one of the most impassioned debates in modern science, Helmholtz and Hering clashed over such issues as space perception, color blindness, optical illusions, and the therapeutic practices of clinical opthamology (Turner, 1994). Helmholtz was particularly interested in discovering the minimum number of primaries from which one could obtain all colors of the spectrum. Initially, he argued against Young's belief in three primaries, opting instead for five: red, yellow, green, blue, and violet.

The experimental work favoring Young's trichromatic theory was not done by Helmholtz but by James Clerk Maxwell (1831–1879), the great Scottish physicist. With sophisticated experimental techniques, Maxwell demonstrated that he could match any spectral value with mixtures of red, green, and blue. Subsequently, Helmholtz embraced the trichromatic theory of Young and the theory has been known ever since as the **Young-Helmholtz trichromatic theory.** A more appropriate name might have been the Young-Maxwell-Helmholtz theory, or even the Young-Maxwell theory. Helmholtz's contributions to color theory, however, are not to be minimized. He tied Young's theory explicitly to possible physiological mechanisms and, in the words of Beck (1968), "extended the theory to account for color blindness, negative afterimages, and successive contrasts" (p. 347). The Young-Helmholtz theory remains an important theory in color science.

Acoustics and Hearing. Helmholtz's great breadth of interest in physics, physiology, and psychology are evident in his original work *On the Sensations of Tone.* His resonance theory of hearing, for example, attempted to identify possible physiological structures for pitch perception. Helmholtz observed that a string on a musical instrument such as a harp or piano is activated by an external sound source of the same frequency as the one to which it is tuned. Helmholtz speculated that fibers in the basilar membrane of the inner ear, like the strings of a piano or harp, may also resonate to specific frequencies. Thus, pitch discrimination is based on vibration of fibers in sympathy with external sources. In yet another extension of Müller's doctrine of specific energies, Helmholtz argued that separate specialized nerves are activated by each discriminable pitch.

Helmholtz also advanced theories attempting to account for the timbre or quality of sound. He reasoned that a specific pitch, say middle C, sounds different on different instruments because of the harmonics or overtones produced by the structural properties of the instrument.

Beck (1968) pointed out, "From the perspective of posterity . . . Helmholtz made his most significant contributions to the fields of sensory physiology and psychology. In particular, he laid the foundations for the experimental investigation of the sensory processes in audition and vision" (p. 345). These contributions, coupled with his measurement of the speed of the nervous impulse and his commitment to the doctrine of the conservation of energy, mark him as one of the most pivotal figures in the history of psychology (Stumpf, 1895).

WILHELM WUNDT

The formal beginnings of modern experimental psychology are traced to the year 1879, when Wilhelm Wundt established a laboratory at the University of Leipzig. Many of the conceptual and

Wilhelm Wundt

methodological tools for the new discipline had already been established by Weber, Fechner, and Helmholtz. What remained was for someone with a vision, and with knowledge of the available tools, to tackle the difficult and risky business of agitating for institutional space and recognition. Wilhelm Maximilian Wundt (1832–1920) had the requisite vision, knowledge, and energy for such an undertaking. To be sure, Wundt faced an uphill battle because typically conservative university officials were less than enthusiastic. There were even administrative concerns that Wundt's introspective methods might cause students to suffer mental breakdowns. To say the least, the outlook for the new laboratory was not optimistic.

But Wundt's efforts were to have monumental consequences. From a single laboratory room on the Leipzig campus, Wundt became the key player in launching a new discipline that was to be international in scope. Who would have predicted that, within a century, a course in psychology would be required for many university majors or that psychology as a major subject would be among the most popular on university campuses? None of this is meant to imply that Wundt was solely responsible for the popularity of psychology after the formal founding. More than any other, however, he had the vision, talent, organi-

zational skill, and enthusiasm for establishing the formal disciplinary status of psychology. Accordingly, he occupies a singular place in the history of the discipline.

Wilhelm Wundt was born August 16, 1832, in Neckarau, a small village located in a German principality close to the present city of Heidelberg. Wundt was the youngest of four children of Maximilian Wundt (1787–1868) and Marie Friederike née Arnold (1797–1868). Typical for the times, only two of the four children survived, Wilhelm and his older brother Ludwig (1824–1902).

Maximilian was a Protestant minister known for his moderate or even liberal theology. Marie was a highly competent, energetic, and thrifty individual who took a strong hand in the management of household economic matters. Both parents came from families of professionals, including several physicians and university professors.

Diamond (1980) noted that "Wundt grew up in effect as an 'only child'" (p. 10). His brother Ludwig, who was eight years his senior, started work in the gymnasium at Heidelberg when Wilhelm was only two years old. Wundt's earliest years were marked by loneliness and poor health (he had a severe case of malaria in his first year). As a consequence of isolation from other children and loneliness, he reveled in his own fantasy world. Indeed, his habit of daydreaming apparently interfered with his high school and early college studies.

In 1836 Maximilian received an appointment to a large parish in Heidelsheim, a rough town that did nothing to allay Wilhelm's shyness or his fear of other children. He had but one friend his own age, a gentle handicapped boy with severe speech deficiencies.

Wundt entered grammar school at age six, but the poorly socialized youngster was ill-prepared to attend to lesson materials. The oppressive atmosphere of the school forced him to withdraw even more into his own thoughts. Wundt's personal difficulties were compounded at age eight, when his father had a severe stroke. The resulting hardship for the family had a dramatic effect on Wundt's early education.

As a consequence of the stroke, Maximilian's young assistant, Friedrich Müller, assumed a large share of the parish responsibilities, and also took an interest in young Wilhelm. According to Bringmann, Bringmann, and Balance (1980), Müller "made his appearance when the boy must have been under considerable stress. His grandfather had just died, his brother remained away from home, and his mother's time was taken up with the care of her crippled husband" (p. 18).

Müller, who shared a room with Wilhelm in the parsonage, assumed the responsibilities of tutor. He assigned and graded lessons and often discussed the youngster's performance. Their bond was so intense that Wundt was overcome with grief when Müller was assigned to a church in Münzesheim. Wundt was then twelve years old and was allowed to go to Münzesheim to live with his tutor. Later he enrolled in the gymnasium in Bruchsal. Again, the result was disastrous. Wundt, enrolled in the equivalent of the first year of high school, and promptly failed. His teachers regarded him as lazy, inattentive, and poorly fitted for anything but an undemanding career. Wundt became all the more deeply embittered and withdrawn.

Wundt's academic prospects were dim, to say the least, following the disastrous year at Bruchsal. Within one year, however, a radical transformation had taken place. Diamond (1980) stated, "Wundt's family—which is to say, his Mother's family—saw to it that he was given another chance. At thirteen, he joined Ludwig in their aunt's home, to attend the Heidelberg gymnasium and do his studying in the same room with his industrious brother, with no daydreaming nonsense allowed" (p. 13). For whatever reasons (e.g., greater maturity, the presence of a good role model, new determination), Wundt's prospects improved. His attention was gradually directed outward, as evidenced by a newfound ability to make friends. His academic performance improved, but was still below expected standards.

Following graduation from the Heidelberg Lyceum in 1851, Wundt was still undecided about a career. However, he was accepted as a premedical student at the University of Tübingen where his uncle, Friedrich Arnold, taught anatomy. Following a year at Tübingen, Wundt was accepted for premedical studies at the University of Heidelberg. For the first time in his troubled academic

career, Wundt gave himself unreservedly to his studies. As a result, he completed the medical program in three years, obtaining his M.D. in 1855 with highest honors.

Wundt quickly discovered that he had little interest in the practice of medicine. As a consequence, in 1856, he sharpened his research skills in physiology in postdoctoral work at the University of Berlin under Johannes Müller and Emil DuBois-Reymond. Back at Heidelberg, later in the year, he was hired as a docent with teaching and research opportunities. The monetary reward was meager, but Wundt at last found work suited to his interests. In 1858, Wundt published his first book, *The Doctrine of Muscular Movement.* In that same year, he applied for a position in Helmholtz's physiology laboratory. He was given the appointment and remained as Helmholtz's assistant for eight years. During this period, Wundt conducted research, instructed medical students, and offered courses of his own. In 1862, he taught a course entitled "Psychology as a Natural Science."

During this period, Wundt's research interests were shifting from physiology to psychology. Two of his most important psychological contributions from the period include *Contributions to a Theory of Sensory Perception* (1862) and *Lectures on Human and Animal Psychology* (1863). The introduction to the book on sense perception included an announcement of a need for a new discipline: experimental psychology.

Wundt remained at Heidelberg for almost a decade after leaving Helmholtz's laboratory. The period from 1865 to 1874 was enormously productive, but the most noteworthy academic achievement was the 1873 publication of Volume I of Wundt's classic *Principles of Physiological Psychology.* The second volume was published in 1874. The period from 1865 to 1874 was noteworthy in another way; after several years of engagement, Wundt married Sophie Mau in 1872.

In 1874, Wundt accepted an appointment as chair of inductive philosophy at Zurich, but in less than a year received a call to the larger, more prestigious University of Leipzig. Wundt's call to Leipzig was prompted by his growing reputation in psychology. According to Bringmann, Bringmann, and Ungerer (1980), the dean at Leipzig hoped that Wundt would bring prestige and recognition to the university. In one of his letters, the dean wrote "I hope that your call to the university will one day be viewed as [the beginning of] an epoch in the history of German philosophy, especially of psychology and epistemology" (p. 128). The dean's hopes were realized when Wundt, already forty-two years old at the time of his appointment, was to embark on the phase of his career for which he is so well remembered.

In his first four years at Leipzig, Wundt taught an average of two courses per semester, including psychology, anthropology, logic and methodology, history of modern philosophy, brain and nerve physiology, and cosmology. Wundt also supervised dissertations and conducted his own research. He averaged almost two publications a month during his first four years at Leipzig—eighty-eight publications in the four-year period, including four books. Few scholars in any field or period of history have matched Wundt's record of productivity.

In 1879, Wundt established the psychological laboratory at Leipzig. Much of the early equipment was provided by Wundt himself. By December, the first experiments were underway, and within a short period, Wundt joined several students as subjects.

Wundt recognized the need for a scholarly journal to publish the numerous research papers coming out of his new laboratory. The new research was not quite appropriate for established journals in physiology or philosophy. So, in 1881, Wundt published the first issue of *Psychological Studies.* Immediately, the title was changed to *Philosophical Studies* to avoid confusion with a parapsychology journal, published under the title *Psychological Studies.* Wundt's journal was primarily an outlet for research from the Leipzig laboratory.

Despite his late start, Wundt's work stretched over the next four decades, and the high productivity in the first four years was indicative of the promise of coming research. In his years at Leipzig from 1875 to 1920, Wundt directed 186 doctoral theses (see Tinker, 1980). Wundt revised his magnum opus, *Principles of Physiological Psychology,* through six editions, the last being issued in 1911. If all this were not enough, Wundt taught

large classes. Indeed, Angell (1921) reported "that there was no lecture room in the university large enough to hold the audience that 'subscribed' to the lectures on psychology" (p. 164). Wundt devoted much of his later years to his long-term interest in sociocultural psychology (*Völkerpsychologie*). The result was a ten-volume work covering areas in anthropology, psycholinguistics, forensic psychology, the psychology of religion, personality, and social psychology. Examples of topics covered included the origin of belief in gods, the growth of complexity of rewards and punishments, the development of legal systems, marriage and family systems, the beginnings of language, and primitive societies. Part of the *Völkerpsychologie* is available in English (see Wundt, 1916).

In view of his enormous scholarly productivity, one might reasonably conclude that Wundt must have been a social recluse, but such is not the case. He was active in politics twenty years before founding his psychology laboratory. In Heidelberg, he was even elected to a parliamentary seat, which he held from 1866 to 1869. He was keenly interested in pressing social concerns of his day, such as improving education and working conditions. Though he seldom traveled, Wundt had a busy social agenda. He and his wife enjoyed hosting dinner parties for laboratory assistants, evening concerts, and time with their children.

Wundt's adult personality is a matter of considerable interest, especially in view of his troubled, withdrawn childhood. Despite his dramatic turnaround and successful years in the M.D. program, the young scientist was still a misfit. Indeed, Titchener (1921) referred to his Heidelberg period as "seventeen years of depression" (p. 171). The childhood and early adult years did not provide grounds for an optimistic projection of Wundt's later development. Did Wundt's early difficulties leave noticeable scars?

The answer is not simple. Wundt did have difficulties with colleagues and was overly reactive to criticism (see Diamond, 1980). However, these negatives are balanced by many positive personal qualities. Wundt was patient and helpful with his students. He genuinely cared about their progress and success. Although friendly and warm, he never allowed students to lose sight of the formal master–student relationship. He was generous in the time he devoted to student laboratory projects and theses. Wundt's student Edward A. Pace (1921) celebrated Wundt's lack of ostentation even when students from around the world were flocking to his laboratory. Howard Warren (1921) and Walter Dill Scott (1921) commented on his encyclopedic knowledge and breadth of vision. A documented perspective on graduate study with Wundt was provided by Sokal (1980a).

Wundt's legacy was summed up by Walter Dill Scott (1921) as follows: "When he began his work psychology was thought of as a branch of philosophy. His work changed it into an experimental science" (p. 183). Wundt's life and work thus mark a turning point in intellectual history. At the time of his death in 1920, the formal discipline he established was firmly rooted in major universities around the world. By that time psychology was both an experimental science and a fledgling professional discipline with branches extending into education, industry, the military, and the clinic.

General Characteristics of Wundt's Thought

Several general characteristics distinguish Wundt's philosophical and psychological vision. Although Wundt often changed his position on specific topics in psychology, many of the broader philosophical underpinnings of his thought remained stable.

Mind and Body. In the *Principles of Physiological Psychology,* Wundt speculated about the evolution of mental function. He rejected the extreme positions of **hylozoism** (the view that mind is manifested in *all* material movement—for example, even the falling of a rock) and the dualistic Cartesian view that only humans have mental functions. Wundt believed that the lower limits of mental function are illustrated in movements that have a voluntary basis. He pointed out that voluntary movements, unlike simple reflexes or vegetative functions (like respiration), "are varied to suit varying conditions, and brought into connection with sense-impressions previously secured" (Wundt, 1910/1969b, p. 28). He gave an unlikely example: "The amoeba, which is regarded mor-

phologically as a naked cell, will sometimes return after a short interval to the starch grains that it has come upon in the course of its wanderings" (p. 29). Wundt noted that such a phenomenon argues for continuity in mental processes. He believed that the origin of mental processes dated to the origin of life itself.

Wundt also speculated about the metaphysical or ontological status of mental processes. He recognized the popular assumption that mind is a substance or a real being, but argued that such an assumption is unnecessary. He noted that we do not treat virtue or honor as substances, yet that does not prevent our doing intelligent and logical work with these topics. In a similar manner, we may simply treat mind "as the logical subject of internal experience" (Wundt, 1910/1969b, p. 18).

In Wundt's psychology, experience is central. Mind is one meaningful subject of discourse and the physical system is another meaningful subject of discourse. Mental *and* physical processes are both known in experience, but psychology cannot, in its immaturity, specify the metaphysical basis of either process. Wundt believed strongly in the unity and interdependence of mental and physical processes. Thus, he was not a mind–body dualist. In many respects, his position was similar to the double-aspect monism of Spinoza.

Breadth of Vision. Another general characteristic of Wundt's philosophical and psychological vision was its enormous scope. We already noted the unusual range of Wundt's teaching assignments (e.g., cosmology, anthropology, logic and methodology, psychology of language, history of modern philosophy, brain and nerve physiology, and psychology). His scholarly publications in such fields as ethics, logic, sociocultural psychology, and physiology illustrate not only breadth but also depth. Frank Angell (1921), one of Wundt's students, said, "For depth and range of learning, for capacity for generalization, for power of scientific imagination, he was the ablest man I ever met" (p. 166). Wundt's breadth of vision for the new psychology was illustrated in several ways. First, he employed a variety of methods. It is true that much of the work of the laboratory for which he is remembered was based on a rigorous form of what we often call introspection; however, he was quick to recognize other methods, including naturalistic observation such as one encounters in astronomy or field biology. He also recognized the historical methods employed in archeology and geology. In his laboratory work, Wundt emphasized precise measurements and the importance of being able to replicate findings. While Wundt's laboratory work focused largely on sensory processes, perception, and reaction time, he nevertheless had the vision of a wider psychology that included studies of social and cultural variables.

Voluntarism.   The name Wundt preferred for his system of thought was **voluntarism.** At the outset, it is important to point out that voluntarism is not the same thing as free will. Wundt wrote in his *Ethics* (1892/1901) that "To be free, an action must be voluntary" (p. 38). It does not follow, however, that all voluntary acts are free. Wundt specifically declared that volition was not a sufficient condition for freedom. Thus, "an insane person may balance motives one against another, and proceed with thoughtful circumspection, yet we do not call his decisions free" (p. 38). Wundt did in fact believe that some human beings possess a free will, but free will is possible only when we can get beyond mere self-consciousness to a truly reflective self-consciousness. True reflective self-consciousness, according to Wundt, is not a mere given. It is based on very wide and deep cognitions that are hard won through experience. Such a free will could hardly be expected to exist in children, the insane, the mentally handicapped, or those who are under unusual duress.

If voluntarism is not the same as free will, then what is it? A *voluntaristic psychology* is one that emphasizes psychological causality. For example, one may stand at the ice cream counter and choose chocolate over vanilla. Asked why, the individual may say, "Ah, I love both, but it has been much longer since I've had chocolate, and besides I caught a whiff of it, and it has a particularly wonderful fresh chocolate aroma." Wundt did not deny that there are underlying material and efficient physiological and biochemical causes for a choice.

But, as psychologists, we study psychical motives, or in Wundt's (1892/1901) words, "ideas accompanying the voluntary act" (p. 52). Such ideas are the stuff of psychical causality. In one sense, Wundt's voluntarism simply affirms the legitimacy, even the primacy, of the world of experience and the causal forces we encounter in that world.

Wundt's voluntarism specifies the scope of psychological investigation. We study those experiences and behaviors that are varied to meet changing circumstances on the basis of past learning, or as Wundt (1910/1969b) said, in "connexion [sic] with sense impressions previously secured" (p. 28). Wundt argued that voluntary actions are not mechanical; rather, they adapt in a flexible manner to changing circumstances. By such a definition, the quest for food in most species provides an example of voluntary behavior. The successful hunter must display a proper sense of camouflage, timing, inhibition, and appropriate speed. The hunting animal must be flexible and adapt quickly to subtle clues. Hunting behaviors are highly purposeful and goal directed, but not necessarily examples of free will. Such behaviors are varied, however, to meet changing circumstances and are thus examples of voluntary behavior.

Wundt and Darwin.   Wundt's emphasis on volition, with its obvious implications for adaptation, might hint at the influence of Darwin. Such a conclusion, however, is unwarranted without further research. Though there are some parallels between Darwinian theory and Wundt's system (e.g., see Richards, 1980), it is not clear that Darwinian thought was assimilated into Wundt's system. References to Darwin in Wundt's major works are sparse and those that do occur are sometimes critical.

An example of a critical treatment of Darwin is found in Wundt's *Lectures on Human and Animal Psychology.* Wundt agreed with Darwin on the importance of the principle of adaptation; however, he argued that his notion of voluntary action supplements and adds to Darwin's concept of adaptation. He pointed out that adaptation, as conceived by Darwin, is a passive concept and is not necessarily directed toward an object. Plants, for example, are altered by the interplay of environmental forces and adapt or die out. The same thing happens to animals, but in addition to passive adaptation, animals display a more active adaptation. In animals, volition has an object toward which it is directed and there is an "interaction of external stimulus with affective and voluntary response" (Wundt, 1863/1907, p. 409). Thus, the animal is not merely passive but acts on its world on the basis of affect and past associations. Acting on the world does not, of course, necessarily imply that animals have free will.

The Laboratory and the Broader Vision

Wundt's work in the laboratory was typically directed toward manageable, well-defined problems that lent themselves to the techniques and equipment available in that day. The goals of laboratory investigation were somewhat modest, but the basic canons of scientific research were not compromised. Wundt's broader vision included many topics (e.g., linguistics, social influences on behavior, etc.) that did not lend themselves to experimental laboratory research as he conceived it. Unfortunately, Wundt's larger view of psychology is often portrayed simply in terms of the work of the laboratory. The result is that his system has often been represented as narrow in terms of methodology and subject matter. There are now numerous helpful criticisms of the stripped-down versions of Wundt presented in early history texts (e.g., see Blumenthal, 1975; Danziger, 1979; Farr, 1983; O'Neil, 1984).

Representative Laboratory Research. Understanding Wundt's experimental psychology is facilitated if we examine concrete examples of his research. The following examples on the speed of reflexes, associations, and vision are typical of the many experimental studies that Wundt conducted or supervised during his years at Leipzig.

In an early article published in the journal *Mind* before the formal founding of the laboratory, Wundt (1876) presented his research on the speed of different types of reflex action. The creation of scientific technology became a hallmark for the "new psychology of the laboratory" (Evans, 2000).

Wundt contributed to this trend by conducting research on reflex action with the assistance of the *pendulum myograph,* an instrument that permitted rather precise measures of stimulus and response. In this case, the stimulus was an electric current and the response was reflex activity of a frog. Among the topics investigated, Wundt compared unilateral spinal conduction, transverse conduction, and longitudinal conduction. In unilateral conduction, excitation is from the sensory root to its corresponding motor root on the same side. Transverse conduction is from the sensory root on one side to the motor root on the opposite side. Longitudinal conduction follows the spinal axis from a lower sensory root to a higher motor root, or vice versa. Longitudinal conduction can follow unilateral or transverse paths. Wundt also studied the effects of temperature on the speed of reflexes. In addition, he examined the reflex process when adjacent nerves were receiving simultaneous stimulation.

Among the findings, Wundt reported that transverse and longitudinal reflexes were slower than unilateral reflexes. He also found that lowering body temperature increases the magnitude of the reflex, but the reflex is slower than that encountered when body temperature is normal. Wundt found that simultaneous stimulation of neighboring nerves had mixed effects on reflex activity. Simultaneous stimulation or compounding of stimulation may have excitatory or inhibitory effects.

This latter finding was important because it demonstrated the critical role of inhibitory processes in the nervous system. Wundt saw inhibition as an equal partner with excitation in lower and higher mental processes. For example, ordered voluntary behavior is based on a mix of inhibitory and excitatory processes. Wundt realized that the growth of inhibition is central to adaptive and voluntary behaviors. One of his abiding curiosities concerned the physiological and psychological nature of inhibition (see Diamond, Balvin, & Diamond, 1963, pp. 40–42, 159–164).

Edward Scripture's (1864–1945) dissertation is another striking example of research conducted at Leipzig. Scripture's work, as described by Titchener (1892), involved the presentation of visual, auditory, tactile, olfactory, and gustatory stimuli to subjects comfortably seated in a darkened and quiet room that was designed to be as free as possible from sensory distractions. Scripture was primarily interested in the nature and quality of associations to his test stimuli. Specifically, he hoped to discover components of the association process. Based on the introspective reports of his subjects, Scripture identified four processes in the act of association; he called them preparation, influence, expansion, and after-effect.

Preparation is the most subtle of the four processes. In the first instance of exposure, it may be that several ideas compete for "center stage" in consciousness. Careful introspection reveals that, in addition to the idea actually evoked by the stimulus, there were others that did not cross threshold. The subject may not be able to articulate what the others were, but subjects did report a sense of competition of ideas. The second stage, *influence,* simply means that an idea or association crosses a threshold and thus alters consciousness. *Expansion* occurs when additional ideas or associations complement the main idea. *After-effect,* as a distinct stage in the association process, may include thoughts about the nature of expansion or further interpretations of a specific association. A reflection such as "I wonder why I had that association instead of this one" might be part of an after-effect.

Scripture believed that his research demonstrated unconscious influences on associations. In one condition, he presented a primary stimulus (e.g., a picture) along with a very brief exposure of a simple stimulus (e.g., a color or a letter). The exposure was in peripheral vision and so brief that the subject knew only that something had been presented but could not clearly identify it with certainty. Scripture found the secondary (briefly exposed) stimulus was correctly associated with the primary picture 34 percent of the time.

Furthermore, Scripture found that the first association to some stimuli, particularly colors, was not an idea per se but a feeling. Such a finding fueled speculation about the status of feelings as compared to cognitions. Some early theorists believed that feelings are always conditioned or added on to existing ideas. Thus, what is primary is cognition denuded of affect. An opposite orientation is that feelings are as primary as cognitions.

A final example of work conducted in Wundt's laboratory was a dissertation project by August Kirschmann on light sensitivity in the retina. He found that central vision involving the fovea results in clearer images, but sensitivity to brightness is greater in parts of the peripheral retina. The somewhat paradoxical nature of the finding is discussed by Titchener (1892), who noted that "the objective brightness of the retinal image decreased from centre to periphery; or in other words, the quantity of reflected light which affects the lateral parts of the retina during fixation is less than that which reaches the *fovea central.* One would, therefore, expect that laterally seen objects would appear less bright than those centrally seen" (p. 209). Titchener provided illustrations of greater sensitivity to brightness in the peripheral parts of the dark-adapted retina. The best-known example is that dim stars increase in brightness if we do not fixate on them directly. That is, the apparent brightness of the star increases if we fixate to the side of the dim star.

Kirschmann's work is typical of laboratory projects that investigated conscious or experiential phenomena in relation to specific physiological structures. Wundt's work inspired extensive research on the structural underpinnings of conscious experiences. There was a large systematic attempt to catalog the range of experiences within specific sensory modalities and then to identify the physiological correlates of those experiences. This approach is still used by researchers who investigate relationships between psychological and physiological processes.

Wundt's laboratory research was focused largely on sensation, perception, and reaction time. Nevertheless, studies were conducted on such topics as attention, emotion, association, and dreams. Wundt also directed many dissertations in philosophy.

Some Key Concepts in Wundt's System

Certain terms occur again and again throughout the corpus of Wundt's experimental work. Such terms represent themes in his thinking and are keys to understanding the work of the laboratory. However, it is well to be reminded that the laboratory work is but one phase of Wundt's larger psychological perspective. To use a metaphor once employed by Freud, it is as if Wundt recognized that the house has more than one floor. Insofar as the work of the laboratory was concerned, Wundt was content to remain on the lower floor. The constructs to which we now turn are those that pertain to this lower floor.

Definition of Psychology.   As far as the laboratory is concerned, Wundt defined *psychology* as a science that investigates "the facts of consciousness" (Wundt, 1912/1973, p. 1). He pointed out that psychology has two tasks: The first is to discover the elements of consciousness and the second is to discover the combinations that elements undergo and the laws that regulate combinations. He referred to a combination of elements as a psychic compound (see Wundt, 1912/1973, p. 44).

Elements.   The term **element** in Wundt's thinking is a somewhat difficult abstraction that requires further comment. We normally think of an element as something simple, pure, and irreducible. Wundt believed that there are mental elements, or pure sensations such as the sensation of the beat of a metronome. However, he recognized that a single simple sensation on the psychological side—that is, a psychological element—is by no means simple on the physiological side. Nevertheless, we may treat simple sensations (e.g., blueness, redness, sweetness, etc.) as elements.

Sensations and Perceptions.   Wundt (1912/1973) defined **sensation** as an element of consciousness (p. 45). In addition to sensations there are perceptions and ideas. He noted that the term *perception* generally refers to combinations of outward sense impressions (e.g., an object of a particular shape and color may be called an apple). An *idea,* by contrast, generally refers to combinations that may come from memory, previous associations, and so on. Wundt questioned the validity of the distinction between *idea* and *perception.* In both cases we observe compounds or combinations and both can be equally lively as experienced phenomena.

Association and Apperception.   Wundt believed that compounds or combinations of elements may be passive or active. He described *passive combinations* as associations and *active combinations* as apperceptions. The distinction between *association* and *apperception* is important in Wundt's thought and carries implications for his larger psychological system.

Association and apperception are illustrated in the distinction between mere rote memory and memory with real awareness. Wundt (1912/1973) pointed out that in rote memory, separate words "are joined to each other by mere association. In the consciousness of the child they do not form a unified whole" (pp. 127–128). Association is manifested in the flight of ideas of a mental patient or in the immediate response to a simple stimulus. Wundt pointed out that a simple series of words such as *school, house, garden, build, stones, ground, hard, soft, long, see, harvest, rain, move,* and *pain* illustrate association. He then asked the reader, "Compare with this a context like the following out of the seventh book of Goethe's *Wilhelm Meister:* 'Spring had come in all its glory. A spring thunderstorm, that had been threatening the whole day long, passed angrily over the hills' " (124–125). What is the essential difference between these series? The first illustrates associations, but they are haphazard, aimless, not well connected, and only moderately intelligent. The second illustrates **apperception** marked by intelligent direction within a larger context. Apperception is characterized by activity with intelligent direction and inner unity—these are lacking in association. Wundt criticized British empiricism and associationism for failing to grasp the important distinction between association and apperception.

The Tridimensional Theory of Feeling.   In addition to studying cognitive concepts such as sensation, perception, ideas, associations, and apperceptions, Wundt was deeply interested in feelings. Wundt (1912/1973) warned that feelings must not be overlooked because they are tied to more complex psychological processes such as apperception, memory, imagination, perception, and cognition.

Through introspective studies, Wundt developed a **tridimensional theory of feeling** based on three dimensions: pleasure and pain, strain and relaxation, and excitation and quiescence. Certain sensations result in specific feelings. Thus, a bitter taste or a smell like ammonia is unpleasant almost to the point of pain, whereas sweetness is usually pleasurable. Wundt noted that red is exciting and blue is quieting. Colors, like music, may produce relaxation or strain.

Rarely are feelings isolated or partial with respect to the dimensions specified by Wundt. Instead, they combine to form a meaningful compound. Thus, a given sensation may be pleasurable and exciting or pleasurable and relaxing. Varieties of combinations are possible. So-called emotions such as joy or hope represent pleasurable feelings tied to a particular cognitive content. Anger or fear may represent feelings of strain and unpleasantness tied also to a particular cognitive content.

The Principle of Creative Synthesis. While Wundt hoped to identify the elements of consciousness and to discover the laws that govern connections of elements, he nevertheless believed that there are inherent indeterminations in psychic compounds. In other words, there is real novelty and creativity in higher mental operations. Wundt's term for such novelty is the principle of **creative synthesis.** He wrote that this principle refers to "the fact that in all psychical combinations, the product is not a mere sum of the separate elements that compose such combinations, but it represents a new creation" (Wundt, 1912/1973, p. 164).

Wundt noted that one of the major manifestations of creative synthesis is illustrated in the principle of the **heterogony of ends.** This principle is exemplified in the emergence of new motives during the course of a chain of activities. For example, one may accept the invitation of a friend to attend an art show. Initially, the motive is simply the anticipation of a pleasant evening in good companionship. But in the course of the evening, one encounters a highly desirable work of art and wishes to purchase it. A whole new set of motives enters the picture and now exists alongside and in addition to the original motive (How can I raise the money? Will the artist accept payments? Would I insult her or is it even appropriate to bargain for a work of art? etc.). Wundt also called attention to the changing motivational structure attached to the practice of ancient habits or customs. Original motives for a practice such as a religious rite or ceremony may be obscured or even be replaced by new motives that bear little relation to the original motives. For example, baptism in some Christian religions was once viewed as a way of casting out evil spirits; such motives for the practice are no longer encountered.

Wundt's Legacy

If there is one central dominating figure in the history of psychology, it is Wilhelm Wundt. Under his leadership, psychology gained status as a separate discipline in a major institution of learning. Undergraduates packed into classrooms and graduate students from around the world flocked to the Leipzig laboratory. Under Wundt's guidance, the new discipline was soon on a firm footing and the Leipzig experiment proved a viable model for other schools. Psychology quickly gained recognition in other major universities.

There have been questions about the lasting effects of Wundt's substantive contributions (e.g., theories and laboratory findings). The fact is, however, that many laboratory findings were cited in early textbooks and some results held up remarkably well. For example, the finding, cited earlier, regarding the locus of retinal stimulation and perceived brightness is widely accepted. Blumenthal (1975) also called attention to additional lasting influences. For example, factor analytic studies of feelings have yielded results that correspond closely to the predictions of Wundt's tridimensional theory. His work was also a central influence in the development of applied cognitive psychology (Hoffman & Deffenbacher, 1992). Unfortunately, his rigid view of memory as an imprecise and overly popular concept with little value for scientific psychology served to alienate some of his contemporaries (Danziger, 2001). Still, Wundt's substantive contributions to the new discipline cannot be dismissed. Indeed, additional historical work should be focused on the lasting effects and generalizability of Wundt's many substantive contributions.

Wundt's laboratory emphasis on sensory processes and reaction time was criticized for its narrowness. But, as noted by Wertheimer (1987), "This criticism may be somewhat inappropriate. After all, this was just the beginning of genuine experimental psychology. Wundt can hardly be blamed that there were no studies of learning in the early years at his laboratory; that kind of work was not yet in the Zeitgeist" (p. 69). Besides, as noted earlier, Wundt's larger vision did include a broader and encompassing psychology. It is perhaps no accident that many of Wundt's students helped implement his wider vision.

The Legacy of Wundt's Students in Applied Psychology

The well-known psychiatrist Emil Kraepelin (1856–1926) learned experimental methodology from Wundt and applied it to early scientific studies of mental disorder. According to Blumenthal (1975), Kraepelin advanced a theory of schizophrenia derived specifically from Wundtian psychology. In his major works, Wundt made numerous references to pathological psychology (e.g., see Wundt, 1897/1969a, 1907), so it is little wonder that some of his students pursued his ideas in this area. Wundt (1863/1907) even argued that "pathological psychology has as good a claim to rank as an independent discipline beside normal psychology, as has the pathology of the body to be separated from its physiology" (p. 316). Kraepelin was awarded his M.D. at twenty-two, one year before Wundt established his laboratory at Leipzig. At twenty-seven, Kraepelin wrote a treatise on psychiatry that produced several editions (Boring, 1950). His early studies on the psychological effects of alcohol and morphine established Kraepelin as a pioneer in the field of psychopharmacology (Healy, 1993). In 1883, he published an early taxonomy of psychiatric disorders that anticipated current classification systems and introduced such enduring diagnostic terms as *paranoia* and *manic-depressive psychosis*. However, Kraepelin's clinical term *dementia praecox* (premature

deterioration) was later renamed *schizophrenia* (splitting of the mind) by Swiss psychiatrist Eugen Bleuler (1857–1939) (Palha & Esteves, 1997).

Kraepelin's interest in dementia led to pioneering studies on a disorder that would later be called *Alzheimer's disease*. Prior to the definitive research of the German neurologist Alois Alzheimer (1864–1915), Kraepelin conducted early clinical work on presenile dementia (Weber, 1997). After Alzheimer published his classic description of the disorder in 1907, Kraepelin named it "Alzheimer's disease" in honor of his colleague.

As forensic research made an impact in Europe at the end of the nineteenth century (see Bartol & Bartol, 1999), Kraepelin played a critical role in the development of criminal psychiatry. He was one of the first researchers to claim that criminal behavior should be considered a mental illness, and he became a vigorous opponent of the death penalty (Hoff, 1998). In a sentiment shared with modern clinicians, he urged the use of psychiatric treatment in rehabilitating prisoners. He envisioned a larger role for the psychiatrist in the courtroom and even suggested that clinicians have a voice in judicial decisions regarding the variety and length of imprisonment.

Born the same year as Sigmund Freud, Kraepelin was a staunch opponent of psychoanalysis, which he saw as art but not science. Instead, he believed the root of psychopathology to be largely organic and drew on his findings to educate the German public about the health dangers of aicoholism and syphilis (Engstrom, 1991). Kraepelin's medical work remains a source of ongoing interest to contemporary psychiatrists (Jablensky, Hugler, von Cranach, & Kalinov, 1993). Wundt's interests in pathological psychology were extended in the work of not only Kraepelin but also Lightner Witmer, the founder of clinical psychology.

Lightner Witmer was born June 28, 1867, in Philadelphia. He took a bachelor's degree from the University of Pennsylvania in 1888. Following a brief teaching career, he studied at the University of Pennsylvania, but later transferred to Leipzig, where he took the Ph.D. with Wundt in 1893. He returned to the University of Pennsylvania, where he worked until his retirement in 1937. He died at the age of eighty-nine in 1956.

Following his work at Leipzig, Witmer engaged in experimental work on such topics as the perception of pain and the special learning problems of mentally handicapped children. His work in this area held practical value for early school psychologists (Fagan, 1996). In March of 1896, Witmer opened the world's first clinic headed by a psychologist. In its first year of operation, the clinic handled about two dozen cases, primarily learning disorders (McReynolds, 1996). Later, the caseload increased and a greater diversity of clients was tested and treated (see Levine & Wishner, 1977). In 1907, Witmer founded a new journal, which he called *The Psychological Clinic*. McReynolds (1987) pointed out that "Witmer's opening article in the first issue of his new journal . . . called for a new profession and proposed that it be termed *clinical psychology*" (p. 852). Summarizing Witmer's contributions, McReynolds (1997) noted that he was the first to see that scientific psychology could serve as the basis for a helping professional discipline. In addition to founding the first clinic and clinical journal, Witmer showed by his own involvement in clinical activities how clinical professionals might function independent of the medical profession. He also believed that there should be close ties between scientific psychology and clinical psychology. Some have even suggested that his work anticipated later developments in industrial/organizational and counseling psychology (McWhirter & McWhirter, 1997).

In subsequent chapters, we will encounter additional examples of how students from Wundt's laboratory extended the boundaries of psychology. If such students departed from the strict focus of the Leipzig laboratory, many nevertheless carved out areas of application not inconsistent with their teacher's larger intellectual agenda.

REVIEW QUESTIONS

1. Psychophysics explores the relationships between the properties of stimuli as measured by a physical scale and the psychological or subjective impressions of those stimuli. List and describe two extreme positions about the nature of the relationship of experience to objects in the world.

2. How did early psychophysics challenge the two extremes referred to in the previous question?

3. Define the term *threshold*.

4. List some of the findings that came out of Weber's work on difference thresholds.

5. Write both the Weber formula and the Fechner formula and explain their meanings.

6. Briefly describe three of Fechner's psychophysical methods.

7. Outline the reasons given by E. G. Boring for Rudolph Hermann Lotze's prominent place in the history of psychology.

8. Briefly explain Helmholtz's approach to the understanding of color vision and his approach to audition.

9. Outline four general characteristics of Wundt's thought.

10. Give two examples of representative research coming out of Wundt's laboratory.

11. How did Wundt define *psychology*?

12. How did Wundt distinguish between perception and apperception?

13. Briefly explain Wundt's tridimensional theory of feeling.

14. What did Wundt mean by *creative synthesis*?

15. Briefly outline Lightner Witmer's contributions to the formal development of clinical psychology.

CHAPTER 11

DEVELOPMENTS AFTER THE FOUNDING

How many evils could be remedied . . . by knowledge of the laws according to which a mental state can be modified!

—Franz Brentano (1874/1973)

Following the formal founding of psychology at Leipzig, there was a rapid growth of interest in the new discipline. Within a few years new lecture courses, laboratories, and degree programs began springing up in Europe and the United States. In 1898, Titchener, writing for the journal *Mind,* reminded readers, "It is now twenty years since Prof. Wundt instituted the first psychological laboratory in the University of Leipzig. A revolution, radical and far-reaching, was thus quietly inaugurated. . . . Laboratories have been established in most of the principal universities of Germany and in all the principal universities of the United States" (p. 311). Excitement about laboratories ran high as journals carried descriptions of research plans, announcements regarding the establishment of new laboratories, and descriptions of basic laboratory equipment. Titchener (1898) celebrated the fact that "to carry on the psychological work of a modern university the psychology professor must have acquired a body of what one may call 'technical' knowledge, knowledge of applied mechanics and applied electricity" (p. 311).

There were also numerous alternative systematic perspectives set forth by psychologists who appreciated Wundt's contributions but who quarreled with his approach to the field. European psychologists debated such topics as methodology, the appropriate subject matter of psychology, theoretical positions, definitions, and basic assumptions.

Before we consider alternatives to Wundt's psychology, let us explore the meaning of expressions such as *systematic thought* and *systems of psychology.* Courses in the history of psychology are sometimes called the "History and Systems of Psychology." What do we mean by a system of psychology or, for that matter, a system of anything? The answer moves us into a rich intellectual arena that is relevant to the way humans function in the world.

SYSTEMS

A **system** may be defined as an *organized way of envisioning the world or some aspect of the world.* There are integrated, all-encompassing systems that are nothing less than a "philosophy of life," or what German scholars call a *Weltanschauung* ("worldview"). More commonly, however, we encounter less ambitious single-domain systems that provide an organized way of envisioning a limited dimension of human experience. We have political systems, religious systems, economic systems, philosophical systems, and psychological systems. The latter will serve as the focus for the remainder of the book. All of this will be more insightful after exploring the meaning of a system. The material on Wilhelm Wundt in the preceding chapter gives some hints so let us reconsider what was encountered there.

First, systems provide definitions. Recall that Wundt defined psychology as the "science that investigates the facts of consciousness." Assuredly, we will encounter different definitions of psychology in other systems. We can uncover countless terms in psychology that are defined in multiple ways depending on a given systematic position. For example, the term *reinforcement* was defined in different ways by two notable learning theorists, Clark Hull and B. F. Skinner (see Chapter 14). (By the way, psychology is not alone when it comes to such discrepancies; for years, physicists quarreled over the definition of a positron.)

Second, systems also include assumptions. Wundt thought that humans possess only a limited kind of free will. By contrast, Sigmund Freud built his system of psychoanalysis on the assumption that all mental phenomena are strictly determined. Systems of psychology vary with respect to assumptions about issues of nature and nurture, mind and brain, and free will and determinism. Assumptions are sometimes explicit and other times implicit. The behaviorist John B. Watson preferred to not waste time talking philosophy, but assumptions are nevertheless evident in his system.

A third characteristic of systems is that they prescribe methodologies or ways to investigate the world. Most of us know about the different methods and assumed sources of truth in religious and political systems. The same is true in psychology in which we use a variety of methodologies associated with different systematic orientations. Wundt's psychology placed an emphasis on introspection, but his research team used additional methodologies in the laboratory. Introspection, phenomenology, naturalistic observation, free association, and controlled laboratory experiments are among the many methodological tools encountered in psychology. Presumably, the methodologies employed by scientists result in observations that can be replicated. Thus, the methods of science are associated with certain constraints and expectations that may not always be evident in nonscientific methods.

Fourth, systems also specify the subject matter of a disciplinary area. Among other things, Wundt was concerned with the discovery of the elements of consciousness and the way these elements combine. By contrast, Freud studied the unconscious mind and its influences whereas the behavioral psychology of John B. Watson focused on observable behavior. Humanistic psychology criticized these systems as narrow and insisted that joyfulness, peak experiences, and self-actualization are legitimate topics for study in psychology.

Fifth, a system may be construed as open or closed. An open system is responsive to new and multiple sources of information whereas a closed system restricts or even censors the flow of ideas. Systems of thought also exist in a hierarchical arrangement. For example, one may embrace several single-domain systems, but one is often dominant and serves as a filter for what is acceptable in other systems. Thus, a political or a religious system may serve as a filter for a scientific system or vice versa. A deep and critical awareness of the effects of such a hierarchy can be expected in a more open system of thought.

Sixth, systems of thought sometimes differ with respect to time. Some psychologists explore the past to understand the present. Psychoanalytic theory emphasizes the power of childhood trauma in coloring adult experiences and behavior. By contrast, behaviorism stresses the importance of present facts—new conditioning begins *now,* so there is no need to dwell on the past.

Seventh, systems of thought also vary along a liberal–conservative continuum. Conservative thought seeks to preserve stability by emphasizing traditions that have proved workable in the past. The term *liberal* means "worthy of a free person." Liberals do not reject tradition "out of hand," but they may argue that contemporary problems are not always solved by traditional methods. Systems tell us how to dress, what to eat, what to regard as primary or secondary, what to regard as relevant or irrelevant, and how to interact with others. Systems may also attach special significance to specific times, locations, and symbols. In many cases, our systems of thought even define, for better or worse, who we are.

As noted earlier, a significant part of the following chapters will tackle the major systems of thought in psychology. The journey is more meaningful if the various systems are viewed in comparative perspective. One might compare each system with respect to topical areas such as methodology, definition of psychology, assumptions, and subject matter. For example, a chart with topical areas laid out horizontally and the systems laid out vertically might facilitate comparative analysis. The cells within the chart could specify the stance of the particular system on each topical area. In doing this exercise, one will find a few cells with question marks. Theorists do not always take a clear stance on every topic. For example, historians have often disagreed over William James's stand on the mind–body question.

The materials that lie ahead may also be more meaningful when judged against one's personal metatheory regarding an ideal system. For example, an individual might believe that an ideal system should address the free will–determinism issue. Each system can then be measured against that ideal. One might ask whether each system is comprehensive, integrative, open to change, and internally consistent, or whether systems are friendly to theoretical and applied endeavors. In this spirit, let us look at some alternatives to Wundt's systematic vision.

Edward Bradford Titchener

Edwin G. Boring (1927) noted that "the best key to Titchener's life . . . lies in the fact that he emulated Wundt" (p. 504). One might conclude that Edward Bradford Titchener (1867–1927) had devoted years of study with the master but, in fact, Titchener's studies in Leipzig were limited to the two-year period from 1890 to 1892. The relationship between the two men in that period could be described as businesslike and professional; it was not a personally cordial or intimate relationship. Nevertheless, Titchener identified with Wundt's personal and professional style and with the elementary dimensions of his psychology. Titchener did not admire Wundt's larger philosophical vision, especially his emphasis on social, cultural, and linguistic studies. Rather, Titchener identified with the hard-core scientific work that came out of Wundt's laboratory.

Titchener, more than any other disciple, transported the scientific dimensions of Wundt's thought and work to the United States. Accordingly, the psychology that Titchener delivered has often been

mistaken as a close version of Wundt's psychology. To be sure, there are similarities between the psychologies of Wundt and Titchener, but there are also important differences. Fortunately, historical scholarship clarified the differences between Wundt and Titchener (e.g., see Blumenthal, 1975, 1979; Leahey, 1981) that had earlier been blurred.

For a time, Titchener was a powerful force in American psychology. His books were widely read and, like Wundt, he produced a large number of doctoral students. Even so, his system quickly lost ground following his death in 1927. The reasons that Titchener's system failed to thrive on U.S. soil will soon become evident.

Edward Bradford Titchener was born in Chichester, England, on January 11, 1867, the son of John Titchener and Alice Field Habin. Titchener studied first at Malvern College in Worcestershire and then at Oxford. At Oxford he studied physiology, the classics, and philosophy. He graduated from Oxford in 1890 and proceeded in that same year to Leipzig, where he embarked on his doctoral studies with Wundt. Following the completion of his Ph.D. program in 1892, Titchener returned to England. At that time, job opportunities in psychology were sparse, as England was one of the last of the major European countries to recognize the new discipline. Unable to secure a

Edward Bradford Titchener

British appointment, Titchener accepted a position at Cornell University in Ithaca, New York. He remained at Cornell until his death in 1927.

Despite frustrations in setting up a new laboratory and establishing a new program, Titchener thrived. By 1895, he advanced to the position of full professor—quite an accomplishment for a twenty-eight-year-old. He translated several of Wundt's works into English and produced a steady stream of his own books and articles. His first book was *An Outline of Psychology,* published in 1896. This was followed by *Primer of Psychology* in 1898; *Experimental Psychology* (4 vols.) in 1901–1905; *Lectures on the Elementary Psychology of Feeling and Attention* in 1908; *Lectures on the Experimental Psychology of the Thought Processes* in 1909; *A Textbook of Psychology* in 1913; *A Beginner's Psychology* in 1915; and finally, a work that was never completed, *Systematic Psychology: Prolegomena* in 1929. In all, Titchener published eight books and over two hundred articles, in addition to his many translations.

Titchener also headed one of the most vigorous doctoral programs in the United States. Boring (1927) listed the names of fifty-six doctoral students who graduated from Cornell in the period from 1894 to 1927 (records before 1910 were incomplete, so the actual number of doctoral students may have been higher). Titchener's first graduate student, according to Boring's list, was Margaret Floy Washburn, later to establish a reputation for her work in comparative psychology. In all, nineteen of the fifty-six graduates listed by Boring were women. In the context of the times, this was a remarkable record.

Graduate education at Cornell resembled the classic German model with an emphasis on laboratory research and independent reading. If students wished, they could audit undergraduate courses, if such courses complemented their research interests. Graduate students also enrolled in selected seminars. Dallenbach (1967) pointed out that "many students were unable to survive this degree of freedom; they required the compulsion of a teacher. Those who did survive, who learned to depend upon their own initiative, were the productive scholars of the future" (p. 81). Research

served as the major focus of the doctoral program. Evaluation of student performance centered on the quality of papers, the dissertation, and the oral defense of the dissertation.

Students who took their degrees under Titchener came away with colorful anecdotes about life in the graduate program at Cornell. Boring (1961) remembered that "psychology at Cornell—at least the orthodox psychology that centered in the laboratory—revolved around and was almost bounded by the personality of E. B. Titchener" (pp. 22–23). Titchener took a keen interest in the progress of his students and gave generous time to their research projects. Young (1972) told of "weekly conferences with Titchener in his home" (p. 334). Titchener conducted a small orchestra on Sunday evenings and students who could play an instrument were encouraged to participate. After the music, Sunday evenings were devoted to casual conversation, generally on topics other than psychology.

Titchener's erudition and brilliance are typical themes in the biographies of his students. Boring (1961) stated,

> He always seemed to me the nearest approach to genius of anyone with whom I have been closely associated. . . . He was competent with languages, and could ad lib in Latin when the occasion required it. If you had mushrooms, he would tell you at once how they should be cooked. If you were buying oak for a new floor, he would at once come forward with all the advantages of ash. If you were engaged to be married, he would have his certain and insistent advice about the most unexpected aspects of your problems, and if you were honeymooning, he would write to remind you, as he did me, on what day you ought to be back at work. (pp. 22–23)

Boring noted that Titchener, like Freud, demanded loyalty from his students. At Cornell, there was a strict European code on matters of decorum and conduct and those who violated the code could pay a severe penalty. Most students decided that the benefits of working with such a man as Titchener far outweighed the inconveniences brought about by his pervasive paternalistic concerns. Titchener's closest relationships were with students rather than with colleagues. By temperament, he was not one who thrived in a rugged democratic climate.

After the first decade of the new century, the tide was turning against Titchener's systematic psychology. John B. Watson called for a radical new approach to psychology. The new Gestalt psychology from Germany issued devastating critiques that challenged Titchener's systematic vision. American functionalism provided an approach to psychology with broader appeal than Titchener's narrow approach to the discipline. Titchener died in 1927 and, though he produced many doctoral students, no one carried on his work. Accordingly, his systematic vision died with him. There is interesting speculation (e.g., see Evans, 1972) about how Titchener's system might have evolved had he had a longer life.

Titchener's Psychology

The technical term employed by Titchener for his system of psychology was **structuralism.** Like other systems, structuralism embraced a specific methodology, advanced definitions of the subject matter of psychology, and made assumptions regarding age-old philosophical problems. Titchener continually drew parallels between the physical sciences (especially physics and chemistry) and psychology. He hoped to establish the new discipline on the same conceptual footing that had proved so successful in the established sciences.

The Subject Matter of Psychology.   Titchener (1913) argued that "all the sciences have the same sort of subject-matter; there can be no essential difference between the raw materials of physics and the raw materials of psychology" (p. 6). All science, according to Titchener, begins with experience. Without experience there can be no cognition, no knowledge. Though all the sciences begin with experience, experience itself can be considered from different points of view. For example, we can consider a unit of time, say an hour, from the point of view of physics. The hour, from such a point of view, is a measured unit of time. The

actual unit of measurement has fixed qualities (e.g., 60 minutes, 3,600 seconds, etc.) that are independent of human judgment. But an hour, from the point of view of psychology, may be long or short, pleasant or unpleasant. The subject matter of psychology, thus, is experience, dependent on the experiencing person. Titchener (1913) stated that formal study from the first point of view (stated above) "gives us facts and laws of physics; [the] second gives us facts and laws of psychology" (p. 8).

The Problem of Psychology.   Science, according to Titchener, always seeks to answer three sorts of questions: what, how, and why? *What* questions deal with the basic, most uncomplicated elements of the subject (e.g., what is water made of?). *How* questions deal with the appearances of things. For example, how do the basic elements that compose water combine with each other? Finally, Titchener (1913) stated that "science enquires, further, why a given set of phenomena occurs in just this given way, and not otherwise; and it answers the question 'why' by laying bare the cause of which the observed phenomena are the effect" (p. 37). The first problem for psychology is to identify the basic elements of experience, much as the first task for the physical sciences was to identify basic elements. The second task is to assess the ways in which elements combine. The third is to determine causal relations in these phenomena. We shall return later to a more detailed consideration of these problems.

The Method of Psychology.   The method of psychology, in Titchener's view, is really no different from the method employed by any other science. All scientific work begins with observation of the phenomena that have been designated as the subject matter of a particular science. The type of observation employed by the physicist is called *inspection,* whereas the type of observation employed by the psychologist is called **introspection.** Needless to say, special training is required for the unique observational tasks of any discipline. For an observation to be scientific, it is important that it be possible to isolate it, vary it experimentally, and repeat it. For example, the stimulation of a particular receptor site on the tongue with a particular substance may produce a specific response. Maybe the subject declares that she or he experienced a taste of sweetness. Presumably, the site can be isolated, the substance can be varied many ways (e.g., with respect to quality, concentration, etc.), and the response for a particular isolated stimulus can be repeated. The observation, in this case, is a variety of introspection, but in Titchener's view, this need not be viewed as radically different from inspection.

The Scope of Psychology.   Because Titchener's method was limited to introspection, it might be argued that psychology, in his view, is limited in scope. For example, how can we ask a baby or nonhuman subject such as a cat or a dog to introspect? For that matter, how can we ask a mentally disturbed individual to introspect? Titchener's psychology is limited to the study of normal human beings. Further, it appears superficially, at least, that introspection reveals only the contents of the individual mind and that we are trapped in a kind of solipsism. Titchener was keenly aware of the problem and took specific steps to ensure that his system did, in fact, have considerable scope. To argue that Titchener was interested only in the adult human mind is to advance a caricature of Titchener's system of thought.

Titchener believed that psychologists must make ample use of analogy. Although we have direct access only to our own experience, we have every reason to believe that a specific behavior (e.g., the expression of fear) in another is comparable to our own experience of fear. Such an argument provides the conceptual basis for social psychology and a similar line of argument provides the basis for comparative psychology. On this topic, Titchener (1913) wrote:

> If however, we attribute minds to other human beings, we have no right to deny them to the higher animals. These animals are provided with a nervous system of the same pattern as ours, and their conduct or behavior, under circumstances that would arouse certain feelings in us, often seems to express, quite definitely, similar feelings in them. Surely we must

> grant that the highest vertebrates, mammals and birds, have minds. (p. 27)

In the same passage, Titchener argued that the range of mind seems to be as broad as the range of animal life. His view on the scope of psychology, then, was broader than what might be derived from an uncritical acceptance of his definition of psychology as human experience dependent on the experiencing individual. The architecture of the nervous system and analogies drawn from behavior provide the glue for the breadth of Titchener's vision. Titchener (1913) told his readers that there is

> A psychology of language, a psychology of myth, a psychology of custom, etc; [there is also] a differential psychology of the Latin mind, of the Anglo-Saxon mind, of the Oriental mind, etc.
>
> And this is not all: the scope of psychology extends, still further, from the normal to the abnormal mind. Life, as we know, need not be either complete or completely healthy life. The living organism may show defect, the lack of limb or of a sense-organ; and it may show disorder and disease, a . . . lapse from health. So it is with mind. (pp. 28–29)

As Titchener's thought evolved, he realized the importance of the study of different types of consciousness. For example, he argued that studies of those with sensory impairment or with morbid fears are important in their own right. Furthermore, such studies may shed light on our understanding of normal conscious processes. In fact, the study of normal conscious processes commanded the most attention in Titchener's laboratory. We turn now to some of the major content areas explored by Titchener and his students.

Elementary Mental Processes.   Recall that the first task of any science, according to Titchener, is to investigate the basic elements of its subject matter. Accordingly, Titchener's first concern was the nature and number of the elementary mental processes. Following the Leipzig tradition, Titchener focused largely on the senses as windows to the mind. His most immediate concern was to identify the basic elements associated with each of the senses. According to Titchener (1913), a true element "must remain unchanged, however persistent our attempt at analysis and however refined our method of investigation" (p. 46). The next task of the psychologist is to arrange "the mental elements precisely as the chemist classifies his elementary substances" (Titchener, 1913, p. 49).

Though the senses occupied a central place in Titchener's system, he identified two additional elementary processes: images and affections. Sensations were regarded as elements of perceptions, whereas images were regarded as elements of ideas, memories, and thoughts. Affections were treated as the elementary processes of emotions. The relative emphasis of Titchener on these elementary processes is illustrated in the amount of page space devoted to each. For example, in *A Textbook of Psychology* (1913), Titchener devoted 293 pages to sensation and perception, 70 pages to affection and emotion, and 72 pages to memory and thought. In that same book, 21 pages were devoted to association, 37 pages to attention, and 41 pages to a discussion of reactions and actions.

In addition to the identification and classification of elements, the psychologist, according to Titchener, must discover the **attributes of elementary mental processes.** For example, he found that all sensations, at a minimum, have four attributes: quality, intensity, clearness, and duration. *Quality* is the major identifying property of a sensation— its saltiness, sweetness, redness, coldness, and so on. *Intensity* simply refers to the fact that the sensation exists in some amount or strength. *Clearness* refers to the transparency or the distinctiveness of a sensation; a clear sensation is easily identified. *Duration,* of course, is a temporal attribute. As noted, all sensations share these four basic attributes, but some sensations have additional attributes. For example, certain solutions such as alcohol applied to the skin may have an attribute that could best be described as penetratingness. Such a solution stimulates the surface of the skin as well as areas below the surface.

Titchener also believed that the attributes of quality, intensity, clearness, and duration are associated with images. He found quality, intensity, and duration in association with affections, but clearness was not easily identified as an attribute of affection. Titchener and his students identified other attributes

with specific elements. For example, he noted that "certain sensations have been credited with an attribute of insistence. They are self-assertive and aggressive; they monopolise consciousness. . . . We speak of the penetratingness of odours like camphor and naphthalene; of the urgency . . . of certain pains" (Titchener, 1913, p. 55).

One way to gain an appreciation for Titchener's system is to examine his position on some key issues of the day. We have already sketched his views on science, his position on methodology, his definition of psychology, and his views on the scope of psychology. We turn now to a consideration of his position on other key issues.

Mind and Brain. Titchener admitted that common sense tells us that we lose consciousness as a result of inhaling ether or that we run because of fear. In other words, the physical system influences the mental and vice versa. Titchener's position, however, was "that mind and body, the subject-matter of psychology and the subject-matter of physiology, are simply two aspects of the same world of experience. They cannot influence each other, because they are not separate and independent things" (1913, p. 13). Titchener referred to his position as *psychophysical parallelism,* but it is not completely clear that the label is accurate. Hergenhahn (2001) referred to Titchener as an epiphenomenalist and cited a passage from Titchener's *A Textbook of Psychology* that seemed to support the idea of a one-way causality from the physical to the mental. Titchener could also be viewed as a double-aspect theorist because he declared that mind and body are but "two aspects of the same world of experience." A true psychophysical parallelist would posit the ontic status of both the physical and the mental but deny that the two interact. To be sure, there are some ambiguities in Titchener's position, and Heidbreder (1933) was correct when she declared that Titchener's "emotions were not involved in the problem for its own sake. . . . He is almost perfunctory in his discussion of the topic" (p. 127). Still, because at every turn Titchener emphasized the primacy of experience, and because he studied experience in relation to the physical system, and because he explicitly rejected commonsense interactionism, he is appropriately viewed as a psychophysical parallelist, just as he described himself. His psychophysical parallelism, however, may be of a pragmatic rather than a metaphysical variety. Thus, psychophysical parallelism, for Titchener, is a useful assumption and helps the scientist get on with the more important business at hand.

Attention.   Like many early psychologists, Titchener was keenly interested in the topic of attention. He distinguished between passive or involuntary attention and active or voluntary attention. He referred to involuntary attention as *primary* and to voluntary attention as *secondary.* Both represent types of consciousness that are identifiable at different stages of development. **Primary attention,** according to Titchener (1913), is "an attention that we are compelled to give and are powerless to prevent" (p. 268). It is brought about by strong stimuli, so the attribute of intensity is sufficient to activate it. Titchener believed that certain qualities are irresistible and observed that, in his own case, attention was commanded by such stimuli as the smell of musk, a bitter taste, or the sight of yellow. Examples of other factors that control involuntary attention include novelty and suddenness.

Secondary attention, according to Titchener, involves a focus on a subject that would not normally call attention to itself. For example, he pointed out that "a problem in geometry does not appeal to us as a thunderclap does" (Titchener, 1913, p. 271). Thus, "secondary attention is attention under difficulties, attention in the face of competitors, attention with distraction" (p. 272). Clearly, secondary attention is associated with a more advanced stage of development. The infant is capable of primary attention but may not yet be capable of secondary attention.

Titchener (1913) found still a third stage in attention, and that stage, he tells us,

> consists in nothing else than a relapse into primary attention. As we work our problem in geometry, we gradually become interested and absorbed; and presently the problem gains the same forcible hold over us as the thunderclap has from the moment of its appearance in consciousness. The difficulties have been overcome; the competitors have been vanquished; the distraction has disappeared. There

could hardly be a stronger proof of the growth of secondary out of primary attention than this fact, of everyday experience, that secondary attention is continually reverting to the primary form. (p. 273)

There were numerous investigations of attention in Titchener's laboratory. Topics such as the duration of attention, the effortfulness of attention, the inertia of attention, and bodily conditions conducive to attention were favorites.

Association.   If Titchener's primary experimental focus was on sensory processes, he by no means intended to neglect the importance of association. He acknowledged the debt of psychology to Aristotle and to all those British thinkers from Hobbes to Bain who emphasized the centrality of association. Furthermore, he quoted, with approval, the contention of David Hume that association is to the mental world as gravitation is to physics (see Titchener, 1913, p. 374). The comparison is apparently based on the idea that association, like gravitation, accounts for such a wide range of phenomena.

Titchener recognized traditional attempts to establish laws of association but argued that all association can be reduced to the law of contiguity. He pointed out that even the so-called law of similarity really involves contiguity. In Titchener's (1913) treatment, association is characterized by the following statement: "Whenever a sensory or imaginal process occurs in consciousness, there are likely to appear with it (of course, in imaginal terms) all those sensory and imaginal processes which occurred together with it in any earlier conscious present. This we may term the law of association" (p. 378).

Titchener immediately recognized a possible objection to his law. What about affective processes? Feelings most assuredly play a role in associative processes. Titchener (1913) agreed but noted that feelings play a role in association only "by virtue of their sensory and imaginal components, and not in their affective character" (p. 378). However, Titchener admitted that little is known about feeling and that his position was tentative.

The Experimental Study of Association.   Titchener noted that, prior to the work of Hermann Ebbinghaus on memory, the experimental study of association was confounded because of the presence of previously acquired meanings. In a celebration of Ebbinghaus's contribution, Titchener (1913) offered the opinion that "it is not too much to say that the recourse to nonsense syllables, as means to the study of association, marks the most considerable advance, in this chapter of psychology, since the time of Aristotle" (p. 381). Nevertheless, according to Titchener, the nonsense syllable is not a complete panacea because we human beings find intrinsic meanings everywhere. Thus, even in a set of nonsense syllables, we may find that one has more meaning than another and the one with the greater meaning forms an impression. The impression then helps mediate associations. Titchener argued that associations must be understood in the context of impressions that result from the fact that some stimuli, even some nonsense syllables, have a unique capacity to impress themselves on the brain. Accordingly, impression and associative processes supplement each other. In Titchener's view, the mere study of association without careful introspective analysis of what is taking place is inadequate. He also warned that our knowledge in this area will remain inadequate until such future time as we are able to devise means to study the physiology of association.

Meaning. According to Titchener (1913), "Meaning, psychologically, is always context" (p. 367). In Titchener's view of the **context theory of meaning,** meaning is understood as a function of the laws of attention in combination with the laws of the connection of sensations. An aggregate of sensations will also be supplemented by images that result from memories of previous encounters with the particular aggregate of sensations. The group of sensations and images, according to Titchener (1913), "has a fringe, a background, a context; and this context is the psychological equivalent of its logical meaning" (p. 371).

Titchener acknowledged that many psychologists would not accept such an associationistic approach to meaning:

> A square, they say, is more than four linear extensions, sensibly of the same length, and occupying certain relative positions in the visual field; a square

is square; and squareness is a new character, common to all squares, but not to be explained by attention, or by the laws of sensory connection, or by those of imaginal supplementing. A melody, again, is more than rhythm and consonance and scale; a melody is melodic; we recognize its melodic character as such; the melodic character is something new and unique, common to all melodies, but not found elsewhere. (Titchener, 1913, p. 372)

Titchener noted that he could not find this extra character in his own introspections. That is, he found no need for a new distinct mental content based on a combination or synthesis of the parts. He was nevertheless open to future research on the matter and added that it is "only right to say that the belief in a new mental content, or new mental character, peculiar to perception, is shared by many psychologists of standing" (1913, p. 373).

Emotion. The most widely discussed theory of emotion in Titchener's day was a rather paradoxical theory (see Chapter 12) advanced by William James (1884b) and propounded independently by Carl Lange (1885/1922). Widely known as the James-Lange theory of emotion, the view stressed the dependence of emotions on the vasomotor system. According to the theory, we experience emotions such as fear, anger, or love because of bodily events (e.g., muscular arousal, discharge of adrenaline, increase in heart rate, etc.) that interpose between one mental event and another. Thus, to use one of James's examples, we see a bear, we run, and we are afraid. The experience of emotion is a product of the running and the multitude of physical events that accompany it. We refer to the theory as paradoxical because it contradicts the commonsense idea that we see the bear, are afraid, and then run. The theory will be examined in more detail in the next chapter, but it is sketched briefly here because it serves as a foil for Titchener's position.

Titchener noted that the so-called James-Lange theory was not really new. It had been anticipated, at least in part, by such figures as Malebranche, Descartes, Spinoza, Lotze, and Maudsley. The idea of an organic basis for emotions had been stirring for a long time. Despite its venerable history, Titchener found flaws in the theory.

The first problem, according to Titchener (1913), was that "the bodily changes to which James refers may appear identically in very different emotions. There are tears of joy and tears of rage, as well as tears of sorrow; we may strike in fear or in cruelty, as well as in anger; we may run as hard to overtake a friend as we run from a pursuing bear" (p. 477). Following criticisms such as this, James modified his theory and admitted that stimuli themselves may produce responses with avoidance or approach characteristics (James, 1894).

Titchener also argued that mere sensations of organic conditions can hardly be identified with the richer, more complex experience of an emotion. Titchener did not deny the importance of organic correlates of emotion but argued for a much broader conception. He believed that in some cases instinctive tendencies are automatically toned with **affect**—a position James also accepted. Such affect occurs in an environmental context and is also associated with organic conditions. Affect may also be associated with images or earlier memories. Thus, according to Titchener, the experience of emotion may have multiple causes.

Titchener discussed the difficulties of classifying emotions as well as emotional types. The major difficulty is that any classification scheme may serve only the convenience of the person doing the classifying and have nothing to do with the science of emotions. For example, he referred to the ancient typology advanced by Galen. Recall that Galen's temperamental types included the choleric, the sanguine, the melancholic, and the phlegmatic. Titchener (1913) referred to other possible classification schemes but noted that they are "of interest rather for an applied than for a general psychology" (p. 498).

Titchener (1913) pointed out that the sentiment "represents the last stage of mental development on the affective side, as thought represents the highest level of development on the side of sensation and image" (p. 499). A sentiment, according to Titchener, is more complex than emotion; it includes discrimination, a critical dimension, possible conflicting claims, and so on. For example, if patriotism counts as a sentiment, it includes emotions, but there are also tensions. What are the re-

lationships between loyalty to state, to nation, or to humankind? What is substantive and what is mere symbol? Clearly, the sentiment involves emotion but is a much more complicated manifestation of the affective dimension.

Affect and Emotion. Earlier, we noted that Titchener identified three elementary mental processes: sensations, images, and affections. **Affections** were initially regarded as the elements of emotions. As Titchener's theory developed, the relationship between affect and emotion became increasingly troublesome. Titchener was suspicious that affections are really nothing more than sensations of pleasantness or unpleasantness (see Henle, 1986). The same suspicions had also been directed at the so-called images; perhaps they were but a species of sensation.

In the final years of his life, Titchener moved away from the concept of elements and thinking in terms of the dimensions or attributes of experience. As noted by Evans (1972), "As early as 1918 the system started out from 'the ultimate dimensions' of psychological subject matter" (p. 172). These ultimate dimensions consisted of what were earlier called attributes: quality, intensity, duration, and so on. Titchener's final approach to psychology was much closer to what we find naturally in experience. It could be argued that what is most immediate is a quality such as redness or sweetness or a sense of pleasantness or unpleasantness. Images, sensations, and feelings are not the ultimate elements or dimensions of experience but abstractions discovered through dissection or discrimination.

Though Titchener was moving toward a new organizational approach to psychology, there is no evidence that he would have changed his rigorously scientific approach. Indeed, though his original system did not survive, his rigorous scientific attitude enjoyed prominence among experimental psychologists. In his final years, Titchener celebrated the growing independence of psychology from physiology. The confidence betrayed in such celebration may have had continuing salutary effects on other psychologists who found security in their work in the new discipline.

MARGARET FLOY WASHBURN: A BROADER PSYCHOLOGY

Titchener's first graduate student, Margaret Floy Washburn (1871–1939), became a significant figure among a new generation of psychologists. Washburn had earned a bachelor's degree from Vassar in 1891. Science and philosophy dominated her academic interests, and she believed that the new field of experimental psychology joined her two interests in a near perfect union. Following graduation, she studied psychology at Columbia University under James McKeen Cattell. Columbia, at that time, accepted a few women as "hearers," but did not accept women as degree candidates. Cattell recommended that Washburn transfer to Cornell University, where she would be permitted to work toward an advanced degree. She agreed and arrived in the fall of 1892 just as the twenty-five-year-old Titchener became a new faculty member. Washburn completed her degree with Titchener in 1894 and became the first woman in the United States to be awarded a Ph.D. in psychology. After brief academic and professional positions at Wells College, Cornell, and the University of Akron, Washburn accepted an appointment at Vassar, where she remained for the rest of her illustrious career.

Washburn accepted Titchener's emphasis on the central role of consciousness in psychology

Margaret Floy Washburn

though she doubted that consciousness consisted of irreducible static elements. She was too much of an empiricist, in the classic sense of that word, to reject the mental world or consciousness as a legitimate topic in psychology. In spite of this, she could not accept Cartesian interactionism with its emphasis on a mental substance that can "go it alone" in the body. She accepted epiphenomenalism because it is friendly to both the mental and the physical worlds, but assumes that real causal force always works from the physical to the mental. Nevertheless, in her opinion, we learn about consciousness and its physical underpinnings by relying on introspection and other psychological techniques.

In 1908, Washburn became a leader in comparative psychology with the publication of *The Animal Mind* (she authored substantial revisions in 1917, 1926, and 1936). Her book provided a wealth of information on animal sensory systems, animal memory, intelligence, attention, behavior, and adaptation. The book's strong evolutionary thrust is evident in her speculations about the role of distance receptors such as the eye and the ear in the development of higher cognitive processes. Early species who had only contact receptors could never afford the luxury of the delay involved in our cognitive processes. Physical contact for such organisms demanded an immediate and appropriate response or else the organism would die or lose the chance to acquire food. By contrast, the development of distance receptors provided the luxury of delay because one may see or hear an enemy or prey at a great distance. With delay, adaptation is facilitated by the development of cognitive strategies, memory, discrimination, and plans. If she were alive today, Washburn would relish metaphors for intelligence that rely on visual and auditory imagery—expressions of cognition where we "gain insight," "see through," "truly hear," or develop a "visionary strategy."

As suggested in the title of her book, Washburn (1908) believed that animals possess consciousness that can be accessed via inference, the same way we study human cognition. In her view, animal consciousness is an appropriate research topic for psychologists. Washburn always argued, however, for a rigorous methodology that challenges simplistic and anthropomorphic inferences. She recognized that facts may be distorted by people who attribute human qualities to animal consciousness. Washburn's *The Animal Mind* is a masterful work in comparative psychology as well as a primer in the evolutionary study of higher cognitive processes.

Washburn (1916) is also well known for a book entitled *Movement and Mental Imagery* that set forth a "motor theory of consciousness." According to the motor theory, mental activity has its origin in, and is supported by, subtle neurophysiological movement systems. An example is found in the work of Walter Samuel Hunter, who allowed a hungry but restrained dog to watch as meat was placed inside a goal box. As it stared hungrily at the goal box, the dog displayed what Washburn called "persistent tentative movements" in the direction of the box. We can assume that the dog "anticipates" food as it salivates and strains at the leash. The dog's behavior is "goal directed" and "purposive." If we release the dog, it will scramble toward the food and eat it. But if we introduce a delay, the dog will become distracted by other things and stop straining in the direction of the goal box. If released after losing its postural set, the dog no longer heads directly to the goal box. In other words, incipient muscular movements appear to support ongoing mental activity and purposive behavior has a motor or muscular component. If the movement system is broken up, the behavior (with respect to the goal) is changed. Consider a different example. Even without an instrument, a musician might practice moving her fingers as if playing a piece, engaging in incipient muscular movements that act as a kind of rehearsal for an actual performance. Washburn's motor theory of consciousness is sometimes regarded as counterintuitive, but it becomes more plausible the more it is studied (see Viney & Burlingame-Lee, In Press, for a more detailed explanation of the theory).

Margaret Floy Washburn was one of the leading American psychologists in the first three decades of the twentieth century. She served as president of the American Psychological Association in 1921, the second woman to hold that position. (Mary Whiton Calkins, the first female APA president, will be discussed in the next chap-

ter.) In 1931 Washburn was named to the National Academy of the Sciences, one the highest honors for any scientist (the renowned anatomist Florence Sabin was the first woman named to the Academy). Washburn acted as president of the Psychology Section of the American Association for the Advancement of Science and served on the editorial boards of numerous journals. Scarborough (2000) claims that Washburn was regarded as the best lecturer at Vassar. She was a powerful force not only in the science of psychology but also for the full participation of women in the intellectual community.

FRANZ BRENTANO AND ACT PSYCHOLOGY

Franz Brentano (1838–1917) provided a striking alternative to Wundt's and Titchener's psychology. As early as 1874, his system, known as **act psychology,** rejected the exclusive alignment of scientific psychology with physiology. It also rejected older interpretations of empiricism that emphasized the content of experience and the building of experience exclusively through mechanical associations. According to Brentano, an authentic empirical psychology will find more in experience itself than mere contents or passive associations. A truly empirical psychology will discover that experience is forward looking, active, manipulative, and intentional. A psychology that does not recognize these dimensions of experience is not a true empirical psychology. According to Sussman (1962), Brentano insisted on the Aristotelian approach to empiricism, "reviving the concept of activity as the fundamental essence of empiricism. In this sense is the oft used quote from him: 'Experience alone influences me as a mistress' " (p. 504). Brentano's best-known psychological work is his book *Psychology from an Empirical Standpoint,* first published in 1874.

Standard biographies of Franz Brentano typically emphasize his family's impressive intellectual and cultural achievements. Franz's father, Christian Brentano, and his mother, Emilie Gegner, were both known for their contributions to Catholic religious literature. An uncle, Klemens (Clemens) Brentano, was a well-known poet and novelist, and an aunt, Bettina Brentano, was a famous German romantic writer. Lujo Brentano, Franz's younger brother, was a well-known economist who won the Nobel prize in 1927 for his outspoken opposition to the growth of German militarism.

Franz Brentano, born January 16, 1838, was one of the five children of Christian and Emilie Brentano. Young Franz was educated in the Gymnasium at Aschaffenburg following private tutoring by a Catholic priest. Brentano excelled in language and mathematics but was also drawn to theological and philosophical studies. Rancurello (1968) noted that "The road to intellectual excellence took Brentano in succession to the universities of Munich (1856–57), Würzburg (1858) and Berlin (1858–59), to the Academy of Münster (1859–60), and to the University of Tübingen where in 1862 he was granted the degree in philosophy" (p. 4). After completing the Ph.D., Brentano studied for the priesthood and was ordained in 1864.

Brentano's career as a university professor included a seven-year period at Würzburg (1866–1873) and a twenty-year period at the University of Vienna (1874–1894). Brentano enjoyed unusual success in terms of his ability to inspire students. His better-known students included Christian von Ehrenfels, later known for his wholistic approach to sensation and perception; Edmund Husserl, a philosopher whose work in phenomenology had a profound influence in psychology; Alexius Meinong, the founder of the psychology laboratory at Graz; and Sigmund Freud, who took courses with Brentano at Vienna. Though scholars disagree about the extent of Brentano's influence on Freud, a case can be made (e.g., see Domenjo, 2000; Fancher, 1977) concerning similarities in their thought. Brentano clearly influenced Carl Stumpf, who in turn influenced some of the founders of Gestalt psychology.

Though Brentano was a brilliant teacher, his was by no means an untroubled career. Prior to the December 1867 meeting of Vatican Council I, debates raged in the church about the relative authority of the papacy versus church councils. Some scholars argued that, in selected spiritual matters, the word of the pope should be regarded as infallible. Catholics were deeply split on the issue, and Brentano sided with those who challenged the dogma of papal infallibility. Those opposed to the dogma of infallibility argued that popes had contradicted each other on spiritual matters and that the doctrine of infallibility was not necessary to the Catholic faith.

On July 18, 1870, the council voted 433 to 2 in favor of a doctrine of infallibility. Brentano's former teacher, Ignaz von Dollinger, also opposed the doctrine of infallibility and was excommunicated for his refusal to accept the council's decision. Brentano, like Dollinger, could not subordinate reason to faith, but neither could he suppress earlier theological doubts now exacerbated by Vatican I. As a consequence, Brentano resigned from the priesthood and separated from the church in 1873.

All of this was not irrelevant to Brentano's academic life. He had been appointed to his position on the Würzburg faculty as a priest. As noted by Puglisi (1924), he felt "morally bound to resign his chair" (p. 416). Brentano's former affiliation with the church haunted him in his subsequent position at the University of Vienna. In 1880, at age forty-two, he was engaged to marry Ida Lieben but, as pointed out by Puglisi (1924), she "as a Catholic could not contract in Austria a religious marriage with one who had formerly been an ecclesiastic. Brentano was therefore obliged to assume Saxon citizenship, and consequently to resign the title of *professor ordinarius* in the Austrian university. On September 16 of the same year, 1880, he was married in Leipzig to Miss Lieben" (p. 417). Brentano was allowed to work at the University of Vienna, but his status was reduced to that of lecturer. Brentano remained at Vienna until the death of his wife in 1894. In retirement years, he lived first in Florence and later in Zurich, where he died on March 17, 1917.

Brentano's Psychology

In *Psychology from an Empirical Standpoint,* Brentano (1874/1973) defined *psychology* as "the science of mental phenomena" (p. 100). In an elaboration of the meaning of *mental phenomena,* he referred to John Locke's famous experiment on the perception of coldness and warmth. Locke warmed one hand while simultaneously cooling the other. Then he placed both hands into a pan of lukewarm water. He then experienced warmth in the hand that was previously cooled and coolness in the hand that had previously been warmed. Brentano argued that the experiment "proved that neither warmth nor cold really existed in the water" (p. 9).

Brentano provided other examples of the effects of context on experience and noted that the term *phenomenon* is close in meaning to the word *appearance*. In the example of the water basin, we experience the water as warm or cold, depending on the previous conditions to which the hands have been subjected. Brentano (1874/1973) believed that the succession of mental phenomena follows yet-to-be-discovered lawful patterns and that there is "a vast range of important problems for the psychologist" (p. 12). According to Brentano, mental phenomena are real. He rejected the idea that the only real things are those that exist in the outside world. We know all things through experience.

Brentano was optimistic about what a science of psychology could accomplish. He envisioned the development of a discipline broad in scope. For example, he asked, "How many evils could be remedied . . . by knowledge of the laws according to which a mental state can be modified!" (1874/1973, p. 22). He considered the enormous value of early diagnosis of aptitudes. Brentano argued that "for the individual and even more for the masses, where the imponderable circumstances which impede and promote progress balance each other out, psychological laws will afford a sure basis for action" (p. 24). Brentano saw psychology as the science of the future, a science both theoretical and practical. He repeatedly conveyed optimism about the potential applications of psychology and noted that "the practical tasks I assign to psychology are far from insignificant" (p. 22). Brentano's optimism is seldom appreciated, but in attitude and orientation, he must be considered as a forerunner of applied psychology.

On questions of method, Brentano advocated a pluralistic and developmental epistemology. He recognized that the history of science involves the adaptation of scientific method to ever more complex phenomena. Scientific method is not static and Brentano mentioned several psychological methods that could be valuable. Included are observations on the newborn, studies of primitive societies, studies of those with congenital disorders

such as congenital blindness to assess the effects of sensory deprivation, animal research, and studies of diseased mental states.

In the study of normal phenomena, Brentano advocated a variety of methods such as the use of biographies and what he called *inner perception.* Brentano distinguished between *inner perception* and *inner observation.* The latter term he equated with introspection and declared it an impossibility. We can observe external objects, but it is pretentious to say we observe psychological phenomena in the same manner. We perceive inner events by focusing attention on the immediate past and on the flow of events. Thus, retrospection is involved in inner perception. Brentano noted that all sciences must consult memory in the course of their work, so psychology is not uniquely disadvantaged if it must trust memory to describe mental phenomena.

Brentano provided an example of inner perception by calling attention to the way we might study our own anger. We do not observe it directly, but we can report our perception of the flow of events and their effects. We retrospect about those things that just took place and the things that preceded them and the perceived consequences. We can know about the inner state of others through verbal reports and behavior. Indeed, he argued that behavior or practical conduct is often the most reliable guide to inner states (1874/1973, p. 39). He also recognized involuntary physical indices such as blushing as guides to the nature of inner states.

If the content of Brentano's psychology was broad in theory, it was nevertheless fairly focused in practice. His unique approach is still informative and provocative. Chances are that if Brentano were devising a curriculum in psychology, he would prefer that course titles, where possible, employ verb forms rather than noun forms. Rather than teaching a course entitled Sensation and Perception, we might better give the course a title such as Sensing and Perceiving. The reason for Brentano's preference for the active verb form rather than the passive noun form is based on what he encountered in experience itself. Experience is an active, participatory, creative, and constructive process. It does not consist simply of inert, static, or passive contents.

Fancher (1977) noted that, for Brentano, "physical phenomena are always objects such as sounds or colors, while mental phenomena are always *acts* that 'contain' *objects,* such as hearing a sound or admiring a color" (p. 208). Physical phenomena, such as the sounds of music over a stereo system, are mere facts in consciousness, but mental phenomena are much more. They may include admiration, reflections over the phrasing or rhythms of a passage, memories, comparisons, wishes, and so forth. The unique feature of the mental act is its intentionality, complexity, and involvement. It does not consist of mere awareness.

Brentano was keenly interested in the classification of mental phenomena and provided an excellent overview and critique, beginning with Plato, of the history of classification schemes (Brentano, 1874/1973, pp. 173–193). His classification system divided mental phenomena into presentations, desires, and judgments. **Presentations** are basic because there could be no desires or judgments without them. A presentation is simply an event or a presence in experience. He pointed out that a presentation and a judgment "are two entirely different ways of being conscious of an object" (p. 201). **Judgment** clearly involves belief or disbelief and it helps define our relationship with a presentation. Similarly, **desire** further delineates our relationship to an object and is still another mode or dimension of consciousness. Presumably, one could desire an object in consciousness, such as an item of food, yet judge the food negatively in terms of its nutritional value. One might also encounter positive judgments or beliefs coupled with negative desires.

Brentano argued that the three types of mental phenomena are intertwined. Indeed, in *Psychology from an Empirical Standpoint,* he contended that "there is no mental act in which all three are not present . . . but it is conceivable without contradiction that there might be a form of mental life which is missing one or even two of these kinds of mental activities and lacks all capacity for them as well" (Brentano, 1874/1973, p. 265). Later, Brentano changed his mind and expressed the belief that there are visual and even auditory sensations lacking in affect (see Rancurello, 1968).

Brentano, as much as any theorist in the history of psychology, struggled with the question of the unity of experience. Is experience, as we encounter it, a mosaic of bits and pieces that add together somehow to form the whole, or are all the parts intimate with each other? Brentano was a strong believer in the unity of consciousness and in the existence of a self in possession of experience. To deny such a self would reduce us to a kaleidoscope of sensations, much as we encounter in the philosophy of David Hume. The self, according to Brentano, is a reality that appropriates and integrates other realities. It ties past and present together, along with intentions about the future.

Brentano is a key figure in the history of psychology because he described an alternative approach that placed appropriate conceptual work in higher priority than experimental work. Brentano would have agreed with Descartes, who counseled that in any conflict between the results of an experiment and reason, we should embrace reason. Brentano did not oppose experimentation but believed that it should be preceded by appropriate conceptual homework.

Brentano's influence on the discipline of psychology is remarkable in view of the sparseness of his written work. He is remembered primarily for his *Psychology from an Empirical Standpoint* and his lectures. Nevertheless, he had a direct and profound influence on phenomenological psychology and existential psychology (Gilbert, 1968). There are clear-cut intellectual affinities between his work and the psychology of William James, American functionalism, existentialism, Gestalt psychology, and, arguably, Freud's psychoanalytic thought. Although his ideas about mental phenomena did not always mesh with the positivistic temper of nineteenth-century psychology, Brentano has been rediscovered as a viable alternative to contemporary models of cognition (Macnamara, 1993).

CARL STUMPF

Born on Good Friday, 1848, to a distinguished family of scholars, Carl Stumpf (1848–1936) remarked that "the love of medicine and natural science was

Carl Stumpf

in my blood" (1930, p. 389). Despite a natural interest in science, his childhood passion was music. By seven, he learned to play the violin and, without formal instruction, had taught himself another five instruments. At ten, he composed the words and music for an oratorio. Stumpf's fascination with music proved to be an instrumental part of his professional career.

Stumpf studied law at the University of Würzburg primarily because it was a career that would provide leisure time for his music. His interest shifted after Franz Brentano joined the faculty. Under Brentano's influence, Stumpf became a critical thinker devoted to the study of philosophy and psychology. Following Brentano's advice, Stumpf made scientific studies a priority and engaged in work on chemistry. Unfortunately, he made "some careless reaction" that nearly burned down the chemistry laboratory. Stumpf (1930, p. 392) remembered that the blaze "might have spread over the whole building if the attendant had not come to the rescue."

Brentano encouraged Stumpf to study with Lotze at the University of Göttingen. In addition to research on physics and physiology, he pursued a long-standing interest in Plato as the basis for his 1868 dissertation. One year later, he entered an ecclesiastical seminary at Würzburg. Like Brentano,

Stumpf lost faith in orthodox religion and left the ministry before his ordination. A chance encounter with Ernst Weber stirred his interest in psychophysics, as did an opportunity to serve as a subject in G. T. Fechner's studies on aesthetics.

After accepting a teaching position at Würzburg, Stumpf began pioneering work on acoustic psychology. He later accepted a position at Prague and published his classic book *Tonpsychologie* in 1883, followed by a second volume in 1890. In 1894, he went to the University of Berlin and converted three modest rooms into an impressive Psychological Institute; in 1920, the Institute moved into twenty-five rooms in the former Imperial Castle. Although more than a decade younger than Wundt, Stumpf's tenacity helped establish Berlin as a dominant competitor to Leipzig for leadership in European psychology. By the time of Stumpf's retirement in 1921, the Berlin Institute was recognized as a preeminent center for psychological research. Stumpf died on Christmas day in 1936.

As a disciple of Brentano, Stumpf made an impassioned protest against the artificial nature of reductionism and developed an approach to philosophy and psychology that placed emphasis on the value of holism. Stumpf shared Brentano's zeal for the study of mental events from an empirical standpoint, especially one that considered the rich, dynamic quality of human cognition. His work was founded on the holistic assumption that all aspects of consciousness are connected and perceivable as a unity. He was convinced that the attributes of any sensation—such as quality, brightness, or intensity—form a whole rather than a simple aggregate of the parts.

Stumpf made significant contributions to areas such as space and auditory perception, emotion, psychophysics, aesthetics, and phenomenology. However, music remained the central focus of his psychology. Stumpf became a leading figure in the emerging discipline of musicology despite being forced to conduct studies only on a cathedral organ and tuning forks because he lacked sufficient research equipment. The research facilities at Berlin were exceptional, and he took the position largely because he believed the city to be the foremost musical center of the world.

In addition to the two-volume work on tone psychology, he founded an 1898 journal devoted to musicology, *Beiträge zur Akustik und Musik-wissenschaft,* and amassed one of the world's leading ethnomusicological collections, housed at Berlin's Psychological Institute. Founded in 1900, the Phonograph Archives consisted of a large assembly of Edison cylinders containing the musical recordings of a vast number of cultures. Stumpf provided the initial funding himself and named the young Berlin psychologist and musicologist Erich Moritz von Hornbostel (1877–1936) as director of the archives. Under the supervision of Stumpf and Hornbostel, the archives grew from a few wax cylinders to a collection of more than 10,000 gramophone recordings from all over the world (Lewin, 1937). The revolutionary phonographic technology quickly became a popular resource for the psychological and anthropological study of native dialects and the musical culture of indigenous tribes. Stumpf also considered music to be an important tool in the holistic study of mental phenomena (see Ringer, 1969).

The American psychologist William James admired Stumpf's work on tone psychology and, though Stumpf proposed a cognitive-evaluative theory that opposed James's famous theory of emotion, the two enjoyed an extensive correspondence (Reisenzein & Schonpflug, 1992). Like James, Stumpf was a strident critic of Wundt's work, especially his research on acoustics. Stumpf challenged the Leipzig school's assumption that a trained but nonmusical introspectionist could make more valid judgments about tone than a trained musician. For Stumpf, the sophisticated perceptual judgments of musical experts were far superior to those generated in laboratory studies of introspection. Wundt was upset by the critique and engaged Stumpf in a bitter and scathing debate. Decades later, Stumpf (1930) wrote that "Wundt's methods of procedure had been repellent to me even since his Heidelberg days, and continue to be so, although I admire his extraordinary breadth of vision and his literary productivity" (p. 401).

Beginning with studies of his own children, Stumpf devoted considerable time to research on the mental life of children. In 1897, he studied a four-year-old boy with exceptional memory and in 1900 helped found the Berlin Association for Child Psychology. In 1903, Stumpf combined his interest in music with developmental psychology when he began investigation of several musical child prodigies.

Like Brentano, Stumpf's psychology offered a holistic alternative to structuralism that inspired many European scholars, especially the Gestalt psychologists (Sprung & Sprung, 1996). Langfeld (1937) noted that Stumpf's death signaled the "last important link with the early decades of experimental psychology, which produced Wundt, Müller and Ebbinghaus, was broken. It was a great period in which virgin soil was tilled and Stumpf had an important part in guiding the plow and sowing the seed from which our present day psychology has developed" (pp. 316–317).

GEORG ELIAS MÜLLER

There have always been diverse roads to greatness in any intellectual enterprise, but Georg Elias Müller (1850–1934), by placing emphasis on extensive laboratory work, took the road less traveled. Many early psychologists were no strangers to the laboratory, but most were equally interested in providing encompassing systematic visions of the discipline. By contrast, Müller was content to focus on the rigorous experimental investigation of several important problem areas. As a result, some of the most productive work in the new experimental psychology came out of the University of Göttingen. Müller was head of the laboratory there for a fifty-year period from 1881 to 1931 and, according to Boring (1950), "As a power and an institution he was second only to Wundt" (p. 379). Boring also pointed out that Müller, unlike many of the other pioneers, "was little else than an experimental psychologist" (p. 379). His interests were directed almost entirely to problems of a psychological nature.

Müller, born on July 20, 1850, studied first at the University of Leipzig, then at the University of Göttingen. He took his Ph.D. under Hermann Lotze at Göttingen in 1873. In 1881, Lotze gave up his position at Göttingen to accept a position at the University of Berlin. He was succeeded by Müller, who remained at Göttingen the rest of his life.

Müller retired from the university in 1931 and died on December 23, 1934.

Müller was highly regarded for his original experimental work in the fields of psychophysics, memory, learning, and vision. He is also remembered for the students he produced who were later prominent in the field of psychology—examples include Erich Jaensch, known for his work on eidetic imagery; Adolph Jost, one of the pioneers in the use of the method of paired associates now commonly employed in learning studies; David Katz, known for his studies on the phenomenology of color and touch; and Edgar Rubin, remembered for his original studies on the figure–ground phenomenon.

Müller, together with Friedrich Schumann and Alfons Pilzecker, was particularly prolific in the areas of memory and association (McGaugh, 2000). Indeed, as noted by Diamond (1974b), the reports of the work on memory and association "run to over 2000 pages" (p. 271). Müller's early work on memory anticipated later work in the area of retroactive inhibition. For example, in an article published in 1900, Müller and Pilzecker reported studies of memory for an initial learning task along with memory for a second task. With the particular problems employed, memory was always better for the second task. Müller and Pilzecker noted that interpolated material may weaken or inhibit the associations necessary for the recall of the initial material. They went on to say, "For lack of any shorter expression we shall designate this type of inhibition as *retroactive inhibition*" (Müller & Pilzecker, 1900, p. 273).

Müller was also one of the first to conduct extensive studies on the problem of perseveration. He noted that some individuals can shift easily from one task to another, while others tend to perseverate on an initial task. He even speculated about the practical consequences of differences in perseveration. Those who persevere on one task may be better fitted for some occupations, and those who shift quickly from task to task would be better fitted for different occupations. According to Diamond (1974c), Müller's work on perseveration provided "the first experimental breach in the theory that the 'train of thoughts' is determined solely by association, and it also points to the existence

of a separate short-term memory process" (p. 271). Müller noticed that there was perseveration on materials presented to a subject, but there was also rapid decay in attention to the materials. His work is clearly an early precursor of later work in short-term memory.

Müller was one of the first to place strong emphasis on the importance of psychological variables in memorial and associative processes. He believed that performance is not just a matter of the mechanics of association but depends on such variables as the attitude or mental set of the subject along with other tendencies such as the tendency to perseverate.

As noted, Müller conducted extensive work in psychophysics and color vision as well as on memory and association (Haupt, 1998). According to Boring (1950), he helped shape these areas and enjoyed leadership in all these fields. Unfortunately, most of Müller's work has not been translated, and as a result has not received the widespread recognition it deserves.

OSWALD KÜLPE AND THE WÜRZBURG SCHOOL

Oswald Külpe (1862–1915) provided another important European alternative to the psychology of Wundt. Külpe's approach to psychology combined some of Brentano's act psychology with Wundt's experimental approach. Külpe's focus on the experimental investigation of thinking presented a direct challenge to elementaristic psychologies.

Oswald Külpe was born on August 3, 1862, in what is now the Baltic Republic of Latvia in the northwest corner of the former Soviet Union. In his early college years, Külpe was torn between history, philosophy, and psychology. In 1881, he enrolled at the University of Leipzig, intending to pursue a career in history, but was also deeply interested in the new psychology laboratory and the work of Wilhelm Wundt. The period from 1881 to 1887 found Külpe studying first at Leipzig, then at the University of Berlin, followed by a year and a half at the University of Göttingen under G. E. Müller. Finally, Külpe returned to Leipzig, where he took his Ph.D. with Wundt in 1887. He remained at Leipzig to help run the laboratory until 1894,

Oswald Külpe

when he received an appointment at the University of Würzburg.

Külpe established a laboratory at Würzburg and remained there for a fifteen-year period. He later established laboratories at Bonn and Munich. Külpe's dedication to psychology was complete. He never married but once declared that science was his bride. Like William James in the United States, Külpe was regarded as one of the most affable and likable of the pioneering psychologists. He died in Munich on December 30, 1915.

Lindenfeld (1978) pointed out that in his early years, Külpe "was a tough-minded experimentalist whose definition of psychology aroused the objection even of Wilhelm Wundt as being too narrow" (p. 132). In later years, Külpe adopted a different approach to the discipline, and it is this later work for which he is known and to which we will direct our attention.

Külpe's philosophical interests extended to the fields of ontology, epistemology, and aesthetics, and all of these interests complemented his work in psychology. Philosophically, he represented a middle road between the extremes of naive realism and idealism. Külpe assumed the independent existence of objects and processes in the world and argued that such an assumption is basic in all sciences. At the same time, we know about objects in the world only through conscious experience, which contributes to what we understand about the world. Külpe's position might be described as a kind of representational or critical realism in contrast with naive realism.

Some of the best-known work coming out of the Würzburg laboratory was clearly related to Külpe's philosophical realism. The work, on **imageless thought,** was a source of controversy because it challenged the elementary building-block approach. *Imageless thought* refers to the belief that there are objective meanings in experience that are not associated with specific words, symbols, or signs. There are, for example, meaningful abstractions in science that have no direct unambiguous stimulus components or images. The worlds of theoretical physics, theology, and psychology are full of such abstractions (e.g., in psychology, Freudian terms such as *ego, superego,* and *id* illustrate the point). Are all thoughts composed of elementary building blocks called *images,* or are there meaningful thoughts that are not reducible to elementary images? Most of us have likely met someone and then later met the same person on another occasion. Though we met the person earlier, we cannot recall or reconstruct the image of the person's face. We think about the person, but without any clearcut image. When we meet again, we typically recognize the individual with little or no difficulty and may even wonder why we could not recall the image earlier. Lindenfeld (1978) pointed out that Külpe believed that "our ability to recognize something we have seen before . . . is quite independent of our ability to remember an image of it" (p. 133).

The Würzburg researchers might agree that there are images associated with many thoughts. For example, most of us probably experience images in connection with simple noun forms such as *dog, cat, car, pencil,* and *book.* It may be more difficult, however, to find an image in connection with terms such as *ontology* or *epistemology.* Furthermore, in simple word association tasks, the word given as a response to a stimulus word (e.g., *table–chair* or *sky–blue*) may be given rapidly and without any introspective awareness of its image.

Students at the Würzurg school also conducted experiments on the effects of mental set on problem solution. **Mental set** refers to a predisposition to respond in a given manner. For example, Külpe briefly presented stimulus materials that varied along several dimensions. If subjects are given a mental set to look for a specific dimension, such as a color, a pattern, or a number, they inevitably find it and may be only minimally aware of the other dimensions that they were not instructed to see. In time, it was recognized that mental set is a powerful factor that accounts for a great deal of the variation in the way people solve problems. The pioneering studies on mental set at Würzburg inspired many subsequent studies on that problem.

Külpe, like Gustav Fechner, was also interested in experimental aesthetics. It was a natural interest because Külpe loved sculpture and painting and, according to Ogden (1951), "was himself a musician and played the piano expertly" (p. 7). Külpe believed that mental economy played an important role in the perception of beauty. Thus, harmony, orderliness, and symmetry require less perceptual effort than their opposites and are more likely to be associated with objects judged to be beautiful.

Though Külpe's students worked primarily on higher mental operations, he was apparently open to a psychology with a much wider scope. He spoke of a need for animal psychology and social psychology, and argued for openness to a variety of methods. He also argued that *psychogenesis,* or the study of the development of mental phenomena, "forms an indispensable supplement to our knowledge of the developed consciousness" (Külpe, 1893/1973, p. 17).

Külpe's influence on the discipline of psychology was extensive. His name is associated with two productive laboratories and a well-equipped institute. Experimental psychology, once confined to the study of simple sensations and reaction times, now included higher thought processes. Külpe also influenced the discipline through his students. His most famous student was Max Wertheimer, the founder of Gestalt psychology. Other students included Kaspar Ach and Henry Watt, both of whom worked on the effects of mental set on problem solving; Robert Morris Ogden, who was instrumental in introducing Gestalt psychology in the United States; and Kurt Koffka, one of the founders of the Gestalt school, who did postdoctoral studies at Würzburg.

HERMANN EBBINGHAUS

In terms of lasting influence on the field of psychology, Hermann Ebbinghaus (1850–1909) ranks as one of the most important pioneers in the discipline. Such a strong claim is all the more remarkable in view of the fact that Ebbinghaus was not a prolific writer, nor is his fame evident through the works of his students. He is remembered for the development of the nonsense syllable and the first quantitative studies of memory. Postman (1973) pointed out, however, that Ebbinghaus's influence on the discipline was much broader. We will examine this influence and his pioneering studies of memory.

Biographical information of Ebbinghaus is sparse, but we know he was born near Bonn in 1850 and that his early interests were in language, literature, and philosophy. He served in the military in the Franco-German War (1870–1871) and took his Ph.D. in philosophy from the University of Bonn in 1873. He then traveled for several years before taking his first academic position at the University of Berlin. Ebbinghaus worked at Berlin from 1880 to 1893 and then took a position at the

Hermann Ebbinghaus

University of Breslau, where he worked until 1905. His final position was at the University of Halle. He died of pneumonia in 1909, only four years after assuming his position at Halle.

Roback and Kiernan (1969) described Ebbinghaus as "a radiant personality, prepossessing in appearance and cooperative, he was practically the antithesis of Wundt" (p. 73). They also noted that at the time of his death he was "revising his first volume of a textbook which in point of lucidity and literary flavor was of a piece with William James's *Principles of Psychology*" (p. 73).

Ebbinghaus is remembered almost exclusively for his pioneering studies on memory, but the importance of that work should not block awareness of his other important contributions. Postman (1973) outlined several guiding principles in the writings of Ebbinghaus that foreshadowed later developments in psychology. The first is that the discipline of psychology should be divorced from philosophy and take its place alongside the natural sciences. Ebbinghaus valued controlled quantitative studies much more than philosophical speculation. The second guiding principle outlined by Postman is that Ebbinghaus broadened the scope of experimental inquiry. No longer was psychology limited to the study of simple sensations and their relations to physiological structures. Now, higher mental operations could be subjected to experimental scrutiny.

Other principles that Postman identified in the work of Ebbinghaus include methodological and theoretical eclecticism. Ebbinghaus eschewed efforts to find the grand theory and the grand method applicable to the entire discipline. Instead, he focused his efforts on identifying more modest methodological and conceptual tools appropriate to a limited domain such as memory. A final principle in the writings of Ebbinghaus, according to Postman (1973) "is the reconciliation of pure and applied psychology" (p. 223). Ebbinghaus believed that problems were important in and of themselves. It is context that dictates whether a problem will be regarded as pure or as applied, but Ebbinghaus regarded the distinction as somewhat artificial.

Ebbinghaus contributed to applied psychology with work in mental testing. He was a pioneer in

the use of what has been called the *completion test* as a way to assess the cognitive capacities of schoolchildren. Completion tests are still regarded as important measures of intellectual development. Such tests provide a context from which a student is asked to draw a logical conclusion. One form of the completion test is the analogy. Thus, a child might be asked to respond to a simple problem such as "If an elephant is big, then a mouse is [small]." This type of question has found its way into all kinds of assessment instruments, from those used with small children to those designed for adults.

Ebbinghaus's original work on memory is set forth in one of the most important classic works in psychology under the title, *Über das Gedächtnis,* which was translated simply as *Memory*. The original work was published in 1885 and an English translation was made available in 1913 (Ebbinghaus, 1885/1913). The lengthy preexperimental scholarship on memory produced many impressive insights (e.g., see Herrmann & Chaffin, 1988), but until Ebbinghaus did his work, the problems of memory were still largely intractable from a scientific viewpoint.

Ebbinghaus's experimental approach to the study of memory was inspired by reading Gustav Fechner's *Elements of Psychophysics*. In the preface to *Memory,* Ebbinghaus (1885/1913) pointed out that "in the realm of mental phenomena, experiment and measurement have hitherto been chiefly limited in application to sense perception and to the time relations of mental process" (p. v). His goal was to apply Fechner's methods to a new dimension of mental life. In order to achieve his mission, he warned at the outset that "the term, memory, is to be taken here in its broadest sense, including learning, retention, association and reproduction" (p. v).

Ebbinghaus acknowledged the apparently capricious and private nature of the mental realm that prevented it from yielding to the natural science method. Weber and Fechner had faced the same problem in the study of sense perception. We cannot gain direct access to the private sensation of another person, but we can discover the relationship between values as they exist on a physical scale and values as they are reported in experience. In a similar manner, we may not be able to gain direct access to the specific memory of another person but, according to Ebbinghaus, there are external conditions of memory clearly accessible to measurement.

Shortly, we shall consider those external conditions that are accessible to measurement, but first it should be recalled that, prior to Ebbinghaus, memory was typically studied only after it had developed. Then, introspective or retrospective work attempted to assess what had taken place. The new approach of Ebbinghaus involved the memorial process from start to finish. Thus, we may easily count the number of repetitions or amount of time it takes to memorize a list of words. Following a lapse of time, we may count the number of repetitions or the amount of time it takes to relearn the list.

Initial learning of material was extremely important to Ebbinghaus's entire project and he exercised unusual caution in controlling the conditions of initial learning. He recognized that previous associations contaminate speed of initial learning, so he developed the nonsense syllable in an attempt to neutralize the effects of prior associations. Chapter 3 of his book describes other ways in which he attempted to control the conditions of initial learning. For example, he tried to control learning speed by memorizing and reciting to the beat of a metronome. He tried to minimize the effects of intonation or accent by rehearsing with due sensitivity to the stress of the voice. He attempted to control motivation and effort and to reduce any efforts to use mnemonic devices to memorize nonsense syllables. He did his work at the same time each day and attempted throughout to keep all conditions of his life as constant or stable as possible.

Ebbinghaus investigated a variety of problems in memory and opened the door to the experimental investigation of a host of additional problems. One of the more interesting findings came out of his work on the time it takes to memorize as a function of the length of a list. In one study, he learned lists of 7, 12, 16, 24, and 36 syllables to a criterion of mastery (one perfect repetition). Ebbinghaus found that, for him, 7 syllables was the number he could typically recite after only one

recitation. The numbers of repetitions, respectively, to memorize the syllables in each of the lists are presented in Table 11.1. It is clear from an examination of the table that the greatest difference occurs between the list of 7 and the list of 12. It took only one repetition to learn the list of 7, but it took 16.6 repetitions to learn the list of 12 syllables.

Ebbinghaus also found that forgetting of nonsense syllables proceeds rapidly for the first two days after initial learning, but then slows down over subsequent days. The famous **Ebbinghaus forgetting curve** is illustrated in Figure 11.1, which shows rapid initial forgetting followed by a slowing so that, for example, there is little difference in the amount of forgetting after one week versus the amount of forgetting after one month.

Ebbinghaus was a significant early psychologist, not only because of his memory research but also because of the new methodology and orientation he brought to the discipline (Danziger, 2001). Following Ebbinghaus, there was an exciting breadth of vision as to what can properly be included in the new discipline of psychology. Many psychologists might be tempted to agree with Titchener's (1913) opinion when he argued that Ebbinghaus's "recourse to nonsense syllables, as means to the study of association, marks the most considerable advance, in this chapter of psychology, since the time of Aristotle" (p. 381). There can be little question that he is a pivotal figure who changed the discipline.

TABLE 11.1 *Number of Repetitions as a Function of Numbers of Syllables*

Number of Syllables in Series	Number of Repetitions Necessary for First Errorless Reproduction
7	1
12	17
16	30
24	44
36	55

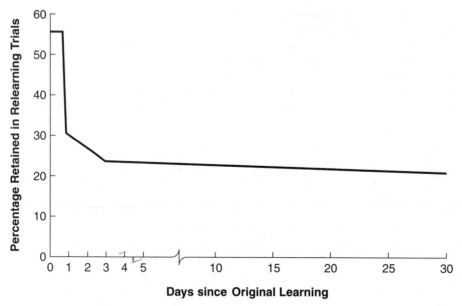

FIGURE 11.1   *Ebbinghaus Curve Illustrating Retention as a Function of Time*

WUNDT'S CONTEMPORARIES
AND APPLIED PSYCHOLOGY

Titchener has seldom been regarded as a friend of applied psychology and it is true that his primary scientific interest was the adult normal mind. At the same time, as noted at the beginning of the chapter, Titchener clearly recognized the importance of abnormal psychology, social psychology, animal psychology, and other subdisciplinary areas. He argued that all of these fields must be "cultivated, if psychology is to progress" (Titchener, 1913, p. 29). He did not find time to include applied areas in his own research programs and clearly placed the greatest value on pure scientific studies. At the same time, he was not closed to the future development of a psychology much broader in scope than he cultivated at Cornell University.

Wundt's other contemporaries also focused largely on basic scientific problems, but were all open to a psychology that would ultimately be larger in scope. Brentano was clearly optimistic about the prospects of applied psychology. As noted, Ebbinghaus thought that the distinction between pure and applied studies is a function of

context and not a basic or logical distinction. In one context, a problem could conceivably be regarded as basic or pure, but in another context, the same problem might be regarded as applied. With the study of an ever larger number of topical areas, it was inevitable that psychology, like the other sciences, would find it impossible to remain in the important but restricted environment of the laboratory. In the next chapter we will encounter a system that, from the beginning, advocated a psychology equally at home in the laboratory and in the world of daily life.

REVIEW QUESTIONS _____

1. Contrast Titchener and Brentano with respect to methodology.

2. Give a typical example of a type of laboratory problem that might have been explored in Titchener's department at Cornell University.

3. Outline Titchener's distinction between primary and secondary attention. Do you regard the distinction as useful?

4. Briefly review Titchener's theory of meaning.

5. What were some of Titchener's criticisms of the James-Lange theory of emotion?

6. What was Washburn's "motor theory of consciousness" and how did her ideas about consciousness differ from Titchener's theory?

7. How did Brentano distinguish between inner perception and inner observation?

8. Outline Brentano's classification of mental phenomena.

9. Briefly describe Stumpf's contributions to the psychology of music. How did his work on tone psychology differ from Wundt's ideas?

10. Outline two of Georg Elias Müller's contributions to psychology.

11. Define *mental set* and show how it plays a role in problem solving.

12. Why was the work at the Würzburg school on imageless thought so crucial to the psychologies of Wundt and Titchener?

13. List five ways, as outlined by Postman, that Ebbinghaus influenced the field of psychology.

14. Briefly describe two important experimental findings coming out of Ebbinghaus's work on memory.

CHAPTER 12

FUNCTIONALISM

Nothing includes everything or dominates over everything. The word "and"
trails along after every sentence.

—William James (1909/1977)

In the early chapters of this book we encountered tensions between process-oriented philosophies such as that advanced by Heraclitus and philosophies of being such as that advanced by Parmenides. The process orientation emphasizes the fluid, changing, mutable, and dynamic nature of the world. The philosophies of being, by contrast, emphasize permanence, unity, and "being" as such. The process orientation is generally more friendly to empiricism, whereas the philosophies of being are more friendly to rationalism. The philosophical tensions between Heraclitus and Parmenides foreshadowed early problems in psychology. Are there fixed or static elements of experience or is the world of experience more like that proverbial stream that is always flowing? Those psychologists in the functionalist tradition emphasized the developmental, adaptive, and dynamic features of experience. The result was a psychology radically different from structuralism. This chapter explores the loosely knit school of thought known as functionalism.

The term **functionalism** is difficult to define, but its meanings should unfold as we proceed. It may help, however, at the outset, if it is pointed out that structuralism was interested largely in *what* questions, whereas functionalism turned attention also to *how* questions. The functionalists were keenly interested in both basic and applied science and adopted a variety of methods. If there was one central focus, it was adaptation. The single most important figure in the historical background of

functionalism is the American psychologist and philosopher William James.

WILLIAM JAMES AND HARVARD UNIVERSITY

The birth and development of psychology in Germany was closely observed by many Americans, but no one was more keenly interested in the new science than a brilliant young American named William James (1842–1910). As early as 1875, James was writing articles for popular American magazines to inform the public about German psychology. For example, in unsigned notices, he called attention to the publication of Wundt's *Principles of Physiological Psychology* (James, 1875) and to developments in applied psychology such as the publication of Franz Von Holtzendorff's work on the psychology of murder (James, 1876a).

James is difficult to characterize as a professional. His degree was in medicine, but he did not practice it. He trained extensively in physiology, but spent little time teaching or researching in that field. He was not formally trained in psychology—indeed, the first lecture he heard on the subject was his own—nor was he formally trained in philosophy. Yet he held professorships in psychology and philosophy and enjoyed world acclaim in both disciplines. If American psychology had a favorite academic son, James would surely be the overwhelming choice.

William James

William James, the first of five children of Mary Robertson Walsh and Henry James (Sr.), was born in New York City on January 11, 1842. The other four children were Henry Jr., born in 1843 and destined to fame as a writer and critic; Wilkinson, born in 1845; Robertson, born in 1846; and Alice, born in 1848. William was named after his grandfather William James of Albany, who migrated to the United States from Ireland around 1789. The prolific and perdurable elder William James, a staunch Calvinist, amassed an enormous fortune and fathered thirteen children by three wives. According to Allen (1967, p. 5) the first wife died after giving birth to twin sons, the second died after giving birth to a daughter. The third wife, Catherine Barber, the grandmother of William James, had seven sons and three daughters.

Henry James (Sr.), the fourth son of William and Catherine, was a lover of nature who found particular joy in hikes through fields and forests. The joy, however, was dampened by the ever-present Calvinistic conscience that produced guilt over any earthly pleasure. The tensions between the God of nature and the God of theology came to a head during a long convalescence that resulted from a tragic accident. Following a severe injury to his leg, Henry endured two amputations without benefit of anesthesia. The second amputation

was necessary because of an infection that followed the first surgical procedure. The period of recovery marked the beginning of a life devoted to philosophy, religion, and introspection.

Though Henry completed a degree in theology and was ordained to preach, he never became a minister. Part of his reluctance was based on a conflict between orthodox Calvinism, with its emphasis on individual salvation, and his growing concern for the social gospel, with its emphasis on the salvation of the human lot. Brennan (1968) pointed out that Henry James's concern was for a truly caring and democratic society in which we seek not "individual salvation but universal salvation" (p. 17). Henry James, independently wealthy through a large inheritance from his father's estate, was able to devote most of his time to philosophical and religious interests. During the course of his life, he published fourteen books, which assured his niche in U.S. religion and philosophy.

In 1840, Mary Robertson Walsh and Henry James were married. It was a marriage that produced a tolerant, stimulating, and even indulgent environment for their children. There was a great deal of travel, the stimulation of famous friends such as Ralph Waldo Emerson, and enrollment in the finest private schools. Moreover, Mary and Henry devoted time to the children, respected their opinions, and encouraged them to think independently. Perry (1954) stated that the James children were "free not only from parental tyranny but, through their parents, from the tyranny of the world. There was a general absence of institutional authority" (p. 42). As a result, according to Perry, "William James began to be William James at a very early age, and began to find and appropriate the food which his characteristic appetites required" (p. 44). When one of the James children spoke of a vocation, Henry James was typically concerned that it be not overly narrowing. In 1860, he reluctantly supported William's decision to study art, but William cut short his attempts to be a painter after deciding that the special genius required for that endeavor was missing.

In the fall of 1861, William enrolled in the Lawrence Scientific School at Harvard University and studied the usual subjects: chemistry, biology, anatomy, and physiology. But, as noted by Perry (1954), "He was perpetually grazing and ruminating, wandering wherever the pasturage was good . . . [James's interests ranged] over the whole field of literature, history, science, and philosophy. They indicate a mind as energetic and acquisitive as it is voracious and incorrigibly vagrant" (p. 71). James's breadth of interest and his extensive travel, including trips to Brazil and Europe, interfered with normal progress toward the medical degree, but helped him refine his own vocational inclinations. He joined Louis Agassiz on a biological expedition to Brazil and discovered a profound distaste for mere collecting and classifying. In Europe, he became acquainted with leading figures such as Emil DuBois-Reymond, Wilhelm Wundt, and Hermann von Helmholtz. He also discovered a distaste for the rigors of routine laboratory work in physiology. James finally completed his M.D. in 1869, submitting a dissertation on the effects of coldness on the human body.

In 1870, James found himself in a state of intellectual and emotional turmoil, still uncertain about his vocational or personal prospects. During this period, he suffered intense anxiety and depression documented in letters to friends and family (brief summaries of some of James's symptoms and his recovery are in McDermott, 1968, pp. 6–8). In 1872, James accepted an appointment as instructor of physiology at Harvard, but by 1873 he was expressing ambivalence about his career. Though a successful teacher, he knew that physiology was not his first love. In 1875, he offered a graduate course on the "Relations Between Psychology and Physiology" and in that same year, founded the psychology laboratory at Harvard. In 1876, James taught his first undergraduate course in psychology, and in 1878, signed a contract with Henry Holt and Company to write a psychology text. In 1878, James also married Alice Howe Gibbens, a twenty-seven-year-old Boston schoolteacher.

Initial plans called for the text to be completed in two years, but James's classic *Principles of Psychology* did not appear until 1890. He was then forty-eight years old. The delay in publication was caused by the usual distractions of settling into a new career and James's wish to produce a truly significant work—not just a summary of existing ideas and findings (King, 1992). Family obligations between 1878 and 1890 were also extensive. In that period, three sons and two daughters were born to William and Alice, and in 1885 their third child, Hermann, died of complications from whooping cough. Thus, for understandable reasons, the gestation of the *Principles* was lengthy, but its success was nearly instantaneous. It quickly became the leading text in the United States and was translated into many foreign languages. A briefer version of the *Principles*, published in 1892, was also a major success. The *Principles of Psychology* influenced generations of psychologists. Over seventy years after its publication, the historian of psychology Robert MacLeod (1969) said that it "is without question the most literate, the most provocative, and at the same time the most intelligible book on psychology that has ever appeared in English or in any other language" (p. iii).

A number of significant major books followed the publication of the *Principles*. They were *The Will to Believe* (1897), *Talks to Teachers* (1899), and *The Varieties of Religious Experience* (1902). After 1900, James's publications were strictly philosophical, though each one returned to specific psychological themes first discussed in the *Principles*. Some of his key philosophical works include *Pragmatism* (1907), *A Pluralistic Universe* (1909), *The Meaning of Truth* (1909), and *Essays in Radical Empiricism,* published posthumously in 1912. The pattern of James's publications reveals the shift of his interest from psychology to philosophy. Even so, James the psychologist remains very much alive in James the philosopher as he returned repeatedly to psychological topics in his major philosophical works. Furthermore, as a philosopher, he remained keenly interested in the welfare of the new discipline he helped found at Harvard University. James retired from Harvard in 1907 and died from a heart condition in 1910.

Appreciative comment for James has always outweighed critical comment. He is typically eulogized for tolerance, industry, warmth, generosity, and intellectual conscience. The most common criticisms of James are directed at inconsistencies in his system. Such criticisms are, to some extent, valid, but less so when James's psychology is understood in the context of his larger philosophical vision. We will now consider some of the general characteristics of James's thought, then focus on selected topics in his psychology.

General Characteristics of James's Thought

James's general philosophical orientation grew out of his sensitivity to people and their problems. Earle (1967) pointed out that "James addressed himself to the people . . . and he listened to the people to find out what life meant to them. He respected not so much their common sense as their common feelings and hopes" (p. 240). What emerged was a philosophy with face validity—a philosophy unique for its openness to differences and its willingness to experiment with methods. It is a philosophy that is well integrated with the character of American thought. It is not overly pessimistic or optimistic—it is, above all, practical—but it leaves ample room for theoretical and nonutilitarian intellectual endeavor. Perhaps its major hallmark is its believability. Seldom is there anything in James that seems strained, overly narrow, or one sided. James's psychology and philosophy are cut from the same cloth, so it is important to grasp the themes that run throughout all his writings. Seven of those themes can be identified.

Individualism. A strong individualistic quality runs throughout James's writings. His emphasis on the importance of the individual was illustrated earlier (Chapter 1) in the discussion of the philosophy of history. Recall that James believed that a purely *Zeitgeist* theory of history causes us to go beyond scientific determinism into fatalism. He believed that individuals are shaped by circumstances but, in turn, individuals also act on the world and shape it in ways that could not have happened without the highly unique contribution of the individual. Thus, individuals *and* circumstances make history.

James's emphasis on the individual was illustrated in his extensive use of biographies and case studies. He believed that experience and reality are not easily separable. Indeed, we come down to reality, as such, in the experience of the individual. When we get away from individual experience, we study abstractions and are thus removed from what is most fundamental. James did not rule out normative analysis, but such analysis should itself be tested against experience.

Multiple Levels of Analysis. Another strand of James's emphasis on individualism is encountered in his fierce denunciation of the impersonal and hollow forces that are often characteristic of large bureaucratic organizations. He has sometimes been portrayed as an insulated academic removed from the concerns of daily life. Coon (1996), however, documents James's active political involvement in the 1890s and his vigorous resistance to the growth of imperializing and dehumanizing forces in government, the military, and large corporations. One of his greatest concerns was that large institutions find ways to honor traditional values of freedom, individuality, and pluralism.

As one trained in physiology and medicine, James was a strong believer in emphasizing the biological and physiological correlates of experience and behavior. But while James repeatedly underscored the importance of physiology he was not a reductionist, because he underscored, with equal vigor, the importance of the more molar psychological world of experience. Experience was James's metaphysical ultimate and, as such, it enjoys a unique status in James's system of thought. For James, there is a real sense in which experience cannot be reduced and cannot be adequately explained by resorting to an alien and abstract biological discourse. The point is well illustrated in his classic book *The Varieties of Religious Experience.* In James's day, it was popular to explain religious experiences in terms of presumed underlying neurological processes. James insisted that the same sort of explanations are applicable to atheistic beliefs and that even if one were to discover the biological basis of belief, that would not undermine the validity of the belief. He argued that the claims of theism and atheism must be adjudicated on other grounds. James clearly affirmed multiple levels of analysis: molecular, biological, psychological, sociological, philosophical—all are legitimate and have their special value and application. The error begins when we believe that all things can be subsumed under any one rubric. This latter point leads to the next major characteristic of James's thought—his pluralism.

Jamesian Pluralism. In *Pragmatism,* James (1907/1975b) argued that the monism–pluralism issue is "the deepest and most pregnant question that our minds can frame" (p. 141). Although James was open to the possibility that there may be only one real thing and that all else is derived from that one reality (monism), he was nevertheless a pluralist and repeatedly referred to himself in that way. (e.g., see James, 1909/1975a, pp. 124–125; 1909/1977, p. 26; 1912/1976, p. 133).

James's **pluralism** had numerous implications for his approach to psychology. The first implication is methodological. If we survey all of James's works, psychological and philosophical, we discover a kind of pragmatic pluralism in which methodology becomes subservient to vision. James embraced a variety of methods and was clearly a methodological pluralist (see Viney, 1989). James's pluralism also had profound implications for his treatment of the subject matter of psychology (see Viney, King, & King, 1992). Though experience is primary in his philosophy, there is no one content area (e.g., learning, sensing, emotion, etc.) that is foundational. James's psychology had enormous scope, including basic and applied problems, the psychology of religion, and even an openness to paranormal phenomena—much to the dismay of his colleagues who believed that psychic research was a pseudoscience that embarrassed the scientific integrity of psychology (Coon, 1992).

Free Will. Few psychologists have struggled with free will and determinism with the intensity that James devoted to the issue. On the one hand he agreed that science, including psychology, may conduct business on the assumption of determinism. At the same time, James (1890/1981) insisted that science "must be constantly reminded that her purposes are not the only purposes, and that the

order of uniform causation which she has use for, and is therefore right in postulating, may be enveloped in a wider order, on which she has no claims at all" (p. 1179). So James leaves room for a methodological determinism for psychology and science. But at the same time, that psychology may proceed on the basis of a methodological determinism, James (1890/1981) argued that we will probably never write a biography on an individual life in advance (p. 1179).

If James reserved a place for methodological determinism in his approach to science, there should be no mistake about his strong rejection of metaphysical determinism. He found it, on personal and intellectual levels, to be an unworkable philosophy. There seems little doubt that in his early years he was a thoroughgoing determinist, but in his period of depression and emotional crisis in the early 1870s he abandoned metaphysical determinism with the declaration, "My first act of free will shall be to believe in free will" (James, 1920, p. 147). The idea for the affirmation of free will by an act of free will came to James through the philosopher Jules Lequier via Charles Renouvier (Viney, 1984; 1997).

James's best-known statement on the free will/determinism issue is in his article "The Dilemma of Determinism" (James, 1884/1979a, pp. 114–140). For James, determinism is more consistent with monism, whereas belief in free will, even a limited free will, is more consistent with pluralism. James argued that the concept of causality, from a philosophical perspective, is as ambiguous as the concept of freedom. He believed that there are genuine ambiguities associated with the future and real possibilities. He believed in regularities, so his was not an untrammeled free will. Indeed, he found that freedom is hard won and exercised only through effortful striving.

Moralistic Psychology and Philosophy. Rambo (1980) has pointed out that James's writings are strongly influenced by his concern with what people *should* or *ought* to do. The point is illustrated in a distinction James makes between easygoing and strenuous moods. In the easygoing mood, we become perfunctory and lazy, but in the strenuous mood, we seize the opportunities for action and work with energy and enthusiasm. James believed we all have the capacity for the strenuous mood, but that capacity must be cultivated. In his famous chapter on habit in the *Principles,* he counseled, *"Keep the faculty of effort alive in you by a little gratuitous exercise every day . . . [;] do every day or two something for no other reason than that you would rather not do it, so that when the hour of dire need draws nigh, it may find you not unnerved and untrained to stand the test"* (James, 1890/1981, p. 130). James seldom lost an opportunity to apply the findings of psychology to daily life. He wanted a basic experimental psychology but also a psychology that made a real and useful difference in our daily lives.

Radical Empiricism.   James lamented the misleading nature of brief names, but indicated that he preferred that his philosophy be called *radical empiricism.* A fundamental postulate of **radical empiricism,** according to James (1909/1975a), is "that the only things that shall be debatable among philosophers shall be things definable in terms drawn from experience" (p. 6). The term *radical* means that things that are experienced must not be ignored. It also implies our right to exclude things that are not definable in terms drawn from experience. James was quick to admit, however, that there may be many real things that are not experienced. He was always open to new possibilities and to borderline phenomena or to things that some people claim to experience and that others claim not to experience. Radical empiricism, for James, meant that we must find a place for everything that is a genuine part of experience. The term *radical* also implies that monism will be regarded as a hypothesis (James, 1897/1979b, p. 5). For James, any monism is a hypothesis and thus open to the test of experience.

James did not believe, however, that monistic conceptions can square with what we encounter in experience. He argued that monism, born in rationalism, tells us what to count and what not to count. Thus, if one is a materialistic monist, the whole mental realm is either not counted at all or is rationalized. If one is an idealistic monist, the physical

realm is intellectualized. James failed to find any monistic vantage point so sufficiently encompassing that it could include everything—hence, his statement at the opening of this chapter: "Nothing includes everything" (James, 1909/1977, p. 145).

Given James's view of process, it is questionable that he could ever believe in the adequacy of any monism. He truly believed that the world is in process, that creation was not an event but is an ongoing process, happening now as always; and for better or worse, we are all participants. He once asked, "What has concluded, that we might conclude in regard to it?" (James, 1910/1978, p. 190). Since the world is in process, there is no vantage point from which one can make the big claim for truth with a capital *T,* because our vantage points are themselves in constant flux. As a consequence, we must be content with provisional and practical truths that are subject to change. James's radical empiricism was nascent in *The Principles of Psychology* (see Crosby & Viney, 1990) and is a key to understanding his system of psychology.

Pragmatism.   The final general characteristic of James's worldview is his pragmatic philosophy. He believed that **pragmatism,** pluralism, and radical empiricism are the closest of intellectual kin, each implying the other. For James, pragmatism is a method, a theory of truth, and a way of thinking about the world. It opposes absolutistic schemes and contents itself with provisional (but workable) concepts and methodologies. James (1907/1975b) instructed his readers as follows: "If you follow the pragmatic method, you cannot look on any such word [e.g., *energy, reason, God*] as closing your quest. You must bring out of each word its practical cash-value, [and view it] as a program for more work" (pp. 31–32). For James, words, theories, concepts, and the like are *"instruments, not answers to enigmas."*

The pragmatic method is illustrated repeatedly in *The Varieties of Religious Experience* in which specific beliefs and practices are always judged by the real work they accomplish in the world. If good work is clearly accomplished, then to that extent a belief or practice is vindicated. James (1907/1975b) rejected the idea that any belief or theory could make the claim to be "absolutely a transcript of reality" (p. 33).

James's pragmatism and pluralistic empiricism found a receptive intellectual climate in the United States. The commonsense nature of his philosophy, his unusual ability to communicate with both academics and the public, and the sheer charm of his personality combined to make him a force and a shaper of psychology. We will now turn to a consideration of selected topics in his psychological thought.

Jamesian Psychology

James (1890/1981) defined *psychology* as "the science of mental life, both of its phenomena and of their conditions" (p. 15). By *phenomena,* James meant feelings, cognitions, desires, and so on. By *conditions of mental life,* he meant bodily and social processes that influence mental processes. Thus, for James, *psychology* was the study of mental processes, but such processes take the psychologist into behavioral, physiological, and cultural dimensions.

Habit. James believed that much of human life is understandable simply in terms of an analysis of habits that have been acquired through learning and education. He stressed the physical basis of habit by pointing out that stimulation seems to follow the path of least resistance in living tissue. For example, a joint once sprained may be more vulnerable to future stress. Similarly, a pathway once established in the nervous system is likely to be used again.

James saw habit in functional terms, as essential to civilization and to the economy of individual action. Most of us carry out our lives by following habitual patterns in manner of dress, ways of greeting and departing, ways of getting to and performing work, ways of eating and even sleeping. In a famous analogy, James suggested that habit does for the individual and for society what the flywheel does for an internal combustion engine. It smooths the operation and keeps the engine running just as habit keeps us in our niche even when circumstances are hard.

James saw it as the goal of education to instill good habits and believed that the success or failure of the individual could depend on the achievement this goal. The commonsense quality of Jamesian psychology is nowhere better illustrated than in his famous chapter on habit. We have, at every turn, an abundance of examples to illustrate the message of the chapter: the accomplished pianist who regularly practiced eight hours a day, the Olympic gold medal winner who tells of years of training, the winner of a Nobel prize who, for years, practiced the eighty-four-hour workweek.

James ended his chapter with practical suggestions for launching into good new habits or breaking old bad ones. He would counsel us to move toward a new habit with great initiative, enlist social support by making a public pledge, and never suffer an exception to occur. We should schedule activities, if possible, to decrease opportunities for the expression of the old habit and to increase the number of opportunities for the expression of the new habit.

The Stream of Thought. James contended that psychologists abandon the empirical method when they attempt to dissect mental life into simple sensations. The reason for this contention is that, in our normal experience, we do not have simple sensations. Rather, according to James, consciousness is marked by continuities, relations, and complexities. The starting point, then, for the study of mental life is not simple sensations but the fact of thinking itself. From such a starting point, James discussed five general characteristics of the **stream of thought.**

First, James found that thoughts are personal and *owned;* they are *your thoughts.* Such a contention appears almost immediately to run headlong into difficulty. We sometimes have dreams or intrusive thoughts that we are reluctant to own and there are obvious cases of pathological dissociation that appear to contradict James's belief in the personal nature of consciousness. James recognized the difficulty and his explanation illustrated his early recognition of unconscious processes. He argued that hysterical anesthesias, automatic writing, and multiple personalities are manifestations of what he called *secondary personal selves* that are sometimes out of touch with the normal self. But James believed that the various forms of dissociation do not constitute an exception to his position that thought tends to be part of a personal consciousness. He noted that within a so-called secondary personality there is some degree of organization and a sense of identity. He also argued that there is some limited communication between primary and secondary personalities.

A second characteristic of the stream of thought is that thoughts are constantly changing. James believed that the experience of constancy is an illusion that results from inattention. He was convinced that our state of mind is always in process; thus, a present state is not exactly like a previous state. It may appear that it is the same view out the window each day, but *we* are a bit different each day, and the view itself is slightly different.

A third characteristic of thought is that it is characterized by continuity rather than division or separation. Again, difficulties arise with such a contention, but James anticipated the difficulties. For example, a loud clap of thunder might appear as a separate and discrete event that breaks in on the continuity of thought. But James argued that what we hear "is not thunder *pure,* but thunder-breaking-upon-silence-and-contrasting-with-it" (1890/1981, p. 234). Time gaps such as we encounter in sleep would appear to contradict James's third characteristic, but he argued that consciousness following a time gap "belongs to" or is sensibly continuous with consciousness before it. It is the same thought that takes up the problem this morning that was put to rest last evening.

A fourth characteristic of human thought is that it conveys a sense that it deals with something other than itself, in other words, it is cognitive. The term *cognitive* is derived from a Latin verb *cognoscere,* which means to know or to become acquainted with. James contended that our belief in an outer reality is conditioned partly by the bridges we build between our past thoughts of an object and our present thought of the same object. From so many separate encounters, we develop the notion of an outer reality and a notion that we are cognitive of, or know, an outer reality.

The final characteristic of thought, according to James, is that selectivity, discrimination, choice, and shifting interests are in its very nature. James believed that selectivity is based on the nature and characteristics of the stimulus, aesthetics, and personal values. He argued that we find it quite impossible to be impartial in terms of how we direct our interest and attention.

The Self. For James, the term *self* includes the totality of all those things that belong to us: friends, children, a home, clothing, a pet, reputation, memory, perception, and a physical structure. He identified three constituents of the self. the material self, the social self, and the spiritual self. In addition to these and in a class apart was the pure ego.

The most intimate part of the material "me" is the body—and some parts are more "intimately me" than others. Clothing is also part of the **material self,** as well as family, furniture, collections, and other possessions. James argued that loss of a possession is a loss of part of the self, so that we truly lose or gain with the ebb and flow of our possessions.

The **social self,** according to James, is not one self but a variety of different selves. He contended that we have a different social self for each person who recognizes us. He also emphasized the importance of context and role playing as determinants of the various social selves. Although we may be shy or polite in the presence of our parents or in the presence of a teacher, we may be "appropriately rude" or assertive in the presence of our friends. For this reason, many of the descriptive adjectives that get attached to us are really names for a particular social self. We are honest, loyal, obedient, courageous, competent, but not all at once and not in every social situation. The football player, brash and courageous on the field, may be weak and inept in front of a speech class. All of us have experienced such duplicity or multiplicity, but James's theory of the self points to a way out of such experiences.

The material and social selves are outward manifestations, but the **spiritual self** is personal, subjective, and intimate. It is an inner citadel that sits in judgment on the other selves. Indeed, the other components of the self belong to the spiritual self and it is more permanent than the rest. In James's view, the spiritual self is a source of effort or will; it is a source of change and desire for change.

James believed that there are some interesting tensions and rivalries among the various selves. There are also tensions among potential selves or selves that we might like to be. Thus, we might like to be wealthy, athletic, scholarly, witty, philanthropic, adventurous, and beautiful. We cannot, however, appropriate the energy to be everything we might like to be. We must be judicious and direct energy in ways that strike a reasonable balance between our ideals and reality.

James argued that our **self-esteem** is a function of the ratio of our success and our pretensions as follows:

$$\text{Self-esteem} = \frac{\text{Success}}{\text{Pretensions}}$$

James pointed out that the greatest burdens are lifted sometimes by adjusting pretensions downward. We sometimes experience great release when we declare that we do not have to be the best at some activity or when we realize that it is acceptable simply to drop the activity. James called attention to the different pretensions associated with the different selves. The material self may find esteem in wealth, the social self may find it in recognition, and the spiritual self may find esteem in purity or moral superiority.

Under the topic of pure ego, James contended that psychology encounters its most puzzling question: What is the nature of personal identity and the sense of continuity that runs through the present self and reaches backward and forward? Is there an arch-ego and, if so, what is its nature? James reviewed spiritualist theories of a substantive soul, transcendentalism, and associationism, finding difficulties in each. He concluded that psychology must content itself for the time with a mere functional approach to the self. Such an approach can do real work in the world and that is scientifically satisfying. For his part, James was always open to the possibility that there may be dimensions of the self and other realities on which science has no special claims. James never demanded that any perspective (science included) provide totality.

The Emotions. James's original paper, entitled "What Is an Emotion," published in 1884, generated extensive comment and controversy. The reaction to the 1884 paper prompted James to publish another paper in 1894, entitled "The Physical Basis of Emotion." James returned to the topic of emotion in *The Varieties of Religious Experience.* The focus of the early papers was on the physiological correlates of emotion, but in the *Varieties,* James emphasized experiential dimensions. James returned to the topic of emotions in many of his later works, including *The Will to Believe, Talks to Teachers,* and *Essays in Radical Empiricism.*

One of the hallmarks of Jamesian psychology is its appeal to common sense, but James's theory of emotion is an exception to the rule. The theory, advanced independently by the Danish physiologist Carl Lange (1834–1900), has come to be called the **James-Lange theory of emotion.** James was quick to admit that his theory departs from a commonsense approach to the emotions. According to common sense, we might, for example, see a bear, experience fear, and then run. According to James's theory, however, bodily changes are indispensable to the experience of emotion. Thus, oversimplified, we see the bear, we run, and then we experience fear. James could not imagine a disembodied emotion. If there were no activation, no arousal, how could there be an experience of emotion? This problem puzzled James.

In his article "The Physical Basis of Emotion," James (1894/1983) pointed out that his theory "assumes (what probably everyone assumes) that there must be a process of some sort in the nerve-centres for emotion" (p. 306). For him, the experience of emotion *is* the experience of the activity of the body. He never denied that stimuli evoke emotional behavior. We see a bear and run! The stimulus provokes emotional behavior. James did not deny the importance of context, either. If we see a bear in a zoo behind bars, or if we see a bear in the wilderness and we are in possession of an adequate weapon, we may not run. In James's view, a stimulus situation (a chance encounter with a bear in the woods or a view of a bear in a cage at the zoo) provokes an adaptive response. We may run or stand in admiration, depending on context.

It might be argued that we could see a bear and freeze in fright or that we could see a bear and run. James would not deny that either reaction is possible but would contend that the emotions associated with freezing would be different from the emotions associated with running. The bodily conditions in the two circumstances are quite different and hence should be associated with different feelings.

James's theory of emotion is still debated in the late twentieth century, and Papanicolaou (1989) has argued that there is still no evidence "indicating that the body is not a necessary condition of emotion. . . . Reports of affect, when detailed, are also reports of somatic sensations" (p. 127). James's larger vision of emotion, as set forth in the *Varieties* and in his philosophical works, emphasized constitutional factors with recognition that some of us are naturally more disposed to an optimistic outlook while others are more disposed to see the darker side of things. James also recognized the difficulty of separating emotion and cognitive processes. The two, in his view, are interwoven in living organisms.

Instincts.   James believed strongly in instincts and was keenly interested in those events that interfere with their uniformity. For example, he pointed out that instincts may be inhibited by habit. Thus, the organism may become partial to the very first stimulus to which it reacted. James illustrated by citing the classic work of Spalding (1873), who demonstrated that chicks born in the absence of a hen "will follow any moving object. And, when guided by sight alone, they seem to have no more disposition to follow a hen than to follow a duck or a human being. Unreflecting lookers-on, when they saw chickens a day old running after me, . . . imagined that I must have some occult power over the creatures; whereas I had simply allowed them to follow me from the first" (p. 287).

James also pointed to the transiency of instincts. For example, the instinct to follow fades

out after a brief but critical period of time. Here, he again cited Spalding, who placed hoods over chicks' heads and showed that they would not follow after being hooded for a period of four days.

James believed that the principle of transiency is important in human and animal life. An instinct is ripe for only a brief period. The mode of expression first utilized is most likely to be followed or fixed and, according to James, there is an optimal moment for attaching an instinct to an appropriate stimulus and this optimal moment or moment of readiness has clear implications for educators. James saw instincts as very important in early development and of less importance later. He believed that behaviors such as sucking, biting, clasping, crying, imitating, and certain fears are instinctive.

Memory.   James opened his chapter on memory with a distinction between primary and secondary memory. **Primary memory,** according to James, is memory for the immediate past or the events that have most recently been in consciousness. He believed there was a close connection between primary memory and afterimages—a topic of considerable interest in perception research. **Secondary memory,** for James, was memory proper. He defined it as knowledge of previous events that are not currently a part of thought or attention. James contended that the exercise of memory presupposes two things: first, the retention of a fact, and second, the demonstration of retention through reminiscence, recollection, reproduction, or recall.

James cited what he called the "heroic" work of Ebbinghaus on memory and concluded his chapter with a section on forgetting. He focused on the utility and the irregularities of forgetting. Under this latter subject, he included such topics as the difficulty of recall that sometimes occurs with strenuous effort and the subsequent ease with which the to-be-remembered material comes back when we relax (psychologists later described such forgetting as the "tip-of-the-tongue phenomenon"). James believed that memory is facilitated by quality of organization, interest, and active (as opposed to passive) repetition. He agreed with French psychologist Théodule Ribot that we have memories rather than memory. He believed that different individuals have different gifts for visual, auditory, tactile, verbal, and muscular memories.

In a lengthy footnote, James described his study on the transfer of learning. Briefly, he investigated whether learning lines from Victor Hugo's "Satyr" would shorten the time to learn lines from a different kind of material (Milton's *Paradise Lost*). He found that the learning of the first task did not facilitate the learning of the second task. This study foreshadowed later transfer of learning studies that proved embarrassing to the doctrine of formal discipline.

James's Legacy

Under James's leadership, the methodological, conceptual, and substantive boundaries of psychology were greatly expanded. Following James, there were attempts to return to narrow unified visions of psychology, but in pluralistic America, such visions, no matter how promising, have always had to suffer at the hands of those permanently infected with a Jamesian suspicion of any grand all-embracing scheme. James left us with a legacy that monism—any monism, be it spiritual, material, political, psychological, scientific, or religious—is but a hypothesis. The positive side of that legacy is that James encouraged us to develop the habit of looking for alternatives. One of the greatest tributes to James is that all of his major works were in print at the start of the twenty-first century. He remains relevant!

The continuing relevance of William James is nowhere better illustrated than in recent scholarship that explores the ecological implications of radical empiricism, pluralism, and pragmatism (see Crosby, 1996; Heft, 2001). Though ecology, as a formal discipline, surfaced long after James's work, some scholars now argue for identifiable affinities between ecological perspectives and Jamesian metaphysics. James did call for the development of a deep and solemn sensitivity to the complexities of our relation to the world. For example, in a speech to a men's club at Harvard, he reminded his audience of the "innocent beasts [who] have had to suffer in cattle-cars and slaughter pens and lay down their lives that we might grow up, all fatted and clad, to sit together here in comfort and carry on this discourse" (James, 1897/1979b, p. 47). James embraced the idea that human experience is not the highest or only type of experience extant in the universe. Neither are humans the only creatures with valuative types of experiences. Humans, he argued, "are tangents to the wider life of things" (James, 1907/1975b, p. 144). To be sure, James was not an ecologist and one can find isolated statements in his work that illustrate insensitivities to things we take for granted a century later. Nevertheless, his mature philosophy, with its strong emphasis on the importance of feelings, relations, particularity, diversity, perspective, and balance, provides a relevant metaphysical frame of reference for ecology.

HUGO MÜNSTERBERG

Though William James founded the first experimental laboratory in the United States, he was temperamentally not suited to direct its activities or conduct experiments. Nevertheless, he was deeply concerned that Harvard maintain leadership in psychology at a time when competing universities were establishing laboratories. A key to Harvard's leadership was to find an outstanding young scholar

Hugo Münsterberg

to direct the laboratory. James was particularly impressed with the early career and promise of a young psychologist by the name of Hugo Münsterberg (1863–1916), who had studied with Wilhelm Wundt. James was aware that Münsterberg was critical of Wundt's work and also that his action theory of behavior was compatible with the James-Lange theory of emotion (Landy, 1992). Largely through James's efforts, an invitation to join the Harvard faculty was forwarded to Münsterberg in 1892. Münsterberg accepted the invitation and remained at Harvard until his death in 1916.

Münsterberg was born in Danzig, East Prussia, (now Gdansk, Poland), on June 1, 1863. He received the Ph.D. under Wilhelm Wundt in 1885 at age twenty-two, and two years later earned the M.D. at the University of Heidelberg. He moved to Harvard following a brief but productive assignment at Freiburg. His major assignment at Harvard was to run the laboratory but, like James, Münsterberg's interests were wide ranging. In addition to his laboratory duties, he was soon involved in a host of activities that would mark him as one of the more important pioneers in applied psychology (Landy, 1992).

Though Münsterberg established residence in the United States well before his thirtieth birthday, he was never able to relinquish his strong German identity. As World War I approached, Münsterberg's German sympathies became increasingly apparent to Americans. He had initially won favor in the United States because he had so clearly demonstrated the utility of psychology, but quickly fell into disfavor because of his public support for Germany (Spillman & Spillman, 1993). Münsterberg died of a stroke in 1916 at the age of fifty-three. His early death may well have been hastened because of the tensions he experienced over his divided loyalties and public rejection.

Münsterberg's Psychology

Though Münsterberg rejected the larger philosophical implications of James's pragmatism, he delivered a psychology that was deeply tuned to the daily lives of people (Morawski, 1983). Indeed, he can be counted as a pioneer in educational psy-

chology, industrial psychology, psychotherapy, and psychology and the law. Münsterberg's applications of psychology to daily life were not grounded in solid experimental work but they helped legitimize a broader vision of what psychology should be about. He argued that psychologists should acquaint themselves with the world of work, the school environment, and courtroom problems and then undertake research on issues encountered in daily life.

Münsterberg's book *On the Witness Stand* (1908) is the standard classic in forensic psychology. The book explores problems associated with such topics as eyewitness testimony, methods of interrogation, suggestibility of witnesses in court, and lie detection. On this latter topic Münsterberg, like others dating back to Galen, was keenly aware of the relationship between physiological arousal and emotional processes. He believed that the emotions associated with telling a lie might be detectable through physiological measures such as respiration and blood pressure. Münsterberg also believed that the day would come when psychological experts would be invited to the courtroom to testify, just like chemists, physicians, and other expert professional witnesses. He anticipated the possibility that there might be a psychological laboratory working specifically on the problems of the courts (Münsterberg, 1913, pp. 292–293).

Münsterberg's text *Psychotherapy* (1909) is remarkably broad in scope. It includes a discussion of the causes of emotional disorders along with a variety of treatment strategies and case histories. It also includes a discussion of the role of religion in treatment, the role of the physician, and the interest of the community. On treatment strategies, Münsterberg advised against a strict systematic approach. He argued that the therapist should adjust the treatment to the special needs and abilities of the patient. Though hypnosis and suggestibility played strong roles in his approach to therapy, he also recognized other techniques. For example, the patient experiencing depression might be asked to go through the motions of joyful expression. Münsterberg (1909, p. 218) believed that such a process, though seemingly artificial, might open "the channels of motor discharge." He also noted that the confidence of the therapist, the capacity of the therapist for empathy, and the expectations of the patient all played crucial roles in psychotherapy.

In his final chapter on psychotherapy and the community, Münsterberg discussed the problems of prevention of emotional disorders. He noted the destructive effects of social and legal injustice and the problem, for the individual and for society, of finding a middle road between the extremes of inhibition and expression. Those extremes, also recognized explicitly by Pavlov and Freud, play pivotal roles in emotional disorders. Münsterberg contended that society should give due attention to those processes that block emotional expression. On the other hand, he recognized that society is impossible without inhibition. In his view, the "middle way is again the real hygienic ideal" (Münsterberg, 1909, p. 397).

Münsterberg's *Psychology and Industrial Efficiency* (1913) is another standard classic in applied psychology (Landy, 1997). His aim, as stated at the outset, was "to sketch the outlines of a new science which is intermediate between the modern laboratory psychology and the problems of economics: the psychological experiment is systematically to be placed at the service of commerce and industry" (p. 3). The book covers many content areas that would later comprise the subject matter of industrial and organizational psychology. He explored such topics as vocational fitness, economy of movement, the problems of monotony and fatigue, job satisfaction, and advertisement. He believed that work can be one of the greatest sources of joy, pride, and satisfaction, but can also produce great depression and discouragement. Thus, few things are as important as the systematic study of work, its conditions, and its relation to personality.

Münsterberg is clearly one of the giants in the history of applied psychology. His most original contributions were in forensic psychology and industrial psychology—two areas that gained momentum in the latter part of the twentieth century (Moskowitz, 1977). Though he did not identify explicitly with functionalism, his sympathies and contributions are more closely related to that tradition than to any other. Münsterberg had no wish

to compromise experimental psychology; he simply had a larger vision of what counts as genuine experimental psychology.

G. STANLEY HALL AND CLARK UNIVERSITY

The functionalist spirit in psychology is nowhere better illustrated than in the work of Granville Stanley Hall (1844–1924) who, according to Averill (1990), explored "every human area and relationship: genetics, childhood, adolescence, family, education, aberration, and religious phenomena" (p. 125). No longer was psychology concerned solely with the dissection of consciousness. Expanding on the pluralistic and pragmatic tradition of his teacher William James, Hall challenged the conservative and somewhat stuffy conventional psychology of his day. In the most deliberate manner possible, he delivered to psychology a process-oriented evolutionary perspective. In his autobiography, Hall (1923) said, "As soon as I first heard it in my youth I think I must have been almost hypnotized by the word 'evolution,' which was music to my ear and seemed to fit my mouth better than any other" (p. 357).

Because of the freshness of his evolutionary perspective and his breadth, organizational skills, energy, and enthusiasm, he was an enormous force in the new discipline. In terms of his influence in U.S. psychology, Hergenhahn (2001, p. 5) placed him "second only to William James."

Granville Stanley Hall was born on February 1, 1844, in his grandfather's house in Ashfield, Massachusetts. He was educated in the rural setting of western Massachusetts. At age sixteen, he was examined by a school committee and awarded a certificate of competence to teach in the public schools. He taught briefly in Chapel Falls, Massachusetts, before enrolling in college preparation studies at Williston Academy in Easthampton, Massachusetts. Hall later entered Williams College, where he received a thorough grounding in Greek, Latin, and mathematics. He graduated from Williams in 1867 at age twenty-three and enrolled that fall in Union Theological Seminary in New York City.

The liberal climate of Union and the cosmopolitan setting combined to challenge his conser-

G. Stanley Hall

vative and orthodox values. In her biography of Hall, Ross (1972, p. 32) called attention to his "clandestine excursions" during the first two years of seminary studies. He attended the theater, sampled a variety of religious services, and immersed himself in New York City's diverse cultural and intellectual opportunities. In 1869, Hall took a leave from the seminary to engage in philosophical studies in Germany. This period of personal and intellectual growth marked a definite shift from theology to natural philosophy. In 1870, Hall was back in New York to complete his final year at Union.

Following graduation, Hall's struggle to follow an academic career was beset with compromises between his real interests and practical financial necessities. His pathway to an academic career included a period of private tutoring and a four-year teaching assignment in the humanities at Antioch College in Yellow Springs, Ohio. With savings from his teaching assignment, Hall, at age thirty-two, was finally able to enroll for graduate studies at Harvard University. He did most of his work with William James but also studied physiology and psychopathology. Ross (1972) noted that his doctorate in 1878 was "the first in the field of psychology to be given in this country" (p. 79). His handwritten dissertation on the muscular perception of space was signed by Francis Bowen, William James, and Frederic H. Hedge.

Following the completion of his doctoral studies at Harvard, Hall returned to Germany where he worked with such luminaries as Emil DuBois-Reymond, Karl Ludwig, Hermann von Helmholtz, and Wilhelm Wundt. In 1881, Hall delivered a series of lectures at Johns Hopkins University, and these were followed by a full-time professorial appointment. At Johns Hopkins, Hall was given space and money for a psychology laboratory that, in his words, was the "largest and most productive laboratory of its kind in the country up to the time of my leaving" (Hall, 1923, p. 227). In addition to founding an important early laboratory, Hall, at considerable personal expense, founded *The American Journal of Psychology,* the first of its kind in English. The first volume was published in 1889.

Within a decade of completing his Ph.D., Hall was such a visible figure in the academic world that he received an invitation to become the first president of Clark University, founded in Worcester, Massachusetts, by Jonas Gilman Clark. As president of a newly founded university, Hall was not hesitant to be chauvinistic for psychology so the program at Clark became a dominant force in U.S. psychology.

Hall was one of the few psychologists to encourage black students to enroll in graduate studies. Under Hall's direction, Francis Sumner (1895–1954) was awarded a Ph.D. from Clark University in 1920, making him the first African American to earn a doctorate in psychology in the United States. Sumner's productive career resulted in more than forty-five publications on such topics as perception, advertising, and the psychology of religion. He proposed strategies for the higher education of African American youth, an issue he struggled with against the smothering backdrop of segregation (Sawyer, 2000). Sumner headed the psychology department at Howard University from 1930 until his death in 1954 (Guthrie, 1998). During Sumner's tenure, Howard was dubbed the "Black Harvard" and played a role in training influential psychologists such as Mamie Phipps Clark and Kenneth B. Clark, later to become the first

African American president of the American Psychological Association (Phillips, 2000). At Columbia University, Otto Klineberg supervised Kenneth Clark's dissertation and encouraged the National Association for the Advancement of Colored People (NAACP) to cite Clark's research "as evidence of the harmful effects of school segregation" (Harris, 1999a, p. 793). After earning their Ph.D.s from Columbia, the Clarks continued to study prejudice and the impact of segregation on children, research that was cited in the 1954 Supreme Court case *Brown v. Board of Education.* Only months before Sumner's death, the Supreme Court's ruling brought a legal end to segregated education in the United States. Although Hall died thirty years prior to the decision, he doubtless would have applauded the outcome.

An overview of Hall's career in psychology during his thirty-one years as president of Clark University is provided by Wapner (1990); some of the more noteworthy achievements include:

1. He founded additional journals such as the *Pedagogical Seminary* (now the *Journal of Genetic Psychology*), the *Journal of Religious Psychology and Education,* and the *Journal of Applied Psychology.*
2. He founded and organized the American Psychological Association (APA) and served as its first president in 1892 and as its thirty-third president in 1924 (Sokal, 1992).
3. He brought Sigmund Freud and Carl Jung to the United States in 1909 and thereby helped introduce U.S. psychologists to psychoanalytic thinking.
4. His department at Clark University was a leader in producing doctoral students in psychology.
5. His enormous scholarly output, consisting of a great many books, articles, and lectures, helped shape the direction of American psychological thought. We will examine this achievement in more detail as we turn to a consideration of Hall's viewpoint in psychology.

Hall retired from the presidency of Clark in 1920 but continued to work on personal and psychological projects. He completed *Senescence* in 1922 and his autobiography entitled *Life and Confessions of a Psychologist* in 1923. He died of pneumonia on April 24, 1924. Ross (1972) noted, "At the small funeral in Worcester, the local minister caused a brief scandal by criticizing Hall for not having appreciated the importance of the institutional church, a scandal which Hall surely would have relished" (p. 436).

Though his accomplishments for psychology were extensive, Hall was tortured by personal difficulties and tragedies. His first wife and an eight-year-old daughter were accidentally asphyxiated in 1890. Later, Hall's second wife was hospitalized with a severe mental disorder. Following the loss of his first wife, Hall lost himself in work and failed to develop a close relationship to his oldest child, Robert Granville Hall. Throughout his life, Hall was torn between passivity and aggression and between depression and intense manic-like periods. He had an apparent need to surround himself with people who were dependent and accommodating. In an informative article, Sokal (1990) discussed this trait and its influence on the development of psychology at Clark. For all of his personal difficulties, Hall ranks as one of the key figures in U.S. psychology. We turn now to a further consideration of some of his contributions.

Hall's Psychology

Hall did not deliver a tightly reasoned system of psychology with clear-cut definitions and rigid methodological prescriptions. However, his published works and the experimental program he advocated had a definite thematic quality. In discussing Hall's experimental laboratory at Johns Hopkins, Pauley (1986) noted that the major topics investigated were "binocular vision, perception of time, coordination of action between the two halves of the body and the relationship between psychological attention and muscular movement" (p. 28). Pauley pointed out that Hall envisioned a much wider experimental program, but most students, in fact, worked on these topics. Hall published in all these areas, but the focus of his early research was on the psychology of childhood (White, 1992). His long-term interest was life-span development.

In the preface to his classic volumes entitled *Adolescence,* Hall (1904) celebrated the "extension of evolution into the psychic field" (p. v). He argued that knowledge of the soul is dependent on knowledge of the history of the soul in the world. Thus, the study of the history of the individual should be complemented by studies of the history of the species. Hall repeatedly expressed the belief that "the child and the race are each keys to the other" (p. vii). He adopted the idea that ontogeny (the history of the individual) recapitulates phylogeny (the history of the species). Such a belief comes ready-made with methodological and substantive prescriptions. On the methodological side, Hall argued that "the animal, savage, and child-soul can never be studied by introspection" (p. vii). The methodology of psychology would have to be broader, more biological. On the substantive side, Hall declared that "we must go to school to learn the folk-soul, learn of criminals and defectives, animals, and in some sense go back to Aristotle in rebasing psychology on biology" (pp. vii–viii). Clearly, Hall's approach to psychology represents a radical departure from the psychology of Titchener. Hall's developmental-evolutionary approach gives concrete expression to ideas that were included in the philosophy of William James, but not always translated into specific programs for action.

Hall's vision for an experimental child psychology was set forth in a popular magazine article entitled "A Children's Institute" (see Hall, 1910). In that article, he campaigned for institutes devoted to broad-based studies of children. Such institutes would have divisions or specializations on a host of topics such as growth norms, language development, special diseases of children, hygiene, juvenile crime, and educational techniques. Much of Hall's personal research was designed to expand the public awareness of what children know and what they do. Thus, he published studies on such topics as what children know (e.g., vocabulary and number concepts) when they enter school (Hall, 1891), children's lies (Hall, 1890), "showing off and bashfulness" (Hall & Smith, 1903), and numerous works on children's concepts (e.g., Hall & Browne, 1903; Hall & Wallin, 1902).

Hall's research work on children covered a variety of additional topics (e.g., fears, pets, curiosity, companions, etc.). A perusal of his bibliography (see Hall, 1923, pp. 597–616) reveals a massive and programmatic effort to understand the mind and behavior of the child. Hall's experimental and conceptual work on children apparently owed much to Theodate Louise Smith, who headed the Children's Institute at Clark. According to Sokal (1990), her interests "meshed effectively with Hall's . . . and contributed to some excellent science" (p. 121). The work of Hall, Smith, and others in the child study movement met a great public need and thus elevated the visibility and status of psychology. Hall's work contributed to the impression that psychology had something important to say about the real problems of living.

The child study movement was by no means restricted to the United States. Indeed, Hall had many counterparts in other countries. In Germany, Wilhelm Preyer (1841–1897) was an important pioneer in childhood studies. His book, *The Mind of the Child* (1882), is one of the great classics in the field. In England, James Sully (1842–1923) wrote numerous books and articles on childhood. In France, Hippolyte Adolphe Taine (1828–1893) wrote an important early paper on lingual development in infancy. These early pioneers and others paved the way for the continuing emphasis on childhood later in the work of such people as Binet, Freud, and Piaget.

As noted earlier, Hall's larger interest was in life-span development from infancy to old age. His final book, *Senescence,* first published in 1922, is a classic work in the study of aging (Cole, 1993). Hall examined the treatment of the elderly in various cultures, along with literature by and on elderly people. He then turned to actuarial and mortality tables and pointed to the inevitable problems associated with the changing age demography, already evident in his day. He reviewed national old-age pension plans in other countries and stated, in 1922, "The United States is the only nation that has no retirement system or provision for old age, even for its employees, save for soldiers and for judges of the Supreme Court" (p. 180). On this matter, Hall was ahead of his time. It had been argued that a national retirement plan would undermine individual responsibility and that it ran counter to the best interests of a capitalistic society. Then, with the Great Depression, previously responsible families were devastated through no fault of their own. As a result of such widespread financial disaster, especially for the elderly, the Social Security Act of 1935 brought the United States into line with other nations. Hall would have approved, because he was deeply aware of the masses of elderly people in his day who were financially destitute.

Hall (1922) called for the creation of a kind of "senescent league of national dimensions" (p. 194) with educational, political, and social divisions that would serve an advocacy role for the elderly. The latter part of *Senescence* presents results of an attitude survey that Hall conducted on such topics as sources of pleasure, belief in an afterlife, death anxiety, beliefs about longevity, and recognition of the signs of aging.

Hall had many other interests, especially in education and pedagogy (Fagan, 1992), the history of psychology (Bringmann, Bringmann, & Early, 1992), and the psychology of religion (Vande-Kemp, 1992). He was especially interested in the effects of religious education on youth. His book *Jesus the Christ, in the Light of Psychology* (1917), represents a kind of "working through" of tensions between his early Calvinistic background and his natural-science approach to psychology.

In terms of his influence on both the basic and the applied dimensions of psychology, his oranizational innovations, his selling of psychology to the public, and his specific developmental-evolutionary perspective and its subsequent influence, Hall must be counted as one of the great psychologists.

FUNCTIONALISM AND THE UNIVERSITY OF CHICAGO

In her classic book *Seven Psychologies,* Edna Heidbreder (1933) referred to the University of Chicago as "the capital of a new school" (p. 201). The term *capital* is appropriate because, while the functionalist slant dominated thought in many U.S. and European universities, it was nowhere more clearly articulated than at the University of Chicago. The two elder leaders of the Chicago school, John Dewey and James Rowland Angell, studied respectively with G. Stanley Hall and William James. The third leader of the Chicago school, Harvey Carr, completed his degree under Angell at Chicago.

John Dewey

Regarded by many as America's most important philosopher of education, John Dewey (1859–1952) played a key role in launching functionalism. Dewey was born on October 20, 1859, in Burlington, Vermont. His early schooling was in Burlington and he graduated from the University of Vermont in 1879. Following a brief teaching career, he enrolled in the graduate program in philosophy at Johns Hopkins University. During that period, he studied with G. Stanley Hall and wrote a doctoral dissertation on the psychology of Immanuel Kant. He took the Ph.D. from Johns Hopkins in 1884 and immediately accepted a teaching assignment in psychology and philosophy at the University of Michigan. In 1894, Dewey accepted an appointment as chair of psychology and philosophy at the University of Chicago. It was during his decade at Chicago that Dewey made his most

John Dewey

visible contributions to the functionalist viewpoint in psychology. In 1904, he moved from Chicago to Columbia University where he focused on the philosophy of education. Dewey's long and productive career came to an end in his ninety-second year, on June 1, 1952.

Dewey's classic article, "The Reflex Arc Concept in Psychology," published in 1896, is so pivotal in the history of the functionalist school that Edwin G. Boring (1953) referred to it as "a declaration of independence for American functional psychology" (p. 146). In obvious celebration of Dewey's general philosophical and psychological orientation, William James wrote in 1903, "It rejoices me greatly that your school (I mean your philosophic school) at the University of Chicago is, after this long gestation, bringing its fruits to birth in a way that will demonstrate its great unity and vitality" (James, 1903/1980, p. 204). What, specifically, were the unique features of Dewey's thought that warranted such praise?

Like James, Dewey believed that philosophy must begin with experience. Furthermore, experience must be understood in a naturalistic context. Dewey was critical of earlier idealistic philosophers whose concepts were not sufficiently wedded to observable events in the world. As with James, Dewey was friendly to a pluralistic view that placed emphasis on the irreducible and unique features of the experiences of individual human beings. Dewey's article, "The Reflex Arc Concept in Psychology," was particularly critical of attempts to dissect experience into artificial piecemeal units. Such dissection is inappropriate even for simple reflexes, let alone more complicated behaviors. Furthermore, such dissection violates what is really found in experience and thus departs from a truly empirical approach to psychology.

Dewey asked his readers to consider the reflex: Do we ever really consider the stimulus as a thing in itself or the response as a thing in itself? Such a distinction is unlikely except in a highly artificial laboratory situation. Dewey (1896) argued that a reflex is not "a patchwork of disjointed parts, a mechanical conjunction of unallied processes" (p. 358). Instead, what we encounter is "a continuously ordered sequence of acts, all adapted in themselves and in the order of their sequence, to reach a certain objective end" (p. 366). The ends we seek (e.g., reproduction, safety, locomotion, etc.) call attention to motivation and to observable behaviors associated with motivation. Shook (1995) has documented Wundt's influence on Dewey's earliest writings. However, Dewey found too much abstraction in the older psychologies and a failure to appreciate the special ends or functions of psychological processes.

Boring (1953) offered the opinion that "after Dewey went to Columbia in 1904 his mission to the new psychology was largely accomplished, like the mission of any parent when the child has grown up" (p. 147). Boring's statement is applicable mainly to Dewey's mission to academic psychology; he continued, however, to have an influence on applied psychology, especially in educational circles (Jackson, 1998). Dewey's continued interest in the applied arena was fueled by a combination of interests in U.S. democracy, economics (Tilman & Knapp, 1999), schools, art (Jackson, 1998), the nature of learning, and his own six children.

According to Soltis (1971), Dewey believed that "democracy was more than a form of government; it was a way of living that went beyond politics, votes, and laws to pervade all aspects of society" (p. 84). Accordingly, Dewey believed that schools should afford firsthand opportunities for children to learn democracy and see it in action. Dewey's cardinal rule of education was that we learn by doing and by reflecting on what happened. Thus, if we want to perpetuate democracy, it should be learned in the schools. Dewey also believed that the educational system should respect individuality but at the same time should challenge our ethnocentrism. He strongly opposed mere imitation, regimentation, and learning only by rote. Such learning, he felt, prepares us not for democracy but for totalitarianism. Dewey clearly was a leading figure in the founding of functionalism and the premier figure in progressive education (Hilgard, 1996).

James Rowland Angell

The pathways of John Dewey and James Rowland Angell (1869–1949) were remarkably similar and crossed on numerous occasions. They were both born in Burlington, Vermont—Dewey in 1859, Angell on May 8, 1869. Angell's college work was at the University of Michigan, where he completed the B.A. in 1890 and the M.A in 1891. Miles (1949) noted that a highlight in Angell's experience at Michigan was "a seminar with Dewey on William James' recently published *Principles of Psychology*" (p. 1). Miles also pointed out that Angell declared that James's "book, more than any other, profoundly influenced his thinking for the next twenty years of his life" (p. 1). Following the completion of his work at Michigan, Angell enrolled at Harvard University where he worked primarily with William James and Josiah Royce. In his autobiography, Angell (1930/1961) spoke of studying Kant with Royce and abnormal psychology with James (see p. 7).

Following his year at Harvard, Angell went to Germany, where he heard lectures by some of the leading scholars in psychology, philosophy, and physiology. A dissertation on the meaning of freedom in Kant's philosophical work was accepted, subject to revision, at the University of Halle. Angell did not revise the dissertation and instead accepted a position as instructor of philosophy and psychology at the University of Minnesota. It is ironic that a man who was instrumental in granting a great many doctorates and who received several honorary doctorates never completed the formalities associated with his own Ph.D.

After completing one year at the University of Minnesota, Angell and Dewey crossed paths again when Angell accepted a position at the University of Chicago. Angell was initially discouraged because, in his words, "For seven years I received no promotion in rank and no advance in salary" (1930/1961, p. 13). He was finally promoted to associate professor in 1901 and to professor in 1904. Angell believed that his promotions came about partly because of outside offers, such as an offer of a professorship at Princeton in 1903. In 1905, Angell became head of the psychology department at Chicago, and in 1911 dean of the Faculties. From 1911 on, Angell was continuously involved in administrative work. He served as dean at Chicago, then acting president. In World War I, he served

with Walter Dill Scott on the Committee on Classification of Personnel. In 1921, Angell accepted a position as president of Yale University, a position he filled brilliantly until his retirement in 1937. Following retirement, Angell worked as an educational counselor for the National Broadcasting Company. He died in New Haven, Connecticut, on March 4, 1949.

Angell's contributions to psychology are all the more remarkable in view of his enormous time commitments to administration. His most visible scholarly contributions to psychology were produced during his tenure in the psychology department at the University of Chicago. In 1904, he published a text, *Psychology,* that quickly went through four editions. In 1907, Angell published an article entitled "The Province of Functional Psychology" based on his presidential address to the American Psychological Association. This work is regarded as a classic exposition of the functionalist school.

Angell argued that functionalism was really not new: It had been around since Aristotle and, in modern times, since Spencer and Darwin. The first mark of the functionalist orientation, according to Angell (1930/1961), is that it involves "the identification and description of mental *operations,* rather than the mere *stuff* of mental experience" (p. 28). The second mark of functionalism is that it is concerned with the conditions or circumstances that evoke a mental state. A mental state does not exist in isolation; it must be understood in social and biological context. Finally, Angell argued that mental states or events must be understood in terms of how they contribute "to the furtherance of the sum total of organic activities, considered as adaptive" (p. 28). In other words, he asked, what contributions do mental events make to our adjustment to the world? These three marks of a functionalist psychology go a long way from a merely descriptive psychology of the stuff of consciousness. According to Angell, the functionalist approach is illustrated in studies of animal behavior, developmental psychology, and psychopathology. A functionalist psychology is inherently social and biological and emphasizes experience and behavior in the service of adaptation.

In his autobiography, Angell commented on other developments taking place in his day. As for the testing movement, he was concerned about its premature application in industry and education but saw it as having definite potential if properly used. As for psychoanalysis, he saw some of its contributions as sound and fundamentally significant but was concerned about the parts of it that seemed romantic and unscientific.

Clearly, Angell and Dewey were forces in U.S. psychology despite the fact that both were torn by other interests. They both served as presidents of the American Psychological Association (Dewey in 1899 and Angell in 1906). Also, both were named to the most prestigious scientific society in America—the National Academy of Sciences. According to Miles (1949), Angell, who was elected in 1920, was the sixth psychologist named to the Academy. Others were James McKeen Cattell (1901), William James (1903), Josiah Royce (1906), John Dewey (1910), and G. Stanley Hall (1915).

Harvey A. Carr

The consolidation and extension of the functionalist position took place under the leadership of Angell's student, Harvey A. Carr (1873–1954). Born in Indiana on April 30, 1873, Carr was educated at DePauw University and later at the University of Colorado where he was influenced by Arthur Allin, a disciple of G. Stanley Hall's. After completing a master's degree at Colorado, Carr enrolled in the doctoral program at the University of Chicago. His dissertation, directed by Angell, was completed in 1905. Carr worked briefly in a high school position in Texas and then at the Pratt Institute before returning to the University of Chicago in 1908. He remained at Chicago from 1908 to 1938, chairing the department through much of that period. Under his leadership, Chicago became one of the leading schools in psychology.

Carr contended that psychology is concerned primarily with mental activity. By *mental activity*, he was referring to "the acquisition, fixation, retention, organization, and evaluation of experiences, and their subsequent utilization in the guid-

ance of conduct" (Carr, 1925, p. 1). Thus, both experience and behavior (conduct) are central features of functionalism as interpreted by Carr. He argued, "The type of conduct that reflects mental activity may be termed adaptive or adjustive behavior" (p. 1). Adaptation or adjustment, according to Carr, involves a response that alters a situation so as to satisfy a motivating stimulus. A motivating stimulus may be a hunger pang, an itch, excessive temperature, pain, and so forth. Clearly, the subject of motivation is elevated in the functionalist system.

Carr accepted a variety of methods, including introspection and objective observation. He questioned whether the methods of all the sciences are really comparable. For example, he noted that "geology, astronomy, and mathematics are usually regarded as sciences, but are they experimental in the usual laboratory sense of the term?" (Carr, 1930/1961, p. 80). Carr expressed doubt "that the experimental method—in the usual sense of that term—is the only scientific method" (p. 81). In his view, psychologists should not be doctrinaire about method, but attend, first and foremost, to the nature of the problem.

Carr, like Angell, believed in a psychology broad in scope, encompassing problems in learning, motivation, psychopathology, education, sensation, perception, and development. Like Angell, he believed that all problems should be examined in terms of biological and social context.

The Chicago functionalists devoted little space to the metaphysical problems that occupied the attention of other psychologists. Carr, in his book *Psychology: The Study of Mental Activity,* discussed various positions on the issue of free will and determinism but seemed most interested in the ways that freedom might have meaning and utility. Such a position is consistent with the functionalist agenda. The metaphysical status of the two positions was not of great interest, but the meaning of the two positions—their utility, the work they accomplish, or the various meanings they convey—were important problems. Believing that freedom is acquired through knowledge, Carr quoted with approval the injunction, "Seek the truth and the truth shall make you free" (Carr, 1925, p. 332).

PSYCHOLOGY AT COLUMBIA UNIVERSITY

We encounter another clear expression of functionalism in the early psychology at Columbia University. Nurtured and developed by James McKeen Cattell, the psychology department at Columbia was to become one of the most visible and productive in the United States.

James McKeen Cattell

One of the more colorful and controversial figures in the history of psychology, James McKeen Cattell (1860–1944) found his way to fame in his chosen discipline via an unusual route. His research program failed and, compared to others, he published relatively few papers. Yet, for a time, he was one of the most visible and powerful figures in the discipline. He won his place in history primarily through editorial and administrative skills. Through his editorial efforts, the experimental and conceptual work of psychologists was brought to the attention of other scientists and the public. The discipline of psychology enjoyed center-stage attention that might not have been possible without Cattell's unique contributions.

Cattell was born on May 25, 1860. He was a gifted student, graduating with honors from Lafayette College in Easton, Pennsylvania, in 1880. Following two years of travel and study in Europe, Cattell returned to the United States to enroll for study in philosophy at Johns Hopkins University. Though he did excellent experimental work in G. Stanley Hall's laboratory at Hopkins, his fellowship for the second year was not renewed. Reasons for the transfer of the fellowship from Cattell to John Dewey are not entirely clear. Sokal (1980b) referred to Cattell's "continual bickering with Daniel Coit Gilman, the university president" (p. 43) and Ross (1972, p. 145) implicated G. Stanley Hall in the decision. For whatever reason, Cattell moved from Baltimore to Leipzig and, as noted by Sokal (1980b), "became the first American to earn a Ph.D. in experimental psychology from Wilhelm Wundt at Leipzig" (p. 43).

Following his work at Leipzig, Cattell went to England, where he worked with Francis Galton. Galton's obsession with the measurement of bodily and mental attributes had a profound influence on Cattell. On the philosophical side, he had earlier been influenced by the Baconian vision and by the enthusiasm of Rudolph Hermann Lotze for an empirical approach to the study of mental processes. Galton's work helped Cattell translate his philosophical biases into an experimental program.

Following work with Galton, Cattell returned to the United States to accept an appointment in 1889 at the University of Pennsylvania. In 1891, he accepted a position at Columbia University, which he held until 1917. Cattell's research programs at Pennsylvania and Columbia focused largely on the development of *mental tests,* a term he coined in 1890 (see Cattell, 1890). In Cattell's day, there were high expectations that mental abilities could be measured and that such measurements would have the most salutary consequences for schools and for industry. The problem was to develop mental tests with demonstrated predictive efficiency. Cattell, following the lead of Galton, measured simple reaction times, complex reaction times, visual acuity, auditory acuity, strength of grip, and the like.

As noted by Sokal (1980b), Cattell's measurements "literally correlated with nothing. The result killed his career as a psychological tester and redirected his efforts away from experimental psychology" (p. 47). As we will see later, Binet, employing a different set of tasks, was able to develop tests with predictive efficiency. Though Cattell's research program failed, he established laboratories at the University of Pennsylvania and at Columbia University. Also, at Columbia, he helped promote one of the most active doctoral programs in psychology.

In 1894, Cattell embarked on his career as an editor—a career that would span a half century. For more than a century, the journal *Science* has been one of the most important periodicals, providing an outlet for research in many fields, including physics, chemistry, biology, geology, and psychology. In 1894, however, the journal was in serious financial difficulty. Cattell took over as editor of *Science* and immediately established policies that rescued the journal and improved its visibility (see Sokal, 1980b). It is noteworthy that such an important outlet for all the sciences was edited by a psychologist. Furthermore, psychology articles increasingly found their way into this prestigious journal alongside articles from the more established scientific disciplines.

In 1893, Cattell joined forces with James Mark Baldwin (1861–1934) to purchase G. Stanley Hall's *American Journal of Psychology* (Sokal, 1997). When Hall refused to sell, Cattell and Baldwin founded the *Psychological Review* one year later, a journal that still occupies a central and visible place in the discipline. In time, Cattell and Baldwin established the *Psychological Review* as America's leading psychology journal and went on to found a family of successful journals including the *Psychological Index* and the *Psychological Monographs.* According to Johnson (2000, p. 1146), Hall's journals had a broader focus whereas "the Baldwin and Cattell journals represented a narrower view of psychology, publishing more specialized experimental articles than general or theoretical articles and considerably fewer applied articles." After years of feuding, Cattell and Baldwin dissolved their partnership in 1903 and the *Psychological Review* journals were sold to the American Psychological Association in 1925.

Cattell edited a great variety of other journals. From 1900 to 1915, he served as editor of *Popular Science Monthly,* a magazine that informed the public about important developments in the sciences. Under Cattell's leadership, *Popular Science Monthly* included many articles on psychology in order to satisfy an ever-growing public demand for information on such topics as child rearing, animal behavior, psychopathology, and mental testing. Cattell also served as editor of the *American Naturalist* from 1907 to 1944 and *School and Society* from 1915 to 1939. Although not exhaustive, this list of his editorial responsibilities does convey the central role he occupied with respect to communication of scientific information. How did Cattell manage the work associated with editing so many journals? He was a capable organizer who employed graduate students and family

members (wife and children) in his science publication machine. Most notably Cattell's wife, Josephine Owen Cattell, played a key role in the publication of *Science.* Indeed, she joined her son, Jaques Cattell, as editor of *Science* following Cattell's death in 1944.

In addition to editorial work, Cattell founded the Psychological Corporation in 1921. The corporation made psychological services such as consulting and testing available in business and industrial settings. Cattell (1937/1992) predicted in the first volume of his *Journal of Consulting Psychology* that professional psychology would thrive in the twentieth century. His Psychological Corporation continues to prosper and, according to Garfield (1992), Cattell was largely correct in his predictions about the future of professional psychology. Another of Cattell's most noteworthy achievements was his work to recognize outstanding achievement in science. He founded the reference series *American Men of Science,* later to become *American Men and Women of Science,* and developed a rating system as a means of establishing eminence (Sokal, 1995). His system, however, was not always received with enthusiasm. For example, in 1903, Cattell asked William James to participate in an exercise to rank psychologists. James complied but expressed his suspicion about fine-tuned rankings. He also argued that the nature of the work of different individuals is not always homogeneous enough to warrant meaningful comparisons. In characteristic Jamesian honesty, he said, "Permit me to say that in my private breast *you* stand lower now than you did before I got this problem from you!" (James, 1903/1986b, p. 313).

Many honors came to Cattell during his life. One of the original founders of the American Psychological Association, he served as its fourth president. As a powerful advocate for science and academic life, Cattell held strong opinions on many issues and did not hesitate to express them. Indeed, his stinging criticisms of key political and university officials ultimately led to his dismissal from Columbia University. Gates (1968) pointed out, however, that "in the course of time the university public, at least, arose to defend and applaud him" (p. 346). Cattell died on January 20, 1944.

Robert Sessions Woodworth

One of the essential features of functionalism is that it broadened the scope of psychological inquiry. Both basic and applied problems were legitimate and there was an extension of research into new basic problem areas. Learning and motivation were especially elevated in importance. A key figure in the development of motivation as a subject area was Robert Sessions Woodworth (1869–1962).

Woodworth was born in Belchertown, Massachusetts, on October 17, 1869. Even as a youngster, Woodworth had broad-ranging academic interests that included music, philosophy, mathematics, and science. Initially, he planned for a career, like that of his father, in the ministry. Upon graduating from Amherst in 1891, he was still considering the ministry but, in order to raise money for additional education, accepted teaching assignments in science and mathematics.

Woodworth's experiences as a teacher caused him to reconsider his vocational plans and, as noted by Poffenberger (1962), "he entered Harvard in the autumn of 1895, fairly well committed to a teaching career in philosophy and psychology" (p. 678). Poffenberger pointed out that, while at Harvard, Woodworth worked with William James and developed friendships with fellow graduate students E. L. Thorndike and W. B. Cannon. He took the M.A. degree from Harvard but then transferred to Columbia, where he graduated with the Ph.D. in psychology in 1899. Woodworth studied in Scotland and in England where he worked with the famous physiologist Sir Charles Sherrington. Woodworth held temporary instructorships before accepting a regular faculty position at Columbia in 1903. With the exception of the brief temporary assignments, Woodworth spent his entire academic career at Columbia University. It was an unusually lengthy career that had spanned six decades when Woodworth died at the age of 92 on July 4, 1962.

Though Woodworth is categorized as a functionalist, he did not think of himself as a member of a school, but as an experimental psychologist seeking to understand cause–effect relationships in experience and behavior. Woodworth's published contributions to psychology extend over two hundred papers and ten books. Though he made substantive contributions in many areas, three areas are especially noteworthy.

First, as noted by Murphy (1963), under Woodworth's leadership, "the term *experimental* was extended to more and more kinds and fields of research endeavor" (p. 131). In the revised version of his classic text, *Experimental Psychology*, coauthored with Harold Schlosberg, Woodworth celebrated the same point. In the introduction, Woodworth and Schlosberg (1954) noted that the field of psychology started with a few scattered experiments conducted by scientists from several other disciplines. Reliable findings were demonstrated in experiments on the senses, but after years of hard work, experimental psychology encompassed the fields of learning, memory, thinking, attention, emotion, and motivation. Woodworth contributed to the growing breadth of perspective about the subject matter of experimental psychology. No longer was it restricted to the senses and to reaction times. Though Woodworth extended experimental psychology to a widening field of subjects, he narrowed the concept of what legitimately counts as an experiment. We will return to this topic later.

Woodworth's second contribution relates to the first but deserves special treatment. Specifically, in his work, we encounter a new and broader emphasis on the concept of motivation. Like the study of emotion, research on motivation had carried over from the last century as a popular topic for psychologists (Edwards, 1999). Woodworth took issue with an exclusively biogenic approach to motivation. He did not believe that all motives have their origin in instincts or in metabolic processes. He drew attention to learned drives and to the idea that there are "activities that have intrinsic incentive value" (Woodworth & Schlosberg, 1954, p. 685). Thus play, manipulation, exploration, and even some forms of work may, in his words, "function autonomously" (p. 686).

The notion of **functional autonomy,** encountered later in the psychology of Gordon Allport

(1937, 1955), refers to the idea that a means or mechanism for satisfying a motive may acquire drive properties. For example, a person may work at a music store as a means of earning a living. In time, however, he or she becomes acquainted with good music and develops a strong drive to spend time each day listening. What started as a mere "means" has now become an acquired motive and is sustained because of its own intrinsic merits.

Woodworth's concept of motivation also extended into the realm of the unconscious. Seward and Seward (1968), for example, pointed out that Woodworth "anticipated Freud in considering the dream to be the result of perseverating wishes; however, his theory rested on a broader base than Freud's, inasmuch as he believed that wishes underlying dreams might pertain to any area of interest" (p. 562). Thus, the wish behind a dream, according to Woodworth, need not be sexual; rather, it might be based on any strong human need such as a need for achievement, recognition, security, and so on.

Woodworth called his approach *dynamic psychology.* The term *dynamic* refers to the importance of understanding the causes of behavior. Woodworth assumed that causes are not always reducible to a simple stimulus-response (S-R) formula. He was famous for arguing that the S-R idea should be replaced by a stimulus–organism–response (S-O-R) concept. The S-O-R formulation emphasizes the crucial role of the organism in the sequence. Examples of organismic variables, according to Woodworth, include learned motives, expectations, readiness to respond, and personal characteristics such as cautiousness or fearfulness.

A third contribution came through Woodworth's influential textbooks. His introductory text entitled *Psychology,* first published in 1921, was widely used, but the text that had the greatest influence on academic psychology was his *Experimental Psychology,* first published in 1938. A revision with Harold Schlosberg as coauthor was published in 1954. Woodworth's *Experimental Psychology* was so influential that it was commonly called "the Bible" (see Winston, 1990). For over two decades the book served as a standard reference for students preparing for graduate school. Noteworthy

for its breadth, Woodworth's text reviewed classic studies and methodologies in a host of content areas including psychophysics, association, emotion, sensation, learning, motivation, memory, and problem solving.

Though Woodworth expanded sensitivity to the scope of experimental psychology, he also narrowed what counted as an experiment with a distinction between correlational and experimental research (Winston, 1990). Woodworth emphasized the importance of independent and dependent variables in true experimental research. An *independent variable* is one that the researcher systematically manipulates. Let us say we are studying the effects of coffee on anxiety. In this case, consumption of coffee is the variable controlled by the experimenter. Presumably, one group consumes no coffee, another may consume a placebo (e.g., a substance that passes for coffee but isn't), and another group actually consumes coffee. The presence or absence of coffee or the administration of a placebo would be counted as the independent variable. Anxiety, as measured by some test, is the *dependent variable.*

Winston (1990) noted that "nearly all textbooks, both introductory and experimental, adopted Woodworth's conceptualization of 'experiment'" (p. 397). Woodworth's definition of an *experiment* elevated the importance of "wet lab" approaches to psychology and enhanced the scientific image of the discipline. In later years, however, the term *experiment* often has broader meanings. Thus, there are activities of astronomers that could possibly be viewed as experimental, even though variables are not manipulated in the usual sense. The discovery of a new planet, for example, may arise from hypothesis testing and controlled observation, but the procedure is not completely comparable to the typical "wet lab" experiment.

Woodworth made many additional contributions to the discipline of psychology. He may be best known for his famous studies with Edward Lee Thorndike on the transfer of training (discussed in Chapter 13). He did extensive editorial work for psychological journals and served as president of the American Psychological Association in 1914. In 1956, the American Psychological Foundation

awarded Woodworth the Gold Medal for his outstanding contributions to the discipline.

MARY WHITON CALKINS

Shortly after 1900, functionalism gained momentum as the dominant orientation in numerous universities. However, some scholars sought
to preserve the best in structuralism and functionalism. One such person was Mary Whiton Calkins
(1863–1930), the founder of one of the early psychology laboratories in the United States.

In the 1880s and 1890s, progressive colleges
and universities encouraged the growth and development of psychology laboratories. Calkins, a
young Greek instructor at Wellesley College, was
given the opportunity to establish a laboratory on
the condition that she take time off and pursue advanced studies in psychology. She explored numerous options but encountered restrictions against
women in most leading institutions in Europe and
the United States. Initially rejected at Harvard, she
was finally permitted to enroll on the condition
that the courses would not count for a degree. She
took a course with William James and later conducted research in Hugo Münsterberg's laboratory. Her work was of a distinguished quality, and
in 1895, she presented a thesis and was given an
unauthorized examination. The examining committee included such distinguished faculty as
James, Münsterberg, and George Santayana. They
affirmed that she met all doctoral requirements,
but Harvard refused to grant the degree. The details of her studies and the controversy over the degree are discussed by Furumoto (1979).

Though she did not receive the Harvard doctorate, Calkins established the laboratory at Wellesley and became a productive scholar. In 1905, she
was elected the fourteenth president of the American Psychological Association. She taught at
Wellesley College until her retirement in 1929.

Calkins believed that *psychology* should be defined as the science of the conscious self. Although
not a popular cause at the time, she was the most
visible advocate of self-psychology for three decades. Wentworth (1999) concluded that Calkins's
vigorous defense of the science of selves was, in

Mary Whiton Calkins

part, rooted in her beliefs about ethics, religion,
and morality. She viewed mind or consciousness
as the ultimate reality and, in that sense, belonged
to the idealist tradition and to a philosophical tradition known as *personalism.* Calkins argued that
if the self is the focus of psychology, then there is
room for a reconciliation between structuralism
and functionalism. Calkins believed that human
consciousness is understood partly in terms of its
environmental contexts. The functionalist engages
in such explorations and thus makes valuable contributions. Consciousness must also be understood
in its own terms as a reality unlike any lower reality from which it emerged. The structuralist is
more likely to provide insights into the unique and
irreducible dimensions of consciousness. Thus,
there is a place for both functionalism and structuralism, a theme echoed in Calkins's presidential
address before the American Psychological Association in 1905.

Calkins made additional contributions to psychology, including early development of the *paired
associate method* as a means of studying retention.
This method required research subjects to learn an
association between a pair of stimulus–response
terms such as *desk–moon* or *orange–hat.* Thus,
when given the stimulus term *desk,* the subject
would be expected to respond with the term *moon.*

Calkins's short-term memory studies anticipated later developments in memory research (Madigan & O'Hara, 1992).

Calkins (1893) also conducted one of the first formal studies of dreams. She kept track of her dreams for fifty-five nights, waking herself up at various intervals to record dreams in a journal. Her colleague, Edmund Clark Sanford, recorded his dreams for forty-six nights, and together they made several insightful findings. She accurately concluded that people dream every night, that four dreams are common in an average night, and that we can, to a degree, control our dreams. Several years later, Sigmund Freud acknowledged Calkins's seminal work in his book the *Interpretation of Dreams*. She is remembered appropriately as one of the pioneers who, in the words of Pratola (1974), demonstrated that "women have a rightful place in scientific and academic endeavors" (p. 780).

THE GROWTH OF APPLIED PSYCHOLOGY

Earlier we encountered Münsterberg's contention that psychological experiments should be placed in the service of practical day-to-day interests. Inspired by functionalism, many psychologists geared their research to problems and issues of daily living. Such research left its mark on public institutions and helped mold public and scientific attitudes about the practical value of psychology. An example of research that attacked and helped change public and scientific attitudes is clearly visible in the work of Leta Stetter Hollingworth.

Leta Stetter Hollingworth

In the late nineteenth and early twentieth centuries, the so-called **variability hypothesis** was used as an explanation for the differential achievements of men and women in science, music, law, and so on. Briefly stated, the variability hypothesis held that men are physically and psychologically more variable than women. Thus, according to the hypothesis, women tended toward averages in all things, whereas males showed more variety; men were thought to be more courageous but also more cow-

Leta Stetter Hollingworth

ardly, more virtuous but more corrupt, more intelligent but more stupid, and more violent but more peaceful. Superficial support for the variability hypothesis was found in the achievements of men compared to women and in the finding that more boys compared to girls were diagnosed as intellectually deficient.

The contention that men are physically *and* psychologically more variable than women is testable and it was altogether fitting that the death blow to this commonly held belief should be delivered by a woman. The story of that woman, Leta Stetter Hollingworth (1886–1939), is told in articles by Benjamin (1975) and Shields (1975). Hollingworth, born Leta A. Stetter, was reared in Nebraska and took her bachelor's degree at the University of Nebraska and her Ph.D. at Columbia University in 1916. Benjamin (1975) called attention to the fact that many early psychologists made claims for the inferiority of women. Such claims were sometimes derived from the predictions of the variability hypothesis.

As a means of investigating the variability hypothesis, Hollingworth compared male and female infants on a variety of physical characteristics such as height, birth weight, cranial circumference, and the like. She found no differences in variability on any of the physical characteristics she explored.

Male infants were slightly larger than females at birth, but were not more variable. Hollingworth acknowledged that more males than females were admitted to institutions for the mentally handicapped, but in early twentieth-century America, more was expected of males and hence a mental handicap was more likely to be detected. She argued persuasively that greater male achievements are the result of unequal educational opportunities. Females had almost no vocational options; hence, achievement was next to impossible.

Hollingworth also conducted research that showed that the perceptual, motor, and mental abilities of women are not adversely affected during the menstrual cycle (Hollingworth, 1914), a discovery that undercut another early twentieth-century myth that women could never compete with men because of a monthly incapacity brought about by menstruation. Hollingworth's studies now count as classics in the psychology of women and made important contributions to the reduction of some prejudices that had prevented equal educational opportunities for women.

Following World War I, Hollingworth became active in clinical research on individual differences in intelligence, an area like the psychology of women that was "fraught with myth and misunderstanding" (Shields, 1991, p. 248). During the course of her prestigious career, Hollingworth focused on two extreme populations of children—"mentally defective" children and gifted children with IQs above 180 (Hollingworth, 1920, 1942). Her work resulted in the celebrated book *The Psychology of the Adolescent* (Hollingworth, 1928) as well as a variety of conceptual issues that remain relevant for contemporary professionals (Klein, 2000).

Helen Wooley

The emphasis of the functionalist school on the usefulness of experimental psychology is encountered in another way in the works of Helen Wooley (1874–1947). Like Leta Hollingworth and Margaret Floy Washburn, Helen Wooley was one of the first generation of women to receive a Ph.D. in experimental psychology (see Furumoto & Scarborough, 1986; Milar, 1999). After receiving her

Ph.D. from the University of Chicago in 1900, Wooley is remembered as a pioneer in the study of sex differences and for her early attempts to explore the consequences of dropping out of school.

Milar (1999) reviewed Wooley's work on a massive longitudinal study of adolescents who remain in school and those who drop out of school to enter the workforce. The consequences of child labor were a major issue in the late nineteenth and early twentieth centuries. The development of child labor laws was a part of the many humanitarian reform movements so prominent at the time psychology was emerging as a new discipline. Wooley served as the director of the Vocation Bureau in the public schools in Cincinnati, Ohio, from 1911 to 1921. In that capacity she worked on numerous problems such as the consequences of dropping out of school and how to best match educational programs with the intellectual and vocational abilities of children.

Because of measurement issues, Wooley's study did not yield clear-cut results and conclusions. Such a disappointing outcome comes as no surprise to those who follow scientific attempts to investigate problems of a much simpler nature (for example, trials on the effects of drugs very often do not yield unequivocal results). Milar (1999) points out, however, that despite the disappointing results of the longitudinal study, Wooley was singled out for praise as a pioneer in childhood education and welfare. Further, "The Vocational Bureau [headed by Wooley] was one of the earliest psychological clinics in a public school and was used to support special education classes of various types and to consult with the juvenile courts" (Milar, 1999, p. 232). Wooley, as a part of the functionalist tradition, helped demonstrate the strengths and limitations of psychology as a means of investigating practical social issues.

Binet and Intelligence Testing

Arguably the measurement of intelligence became the most significant psychological research in terms of its lasting impact on public institutions. Earlier in the chapter, we referred to Galton's work on individual differences and to Cattell's unsuccessful attempts to measure intelligence. Shortly after

1901, the French experimental psychologist, Alfred Binet, declared his intention to measure intelligence by means of special tests. Early in his career, Binet flirted with research on physiognomy, the theory that a person's physical appearance can reveal aspects of character (Collins, 1999). After numerous failures, Binet and his collaborator, Théodore Simon (1873–1961), constructed a scale generally regarded as the first successful intelligence test.

Alfred Binet (1857–1911) is not associated with any of the dominant systems of psychology but, in her biography on Binet, Wolf (1973) argued that "he was in fact completely absorbed by the ideas of the functional viewpoints and terminology, by concerns about the nature of consciousness, and by the need for comparative and developmental studies" (p. 4). As an experimental psychologist, Binet's interests were wide ranging. In addition to work on intelligence, he conducted studies on such topics as hypnosis, attention, creativity, graphology, and eyewitness testimony. He helped found a laboratory for experimental approaches to education and assisted in the founding of the first French journal of psychology, *L' Année Psychologique.*

After considerable trial and error, Binet attempted to measure intelligence in a way that departed from the earlier approaches of Galton and Cattell. According to Wolf (1973), Binet realized that it might be possible to find differences "in complex superior processes rather than in elementary ones" (p. 146). Thus, instead of studying simple reaction times, Binet looked at memory for numbers, ability to solve spatial or conceptual problems, and memory for designs. Test items were directly related to daily tasks. Binet also gathered normative data on types of problems that typical children in various age groups could solve. This approach yielded the first usable intelligence test, published in 1905 and revised in 1908 and again in 1911. The Binet-Simon scales, though ignored and even ridiculed in France, were translated into other languages and hailed as a major achievement (Schneider, 1992).

Wolf (1973, p. 35) quoting Simon, noted that Lewis Terman (1877–1956) purchased the rights to publish the first U.S. version of the Binet-Simon scale for the sum of one dollar. Terman translated the test, made adaptations, and standardized the test on a large group of American children. The first Terman adaptation was published in 1916 and was called the Stanford-Binet Intelligence Scale (the name of the test was based partly on Terman's affiliation with Stanford University). Later editions of the Stanford-Binet were published in 1937 and 1960. Alternatives to the Stanford-Binet test quickly surfaced and often featured special conveniences or applications. For example, in World War I, a paper-and-pencil test designed for group testing and known as the *Army Alpha* was developed by Robert M. Yerkes (1876–1956) and his associates as a means of screening large numbers of service personnel. An alternative, known as the *Army Beta* was designed for illiterate personnel. These tests were used as means of rejecting individuals for service and as an aid in making special assignments. Following the war, a steady growth in the use of intelligence tests led to a proliferation of different tests.

Though many theoretical and practical problems of measuring intelligence were solved early in the century, the social consequences of large-scale testing remained a concern in the latter part of the century. In his book *Even the Rat Was White,* Guthrie (1998) outlined the warnings of African American psychologists about the dangers of mental testing and the pitfalls of cultural biases in tests. In his book *The Mismeasure of Man,* Gould (1981) outlined the history and social consequences of conceiving intelligence as a single thing and of characterizing human beings in terms of an abstract number that serves as a symbol of merit. Numerous additional sources on the history of testing (e.g., Sokal, 1987; DuBois, 1970) are recommended reading.

Walter Dill Scott

Though functionalism created a friendly climate for the development of applied psychology, it is an error to tie the growth of applied interests too closely with one school of thought. Earlier we noted the discrepancy between Wundt's laboratory work and his larger vision of psychology. Perhaps it is no accident that some of Wundt's students became great innovators and leaders in applied psychology. Walter Dill Scott (1869–1955), like some of Wundt's other students, such as Lightner Witmer and James McKeen Cattell, must be counted as one of the pioneers in applied psychology (Landy, 1997).

Scott received his bachelor's degree at Northwestern University in 1895 and his Ph.D. under Wilhelm Wundt in 1900. After completing the doctorate, he returned to Northwestern, where he held a professorial position from 1901 to 1920. He was president of the university from 1920 until his retirement in 1939. He was founder and president of the Scott Company, the first personnel consulting firm, and was elected president of the American Psychological Association in 1919. Among his various honors, Scott received the Distinguished Service Medal for his many contributions to personnel selection and evaluation in World War I. Von Mayrhauser (1989) called attention to the similarities between Binet's and Scott's approaches to intelligence testing and to Scott's crucial role in developing successful group tests.

Strong (1955) argued that Scott "may properly be called the father of applied psychology for no one else applied psychology to such a variety of business problems as he did and at so early a date" (p. 682). If Scott had a favorite topical area in academic psychology, it was undoubtedly motivation, but his interest in theoretical problems in motivation was complemented by an interest in practical motivational problems. Some of his earliest contributions in applied psychology were books and articles on advertising (Kuna, 1976). In an early popular article written for *Atlantic Monthly,* Scott (1904) reviewed the history and growth of advertising and argued that there was a significant role for psychologists in this field. He wrote about the roles of mental imagery, motivation, and suggestion in advertising and showed that psychologists, by virtue of their training, have expertise especially relevant to the field. Scott's other applied interests included the psychology of public speaking, the psychology of argument and persuasion, prediction of vocational interests and skills, methods of improving work efficiency, and management techniques.

Walter Dill Scott and Hugo Münsterberg were not alone in expressing enthusiasm for applied psychology. Despite occasional concerns about premature application, well-known scholars filled books and periodicals with suggestions on how psychology might be useful. For example, Royce (1898) pointed out that psychology might be useful to educators in finding ways to combat fatigue, boredom, and poor work habits. Seashore (1911), in a *Popular Science Monthly* article, offered the optimistic opinion that there was a need for consulting psychologists in a great range of human endeavors, including the arts, science, the professions, and industry. Others wrote on such topics as the value of humor (Kline, 1908), the importance of play and relaxation (Patrick, 1914), and the effects of strong emotions (Cannon, 1922). Psychology, almost from the beginning, had a promising potential that easily captured the attention and imagination of the public.

INFLUENCE OF FUNCTIONALISM: AN EVALUATION

Functionalism grew out of a pluralistic, pragmatic, and radically empirical context and thus, as a philosophical psychology, was more inclined to open doors than to shut them. It entertained a host of interesting problems that affected the daily lives of people: the problems of child rearing, education, aging, the work environment, and emotional disorders. Furthermore, it refused to be restricted by narrow conceptions of the scientific method. Functionalism did not persist as an organized school or system of thought, but its values and vision were incorporated into subsequent schools. Indeed, as we will see in Chapter 13, John B. Watson, the founder of American behaviorism, specifically spoke of the functionalist nature of behaviorism (see Watson, 1913, p. 166).

There are numerous legitimate criticisms of functionalism. One of the more common criticisms is that it seems vague. Indeed, the typical student may read about functionalism and then experience difficulty expressing what the school is all about. A related criticism is that functionalism was eclectic and often inconsistent or even incoherent. The functionalists did not work within a tightly reasoned, rigidly prescriptive system of thought. The resulting looseness and inevitable ambiguities are sources of frustration. Examples abound, but we might illustrate the point by considering the functionalist treatment of freedom and determinism. Many psychologists took clear-cut and unequivocal stands on the issue so that there were no further questions to be asked. James clearly believed in free will, but thought it appropriate that scientists postulate the operation of lawfulness within their investigations. Harvey Carr left his readers with even greater ambiguities than James on the free will and determinism issue. He was perfectly willing to use both positions and to see where they led.

Perhaps one of the appeals of the behaviorist system (which we will review in Chapter 13) is that it was more straightforward. The functionalists were not overly concerned about criticisms regarding their inconsistencies. In the *Principles,* James (1890/1981) argued that absolutism "is the great disease of philosophical thought" (p. 334). He believed that there are genuine ambiguities in the world and that systems that hide or cover up such ambiguities may achieve coherence and consistency, but these are won at the expense of adequacy.

Functionalism was also criticized for ignoring basic problems and focusing instead on applications. It is true that functionalists were interested in applications, but they also valued basic studies. What they rejected was a psychology that focused exclusively on basic science. Their emphasis was on the discovery of facts (basic science) and the understanding of what differences the facts make (applied science). This balance of emphasis quickly became a hallmark of American psychology. In a real sense, much of the mainstream psychology of the late twentieth century can be regarded as functionalist. Some psychologists worked within the tradition of basic science, while others were free to conduct research on practical day-to-day problems. Following the work of William James, G. Stanley Hall, and the Chicago and Columbia functionalists, there was a virtual explosion of interest in applied psychology.

REVIEW QUESTIONS

1. List and briefly describe seven general characteristics of the thought of William James.
2. What advice might James give to someone who wishes to get rid of an undesirable habit?
3. List five characteristics that James found with respect to the so-called stream of thought.
4. What were the constituents of the self, according to William James?
5. Briefly explain James's concept of self-esteem and how self-esteem might be improved.
6. Explain and criticize the James-Lange theory of emotion.
7. What did James mean by the transiency of instincts? Give an example.
8. Distinguish between primary and secondary memory in James's psychology.
9. List five of G. Stanley Hall's major achievements.
10. How did Hall's book *Senescence* anticipate late twentieth-century developments in the psychology and sociology of aging?
11. Outline the essential features of Dewey's arguments in his classic article "The Reflex Arc Concept in Psychology."
12. List three characteristics of functionalism according to James R. Angell.
13. In what way did James McKeen Cattell contribute to the scientific stature and visibility of psychology?
14. Outline three major contributions to psychology made by Robert Sessions Woodworth.
15. What was the variability hypothesis and how did Leta Stetter Hollingworth study it?
16. According to Mary Calkins, how might structuralism and functionalism be reconciled?
17. Discuss three major criticisms of functionalism and explain how a functionalist might respond to each criticism.

CHAPTER 13

BEHAVIORISM

Psychology as the behaviorist views it is a purely objective experimental branch of natural science. Its theoretical goal is the prediction and control of behavior.

—John B. Watson (1913)

Behaviorism started as a system of psychology but has proved to be much more than that. Like evolutionary thought, behaviorism captured the attention of the public and became a favorite subject for lively comment in popular magazines, editorials, books, and sermons. Behaviorism commanded intense loyalties but also stirred harsh polemics by its detractors. Titles such as "Men or Robots?" (McDougall, 1926b), "Does the Behaviorist Have a Mind?" (Johnson, 1927), "Behaviorism and Its Anti-Religious Implications" (Frick, 1928), and "Paradox of the Thinking Behaviorist" (Lovejoy, 1922) betray the concerns of detractors and moralists. On the other hand, enthusiasts were quick to point to the advantages of a more scientific psychology and there were reassurances that behaviorism would not undermine moral and ethical interests. For example, in an article on behaviorism and ethics, Weiss (1928) offered the optimistic opinion that "even the most advanced thinkers on social evolution have [failed] to foresee some of the possibilities of human achievement when scientific mechanism is taken as a fundamental postulate in human behavior" (p. 397).

Understandably, the intellectual ferment generated by behaviorism spilled over into other disciplines such as literature, philosophy, political science, psychiatry, and sociology. Moreover, behaviorism had a sustained influence within some of these disciplines. Indeed, in the late 1980s behaviorism was still a subject heading with a substantial number of entries in the *Philosopher's Index*. It

was also a subject heading, though with fewer entries, in other standard reference sources such as the *Humanities Index* and the *Sociological Abstracts*.

Though behaviorism ultimately revolutionized psychology and attracted widespread attention in other disciplines and in the popular press, its initial reception within psychology was cool or even grudging. The new system was set forth succinctly in a 1913 article by John B. Watson entitled "Psychology as the Behaviorist Views It." Though the article, later called the *behaviorist manifesto,* is now viewed as a pivotal and classic piece in the history of psychology, it was met primarily with criticism by the older conservative psychologists. Samelson (1985) documented the initial cool reception of behaviorism, but, quoting Watson, pointed out that "there was hope. 'The younger students . . . seem to be accepting behaviorism. The public is genuinely interested in it' " (p. 33). Watson made this statement fifteen years after the publication of his manifesto. Within a few more years, behaviorism dominated the American scene and Watson's prominent place in the history of the discipline was secure.

ANTECEDENTS OF BEHAVIORISM

The philosophical antecedents of behaviorism can be traced to the ancient Greek atomic theory set forth by Leucippus and Democritus whereby only the atoms and the void are real. The world, as it appears, is based on the shapes and combinations of atoms. Psychological processes such as sensations and thought are also based on the complex interplay of atoms. Atomic theorists provided the first complete mechanistic and materialistic approach to psychology. Over the centuries, the basic idea was rediscovered, refined, and amplified. The modern philosophical foundation of behaviorism was reinforced by advances in neurophysiology (see Chapter 8).

Wertheimer (1987) pointed out that **behaviorism** is typically viewed as an American school of thought, yet "its predecessors were Europeans rather than Americans" (p. 121). There is much to support such a claim. At every turn, we encounter key ideas in the work of European thinkers that were later assimilated by the U.S. school. We are reminded of materialists such as Condillac, Gassendi, Helvétius, and Hobbes; empiricists and associationists such as Locke and Hartley; and, of course, physician philosophers such as Cabanis and La Mettrie. According to Campbell (1967), the "Bible of all materialism" came from the pen of the German philosopher Paul Heinrich Dietrich d'Holbach (1723–1789). d'Holbach's *System of Nature,* published under the pseudonym *Mirabaud,* set forth a thoroughgoing naturalism containing, according to Campbell (1967), "the first behavioral analysis of mental concepts" (p. 183). Even if d'Holbach's work can be viewed as a first, it is nevertheless the Russians who provided a behavioral approach to mental concepts in terms of actual laboratory work. Their work, especially the research of Ivan Pavlov, is worth detailed consideration.

Ivan Mikhailovich Sechenov

Pavlov's immediate predecessor, Ivan Mikhailovich Sechenov (1829–1905), is commonly regarded as the founder of Russian physiology. Sechenov served as a military engineer in Kiev before embarking on medical studies at the University of Moscow. After completing a medical degree in 1856, Sechenov worked in an intense postgraduate program with such luminaries in physiology as Hermann von Helmholtz, Carl F. W. Ludwig, Johannes Müller, and Emil DuBois-Reymond.

During this period, Sechenov found inspiration in the evolutionary thought of Herbert Spencer and Charles Darwin.

Sechenov's academic work in Russia started with a ten-year appointment at St. Petersburg. This appointment ended abruptly when Sechenov resigned in disgust when the university failed to hire Ilya I. Mecnikov because he was a Jew. Sechenov returned to St. Petersburg after serving at the University of Odessa. His final academic appointment was at the University of Moscow.

Esper (1964) argued that Sechenov "wrote the first 'objective psychology' and became the first 'behaviorist' of modern times" (p. 324). The claim that Sechenov was a precursor of behaviorism is justified partly by his contention "that the psychical activity of man finds expression in external signs" (Frolov, 1938, p. 5). Sechenov argued for an objective psychology based on natural science in an 1863 essay entitled *Reflexes of the Brain.* Brožek (1972) pointed out that "*Reflexes of the Brain* is the work of a young man who had just returned from postgraduate studies abroad. How modern, how daring must have appeared, in 1863, 'an attempt to establish the physiological basis of psychological processes'!" (p. 18). Daring indeed—according to Frolov (1938), the government "imposed a prolonged ban on his book" (p. 4). Brožek (1972) reminded us that while *Reflexes* anticipated the physiological approach to psychological processes, it did not "influence the development of the scientific study of behavior in the west" (p. 19). Indeed, *Reflexes of the Brain* was not published in English until 1965 and few English-speaking psychologists read the Russian edition.

Sechenov's psychological system relied on the philosophical assumption of materialistic monism. Sechenov, as quoted by Frolov (1938), noted that "the new psychology will have as its basis, in place of the philosophizings whispered by the deceitful voice of consciousness, positive facts or points of departure that can be verified at any time by experiment" (p. 6). The positive facts consist of observable movements or events that are measurable. In the final analysis, psychological and cerebral events are reducible to muscular movements.

The fundamental unit of study, according to Sechenov, is the reflex consisting of three parts: afferent activity, central connective processes, and efferent activity. Even so-called voluntary movements are best regarded as complicated reflex chains (see Kimble, 1996). This basic idea was more attractive following the conditioning experiments performed later by Pavlov. For Sechenov, the idea was advanced as a theoretical point of departure.

On the methodological side, Sechenov argued for a scientific approach to psychology based on the methods of physiology. His article, "Who Must Investigate the Problems of Psychology and How?" stresses that physiological methods provide the most promise for understanding psychological phenomena.

In summarizing Sechenov's psychological system, Razran (1968) emphasized "a radical environmentalism: the largest part of thoughts and ideas, 999 parts out of a 1000, as Sechenov would have it, derives from training, and only a minimal part is due to heredity" (p. 130). Such radical environmentalism would hold great appeal later in the Soviet system. American behaviorism under the leadership of John B. Watson would also stress the importance of the environment.

Ivan Pavlov

Ivan Petrovich Pavlov, born in Ryazan, Russia, on September 14, 1849, was the first of eleven children of Piotr Dmitrievich Pavlov and Varvara Ivanova. Pavlov's father was a poorly paid village priest who found it necessary to cultivate large vegetable gardens to feed his family. The Pavlov family had more than its share of difficulty and sadness. Of the eleven children, six did not survive childhood and the youngest son, Sergei, died of typhus during the revolution of 1917. Young Ivan sustained a severe head injury, delaying formal schooling until he was eleven years old. Fortunately, Pavlov's father, a lover of books, took a keen interest in the boy's education, so the injury was not as detrimental as it might have been.

In his autobiography, Pavlov (1955) stated that he received his "secondary education at the local theological seminary, which I recall with gratitude" (p. 41). His gratitude was based on the liberal atmosphere that characterized the seminary at that time. A student who did not excel in one subject was encouraged in other subjects. The seminary was a stimulating environment that encouraged a vigorous exchange of ideas, permitting students to discover their unique talents. Early in his career, Pavlov developed a love of argument—a passion that remained throughout his life. Influenced by Darwin and other Western scientists, Pavlov abandoned his plans for the priesthood and dedicated himself to science (Windholz, 1997).

In 1870, Pavlov entered St. Petersburg University, where he pursued a degree in the natural sciences. After completing the degree in 1875, he enrolled in the Medico-Chirurgical Academy. In his autobiography, he pointed out that he enrolled in the academy "not for the purpose of becoming a physician, but with the idea that after getting the degree of doctor of medicine, I would qualify for a chair in physiology" (Pavlov, 1955, p. 42). Pavlov's doctoral thesis was a study of the role of cardiac nerves in circulation. His medical degree was granted on December 19, 1879. He also won a gold medal and a scholarship for postgraduate studies.

In 1881, Pavlov married Serafina (Sara) Vassilievna Karchevskaya. Their first nine years of marriage were marred by poverty and the death of two children. The first child was lost in a miscarriage and the second died from a childhood disease. In the early years of marriage, Pavlov was in charge of S. P. Botkin's experimental laboratory at St. Petersburg. The laboratory afforded opportunities for Pavlov's early work in digestion that would later earn him a Nobel prize. Unfortunately, the pay was meager. The difficulties for Pavlov's wife were compounded during a two-year period (1885–1886) when postgraduate studies took Pavlov out of the country.

Not until 1890 did circumstances improve for the Pavlovs. At that time, Ivan was appointed chair of pharmacology at the Military-Medical Academy. Five years later, he was appointed chair of physiology. Pavlov could now devote himself unreservedly to science without the financial worries that had earlier plagued his life and work.

In 1904, Pavlov won the Nobel prize for his work on digestion, but even in his acceptance speech he referred to the work on conditioning that would dominate his scientific work. Indeed, Babkin (1949) pointed out that "the last thirty-four years of his life (from 1902 until 1936) Pavlov devoted almost exclusively to the study of the functions of the cerebral cortex by the method of conditioned reflexes" (p. 273).

Pavlov's popularity soared beyond his native Russia as he became one of the most revered figures in science. Despite his international reputation, Pavlov seemed cursed with financial woes. He had deposited the monetary award of his Nobel prize into a St. Petersburg bank only to see it liquidated by the Bolsheviks after the 1917 Revolution. He lost the entire sum of 73,000 gold rubles. Little wonder that Pavlov condemned the Revolution as the "greatest misfortune sustained by Russia" (Babkin, 1949, p. 161). Nonetheless, from Lenin to Stalin, the Soviet regime supported his research with funding and praise. Pavlov was not appeased.

Disenchanted with communism, he flirted with the idea of moving his laboratory to either England or the United States. Recognizing the value of his achievements, the Soviet government denied permission, but allowed a visit to America. In July 1923, he attended a conference in New York City where again financial hardship haunted him. After Pavlov and his son, Vladmir, boarded a train at Grand Central Station, two rough-looking men assaulted the seventy-four-year-old scientist while a third acted as a lookout. Later, Pavlov realized that the men had taken his wallet, stealing perhaps as much as $2,000 in cash (Thomas, 1997).

Undeterred by the experience, Pavlov returned to the United States in 1929 and gave a rousing address before the International Congress of Psychology at Yale University. Pavlov spoke in Russian, then waited impatiently for a translator to relay his words in English. Despite the language barrier, his audience was entranced. Edna Heidbreder, a young historian of psychology in the audience, recalled the animated talk delivered by the eighty-year-old physiologist:

> Pavlov seemed to be speaking with great enthusiasm, and the empathizing audience broke into enthusiastic applause without waiting for the translation. When the translation came the applauded passage

proved to be a description of some apparatus used in Pavlov's laboratory (Heidbreder, quoted in Duncan, 1980, p. 3).

While attending the 1929 Congress, Pavlov toured the facilities at the Yale Primate Center with his host, Robert M. Yerkes, and a group of admiring comparative psychologists. During the visit, a chimpanzee singled out Pavlov and hurled its feces at him. The unflappable scientist glanced at the mortified group and realized he was the only one with facial hair. Turning to Yerkes, Pavlov asked, "How did you condition the chimpanzee only to throw at people with beards?" (Hothersall, 1995, p. 484).

With the exception of a brief illness with gallstones in 1927, Pavlov remained vigorous and in good health until the spring of 1935, when he suffered from grippe complicated by pneumonia. The eighty-five-year-old man, severely weakened, had recurring bouts with flulike symptoms until his death on February 26, 1936.

Pavlov's biographers emphasized his fierce integrity, abundant energy, dedication to facts, and complete devotion to science. His dedication to science was so intense that he was often inept when it came to practical matters. Sara managed the money, bought Pavlov's clothes, and, in general, tended to all family matters (Babkin, 1949). The difficulty of Sara's task was compounded not

Ivan Pavlov

only by her impractical scientist-husband but by the four children born to the couple after the loss of the first two.

Gantt (1928) illustrated Pavlov's complete devotion to science with a story of an assistant who arrived late for work one morning during the revolution. Confronted by Pavlov for his tardiness, the assistant complained about fighting in the streets and his difficulty getting to work. Pavlov's reply was, "What difference does a revolution make when you have work in the laboratory to do!" (p. 25). Pavlov could be short tempered and demanding. Babkin (1949) admitted that "If he had been an ordinary man, he would be considered an egotist, for whom personal interests were of such paramount importance that everyone and everything had to serve them" (pp. 52–53). But then, Babkin added, Pavlov's "interests were not his personal interests in the strict sense of the word but lay outside him, so to speak" (p. 53). He was driven by a faith amply summed up in his classic *Lectures on Conditioned Reflexes:* "Only science, exact science about human nature itself, and the most sincere approach to it by the aid of the omnipotent scientific method, will deliver man from his present gloom, and will purge him from his contemporary shame in the sphere of interhuman relationships" (Pavlov, 1928, p. 41).

Pavlov's Psychological Work.   Pavlov's work on the gastric and salivary glands resulted in unexpected observations that led to work on "higher nervous activity." Pavlov and his colleagues measured the amount and quality of salivary and gastric secretion in relation to the nature of stimulus materials placed in a dog's mouth. Early, there was evidence that secretions are "intelligent" in the sense that their amount and quality are dependent on the nature of stimulus materials. Thus, edible materials stimulate thick and viscous saliva while materials high in acid or salt may result in a more watery fluid. The fundamental fact, in Pavlov's words, was that "the kind of substances getting into the digestive canal from the external world, i.e., whether edible or inedible, dry or liquid, as well as the different food substances, determined the onset of the work of the digestive glands, the peculiarities of their functioning in each case, the

amount of reagents produced by them and their composition" (Pavlov, 1955, p. 131).

Pavlov observed another way in which salivary activity is "intelligent." In his Nobel speech, Pavlov (1955) pointed out that "it has long been known that the sight of tasty food makes the mouth of a hungry man water" (p. 139). He noted that though such an observation is commonplace, its implications and mechanisms had never been investigated. Pavlov and his colleagues repeatedly observed, after several trials, that dogs salivated at the mere sight of the food object being used in the gastric experiments. Furthermore, objects (e.g., containers, noises) associated with the food objects also produced salivation. Salivation produced in early trials, as a result of the direct action of the food, is clearly understandable in terms of classic reflex theory. That is, food has a direct action on the receptor system and the response is understandable in terms of material and efficient causes. But salivation at the mere sight of the food or at the sight or sound of a stimulus associated with the food is a different matter. Pavlov referred to such salivation as **action at a distance** and in his early work also referred to it as a **psychical reflex.** Later, these terms were replaced with more exact terminology.

The concept of *action at a distance* was troublesome for Pavlov in the fields of physiology and psychology just as the same term had been troublesome for other scientists such as Descartes and Newton in physics. The issue in physics centered on the action of magnets, gases, gravitational fields, and the transmission of light. How could such actions be explained in terms of direct action or efficient causes? (See Hess, 1967, pp. 9–15 for a brief but helpful discussion of the problem.) Action at a distance, at least from a superficial standpoint, appeared to challenge material and efficient causality, so central to science as Pavlov conceived it. Specifically, what was it that stimulated the salivary glands when the animal salivated at the mere sight of the food? The expression *psychical reflex* really didn't explain anything; it provided only a name for an observed relationship. Pavlov wanted to know the mechanism responsible for the so-called psychical reflex.

Pavlov's analysis led him to conclude that he was dealing with two kinds of reflexes. The first, the physiological reflex, he regarded as unconditioned. An external stimulus (food) acts directly on the organism by stimulating different nerves, which act on the effectors through connecting nerves. The simple reflex is understandable in terms of material and efficient causation. The second reflex also has its origin in external stimuli, but these activate the eye, ear, or nose (etc.) rather than the receptors in the oral cavity. Pavlov (1955) observed that the new reflex "is permanently subject to fluctuation, and is, therefore, *conditioned*" (p. 144). Pavlov argued that conditioned reflexes, like the unconditioned reflexes, "can be easily conceived from the physiological point of view as a function of the nervous system" (p. 145). The task was then to discover the functional relations between the two types of reflexes.

Pavlov (1928, p. 156) observed that "nervous activity consists in general of the phenomena of excitation and inhibition" and argued that either phenomenon can spread, or irradiate, over the cortex. Such irradiation provides a conceptual basis for connections between stimulus events from various sensory modalities. Thus, through the spread of nervous activity over the cortex, visual, auditory, or other signals may be associated with the unconditioned reflex.

In time, Pavlov's basic paradigm was elaborated in terms of an **unconditioned stimulus (UCS)** that reliably produces an **unconditioned reflex (UCR).** The unconditioned stimulus is a biologically adequate stimulus that has the capacity automatically to induce the reflex activity that terminates with the unconditioned reflex. The unconditioned, or unlearned, reflex has a high degree of automaticity. The **conditioned stimulus (CS)** was at one time a neutral stimulus, but after repeated pairings with the UCS, the CS produces a reflex similar to the UCR, **the conditional reflex (CR).**

The temporal relations between the UCS and the CS resulted in some findings that surprised Pavlov and his coworkers. They discovered that conditioning was optimal when the CS just precedes the UCS by a fraction of a second (see Figure 13.1 A). This arrangement of the CS and the UCS is called *delayed conditioning.* Another temporal arrangement, much less efficient than delayed conditioning, is called *simultaneous conditioning*

(Figure 13.1 C). The most interesting discovery regarding the relationship of the CS and the UCS is called *trace conditioning.* In this arrangement, the CS and the UCS are initially paired, as in Figure 13.1 A, but then the temporal interval between the two is increased so that the CS occurs prior to the UCS and is terminated before the UCS occurs (Figure 13.1 B). As the temporal interval between termination of the CS and the onset of the UCS increased, Pavlov's dogs sometimes became drowsy or even fell asleep. Pavlov argued that the CS may be associated with local cortical inhibition and that, in the absence of the excitatory UCS, the inhibition associated with the CS may irradiate over the surface of the cortex. Sleep was explained as the result of the spread of inhibition.

Pavlov also conducted pioneering work on other topics that inspired learning research in the twentieth century. Some of the key areas are **extinction, spontaneous recovery, disinhibition, stimulus generalization,** and **discrimination.**

Extinction. When the CS is presented repeatedly in the absence of the UCS, Pavlov found that the CS loses its ability to produce salivary activity.

Spontaneous recovery. As just mentioned, the CS loses its ability to produce the CR if it is presented repeatedly in the absence of the UCS. But, following a period of rest, the CS may again elicit the CR; Pavlov called this phenomenon spontaneous recovery. The CR, however, is quickly extinguished if the CS is again presented several times without the UCS.

Disinhibition. An animal that has stopped salivating in the presence of the CS may salivate in the presence of a different sudden or unexpected stimulus. Pavlov assumed that the CS is associated with inhibition. An unexpected stimulus may release the inhibition and the animal will then salivate.

Stimulus generalization. Stimuli similar to the original CS may also elicit the CR. Thus, if the original stimulus is a bell of a given pitch, then a bell of a similar pitch may also elicit the CR.

Discrimination. Pavlov observed that discriminations, sometimes even remarkably fine ones, can be

Type of Conditioning   **Temporal Relation of CS and UCS**

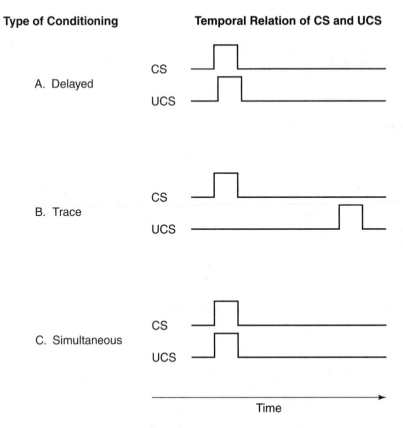

FIGURE 13.1   *Temporal Relations between the CS and the UCS in Classical Conditioning*

conditioned. Thus, a circular shape may be reliably associated with food (the UCS) while an ellipse may never be associated with the UCS. The dog soon learns to salivate to a circle, but not to an ellipse. If the ellipse is gradually changed so that it looks more and more like the circle, the discrimination becomes difficult. Such a procedure tests the discriminatory capacity of the animal. It also serves as a major frustration, especially if it is important to make the discrimination, as it may well be for a hungry dog. The behavior of the dog in difficult discrimination tasks became a major curiosity for Pavlov and contributed to his interest in the problems of psychiatry (Wolpe & Plaud, 1997). Before turning to this topic, it is important to examine another dimension of his theory.

Temperament.   As noted earlier, Pavlov believed in two fundamental processes in the nervous system: inhibition and excitation. Both were distributed differently in different temperaments. He observed that some dogs, like the terrier types, are nervous, easily excitable, quick, short tempered, and very alert. Pavlov believed that such dogs have more excitation than inhibition. By contrast, other dogs are timid, hesitant, and shy. He believed that such dogs (perhaps the collie) are dominated more by inhibition than excitation. Other dogs are warm, friendly, and affable. They represent a balanced temperament marked by an even mix of inhibition and excitation.

Pavlov believed that Galen's classification of temperaments are true for both humans and dogs.

Pavlov's version of Galen's scheme is illustrated in Table 13.1.

In accepting the idea of temperamental differences, Pavlov departed from the radical environmentalism of Sechenov. Pavlov's laboratory work led to the conclusion that temperamental differences interact with learning processes. More importantly, temperamental differences dictate how a dog will respond to laboratory-induced stress caused from difficult discrimination problems.

Experimental Neurosis. Beginning in the 1920s until his death, Pavlov's interests shifted to clinical problems (Windholz, 1990). Pavlov (1941) found that almost any assault on the nervous system might produce discernible consequences. Severe conflict, coupled with a rundown physical condition caused by periods of long work, lack of sleep, or physical illness, had an especially powerful effect. Resistance to stress was clearly a function of general health and temperament. Some dogs were naturally more resistant to stress than others.

Pavlov found that severe stress-producing situations resulted in what he called ultraboundary or **ultramaximal inhibition.** The effects of such inhibition can be thought of as somewhat comparable to the effects of shock, which may also result from a severe biological insult. Just after a severe crash or a severe and life-threatening explosion, an individual may show shocklike symptoms. Such symptoms may be marked by a vacant stare, unresponsiveness, or stereotyped responding. Pavlov believed that a powerful assault on the nervous system may convulse the brain in inhibition. If the entire cortex is in an inhibitory mode, then one could expect that the organism would be unresponsive. In the face of overwhelming threat, inhibition can be protective, at least in the sense that it may block the input of still more threatening stimulation.

Laboratory studies revealed three different after effects of ultramaximal inhibition. First, some animals display the **equivalent phase,** whereby the dog responds with the same amount of saliva regardless of the strength of a stimulus. Sargant (1957) pointed out that "the observation is comparable to the frequent reports by normal people in periods of intense fatigue, that there is little difference between their emotional reactions to important or trivial experiences" (p. 64).

Following a more profound biological or psychological insult, the dog may display the **paradoxical phase.** In this phase, a strong stimulus produces a weak response (very little saliva) and a weak stimulus produces a strong response (much saliva). The paradoxical phase has counterparts in humans in stress situations. A whisper may produce an explosive outburst, whereas a shout may result in little more than an eyeblink. The paradoxical phase makes sense in terms of Pavlov's notion of ultramaximal inhibition. Perhaps there are circumstances in which a weak stimulus gets through the inhibitory barrier and is fully processed, while a strong stimulus does not get fully processed. If such were the case, then one might predict a weak response to a strong stimulus and a strong response to a weak stimulus.

Pavlov had the most interest in the **ultraparadoxical phase.** Following severe trauma, Pavlov observed a radical shift in the personality of the dog and its response system. In this phase, stimuli that previously produced a positive response now produced a negative response and vice versa. Sargant (1957) observed that in this phase the dog may "attach itself to a laboratory attendant whom it had previously disliked, and try to attack the master whom it has previously loved" (p. 65). The ultraparadoxical phase is all the more interesting in that its effects may be longlasting. In his book,

TABLE 13.1 *Galen's Classification of Temperaments*

Temperamental Type	General Characteristics
Choleric	Excitable, touchy, quick tempered; marked by excess of excitation
Sanguine	Marked by warmth, balance of excitation and inhibition
Phlegmatic	Not easily excited, also balanced between excitation and inhibition
Melancholic	Tendency toward depressed moods, excess of inhibition

Battle for the Mind, Sargant (1957) showed how the ultraparadoxical phase may explain political and religious conversions, especially when such conversions follow an intense assault on the nervous system. Such an assault, at the human level, may include threats of damnation or death given in an atmosphere in which individual adequacy and judgment have already been undermined.

Pavlov became more and more concerned that inhibition and excitation interact with temperament to produce a variety of psychiatric illnesses. He believed that choleric (predominantly excitatory) and melancholic (predominantly inhibitory) individuals are more vulnerable to breakdown, whereas sanguine and phlegmatic (balanced types) were more resistant to stress. However, any individual, subjected to sufficient stress, would likely break down. Pavlov's work in this area had a major impact on the field of neuroscience (Gray, 1999; Grimsley & Windholz, 2000; Pickenhain, 1999) as well as the development of behavioral therapy in Russia and abroad (Sukhodolsky, Tsytsarev, & Kassinove, 1995; Wolpe & Plaud, 1997).

Problem Solving.   In his final years, Pavlov became increasingly interested in the nature of problem solving. The Gestalt psychologist Wolfgang Köhler (see Chapter 15) had argued that higher primates do not solve problems in a mechanical stimulus–response fashion. Rather, in open situations, such as field settings, primates show evidence of true insight achieved not through mechanical means but through creative, novel, and flexible response modes. Such a wholistic approach to problem solving represented a direct challenge to Pavlov's mechanistic and reductionistic system. As a consequence of Köhler's work, Pavlov initiated research on chimpanzees from 1933 to 1936 (see Windholz, 1984). Pavlov replicated some of Köhler's experiments but offered his own explanations in terms of the mechanics of conditioning and trial and error.

Pavlov's conflict with the Gestalt psychologists was illustrated in polemical comments that came out of his Wednesday meetings with staff and colleagues. Pavlov's respect for and concern about Köhler's work is evident in a lecture from January 23, 1935:

Now gentlemen, we shall pass from peaceful affairs, if we may say so, to matters of war, to Mr. Köhler. We are at war with him. This is a serious struggle against psychologists. Köhler is professor of psychology at Berlin University. A scientist of minor authority would hardly be elected to a chair in Berlin University; they respect hierarchy there. (Pavlov, 1955, p. 606)

Such a statement reflects Pavlov's tight systematic worldview and his sensitivity to storm clouds on the horizon that threatened that view. The tension between Pavlov's mechanistic view and Köhler's wholistic view would dominate the intellectual agenda in psychology for years to come.

In his autobiography, Pavlov relished the happiness and success he found in science. "I devoted myself to the laboratory. I have renounced practicality in life with its cunning and not always irreproachable ways, and I see no reason for regretting this; on the contrary, precisely in this I find now certain consolation" (Pavlov, 1955, p. 44). Pavlov did not live to witness the enormous influence of his system, but the later success of his work and its extensive heuristic value would doubtless have been a source of even greater satisfaction.

Other Russian Psychologies

There was not unified viewpoint on psychology in Russia until well after the Marxist-Leninist revolution of 1917. Prior to that time, several competing schools of thought emerged with at least two belonging to the intellectual tradition that shaped behaviorism.

Reflexology.   Vladimir Mikhailovich Bekhterev (1857–1927), a contemporary of Pavlov, advanced an objective psychology based on the idea that the reflex is the fundamental category of inquiry. Bekhterev received his medical degree from the Medical and Surgical Academy of St. Petersburg in 1881. He also did postdoctoral work with Charcot, Paul Emil Flechsig, and Wundt before embarking on his own career in psychiatry and neurology.

Many of Bekhterev's contributions to psychology are set forth in his three-volume *Objective Psychology,* published from 1907 to 1910, and *General Principles of Human Reflexology,* published in 1917. Instead of working with salivation as a conditioned response, Bekhterev focused on more molar responses. His pioneering work on (an aversive) UCS (shock) helped establish the experimental paradigm for later work on escape and avoidance learning. Bekhterev also extended his **reflexology** to collective or group behavior.

He helped establish the Bekhterev Psychoneural Institute, a research center dedicated to pedagogy, law, criminology, medicine, and experimental psychology (Zhuravel, 1995). In later years, he reconciled his reflexology with Marxist-Leninist thought, but as noted by Misiak and Sexton (1966), Bekhterev's system "gradually lost favor because of the ideological struggle in the Soviet Union for a more dialectical psychology" (p. 267).

A more sinister factor may have caused disfavor with the Soviet government. Bekhterev examined Joseph Stalin and later described the Communist dictator as a "paranoiac with a withered arm." Never popular with the Bolsheviks, Bekhterev found himself in the center of controversy. In 1927, he attended a convention of the All-Union Congress of Neurologists and Psychiatrists in Moscow where he died suddenly after attending the theater with his wife. Only his skull was offered for autopsy. His body was hastily cremated. The circumstances of his untimely death remain a mystery, prompting conspiracy theorists to suggest that Bekhterev's careless remarks about Stalin may have cost him his life (Shereshevskii, 1994).

Reactology. Konstantin Nikolaevich Kornilov (1879–1957) worked valiantly to articulate a psychological system that complemented the larger Marxist-Leninist political vision. Educated at Moscow University, Kornilov for a time was one of the most visible figures in Soviet psychology. He served as editor of the journal *Psychology* and wrote systematic books such as *The Study of Man's Reactions or Reactology* (1922) and *Textbook of Psychology from the Standpoint of Dialectical Materialism* (1926).

Kornilov, like Pavlov and Bekhterev, argued for an objective psychology, but rejected the reflex as the fundamental unit of analysis. Indeed, he emphasized voluntary behavior in social context.

Kornilov's theory of **reactology** stressed the importance of social and economic forces in shaping human reactions. In his treatment, psychology was not just a natural science; it was also a social science, and the behavior of the whole person in social context was emphasized.

Misiak and Sexton (1966) pointed out that Kornilov's system was discredited "soon after the publication of Lenin's *Philosophical Notebooks* (1929–1930), which claimed that man was active not simply reactive" (p. 271). Psychology was not alone in its search for a system consistent with Marxist-Leninist thought. The same search took place in other disciplines such as physics and biology. (For an excellent discussion of Russian science and ideology, see Joravsky, 1989.)

Edward Lee Thorndike

In the United States, the work of Edward Lee Thorndike (1874–1949) can also be regarded as an important antecedent of behaviorism. Thorndike was educated in the functionalist tradition and remained sympathetic to the tolerant spirit and openness of functionalism. Nevertheless, his personal preference was for an objective psychology that focuses on the observable actions of living organisms. Thorndike was often critical of the method of introspection and the study of people's minds (or inner states) as the appropriate subject matter for psychology. He believed that anything that exists, exists in some amount, and is thus quantifiable. He believed in the methods of the other sciences and vigorously applied those methods to such a host of problems that he has been referred to as "America's most productive psychologist" (Jonçich, 1968). From a broad philosophical standpoint, Thorndike can be considered a functionalist, but his practical work can be viewed as a precursor to behaviorism.

Thorndike was the second of the four children of Edward Roberts Thorndike and Abibie Brewster Ladd. Edward abandoned law in favor of the Methodist ministry. The atmosphere of the Thorndike home was austere and serious, with emphasis on duty, industry, independence, discipline, honesty, and propriety. Many of the values of Thorndike's home were put to productive use in his adult

Edward Lee Thorndike

years. Thorndike appropriated a moral code of his own that was more liberal than his family's, at least in matters of religion.

Thorndike entered Wesleyan University in Middletown, Connecticut, in 1891 and graduated from that institution in 1895. Later, he received a master's degree in psychology from Harvard, where he developed a strong friendship with William James. Following his work at Harvard, Thorndike enrolled in the graduate program at Columbia, where he studied with James McKeen Cattell. He graduated with the Ph.D. from Columbia in 1898. After holding a brief faculty position at Western Reserve University, he accepted an appointment at Columbia, where he remained until his retirement in 1941. During his long and productive career, Thorndike was president of the American Psychological Association in 1912, was elected to the National Academy of Sciences, and won a gold medal award from Columbia for his distinguished research contributions to education. Thorndike died in Montrose, New York, on August 9, 1949.

Thorndike's Work. Thorndike's contributions ranged over a variety of problems in psychology and education (Hilgard, 1996). He was a pioneer in the experimental study of animal behavior and advanced one of the earliest theories of learning.

Many of the details of Thorndike's theory of learning grew out of his laboratory research. The theory is best understood in the context of Thorndike's view of human nature.

Though Thorndike had one foot in the camp of associationists and empiricists such as David Hartley and John Locke, the other foot was planted firmly in the camp of Francis Galton, who emphasized the importance of heredity in human life. Thorndike did not believe that all knowledge can be transmitted to all human beings by simple social engineering of rewards and punishments. His own research convinced him that heredity plays a powerful role in human life. He compared identical twins on various tasks (see Thorndike, 1905) and was struck by the similarities in their performance. He also observed that correlations between identical twins were greater than correlations between siblings. Jonçich (1968) noted that Thorndike believed in individual differences, but "Thorndike's individual is already armed, well or poorly, by . . . genes" (p. 333). The role of learning is extremely important to the individual and to society, but learning alone will not achieve all things. In Thorndike's view, genetic principles are even more important than learning and must not be neglected.

As noted, Thorndike's views on learning grew out of his early laboratory studies (Chance, 1999). His doctoral dissertation at Columbia was based on his work with cats and was published in 1898 under the title *Animal Intelligence.* In his dissertation, Thorndike rejected earlier anecdotal and anthropomorphic work on animal study in favor of groundbreaking methods that remain the basis for comparative psychology more than a century later (Galef, 1998). This work, now a classic in the psychology of learning, set forth the basics of a theory of learning known as **connectionism.**

Thorndike conducted extensive studies on the behavior of cats confined in simple "puzzle boxes." In a confined space, a cat immediately engages in escape behaviors that initially appear to be of a random or trial-and-error variety. At some point, the cat activates a latch or a key in an appropriate way and escapes. The desirable consequence of the cat's own behavior is slowly associated with a highly specific series of movements. In time, irrelevant movements drop out and the correct set of movements produces the desired set of consequences.

Thorndike emphasized the connections or bonds between sense impressions and response patterns. Learning, in his view, involved the strengthening of these bonds or connections, which he believed were ultimately grounded in physiology. This was one of the earliest and most influential of the stimulus–response or S-R psychologies. In his theory, Thorndike formulated the **law of exercise,** which states that connections are strengthened through repetition or use and weakened through disuse. He believed that connections are also strengthened or weakened as a result of their consequences. He referred to the consequences of actions as the **law of effect.** In its early expression, the law of effect asserted that a connection is strengthened when it is followed by a "satisfying" state of affairs and weakened when it is followed by an "annoying" state of affairs. Thus, reward or reinforcement strengthens a connection and punishment weakens it. These two principal laws laid the foundation, in part, for Thorndike's system of behavior analysis (Donahoe, 1999). Thorndike also recognized the importance of factors such as maturation or readiness to respond, the ability to generalize, and mental set or attitude.

In the early 1930s, Thorndike modified both the law of exercise and the law of effect. He became convinced that exercise by itself (as mere blind repetition) does not strengthen a connection. Rather, it is exercise in conjunction with other conditions that strengthens connections. For example, if each repetition of a response is accompanied by information about whether the response is more or less accurate, then a connection might be strengthened. The modified law of effect, sometimes called the **truncated law of effect,** casts doubt on punishment as a means of weakening connections. Thus, the truncated law of effect simply holds that responses that are followed by a satisfying state of affairs will be strengthened. Thorndike's doubts about the efficacy of punishment were based on research in which subjects matched one of five English words with a Spanish equivalent. When subjects chose correctly, the experimenter rewarded them by saying *Right.* When

subjects chose incorrectly, the experimenter employed punishment by saying *Wrong.* It was found that punished connections did not tend to drop out, but rewarded connections tended to be retained. Thorndike explored the efficacy of punishment in other ways and concluded that it was not an effective means of weakening connections.

Some of Thorndike's most visible research was carried out in collaboration with Robert S. Woodworth on the subject of transfer of training. Conventional wisdom held that knowledge of certain academic subjects improved intellectual ability in general. For example, the study of Latin was thought to enhance logic and reasoning skills over and above the specific advantages of knowing the ancient language in its own right. The idea that certain subjects held such special beneficial effects on the mind was called the **doctrine of formal discipline.** This doctrine assumes that the mind is somewhat like a muscle and that certain exercises can strengthen the "mental muscle."

The opposite view does not deny the importance of the exercise of intellectual functions, but holds that the transfer of abilities is more specific than assumed by the doctrine of formal discipline. This opposite view, sometimes called the **identical elements transfer theory,** emphasizes the degree of identity between the first and second tasks. Thorndike and Woodworth (1901) demonstrated that the amount of transfer is a function of the similarities between two tasks. Transfer is sometimes surprisingly small even when the tasks are fairly similar. For example, improvements in the accuracy of judgments of line lengths of .5 to 1.5 inches did not result in better subsequent judgments of line lengths of 6 to 12 inches.

Working with simple perceptual problems, Thorndike and Woodworth supported the identical elements transfer theory, but there were still concerns that subjects such as Latin and geometry might have general transfer values in the real world. Thus, a series of studies was conducted on the transfer effects of specific subjects studied in high school. Thorndike (1924), over 20 years after his early work with Woodworth, conducted a classic study on the transfer effects of specific high school courses. Using 8,564 high school students as subjects, Thorndike investigated the relative effects of a great variety of courses (e.g., algebra, physics, psychology, Latin, French, biology, etc.) on subsequent problem-solving ability. There were surprisingly small transfer effects of the various subjects on later problem-solving ability. A very significant finding, however, was that students in the upper levels of ability at the beginning of the study gained far more than students who entered the study with lower levels of ability. The work of Thorndike had far-reaching implications for educational planning.

The emphasis following the work of Thorndike was on the relationship between the content of a subject in school and the demands of daily life. The new educational rule was simple and practical: If you want to know English, study English; if you want to know algebra, study algebra; and so forth. Studies in the transfer of training remain an important area in the psychology of learning.

Thorndike's Other Interests.   As noted at the outset, Thorndike had interests in a host of topics in psychology and education. His publications on the psychology of labor (Thorndike, 1922) and the psychology of the profit motive (Thorndike, 1936) are important early contributions to industrial psychology. On the subject of labor, Thorndike argued that work is not necessarily aversive and encouraged research on worker satisfaction and dissatisfaction. He was deeply interested in ways to humanize capitalism. He believed in values from the profit motive but also social problems associated with the profit motive that psychology might address.

Another area of interest for Thorndike, perhaps stemming from his early religious background, was the meaning of education in a scientific and technological age. Thorndike (1920) expressed concern that the twentieth century held such widespread belief in magic, so much dogmatism, and so many beliefs guided by emotion rather than intellect. His concern was based on his conviction that our great task is to improve quality of life. This belief fueled his mature work on the effects of social context on quality of life. His books, *Human Nature and the Social Order* (1940), *Man and His Works* (1943), and *Your City* (1939), all demonstrate his social psychological interests and

optimism about psychology's role in addressing the problems of daily life. Thorndike was a "sane positivist" who believed that a science of values could be used as a guide for moral assessment, social policy, and the betterment of humanity (Beatty, 1998; Dewsbury, 1998).

Thorndike's work and methodology was singled out for praise by John B. Watson (1878–1958), the founder of American behaviorism. As noted by Jonçich (1968, p. 414), Watson seldom praised the work of others but did admire the way Thorndike conducted his investigations. For his part, Thorndike was friendly to much of Watson's behaviorist program, but in the Jamesian spirit, he worried that behaviorism could become a "restrictive orthodoxy" (see Jonçich, 1968, p. 418).

FORMAL FOUNDING OF AMERICAN BEHAVIORISM

American behaviorism was rooted in the philosophical and scientific soil familiar to the history of ideas in the early twentieth century (O'Neil, 1995). Yet, when the entire systematic vision was set forth by John B. Watson in 1913, it had a fresh, simple, and even revolutionary quality. As with many revolutions, it had a promising dimension and represented a significant break from the dominant psychologies of the day. Part of behaviorism's appeal was that it was set forth in a direct and unambiguous fashion. Watson's message promised a new and better way to do things—a way that offered hope for cutting through vexing complexities of the past.

John B. Watson

Watson's straightforward and unpretentious style is evident in his autobiography, in which he described himself as a lazy and insubordinate youth. He seldom made above a passing grade in grammar and high school and was arrested twice, once for fighting and once for shooting a firearm in the city.

Watson was born in Travelers Rest near Greenville, South Carolina, on January 9, 1878, the last of the four children of Pickens Butler Watson and Emma Roe. Pickens was a handsome man with powerful lusts for hard liquor and women. He ran

John B. Watson

a sawmill in Greenville, but, according to evidence cited by Brewer (1989), devoted weekends to his own pleasures. John's mother was a study in contrast with Pickens. She was very much at home in the conservative atmosphere of Southern Baptist country. Her evangelical efforts apparently influenced an older son, but were lost on Pickens and John B. Watson. Watson was torn by ambivalent feelings toward his mother and father. In many respects, John was like his father, but experienced deeply the consequences of his father's lack of responsibility. According to Buckley (1989), Emma Watson "singled out John Broadus Watson for a special destiny. Emma had named her son after John Albert Broadus, a prominent Baptist minister" (p. 4). Brewer (1989) noted that Emma once extracted a promise from John that he would enter the Baptist ministry. After Emma's death in 1900, however, Watson showed no interest in religion.

In the fall of 1894, Watson enrolled in Furman University. He worked his way through school, improving academically though still not outstanding (Harris, 1999b). In his autobiography he explained why he took five years and graduated with an A.M. instead of taking four years and graduating with an A.B. One of Watson's professors declared that, "if a man ever handed in a paper backwards, he would flunk him" (Watson, 1961,

p. 272). Watson inadvertently handed his paper in backwards and the professor kept his word!

Watson's decision about where to pursue the Ph.D. was made partly on the basis of language requirements. He decided to attend the University of Chicago when he learned that Princeton still required reading knowledge of Greek and Latin. At Chicago, Watson studied with an all-star cast: John Dewey, the neurologist Henry Donaldson, and the well-known physiologist Jacques Loeb. However, James Rowland Angell had the most influence on Watson. Indeed, Angell was a father figure, and some years later Watson discovered the pain of breaking intellectual ties with such a powerful mentor.

Watson developed rigorous work habits at Chicago that stayed his entire life. His work was so intense, however, that it may have contributed to a nervous breakdown in his third year there. He called it "a typical Angst," marked by sleeplessness and fear of the dark. Watson noted that his breakdown caused him "to accept a large part of Freud, when I first began to get really acquainted with him" (Watson, 1961, p. 274). He quickly recovered, completed his dissertation, and graduated magna cum laude in 1903.

After graduation, Watson was appointed as a laboratory assistant at Chicago, a position he held for five years. The year 1903 was pivotal for Watson in another way. A young student named Mary Ickes had fallen in love with her handsome and intellectual laboratory instructor. Watson's salary was hardly adequate to support a family, but emotion triumphed over practical considerations. The marriage was apparently successful for a number of years and brought forth two children, John and Polly.

In 1908, Watson accepted an offer as chair of psychology at Johns Hopkins University. He had already achieved considerable recognition for his research and was viewed as one of the most promising young psychologists in the country. Interestingly, despite his poor salary at Chicago, Watson had a difficult time deciding to leave James Rowland Angell. Watson's point of view in psychology was steadily departing from that of his teacher, so the anxiety of separation had both a physical and an intellectual dimension.

In his early years at Hopkins, Watson developed the essentials of behaviorism. In the classroom, he "taught a modified James type of general psychology" (Watson, 1961, pp. 276–277), but his research focused on animal behavior. In the postdoctorate years, Watson carried on dialogue with other psychologists such as Robert Yerkes, Knight Dunlap, and Karl Lashley about the subject matter of psychology. With these friends, he felt secure in exploring the ideas that later formed the foundations of behaviorism (O'Donnell, 1985). Surprisingly, Watson remained friendly to Freud's work and even proclaimed in 1912 that "I believe thoroughly in the method of psychoanalysis" (cited in Rilling, 2000a, p. 304). Before long, though, his views on Freud would harden, leading him to predict in 1924 that "20 years from now an analyst using Freudian concepts and Freudian terminology will be placed in the same category as a phrenologist" (Watson, 1924a, p. 243).

Inspired by Pavlovian conditioning, Watson designed behaviorism as a new method to compete with Titchener's method of introspection and Freud's method of psychoanalysis (Rilling, 2000b). In 1913, the *Psychological Review* published Watson's classic article, "Psychology as the Behaviorist Views It." It was no easy matter for Watson to publish a paper that attacked the method of introspection and the old view that psychology is the study of consciousness. The reaction of Angell was predictable. Indeed, Cohen (1979) told of a letter from Angell to Titchener in which the former declared, "I shall be glad to see him [Watson] properly spanked even though I cannot join the ceremony" (p. 79). So, five years after Watson joined the Hopkins faculty, the die was cast—the new system was launched.

Watson's work at Hopkins was interrupted by World War I. He was inducted into military service and was soon in charge of aviation examining boards. A major task for such boards was the selection of pilots for World War I fighter planes. He also worked on the use of homing pigeons in delivering military messages. Late in the war he worked on a medical project on oxygen deprivation, but ran into trouble with his supervisors. It was recommended that he be "sent to the line" which conveyed, according to Watson's assessment, a wish on the part of his supervisors that he be killed! Fortunately, the war ended before Watson got to the line. He was back in civilian clothes as fast as possible.

In his autobiography, Watson summed up his whole army experience as a nightmare. "Never have I seen such incompetence, such extravagance, such a group of overbearing, inferior men" (Watson, 1961, p. 278). He claimed that after his army experience he understood how it was that some officers fail to return from missions even when not engaged by enemy troops.

At Johns Hopkins the academic career of the founder of behaviorism would soon be brought to a sudden and dramatic halt. Watson fell hopelessly in love with a new graduate student, Rosalie Rayner. Rosalie came from a distinguished Baltimore family and was a recent graduate of Vassar. Needless to say, the affair between the well-known professor and the daughter of a distinguished local family created a scandal in Baltimore. The event became all the more focal when copies of love letters were discovered and published in the local newspapers. University officials saw no other recourse than to ask Watson to resign his position. So his career in academia came to an abrupt halt in 1920. In 1921, after divorcing his first wife, the forty-two-year-old Watson married Rosalie. Watson was deeply embittered by the loss of his academic position. Apparently, in his view, an affair between consenting adults should not constitute grounds for dismissal, but university officials obviously saw the matter from a different perspective.

In his autobiography, Watson told of the hardships of the first few months after resigning from Hopkins. "I went to New York, stranded economically and to some extent emotionally. I lived the summer and fall out with William I. Thomas. What I should have done without his understanding counsel and his helpfulness on the economic side, I do not know. I was a product of schools and colleges. I knew nothing of life outside the walls of a university" (Watson, 1961, p. 279).

Watson went on to explain that Thomas introduced him to Stanley Resor, president of the J. Walter Thompson Company. Watson was given a temporary assignment to study the rubber boot market. Soon he was ringing doorbells and canvassing to determine preferences for boots. Following this work he was given a permanent position that placed him in charge of Yuban coffee sales and Pond's facial creams. Watson reported that within a year he had "found himself," which means that he was finding it "just as thrilling to watch the growth of a sales curve of a new product as to watch the learning curve of animals or men" (Watson, 1961, p. 280). Watson's behavioristic approach did not signal a revolution in advertising, though he rejected popular catchy slogans in favor of appeals to consumer attitudes about prestige and image (Coon, 1994). By 1924, Watson was vice president of the J. Walter Thompson Company. He was soon a wealthy man whose pioneering contributions to advertising and sales were as noteworthy in the business world as his contributions in psychology were to academia.

Watson and Rosalie Rayner had two children, William and James. Brewer (1989) suggested that the two first names of the boys may have been no accident, because Watson was a great admirer of William James. Though Watson never returned to academia, he continued to write books and articles on psychology (Harris, 1999b). His writings after 1920, however, were increasingly geared for popular consumption. There can be little doubt that the later writings lacked discipline and were too bold in their claims.

In 1936, Rosalie Rayner died of dysentery. Watson, now with the William K. Esty Company, continued with his advertising work until retiring in 1947, but much of the creative spark was gone with Rosalie's death. Watson withdrew more and more, though he attempted to be a good father for Billy and Jimmy, who were teenagers. He also remained in touch with a few colleagues from his days in academia, especially Karl Lashley (Dewsbury, 1993).

In an article looking back over the contributions of the founder of behaviorism, Bergmann (1956) declared that John B. Watson was second only to Freud as "the most important figure in the history of psychological thought during the first half of the century" (p. 265). His contributions were indeed extensive. First, of course, was the systematic objective approach to the discipline. His conceptual approach was also tied to impor-

tant experimental work in comparative psychology, learning, and emotional conditioning in children (Morris & Todd, 1999). This later work had a direct influence on the development of behavior therapy. All of this was accomplished in the relatively short span of Watson's academic career, from 1903 to 1920—a time interrupted by his service in World War I. Watson also influenced the world of advertising and, with his many popular articles, contributed to public awareness of psychology. His remarkable career came to an end when Watson died on September 25, 1958.

Watson's Psychology. In his book *Behaviorism,* Watson (1924a) argued that "behaviorism is new wine and it will not go into old bottles; . . . therefore . . . I am going to ask you to put away all of your old presuppositions" (p. 10). Watson despaired that "literally hundreds of thousands of printed pages have been published on the minute analysis of this intangible something called 'consciousness'" (p. 5). Furthermore, almost all the psychologies of the day—the psychologies of Angell, Dewey, James, Titchener, and Wundt—studied consciousness through the revered method of introspection.

Despite inconsistencies in his own work (see Salzinger, 1994), Watson's criticisms of the subject matter and method of the older psychology were extensive. Some of the strongest criticisms were as follows:

1. *The divisions of consciousness are arbitrary.* In his famous article "Psychology as the Behaviorist Views It," Watson (1913) asked the reader to consider "the question of the number of isolable sensations. Is there an extremely large number of color sensations—or only four, red, green, yellow and blue?" (p. 164). He argued that if we count each just noticeable difference then "we are forced to admit that the number is so large and the conditions for attaining them so complex that the concept of sensation is unusable, either for the purpose of analysis or that of synthesis" (p. 164).

2. *Psychology is too human centered.* Another major criticism of the older psychology was that it had little use for observed facts unless they refer to human consciousness. As a result, animal behavior and comparative psychology were embarrassments. In effect, the old psychology was too human centered; he argued that the same situation had dominated early biology. Watson (1913) pointed out that "the whole Darwinian movement was judged by the bearing it had upon the origin and development of the human race" (p. 162). When the emphasis shifted to the experimental study of adaptation and descent, biology was rescued from its anthropocentrism. By the same token, with behavior as the primary focus of interest, psychology too could be rescued from anthropocentrism.

3. *Introspection is unreliable and esoteric.* Watson (1913) noted that if one person cannot replicate another's results, it is commonly assumed that the introspectionist was not adequately trained. Thus, "the attack is made upon the experimental setting. In physics and chemistry the attack is made upon the experimental conditions. The apparatus was not sensitive enough, impure chemicals were used, etc. In these sciences a better technique will give reproducible results. Psychology is otherwise. If you can't observe 3–9 states of clearness in attention, your introspection is poor. If, on the other hand, a feeling seems reasonably clear to you, your introspection is again faulty. You are seeing too much. Feelings are never clear" (p. 163).

4. *Older psychologies are dualistic.* Watson (1913) pointed out that the older psychologies were typically concerned about the relative merits of parallelism and interactionism. He then declared, "I should like to bring my students up in the same ignorance of such hypotheses as one finds among the students of other branches of science" (p. 166). He believed that if behavior is the subject matter of psychology, then mind–brain positions should be of no greater interest to the psychologist than to the chemist or physicist.

Watson made it clear that his quarrels were with structuralists as well as functionalists. "I have done my best to understand the difference between functional psychology and structural psychology. Instead of clarity, confusion grows upon me. The terms sensation, perception, affection, emotion, volition are used as much by the functionalist as

by the structuralist. The addition of the word 'process' . . . after each serves in some way to remove the corpse of 'content' and to leave 'function' in its stead" (Watson, 1913, p. 165). Both structural and functional psychologies were equally vague. What was required, according to Watson, was a radical break with both. What is the nature of that radical break?

Definition of Psychology. Watson (1924a) argued that "the definition of any one science, physics, for example, would necessarily include the definition of all other sciences" (p. 11). Then we "mark a ring around that part of the whole of natural science that we claim particularly as our own" (p. 11). Just like the physicist, the psychologist studies reactions, adjustments, movements, activities, and behaviors. Watson maintained that psychology is a behavioral science.

Relation to Other Sciences. Watson (1913) declared in the opening of his manifesto that "psychology as the behaviorist views it is a purely objective experimental branch of natural science" (p. 158). In *Behaviorism* (1924a), he pointed out that "its closest scientific companion is physiology. It is different from physiology only in the grouping of its problems, not in fundamentals or in central viewpoint" (p. 11). He also acknowledged the importance of studying behavior in social and cultural context, thus recognizing that psychology is also allied with the social sciences.

Goals of Psychology. As with any other science, the "theoretical goal is the prediction and control of behavior" (Watson, 1913, p. 158). On the practical level, Watson (1924a) pointed to the time when "we will have a behavioristic ethics, experimental in type, which will tell us whether it is advisable from the standpoint of present and future adjustments of the individual to have one wife or many wives; to have capital punishment or punishment of any kind; whether prohibition or no prohibition; easy divorce or no divorces" (p. 7).

Watson believed that such prediction and control was best accomplished though an understanding of the environmental conditions that influence behavior. He was confident that the environment played a critical role in shaping both human and animal behaviors. During a Clark University address, Watson (1926) dramatically expounded on his radical environmentalism with the bold claim

> I should like to go one step further tonight and say, "Give me a dozen healthy infants, well-formed, and my own specified world to bring them up in and I'll guarantee to take any one at random and train him to become any type of specialist I might select—a doctor, lawyer, artist, merchant-chief and, yes, even into beggarman and thief, regardless of his talents, penchants, tendencies, abilities, vocations and race of his ancestors." I am going beyond my facts and I admit it, but so have the advocates of the contrary and they have been doing it for thousands of years. (p. 10)

Methods of the Psychologist.   Unlike the structuralist method of introspection, Watson's behaviorism dovetailed with technoscientific ideals in the United States that stressed the importance of quantification and standardization (Coon, 1993). There was no place for introspection, but Watson did acknowledge a variety of methods consistent with the behaviorist program. Like all sciences, the object is to gather facts, verify them, and subject them to logical and quantitative analysis. Watson recognized the legitimacy of conditioning techniques such as those employed by Pavlov. He also accepted psychological tests so long as they are not called "mental" tests. "To the behaviorist tests mean merely devices for grading and sampling human performance" (Watson, 1924a, p. 35). He approved of a great variety of tests and considered them important assessment tools. Watson also approved technical forms of social experimentation and naturalistic observation. His chapter "How to Study Human Behavior" in *Behaviorism* includes a rather broad methodological agenda. The acid test for methods is that they be truly public and lead to measurable results.

Scope of Psychology.   Watson (1913) pointed out that the behaviorist "recognizes no dividing line between man and brute. The behavior of man, with all of its refinement and complexity, forms only a part of the behaviorist's total scheme of investigation" (p. 158). Psychology, then, according to Wat-

son, has affinities with all the sciences and shares with biologists an interest in all life forms.

Selected Content Areas.   As noted by Samelson (1994), the focus of Watson's research interests shifted across several content areas during the course of his career. Habit and learning were the foundation areas for behaviorism, but other topical areas were also important.

Habit.   The central concept of Watsonian behaviorism was habit. Watson (1924a) declared that at birth there is a stream of unlearned activities, but some of these activities begin to be "conditioned a few hours after birth" (p. 218). Ultimately, personality is to be regarded as a complex system of habits—and this applies to each arena of life. As an example, Watson asked what it means to say that a human being is religious. It may mean that the person goes to church regularly, reads the appropriate religious literature, says grace at meals, and perhaps tries to convert others. "Let us put all of these separate activities together and call them the *religious habit system* of the individual. Now each of these separate activities making up this system has a dating back in the individual's past and a history" (p. 219). Watson went on to show how the child may have been taught to pray, rewarded for memorizing Bible verses and attending church. Watson would not, of course, rule out sudden conditioning, perhaps through fear.

Watson argued that the so-called normal personality is one who has grown up with a certain consistency of conditioning patterns. The person with the normal personality may have been fortunate enough to have been reared in an environment free from excessive punishment and trauma. Weaknesses in personality or even illnesses result from habit conflicts. He quarreled with expressions such as *mental illness* or *mental disturbance.* Watson (1924a) pointed out that in many functional psychopathologies "there are no organic disturbances of sufficient gravity to account for personality disturbance. There may be no infections, no lesions anywhere, no absence of physiological reflexes (as there often is when there are organic diseases). And yet the individual has a sick personality" (p. 244). Watson argued that the expression *mental illness* raises the ghost of interactionism. His preference would be to emphasize the role of conditioning in the acquisition and extinction of personality disturbances. The details of his position in one situation are illustrated in his classic studies on fear conditioning.

Fear Conditioning.   One of the most extensively cited studies in the history of psychology is "Conditioned Emotional Reactions" by Watson and Rosalie Rayner (1920). Harris (1979) pointed out that "this work was the final published project of Watson's academic career, although he supervised a subsequent, related study of the deconditioning of young children's fears" (p. 152). Watson and Rayner conducted experimental work with an infant named Albert B. who had been reared by a wet nurse in a hospital environment. Albert was described by Watson and Rayner (1920) as "healthy from birth and one of the best developed youngsters ever brought to the hospital. . . . He was on the whole stolid and unemotional. His stability was one of the principal reasons for using him as a subject in this test" (p. 1). When he was about nine months of age, Watson and Rayner presented Albert with "a white rat, a rabbit, a dog, a monkey, with masks with and without hair, cotton, wool, burning newspapers, etc." (p. 2). Albert showed no fear of any of these things. Also, at about nine months of age, Albert was tested to determine his reaction to a loud sound created by striking a four-foot-long suspended steel bar with a hammer. The sound characteristics (e.g., decibel level, etc.) were not specified, but sharp blows to the bar did result in a violent reaction, including crying and the usual symptoms of fear.

The stage was then set to determine whether a conditioned emotional response could be established. Watson and Rayner were initially hesitant for ethical reasons, but finally concluded that conditioned emotional responses take place in the world all the time anyway. If such responses were to be understood, they would have to be examined experimentally. So, when Albert was eleven months and three days old, the white rat was presented and, as Albert reached for the rat, the loud noise was sounded. Albert jumped but did not cry. After seven repetitions, Albert displayed a conditioned emo-

tional response to the rat. That is, when the rat was presented alone, Albert began to cry and crawled away. Watson and Rayner also showed that Albert then avoided other objects (e.g., the rabbit, the fur coat, the dog). Though there were many methodological problems (see Harris, 1979) in the Watson and Rayner experiment, it was generally accepted as a demonstration of fear conditioning. The study was also a demonstration of the generalization of the fear response from the original conditioned stimulus (the rat) to other stimuli.

Watson and Rayner chided the Freudians, who they declared would likely analyze a twenty-year-old Albert's fear of a seal skin coat in terms of his repressed memories for a time when he was scolded for attempting to play with his mother's pubic hair. They argued, "Emotional disturbances in adults cannot be traced back to sex alone" (Watson & Rayner, 1920, p. 14). It should be noted that Watson and Rayner did not attempt to decondition Albert or desensitize him. Later, Watson supervised research by Mary Cover Jones (1924a, 1924b) that was concerned with the experimental elimination of fear in another boy.

Emotions.   The preceding material shows that Watson believed that most emotional attachments occur through conditioning. Thus, fears, anxieties, and phobias may result from unfortunate early conditioning experiences. The same may be said for positive attachments. Love for another person, objects, animals, and so on occurs through associations of pleasant circumstances with the loved object or person.

Watson quarreled with earlier psychologists on the unlearned beginnings of emotional reactions. He argued that there are only three responses—fear, rage, and love—that can be brought forth in the infant. He cautioned, however, that these terms must be stripped of their old connotations. Fear is brought forth naturally by sudden or unexpected stimuli such as a loud sound. Fear is also initiated by a sudden loss of support. Rage is observed when bodily movement is hampered or a goal-directed activity is blocked. Watson pointed out that stimuli that provoke "love responses" include "stroking of the skin, tickling, gentle rocking, patting" (Watson, 1924a, p. 123). In each of these cases—fear, rage, and love—Watson was referring to rather broad, undifferentiated response patterns. Such patterns are later differentiated in highly specific ways through conditioning. In their earliest expressions they are somewhat diffuse yet easily distinguished from each other. For example, the cry of rage is easily distinguished from the cry of fear.

Instincts.   Watson's position on the existence of instincts changed dramatically over the course of his career. In an early article on instinctive activity in animals, Watson (1912) argued that "there are at least three great divisions or classes into which we may provisionally throw the acts of animals: Instincts essentially perfect upon their first appearance; instincts which must be supplemented by habit; and finally, random activity of instinctive origin" (p. 377). Watson found evidence for the first type of instinct in his early field studies on noddy and sooty terns. He argued that very young terns eat food in the same species-specific way with or without the parents as models. The same was true for other characteristic behaviors such as preening feathers. Watson also believed that fear responses, fighting, and nest cleaning are examples of congenital instincts. He argued that pecking is an example of the second class of instincts; it improves dramatically with practice. Examples of the third class are random responses to indefinite stimuli such as hunger, thirst, light, dark, warmth, and cold. More specifically, increased activity is normal when the organism is hungry. Random activity associated with hunger drops out when the right movements bring success.

Seven years after making these observations about instinct, Watson (1919) argued that "there is no sharp line of separation between emotion and instinct. Both are hereditary modes of action" (p. 231). In "Psychology from the Standpoint of a Behaviorist," Watson (1949) defined *instinct* as "a hereditary pattern reaction, the separate elements of which are movements principally of the striped muscles" (p. 231). Watson contended that at the human level it is almost impossible to classify instincts, but that at the animal level there are meaningful classifications. Classification at the human level is difficult because habit quickly dominates human actions.

Five years later, Watson devoted two chapters in *Behaviorism* to the topic of instincts, but the chapter title "Are There Any Human Instincts?" betray a new skepticism. Watson admitted that we inherit structures that interact with conditioning to determine what we can accomplish. He also admitted that there are unlearned responses such as hiccuping, crying, smiling, and grasping. He asked, however, whether there is any real utility in the concept of instinct. Smiling, for example, he says. "It begins at birth—aroused by intra-organic stimulation and by contact. Quickly it becomes conditioned, the sight of the mother calls it out, then vocal stimuli, finally pictures, then words and then life situations either viewed, told or read about" (Watson, 1924a, p. 104). He next raised the question of whether the whole concept of instinct is not meaningless. What is really important is conditioning and habit. Four years later, in *Psychological Care of Infant and Child,* Watson (1928) asserted, "There are no instincts" (p. 38). At least at the human level, he was embracing the Lockean viewpoint when he declared that "we build in at an early age everything that is later to appear" (p. 38).

The 1920s and 1930s afforded a friendly climate for Watson's skepticism about the utility and scientific legitimacy of instinct. Anti-instinctivism flourished in the early part of the century and may have served as a corrective to psychologies that placed too heavy an explanatory burden on instincts. An example is found in the work of William McDougall (1923, 1926a). The anti-instinct movement may also have flourished because of newfound optimism about the power of conditioning and the importance of the environment. For whatever reasons, the 1920s and 1930s witnessed an outpouring of argument against the concept of instinct. Representative works included Kuo's (1924) paper "A Psychology without Heredity" and Bernard's (1924) book *Instinct: A Study in Social Psychology.* Even by midcentury, questions remained about the usefulness of the concept of instinct (e.g., Beach, 1955). However, at the same time, behaviorists trained in zoology, often called *ethologists,* were marshaling powerful evidence for the role of instincts in animal behavior (e.g., Hess, 1962). For good overviews of the history of the concept of instinct, see Diamond (1971, 1974a).

Thinking and Speech.   In his book *Behaviorism,* Watson (1924a) warned readers that they have been taught to believe "that thinking is something peculiarly uncorporeal, something very intangible, very evanescent, something peculiarly mental" (p. 191). He further warned that "there is always a strong inclination to attach a mystery to something you can't see" (p. 191). It appears, at least superficially, that thinking would present a problem to a psychology that denies the existence of mental events. Yet Watson argued that a natural-science approach to thinking is both possible and productive. Watson (1924b) admitted that "thinking, with the behaviorist, is and must remain until the advent of experimentation partly a logical formulation" (p. 339). He was confident, however, that with the advancement of science, there would be "fewer and fewer phenomena which cannot be observed" (Watson, 1924a, p. 191). Accordingly, more and more scientific experimentation on thinking would be possible. What, then, was the behaviorist view of thinking?

In an article entitled "The Unverbalized in Human Behavior," Watson (1924c) noted that a person "learning to play golf learns (usually) simultaneously to talk golf" (p. 273). Words can substitute for actions as well as for objects. The utility of the substitutability or equivalence of words for actions or objects is obvious.

Watson pointed out that as we develop we soon have verbal organizations for every object or situation we have encountered. He compared verbal habits or organizations with the kinesthetic organization of playing a tune on the piano. Initially, one must look at each note on the score and carefully find the corresponding key on the piano. Soon, however, the initial stimulus note may trigger a response chain. One may even take the music away or play in the dark. Watson (1924a) argued that "the same thing happens in word behavior" (p. 188). After a few repetitions, the first line of a poem or a fairy tale may trigger a repetition of the entire passage.

Watson believed that we learn muscular habits when we learn to speak. Thus, speaking is not just a central process, it is also a peripheral process. We speak as a consequence of the interaction of the brain and the musculature. The primary muscle groups involved in speech are those associated with the larynx, but Watson (1924a) was aware that "removal of the larynx . . . does not destroy whispered speech" (p. 191). Hence, he believed that we really speak with our whole body—our hands, shoulders, tongue, facial muscles, throat, chest, and so on. The brain does not function in isolation from the rest of the physical system.

Another component in Watson's theory of thinking and speech grew out of his observations of children at play. When young children play by themselves, they typically talk to themselves. Watson (1924a) pointed out that even "deaf and dumb individuals who when talking use manual movements instead of words use the same manual responses they employ in talking, in their own thinking" (p. 193). In time, young children cease to talk aloud, but "talking" goes on nonetheless, behind the lips. "Behind these walls you can call the biggest bully the worst name you can think of without even smiling" (Watson, 1924a, p. 193). In an article entitled "The Place of Kinesthetic, Visceral and Laryngeal Organization in Thinking," Watson (1924b) declared, "The behaviorist has preferred to call all verbalization that goes on behind the closed door of the lips 'thinking,' regardless of whether new verbal adjustments are effected or only old habits rehearsed" (p. 340). Thinking, then, as the behaviorist views it, is closely tied to speech. Indeed, thinking could be defined as subvocal speech.

Watson anticipated an important question about his theory. Do we think only in words? His answer was, "Yes, or in word substitutes, such as the shrug of the shoulders or other bodily response. . . . When the individual is thinking *the whole of his bodily organization is at work*—even though the final solution shall be a spoken, written or subvocally expressed verbal formulation" (Watson, 1924b, p. 341).

Under Watson's treatment, thinking and all other psychological processes are subject to investigation by the established methods of the natural sciences. By deemphasizing the role of central (brain) processes in thinking, he opened the door to the use of new response measures (e.g., throat movements, verbalization) in the study of thinking. Following

Watson, there were many studies on the role of peripheral processes in thinking. Watson may have had a small impact on the literature on thinking, but his narrow approach to the topic had a truncating effect on the types of questions that were raised. In the end, a broader, more cognitive approach proved more productive. The broader approach made room for the investigation of topics such as the role of cognitive strategies in problem solving, the effects of the structure of a situation on problem solving, and problem solving as a function of the capacity to transform and rearrange parts or to see alternatives. The Watsonian approach to thinking was driven by the dictates of the larger behavioristic vision rather than by the special nature and requirements of the phenomenon in question.

BEHAVIORISM AND APPLIED PSYCHOLOGY

In his classic article, "Psychology as the Behaviorist Views It," Watson (1913) declared that "One of the earliest conditions which made me dissatisfied with psychology was the feeling that there was no realm of application for the principles which were being worked out" (p. 169). In that same article, he pointed out that if psychology would follow his system, "the educator, the physician, the jurist and the business man could utilize our data in a practical way, as soon as we are able experimentally to obtain them" (p. 168). Watson lamented the sterility of the older psychology that explored such problems as the number of discriminable shades of gray. Watson (1913) argued that he would rather explore such problems as the relative advantages of whole versus part learning, "the effect upon behavior of certain doses of caffeine . . . [and] the effects of recency upon the reliability of a witness's report" (p. 169). He stated boldly "that *behaviorism* is the only consistent and logical functionalism" (p. 166).

In terms of the systems examined in this book, behaviorism ranks high in its contributions to applied psychology. Both Pavlov and Watson were deeply concerned with practical problems. Indeed, the later parts of Pavlov's career were devoted extensively to an understanding of clinical problems and Watson supervised the earliest studies on

the counter-conditioning of fear (see Jones 1924a, 1924b). Following Watson, there was an explosion of interest in behavior therapy techniques. Such interest was manifested in the founding of scholarly journals such as *Behavior Research and Therapy, Journal of Applied Behavior Analysis,* and *Behavior Therapy.* Numerous scientific and professional organizations were also founded as vehicles for the exchange of ideas on behavioral therapy. Such organizations include the Association for the Advancement of the Behavioral Therapies, the Association for the Behavioral Treatment of Sexual Abusers, the Association for Behavior Analysis and the Society of Behavioral Medicine.

Watson's contributions to applied psychology also extended into the field of advertising (see Larson, 1979). Watson understood that people buy products on the basis of needs and motives. In addition to the product itself, we buy ideas associated with the product. Hence, the successful advertising agency will show how a product can satisfy basic human needs such as security, adventure, and fame. The extent of Watson's contributions to the psychology of advertising and sales is still not sufficiently appreciated.

The interest of behaviorism in applied problems was inevitable because this was a psychology that investigated what people actually do in the world. In contrast with psychologies that examined the mind, this was a matter-of-fact, rough-and-ready psychology that emphasized identifiable stimulus–response connections. If a person was looking for philosophical subtleties and refinement, this was the wrong psychology, but if a person was impatient to get on with a solution to immediate practical problems, then behaviorism was a psychology deserving of loyalty.

REVIEW QUESTIONS

1. Briefly outline some of the important intellectual antecedents of behaviorism.

2. Summarize Ivan Sechenov's approach to psychology.

3. Why was the concept of *action at a distance,* or *psychical reflex,* troublesome to Pavlov?

4. Define the terms *unconditioned stimulus, conditioned stimulus, unconditioned reflex,* and *conditioned reflex.*

5. Outline some of the possible temporal relations between the conditioned stimulus and the unconditioned stimulus.

6. What are the four temperament types included in Pavlov's system?

7. Define *extinction, spontaneous recovery, disinhibition, stimulus generalization,* and *discrimination.*

8. Discuss Pavlov's approach to experimental neurosis and specify the meaning of terms such as *ultramaximal inhibition, equivalence phase, paradoxical phase,* and *ultraparadoxical phase.*

9. Briefly outline the approaches to psychology in the works of Vladimir M. Bekhterev and Konstantin Kornilov.

10. How did John B. Watson define *psychology* and what methods did he advocate?

11. Outline Watson's critique of older systems of psychology.

12. Outline Watson and Rayner's classic work on fear conditioning.

13. Describe Watson's treatment of thinking. What criticisms can you offer of his approach?

14. Discuss the evolution of Watson's ideas on instinct.

15. Outline some of the contributions of behaviorism to applied psychology.

16. In what sense can Thorndike be considered a functionalist and in what sense can he be considered a behaviorist?

17. Distinguish between Thorndike's early law of effect and his later law of effect. Do you think he was correct in modifying the law of effect?

CHAPTER 14

OTHER BEHAVIORAL PSYCHOLOGIES

The term existence is only a synonym for movement.
—Paul Weiss (1924a)

Shortly after publication of Watson's behaviorist manifesto, it might have been possible to offer the optimistic assessment that psychology was destined to become a coherent discipline or, in the words of Kuhn, a "paradigmatic science." There was optimism, especially in the younger generation, that psychology, at last, was achieving scientific status. The methodology of psychology as viewed by the behaviorists was, after all, the same as that of other sciences and the subject matter was observable and quantifiable. Yet, shortly after the founding, the behaviorist school was far from coherent. Even as behaviorism came to dominate American psychology (Mills, 1998), it was a house divided over many substantive and methodological issues. On the other hand, there was some fundamental agreement among those psychologists who regarded themselves as behaviorists.

This chapter examines several behaviorist systems that represent alternatives to Watson's classic system. Before looking at specific alternatives to Watson, we will examine some of the threads of thought that are more or less common to behaviorist systems.

IMPORTANCE OF LEARNING

What do we know that we have not learned? Reflection on such a question demonstrates the central role of learning in human life. We are aware that we have learned a specific language and that skills such as swimming, riding a bicycle, and playing tennis are also acquired through learning. It is also true that attitudes, fears, self-concepts, political orientations, and philosophical positions are subject to learning. The behaviorist psychologies regarded learning as foundational to psychology. The study of learning held extraordinary promise as a means of understanding and controlling behavior. For example, if an irrational fear is conditioned, perhaps it could be as easily extinguished if we understand the processes. If a prejudicial attitude is acquired, perhaps through learning principles we could find efficient ways to change it. Unlike earlier psychologies that concentrated largely on reaction time, sensation, perception, and attention, behaviorism focused on learning as the foundation on which the science of psychology should be built. Of course, determinism remained a cornerstone in the foundation of learning theory since its inception, giving rise to a variety of deterministic orientations in the behaviorist literature (Slife, Yanchar, & Williams, 1999).

IMPORTANCE OF PRECISION AND CLARITY

Behaviorists often disagreed with each other over exact meanings of essential terms such as *learning, reinforcement, discrimination,* and *extinction.* Nevertheless, there was agreement among behaviorists on the importance of linking such concepts to experimental procedures. Thus, if an expression such as *hunger drive* were employed, there was agreement that such an expression should be treated as if it had no transexperimental meaning. Instead, the expression was tied to a specifiable metric employed in an experiment. *Hunger drive,* for example, might be defined in terms of hours of food deprivation, and a group that had gone, for example, for twelve hours without food would, by definition, have more hunger drive than a group that had gone for only six hours without food.

The importance of establishing empirical meanings for scientific terms is found in the work of the Nobel prize–winning physicist Percy W. Bridgman (1882–1961). In his classic book, *The Logic of Modern Physics,* Bridgman (1927) set forth the principles of operationism. As envisioned by Bridgman, **operationism** is a programmatic attempt to tie scientific terms to the measurements or operations of an experiment. For example, in physics, linear distance is linked to the procedures of measurement. Various measurement alternatives are usually available (e.g., use of a rigid rod, calculation of the speed of an echo from a sonic source, etc.). In psychology, one may measure a concept such as hunger drive in terms of hours of food deprivation, number of stomach contractions in a specified time period, blood chemistry changes, or number of approaches to a food container in a specified block of time.

Operationism, in its original form, challenged the idea that there are absolute meanings or intrinsic meanings. The assumption was that all meaning is relative. For example, Bridgman argued that there is no absolute time; rather, time is an arbitrary temporal interval marked off by the pointer readings on a clock. Bridgman also argued that the most meaningful references to topics such as energy, temperature, and light are cast in terms of the measures we employ. Many psychologists, most notably S. S. Stevens (1951), argued that the same must be true of psychological concepts.

Criticisms of operationism appeared after 1927 but were slow to capture the attention of psychologists. Indeed, operationism enjoyed considerable longevity in psychology (see Rogers, 1989). One criticism was that operationism described nothing new; it merely provided a label for a practice that had long been in use. Bridgman recognized the legitimacy of the criticism but contended that explicit clarification of scientific procedure is always useful.

A more damaging criticism was the intuitively appealing idea that measurement, in fact, points to something beyond itself. A major problem with operationism is that it leaves us with a truncated theory of meaning. Untrammeled operationism even runs the risk of prescribing a rigid absolutist stance about the meaning of meaning. The difficulty is illustrated by the idea that one operational definition can be better than another. If "better than" implies something other than mere ease of administration or utility of procedure, then such a statement may reveal an implicit assumption that there is a relationship between a set of operations and a concept that is "other than" that set of operations. In fact, most scientists probably do not believe that concepts such as length, drive, intelligence, and so on are nothing but a set of operations. Operationism is beset with the problem of what Hodgson (1988) has called the "intransigence of evaluative concepts" (p. 321).

In a symposium that examined the status of operationism about twenty-five years after the formal founding, Bridgman (1954) agreed with critics who argued that scientists should pay more attention to "what it is that makes an operation 'good' for the purposes of the scientist" (p. 225). Such attention inevitably forces the scientist to go beyond operationism. At the same time, Bridgman continued to find value in operationism and believed that a sophisticated application of that point of view does not necessarily restrict the intellectual freedom of the scientist. Bridgman regretted the way operationism had sometimes become dogma. In such cases, he compared it to a Frankenstein monster that had escaped from him. Debate still rages today about the success or failure of operationism in behaviorism as well as in later research by cognitive scientists (see Bickhard, 2001; Grace, 2001; Green, 2001a; Leahey, 2001).

The neobehaviorists were influenced by operationism and also by a related movement in philosophy called **logical positivism.** Logical positivism's impact on neobehaviorism further illustrates the emphasis on precision and clarity in these schools of thought.

Logical positivism, sometimes also called *critical empiricism* or *scientific empiricism,* grew out of a school of philosophy referred to as the Vienna Circle. The Vienna Circle was a discussion group including such scientists and philosophers as Moritz Schlick, Otto Neurath, Rudolf Carnap, Herbert Feigl, and Philipp Frank. The members of the Vienna Circle dreamed of a unified science, devoid of ambiguous and meaningless metaphysical concepts. Such a science would be based on the finest empirical traditions and would insist first and foremost on clarity of expression in scientific work.

The logical positivists argued that many concepts are devoid of scientific meaning because they cannot be explicitly verified or confirmed. Such concepts are thus little more than collections of words without clear-cut references. The positivists were not referring to random collections of words that anyone might see as meaningless but to coherent statements with the power to evoke feeling or trigger past associations. For example, a statement such as *The rat is happy* illustrates the point. The statement may be coherent and may evoke past associations, yet it is scientifically meaningless. Why? Because, according to the logical positivists, we cannot scientifically study an inner world devoid of clear and explicit references. We could, of course, operationalize *happiness* and study such behaviors as vigor of response, amount of food consumed, or number of intromissions in a sexual episode. Each is measurable and confirmable by independent observers. By contrast, an expression such as *The rat is happy* calls for an assessment of the inner world of the rat. Such an expression cannot yield the same kind of quantitative, publicly verifiable data as, for instance, amount of food consumed.

The emphasis of the logical positivists on the importance of publicly confirmable propositions and their suspicion of inner experience was entirely consistent with the thinking of most behaviorists. Though logical positivism would later succumb to its critics, its influence on behaviorism was extensive.

IMPORTANCE OF EXPERIMENTATION

Still another value shared by almost all neobehaviorists was the importance of experiment as a means of testing major concepts and theories. In general, there was agreement that theories and hypotheses must be subjected to active and vigorous experimental scrutiny. During the reign of neobehaviorism in the 1930s, 1940s, and 1950s, there was an unprecedented outpouring of experimental research. Such research typically incorporated the latest design techniques made possible by the rapid growth of new statistical procedures.

Neobehaviorists were often accused, however, of placing sophistication of design in higher priority than the significance of the problem. It is clear that scientists can employ powerful methodologies to explore trivial problems. Koch (1969) warned that it is a mistake to assume that the tools of scientific inquiry can "displace their human users" (p. 14). There was concern in many quarters that neobehaviorists were guilty of studying problems that were relevant only in the context of their own rather insular and esoteric programs.

The reply to such a criticism is that it is preferable to gain sure knowledge of simple events, even if such events seem trivial, than to have speculative knowledge of larger, more significant events. Some of the basic experiments in the young science of physics (e.g., rolling balls down inclined planes or studying the movements of a pendulum) may have seemed trivial at the time, but later proved valuable as the science progressed. A priori assessments of what is relevant and what is trivial are not distinguished for their accuracy.

Clearly, the behavioristic psychologists shared many beliefs but, as noted earlier, also disagreed with each other on numerous substantive issues. We turn now to a consideration of several behavioristic psychologies and some of the issues that divided them.

EARLY BEHAVIORISTIC PSYCHOLOGIES

The call for a more objective psychology was present from the turn of the century and, as noted earlier, that call had been translated into action in Russia through the work of scientists such as Sechenov and Pavlov. In the United States, several psychologists were identified with objective orientations. Some even preceded Watson in calling for an objective psychology. We will review the work of some of the early behaviorally oriented psychologists. Then we will turn to a consideration of the neobehaviorists—those who were inspired directly or indirectly by Watson but who modified his system.

Max Frederick Meyer

Max Frederick Meyer (1873–1967) was born on June 15, 1873, in Danzig, Germany (now Gdansk, Poland). In 1892, he enrolled in the University of Berlin as a theology student, but by 1894 had shifted to a broader-based curriculum. He studied first with Ebbinghaus and later with Carl Stumpf. He was also influenced strongly by the physicist Ernst Mach. Meyer and Stumpf shared interests in music and the problems of audition. In 1896, Meyer earned his Ph.D. under Stumpf with Max Planck, the theoretical physicist, sitting on the committee.

After a brief sojourn in England and one year at Clark University, Meyer accepted a position at the University of Missouri. His many publications were devoted to the scientific problems of audition, but Meyer also worked extensively on behalf of hearing-impaired people in the state of Missouri.

In 1929, Meyer's undergraduate student O. Hobart Mowrer, later destined for recognition as a learning theorist, constructed a questionnaire designed to fulfill a course requirement in the sociology department. According to Esper (1967), Meyer gave advice to Mowrer about the wording of several questions and provided envelopes to cut down on mailing expenses. The questionnaire explored attitudes on such topics as premarital sex, divorce, common-law marriage, and the effects of working women on the economy.

The questionnaire proved controversial in conservative Columbia, Missouri. Newspapers carried inflammatory editorials on the questionnaire and petitions called for the dismissal of Meyer and the sociology professor under whom Mowrer was studying. Meyer was suspended for one year without pay and the sociology professor was fired.

A year later, Meyer was fired when he made the mistake of presenting his own polemic version of the incident at a professional meeting. Numerous colleagues protested the dismissal of a man who had devoted so much to the University of Missouri and had worked so diligently on behalf of the hearing impaired. In an obituary, Hirsh (1967) declared that the whole incident "brought more shame on the curators of Missouri University than on Meyer himself" (p. 645). Meyer spent the last years of his life teaching and conducting research at the University of Miami. He died on March 14, 1967.

Meyer's Work.   Much of Meyer's work was on the mechanisms of the inner ear and on the psychology of music, but his broader vision for the discipline of psychology had a decidedly behavioristic cast. Indeed, early in his career, Meyer, as quoted by Esper (1966), said, "I am by nature a follower of every line of positivistic philosophy" (p. 347). In 1911, two years before the publication of Watson's famous behaviorist manifesto, Meyer published a book entitled *The Fundamental Laws of Human Behavior.* This was one of the first works to employ the term *behavior* in its title.

In his best-known book, *The Psychology of the Other One* (1922), Meyer emphasized the importance of restricting oneself, as a scientist, to that which can be measured. He noted that in earlier times people turned to psychology when they wanted to know something about the self or the soul, but he argued that a science of such topics is an anachronism. He pointed out that other sciences had also been plagued with similar kinds of anachronisms. For example, "Man tried in vain to explain the heavenly bodies, the weather, the land, the water, the animals and the plants by regarding them as Selves: Jupiter, Apollo, Neptune, and so forth" (Meyer, 1922, p. 3). Meyer underlined his point about the importance of measurement by declaring, "Modern science owes its triumphs to the fact that it has learned to restrict itself to describing merely that which one can measure" (p. 3).

Meyer's objective approach is further illustrated by his declaration that psychology should ask only about what human beings actually do, in contrast with older psychologies that explored the contents of consciousness. He believed that psychology should investigate both basic and applied topics. Meyer's behaviorism lacks the radical flavor encountered in the writings of Watson. Indeed, Meyer's moderate approach may have prevented it from capturing the public imagination. Watson's more dramatic statements, by contrast, likely gave his system visibility.

William McDougall

In his *Outline of Psychology,* William McDougall (1871–1938) referred to behaviorism as "a most misshapen and beggarly dwarf" (1923, p. ix). Nevertheless, McDougall argued that the behavior of human beings is the major practical topic of interest for psychologists. Therefore, according to McDougall, "All psychology is or should be behaviouristic" (1942, p. 16). The "misshapen and beggarly dwarf" in the above quotation reflects his disdain for Watson's metaphysical behaviorism. In contrast, McDougall advocated a moderate pragmatic behaviorism marked by methodological and metaphysical openness.

McDougall was born in Chadderton, England, on June 22, 1871. His education at Manchester and Cambridge Universities was noteworthy for its breadth and quality. Prior to earning a medical degree, he was recognized for his meritorious work in biology. He held academic positions at Cambridge, London, and Oxford. Later he moved to the United States and joined the faculty at Harvard University and became head of the psychology department at Duke University. During the last month of his life, McDougall kept a journal detailing his experiences with pain and the looming threat of death. Researchers have examined this work as a model of the dying process (Kastenbaum, 1995). McDougall died on November 28, 1938. He published 24 books and over 165 articles, ranging over a great variety of subjects in anthropology, psychology, and philosophy.

McDougall emphasized the centrality of activity, conduct, and behavior throughout his published works in psychology. Indeed, he preceded Watson in defining *psychology* as a positive science concerned with conduct (see McDougall, 1905, p. 1). McDougall argued, however, that the study of conduct or behavior need not blind us to what we encounter repeatedly in common sense and common speech; namely that there are mental activities that are part of a whole system of functions encountered in living organisms. Thus, psychology studies both experience (mental activity) and behavior, especially in relation to social and physiological correlates. McDougall's early books, *Physiological Psychology* (1905) and *Introduction to Social Psychology* (1980), reflect his breadth of vision.

According to McDougall, goal seeking or purposeful striving, is the central feature of mental activity and behavior. McDougall used the term **hormic,** from the Greek *horme* meaning urge, to refer to this central feature of animal and human life. From the lowest organisms to humans, we encounter, at every turn, behavior directed toward objects in the environment that satisfy needs. He noted with regret that most psychologists of his day ignored the hormic nature of organismic activity.

While McDougall emphasized the purposeful nature of organismic activity, he did not neglect the importance of mechanistic explanations based on material and efficient causation. In his book *The Energies of Men,* McDougall (1942) argued for "the validity of both the mechanistic and the purposive principles of explanation, each in its own sphere" (p. 22). Thus, one might explore the correlates of experience considered from a purposive standpoint and neurological activity considered mechanistically. Uytman (1967) pointed out that McDougall's task was "to reconcile a presumably purposive mind with an apparently causally determined body" (p. 227). McDougall explored the possibility of such a reconciliation through a kind of monadology similar to that advanced earlier by Leibniz (see Chapter 7).

Because of the complexity of its subject matter, psychology, according to McDougall, should employ all possible methods: laboratory methods, paper-and-pencil tests, introspection, free association, dream analysis, comparative methods, statistical methods, and field studies (see McDougall, 1942, p. 23). He was as pluralistic methodologically as William James and more explicit than James about the variety of methods that should be employed in psychology. McDougall insisted that psychology should not imitate other sciences; rather, psychology should have the courage to employ methods appropriate to its unique subject matter.

Unfortunately, McDougall was almost always out of step with the mainstream psychology of his day. At a time when most psychologists preferred mechanistic explanations, he advocated a purposive behaviorism. He emphasized the role of instincts in animal and human behavior during a time of radical environmentalism. He welcomed studies of paranormal phenomena (e.g., mental telepathy and clairvoyance) and helped establish the parapsychology laboratory headed by J. B. Rhine at Duke University. He also embraced a Lamarckian approach to evolution and even conducted experiments designed to provide evidence for the inheritance of acquired characteristics.

If McDougall championed many unpopular causes, he was also one of the first to emphasize the importance of social psychology. In this context, he drew upon the political climate of the early 1900s in reconciling "crowd psychology" with his views on democracy (see Allett, 1996). He also wrote an early text on abnormal psychology. Arguably, McDougall's most important influence was on neobehaviorist Edward Tolman (treated later in this chapter).

Edwin Bissell Holt

Edwin Bissell Holt (1873–1946) was born in Winchester, Massachusetts on August 21, 1873. Though his father, a congregational minister, died when Holt was a young man, his mother continued to encourage him in his studies. In 1896, Holt received his bachelor's degree magna cum laude from Harvard. Five years later, he received his Ph.D. from the same institution.

Holt was deeply influenced by William James. Langfeld (1946) noted that Holt "was probably more like James than any other of James's disciples in the quality of his intellect, in his dislike of sham and outworn convention, in his independence of thought and criticism, in his brilliant conversation and originality of expression, and in his generosity in helping and encouraging little known but promising writers" (p. 251).

Holt was an assistant professor at Harvard, where he assisted Münsterberg with the psycho-

logical laboratory. Later in his career, Holt taught at Princeton, where his course in social psychology was one of the most highly regarded on campus. In 1936, Holt retired from active teaching and devoted himself exclusively to historical studies and his psychological projects. He died on January 25, 1946.

Holt's Psychology. Holt agreed with Watson that psychologists should study behavior, and in that narrow sense can be counted among the behaviorists. Holt's view of behavior, however, was much broader and more philosophical than Watson's. Unlike Watson, Holt argued that organisms are goal directed and that movement toward goals is based on purposes, wishes, and plans.

Holt's emphasis on purposes and wishes may remove him from the behaviorist camp, but Holt denied this. He claimed that behavior is not random or without purpose or chaotic. Behavior is, above all else, purposive and goal directed. Unlike Watson, Holt did not deny the scientific legitimacy of consciousness and mental phenomena; instead, he attempted to provide a new interpretation of such phenomena. According to Holt, consciousness is inextricably linked with neurophysiological processes and with physical objects.

Holt's best-known book, published in 1931, was *Animal Drive and the Learning Process: An Essay Toward Radical Empiricism.* This book, plus other major works such as *The Concept of Consciousness* (1914) and *The Freudian Wish and Its Place in Ethics* (1915), delivers a philosophical and dynamic behaviorism that focuses on what organisms do in their environments. Holt's emphasis was on molar behavior. The term *molar* is distinguished from *molecular* and refers to large behavioral units, to things that organisms do such as building a nest, running a maze, driving a car, and so forth. The major characteristic of molar behavior is that it is purposive or goal directed. We will see later how this line of thought developed in the work of Holt's student, Edward Chace Tolman.

Albert Paul Weiss

Albert Paul Weiss (1879–1931) proposed an exceptionally strict, unyielding behaviorism of the purest variety. Elliott (1931) pointed out that "no behaviorist could ever be more zealous or thorough-going than Weiss in eliminating subjective categories from psychology while holding a primal faith in the competence of mathematics and scientific method to record and define a monism of physical substance" (p. 708).

Albert Paul Weiss was born in Steingrund, Silesia, on September 15, 1879, but when he was still quite young, the family moved to the United States. Weiss studied with Max Meyer at the University of Missouri, where he completed the Ph.D. in 1916. Weiss's entire scientific-professional career was at Ohio State University. His career was cut short by a heart ailment that left him incapacitated for the three-year period before his death on April 2, 1931.

Weiss's Work. Weiss believed that behavior should be understood in terms of social and physiological components. With sufficient attention to both sets of determinants there was no reasonable basis, in his opinion, for invoking consciousness, agency, or any type of "ghost in the machine." According to Elliot (1931), "Weiss used both his physiology and his sociology to serve the same end, to exorcise the psychic fiend from the science of behavior" (p. 709). Weiss clearly stands in the materialistic tradition of La Mettrie, Pavlov, and Watson.

One of Weiss's clearest expositions of his systematic position was published in two articles in the *Psychological Review* (1924a, 1924b) under the title "Behaviorism and Behavior." In the first of these articles, Weiss declared that the behavioristic system is set forth "in the statement that all human conduct and achievement reduces to *nothing but:* (a) different kinds of electron-proton groupings characterized according to geometric structure; [and] (b) the motions that occur when one structural or dynamic form changes into another" (p. 39). Weiss argued that psychologists, like physicists, should refuse to employ any psychical explanatory principle until all mechanical explanations are completely exhausted. Psychology, according to Weiss, reduces to the study of movement. In one of the boldest statements ever made on the centrality of movement, Weiss (1924a) declared that "the term existence is only a synonym for movement" (p. 40).

Weiss may qualify as the most radical and uncompromising behaviorist. He was committed to a complete physical monism and to a psychology at one with sciences such as physics and chemistry. Weiss's psychological interest touched on theoretical, basic, and applied topics. On the latter subject, he was one of the pioneers in the study of human–machine interactions. His book *Psychological Principles of Automobile Driving* (1930) is one of the early classics in the study of human–machine systems.

Walter Samuel Hunter

If Meyer and Weiss represent the conservative side of behaviorism, Walter Samuel Hunter (1889–1954) could be counted with Holt as one of the liberals of the movement. Although a behaviorist, Hunter avoided extreme positions marked by the use of such terms as *nothing but, all,* and *every.*

Walter Samuel Hunter was born in Decatur, Illinois, on March 22, 1889. He earned a bachelor's degree at the University of Texas in 1910 and was immediately accepted for graduate work at the University of Chicago, where he earned a Ph.D. under the direction of Harvey Carr in 1912. Hunter's dissertation, entitled *Delayed Reaction in Animals and Children* (1913), was immediately regarded as an important work and was widely quoted in psychological literature.

After completing his Ph.D., Hunter accepted a position at the University of Texas. His four years at Texas were productive and happy, but were marred by the death of Hunter's wife in 1915. He was left with a daughter, born in 1914.

In 1916, Hunter accepted a position at the University of Kansas. In his autobiography, he remembered that James Angell, although supportive, expressed concern that Hunter "might be getting promoted too fast for [his] age" (Hunter, 1952, p. 169). At Kansas, Hunter enjoyed excellent laboratory facilities, remarried, and spent nine years as professor with sixteen months off for military duty in World War I.

In 1925, Hunter accepted a position at Clark University until 1936, when he became department head at Brown University. In 1930, Hunter served as president of the American Psychological

Association. He was also one of those rare individuals honored with membership in the prestigious National Academy of Sciences. His work at Brown was interrupted by World War II, when he served as a member of the Emergency Committee on Psychology and as chief of the Applied Psychology Panel of the National Defense Research Committee. For his work in World War II, Hunter was honored by President Truman with the President's Medal of Merit. After the war, Hunter devoted his full attention to his academic career at Brown University until his death in 1954.

Hunter's Work. In the preface of his book *Human Behavior,* Hunter (1928) instructed the reader as follows: "The present discussion is written from what is generally called the behavioristic point of view, which I prefer to call the viewpoint of anthroponomy, the science of human behavior" (p. v). Hunter preferred the term *anthroponomy* to *psychology* because of the mentalistic connotations of psychology. The term **anthroponomy** comes from the Greek *anthropos,* meaning man, and *nomos,* meaning law. The term anthroponomy never did catch on; years later, in his autobiography, Hunter (1952) said that he "was never under any delusion that the designation of the science would be changed to anthroponomy, but the path of our science would have been much smoother in its public relations had some nonpsychic term designated it" (p. 172). Many would agree with Hunter, but alternative designations such as anthroponomy, behavioral science, or cognitive science have never gained unanimous approval.

Although Hunter argued that the subject matter of psychology is behavior, he was open to a variety of methods such as field observation methods, clinical methods, and the experimental method.

Hunter was interested in a broader range of problems than were most behaviorists. Though he worked with animals, he was deeply interested in human behavior. He emphasized the importance of basic studies, but also stressed applied studies that are relevant to education, the workplace, everyday adjustment, and the military.

Hunter's most famous work was on delayed reactions in animals and in children (Schlosberg,

1954). The work provided important information on representational processes in a variety of species. The delayed reaction experiment allows a subject to see a stimulus (a light) above one of three doors equidistant from a holding cage. The light signals the presence of food. The problem is that there is a delay between turning off the light and the release of the animal from the holding cage. Hunter found that rats and dogs tend to make the correct response (i.e., choose the correct door) if the delay was not so long that they lost their bodily orienting response. In other words, rats and dogs make the correct response if their muscular orientation remains intact. If the muscle orientation toward the correct door dissipates (during the delay period), the animal tends not to make the correct response. Hunter found that racoons could handle much longer delays. The delayed reaction experiment was one way of testing cognitive or representation processes in a variety of species. The practicality of the approach has a certain intuitive appeal because everyone has been confronted with the task of remembering the location of an object after a delay period.

In World War II, he was called on to recommend psychologists who could conduct studies on human–machine systems. He was adamant that it was not just a war of machines. He pointed out that "men must operate machines and that their efficiency and morale are after all the fundamental factors" (Hunter, 1952, p. 182). Thus, he was one of the first to address the human–machine problem.

Because of his breadth of vision and pluralistic approach to methodology, Hunter added to the vitality of the behavioristic movement (Plaud & Montgomery, 1993). His work contributed to the growing perception that this was not a sterile psychology restricted only to the laboratory or a single content area such as learning but a psychology with a promising agenda.

Karl Spencer Lashley

Karl Lashley (1890–1958) was strongly influenced by John B. Watson and was sympathetic with behaviorism. He was not, however, inclined to devote energy to the systematic or philosophical defense of behaviorism. Instead, he focused on specific problems in learning and their experimental investigation. His major interest was the cerebral localization of learning and discrimination. Although Lashley identified with behaviorism, his work on cerebral localization was more consistent with Gestalt psychology than with behaviorism.

Karl Lashley was born on June 7, 1890, to Charles Gilpin Lashley and Maggie Blanche Spencer. His father was a successful businessman and his mother, a descendant from the American Calvinist theologian-philosopher Jonathan Edwards, was a former schoolteacher. In his early years he had an unusual fascination with the biological world, so it was no surprise that he majored in zoology in college. He graduated from the University of West Virginia in 1910 and proceeded to the University of Pittsburgh, where he earned a master's degree in biology. In 1914 he received his Ph.D. in biology with an emphasis in genetics from Johns Hopkins University. Throughout his education Lashley took only one formal course in psychology, but at Hopkins he worked with John B. Watson and the psychiatrist Adolph Meyer. As a result, Lashley's interests turned more and more to psychological topics.

Lashley's academic career included a twenty-year appointment at Harvard University and a thirteen-year appointment at the Yerkes Laboratory of Primate Biology. He served as president of the American Psychological Association in 1929 and received numerous honorary degrees and medals in recognition of his research.

There are few people in science whose diligence and integrity matched that of Lashley. Morgan (1968) noted that Lashley "did all his own research, 'running' his animals, doing data analysis, making histological reconstructions, and writing his own papers" (p. 29). Morgan also noted that Lashley was dismayed at the new funding trends for scientific research. He was fearful that ever larger dollar amounts would create pressures that would undermine scientific honesty and the integrity of the scientific process.

Lashley retired in 1955 and served as emeritus professor at the Yerkes Laboratories from 1955 to 1958. He died on August 7, 1958.

Lashley's Work. Lashley conducted work on instinct and on color vision, but it was his work on the cortical basis of learning and discrimination that was most influential. Following the completion of his Ph.D., Lashley engaged in postdoctoral studies with the physiological psychologist Shepherd Ivory Franz (1874–1933). Franz, working with brain-damaged human subjects and with cats and monkeys, discovered that many habits that were lost following brain injury could be relearned. If old pathways were destroyed by brain injury, then relearning must be based on establishment of new pathways laid down in a new cortical site. These findings raised doubts about the concept of a precise cortical localization for behavioral functions.

Just after the turn of the century, there was a tendency to think of brain functions in terms of strict point-for-point connections after the model of the telephone switchboard. In that day, the telephone switchboard, with its millions of point-for-point connections, was viewed as a modern miracle of technology and surely a suggestive model of how the brain might operate. Lashley believed that point-for-point connections should have a precise locus in the brain and that destruction of such connections should reveal important information about the neurophysiological underpinnings of behavior.

Lashley's method was to teach an animal, typically a laboratory rat, to perform a specific task. As a part of this phase of the research, Lashley developed the jumping stand, an apparatus that was later to bear his name. The jumping stand consisted of an elevated platform situated in front of two stimulus cards. If the rat jumped to the correct stimulus card, the card fell over and the rat received a food reward. A jump to the wrong card resulted in a fall into a net situated immediately below the cards. Thus, the task of the rat was to establish a habit of jumping to the correct card (perhaps a black card as opposed to a white card). In a later phase of the experiment the rat was tested for its ability to recall which of the cards would lead to reward.

After a habit was established, Lashley would extirpate various sites in the cortex of the brain. In subsequent testing he could ascertain the effects of the extirpation on retention of the previously acquired habit. Lashley's results, in experiment after experiment, came as a surprise to those who believed in a strict point-for-point connection between stimuli and responses. Though it is clear that some parts of the nervous system are "hardwired" in a point-for-point fashion, Lashley failed to find evidence of localization of function for the learning tasks he studied.

Lashley found that his subjects retained previously acquired habits even when every conceivable pathway had been destroyed. To be sure, brain damage impaired performance, but Lashley's data suggested that a field theory approach to brain function characterized intelligent behavior more accurately than did a rigid connectionism. By 1926, Lashley rejected the connectionist model because of its failure to account for the complexity of his findings (Bruce, 1998). It was clear that certain functions, especially certain sensory and motor functions, are highly localized, but Lashley's data suggested that there is no so-called learning center or intelligence center.

Two principles that grew out of Lashley's work have been enduring. **Mass action** refers to the idea that the rate, efficiency, and accuracy of learning depend on the amount of cortex available. Thus, it is not so much the locus of an injury that is important; rather, the amount of cortex damaged is more critical to the resulting deficit in learned and intelligent behavior. **Equipotentiality** refers to the idea that one part of the cortex can take over the function of another part. Thus, some functions that are lost following brain damage can be restored through relearning using other regions of the brain.

During his career, Lashley was cautious about making any broad claim or sweeping generalization. His was a measured and admirable approach to science.

NEOBEHAVIORISM

All of the psychologists covered thus far in the chapter were in the behavioristic tradition. The ones we now consider were clearly influenced by Watson but established well-elaborated systems that commanded considerable attention and that represented alternatives to Watson's systematic position. Their systematic influence was very powerful in psychology just before midcentury.

Clark Leonard Hull

Clark Hull (1884–1952) was probably the dominant figure in academic psychology from about 1930 to 1950. According to Logan (1968), Hull's dominance can be attributed to the fact that he "presented his theoretical ideas with a degree of rigor and analytic detail then unfamiliar in psychology" (p. 535). Logan also pointed out that Hull's theory drew from dominant influences of the day—Watson, Pavlov, Darwin, Thorndike, and even Freud. The latter's emphasis, according to Logan (1968) on "the central role of motivation in behavior [was] a position Hull increasingly adopted" (p. 535). Hull's theoretical approach to learning and behavior, as we will see, can be characterized as mathematical and deductive. The theory is set forth explicitly in terms of quasi-mathematical postulates and corollaries that lend themselves readily to experimental procedure.

Hull was born in a rural area of New York close to Akron on May 24, 1884. As a youth, he had to overcome a severe case of typhoid fever and poliomyelitis. The latter, contracted in his second year of college, left one leg paralyzed.

Despite hardships, Hull graduated from the University of Michigan in 1913, where he studied with Walter B. Pillsbury. After teaching for a year, Hull enrolled at the University of Wisconsin, where he received his Ph.D. in 1918. Hull continued to work at the University of Wisconsin, focusing largely on aptitude testing. Later, his interests changed to suggestibility and hypnosis.

In 1929, James Rowland Angell hired Hull to work at the Institute of Human Relations at Yale University. During this time, he produced his monumental work in behavior theory. Hull was recognized with many honors during the course of his academic career including election as president of the American Psychological Association in 1935.

Hull had a singular impact on experimental psychology and expanded the scope of S-R psychology (Rashotte & Amsel, 1999). One of Hull's

Clark Leonard Hull

best-known students, Kenneth W. Spence (1952), claimed that 70 percent of all experimental studies on learning and motivation "reported in the *Journal of Experimental Psychology* and the *Journal of Comparative and Physiological Psychology* during the decade 1941–1950 made reference to one or more of Hull's publications" (p. 641). Hull clearly enjoyed a position of leadership along with others, such as Pavlov and Watson, who also conceived of psychology as a natural science. Hull died of a heart condition on May 10, 1952.

Hull's System.   As noted earlier, Hull had an early interest in the fields of aptitude testing and hypnosis. His books *Aptitude Testing* (1928) and *Hypnosis and Suggestibility* (1933) represent substantial contributions in these fields. In his autobiography, Hull (1952) noted that he became pessimistic about the future of aptitude testing, so he left the field. Despite such misgivings, he remained interested in mental testing and challenged Lashley's views on heredity and intelligence (Weidman, 1994). His departure from the experimental investigation of hypnosis was not completely voluntary. Hull worked in the field of hypnosis at Wisconsin for about ten years and his work, together with that of his students, resulted in thirty-two published papers. When he moved to Yale,

however, members of the medical community opposed his work. Experimental work in progress at that time was completed by Hull's students and collaborators in the midwest where, according to Hull (1952), "the superstitious fear of hypnosis was not nearly so great" (p. 152). *Hypnosis and Suggestibility* was published four years after Hull joined the faculty. In his words, "Despite its technical nature this book seems to have been read quite widely, not only by academic persons but by the general public as well" (p. 153). Hull's book is a classic in the field of hypnosis.

The intellectual background for Hull's general behavior theory was partly his love for quantitative predictions and his quest for scientific unity (see Mills, 1988). The theory is set forth in four books and a large number of scientific papers. His major books include *Mathematico-Deductive Theory of Rote Learning,* published in 1940, followed by the classic *Principles of Behavior* (1943). Eight years later, *Essentials of Behavior* (1951) showed the maturity of Hull's system. Hull's final book, *A Behavior System* (1952), was published posthumously. According to Logan (1968), another book on "application to social and cultural problems remained to be written at the time of Hull's death in 1952" (p. 536).

Hull was central in the development of quantitative approaches to behavior. The anchoring events for the terms in his theory are stimuli and responses, but these are assumed to be bridged by intervening variables such as **drive,** fatigue, **habit strength,** and **incentive.** Hull attempted to establish hypothetical quantitative connections between such intervening variables and observable stimulus and response events. An example is provided by the following formula:

$$_sE_R = {}_sH_R \times D \times V \times K$$

$_sE_R$ refers to action potential in a given situation; $_sH_R$ refers to habit strength or number of previous trials in the situation; D is drive strength (e.g., the number of hours of deprivation); and V refers to **stimulus intensity dynamism.** This last term recognizes that some stimuli have a stronger influence on behavior than others. For example, the rat, a nocturnal animal, might run more readily in a darkened runway than in a well-lighted runway. Thus, V would have a greater value in the darkened runway. Finally, K refers to incentive motivation. For example, a child might work harder for a marble than a button. Presumably the marble would have more K, or incentive value.

Hull's formula indicates that reaction potential is a joint multiplicative function of habit strength, drive level, the nature of the stimulus, and incentive motivation. Thus, a rat might be expected to be vigorous in a familiar slightly darkened runway working for a preferred food object under relatively high drive. The foregoing formula is somewhat simplified but provides a general sense of Hull's approach. Hullian formulas were highly suggestive and often made rather precise predictions about what subjects would do in specific situations.

Hull's work in psychology began with simple observations (e.g., performance improves with practice, we learn better under some circumstances than others, and under certain circumstances we quit engaging in what was once a well-established response). The terms Hull used as intervening variables (e.g., *drive, incentive,* and *habit strength*) all have intuitive appeal and are tied precisely to observable behaviors and observable stimulus events. Let us now consider Hull's position on several specific problems in behavior theory.

Reinforcement.   **Reinforcement** played a key role in Hull's behavior system. He spoke of the law of reinforcement, which meant that stimuli that reduce drive stimuli are reinforcing. Thus, food reduces hunger stimuli produced by the depletion of solid material in the stomach, just as escape from shock reduces shock stimuli. Further, Hull recognized the crucial role of "secondary" reinforcement in the control of behavior: Any stimulus consistently associated with primary reinforcers takes on reinforcing properties. As noted earlier, Hull also recognized the role of incentive as an important dimension of reinforcement.

Experimental Extinction.   Because of its theoretical and possible practical applications, the study of experimental extinction has been a topic of continuing interest from the time of Pavlov and Thorndike. The usual procedure is to establish a response through conditioning and then study the persis-

tence of the response once reinforcement is terminated. The speed of extinction, the conditions that accelerate or retard it, and the explanations for why it occurs have occupied a prominent place in the literature of behavior theory.

Hull argued that each response generates some degree of inhibition. Such inhibition is an after-effect of the response and akin to a negative drive, like fatigue or pain. Hull referred to the inhibitory potential associated with each response as I_R, or *reactive inhibition.* Hull assumed that I_R dissipates with the passage of time, so it is a temporary state of affairs that follows each response. When responses are massed close together or when responses require high effort, I_R should be increased.

A second component of Hull's theory of extinction is called *conditioned inhibition,* or $_SI_R$. Hull assumed that $_SI_R$ builds up during the dissipation of I_R. To illustrate, assume that a rat during extinction has pressed an eighty-gram counterweighted bar several times. Such a bar would be fairly heavy for the typical laboratory rat. After such a response burst, the rat has presumably generated much I_R, or fatigue. Now the rat rests and the act of resting is reinforcing. In other words, the dissipation of I_R is reinforcing. So $_SI_R$, or conditioned inhibition, gets built up. Hull accounted for permanent extinction in terms of conditioned inhibition. Hull's predictions on the roles of effort and inhibition in extinction have received support in the literature, but it is unlikely that inhibition in its various forms is sufficiently robust to provide a complete account of extinction of responses.

The Role of Insight in Learning.   Hull believed that learning proceeds in a continuous fashion and "the organism's own responses furnishes the surrogates for ideas" (Hilgard & Bower, 1966, p. 183). Hull attempted to understand behavior mechanistically in terms of material, efficient, and formal causation. While he did not deny that terms such as *purpose,* **insight,** and *intention* can be attributed to the behavior of organisms, his hope was to show that such terms are "secondary principles" that can be deduced "from more elementary objective primary principles" (Hull, 1943, p. 26).

How Does Learning Occur?   As noted earlier, Hull believed that reinforcement plays a crucial role in learning. Hilgard and Bower (1966), in summarizing Hull's position, pointed out that "mere contiguous repetition does nothing but generate inhibition; all improvement depends upon reinforcement . . . [and] the number of reinforcements is the basic variable in acquiring habit strength" (p. 182). Nevertheless, Hull's theory is by no means a single-factor theory. Reinforcement may be necessary for learning in Hull's system, but it is not sufficient, nor is any other element, such as contiguity, sufficient. Hull's theory accounts for learning in terms of a complex interaction of a variety of organismic and environmental variables.

Appraisal of Hull's Theory.   Although a leading figure in neobehaviorism during his lifetime, Hull's visibility in the psychological literature diminished after his death (Webster & Coleman, 1992). A number of critics outlined potential concerns in Hull's system. However, Spence (1952) stated that "no account of Hull's point of view would be complete which failed to emphasize his appreciation of what it was necessary to do in order to develop a science of psychology" (p. 646). Hull has even been criticized for the very scientific quality that some psychologists count as a virtue. Specifically, critics have argued that the approach is sterile, artificial, and irrelevant to real-life concerns. Spence (1952) effectively replied to such criticism by writing, "Hull fully realized that, just as the physicist found it necessary to introduce such unworldlike conditions as the vacuum and the biologist such unnatural situations as an isolated piece of tissue 'growing' in a test tube, so likewise the psychologist must not hesitate to observe behavior, whether animal or human, under controlled conditions, artificial or otherwise" (p. 646). The comparison with early physics and biology is provocative, but it is perhaps still too early to gauge its legitimacy.

Edwin Ray Guthrie

Sheffield (1959) pointed out that Edwin Guthrie (1886–1959) "did not follow a conventional route to distinction in psychology" (p. 643), nor did he follow a conventional path to the behaviorist viewpoint. Guthrie came to psychology from mathematics, formal logic, and philosophy.

Edwin Ray Guthrie

Edwin Ray Guthrie was born in Lincoln, Nebraska, on January 9, 1886, the eldest of the five children of Edwin Ray Guthrie and Harriet Pickett Guthrie. From his early years, Guthrie showed scholarly promise. He remained in his home state to take a bachelor's degree in mathematics and a master's in philosophy from the University of Nebraska. In 1912, Guthrie obtained his Ph.D. under E. A. Singer at the University of Pennsylvania.

Guthrie's first academic appointment was at the University of Washington in philosophy, but after five years he shifted to psychology. His academic career was interrupted by service in World War I and World War II. His final regular academic position at the University of Washington was as dean of the graduate school. He retired in 1956 and died in 1959.

Guthrie, like Hull, received many honors during his academic career. He served as president of the American Psychological Association in 1945, and in 1958 the American Psychological Foundation awarded Guthrie the Gold Medal Award for his distinguished contributions to the science of learning.

Guthrie's Behaviorism.   Unlike Hull, Guthrie avoided technical language and formal theory construction. Sheffield (1959) noted that Guthrie's "avoidance of formalized theory was apparently deliberate, motivated not only by a general skepticism of the ultimate validity of deductively proven 'truths' but also by a belief that construction of formalized scientific systems hampered the search for new knowledge" (p. 648). More than Hull, Guthrie was suspicious of intervening variables or hypothetical constructs. Perhaps more than any other behaviorist, he restricted himself to accounts of the actual behaviors of the organism in the world. He was wary of hypothetical central processes (e.g., inhibition, drive, etc.) even when such processes were tied to physiology. Let us take a look at Guthrie's position on some key behavioristic issues.

Reinforcement. Guthrie believed that reinforcement per se has no direct logical or causal relationship to learning. Even reinforcement theorists must question possible causal relationships between a learned connection and, for example, the consumption of food. What possible physiological connections could there be between reinforcers and the establishment of connections involved in learning?

A major problem with reinforcement and drive-reduction theories, as noted by Voeks (1968), is that they may produce "an ever-lengthening list of motives (conscious and unconscious) or drives (primary, secondary, tertiary) or needs, in an attempt to account for seemingly dysfunctional learning" (p. 297). Consider the teenager who fails to hang her coat up when entering the house even though she has been reprimanded time and again. Drive-reduction explanations of such behavior could lead to questions about whether the teenager may have hidden motives (e.g., maybe she enjoys annoying her parents). Guthrie suggested an approach that did not rely on the concepts of reinforcement, drive reduction, or hidden motives.

The Law of Contiguity. Although the teenager in the above example has been reprimanded for failing to hang up her coat, the reprimands have changed nothing. Guthrie suggested a different approach. A careful study of the sequence of events may reveal that closing the door is inevitably followed, for example, by a turn to the right in the direction of the sofa, instead of a turn to the left in the direction of the closet. The coat is then thrown on the sofa. Now the young woman is asked to put

the coat back on, go back out, and go through the sequence of movements of coming into the house, but this time she is asked to close the door and turn to the left. Turning to the left brings her to the closet door, which she is now asked to open. She may now hang up her coat. Guthrie believed that such an approach to establishing a new habit or breaking an old one can have remarkable effects. Why?

According to Guthrie, there is but one law of learning, and that is the *law of contiguity*. We learn connections when stimuli are arranged so that they can be effective cues for a desired response. **Contiguity** is a necessary and sufficient condition for learning based on close temporal or spatial conjunction. Reinforcement has nothing to do with learning per se, but a reinforcer, as a strong stimulus, may keep an organism in a situation so that the necessary cues are attached to the appropriate response.

Guthrie's position emphasized the importance of recency in learning situations. Thus, it is the last thing we do in one situation that sets the stage for what is to come next. In the example of the teenager and the coat, what is important is that closing the door becomes the cue for a left turn instead of a right turn. Many athletes have an intuitive feel for Guthrie's emphasis on recency: Never end a practice session on a failure; rather, end on a success, because we tend to repeat what we last did in a situation. If the last response ended in failure or fear, there is an increased likelihood that such failure or fear will become conditioned to the situation.

One-Trial Learning. Almost all learning theorists have stressed the importance of practice effects and repetition. Guthrie offered a new interpretation of why practice or repetition appears to work. Learning, according to Guthrie, takes place in one trial. Thus, when there is appropriate conjunction between stimulus and response, a connection is immediately established. The idea that we learn in one trial is not completely counterintuitive, because most of us have experienced what seems to be one-trial learning. At the same time, we experience the beneficial effects of practice and we observe trials when no apparent connections are made. So how are we to resolve the apparent discrepancies between Guthrie's idea that learning occurs in one trial and the obvious benefits of practice?

According to Guthrie, we simplify the meanings of the terms *stimulus* and *response*. What we call a *response* is actually many smaller responses consisting of a large number of postures and movements. Similarly, what we call a *stimulus* is usually a multifaceted affair. What we learn, according to Guthrie, is learned in one trial, but sometimes many small connections must be established to produce what we have designated to be the appropriate response. When all smaller connections are established (and each one, according to Guthrie, is established in one trial), then we may observe what we have designated to be the appropriate response.

How does Guthrie account for trials that seem fruitless or empty? Connections that are made in a single trial are not always visible. Guthrie also emphasizes the idea that we may make the wrong connections and thus retard progress. One of the most important functions of a teacher is to monitor learning and provide feedback when connections are not headed in the desired direction.

Extinction.   According to Guthrie's theory, responses are not weakened by the mere passage of time. Furthermore, the withdrawal of reinforcement has no direct bearing on the extinction of a response. What we call **extinction** really amounts to new learning that results from the process of establishing new responses to old stimuli. Experimental extinction is brought about by rearranging the stimulus situation. Going back to our example about hanging up the coat, we could focus on how we have extinguished the habit of throwing the coat down. But old responses were replaced by new responses, so extinction cannot easily be separated from new learning. What is important for extinction is the same thing that is important for any learning: namely, contiguity of stimulus and response. Withholding reinforcement changes the stimulus complex and contributes to the probability that new responses will be learned. Thus, the withholding of reinforcement has only an indirect bearing on the extinction or new learning process.

Insight.   Guthrie rejected mentalistic interpretations of insight but was impressed with experiments on insight conducted by the Gestalt psychologist Wolfgang Köhler. Working in open field situations, Köhler found ways to arrange stimuli so as to maximize the probability of a connection. Though Köhler and Guthrie would disagree on interpretations of so-called insightful learning, they would share interests in experimental and practical conditions that facilitate such learning.

Appraisal of Guthrie's Theory.   One appeal of Guthrie's theory is his use of illustrations from everyday life. He was interested in psychotherapy, the problems of habit breaking, and a host of educational problems. His anecdotes contributed to the impression that the theory is relevant to important issues of life. Such an impression is premature, however, until the theory proves its mettle in rigorous experimental tests.

Fortunately, some of Guthrie's students and admirers (e.g., Estes, 1950; Voeks, 1950) formalized the theory so it could be more readily subjected to experimental scrutiny. Voeks restated many of Guthrie's ideas in the form of testable theorems and postulates while Estes advanced a formal statistical theory of learning.

Perhaps more than any behaviorist after Watson, with the exception of Skinner, Guthrie was concerned about the transitions from the laboratory to the world. Guthrie's practical interests are illustrated in his book *The Psychology of Human Conflict* (1938), an attempt to apply learning principles to the problems of psychopathology. His practical interests are further illustrated in his book *Educational Psychology* (1950), coauthored with Francis Powers, and his paper "Personality in Terms of Associative Learning" (Guthrie, 1944).

Guthrie's applications of learning foreshadowed major developments in that same area in the 1960s. The weakness of the theory—namely, its anecdotal nature—may also have been a strength because the anecdotes, drawn as they were from real-life situations, contributed to the idea that learning does not have to be an insular and narrow subdiscipline of psychology. Indeed, in Guthrie's hands, learning is not just a sterile laboratory discipline. It is a vital and all-encompassing way of thinking about behavior in educational, clinical, industrial, and daily-life situations.

Edward Chace Tolman

Edward Chace Tolman (1886–1959) developed a "new formula for behaviorism" (see Tolman, 1922) that accepted behavior as the proper subject matter of psychology but rejected Watson's stark stimulus–response system. Tolman was deeply influenced by Edwin B. Holt, his teacher at Harvard; William McDougall, with his emphasis on the role of purpose in living organisms; and Gestalt psychologists, particularly Kurt Koffka and Kurt Lewin. These influences are clearly evident in Tolman's system of psychology, which focused on the role of cognition and purpose in animal and human life.

Edward Chace Tolman

Tolman was born to an upper-middle-class family in Newton, Massachusetts, on April 14, 1886. Tolman graduated from Massachusetts Institute of Technology and immediately enrolled in philosophy and psychology courses at Harvard, taught by Ralph Barton Perry and Robert M. Yerkes. Tolman thought he might want to be a philosopher, but after taking Perry's course, Tolman (1952) declared, "I decided then and there that I did not have brains enough to become a philosopher (that was still the day of great metaphysical systems), but that psychology was nearer my capacities and interests" (p. 323). Instead, Tolman leaned toward the work of Yerkes, a pioneer in animal research and an early supporter of Pavlov's work (Wight, 1993). After his first year at Harvard, he spent part of a summer at Giessen with Kurt Koffka. That brief experience made Tolman receptive to Gestalt ideas when they entered the American literature. Indeed, in 1923, Tolman went back to Giessen for more instruction in the Gestalt perspective.

Following graduation from Harvard, Tolman worked for three years at Northwestern before taking the position at Berkeley that he would hold the rest of his life. Tolman's life and work at Berkeley were highly rewarding until the early 1950s, when McCarthyism swept the country. It was a time when a paranoid fear of subversive activity resulted in the demand for loyalty oaths. Those who refused to sign were subjected to publicized personal attacks,

intimidation, and threats. Tolman, though normally a shy individual, assumed a position of leadership in the fight for academic freedom. In the words of Krech (1968), "It was Tolman (a member of the national board of the American Civil Liberties Union) who led the faculty in full battle against the university—a battle that saved academic freedom at the university" (p. 95).

Crutchfield (1961) pointed out that "Tolman's distinguished career as a creative scientist and as a leader in the academic and social community spanned four decades from 1918, when he came to the University of California in Berkeley as an instructor in psychology, until his death in Berkeley on November 19, 1959" (p. 135). Like other neobehaviorists covered in this chapter, Tolman enjoyed many honors in his lifetime. He served as president of the American Psychological Association in 1937. In 1957, Tolman received the Distinguished Scientific Contribution Award from the American Psychological Association.

The citation for the Distinguished Scientific Contribution Award provides a fitting introduction to Tolman's work. It reads as follows:

> For the creative and sustained pursuit of a theoretical integration of the multifaceted data of psychology, not just its more circumscribed and amenable aspects; for forcing theorizing out of the mechani-

cal and peripheral into the center of psychology without the loss of objectivity and discipline; for returning [the human being] to psychology by insisting upon molar behavior purposely organized as the unit of analysis, most explicitly illustrated in his purposive-cognitive theory of learning. (*American Psychologist,* 1958, p. 155)

Tolman's Cognitive Behaviorism. One of Tolman's first concerns was to construct a system of psychology sensitive to the range of events we encounter in our daily lives. One major complaint against Watsonian behaviorism was that it achieved scientific status at the expense of believability. Watson's system was hard to accept because it left so much out. Topics such as cognition, belief, and goal directedness were either banished altogether or redefined in ways that defied common sense. In contrast, Tolman delivered a psychology with true breadth of perspective that retained the desirable objectives of classical behaviorism.

Tolman characterized his system as a true behaviorism because the focus was on behavior rather than consciousness and on objective observation rather than introspection. He also characterized his system as a **molar behaviorism** in contrast with the molecular behaviorism of Watson. The term *molar* referred to large units or the kind of global behavior that we observe in the everyday world. Tolman believed that behavior is a legitimate scientific topic of inquiry in its own right. Thus, we gain no additional scientific respectability by correlating behavior with physiological processes. This theme was later amplified in the work and thought of B. F. Skinner.

Tolman also referred to his system as a **purposive behaviorism.** One of the most immediately striking features of the behavior of animals and humans is that such behavior is directed toward goals (Innis, 1999). Furthermore, such goals have clear-cut, observable qualities and can thus be objects of scientific analysis. We need not get lost in the philosophical subtleties of teleology in order to account for behavior in terms of its goal-directed features.

According to Tolman, **molar behavior** has a purposive quality but it is also *cognitive* and *docile.* These two terms distinguish molar behavior from rigid, reflexive pathbound mechanical behaviors. Molar behavior is not like a reflex. A major difference is that molar behavior has a multitude of causes; it has an intelligent "teachable" quality, and it is not blind. The term *teachable* is close in meaning to Tolman's term *docile.* The term *cognitive* refers to such abilities as the capacity to discriminate, the sense of locations, a sense of what leads to what, and the capacity to form expectations.

Intervening Variables. Tolman believed that we can identify meaningful psychological concepts that help account for the behavior of living organisms. In other words, Tolman was not content to describe simple stimulus–response relationships. He believed that psychological processes intervene between stimuli and responses. Such psychological processes are inferred from behavior and meaningfully tied to behavior. The expression **intervening variable** refers to psychological processes that direct behavior and mediate between environmental stimuli and observable responses. Examples of intervening variables include cognitions, expectancies, purposes, hypotheses, and appetite. To illustrate, consider the term *expectancy.* According to Tolman, an expectancy develops when a reward follows each successful response. Humans and animals develop expectancies any time there are regular relationships between responses and environmental stimuli. Once developed, an expectancy is involved in directing and controlling behavior. Many of Tolman's intervening variables had a decidedly mentalistic ring yet were always tied to observable events. We turn now to a consideration of Tolman's position on some key issues in learning.

Reinforcement. What we normally think of as a reinforcement (e.g., a food object) has nothing to do with learning as such, but reinforcements do regulate the performance of learned responses. Tolman, more than any theorist, drew a sharp distinction between learning and performance. Classic experiments on **latent learning** illustrate Tolman's position on the relationships among reinforcement, learning, and performance.

In a typical experiment (e.g., Tolman & Honzik, 1930), one group of rats is given a food reward following each successful run through a maze. The speed of running quickly increases and the number of errors decreases. Another group of subjects receives no food in the maze. After spending time in the maze each day, subjects in this group are removed and returned to their home cage. Speed of running and number of errors for this group does not improve significantly. At this point, one might conclude that the group that had been rewarded had learned while the group that had not been rewarded did not learn. Such an interpretation, however, is apparently incorrect. Perhaps the group that had not been fed had also learned the maze but had no reason to show that they knew it. So, on day eleven, Tolman and Honzik introduced food in the reward box for subjects that had not previously been rewarded. Their running speeds and error scores improved dramatically—so dramatically that it is reasonable to conclude that there was latent learning during the nonrewarded trials.

Tolman argued that rats learn spatial relationships or even develop a so-called cognitive map of a maze by virtue of sheer exposure. Reinforcement influences motivation and hence performance, but learning itself is an independent process. For practical purposes, we still use reinforcement because of the important role it plays in motivation.

Experimental Extinction. Extinction occurs largely because of changes in expectancies. Response strength remains high so long as conditioned stimuli continue, in a majority of cases, to serve as signs that food will be forthcoming. When stimuli no longer have value as signs, expectancies change and so do responses. One implication of Tolman's position is that extinction, in theory, can be a cognitive affair; that is, it could occur without responding. If one were in a position to see clearly that a sign will no longer lead to a reinforcement, extinction could be accomplished without the necessity of responding. Experiments on latent extinction have provided evidence for cognitive interpretations of extinction.

In the typical experiment, subjects are repeatedly placed in an unbaited goal box that was once a place where they had obtained reinforcement. Subjects who are exposed to an unbaited goal box

extinguish much faster in subsequent extinction trials than do subjects who have had no such prextinction exposure to the unbaited goal box. Extinction, according to Tolman, results from changing cognitions that are influenced by sign stimuli in the environment. Such a position is in marked contrast with Hull's response-produced inhibition theory.

Cognitive Maps. The emphasis in many early learning theories was on connections between stimuli and responses. Tolman accepted the idea that some kinds of learning do involve stimulus–response connections, but also emphasized the importance of stimulus–stimulus connections. Complicated stimulus–stimulus connections are vital components in Tolman's concept of the **cognitive map.**

Consider the complicated maze that the typical college student must run in order to get from a dorm room to a classroom. The maze may involve many left and right turns, some diagonal pathway, stairs, or even elevators. In animal laboratories, comparable situations are sometimes created for the white rat. When the maze is successfully traversed, we may ask ourselves what it is that has been learned. Have we learned a complicated chain of stimulus–response connections? According to Tolman, the answer is no. In such a situation we learn a cognitive map.

For example, we do not learn that we must make three successive left turns, followed by two right turns, followed by a left turn, and so on. Instead, we develop a cognitive map that includes, at first, a vague sense of location and a sense of the layout of the situation, including many possible pathways connecting various locations. In other words, there is a cognitive representation of the world in which we work. We do not move about our world in a mechanical highly fixed fashion; rather, we move in a more flexible fashion, following first one pathway then another. Simpler organisms such as the white rat do the same thing. Again, Tolman did not deny that some learning involves stimulus–response connections, but in addition to such learning, he also insisted that we learn stimulus–stimulus connections and that such connections are vital to the development of complicated cognitive maps.

The Role of Insight in Learning. Tolman accepted the idea that learning is often marked by radical discontinuities. Most learning is not of the blind trial-and-error variety discussed in the early classic work of Thorndike. Tolman believed in the "*capacity* for grasping field-relationships" (Tolman, 1932, p. 200). He referred to such a capacity as a *means–end capacity.* This expression refers to innate and acquired abilities to engage in intelligent commerce with pathways, routes, barriers, and various temporal and spatial characteristics of a field. Tolman spoke of the capacity for *inventive ideation,* which referred to "running back-and-forth, attempting alternatives, and making behavioral adjustments." While Tolman generally avoided the term *insight* as used by the Gestalt psychologists, he was largely friendly to the term's meaning. Along with the Gestalt psychologists, he rejected the idea that learning is a continuous, gradual, mechanical process.

Appraisal of Tolman's System.   Tolman demonstrated that the desirable methodological rigor of classical behaviorism could be coupled with a richer, more believable psychology that recognizes the complexities and subtleties of human and animal life. His system provided much of the intellectual spadework necessary to the cognitive movement that became so dominant in the 1960s. Hilgard and Bower (1966) noted that Tolman "gave a new cast to behaviorism by insisting that it be open to the problems created by cognitive processes, problem solving, and inventive ideation" (p. 228).

Finally, Tolman's work can be viewed as a springboard for developments in the 1950s and 1960s in such diverse areas as motivation (e.g., Festinger, 1962; Lawrence & Festinger, 1962), clinical psychology (e.g., Rotter, 1954), neuropsychology (e.g., Olds, 1954), and mathematical learning theory (e.g., Bower, 1962; MacCorquodale & Meehl, 1954). He was the first to publish research on selective breeding for maze-learning ability in rats, work that inspired his students such as Robert

Choate Tryon (1901–1967) and influenced the field of behaviorial genetics (Innis, 1992). Tolman's work is undoubtedly one of the most important bridges between classical behaviorism and contemporary psychology (Goldman, 1999).

Burrhus Frederic Skinner

Hull, Guthrie, and Tolman were not, of course, the sole champions of neobehaviorism. In fact, the behavioristic viewpoint in many of its classical characteristics was set forth in the work of B. F. Skinner (1904–1990), one of the most prominent and celebrated figures in psychology in the latter half of the twentieth century.

Burrhus Frederic Skinner was born on March 20, 1904, in Susquehanna, Pennsylvania. He lived a pleasant childhood surrounded by a cordial family. However, occasional developmental events were instructive about the influence of aversive conditioning. Skinner (1967) recalled that he was never physically punished as a child. Nevertheless, he often heard lectures about the horrors of hell and the terrible consequences of antisocial behavior.

Skinner was a student of the humanities, though initially he was encouraged to pursue a career in law. (Skinner's birth announcement in the local newspaper predicted succession to his father's legal

Burrhus Frederic Skinner

practice: "The town has a new law firm: Wm. A. Skinner & Son" [Skinner, 1967, p. 394].) Skinner, however, hoped to become an author and, though a careless student, made an active study of literature at Hamilton College in New York. He ultimately decided against a writing career despite a favorable appraisal of his work by Robert Frost.

While at Hamilton, Skinner read Ivan Pavlov's *Conditioned Reflexes*, Bertrand Russell's *Philosophy,* and John B. Watson's *Behaviorism.* Though lacking an undergraduate course in psychology, he enrolled in the graduate program at Harvard University. Edwin G. Boring was the principal figure in an academic climate largely untouched by behaviorism; the only seminar on the subject was offered by Walter S. Hunter, who traveled from Clark University as a guest lecturer (Plaud & Montgomery, 1993).

Despite the minimal emphasis on behaviorism, the graduate program at Harvard allowed Skinner great autonomy in developing his research interests. He completed all requirements for his master's degree in 1930 and received his Ph.D. the following year. From 1933 to 1936, Skinner continued his research in the prestigious position of junior fellow of the Harvard Society of Fellows.

In 1936, Skinner joined the faculty of the University of Minnesota. His appointment proved productive in both laboratory and classroom activities. He contributed to wartime research while developing his notions about operant conditioning. His success in teaching was enhanced by the exceptional quality of his students. Skinner (1983a) later recalled that over 5 percent of his students at Minnesota subsequently earned Ph.D. degrees in psychology. In 1945, he assumed the chair of the psychology department at Indiana University. After three years, he returned to Harvard University.

In 1958, the American Psychological Association honored Skinner with its Distinguished Scientific Contribution Award. In the same year, he was appointed to the prestigious Edgar Pierce Professorship, named in honor of the affluent Harvard alumnus who established the William James lecture series. Skinner, however, found little gratification in such veneration. Indeed, there was a marked lack of ostentation in his style of life. He answered his own phone, refused to display medals or trophies,

and stored his honorary degrees in a box in the basement of his home. When he allowed himself to be interviewed or when he appeared on talk shows (such as a 1971 debate with the physicist Donald MacKay on the TV program *Firing Line*), it was not for self-aggrandizement but for the promotion of behaviorism (Washburn, 1997).

Skinner retired in 1974 to become Professor Emeritus of Psychology and Social Relations. In August 1990, the American Psychological Association presented Skinner with the unprecedented Citation for Outstanding Lifetime Contribution to Psychology award. B. F. Skinner died from leukemia on August 18, 1990, a mere eight days after accepting the APA award.

For six decades Skinner was a prolific and animated defender of behaviorism. His experimental behavior analysis was set forth in numerous scientific and nontechnical books, including *The Behavior of Organisms* (1938), *Walden Two* (1948), *Science and Human Behavior* (1953), *Verbal Behavior* (1957), *The Technology of Teaching* (1968), *Beyond Freedom and Dignity* (1971), and *About Behaviorism* (1974). In addition, he published a three-volume autobiography: *Particulars of My Life* (1976), *The Shaping of a Behaviorist* (1979), and *A Matter of Consequences* (1983a). Although his research was often marked with controversy and criticism (Rutherford, 2000), Skinner refused to answer his critics. His preference was to collect data and work out the details of his position.

Precursors to Skinner's Behaviorism.   Toward the end of the 1950s, Skinner's agenda for experimental behavior analysis was gaining popularity. Before considering the primary tenets of Skinner's work, we should briefly survey other scholars to whom he owed a conceptual debt.

Although Bacon, Sherrington, La Mettrie, and other figures comprise part of Skinner's intellectual history, five names seem particularly prominent. Charles Darwin's insistence on the continuity of species reinforced the belief that data from animals were meaningful for all organisms. C. Lloyd Morgan's canon of parsimony counseled Skinner to neglect grandiose explanations in favor of simple, descriptive ones. Edward L. Thorndike's puzzle box experimentation demonstrated that complex behavior could be studied in an objective manner without reliance on mentalism. Ivan Pavlov's research established the precedent for a controlled laboratory investigation of lawful conditioning. Finally, John B. Watson's behaviorism inspired Skinner to adopt the scientific study of behavior as an alternative to the study of consciousness.

While applauding the 1913 behaviorist manifesto, Skinner (1963) observed that Watson failed to support his position with a solid research program. Skinner, by contrast, was clearly more successful than Watson in generating data for behaviorism. In an effort to promote research on behavior analysis, the *Journal of the Experimental Analysis of Behavior* was founded in 1958, the year of Watson's death. The endurance of the journal is a singular tribute to Skinner's influence on the psychology of learning. His influence is further reflected in professional organizations such as APA Division 25, a collective body of researchers interested in the experimental analysis of behavior (Lattal, 1992). For a better understanding of Skinner's work, it is important to examine the basic assumptions of his behavior analysis.

Skinner's Philosophy of Behaviorism. Skinner was a resolute positivist devoted to psychology as an objective natural science. According to Skinner (1963), behaviorism was more than the study of behavior; it was a philosophy of science. Like Watson, Skinner saw psychology as a natural science and, like Watson, was a thoroughgoing determinist. Skinner (1971) insisted that behavior is lawful and argued that the romantic notion of free will is counterproductive both to behavioral science and to society at large.

Though Skinner's writings gave the impression of hard determinism, his research on reinforcers that increase the probability of a future response suggests an interest in probabilistic lawfulness rather than strict determinism. Nevertheless, emphasis on prediction and control was central to Skinner's entire system of thought. Furthermore, his goal was to demonstrate the detrimental features of aversive control and the advantages of positive control. Skinner strongly believed that individuals and society and its institutions can progress most effectively through a "technology

of behavior" drawn from the principles of behavior analysis.

Like most other neobehaviorists, Skinner was a student of behavior rather than of mental events. Although previous neobehaviorists adhered to methodological behaviorism (the emphasis on controlled, observable experimentation with falsifiable and replicable conclusions), Skinner went a step further as he complemented methodological behaviorism with a radical behaviorism—a philosophy supporting the experimental analysis of behavior. According to Skinner (1974), "The position can be stated as follows: what is felt or introspectively observed is not some nonphysical world of consciousness, mind or mental life but the observer's own body" (p. 17). He claimed that three obstacles stand in the way of radical behaviorism: third-force psychology, psychotherapy, and cognitive psychology. Skinner (1987a) argued, "By their very nature, the antiscience stance of humanistic psychology, the practical exigencies of the helping professions, and the cognitive restoration of the royal House of Mind have worked against the definition of psychology as the science of behavior" (p. 784). Although he mourned the damage of these approaches, Skinner remained confident that radical behaviorism would deliver psychology from pseudoscientific factions. In his final article, completed the evening before his death, Skinner (1990) adamantly declared that a scientific psychology can only be an analysis of behavior and not a study of the mind.

Unlike Clark Hull, Skinner eschewed grandiose theory construction in favor of descriptive observations of behavior. More than any behaviorist, Skinner (1956) followed in the critical inductivist tradition of Bacon. He denied that he constructed hypotheses or that he tested formal theorems or models. He assumed that behavior was lawful and understood the difficulty of discovering its laws. We turn now to a consideration of some of Skinner's specific contributions.

Operant Conditioning. Skinner (1938) established the principal notions of experimental behavior analysis in his classic work *The Behavior of Organisms.* Based on his published research since 1930, this book presented a comprehensive system of methods for the **operant conditioning** of animals. Although some critics attacked Skinner for making no effort to tie his ideas to existing data and concepts, *The Behavior of Organisms* was hailed as a significant contribution to the psychology of learning (Knapp, 1995). As far back as 1932, Skinner had distinguished between two major types of conditioning, and five years later introduced the term *operant* in contrast with Pavlovian **respondent conditioning** (Coleman, 1981).

Pavlovian conditioning probed the correlations between unconditioned and conditioned stimuli, whereas Skinner stressed the relation of the response and reinforcement. Thus, Skinner referred to Pavlovian conditioning as *Type II* or *Type S* (reinforcement correlated with a stimulus) and operant conditioning as *Type I* or *Type R* (reinforcement correlated with a response). Type S encompassed conditioning of autonomic behavior, whereas Type R was conditioning of voluntary behavior.

From its genesis, the familiar premise of operant conditioning centered on the modification of behavior as a consequence of reinforcement. Any consequence that increased the probability of a future response was deemed a reinforcer. A positive reinforcer (e.g., food, money) entails a stimulus that increases the likelihood of a future response. A negative reinforcer involves removal of an aversive stimulus to increase the probability of a future response (e.g., a termination of electrical shock or extreme heat). Thus, operants comprise a class of behaviors strengthened by a class of consequences, or reinforcers.

Because Skinner was not concerned with the antecedent association between stimulus and response, his work is not in the tradition of S-R psychology. Skinner clearly denied this heritage: "I do not consider myself an S-R psychologist. The stimulus is only one among a lot of different variables. As it stands, I'm not sure that response is a very useful concept. Behavior is very fluid; it isn't made up of lots of little responses packed together. . . . It is a mistake to suppose that there are internal stimuli and to try to formulate everything as S-R psychology" (quoted in Evans, 1968, pp. 20–21).

The observant student will note the similarity between the research of Skinner and of Edward L. Thorndike (Chance, 1999). In a letter to Thorndike, Skinner (1967) acknowledged that his work was an elaboration of the former's puzzle box research. As in Thorndike's revised law of effect, Skinner favored reward over punishment in the strengthening of behavior. Intermittent punishment may produce unfortunate by-products and only short-term gains. Nevertheless Skinner (1953) asserted that society had made progress in diminishing the aversive influence of punishment. He celebrated the demise of angry avenging gods and threats of hellfire that terrorized previous generations. He was also pleased that the "dunce cap" and birch rod in schools were replaced by more enlightened positive incentives to learn. Skinner verified reinforcement principles with data collected from various technological innovations. Indeed, his modification of ice chests into operant chambers revolutionized the study of animal behavior. The chamber allowed an animal subject to demonstrate a learned behavior (e.g., a bar press or pecking at a lit disk) that could be rewarded by a food dispenser. Interestingly, the operant chamber was branded with the infamous title the "Modified Skinner Box" by Clark Hull, although in characteristic modesty, Skinner (1983a) protested usage of the eponym.

Skinner also constructed the cumulative recorder, a mechanical device that monitored patterns of operant behavior from a single animal subject. By the mid-1950s, operant instrumentation was manufactured by several companies. His experiences with operant technology occasionally led to new discoveries, such as the influence of different schedules of reinforcement on behavior (Crossman, 1991). Skinner (1956) reported that practical necessity motivated some of his early interest in schedules of reinforcement. One day it was clear that he was going to run out of food pellets, so he reinforced his subject once every minute. He saved his supply of pellets and observed a rather constant rate of responding. This serendipitous finding led to the study of fixed intervals and other schedules of reinforcement. Together with Charles Ferster, Skinner published a book containing over nine hundred figures on the specifications of these experimental reinforcement schedules (Ferster & Skinner, 1957).

Skinner's fundamental vision of operant conditioning did not radically change in the ensuing fifty years (although ideas about drive and reflex were abandoned after the 1930s). However, Skinner's contribution extends beyond research on animal learning. In fact, the broad implications of his research on operant conditioning have served as the impetus for numerous applications.

Skinner's Applied Research. One hallmark of B. F. Skinner's legacy is an effort to generalize his ideas from the domain of the laboratory to the complexity of the external world. Though initially he found little interest in the applications of operant conditioning (see Skinner, 1938, pp. 441–442), he was later to change his position. Indeed, the 1968 debut of the *Journal of Applied Behavior Analysis* signaled one of many applications of the experimental principles of behavior analysis. We shall consider a few of Skinner's more prominent applications in greater depth.

Verbal Behavior. One of Skinner's earliest applied efforts, started in 1935, was an analysis of verbal behavior. Although a disciple of Darwinian continuity, Skinner (1938) admitted, "The only differences I expect to see revealed between the behavior of rat and man (aside from enormous differences of complexity) lie in the field of verbal behavior" (p. 442). Skinner revealed his concept of language acquisition in his 1948 William James lectures, which were expanded into the controversial 1957 publication *Verbal Behavior.* He claimed that verbal behavior is learned and, like any operant behavior, is modified by ensuing consequences from a given community.

Critics, most notably psycholinguist Noam Chomsky, argued that Skinner's reinforcement explanation of linguistic development was simplistic and reductionistic. Chomsky (1959) believed that language was an abstract, rule-governed system. Chomsky's scathing review generated considerable attention while Skinner's work was largely neglected (Andresen, 1991). However, Skinner was

convinced that Chomsky misunderstood the book and declined rebuttal to the psycholinguist's critique. Kenneth MacCorquodale (1970) later defended Skinner's verbal behavior perspective within the context of the nativism (Chomsky) versus environment (Skinner) debate. Despite criticism of the book, Skinner continued to support the reinforcement explanation of verbal behavior.

Developmental and Educational Applications. While at Indiana, Skinner gained notoriety for his invention of the aircrib, a large well-lit chamber with proper temperature control for child rearing (Benjamin & Nielsen-Gammon, 1999). Originally called the baby-tender, Skinner employed the chamber during the upbringing of Deborah, his second daughter. Contrary to rumors about hardships resulting from her upbringing, Skinner (1967) proudly noted that his daughter was a college graduate and an accomplished artist. Furthermore, Julie, his oldest daughter and an educational psychologist, raised Skinner's granddaughter in an aircrib.

Skinner also took an active interest in his children's education. After observing that education was often the product of inappropriate consequences, Skinner (1958, 1968) proposed a solution by way of programmed instruction. In the 1920s, Sidney L. Pressey had constructed programmed machines for testing intelligence. Skinner revised Pressey's idea by designing programs that dispense immediate feedback for each student response. Skinner's programmed instruction promoted sustained activity with self-paced mastery of the material. The idea generated a great deal of media attention (Rutherford, 2000). Although IBM and other companies were interested in marketing teaching machines, negotiations collapsed along with Skinner's dream of reforming American education (Bjork, 1993); nonetheless, Skinner clearly anticipated computer-assisted instruction by several decades. His programmed instruction inspired other researchers to develop innovative educational methods. Most notably, Fred S. Keller formulated a Personalized System of Instruction (PSI), which emphasized the individual student's responsibility for mastering the material (Keller & Sherman, 1974). Despite such pedagogical innovations,

Skinner (1984) remained dissatisfied with the direction of U.S. education.

Finally, Skinner explored the process of aging. Together with Harvard colleague Margaret Vaughan, he published a nontechnical book entitled *Enjoy Old Age* in 1983. This book contained practical suggestions and insights on such gerontological concerns as diet, exercise, retirement, forgetfulness, sensory deficiencies, and the fear of death. Ironically, Skinner (1983) recalled the rigorous composition of the book: "We met a self-imposed deadline and finished it in three months, thereby violating, for me, one of its basic principles: avoid fatigue. I was scarcely enjoying old age when we finished the book, but I soon recovered" (p. 394).

Military Applications.   Perhaps Skinner's most unconventional idea was his so-called Project Pigeon research during World War II. With the assistance of several outstanding students from the University of Minnesota (including Keller and Marilyn Breland and William K. Estes), Skinner trained pigeons to navigate an armed glider named the "Pelican" (so named because like the bird, the glider had a large frontal store with a considerably smaller body). The enthusiastic researchers demonstrated the efficiency of their automated bombers to government officials but with disappointing results. Ironically, Skinner (1960) claimed that one military authority declared that the pigeons were more accurate than radar. Despite Skinner's certitude about the effectiveness of his "crackpot idea," the government rejected further support for the project. Despite initial funding by General Mills, the decision was made to discontinue funding in favor of other military projects.

However, the classified research did demonstrate the efficacy of operant conditioning. Skinner kept thirty pigeons and demonstrated immediate and accurate target strikes even after six years of inactivity. The research was later resurrected by Franklin Taylor under the auspices of the Naval Research Laboratory in Washington, DC. Currently, a missile nose cone from Project Pigeon resides with a teaching machine in the Smithsonian Institution (Skinner, 1983b). Skinner's ideas were also implemented in an aerospace program that sent two bar-pressing chimpanzees into space (Rohles, 1992).

Walden Two: Another Behaviorist Utopia.   In an essay on "A Behaviorist's Utopia," John B. Watson conceived of a society that controlled childcare and social relationships from the time of birth to maturity (Buckley, 1989). Although far removed from Watson's utopia, Skinner proposed in detail an institution based on behavioral principles of reinforcement. In his 1948 novel *Walden Two,* he described life in a hypothetical experimental colony designed by behavioral engineering. The novel centered on a Professor Burris, who is reacquainted with T. E. Frazier, a maverick colleague from their graduate school days. Frazier is the founder of Walden Two, a community maintained and established on positive reinforcement. Workers labor for four hours daily, have a credit system of payment, and enjoy numerous opportunities for creative relaxation. Through the observations of Burris and Frazier, the reader is allowed insight into Skinner's vision of a behaviorist utopia.

Written in a mere seven weeks, *Walden Two* became one of Skinner's most popular books, especially during the quest for alternative lifestyles in the 1960s. The controversial nature of a behaviorally designed community aroused curiosity among the general public, college students, movie studios, and even the Central Intelligence Agency (Skinner, 1983). An experimental community based on *Walden Two* was established in 1967 in Twin Oaks, Virginia. The community proved only marginally successful, but led Skinner (1967) to reformulate the role of incentive, education, and sexuality in a behaviorist community. Although fictional, Skinner's *Walden Two* provides an intriguing glimpse of behavioral engineering.

Clinical Application.   Skinner's experimental behavior analysis has also found application in psychotherapy. During the 1930s, he had an interest in employing operant techniques with psychotic patients but was prevented from doing so by a rigorous schedule. In 1948, he delivered a series of lectures at Worcester State Hospital but was again unable to initiate a research program on psychotic behavior modification.

Finally in 1952, Skinner initiated a behavior therapy program at the Metropolitan State Hospital in Waltham, Massachusetts. Ogden Lindsley, one of Skinner's students, engaged in six hundred hours of successful behavior modification with psychotic patients using candy, cigarettes, and pin-up posters as reinforcers (Skinner, 1983b). In November 1953, Skinner and his colleagues presented their research in the paper "Studies in Behavior Therapy," marking the first usage of the term *behavior therapy.* Today, behavior therapy and modification remain an enterprising field of psychotherapy.

Critical Appraisal of Skinner's Behaviorism. The praise for Skinner's work has been joined with dissension from both public and scientific sectors. Following the 1971 publication of *Beyond Freedom and Dignity,* Skinner reached the height of his public exposure and found himself embroiled in controversy that spilled into the *New York Times* among other media (Rutherford, 2000). His ideas usually provoked skeptical or condemnatory reaction and, at times, detractors perceived him as a sort of "scientific despot." A legion of critics from psychotherapist Carl Rogers to former Vice President Spiro Agnew damned Skinner's ideology. He was branded a fascist and a Nazi, his talks were picketed by protestors, and his image was hung in effigy. His open criticism of the Vietnam conflict during the 1960s nearly jeopardized government funding of his research and made him the target of an FBI investigation (Skinner, 1983; Wyatt, 2000).

Skinner also provoked criticism from colleagues within the scientific community. Critics such as Chomsky contended that Skinner's "simplistic explanations" appear sound in an artificial laboratory context, but have little validity in the real world. Furthermore, behavior analysis has been accused of indifference toward topical areas such as the self, personality, cognition, feelings, purpose, creativity, and nativism. Skinner has also been blamed for advancing a mechanistic science that dehumanizes the individual. In addition, Mahoney (1989) charged that the radical behaviorist's intolerant opinion of contemporary psychology has

jeopardized its future, and called for a tempering of ideology if the discipline is to progress.

Despite voluminous objections, Skinner (1987b) remained puzzled about the controversy surrounding his research. After all, anybody could test his results for themselves. If there were errors, they could be corrected by research.

Beginning in the 1980s, the controversy began to cool as Skinner's extraordinary contributions enjoyed greater credibility. Rutherford (2000, p. 391) observed a "shift in public opinion and a more philosophical evaluation of his impact on the popular culture of psychology" following Skinner's death in 1990. Although his ideas generated opposition, there can be no denying his pervasive influence on psychology in the latter half of the twentieth century. His contributions to both experimental and clinical psychology are a monument to his influence on the discipline.

FURTHER CONTRIBUTIONS TO APPLIED PSYCHOLOGY FROM NEOBEHAVIORISM

Classical behaviorism has always emphasized the applications of psychology to the problems of daily life. Indeed, one of Watson's criticisms of earlier psychologies was that they were too sterile, too far removed from the problems of law, business, education, medicine, and interpersonal relations. Watson embraced that part of functionalism that explored the daily problems of life, but hoped to move beyond functionalism with a down-to-earth psychology that dealt primarily with the tangible world. Other behaviorists shared Watson's interest in the problems of living. Though the bulk of the laboratory work of the behaviorist schools was devoted to the psychology of learning, representatives of those schools had unmistakable interests in a larger agenda.

Examples of the contributions of behavioristically oriented psychologists to applied problems abound. Earlier, we noted Max Meyer's practical work with hearing-impaired people and Albert P. Weiss's work on human–machine interactions. Walter Samuel Hunter was also heavily involved in the study of human–machine systems in World War II. Karl Lashley's work with brain-damaged subjects represents a pioneering effort to find ways to restore functions lost through injury and disease. Lashley's work foreshadowed the field of behavioral neuroscience with its emphasis on basic and applied problems associated with the structural and functional properties of the nervous system.

The neobehaviorists who followed most directly in the intellectual tradition of John B. Watson also worked on a variety of practical problems. Though he was keenly aware of the problems of assessing human ability and potential, Hull's book *Aptitude Testing* (1928) is a classic in that area. His book *Hypnosis and Suggestibility* (1933) is also one of the most informed and substantial books on the topic of hypnosis.

As we have seen, Skinner was dedicated to the application of operant conditioning to a broad range of areas including education, linguistics, development, and military and clinical psychology. Along with Skinner, Guthrie had the broadest range of interests in applied problems. Guthrie's major works are filled with practical anecdotes on how to apply his learning theory to daily problems. His book *Educational Psychology* (1950), published with Francis Powers, is an application of learning theory to the classroom. He also wrote on the topics of personality, psychotherapy, leadership, the evaluation of faculty performance, and the function of the state university. His interests were by no means restricted to the issues of learning theory. However, when Guthrie thought about the basic problems of learning, he seemed to be led irresistibly to place these problems in a larger practical context. His was truly a functional behaviorism.

Though most of Tolman's published works dealt with theoretical issues in learning, his cognitive emphasis brought new breadth to behaviorism. His was a more psychological behaviorism and his followers explored a larger range of problems while retaining much of the methodological rigor that had always been a virtue of behaviorism. Tolman's book *Drives Toward War*, published in 1942 just after the United States' involvement in World War II, illustrates his interest in the psychological sources of conflict. The book focuses on some of the psychogenic or learned needs that contribute to human conflict and war.

Behaviorism was the dominant force in U.S. psychology from the 1920s to the late 1950s. Though most behaviorists viewed learning as foundational to the field of psychology, their interests ranged broadly from the problems of psychopathology to the problems of social psychology. Even so, by the 1960s, there was a growing consensus that their vision was too narrow, that both methodologically and substantively, they had closed too many doors. Their many positive contributions, however, were carried on in new broader approaches to the discipline.

REVIEW QUESTIONS

1. Briefly discuss three values that are more or less common to all behavioristic psychologies.

2. What is *operationism* and what are some of the common criticisms of it?

3. How did Max Meyer's behavioristic system differ from that advanced by John B. Watson? How did Edwin B. Holt's system differ from Watson's approach?

4. According to Albert P. Weiss, what was the subject matter of psychology? Do you agree or disagree with his position? Why?

5. Outline two of Walter S. Hunter's contributions to psychology.

6. Define Lashley's concepts of equipotentiality and mass action.

7. Contrast Hull, Guthrie, Tolman, and Skinner with respect to their views on the subject of reinforcement.

8. What practical advice on the extinction of responses might come out of the theoretical work of Hull? Guthrie? Tolman?

9. Briefly explain the significance of the latent learning experiments.

10. What did Tolman mean by the expression *intervening variable*?

11. Briefly describe some of the applied interests of the psychologists covered in this chapter.

12. Contrast Skinner and Hull with respect to their views on the role of theory in science.

13. According to Skinner, what are the essential differences between Type S and Type R conditioning?

14. Discuss Skinner's philosophy of punishment and state why you think he is right or wrong on the issue.

15. Discuss three applications of Skinner's research.

CHAPTER 15

GESTALT PSYCHOLOGY

Is the human mind to be regarded as a domain of mere indifferent facts? Or do intrinsic demands, fittingness, and its opposite, wrongness, occur among the genuine characteristics of its contents?

—Wolfgang Köhler (1938/1966)

The demand for a radically different orientation to psychology surfaced in Germany in 1910. The new orientation, called *Gestalt psychology,* was headed by Max Wertheimer (1880–1943) and his close associates Wolfgang Köhler (1887–1967) and Kurt Koffka (1886–1941). Wertheimer, Köhler, and Koffka called for a much broader conception of the subject matter and the methods of psychology. Initially, the Gestalt revolt was against the elementary dimensions of Wundt's psychology but later the revolt was directed against American behaviorism. Indeed, in later classical works, Gestalt psychology attacked behaviorism more than the psychologies of Wundt and Titchener.

There is no exact English counterpart for the German word **Gestalt,** but *configuration, form, holistic, structure,* and *pattern* are commonly employed in attempts to provide a usable translation. While none is an exact equivalent, they provide intellectual openings into a complex and fascinating system of thought. However, we should avoid the trap of relying too heavily on any one English word as an equivalent for the term *Gestalt.* For example, it is an error to treat Gestalt psychology as nothing but holistic psychology. Michael Wertheimer (1983) pointed out that there have been many holistic psychologies, but most lack the precision and rigor that have characterized Gestalt psychology. Hence, it can be misleading to translate the term *Gestalt* as holistic.

This chapter begins with a review of biographical materials on the leaders of the school then examines historical antecedents and major themes in the Gestalt system. The chapter closes with an estimate of the impact and continuing relevance of this important system.

MAX WERTHEIMER

Max Wertheimer was born in Prague, Austria-Hungary, later Czechoslovakia, on April 15, 1880, the second son of Wilhelm Wertheimer and Rosa (Zwicker) Wertheimer. Max's father was a prominent educator who pioneered a "kind of personalized system of instruction, a tutorial approach for the teaching of business practice, typing, accounting, shorthand, and the like" (Wertheimer, 1980b, p. 6). Following high school, the young Wertheimer attended Charles University in Prague, initially to study law, but he foraged widely in other fields such as philosophy, music, physiology, and psychology. Max's son, Michael Wertheimer (1980b), called attention to the likelihood that "among his most important teachers at this time was the philosopher-psychologist Christian von Ehrenfels, from whom Max took several courses" (p. 9).

In the end, it turned out that Max's interests were too wide to continue his studies in law. A practical career in law did not appeal to him, though more abstract treatments of justice, values, and ethics were of deep and lasting concern. As a consequence of the breadth of his interest, Max shifted from law to philosophy, which he studied first at Prague and then at Berlin. At Berlin, he

Max Wertheimer

worked in the company of such notable figures as Carl Stumpf; Friedrich Schumann, the codeveloper with Georg Elias Müller of the memory drum; and Erich von Hornbostel, a musicologist. Following his work at Berlin, Wertheimer enrolled in the Ph.D. program at Würzburg, where he took his degree in 1904 with Oswald Külpe.

Wertheimer's academic career started with a position at an institute in Frankfurt (later to become the University of Frankfurt). From 1916 to 1929, he worked at the Berlin Psychological Institute and in 1929 moved back to Frankfurt as a full professor. With the advent of the Nazi movement and subsequent losses of academic freedom (see Henle, 1978b), there was a mass exodus of Germany's brightest and most capable scientists and other academics. The magnitude of the emigration of German intellectuals is outlined in Ronald Lewin's book, *Hitler's Mistakes* (1984). Such notable figures as Albert Einstein, John von Neumann, Edward Teller, and Max Delbrück were among the émigrés from Germany to the United States.

Lewin (1984) noted the quality of the loss to German science by pointing out that "five of those who transferred to the United States had already won the Nobel prize and six were subsequently to do so" (p. 56). Included in the émigrés from Germany was the fifty-three-year-old Max Wertheimer, his wife, Anne, and their three children,

Valentin, Michael, and Lise. Wertheimer accepted a professorial position in New York City at the New School for Social Research. He held his position at the New School from 1933 until his death in 1943. His ten years in the United States were productive, resulting in papers that extended the Gestalt vision into such areas as the meaning of truth (1934), ethics (1935), democracy (1937), and freedom (1940). We will see that the Gestalt vision advanced by Wertheimer is more than a system of psychology—it is a worldview with implications for other intellectual arenas, such as philosophy, science, and education.

In October 1988, the German Society for Psychology conferred the Wilhelm Wundt plaque posthumously upon Max Wertheimer. The Wilhelm Wundt plaque, accepted on his father's behalf by Michael Wertheimer, is the highest honor the society can bestow. In presenting the award, the society recognized Wertheimer's experimental investigations, his systematic contributions, and his abiding philanthropic and humanistic concerns. Such a posthumous tribute is one of many indicators of the recognition of the continuing relevance of the system that grew out of Wertheimer's work.

WOLFGANG KÖHLER

Wolfgang Köhler (*KUR lur*) was born on January 21, 1887, in Reval, Estonia, but his early formal education was in Germany at the Gymnasium at Wolfenbüttel. He earned his Ph.D. in 1909 at the University of Berlin under Carl Stumpf. Following his doctoral work at Berlin, Köhler took a position as assistant in the psychology laboratory at the Frankfurt Academy, soon to become the University of Frankfurt. From 1913 to 1920, he was director of the Anthropoid Research Station on the Island of Tenerife located in the Canary Islands. His work on Tenerife resulted in one of the classic works in Gestalt psychology, *The Mentality of Apes,* first published in English in 1924.

Following his work on Tenerife, Köhler returned to Germany to take a position as professor at the University of Göttingen. In 1922, he accepted a position as professor and director of the Psychological Institute at the University of Berlin. Henle (1978b) pointed out that the institute, under

Wolfgang Köhler

Köhler's direction, included an "all-star cast of characters." Faculty members present during all or part of Köhler's tenure included Max Wertheimer, Karl Duncker, Kurt Lewin, Otto von Lauenstein, and Hedwig von Restorff.

The 1920s and early 1930s at the Berlin Institute were highly productive years, but the delicate climate that encourages scientific creativity was shattered in 1933 when the Nazi regime came to power. Hitler immediately invoked changes that wreaked havoc in the entire German university system. Jewish professors and any professors who were unfriendly to national socialism were dismissed. Scientific theories, methods, and problems were increasingly selected on the basis of their agreement with political authority (Ash, 1995). Professors found it difficult to obtain funds and the scientific enterprise was burdened with an unreliable bureaucratic structure marked by infighting and a continual breakdown of authority. Lewin (1984, p. 55) remarked that as early as 1933, the great mathematician John von Neumann lamented, in a letter to a friend, that the Nazis would ruin German science for a generation. Psychology did not, however, disappear under national socialism; in fact, professional psychology grew rapidly during the Third Reich (Geuter, 1984/1992).

In a thoughtful article entitled "One Man Against the Nazis," Henle (1978b) called attention to Wolfgang Köhler's heroic struggles against the Nazis. Among many activities of resistance, Köhler wrote a powerful letter to protest the dismissal of Jewish professors. When the regime demanded that professors begin classes with a Nazi salute, Köhler did a caricature of the salute and followed this with a speech declaring that his salute did not come with ordinary meanings attached to it. Henle pointed out that Köhler's comments were greeted with thunderous applause. The Nazi brownshirts in the crowd were undoubtedly not among those in agreement. Köhler's work at the Berlin Psychological Institute continued until 1935, but by that time conditions were all but unbearable. Finally, Köhler resigned his position and emigrated to the United States, where he accepted a position as professor of psychology at Swarthmore College.

Köhler was a prolific writer and spokesman for the Gestalt movement. In 1929, he published *Gestalt Psychology,* a classic statement that opened with a trenchant attack on behaviorism. The book brings to focus the extent to which behaviorism is based on the atomism and mechanism of nineteenth-century physics. Köhler then set forth the Gestalt position that took its lead from the newer concepts of field physics. He published *The Place of Value in a World of Facts* in 1938 and *Dynamics in Psychology* in 1940.

Many honors came to Wolfgang Köhler. Among the most significant were his delivery of the William James lectures at Harvard University and his delivery of the Gifford lectures at Edinburgh in 1958. He was named research professor of Philosophy and Psychology at Swarthmore College in 1946 and was elected president of the American Psychological Association in 1958. A year before being elected to the presidency of the American Psychological Association, he received the Distinguished Scientific Contribution Award from that association. He received honorary doctorates from numerous universities in this country and abroad. The estimate of his biographers is noteworthy. Asch (1968) said, "There are few in any generation of his stature" (p. 119) and Henle (1978b), referring to Köhler's struggles with the

Nazis, said, "It shows us once more what a human being can be" (p. 944).

Wolfgang Köhler made his home in Enfield, New Hampshire, following his formal retirement from Swarthmore. In his later years, he continued to write, give lectures, conduct research, and consult with interested students and colleagues. He died in Enfield on June 11, 1967.

KURT KOFFKA

Kurt Koffka was born on March 18, 1886, in Berlin, Germany. There were family expectations that Koffka would follow in the footsteps of his father and enter the legal profession. But, like Wertheimer, Koffka's interests were wide-ranging and theoretical. When he entered the University of Berlin in 1903, it was as a philosophy major; later he shifted to psychology. With the exception of a year of study at Edinburgh, Koffka worked at Berlin, earning a Ph.D. in 1909 under Carl Stumpf. Koffka's formal degree studies were followed by a year of work as an assistant in the laboratory of Johannes Von Kries of Freiburg and another year as assistant to Oswald Külpe at Würzburg. Beginning in 1910, Koffka worked for three semesters at Frankfurt with Wertheimer and Köhler.

In 1912, Koffka accepted a position at the University of Giessen in central Germany. After several visits to the United States in the mid-1920s and after holding some visiting professorships, Koffka accepted a position at Smith College in 1927. He remained at Smith until his death in 1941.

In 1924, Koffka published *Growth of the Mind,* a creative and influential book that demonstrated the relevance of Gestalt principles in the field of developmental psychology. In 1935, he published *Principles of Gestalt Psychology,* a major systematic treatise on Gestalt psychology. Koffka was the first to write an article in English on Gestalt psychology. The article, "Perception: An Introduction to the Gestalt-Theorie," was published in the *Psychological Bulletin* in 1922. Unfortunately, the article left the impression that Gestalt theory was concerned only with perception. To the contrary, the first problem addressed by Gestalt psychologists was thinking. But, as discussed earlier, it is a system of psychology with a broad vision and an interest in a host of topics that extend beyond the borders of psychology.

INTELLECTUAL BACKGROUND OF GESTALT PSYCHOLOGY

Appreciation for the Gestalt school is enhanced by reviewing the philosophical, scientific, and psychological traditions that influenced its founders. There are clearly identifiable intellectual influences that helped shape the thinking of the Gestalt psychologists, but there are also unique features in the system that cannot be easily identified with any one antecedent influence. We will now turn to some of the traditions in philosophy, science, and psychology that left their mark on the Gestalt psychologists.

Philosophy

It will be recalled that the philosopher Immanuel Kant (1724–1804) argued that many of our mental processes are organized in an a priori fashion. Thus, meaningful experiences are not always the result of the mechanical laws of association. Instead, there are ordering principles such as intuitions of causality, time, and space that actively interact with sense experience. Sensory experiences are not necessarily disjointed affairs that await an external connecting principle; rather, organization is a natural ongoing process and meanings are often given in experience itself.

Kant also believed that experience is the foundation upon which knowledge is built. As noted in an earlier chapter, he is regarded as a rationalist, but his emphasis on the key role of experience in knowledge shows that he was seeking a more moderate position between the extremes of rationalism and empiricism.

Gestalt psychology is also often regarded as a system that is more akin to rationalism rather than empiricism. This is an error. Gestalt psychologists challenge us to a more adequate empiricism—an empiricism that is based on those things that are most real in our experience. Gestalt psychologists would argue that an adequate empiricism could hardly lead us to the conclusion that all of our meaningful experiences are built mechanically out of separate elements held together by the glue of association. The Gestalt position emphasizes conjunctions, meanings, and patterns that are simply given in the natural flow of experience. We will later examine the detailed arguments for this position. For the time being, we will simply note that the Gestalt school should not be placed in either of the philosophical extremes of rationalism or empiricism. The starting point for this school is experience, and thus Gestalt psychology is empirical, but proper attention to experience itself will lead to a confirmation of some of the claims of the rationalists.

Science

In the latter part of the nineteenth century and the early twentieth century, there were powerful new currents of thought in the scientific world that had a direct influence on the founders of the Gestalt school. Wolfgang Köhler had a strong background in the physical sciences and had studied with the great theoretical physicist Max Planck (1858–1947). There were personal and intellectual similarities between Planck and Köhler. On the personal side, they both openly resisted the Nazi movement. Planck also resisted Hitler by demanding the release of German scientists imprisoned because of their political or religious beliefs. Because of his resistance, Planck was dismissed as president of the Berlin Physical Society. Later, the Nazi regime imposed a brutal penalty on the famous scientist by forcing him to attend the execution of his son, a member of the Hitler resistance movement.

Planck's approach to science, which included a critique of strict empiricism, also left its mark on Köhler. Planck argued that scientific progress is nurtured by creative theoretical work. An obsession with measurement for its own sake will interfere with scientific progress. Planck's emphasis was on the nature of the events and specific processes that underlie a measured effect. Like his teacher, Köhler was also deeply critical of the premature elevation of measurement. His position is illustrated in a scathing attack on operational definitions of in-

telligence defined as that which an intelligence test measures (see Köhler, 1947, pp. 44–48).

Albert Einstein also influenced Gestalt psychology. This influence may have grown out of the close friendship of Einstein and Max Wertheimer. They spent long hours in conversation about such topics as the nature of science and creativity. Einstein once sought the company of Wertheimer and another friend, Max Born, to help him intervene in a dispute between the student council and the administration of the University of Berlin (see Clark, 1971, p. 198). The larger intellectual implications of Einstein's work in physics undoubtedly left their mark on Wertheimer. Indeed, more than any other psychological system, Gestalt psychology is sensitive to the importance of the context of the observer or the so-called frame of reference. These concepts grew directly out of Einstein's work on electrodynamics of moving bodies. Wertheimer and Köhler were also influenced by the concept of field forces in the new physics. The concept can be illustrated with a magnetic field, as when small iron filings sprinkled on a sheet of paper are distributed into a definite configuration when a magnet is placed under the paper. The focus of the scientist is as much on the field or the pattern as on single elements within the field.

Gestalt psychologists were also influenced by the work of the physicist Ernst Mach (1838–1916) on sensation. Though there was much in Mach's empiricism that was disagreeable to Gestalt psychologists, his book, *The Analysis of Sensations* (1886), was a source of inspiration. Mach argued for space-form and time-form sensations that are essentially configural. An example of a time-form sensation is a melody, which is something different from its several elements. The elements, or individual notes, can all be changed, as when one transposes to a different key signature, and yet the melody remains. In other words, the melody is not just a collection of so many different or separate elements; instead, it is a pattern with a clear identity of its own. Similarly, a visual or space-form sensation maintains an identity independent of the elements. The form quality of a triangle persists regardless of one's spatial orientation to the triangle. Triangularity as a space form is thus something different from just lines that serve as the elements.

Psychology

The concept of form qualities was further elaborated in the work of Christian von Ehrenfels (1859–1932), a philosopher-psychologist associated with the Austrian school of act psychology. Ehrenfels agreed with Mach that form qualities are different from the elements of which they are composed. In a pivotal paper published in 1890 and entitled "On Gestalt Qualities," Ehrenfels took the position that form qualities are given immediately in experience and may persist even when the elements change. Ehrenfels held a position at the University of Prague after 1896 and the young Wertheimer took several courses from him in the period from 1898 to 1901. Ehrenfels undoubtedly helped focus the attention of Wertheimer on the part-whole problem, though it would be over a decade after studying with Ehrenfels before Wertheimer would propose a solution to the problem that was to be radically different from the solution embraced by his teacher.

Ehrenfels, in accord with holistic psychologists, agreed that the whole is *more* than the sum of its parts, but the whole was still viewed as derivative or as another element. The unique feature of the Gestalt system, as noted by Michael Wertheimer (1983), is "the radical view that *the whole is psychologically, logically, epistemologically, and ontologically prior to its parts. A whole is not only more than the sum of its parts, it is entirely different from a sum of its parts: thinking in terms of a sum does violence to the very nature of the dynamics of genuine wholes*" (p. 43).

The relationship between the psychology of William James and Gestalt psychology calls for more detailed scholarly review than it has received to date (Woody, 2001). The leaders of the Gestalt movement quoted from James's psychological and philosophical works and found some points of agreement, but also found much with which to disagree.

James's powerful attacks on atomism mark a point of agreement. In particular, James's mature philosophical vision, especially his radical empiricism, reveals rich parallels with the Gestalt school. In a compelling analysis of common sympathies between the two approaches, Woody (2001, p. 40) observed that "both Gestalt psychologists and William James begin investigations with experience, argue that science and other epistemological endeavors should be grounded in experience, experientially evaluate the truth of a given claim, emphasize the personal nature of experience, and embrace experienced relationships across many levels." And just as experience plays a critical role in epistemology, James and the Gestalt school agreed that methodological pluralism offers real promise for a robust science of psychology (Woody, 2001). The range of topical areas was clearly broader in these two systems than in many other systems.

As noted, the Gestalt psychologists found much in James's psychology to criticize. For example, Koffka (1924/1980, pp. 90–97) took issue with James's view of instincts as a series of chained reflexes. Köhler (1947) criticized James's emphasis on the idea that boundaries in sensory experience have a pragmatic basis. James's interest in the boundaries of sensory experience also shows, however, that he was deeply interested in the part-whole problem. Köhler (1947) recognized that James was sensitized to the same kinds of problems that concerned the Gestalt psychologists, but Köhler was largely critical of James's approach. Though James wrote extensively on the part-whole problem, the extent of his influence on Gestalt psychologists, if any, remains to be uncovered by further scholarship.

THE FUNDAMENTALS OF GESTALT PSYCHOLOGY

The formal founding of Gestalt psychology can be dated to 1910 when Max Wertheimer initiated experiments on the **phi phenomenon.** The results of the experiments were published in Wertheimer's classic paper entitled "Experimental Studies on the Perception of Movement" (1912). The phi phenomenon, or apparent movement, is illustrated in the simplest form by two discrete lights. If the lights are flashed onto two different locations on the retina and if one light succeeds the other by a very brief time interval, then the subject sees movement. Though the lights are stationary and though they represent two discrete points, the subject sees a sweeping movement in a direction from the first flash to the second. In this case, the observer does not see two separate elements or two local events. What is seen is radically different from the elements. Indeed, one could study the elements separately, but fail by such a procedure to provide an adequate understanding of the experience of movement. Max Wertheimer, working with Köhler and Koffka as subjects, collected data that formed the basis of the 1912 paper on the perception of movement that launched the Gestalt movement.

The standard explanation of the phi phenomenon was that movement is perceived because the eye itself moves in response to the successive flashes of light. The movement we experience is based on the kinesthetic feedback from the movement of the eye. But if a light is projected in the center of a field and if this light precedes two lights located on either side of it, the subject will see two movements simultaneously going in opposite directions. Such a finding proves embarrassing to the explanation based on eye movement. The eye could hardly move in two directions at the same time.

The phi phenomenon represents a particularly elegant demonstration that the quality of the whole is *different* from the sum of the parts. In this case, the parts are static elements, simply two stationary flashes of light. But given appropriate temporal and spatial relationships, we see something fundamentally and qualitatively different. Gestalt psychologists believed that the whole could never be understood by piecemeal examination of the isolated elements. Thus, a piecemeal approach from part to whole would prove inadequate to the understanding of experience.

By contrast, analysis that begins with what is given in experience will lead to a more adequate and believable psychology. The Gestalt psychologists took the position that the whole is prior to its parts and thus part processes are governed by the nature of the whole. If this position seems unten-

able, consider the phi phenomenon again. What we see is movement; we do not see the isolated elements. In our immediate experience, the whole is quite literally prior to its parts. Starting with what is given in our experience, we may then proceed "from above" and discover the natural parts and their relations.

Consider another illustration. If a theoretician of music asked for an analysis of a melody, we would begin by focusing on the melody itself. The melody, like the phi phenomenon, has a clear identity in our experience. With that identity as a starting point, we may proceed with a meaningful analysis of the relative arrangement of the parts. According to Köhler (1947), "One of the main tasks of Gestalt Psychology is that of indicating the genuine rather than any fictitious parts of wholes" (p. 168). We will now turn to an examination of Gestalt principles applied to various topics of psychology.

Thinking

As noted earlier, it is a common mistake to believe that Gestalt psychologists were interested first and foremost in perceptual processes. Michael Wertheimer (1980b) pointed out that the earliest Gestalt orientation of Max Wertheimer is found "in the psychology of thinking or in 'Völkerpsychologie' rather than in perception" (p. 13). Many of Wertheimer's contributions to the psychology of thinking are found in his classic book *Productive Thinking,* published posthumously in 1945 and reprinted in 1959 and in 1982 in enlarged editions that include fragments and additions found in Wertheimer's unpublished papers.

Wertheimer was keenly interested in the distinction between *reproductive* thinking and *productive* thinking. The former is associated with mere repetition, conditioning, drills, habits, or the routine retracing of familiar intellectual territory. The latter, by contrast, results in new ideas, breakthroughs, or insights that make a difference. What really happens, asked Wertheimer, when productive thinking takes place? What are the conditions that foster it or that block it? How can we nurture it?

Wertheimer opened his book by reviewing traditional approaches to thinking. There had been widespread belief that thinking is nurtured by training in traditional logic. Wertheimer encouraged such training because it stimulated rigor and a critical orientation, but he concluded that logic in and of itself does not give rise to productive thinking. One can be logical without being creative. He criticized associationist theories of thinking, pointing out that blind trials, drills, repetitions, and chance connections can hardly be construed as sensible thinking. He recognized the historical importance of Hegelian, Marxist, and functionalist approaches, but found that they do not leave us with satisfactory solutions to the problem of productive thinking.

Wertheimer declared that his approach to thinking would be in terms of field principles. He proceeded with a very comprehensive examination of thinking in a rich variety of topical areas. For example, he explored the thinking of Albert Einstein that led to relativity theory and the thinking of Galileo that led to the law of inertia. His interest in the Gestalt process of discovery inspired his students. While directing the psychology department at Frankfurt, Germany, in 1932, Wertheimer challenged his students to write a paper on productive thinking and offered an award for the most outstanding work (Fromm, 1998). One student, Erika Fromm (then Erika Oppenheimer), wrote to one hundred prominent scientists and philosophers, asking them about the productive thinking that led to their intellectual discoveries. Although she did not win the award, more than forty scholars responded to her survey including Einstein and Freud. Einstein described his discovery process as "comparable with the attitude of somebody who wants to solve a puzzle or a chess problem, who is convinced that the solution exists, because the creator of the problem possesses the solution" (cited in Fromm, 1998, p. 1198).

In more common examples of productive thinking, Wertheimer explored such diverse problems as finding the areas of various geometric shapes to the thinking underlying the way we see ourselves in various social situations. *Productive Thinking* is filled with illustrations of alternative solutions to specific problems. For instance, the story is told of a teacher in the eighteenth century who presented this simple addition problem to a class of youngsters:

$$1 + 2 + 3 + 4 + 5 + 6 + 7 + 8 + 9 + 10 = ?$$

Do you know the answer? Carl Friedrich Gauss (1777–1855), later to become a famous mathematician, but then only six years old, announced almost immediately that the answer is 55. Perplexed by his quick solution, the teacher asked young Gauss how he had done it. While other students added $1 + 2 + 3$ and so on, Gauss looked at the whole string of numbers and observed a pattern of 5 11s. In Gauss's novel solution, he combined $1 + 10$, $2 + 9$, $3 + 8$, and so on. Gauss's solution illustrates Wertheimer's point that productive thinking results when we look for structural truths rather than piecemeal truths.

Wertheimer argued that productive thinking is based on the capacity to grasp structural features and to envision structural reorganization. In the preceding problem, Gauss broke out of the usual lock-step approach to addition. He looked first at the whole problem, then he structurally transposed by looking at the two extremes and found the number 11. He then found that the number 11 repeated itself four more times.

As noted, *Productive Thinking* is filled with examples of problems that arise in human life. The book's continuing relevance is illustrated in contemporary emphasis on schemas, plans, and knowledge structures—all reminiscent of Wertheimer's approach to thinking (German & Defeyter, 2000).

Principles of Perceptual Organization

Wertheimer found that the Gestalt principle held up in many intellectual and sensory domains. Whether we are listening to a melody, perceiving movement, observing objects, or attempting to grasp an idea, we perceive our world in terms of meaningful patterns or unified wholes. Organization is a given in our experience and not something that has to be added on by association to a collection of elements. The parts or elements are not what is most basic; what is most basic in our phenomenal world is the pattern or organization. In studying perceptual organization, the Gestalt psychologists discovered several principles that clarify the process. Some of the most important Gestalt principles are as follows:

1. *Figure–ground.* The Danish psychologist Edgar Rubin (1886–1951) argued that there are two components in perception. There is that which stands out or that dominates or that has a "thingness" about it. Rubin referred to this component of perception as *figure.* Other things recede into the background and Rubin referred to these as *ground.* He observed that there are sometimes reversible **figure–ground** relations, as observed in Figure 15.1A. The Gestalt psychologists did not always agree with Rubin about some of the interpretations or the technical features of figure–ground phenomena, but the finding has persisted as a recognized principle of organization and has become a mainstay in psychological literature.

2. *Similarity.* One of the standard features of perceptual organization is that similar things (gestalten) tend to be grouped together. This principle is illustrated in Figure 15.1B.

3. *Proximity.* According to this principle, close temporal or spatial conjunction leads to a perception of togetherness. In Figure 15.1C, we tend to see three groups of three instead of nine squares.

4. *Closure.* According to the principle of **closure,** we tend psychologically to complete that

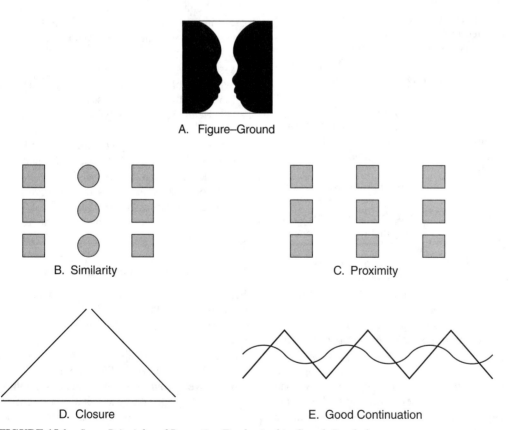

A. Figure–Ground

B. Similarity

C. Proximity

D. Closure

E. Good Continuation

FIGURE 15.1 *Some Principles of Perception Emphasized in Gestalt Psychology*

which is incomplete. If there are gaps, we fill them in. In Figure 15.1D, we tend to see a triangle rather than a series of disconnected lines.

5. *Good continuation.* In Figure 15.1E, it would be possible to see a series of broken lines if we transferred back and forth away from the wavy to the straight lines. However, we tend to see a **good continuation** of the wavy lines and a good continuation of the angular lines.

All of these principles of organization contribute to what Wertheimer called the **law of Prägnanz.** According to this law, perceptual organization tends to be as good as possible under prevailing conditions. Thus, we see our world in as orderly, coherent, and economical a way as conditions permit.

It is important to emphasize that these principles of organization are givens in perceptual experience. Gestalt psychology does not deny that learning, association, and motivation influence perception, but it is primarily concerned to point to the importance of understanding what is given in experience. The Gestalt psychologists also argue that the organization that we find in psychological experience resembles physiological organizations. This topic will surface later in the discussion of the Gestalt treatment of the mind–brain problem.

Learning

Earlier, it was pointed out that the Gestalt psychologists launched many of their attacks against behavioristic psychologies. Specifically, they opposed the connectionism of Thorndike, the reflexological emphasis of Pavlov, and the S-R psychology of Watson. Their opposition to these schools focused on learning theories that emphasized blind or mechanical connections as well as on artificial methodologies. Some of the most creative and challenging research is found in the Gestalt literature on learning.

One could select many points of entry into the Gestalt studies on learning, but we choose here some important experiments conducted by Karl Lashley (1942) and independently by Wolfgang Köhler (1929/1947, pp. 199–200) without knowledge of Lashley's work. The study begins by training a subject to select the darker of two shades of gray. Thus, as indicated in Figure 15.2, the subject is rewarded when it selects object 2, the darker of the two objects. The two objects are, of course, randomized with respect to position (left versus right) so that the animal soon learns to respond to number 2 whether it appears on the left or the right. In phase 2, the formerly rewarded object is now paired with a new object 3 that is darker than number 2. The brightness interval between 2 and 3 is the same as the brightness interval between 1 and 2. Now confronted with 2 versus 3, subjects choose 3 in most cases.

Notice that number 3 has never been rewarded in the past, whereas number 2 has consistently been associated with reward. Yet the preference is for number 3. Such a finding is embarrassing to a strict connectionism or an S-R theory. In view of the reinforcement history with number 2, it should be the object that is firmly connected to the response. Yet the subject selects an object that has never been rewarded and ignores the one that has always been rewarded. Köhler's interpretation is that in the total configuration, the subject learns a relational discrimination "darker than" rather than a response to an absolute stimulus value. If that is the case, then the stimulus for the subject is not what the behaviorist defines it to be. Furthermore, the established connection is not a hardwired connection between object 2 and the response.

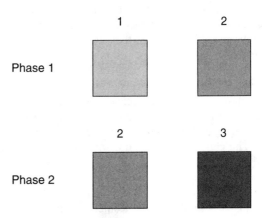

FIGURE 15.2 *Discrimination Problem Demonstrating the Learning of Relationships as Opposed to Absolute Stimulus Values*

Instead, the subject sees the pattern of the relationship rather than an isolated element. If that perception of a relationship is established in the first problem, then the subject simply transposes from the first problem to the second one. In the transposition, it is "darker than" that wins. The most parsimonious interpretation, according to Gestalt theory, is that relationships outweighs absolute stimulus values. The data suggest that what is learned is a cognitive structure rather than a response to an absolute stimulus value.

Insight: A Further Challenge to the S-R Formula

The best-known work on learning in the Gestalt literature is Köhler's classic book *The Mentality of Apes* (1925/1976). In that book, Köhler describes studies he conducted while on the Isle of Tenerife. These studies demonstrated that animals often solve problems by envisioning a whole situation and then restructuring various parts of the situation so as to attain a goal. Without such restructuring, the goal would be unattainable.

For example, Köhler suspended a banana by a string several feet above the head of a chimpanzee. Jumping is ruled out as the banana is higher than the chimpanzee can jump. If boxes were lying on the ground in the vicinity of the banana, the chimpanzees found a solution to their problem. The situation can be restructured by dragging boxes to a point beneath the banana. Though chimpanzees understand little of statics and though they are rather awkward builders, they were nevertheless capable of crude building efforts that helped them achieve their objective. One of Köhler's chimpanzees named Grande even built a four-story structure of boxes. It was clear to Köhler that the restructuring of a field progresses without any evidence of reinforcements for discrete responses.

The chimpanzees did not solve problems by blind trial and error or in a mechanical fashion by which every response is followed by a reward. Given an open situation (the ability to see the relevant parts of the field), Köhler's chimpanzees demonstrated the ability to solve problems in inventive and insightful ways. Köhler's stated criterion for insight is "the appearance of a complete solution with reference to the whole layout of the field" (Köhler, 1925/1976, p. 190).

Köhler argued that behavioral studies are often structured to preclude the possibility that animals could see the layout of the whole field. In a typical maze, the possibilities of visualization are limited and there is little way to learn except by trial and error. A human in a maze would also learn by trial and error, but imagine how different that learning curve would be if the entire maze were viewed, even for a brief moment, from the air (an optically given situation in Köhler's language). Most natural learning occurs in field situations in which there are possibilities for pattern recognition and restructuring. Artificial laboratory situations may lead to false conclusions about crucial questions such as what it is that gets learned, what the conditions are that facilitate learning, and what the capacities of the learners are.

Developmental Concepts

As noted earlier, Koffka's book *Growth of the Mind* provided a wider application of Gestalt principles by showing their operations and applications in developmental processes. The major emphasis of the book, in Koffka's (1924/1980) words, is "upon the evolution of the child's mind" (preface). Koffka pointed out that without sound developmental and comparative psychologies, the psychology of normal adults will be defective. Koffka observed that the extreme positions of empiricism and nativism had undercut the study of development. Thus, rather than attempting to understand the problems of mental growth as we find them, the empiricists and nativists searched for those things that fit their preconceptions.

Methodological Considerations in Developmental Psychology. Koffka distinguished between the view *from without* and the view *from within*. The view from within is a descriptive concept (i.e., I know my toothache, my headache, or my feeling of elation; when someone else has a toothache, I cannot get out of my skin and know it directly). But Koffka contended that if people weep, we may be assured they are sorrowful; if they laugh, they are happy; if they are animated, we may have certain confidences about their experience of energy and well-being. When we say that someone is animated or active, we are using behavioral concepts, but such concepts are also functional in that they refer to underlying experiences. Functional concepts assume an intimate relationship between observable behavior and experience. When we study infants and young children, we employ functional concepts, but with the assurance that if an infant smiles and coos, its behavior corresponds to experiences of well-being. We will now turn to some examples of Koffka's work in developmental psychology.

The Growth of Learning.   Koffka believed that much of early learning is what he called *sensori-motor learning.* An illustration of sensorimotor learning is found in the maxim, "The burnt child shuns the flame." Koffka (1924/1980) argued, "The withdrawal of the burned hand is naturally reflexive, but what is learned is not to withdraw the hand, but to avoid the fire in the future" (p. 302). What is learned is a configuration relating fire and pain, not a reflex that occurs naturally. If there were no attention, the child would not learn and then the experience would have to be repeated. So even in so-called sensorimotor learning, we do not learn mere connections; rather, what is learned is a constructive achievement with future adaptive significance.

Imitation.   In addition to sensorimotor learning, Koffka argued that a great deal of learning occurs by imitation. Such learning occurs in natural settings, but is less likely in artificial settings such as many laboratory experiments on learning. Koffka contended that there is no need to explain imitation or its purposes; it simply occurs in the natural flow of events. What often is imitated is complex configurations, whether these be auditory or visual. We can observe children attempting to perfect their imitations. Koffka believed that the perceptual and motor systems are closely related so that configural recognition or transfer can go naturally from one to the other. Koffka was not talking about mere observational learning. Rather, for him, imitation implied a capacity to discern relevant relations.

Ideational Learning.   The highest type of learning in Koffka's developmental scheme is ideational

learning, a type of learning that makes use of language. Koffka pointed out that it is a pivotal time in children's development when they grasp the idea that things have names. In early experience, the name is thought to inhere in the thing itself as an attribute. Koffka illustrated with a bit of humor that comes from an argument about the best language. One of the participants says, "The English language is the best, and I can prove it to you. Take the word *knife;* the French call it *couteau;* the Germans *Messer,* the Danes *kniv,* while the English say knife, and that's what it really is" (Koffka, 1924/1980, p. 324).

Following the naming stage, children enter a period marked by a remarkable new flexibility with respect to the application of language. A word, for example, that was originally associated with only one thing or event may now be applied to other things. Koffka related the case of Hilda Stern, who, after learning the word *nose,* applied it to the tips of her shoes. Such inventive manipulations are common in young children. Children also often generate words of their own in a playful manner. Thus, four-year-old Karen Wertheimer preferred to refer to a butterfly as a *flutterby.* Such a rearrangement illustrates verbal generation of ideational material that can play a role in learning. The new term *flutterby* is descriptive; it conveys an idea about the object that is not captured in the term *butterfly.* From a multitude of possible verbal rearrangements and new symbolic representations we have a powerful tool that greatly extends our capacity to learn and to solve problems. We turn now from learning modes to one of Koffka's most speculative but interesting suggestions regarding developmental phenomena.

Primitive Phenomena

Koffka (1924/1980) suggested that the behavior of infants disputes the idea that "single mental units called sensations are aroused in a simple manner by stimulation, and from them every other kind of experience is derived by a process of association" (p. 132). Instead, Koffka believed he found evidence that the most primitive phenomena are complex configurations upon a ground. He argued, "It is not the stimuli the psychologist takes to be simple, because they correspond to . . . elementary sensations, that are most influential in the behavior of a baby" (p. 133). Quite the contrary, it is human faces and human voices in all their complexity that are most influential.

Koffka even suggested that the most primitive phenomena are both perceptive and affective. Such a contention was, and to some extent still is, unorthodox. Standard treatments of affect have typically emphasized *add-on* approaches. Thus, affect gets added on to cognition through association. Koffka (1924/1980) suggested, however, that "the primitive world of experience embraces affective determinations just as it does those we are accustomed to characterize as objective" (p. 135). Such a contention represents one of the most significant departures from simplistic approaches that called for the separation of affect and cognition. Yet, Koffka's position may be more biologically sound—more consistent with evolution. Absence of primitive affect or its delayed development in response to dangerous (life-threatening) configural patterns would be fatal for all but the most sheltered and protected organisms.

GESTALT PERSPECTIVES ON SCIENTIFIC METHOD

The approach of Gestalt psychologists to scientific methodology helps illustrate the thoroughness of their revolt against established psychology. In his book *Gestalt Psychology,* Köhler accused the established psychologies, particularly behaviorism and structuralism, of attempting to emulate the physical sciences in their most advanced form. Such imitation, he argued, resulted in an overemphasis on the value of quantitative methods per se and a failure to pay attention to qualitative considerations that often precede quantification. Köhler argued that psychologists should attend to the early development of the physical sciences. In early stages, prior to the emergence of sophisticated quantitative procedures, physical scientists attended to the experiences of everyday life. As an example, Köhler called attention to the work of Henry Cavendish (1731–1810) on electrical resistance. Prior to developing exact quantitative mea-

sures of resistance, Cavendish directly experienced shocks to his arm delivered through varying pieces of material inserted in an electrical circuit.

Köhler called attention to the danger to the new psychology in copying the advanced quantitative form of the established sciences without first attending to the demands inherent in psychology's unique subject matter. One of the foremost dangers of premature emphasis on measurement is that such an emphasis may cause us to overlook important processes and phenomena. The net result is that we focus on those things that lend themselves to measurement but overlook things that may be of greater importance but not yet amenable to precise quantitative techniques. Köhler (1929/1947) argued that "narrowness in observation protects narrowness in theory" (p. 54). An overvaluing of quantitative techniques restricts the range of legitimate problems in the new discipline.

One of Köhler's (1929/1947) major concerns was that psychologists would conduct elegant but fruitless experiments. Indeed, he found evidence of that very problem in the field of psychophysics in which he charged "that thousands of quantitative psychophysical experiments were made almost in vain. No one knew precisely what he was measuring. Nobody had studied the mental processes upon which the whole procedure was built" (p. 44).

What, then, was the Gestalt solution to the methodological criticisms set forth by Köhler? First, according to Köhler (1929/1947), "A method is good if it is adapted to the given subject matter; and it is bad if it lacks regard for this material, or if it misdirects research" (p. 37). He also warned that a methodological procedure may work in one science and be all together useless in another science. It follows that methodology should be adapted to the subject matter of a discipline rather than the other way around.

Köhler believed that Gestalt psychology occupied a central place among the natural sciences (Henle, 1993). Not surprisingly, we encounter a variety of adaptations of scientific procedure within the Gestalt literature. For some types of problems, the Gestalt psychologists worked like astronomers or field biologists, employing the method of naturalistic observation with a minimum of intrusion into the ongoing activities of their subjects. In other studies, Gestalt psychologists worked more like scientists in a wet-lab situation, carefully manipulating and controlling variables.

Gestalt psychologists were also pioneers in the use of the phenomenological method, and they would likely be open to well-conceived interview and questionnaire techniques so long as these methods are meaningfully tied to the problems under investigation. Their broad approach to methodology is close to that embraced by William James, and as was true for James, it was vision, not method, that inspired their science. The Gestalt psychologists argued for a greater metaconsciousness of science. They were aware of the dangers of losing critical perspective on methodology: The range of legitimate problems may be restricted, there is a risk of generating misinformation, and the scientific enterprise may be trivialized as it is removed from the flow of meaningful events.

The methodological concerns of the Gestalt psychologists should not be interpreted as having anything to do with the split between mission-oriented (applied) research and basic research. Indeed, the dichotomy would be deemphasized with an informed philosophy of science as envisioned by the Gestalt school. The dichotomy might even disappear because a truly basic science would yield sensible findings. Even if such findings are not immediately applicable, they would not strain credulity with respect to their eventual potential to make a difference somewhere in the world of our experience.

MIND AND BRAIN

In 1876, just three years before the founding of the psychology laboratory in Leipzig, a patent for an electric speaking telephone was granted to the U.S. inventor Alexander Graham Bell. By 1877, the first telephones were being produced, and by the turn of the century, complex central telephone switchboards were mechanically connecting the messages of thousands of callers from distant points. A visit to a central telephone switching station in any large city was a memorable experience. The literally thousands of miles of wire and the sheer complexity of the circuitry were nothing short of a modern miracle. It was difficult to resist the temptation to compare the human brain with the telephone switchboard with its tens of thousands of wires and switches linking an almost unimaginable number of points in big cities. Perhaps the enormous telephone exchange could somehow be informative as a model of the human brain. The model was as compelling at the beginning of the century as the computer model is at the end of the century or the hydraulic model in Descartes's day.

There are problems, however, with a mechanical model that emphasizes hardwiring or rigid point-for-point connections. Not the least of the problems is the question of how a rigid mechanical model of the brain could explain perceived constancies of color, size, and shape. Perceived constancies strongly suggest that sensory experience cannot be explained solely on the basis of local stimuli alone. For example, an image of a person standing nearby may be twice as large on the retina as when the person is positioned a few feet back, yet the person is seen as the same size in both instances. We may also question whether natural systems are organized in the rigid mechanical fashion of artificial systems.

These and other questions led the Gestalt psychologists to a rejection of the telephone switchboard model and other machine models. Köhler (1929/1947, p. 124) acknowledged that arguments in favor of machine theory are compelling because of their simplicity and the consequent ease with which they are understood. But simplicity and ease of understanding alone are not adequate criteria for adopting a model. According to Gestalt theory, the best clues as to how the brain functions are not to be found in mechanical models but in natural systems and more specifically in the brain itself. Many natural systems are characterized most meaningfully in terms of *free dynamics*. Thus, whether we are talking about electrons, magnetic fields, chemical solutions, or molar behavior of living organisms, we do not observe machinelike connections. To be sure, we observe regularities, but such regularities are best understood in terms of patterns or configurations that occur within a field.

If we place a drop of oil on water, we observe a segregated pattern within a large field. Another drop of oil will also result in a pattern. If we produce soap bubbles, we observe segregated and organized entities floating in a field. The parts are not indifferent to each other or to the whole. On the contrary, local regions are profoundly dependent on other local regions. A change anywhere can produce changes everywhere. The organized natural entity displays regularities or, as Michael Wertheimer (1987) pointed out, "Physical forces, when released, do not produce chaos, but their own internally determined organizations. The nervous system, similarly, is not characterized by machine-like connections of tubes, grooves, wires, or switchboards, but the brain too, like almost all other physical systems, exhibits the dynamic self-distribution of physical forces" (p. 137). We will now turn to a more detailed consideration of the Gestalt approach to the mind–brain problem.

Isomorphism

The Gestalt view on the mind–brain problem has been called **isomorphism.** Köhler (1929/1947) defined the term as follows: "Experienced order in space is always structurally identical with a functional order in the distribution of underlying brain processes" (p. 61). Literally, the word *isomorphism* means having the same appearance or the same form. In chemistry, two substances may be said to be isomorphic if they share certain similarities with respect to atomic structure. The term *isomorphism* in Gestalt psychology refers to the structural correspondence between experience and underlying brain processes. Thus, the ordered nature of an experience does not exist in isolation but corresponds to an ordered distribution of cortical events. If we experience an auditory temporal sequence (a rhythm), we may also expect a pattern of events in brain processes that are isomorphic with the experience.

There are many misrepresentations of isomorphism (see Henle, 1984), but one of the most common is that it means that we have pictures in our heads corresponding to physical structures. Some people have even criticized isomorphism by asking whether color in the external world is isomor-

phic with some part of the brain that matches that color (Gregory, 1974, pp. 255–256). What is missed in many misrepresentations of isomorphism is the importance of the word *functional*. Köhler (1938/1966, p. 195) took pains to point out that the *functional* cortical counterpart of a color would not have to be a color; neither would the functional cortical counterpart of a sound such as the sound of a violin have to replicate the physical features of such a sound. The "pictures in the head" misrepresentation misses something even more fundamental. Isomorphism, as used by the Gestalt psychologists, does not refer to a correspondence between physical events and brain processes. It is not a theory about the relationship of brain processes and physical events but is a theory about the relationship between experience and brain processes. The position expresses a kind of faith in the fundamental structural similarity of two realms (experience and brain) that are of vital importance to the work of psychology.

THE INFLUENCE OF GESTALT PSYCHOLOGY

By the early 1920s, Gestalt psychology had become a vital force in Germany. The largest center of activity was at the Psychological Institute headed by Wolfgang Köhler at the University of Berlin. Henle (1977) pointed out that "graduate students were coming to the Institute from a number of countries; the *Psychologische Forschung,* the journal of the Gestalt Psychologists, was founded, and work was progressing in many directions" (p. 3). During this time, Gestalt theory influenced psychologists in other cultures including Italy and Japan (Sakuma, 1999; Verstegen, 2000). Historians can only speculate about the outcome had the Berlin Psychological Institute been allowed to prosper in a friendly environment. Undoubtedly, a continuing research program and the production of doctoral students would have formed the core of a significant research force—something Gestalt psychology never enjoyed.

Unfortunately, when Hitler came to power in 1933, the world could no longer look to Germany as a rich source of scientific ideas. The small nucleus of Gestalt theorists split into isolated colleges that did not offer major doctoral programs (Koffka at Smith College, Köhler at Swarthmore, and Wertheimer at The New School for Social Research). The Gestalt movement faced an uphill battle in another way. The major leaders, isolated from each other and from graduate students, were on foreign soil in a country already captured by the behavioristic revolution. The vicissitudes of Gestalt psychology in the United States are discussed in thoughtful articles by Sokal (1984) and Ash (1985).

In spite of the obstacles, however, the sheer force of Gestalt research, argument, and theory had a telling and continuing influence. The influence was felt in three important ways:

1. There were systematic approaches to subdisciplinary areas such as motivation, personality, and social psychology inspired by Gestalt psychology though not a part of the classic core of Gestalt thought.
2. Gestalt concepts and research discoveries found their way into the textbooks that convey the mainstream of psychological knowledge.
3. Gestalt research findings served as a powerful stimulus for other systems, often forcing modifications in their positions.

We turn to an examination of an influential system that had roots and inspiration in Gestalt psychology.

KURT LEWIN AND FIELD THEORY

Wertheimer, Köhler, and Koffka worked primarily in the areas of thinking, perception, learning, and development. As noted earlier, however, there is great breadth in the Gestalt vision—it is a world view that extends beyond the boundaries of psychology itself. Following the initial statements of the Gestalt position, there was much work to be done to explore Gestalt applications in other subdisciplinary areas of psychology. Kurt Lewin (1890–1947) was a figure among those who wished to broaden the base of the Gestalt position. His interests were in motivation, personality, social psychology, and conflict resolution. There can be little debate that he drew his initial inspiration from the classic work of Wertheimer, Köhler, and Koffka.

Lewin was born in Mogilno, Prussia (now part of Poland), on September 9, 1890. When he was age fifteen, the family moved to Berlin, where Lewin completed his high school studies at the Kaiserin Augusta Gymnasium. After a semester at the University of Freiburg and another at the University of Munich, he enrolled at the University of Berlin. He completed the requirements for a Ph.D. in psychology at Berlin under the direction of Carl Stumpf.

Following graduate studies, Lewin enlisted in the German army and served through World War I. He was awarded the Iron Cross after being wounded in battle. Students of Lewin's thought (e.g., see Marrow, 1969, p. 11) have pointed out that his experiences in World War I served as a basis for his later psychological field theory. Concepts such as *boundary, force,* and *zone* are very real on the battlefield as well as in ordinary human experience.

Upon completing his military tour of duty, Lewin took a position at the Psychological Institute at the University of Berlin, where he worked with Wertheimer and Köhler. Marrow (1969) pointed out that "Gestalt holism impressed Lewin. Though he was never a completely orthodox Gestaltist, he did become a vital force in the new movement and contributed to it his own special insights" (p. 13). Marrow also noted that Lewin was impressed with the psychoanalysts because they were working with real-life problems, but believed that the methods of psychoanalysis were flawed (Marrow, 1969, p. 29). Lewin's work at the Berlin Institute continued with but minor interruptions until 1933. By that time he had gained international visibility and an impressive publication record approaching forty scholarly articles. Several articles attracted the attention of the psychological world and one, in particular, which contrasted Aristotelian and Galilean thought modes (see Lewin, 1931), brought widespread recognition.

In 1933, Kurt Lewin joined the large exodus of intellectuals from a country caught in the grip of Nazi madness. Lewin declared he could not continue to teach in a university where his children would not be welcome as students (see Marrow, 1969, p. 68). In the fall of 1933, he took a temporary position at Cornell University. In 1935, he accepted a position at the Child Welfare Research

Station at the University of Iowa, a position he held until 1944. In 1944, he was named director of the Research Center for Group Dynamics at Massachusetts Institute of Technology (M.I.T.). He died of a heart seizure at his home in Newtonville, Massachusetts, on February 12, 1947.

Like William James, Lewin could be characterized as an intellectual democrat. He took ideas too seriously to demand intellectual conformity or loyalty. Many students were attracted to him and, as noted by Marrow (1969), they could move in and out of his circle without feeling guilt or being accused of disloyalty (p. 89). Lewin's openness could be characterized as a logical outgrowth of his philosophy of science. He was strongly committed to the idea that science must continually change. He argued that "the idea of an eventual unification of all sciences is wishful thinking" (Marrow, 1969, p. 19).

Lewin's Field Theory

Lewin's psychology can be interpreted as a corrective for earlier systems of thought that placed emphasis on traits, inherited predispositions, learning, agencies, or other intrapsychic events or processes. In contrast with extreme individualistic approaches, Lewin's **field theory** emphasized the interdependence of the person *and* the environment. His most characteristic formula, $B = f(p,e)$, states that behavior is a function of person *and* environment. According to the formula, an adequate psychology can be developed only by appreciating the full scope of forces that play a role in human life. Lewin believed that earlier psychologists had placed too large a burden on the explanatory role of association and other limited concepts. He also believed that earlier psychologies had seriously neglected the roles of affect, motivation, and social forces.

One of the key concepts in Lewin's psychology is the **life space,** which refers to every psychological fact that is influential in the life of an individual at a given time. In any one slice of time, the life space consists of physical events (an impending storm, a new car, a cup of coffee, the aroma of cinnamon, a book), personal and biological facts

(a toothache, a memory, fatigue, the exhilaration of a workout), and social facts (another person, membership in a group). It consists of the extensity of experience at a given moment. The life space of the child is limited both spatially and temporally, but with growth, the space expands. Lewin believed that the task of education is to extend the life space so that we can strive for goals that are further and further removed in time. Young children typically strive only for that which is concrete and visible. With education and growth, the present can become more spacious, the future more pregnant with possibilities, and the past more enlarged. Lewin quoted with approval Goethe's famous statement, "Who cannot give an account of three thousand years remains in the darkness of inexperience, can live only from one day to another" (see Lewin, 1935, p. 173).

It is important to point out that the life space is not static. At a given time, its focal features may consist of a small group of people, a physical setting, some food, and pleasant conversation. In the midst of all that, a phone call may bring salient information that radically changes the focus of attention and hence the life space.

Lewin referred to positive or negative features of objects in the life space as **valences.** A *positive valence* simply refers to the attractive or desirable qualities that reside in an object. In general, objects that satisfy a need possess positive valence and objects that frustrate or frighten have a negative valence. Valences fluctuate dynamically with needs. Thus, a food object will have a higher positive valence for a hungry child, but after a meal, a favored toy may have a higher positive valence.

Lewin's emphasis on positive and negative valences led to some of the most productive work in the history of psychology on the nature of conflict. In the day-to-day world, we rarely encounter a simple pathway to a simple goal. Instead, we encounter complexities that require adjudication and choice. Lewin and his students called attention to common types of conflicts.

First, we may be caught between two objects with comparable positive valences. Though there may be considerable vacillation in such a circumstance, this type of conflict is usually regarded as fairly easy to resolve. Second, another type of conflict occurs when an object has positive *and* negative valences or when an object with a positive valence is surrounded by a physical or psychological barrier. The dynamics of conflict resolution in this type of situation are complex and depend ultimately on the relative weights of the positive and negative valences and the capacities of the individual. Lewin observed that individuals may attempt circuitous routes to the goal or, when the conflict is too intense, the individual may leave the field and search for an alternative goal. The third type of conflict surfaces when we are caught between two regions that both have negative valences. Lewin gave the example of the child who is required to perform an undesirable task and failure to do the task will result in punishment. This is a very severe type of conflict, especially if escape from punishment is impossible and if the task is sufficiently repugnant.

These types of conflict are easily recognized as part of the mainstream of psychological literature under the labels of **approach-approach conflict, approach-avoidance conflict,** and **avoidance-avoidance conflict.** Lewin's original work on conflict has inspired a great deal of research on simple conflict situations and on more complicated real-life situations in which there are multiple positive and negative valences associated with many regions.

Tension Systems and Recall

Lewin believed that needs are associated with tension systems and that the satisfaction of a need is associated with the dissipation of tension. One of the implications of this idea was tested by Lewin's student, Bluma Zeigarnik. The subjects in Zeigarnik's research were given a series of simple tasks. In some instances the subjects were interrupted before they could complete a task, and in other instances they were allowed to carry the task through to completion. The assumption was that tension is dissipated when a task is completed, but when a task is interrupted, tension persists for a longer period. Zeigarnik tested this assumption by asking subjects to recall the various tasks they had performed. Because of the persistence of tension associated with the interrupted tasks, Lewin predicted that there would be better recall for interrupted compared with completed tasks. The findings supported Lewin's prediction. Better recall for uncompleted compared with completed tasks came to be known as the **Zeigarnik effect.**

One explanation for the Zeigarnik effect is that tension remaining from an uncompleted task may cause subjects to persevere or rehearse the materials associated with that task. On the other hand, the completion of a task may free the subject to turn attention to other things. In other words, the uncompleted task serves as a barrier to interference. Regardless of why it works, the Zeigarnik effect suggests that a study unit might be ended most effectively with a question. A compelling question, by its very nature, means that something is not complete or that something is unanswered. A good question should result in a tension system that will keep the learner on task for a longer period of time than would be the case without the question.

Group Dynamics

Earlier it was noted that in 1944 Lewin was named director of the Research Center for Group Dynamics at M.I.T. In his later years, Lewin focused his research efforts on group dynamics—a problem that had been of long-standing interest. The expression **group dynamics** is not easily defined, but in general it includes the study of the effects of groups on individuals and individuals on groups. Groups modify individual behaviors and perceptions, and individuals modify groups. Group dynamics also includes studies of the structures of groups with respect to leadership (e.g., democratic vs. authoritarian) and the effectiveness of leadership structures in various kinds of tasks and contexts.

Lewin's interests extended to wide varieties of groups, including industrial work groups, educational groups, and casual interest groups. He was also interested in community action programs where psychological theory could be tested in the day-to-day world. Representative of this interest was an experiment on integrated housing inspired by Lewin but conducted by his students after his death. Deutsch and Collins (1951) studied housing projects in which blacks and whites were integrated in a random fashion. That is, houses were available on a first-come, first-served basis. In another condition, blacks and whites were segregated in a block-type or checkerboard pattern. Results showed that integration resulted in more positive and accepting interracial attitudes. Segregated housing patterns resulted in increased resentment, prejudice, and a desire for even greater segregation. It can be assumed that within integrated neighborhoods, there were more opportunities to build friendships and gain a sense of the basic humanity of members of other ethnicities.

Lewin's Influence

The extent of Lewin's influence on psychology should not be underestimated. One mark of that influence, as noted by Marrow (1969), "was the setting up of an annual Kurt Lewin Memorial by the Society for the Psychological Study of Social Issues" (p. 228). A large number of eminent psychologists, including such notable figures as Gordon Allport, Edward Chace Tolman, Fritz Heider, and Leon Festinger, have commented on the fertility and durability of Lewin's work. Lewin, along with the founders of Gestalt psychology, must be counted among the great psychologists.

The Second Generation of Gestalt Psychologists

Aside from the contributions of Wertheimer, Koffka, Köhler, and Lewin, a legion of second-generation Gestalt psychologists greatly enhanced the work of their mentors. Students of Gestalt psychology enjoyed a time of great productivity in Germany during the 1920s. Among the more influential students were Karl Duncker (1903–1940), Hedwig von Restorff (1903–?), and Solomon Asch (1907–1996).

Karl Duncker. Karl Duncker was born on February 2, 1903, in Leipzig. Although his early training was in the German educational system, Duncker also studied in the United States and received his master's degree at Clark University in 1926. He returned to Germany and earned his doctorate in psychology at the University of Berlin in 1929. Following completion of his degree, he stayed at Berlin as a research assistant for Wolfgang Köhler until 1935, when Duncker was dismissed by the Nazi government for political reasons (King, Cox, & Wertheimer, 1998). In 1935, Duncker emigrated to England and worked for a year at Cambridge University with the eminent psychologist Frederick C. Bartlett. In 1938, Duncker emigrated to the United States, where he served as instructor in psychology at Swarthmore College. Regrettably, Duncker committed suicide on February 23, 1940, twenty-one days after his thirty-seventh birthday.

Despite a brief career, Duncker made several impressive contributions to the domain of Gestalt psychology. In early research, Duncker (1929/1950) found that people tend to perceive personal movement if their body is stationary but another object in their perceptual field is in motion. For example, standing at the middle of a bridge looking down at a passing stream may give the distinct impression that the perceiver, rather than the water, is in motion. This so-called *induced motion* was the basis of Duncker's research which proved an excellent addition to the Gestalt literature on perception.

Under Wertheimer's direction, Duncker also conducted an ingenious series of experiments on problem solving. Originally published in German in 1935, Duncker's research was translated a decade later into English (Duncker, 1935/1945). After conducting numerous experiments, Duncker found that many subjects exhibited a **functional fixedness,** that is, an inability to find productive solutions to new problems. Duncker's research has continued to influence problem-solving research (German & Defeyter, 2000; Newell, 1985). According to Mandler and Mandler (1969), "Apart from the personal tragedy, there is reason to believe that [Duncker] was the most brilliant of the Gestalt group.... His main contribution has made a continuing impact on the psychology of thinking, both in the United States and elsewhere" (p. 393).

Hedwig von Restorff.   A further contribution to the Gestalt theory of memory came from the work of Hedwig von Restorff, who was born in 1903 and had a brief but notable career. After receiving her Ph.D. in psychology, von Restorff served as a research assistant for Köhler at the Psychological Institute in Berlin. Like Duncker, she was dismissed by the Nazis in 1933. Little more, including the exact date of her death, is known about her.

In a classic experiment, Köhler and von Restorff found that isolated items are recalled better than a series of homogenous items. Subjects in one of their experiments learned a list of nonsense syllables. However, when an individual three-digit item was presented with the nonsense syllables, subjects had superior recall for the three-digit number than the nonsense syllables. According to Köhler and von Restorff (1935), the three numbers acted as the figure to the ground of the homogeneous nonsense syllables. This phenomenon has been popularized with the eponym of the *Köhler–von Restorff effect* or the more inaccurate **von Restorff effect.** According to Baddeley (1990), the British Post Office even employed the research of Köhler and von Restorff in the design of its postcode. The von Restorff effect remains a viable research construct (Kelley & Nairne, 2001).

It is an unfortunate circumstance that many of the heirs of Gestalt psychology were severely affected by the Nazi regime. Henle (1986) lamented, "By the end of World War II, the first generation of young Gestalt psychologists was essentially wiped out" (p. 119). Some were lost in the war, but most had moved to other countries. Despite the turbulent events of World War II, several researchers did further the discipline of Gestalt psychology in the United States. In particular, Solomon Asch found great success in the incorporation of Gestalt theory into his research in the United States.

Solomon Asch.   Solomon Asch was born in Warsaw, Poland, in 1907. He emigrated with his family to the United States in 1920. Asch was an introverted child who mastered English after an intensive reading of Charles Dickens's novels. He quickly flourished in his studies and earned his master's degree under Robert Sessions Woodworth

at Columbia University. Asch received his Ph.D. from Columbia in 1932. He was captivated by the Gestalt orientation and became acquainted with Max Wertheimer shortly after his emigration to the United States. In the early 1940s, Asch joined Rudolf Arnheim in editing drafts of Wertheimer's *Productive Thinking.* Two years after Wertheimer's death, Asch, Wolfgang Köhler, and Clara Mayer (dean at the New School for Social Research) edited the first edition of *Productive Thinking* (Wertheimer, 1945). Asch stayed at the New School until moving to Swarthmore College in 1947, where he established a strong relationship with Köhler. In 1966, he headed the Institute for Cognitive Studies at Rutgers University, then moved to the University of Pennsylvania where he retired in 1979. He died in February 1996.

Asch's contributions to cognition, learning, personality theory, and perception all carry a Gestalt flavor (Gleitman, Rozin, & Sabini, 1997). Arguably, his most enduring work was in social psychology when he substituted "the dichotomy of individual and group with an integrated view of social interaction and its intrinsic dynamics" (Arnheim, 1986, p. 34). Asch's landmark research on group pressure and the judgment of line length is a classic in social psychology (Asch, 1955). The ideas of Solomon Asch have implications on contemporary research on cognition and social psychology (Rock, 1990; Rozin, 2001).

In a more indirect fashion, the work of other psychologists reflects the principal tenets of Gestalt psychology. Edward Chace Tolman, though a behaviorist, acknowledged that Gestalt psychology had been a major source of inspiration for his cognitive approach to learning. Muzafer Sherif's (*Sher uhf*) conceptual approach to psychology, his experiments on the autokinetic effect, and his well-known boys' camp experiments (which incidentally were the source of inspiration for the novel *Lord of the Flies*) are best appreciated within a Gestalt orientation. Kurt Goldstein's organismic personality theory was directly influenced by Gestalt theory, as was Andras Angyal's theory of personality. Other theorists such as Hans Wallach, Fritz Heider, Wolfgang Metzger, and Herman Witkin drew inspiration from the Gestalt school. Henle (1985) has also demonstrated that contemporary cognitive psychology owes a large, and often unacknowledged, debt to Gestalt psychology. Other influences of Gestalt psychology are outlined by Rock and Palmer (1990).

SOME COMMON MISUNDERSTANDINGS OF GESTALT PSYCHOLOGY

There is perhaps greater complexity and subtlety in the Gestalt system than in any of the systems we have covered thus far. For this reason, there are more misunderstandings of this system than any other. We will briefly summarize some of the most common misunderstandings.

Gestalt Psychology and Gestalt Therapy

Because of similarities in terminology, it would be reasonable to assume that Gestalt therapy, which had its origin in the work of Fritz Perls, is somehow related to Gestalt psychology. In an article entitled "Gestalt Psychology and Gestalt Therapy" Mary Henle (1978a) examined **Gestalt therapy** and found it to be in marked contrast with the teachings of the Gestalt psychologists. Henle concluded that the terms Perls borrowed from Gestalt psychology are stretched beyond recognition and that the psychology advanced by Perls "is *not* Gestalt psychology" (p. 31). Agreeing with Henle, Michael Wertheimer (1987) found "*no* conceptual relationship between Perls' neoanalytic 'gestalt psychotherapy' and Gestalt psychology in the sense of the Wertheimer-Köhler-Koffka theory" (p. 139).

Gestalt Psychology and Scientific Analysis

Another common misunderstanding is that Gestalt psychology opposes analysis. This accusation is set forth most vividly in Pavlov's polemics against the Gestalt school (see Gibbons, n.d.). Earlier, we pointed out that Gestalt psychology should not be confused with holistic psychologies that do oppose analysis. Gestalt psychology has never rejected analysis of the natural units of the phenomenal field. Thus, if a unit is a genuine part of a whole, it is a legitimate task of the scientist to under-

stand that unit. Köhler (1947) said, "Analysis in terms of genuine parts is a perfectly legitimate and necessary procedure in Gestalt psychology" (pp. 168–169). From a Gestalt perspective, analysis starts with a phenomenal event then proceeds to its natural parts and their relations.

Gestalt Psychology and Nativism

Another common misunderstanding is encountered in the belief that Gestalt theory is a nativistic psychology, meaning that it places heavier emphasis on heredity than on environment. In fact, Gestalt psychologists reject the nature–nurture dichotomy and argue that it is misleading to treat events in the psychological world as if they were *simply* inherited or learned. In his last book, Köhler (1969) declared it an error to treat "the terms 'learned' and 'inherited' as though these words indicated an 'either-or' alternative" (p. 89).

The Gestalt position goes back to an often neglected feature of evolutionary theory—namely, that the physical-chemical forces of nature are applicable to living organisms. Thus, physical conditions (e.g., gravitational forces, pH values, ambient temperature) and principles (e.g., conservation of energy) all contribute to the dynamic distributions or possibilities. For example, at a relatively low ambient temperature, gelatin is a semisolid, but at a higher temperature, it is a liquid. The dynamic distribution and movement of particles is a function, among other things, of temperature. Temperature is associated with limits or constraints within which we observe invariant dynamics.

Köhler (1969) argued that "it is three factors (not two) by which events in organisms, and therefore also in nervous systems, are generally determined. First, the invariant principles and forces of general dynamics, secondly, anatomical constraints which evolution has established, and thirdly, learning" (p. 89). If we focus only on what is learned or inherited, we neglect attention to what Köhler called *invariant dynamics,* something we share with the inorganic world. Köhler (1969) asked whether "processes in our nervous system follow the laws of nature because some genes compel such processes to do so" (p. 69). The answer is clearly no.

The upshot of the Gestalt position is that it calls for a psychology informed by life sciences *and* physical sciences.

The Role of Past Experience

A final misunderstanding of Gestalt psychology is that it neglects the role of past experience. Gestalt theory has been accused of neglecting history because it stands in sharp contrast with other systems that overemphasize the importance of the past. If thinking, learning, and perception work as the Gestalt theorists believe they do, then present facts are important, though the past is by no means unimportant. If the Gestalt position is correct, we may not be tied in a blind and mechanical way to our individual and collective histories, because of insight and productive thinking. Both **insight** and productive thinking would be impossible without the ability to integrate the past into ongoing activities.

Recall that Lewin quoted with approval Goethe's statement, "Who cannot give an account of three thousand years remains lost in the darkness of inexperience." Gestalt concepts such as insight and productive thinking give a new intimacy with the past. We are hardly intimate with the past if its events dictate (either through conditioning or unconscious motivations) the present flow of events. In the Gestalt perspective, the present is elevated in importance but the past and the future are not neglected. Indeed, time perspective may have greater breadth within a Gestalt framework than in any other system of psychology.

GESTALT PSYCHOLOGY AND APPLIED PSYCHOLOGY

Although focused on the study of perception, thinking, learning, development, and social psychology, Gestalt psychology was actively applied to topics such as the psychology of art, education, and psychotherapy. Behrens (1998) argued that the work of Cubist artists such as Pablo Picasso had an impact on Gestalt theory. Likewise, several illustrious artists including Paul Klee, Vassily Kandinsky, Josef Albers, and M. C. Escher found inspiration in the tenets of Gestalt theory (King, Wertheimer, Keller, & Crochetière, 1994). Like his mentor Max Wertheimer, Rudolf Arnheim (1943) saw the principles of Gestalt theory in the natural world, not only in the rigorous constraints of the laboratory. Arnheim earned his Ph.D. from Wertheimer at the University of Berlin in 1928. In 1933, he emigrated to Italy and later to the United States where he held positions at Sarah Lawrence College, Harvard University, and the University of Michigan.

Arnheim's greatest contribution involved his use of Gestalt theory to explore the psychology of art. His scholarly activities ranged from a molar study of architecture, music, film, radio, poetry, theater, and sculpture to a detailed, Gestalt-inspired analysis of Picasso's creative thinking during the painting of his *Guernica* (Arnheim, 1962). Indeed, the majority of his books on the psychology of art bear the unmistakable stamp of Gestalt theory (Arnheim, 1966, 1974, 1986). Mandler and Mandler (1969) claimed that

> Arnheim's investigations in the psychology of art within the Gestalt framework, in part because of the sin of omission by the mainstream of American psychology, became the dominant influence in the psychology of art. His work has been central and seminal and is certainly one of the milestones in the contribution of Gestalt psychology to American culture. (p. 394)

The Gestalt model also held important implications for education and teaching. In the fall of 1934, Wertheimer offered a seminar on the "Consequences of the Gestalt Theory of Psychology for Education and Teaching." The Gestalt perspective paralleled closely the functional ideology of progressive education as opposed to a more traditional, structural orientation. Wertheimer's vision of a Gestalt theory of education had a profound influence on two of his students, George Katona and Catherine Stern.

Although he earned a Ph.D. under G. E. Müller at Göttingen, George Katona came under the influence of Wertheimer and Köhler while studying in Berlin. In 1933, he emigrated to the United States and taught at the New School for Social Research from 1938 to 1942. He later taught at the University of Michigan. Katona was a prolific researcher, particularly in the area of behavioral economics, in which he successfully applied field theory to the study of economics in numerous books and articles.

Katona's most dynamic contribution to Gestalt psychology was a book on memory and education titled *Organizing and Memorizing* (1940). Like Duncker's research on problem solving, Katona's book complemented Wertheimer's work on productive thinking but with a greater application to educational psychology. Katona (1940) demonstrated that understanding of information based on insightful grouping (*meaningful* learning) would yield superior results to memorization of unorganized materials (*senseless* learning). Katona concluded that memorization would yield faster rates of forgetting than understanding and was less likely to transfer to learning of new tasks. He even challenged the utility of Ebbinghaus's retention curve by noting that the data were derived from nonsensical stimuli rather than meaningful material. Katona's work stands as an important precursor to research on organization in learning and memory (Baddeley, 1990).

In addition to Katona, Catherine Stern borrowed Wertheimer's ideas and applied them to the basics of mathematical education. She developed Structural Arithmetic, an education program based on her research and Wertheimer's ideas about productive thinking. In opposition to drill and associative learning, Stern constructed situations in which the structural characteristics of the number system were understood, rather than memorized, by children. In 1949, she published *Children Discover Arithmetic: An Introduction to Structural Arithmetic,* a book dedicated to Wertheimer. In later years, Stern examined other facets of education based on the learning methods of discovery and insight (Stern & Gould, 1955). In particular, she concluded that the teaching of alphabetic characters was, like arithmetic, based on memorization and drill (or the *sight method*). As a remedy, Stern designed a program of "Structural Reading" in which students grasp structural characteristics common to whole groups of words and sentences rather than piecemeal elements (Stern & Gould, 1968). Stern's work stands as an ambitious effort to extend Wertheimer's research into the realm of education.

The Gestalt contribution to psychotherapy is less evident than its applications to art and education. Although Wertheimer dismissed Freud's work as excessively associative and unscientific, several psychologists linked Gestalt theory with psychoanalysis and other psychotherapies. As with Fritz Perls's Gestalt therapy, most efforts bore no intellectual resemblance to the Gestalt theory of Wertheimer, Köhler, and Koffka (King et al., 1994).

However, the Gestalt psychologists were not adverse to the application of their ideas to a clinical setting. Select passages in Wertheimer's *Productive Thinking* reveal an interest in psychopathology. In the 1920s, Wertheimer supervised a student named Heinrich Schulte on a Gestalt theory of paranoia. According to Levy (1986), the Wertheimer-Schulte theory has relevance because it "claims to account for *all* forms of paranoid developments, regardless of whether they are exogenous or endogenous, psychogenic or somatogenic, and so offers a general theory which at present we do not seem to have" (p. 248). Furthermore, the work of Adhémar Gelb (1887–1936) and Kurt Goldstein (1878–1965) on brain injury and agnosia reflects the influence of Gestalt psychology. Despite Gestalt therapy's mistaken identity, the Gestalt model can serve as a fruitful resource for the clinical psychologist (Crochetière, Vicker, Parker, King, & Wertheimer, 2001).

THE CONTINUING RELEVANCE OF GESTALT PSYCHOLOGY

In an address at a conference on the worldview of contemporary physics, the theoretical physicist Fritjof Capra (1988) contrasted the paradigm that has been dominant in the sciences and in society for the past several hundred years with an emerging new worldview. The old paradigm, according to Capra, included beliefs in a mechanical universe consisting of elementary building blocks, the human body as a machine, unlimited material progress through technological and economic growth, life as a competitive struggle, and the natural domination of the male over the female. Capra characterized the emerging new worldview under five points:

1. A shift from the part to the whole
2. A shift from structure to process
3. A shift from "objective science" to "epistemic science"
4. A shift in scientific metaphor from knowledge as a building block to knowledge as a network
5. A shift from truth to approximate description

Although there are many differences between Gestalt psychology and the new perspectives as outlined by Capra, there are also some important similarities. Long ago, Gestalt psychology rejected the view of the universe as a mechanical system consisting of elementary building blocks and the view of the human body as a machine. Gestalt psychologists could also offer a great deal of informed comment to all those who agree with Capra that there should be a shift of emphasis from the part to the whole, from structure to process, and from objective science to epistemic science.

The continuing relevance of Gestalt psychology is manifested in other recent scientific developments. Recall that one of the major positions of the Gestalt system is that there are internally determined organizations within physical forces. As stated by Henle (1985), "Physical interactions do not occur indiscriminately, but depend on the properties of the interacting events" (p. 105). In recent years there is increasing awareness of this very point and its implication that there is latent order within apparent disorder. For example, there are repeated orderly patterns in chaotic physical events such as shattered glass, a rising heat current, and the distribution of matter in an explosion. The Gestalt concept of free dynamics is applicable to these and other physical events. In some cases, computer-generated models of chaos (e.g., see Gleick, 1987) reveal striking repetitions of consistent and orderly patterns and shapes occurring on large and small scales.

The continuing relevance of Gestalt theory is evident in a number of contemporary fields including memory and cognition (German & Defeyter, 2000; Kelley & Nairne, 2001; Murray, 1995), perception (Chen, 2001; Kellman, 2000), evolutionary psychology (Murray & Farahmand, 1998), visual neuroscience (Westheimer, 1999),

and artificial intelligence (Guberman & Wojtkowski, 2001). In an article entitled "Rediscovering Gestalt Psychology," Henle (1985) called attention to the parallels between Gestalt concepts and concepts such as contextualism, top-down processing, and subjective organization.

Though psychologists today do not typically claim allegiance to the Gestalt school, there is much in this school that is consistent with the scientific orientations that prevailed near the end of the twentieth century. Indeed, Gestalt theory is undoubtedly more consistent with the scientific worldview of the twenty-first century than that of the 1940s. In an era marked by interest in ecological concerns and suspicion of reductionism, it would not be surprising if Gestalt theory continues to be rediscovered.

REVIEW QUESTIONS

1. Trace some of the key influences on Gestalt theory coming out of science, philosophy, and psychology.
2. The standard explanation for the phi phenomenon was based on the idea that there was kinesthetic feedback from the movement of the eye. Describe a demonstration that proved embarrassing to the standard explanation. Why was the phi phenomenon so important to Wertheimer?
3. Distinguish between productive thinking and mere reproductive thinking.
4. What is the law of Prägnanz and how can it be illustrated?
5. Briefly review the evidence that learning is not based on strict point-for-point mechanical connections.
6. Outline three types of learning discussed in the work of Koffka.
7. What did Koffka mean by primitive phenomena? Do you think he was correct? Why?
8. Discuss the Gestalt approach to the scientific method. Contrast this approach to the behavioristic approach. Which do you believe to be more adequate? Explain your reasons.

9. Explain the Gestalt approach to the mind–brain problem. Why is the concept of "pictures in the head" a misrepresentation of isomorphism?

10. Explain Lewin's concept of the life space and why it was important to his overall conceptual approach to psychology.

11. What is the Zeigarnik effect and what are some of its practical implications?

12. Discuss Lewin's concept of motivation and its relationship to his approach to conflict.

13. Outline four common misunderstandings of Gestalt psychology.

CHAPTER 16

PSYCHOANALYSIS

The ego is not master in its own house.
—Sigmund Freud (1917/1955)

Like behaviorism, psychoanalysis is more than a system of psychology. It is an intellectual movement that has had a deep and pervasive influence in many fields, including literature, philosophy, art, religion, and history. Psychoanalysis, also like behaviorism, has had an unusual capacity to provoke loyalty and hatred; neither is there agreement about the continuing impact of psychoanalysis on psychology (see Crews, 1996; Horgan, 1996). We can find those who believe that the influence of this school is in decline and those who argue that psychoanalysis is alive and well. In terms of the sheer numbers of professional organizations and journals, the weight of the evidence is with the latter. We begin our consideration of the classic psychoanalytic system with a biographical sketch of Sigmund Freud (1856–1939) and then turn to a discussion of his system of thought.

SIGMUND FREUD

Sigmund Freud was born on May 6, 1856, in Freiberg, Moravia, a small town of approximately 5,000 people. His father, Jakob Freud, was a wool merchant who had two sons by a previous marriage. Sigmund was the first of the eight children of Jakob and Amalie Nathansohn. In 1860, Jakob and Amalie settled in Vienna, a city that was to be Freud's home for the next seventy-eight years. Although Freud was raised and educated in Vienna, it was not a location that could inspire his loyalty. Prevailing anti-semitism undermined the quality of day-to-day life and severely narrowed

the range of vocational choices for Jews. In his standard biography of Freud, Jones (1953) relayed the story of a ruffian who knocked Jakob Freud's new hat into a puddle of mud with the demand, "Jew get off the pavement" (p. 22). Jews were repeatedly the victims of demeaning acts and hostile humor. Understandably, such a climate had a profound effect on the thought and character of Sigmund Freud (e.g., see Bakan, 1958; Miller, 1981; Roith, 1987).

Freud, always a precocious student, graduated from high school summa cum laude at age seventeen. He loved literature, history, science, and

Sigmund Freud

language. His facility with languages was demonstrated by his knowledge of Latin, Greek, French, English, Italian, Spanish, and Hebrew. In 1873, Freud matriculated in the University of Vienna, where he pursued a degree in medicine. Like William James, however, his interests ranged over the entire curriculum. He attended courses in philosophy and psychology taught by Franz Brentano, a course on evolution taught by Carl Claus, and a course on the physiology of voice and speech taught by Ernst Brücke (1819–1892).

From 1876 to 1882, Freud worked in Brücke's laboratory, where he met a respected physiologist fourteen years his senior named Joseph Breuer (1842–1925). In December 1880, Breuer began treating Bertha Pappenheim, a remarkable twenty-one-year-old woman who had developed hysteria while caring for her dying father. Breuer tried to find the psychological cause for Pappenheim's headaches, loss of sensation, partial paralyses, and vivid hallucinations about skeletons and black snakes.

Breuer first described Pappenheim's case to Freud in 1882. Breuer hypnotized her and found that she could relive traumatic events that had seemingly escaped conscious memory. Breuer noted that she made dramatic progress after giving conscious expression to disturbing memories and emotions, and he referred to this process as catharsis; Pappenheim called it her *talking cure* or *chimney sweeping* (Gay, 1988). After several years of therapy and significant progress, Pappenheim announced that she was pregnant with Breuer's child. Although the false pregnancy was another symptom of her hysteria, he stopped working with her and left her in the care of a colleague. In time, she overcame the hysteria and became one of Germany's first feminists and a pioneer in the field of social work.

Freud was fascinated by Pappenheim's case and described it in a book he wrote with Breuer entitled *Studies in Hysteria* (1895). The authors used the pseudonym *Fräulein Anna O* rather than Pappenheim's real name. They also shrouded the details of her false pregnancy and actual recovery (in a previously unpublished letter discovered by Forrester and Cameron [1999], Freud described the case of Anna O as a "cure with a defect").

Nonetheless, Anna O became the first case study in psychoanalysis and formed the basis for Freud's early ideas about therapy.

In his third year at the university, Freud was the recipient of a grant that paid for two brief trips to Triste, where he engaged in research in marine biology. Freud's interests centered mainly on research in anatomy and physiology. Indeed, it would have been his preference to have worked as a researcher in Ernst Brücke's physiology laboratory, but dismal prospects for advancement as well as personal financial exigencies forced him into a medical career. He served as a resident in the Vienna General Hospital from July 31, 1882, to August of 1885. During this period, he gained experience in surgery, internal medicine, dermatology, and ophthalmology, but had little enthusiasm for any of these fields. His interests picked up, however, when he worked in Theodore Meynert's psychiatric clinic and in Franz Schol's Department of Nervous Diseases.

In September of 1885, Freud was appointed *Privatdozent* (a lecturer paid only by student fees) in neuropathology. Subsequently, he worked five months in Jean-Martin Charcot's (1825–1893) clinic in Paris, where he developed an interest in hysteria and hypnosis. Freud's experiences were pivotal because the emphasis in Paris was on the psychological nature of emotional problems, whereas the emphasis in Vienna had been on physical interpretations. Following his work in Paris, Freud returned to Vienna and set up a private practice on April 25, 1886. In that same year, after a long engagement, he married Martha Bernays.

The system of treatment that, among other things, gave Freud such a prominent place in history did not develop suddenly. Indeed, the term **psychoanalysis** did not appear until 1896, fully ten years after Freud had established his practice (Jones, 1953). In the earliest phases of his practice, Freud used physical methods such as electrotherapy (which is not to be confused with electroshock). *Electrotherapy* consisted of passing small currents of electricity through the skin and muscles of the head on the assumption that such currents would improve circulation. Deficiencies in circulation had long been assumed to be implicated in mental disorders. Later, Freud used hypnotic

The 1909 Conference at Clark University played host to some of psychology's most influential pioneers. In the front row, Clark's president G. Stanley Hall (center, hat in hand) stands next to Sigmund Freud (hat and cane); Carl Jung stands at Freud's right. E. B. Titchener stands in the front row, second to the right. On his right is William James (holding hat and coat) and J. M. Cattell appears behind James's right shoulder.

suggestion and still later the cathartic method. The technique of free association was developed partly because of Freud's disillusionment with other therapeutic methods. Freud gradually introduced changes in the method on the basis of his clinical experience and comments from his patients.

The Interpretation of Dreams, published in 1900, is Freud's best remembered book. Here, Freud advanced his well-known position that dreams represent wish fulfillments in disguise. The book, now regarded as a classic in psychology, did not bring instantaneous fame to its author (Fancher, 2000). Indeed, initial reaction was hostile, especially in some Viennese circles. Slowly, however, the book attracted attention and within ten years after its publication Freud's fame was assured.

Freud's bibliography following *The Interpretation of Dreams* reveals an impressive output of major books, shorter papers, and case histories that elaborate and extend his system of psychological thought. So prolific were his writings that the collected works are now contained in twenty-three volumes with an additional volume devoted to indexes and bibliographies (see Strachey, 1953–1974). The entire corpus established Freud as one of the great psychologists and a pioneer in aspects of the discipline that were ignored in other systems of psychological thought.

Freud accepted G. Stanley Hall's invitation to speak at Clark University in 1909. In addition to receiving an honorary doctoral degree, the invitation satisfied Freud's craving for international recognition. Gay (1988) observed that prior to his American lectures, psychoanalysts "represented a small, embattled minority in the psychiatric profession; Freud's ideas still remained the property of the few, and a scandal to most" (p. 206). Hall's interest, however, bolstered the visibility of psychoanalysis and prompted Freud to regard the Clark University ceremony as the "first official recognition of our endeavors" (Jones, 1955, p. 57). William James was one of the many luminaries who attended Freud's five lectures. The two men later met for a walk but were interrupted when James experienced pain from the aggravated heart condition that would claim his life almost one year later. Inspired by James's stoicism, Freud (1924/1959a) later wrote, "I have always wished that I might be as fearless as he was in the face of approaching death" (p. 52).

Freud's biographers paint the picture of a brilliant thinker with a complex personality (Gelfand & Kerr, 1992). On the one hand, he could appear shy almost to the point of lacking confidence, but the shyness was often only an appearance. Freud had brief periods of depression, but could also be joyful, enthusiastic, or even jubilant. His creativity was by no means consistent. There were times of inhibition, or even dullness, when he seemed quite incapable of being productive. But such times were followed by bursts of creative activity and productivity.

Freud had a strong devotion to his family and a considerable capacity for commitment. Although he worked unusually long hours, he nevertheless found time to be with Martha and their five children. His tastes in music were severely truncated, but he had an enormous appreciation of art, especially sculpture. His major indulgence was a collection of antiquities (sculptures of ancient figures) that afforded great intellectual and aesthetic pleasure.

Freud's last days were spent in exile in London, England. Austria had been invaded by the Nazis in 1938 and Freud, at first defiant, was finally persuaded by friends to leave Vienna. His affiliation with B'nai B'rith, as well as his theories, made him a prime target for Nazi hostilities. Indeed, Gay (1988, p. 592) reports that Freud's books, along with those of other intellectuals, were burned by the Nazis in numerous public squares on May 10, 1933. Freud's theories have never been popular in totalitarian regimes, possibly because of the psychoanalytic emphasis on the unconscious determinants of cognitive processes. In any case, Freud, already a sick man and dying from cancer of the jaw, was forced from his home by the Nazi invasion. He died in London on September 23, 1939.

General Characteristics of Freud's Thought

Though Freud's system of psychology evolved over time, there are several major philosophical assumptions that consistently guided his work. We review here six characteristics of his theory and then turn to a consideration of the principal details of his systematic position.

Determinism. Unlike William James, Freud devoted no essay explicitly to the free will/determinism issue. Nevertheless, he repeatedly expressed his preference for theoretical determinism and for a methodology that assumes natural causes for all mental events (MacMillan, 1991). Gay (1988) wrote, "It is a crucial point in Freud's theory that there are no accidents in the universe of the mind" (p. 119). Sulloway (1979) noted that "Freud's entire life's work in science was characterized by an abiding faith in the notion that all vital phenomena, including psychical ones, are rigidly and lawfully determined by the principle of cause and effect" (p. 94). Other scholars (e.g., Brown, 1964, p. 3; Jones, 1953, p. 304; Wisdom, 1943) have also emphasized Freud's strong commitment to determinism. As we will see later, however, there are some possible meanings of freedom that surface in Freud's system of thought.

Belief in the Continuity of the Animal Kingdom. In his autobiographical study, Freud (1924/1959a) noted that Darwin's theory had a powerful influence on his thinking because it suggested that our understanding of the world may grow through knowledge of natural processes. In an open letter to Albert Einstein on the subject of war, Freud (1932/1964a, p. 204) insisted that human beings have no grounds for excluding themselves from the animal kingdom. According to Jones (1953), Freud subscribed to the evolutionary position that "no spirits, essences, or entelechies, no superior plans or ultimate purposes are at work. The physical energies alone cause effects—somehow" (p. 42). Freud believed that there were distinct advantages in a thoroughgoing naturalistic approach to the study of human nature.

Role of Unconscious Influences.   One of the unique features of Freud's systematic approach to psychology is his belief in the importance of unconscious processes. He strongly believed that rational processes may actually serve unconscious motives. He understood that his position struck a blow at human narcissism and that it challenged our cherished belief in human rationality. According to Freud (1917/1955), "the ego is not master in its own house" (p. 143). Nevertheless, Freud believed that human beings need not remain in bondage to unconscious influences. Indeed, as we will see later, Freud's goal of psychoanalysis is to return back to the ego "its mastery over lost provinces of . . . mental life" (Freud, 1938/1964b, p. 173).

Developmental Emphasis.   A hallmark of classic psychoanalytic theory is the importance it gives to development and growth. Freud was deeply sensitized to the idea that needs and abilities vary as a function of age. He also believed that there are critical periods, or periods of maximal sensitivity to certain qualities of stimulation. According to Freud's theory, events early in life are consequential to later adjustment. Furthermore, he believed that there are identifiable developmental stages that must be successfully negotiated if the individual is later to enjoy psychological health and well-being.

Emphasis on Motivation.   The major systems of psychology are often associated with preferred areas of study. For example, structuralism placed its strongest emphasis on the study of the senses, whereas behaviorism emphasized learning. The content area that is privileged in Freudian psychology is motivation. Freud repeatedly refers to the centrality of pleasure in human life and to specific determinants of its expression. Furthermore, his discussions of his patients and their problems are inevitably couched in the language of motivation. Though Freud did not deny the crucial roles of learning, perception, and social influence in human life, clearly his emphasis was on motivation.

Applied Psychology.   A final emphasis in the psychology of Sigmund Freud is on application.

Freud's theoretical interests ran deep, but he was equally interested in developing a psychology that could speak effectively to the daily problems of life. Thus, a great deal of his intellectual energy was devoted to the problems of effective intervention and treatment. Indeed, the very term *psychoanalysis* refers simultaneously to a system of psychology and to a psychotherapy.

FREUD'S SYSTEM OF PSYCHOLOGY

Psychoanalytic theory and practice changed and developed, sometimes rather dramatically, over the forty-three years of Freud's professional career. In fact, one of his initial ambitions was to advance a psychology thoroughly anchored in neurology and physiology—a psychology that would be worthy as a natural science (Connors, 2000). Freud's efforts along these lines resulted in a paper entitled "Project for a Scientific Psychology." He quickly realized that it was premature to attempt to establish rigorous connections between the world of physiology and the world of experience, so he abandoned the project. Thereafter, Freud showed some distrust about experimental attempts to validate his clinical concepts (Rosenzweig, 1997).

Many times he followed false leads and had to backtrack and start over. Thus, the development of psychoanalysis was not marked by a smooth linear progression of ideas. In what follows, we begin with some of Freud's most mature thought. Such thought, advanced during the later years of his life, provides the broadest possible picture of his approach to psychology. We then work back to his earlier ideas to fill in some of the details of his theory.

Life's Major Goal and Its Inevitable Frustration

In his book *Civilization and Its Discontents,* Freud (1930/1961a) stressed his belief that the **pleasure principle** dominates psychological processes. From the very beginning of life we seek to experience pleasure and to avoid pain. He noted that pleasure results from the satisfaction of needs, but while we seek pleasure through the satisfaction of needs, we find that the world is not very coopera-tive with our efforts. Furthermore, our own con-stitution works against sustained pleasure. Freud observed that we know pleasure only through con-trast, but we have a constitutional incapacity to experience contrast for sustained periods. For ex-ample, we may know intense pleasure when we submerge ourselves in a bath after shivering from the cold, but such pleasure is short lived. The con-stancy of the bath would itself become aversive if we remain in it too long. Freud (1930/1961a) reminded his readers of Goethe's warning that "nothing is harder to bear than a succession of fair days" (p. 76). In addition to the constitutional con-straints on happiness, Freud outlined three great sources of suffering that inevitably work in greater or lesser degree against the pleasure that we so highly prize.

The first source of suffering is our own body, which is the material medium for pleasure and pain. The body, doomed to progressive deteriora-tion, sends a relentless succession of signals or warnings of its frailty and inevitable demise. The second source of suffering, the outer world, rages against us with unrelenting insults. Even the best of niches is beset with natural disasters and with bacterial and viral invasions that are a constant threat to life. Finally, by far the greatest source of suffering is other people. Freud was deeply tuned to the social sources of pain and unhappiness—war, rape, theft, assault, prejudice, child and spouse abuse, daily insensitivities and hostilities, dishon-esty, authoritarian structures and attitudes—these are but a few of countless possible examples of this third source of pain and suffering. In view of all of the sources of unhappiness, Freud (1930/1961a) wondered openly whether we are not justified in feeling that it was never intended that human beings should be happy. He concluded that some people find a modicum of happiness in the simple fact that they have temporarily escaped unhappiness.

After outlining the sources of suffering, Freud turned to the remedial actions that are open to human beings. Though these actions seek to pre-serve pleasure, they are all temporary in their ef-fects and are thus flawed. Nevertheless, some are more economical than others and some more ad-mirable. Freud discussed attempts at unbridled sat-

isfaction of needs and noted that this method sets us at odds with others and is therefore not toler-ated by society. One of the great growth tasks con-fronting every child is that of learning to delay gratification or to substitute one kind of gratifi-cation for another. Another method is to withdraw from the world and thus savor whatever satisfac-tion can be found in self-imposed isolation. Still another method, highly prized because it produces a small portion of happiness and independence from the world, is the method of intoxication. Freud was not, however, impressed with the men-tal economics of artificial intoxications because it represents an essential withdrawal from reality and requires energy that could have been put to better use.

Freud also included religion as one of many de-fenses we erect as a means of coping with the world. He compared religion to intoxication arguing that, in both cases, the individual escapes from reality. Religion, he believed, places us in a state of men-tal infantilism that depreciates the value of this world and at the same time promises the illusion of a better world to come. Freud's major critique of religion is contained in his well-known book *The Future of an Illusion* (Freud, 1927/1961c).

Other defenses outlined by Freud included lov-ing and being loved, enjoyment of works of art, and the flight into mental illness. According to Freud, hard work and science are the most ad-mirable defenses against the sources of suffering. Through hard work and science, there is great po-tential to make lasting contributions for the good of others; yet Freud pointed out that work is sel-dom valued by the masses of people.

Freud acknowledged that his enumeration of the strategies for attaining happiness and the de-fenses against suffering were incomplete. He ar-gued that we are fighting a losing battle and that the demands of the pleasure principle cannot be fulfilled. He believed that the different alternatives we attempt must ultimately be judged in terms of a kind of complicated equation that is duly sensitive to short-term and long-term interests and to individual and social interests. The difficulties, complexities, and ambiguities involved in the intelligent pursuit of happiness confront every human being. Freud's views on the pleasure principle and its vicissitudes provide an important backdrop for understanding his views on the structure of personality and the nature of the stresses that all human beings face.

The Structure of Personality

Freud conceptualized the structure of human personality in terms of three interrelated systems called the *id, ego,* and *superego* (meaning, respectively, the *it, I,* and *over-I*). The three systems are in more or less continuous conflict—a conflict with which all human beings must successfully cope if they are to adapt to the world. The psychological adjustment of the individual depends on the maintenance of a reasonable balance among the three systems. Indeed, severe consequences result if any of the three are unduly weakened. The three systems offer differing strategies for coping with the problem of the pleasure principle (discussed in the previous section). Freud's views on the structure of the personality must be viewed in the context of his views on the meaning of life's purpose. It should be noted that Freud often spoke of the id, ego, and superego almost as if they were localizable entities, but intended them to be viewed as hypothetical systems that describe major functional areas of the human personality.

The Id.   The **id** is the most primitive and, developmentally, the first component of personality. It is driven by powerful biological needs necessary to the physical survival of the individual. The needs that the id represents are common to all animal species and seek expression in the most direct, biologically efficient manner. The id is not constrained by customs, morality, values, conventions, or ethics. On the contrary, it impulsively and reflexively seeks immediate gratification. The id, according to Freud, operates purely on the basis of the pleasure principle in its most unconstrained manifestation.

The id is represented directly in impulsive and reflexive activity, but it is also expressed in what Freud called the **primary processes,** which include images or memories of objects that satisfy needs. For example, if one dreams of a sexual encounter and the dream is rich in imagery, then such imagery may be an example of primary processes. Such processes present themselves without the embellishments of polite social conventions and norms.

Freud believed that the id is true psychic reality serving the pleasure principle. He employed the term *libido* to refer to psychic energies that are directed toward need gratification. The libido, or libidinal energy, is usually directed toward loved or desired objects in the world (object libido) but may attach itself to the ego. When this happens, self-love, or narcissism, replaces object love.

The Ego.   The **ego** is the *I* or *me* of the personality—the center of organization and integration. While the id is closely connected to the demands of the pleasure principle, the ego must adapt to the demands of reality. The ego is thus caught between powerful forces and, as such, must serve as a kind of administrator or executive. It cannot ignore the demands of the id, but unlike the id, neither can it ignore the demands of the world of social convention. Caught between such powerful forces, it learns to appropriate, compromise, substitute, and delay. Through such techniques it serves to protect the individual and the social order by finding appropriate and acceptable channels for the demands of the id. The ego makes use of plans that Freud referred to as the **secondary process.** The secondary process assists the primary process of the id by devising strategies through which drives can be satisfied in a socially acceptable manner. It goes without saying that the ego must be strong and durable to withstand the severe and continuous conflict imposed by the contradictory demands of the id and society. This is not the complete story, however; the ego must cope with still another force: the superego.

The Superego.   The **superego** consists of internalized social norms, ideals, and standards to which the individual has been conditioned. The superego, like the id, is not rational; instead of serving the goal of pleasure, it serves the goal of perfection. The superego is a kind of conscience with an inhibitory function, but over and above this, facilitates action toward achievement of higher values embraced by society. In terms of its demands on the ego, the superego is no more realistic than the id; both systems make irrational and impossible demands.

The inevitable tensions among the id, the ego, and the superego were highly important to Freud. Indeed, he believed that the relationship among these systems had far-reaching consequences for the health of his patients. All three serve important roles and each system must find legitimate and acceptable expression. The id represents an important dimension of biological life that cannot be ignored. On the other hand, if we are to live with other people in civilization, there must be inhibition and restraint. If the id dominates the ego, antisocial behavior results and society must then take action to isolate and correct such behavior. Likewise, a superego that is too powerful may block the expression of basic biological needs. Freud believed that the repression of biological drives results in the varieties of emotional difficulties that are so common in civilized societies. We will return to this topic later. According to Freud, the ego must have sufficient strength to deal with the complex and sometimes capricious demands of the external world while at the same time permitting the compromised expression of both the id and superego.

Motivation and Unconscious Processes

Orgel (1990) pointed out that "the core idea of psychoanalysis begins with the assumption that in every human being there is an unconscious mind" (p. 1). Some of Freud's early experiences with hypnosis in H. M. Bernheim's clinic in 1889 had particularly important effects on the development of his theory. Specifically, in a typical demonstration, a patient was hypnotized and given a suggestion that was to be carried out later (i.e., after the patient had been awakened from the trance). The suggestion was that the next time the physician and the physician's assistants entered the room, the patient would open the physician's umbrella (which had purposefully been left in the corner of the room) and hold it over the physician's head. Predictably, when the physician and the assistants returned to the room, the patient greeted the company, opened the umbrella, and held it over the physician's head.

After the patient carried out such a posthypnotic suggestion, the physician would talk to the patient and ask why he or she had engaged in such behavior. The patient, typically embarrassed, offered a rationalization. For example, the patient might claim that the weather forecast had called for rain and that it seemed a good idea to open the umbrella and inspect it to make sure it does not leak. The fact is, patients were unable to explain their behavior because they could not consciously recall what had taken place during the hypnotic trance. The patient might even experience the opening of the umbrella as a free act and even defend the act with a rationalization. But other observers knew there were unconscious forces that had contributed to the act.

Commenting on such demonstrations, Freud, as quoted by Jones (1953), noted, "I received the profoundest impression of the possibility that there could be powerful mental processes which nevertheless remained hidden from the consciousness of man" (p. 238). Patients, in fact, did not seem to understand the basis of their behavior. The demonstrations of such hypnotic phenomena provided graphic examples of mental processes that are clearly not in conscious awareness but are nevertheless powerful determinants of behavior. At the same time, conscious explanations of the behaviors in question were demonstrably inadequate—one might even say illusory.

Bernheim's work with hypnosis, which Freud described as astonishing, clearly had a major influence on the development of psychoanalytic thought. No longer could conscious processes be viewed as autonomous, nor could we be certain that we are aware of all that is in the mind. Freud viewed it as a mistake to equate mental processes with consciousness alone. To defend the powerful role of unconscious forces in human life, he drew from hypnotic phenomena, dreams, slips of the tongue, and everyday purposeful forgetting such as the forgetting of a dental appointment. No conscious event was sacrosanct—not even a religious experience. Freud provided an interesting case study to illustrate this last point.

The case study, entitled "A Religious Experience" (Freud, 1927/1961d), tells of a young medical doctor who wrote to Freud to share the story of his religious conversion. The young doctor knew that Freud was an atheist and had hoped to convince Freud of the reality of God. The doctor's letter told of seeing the body of an old woman on a cart being taken to a dissecting room. He was suddenly overwhelmed by the apparent injustice of death and the final disposition of the remains of the old woman. He told Freud that he decided then and there to abandon his belief in God. But later as he was reflecting on the matter, he reported that a voice "spoke to my soul that 'I should consider the step I was about to take'" (Freud, 1927/1961d, p. 169). Following that event, the young doctor was overcome with fear and remorse and was converted to a complete acceptance of the Bible and the teachings of Jesus Christ.

In relaying this experience, the young doctor beseeched Freud to abandon his atheistic beliefs. Freud sent a polite reply to the doctor's letter and then proceeded to analyze the religious experience. The analysis raised a particularly cogent question at the outset. Why had the young doctor been so outraged and why had he renounced God at the sight of the old woman being carried away for dissection? The question is cogent because doctors see far more horrible sights than a corpse destined for autopsy. It must be a peculiarity, even for a non-Freudian, that this particular event should initiate a renunciation of belief in God and a subsequent religious conversion. It would have been more reasonable if belief in God had been challenged by the protracted suffering of a young person, the senseless death of a child, or the heart arrest of a young adult undergoing routine surgery. Doctors see tragedies far worse than that of the corpse of an old person being taken to a dissecting room.

But Freud reasoned that this particular event was well suited to initiate the doctor's conversion because the event aroused unconscious associations and motives. Freud argued that the sight of the old woman triggered associations of the doctor's mother. In this case, the cruel fate of the mother is the work of God the father. In a cry of outrage, the doctor then rebelled against the source of the indignity and injustice. He would no longer believe in God. But why, then, was the doctor so

quickly converted? Conversion, in this case, represents surrender to the same God and father who only hours before is renounced. The reason for the conversion, according to Freud, is found in an unconscious conflict that most human beings experience at an earlier stage in their lives. Furthermore, this conflict can be reexperienced symbolically at later stages in life.

Freud believed that Sophocles's Greek tragedy *Oedipus Rex* is characteristic of conflicts that young children experience. A child may build a strong emotional attachment to the parent of the opposite sex, but the child must then resolve the tensions such emotional attachments create in relations with the parent of the same sex. For example, a boy with strong attachments to his mother may feel hostility toward his father because the father is viewed as a usurper who possesses the mother and thus robs the boy of exclusive rights to the pleasure provided by the mother. But hostility toward the father is fraught with danger—the father is awesome and, by comparison, the boy is completely powerless. The Oedipus situation is resolved as the boy gradually or suddenly abandons his competitive stance and identifies with the father. Identifying with power, even aggressive power, is a well-known psychological phenomenon. According to Freud, the Oedipus conflict is not fully resolved in early years, hence it may recur at later times in life.

Following Freud's line of argument, it is no accident that the young doctor could not maintain his indignation at God. In the doctor's belief system, God was too powerful, and the mere suggestion that he should consider the step he was about to take quickly led to fear followed by remorse for his rebellion. Resolution is achieved through a complete identity with God the father and a religious conversion was the end result.

Predictably, the adequacy of Freud's explanation of conversion experiences and of his approach to religion generally have been challenged (e.g., see Kovel, 1990; Meissner, 1984; Zilboorg, 1961). That issue notwithstanding, the case history just reviewed provides a particularly graphic example of Freud's position with respect to the pervasive role of powerful unconscious forces in human mental operations. Initially, the young doctor might have justified his renunciation of God in terms of his indignation at the fate of the old woman. But, according to Freud, the conversion was hardly the result of rational processes and the doctor's explanation of the conversion cannot be taken at face value. Our so-called rational explanations may themselves be conditioned by forces outside the realm of immediate consciousness, as illustrated by the earlier example of posthypnotic suggestion.

The idea that rational processes may serve unconscious motives is a blow to many human pretensions. It is little wonder, then, according to Freud (1917/1955), that "the ego does not look favorably upon psychoanalysis and positively refuses to believe in it" (p. 143). Freud, like Copernicus and Darwin, challenged human narcissism. With Copernicus, we were no longer on center stage in the cosmos; with Darwin, we were no longer products of special creation. Our self-confidence and pride, however, received still another blow when Freud argued against our long-held and cherished belief that we are rational creatures with a free will that places us fully in charge of our own agendas.

Though Freud emphasized the role of unconscious forces in human life, his larger vision of human motivation was much more complicated and multidimensional. We turn now to consider some of the additional dimensions of his theory as set forth in an important work entitled "Instincts and Their Vicissitudes" (Freud, 1915/1957a). Unfortunately, the English term **instinct** is not a satisfactory equivalent for the German term *Trieb* used in Freud's original work. The term *drive,* as that term is used in American psychology, may be closer in meaning to the term *Trieb* as employed by Freud. Whatever the most appropriate translation, Freud's concept of *Trieb* is an important key to his larger approach to motivation.

Trieb.   Freud argued that *Trieb* has its origin in a stimulus that, unlike external stimuli, is not momentary. Indeed, it persists until it finds satisfaction. Freud pointed out that the term *need* may be the best word to describe the nature of such a stimulus. Freud argued that there are four components

associated with an instinct. (With the above cautionary note, we will use the term *instinct* for the German *Trieb*.)

The first component is the *source,* which refers to somatic processes that give rise to the stimulus in the first place. The somatic processes are mechanical or chemical changes in the body. Such changes constitute an initiating stimulus that will persist and intensify. For example, hunger is initiated by a variety of mechanical and chemical changes and will persist until the source is abolished. Satisfaction, however, is always temporary because instincts have a cyclical nature.

Freud anticipated the question that any reader might raise: How many instincts do we have? His reply was "There is obviously a wide opportunity here for arbitrary choice" (Freud, 1915/1957a, p. 124). He saw no reason, for example, why one might not posit instincts for such activities as play or aggression. Elaborating on the arbitrary nature of classification systems, Freud (p. 124) expressed doubt that there is a decisive basis for the distinction and classification of instincts. He went on to note that psychoanalysis had focused largely on the sexual instincts.

The second characteristic of an instinct is what Freud called the *impetus.* He used this term to refer to the amount of energy associated with the activity in question. He also used the expression *motor element* to define the term *impetus.* Presumably, the impetus of the instinct grows as a function of the amount of time that has lapsed since the initiating source of the instinct was first felt.

The third characteristic of an instinct is its *aim.* Freud (1915/1957a) noted that instincts always seek satisfaction through altering the stimulation that gave rise to them in the first place. Though satisfaction is the final goal of every instinct, there may be more than one possible means by which such satisfaction is attained. Further, there may be compromises, temporary delays, substitutes, and so forth. The ego obviously plays a crucial role in assisting with the aim of instincts.

The final, and perhaps the most interesting, component of an instinct is its *object.* It is through the object that the instinct achieves its aim. Freud (1915/1957a) argued that the object of an instinct is highly variable. A single stimulus may serve more than one instinct and a given instinct may become attached to a variety of stimulus objects. A particularly strong attachment to a specific stimulus is called a **fixation.**

Freud observed that instincts undergo a variety of vicissitudes. For example, instincts may be sublimated, repressed, or even reversed into their opposites. The mode of their expression has far-reaching consequences for the adjustment and health of the individual, so this was a topic of great interest to Freud. Some of the vicissitudes of the instincts will become evident as we now turn to some additional dimensions of Freud's theory.

Anxiety

One of the interesting features of Freud's psychology is its emphasis on the interplay of tensions that confront every human being. Thus, there are tensions among various components of personality, tensions among competing drives, and tensions from the sources of pain and suffering covered at the beginning of our treatment of Freud's system. Freud believed that there are specific varieties of anxiety associated with some of the important and pervasive tensions that we all must face.

Objective Anxiety.   A common anxiety is that associated with objective threats to our well-being. As noted earlier, the outer world can rage against us, our body is vulnerable to assaults from within and without and, most of all, we can be hurt by other people. Freud acknowledged that many of our anxieties have a real basis from objective threats. He referred to such anxiety as **objective anxiety.** It is part of the wear and tear of living in a world that is not always friendly. It arises when the ego is threatened by objective forces in the world. Its force is a function of the strength of the ego in relation to the power or perceived power of the objective threat.

Neurotic Anxiety.   Freud was particularly concerned with **neurotic anxiety,** which arises when the ego is threatened by the irrational forces of the id. Thus, unlike objective anxiety, the source of the threat is from within our own personality. Because the source of threat is from within, there is no ob-

vious escape and no clearly identifiable cause. Neurotic anxiety can therefore have a ubiquitous quality in the sense that it can appear, for no apparent reason, at any time or place. The individual may suddenly have a vague sense of impending doom or a feeling of panic. Neurotic anxiety is more likely when basic drives are persistently thwarted or bottled up. In the Victorian culture of Freud's days, there were particularly strong prohibitions and rigid prescriptions regarding the expression of sexuality. A major emphasis in Freud's theory is that if such a powerful drive is stifled at every turn, then it will find another mode of expression. Neurotic anxiety is one manifestation of powerful instinctual energy threatening to overcome the ego.

Moral Anxiety.   The final type of anxiety, **moral anxiety,** is a kind of counterpart of neurotic anxiety; however, in this case, it is the irrational demands of the superego that overwhelm the ego. Like neurotic anxiety, the source of moral anxiety is within the personality, so there is no escape. Originally, the sources of moral anxiety were in the outside world, but in time, the superego incorporates norms, values, customs, and prohibitions of society. The superego becomes a kind of internal substitute for the punishment that was once threatened by the parents. Now, moral anxiety is experienced as guilt over real (or even imagined) departures from internalized values. Obviously, the stronger the superego, the greater the likelihood of moral anxiety. Furthermore, sometimes the most virtuous and exemplary people experience the greatest moral anxiety. On the opposite extreme, there are those who experience almost no moral anxiety, but such people run the risk of placing their own instinctual needs ahead of the rights of others. Such people obviously risk being isolated by one means or another. Those with excessive moral anxiety risk living a colorless, truncated, overly controlled, and hollow existence.

The varieties of anxiety with their various trade-offs illustrate the importance of balance in the three systems of personality. The health and adjustment of the individual require a channeled flow of energy from the id and the superego. The ego must also have sufficient strength to deal with the harsh demands of the world and with the persistent demands of its ever-present internal companions. We turn now to some of the strategies employed by the ego as it goes about the task of coping with the great range of rational and irrational forces that play on it.

Defense Mechanisms of the Ego

Earlier, we discussed Freud's belief that work is the most admirable defense against the sources of pain and suffering that we all encounter. Freud believed that nothing ties us so closely to reality as our work. The capacity to work with vigor and joy is, in his view, a mark of health. Freud believed that the ego can employ admirable methods as it copes with dangers and anxieties. The ego may also employ unfortunate defensive strategies that make use of disguises, distortions, falsifications, denials, and misrepresentations of reality. We now consider some of these strategies.

Repression.   There is no concept more central to psychoanalysis than repression. Indeed, Freud (1914/1957c) pointed out that "the theory of repression is the cornerstone on which the whole structure of psychoanalysis rests. It is the most essential part of it" (p. 16). The theory of repression, of course, also implies the existence of unconscious mental processes. **Repression,** as a defense, means that dangerous or anxiety-provoking thoughts, memories, or perceptions are forced out of consciousness and into the unconscious realm. The content of the unconscious mind is largely repressed material. In describing the unconscious arena, Gay (1988) compared it to "a maximum-security prison holding antisocial inmates . . . [such inmates are] heavily guarded, but barely kept under control and forever attempting to escape" (p. 128). For most of us, the inmates or their representatives do in fact escape on a continuing basis and are manifested in dream content, slips of the tongue, forgotten appointments, and humor. Freud also believed that repression is involved to some degree in other defense mechanisms.

Though the ego makes use of repression, it may be aided by the superego. There is also a kind of

repression that occurs with minimal involvement from the ego. Freud referred to this process more as *primal repression,* which refers to a class of ideas so painful and unthinkable that they are normally barred from consciousness in the first place. Ideas of incest and aggression against the opposite-sexed parent are included in this group.

Projection.   **Projection** occurs when personal faults or weaknesses are externalized or ascribed to objects, events, or other people. When personal motives or ideas are unacceptable or when they provoke anxiety, they may be repressed. The repressed materials may then be expressed in the claim that the repudiated motive is operating in others. For example, a marital partner tempted to be unfaithful may accuse the other partner of having unfaithful fantasies. Aggressive individuals or even aggressive groups may claim that the real source of aggression is in others. Those with repressed voyeuristic curiosities may worry about the moral breakdown of society and the excessive interest of others in pornography. In projection, the ego is protected because it does not have to own the motives and ideas that provoke anxiety. The price for such protection, however, is high because reality is severely distorted. What could have been faced as neurotic or moral anxiety is now disguised as objective anxiety. For example, the anger over the perceived unfaithfulness that one now projects onto another will exact its own price in anxiety.

Regression.   **Regression** involves the return or retreat to an earlier stage of development and the reinstatement of attitudes and behaviors that were characteristic of that earlier stage. Regressions may be brief and episodic or, in the face of overwhelming threats, may be of longer duration. Brief or episodic regression may be manifested in dreams or daydreams in which one returns to an earlier, more secure stage in life. Regression may also be illustrated in activities such as temper tantrums, easy submission to authority, masturbation, the need to be babied during an illness, or taking drugs as an escape from responsibility. The ego is less accountable if it is temporarily operating in an earlier mode. In severe regression, the ego is removed from adult responsibility and is literally aided and assisted as in childhood.

Reaction Formation.   In "Instincts and Their Vicissitudes," Freud (1915/1957a) talked about paradoxical situations in which the instinct may undergo a reversal into its opposite. Freud believed that mental life is marked by the existence of polarities and that reversals are always a distinct possibility. Love may turn to hate, pleasure to pain, passivity to activity, and so forth. In the reaction formation, we encounter a defense in which the ego masks awareness of an anxiety-provoking motive by emphasizing its opposite. For example, a parent who harbors a great deal of hostility toward a child may mask the hostility by being overly indulgent and overprotective. A person threatened by homosexual inclinations may cover the threat by developing a phobia for homosexuality. In reaction formations there are clear denials of certain motives. Such denials are made all the more plausible by engaging in activities that are in opposition to the threatening motives. Like other defense mechanisms, reaction formations purchase some degree of relief from anxiety, but the opposite extremes produced by this defense generate anxieties of their own.

Other Defenses.   There are many additional defensive strategies employed by the ego. Some involve far less repression than those just mentioned and are thus more realistic and adaptive. Freud talked repeatedly about **sublimation,** or the substitution of a socially acceptable goal for one that is less acceptable. Many activities such as work, sporting events, art, and even philanthropic activities may represent the rechanneling of sexual energy into socially acceptable activities. Freud saw sublimation as important to the overall goals of civilized life. Another defense, **rationalization,** is the commonly encountered practice of employing false but logical and even plausible explanations designed to excuse weaknesses or errors. Still another defense, **identification,** covers weakness by imitating or becoming like more successful and adequate role models. One may imitate lifestyles, clothing styles, gestures, or even the voice of the

model. If the ego is not adequate in itself, it can at least borrow from or attempt to steal from the adequacy of another. In extreme cases, involving real pathology, the distinctions between the self and the model break down so that one falls into the delusion that one is, in fact, the object of identification.

There are numerous other defenses that serve to assist the ego with its internal and external adversaries. In his work entitled *The Ego and the Id,* Freud (1923/1961b) described the ego, as "a poor creature owing service to three masters" (p. 56). Since those masters—the id, the superego, and the external world—are so powerful and uncompromising, the ego must amass a great psychological arsenal of its own. Yet it cannot make all the necessary acquisitions without help. It must be nurtured and assisted in a supportive environment. Few psychologists have been as sensitive to the issues of growth and development as Freud. We turn now to a consideration of his views on development.

Stages of Psychosexual Development

Freud believed that the quality of adult experience is connected to the quality of experience in childhood. Hence, the development of the child was a key focus in his work and he could not separate development in the larger sense from sexual development. On this latter topic, Freud is often accused of advancing an overly narrow view of sexuality and a narrow view of psychology based exclusively on sexual motivation. Freud argued, however, that it is the common view of sexuality that is narrow. According to the common view, the idea of sex is limited to genital contact with a member of the opposite sex. Freud pointed out that such a view ignores the clear fact that there are object attachments, sexual in nature, not associated with the genitals of the opposite sex. He believed that all surfaces of the body, not just the genitals, are erotogenic. Some surfaces (e.g., the lips) are especially erogenous. Freud tied sexuality closely to the pleasure principle and thus viewed the subject in very broad terms. Sexuality, for Freud, was not just one thing. As we discussed earlier, Freud noted that object is the most flexible characteristic of an instinct. Furthermore, he referred to sexual instincts in the plural. We turn now to Freud's stage theory of psychosexual development.

Oral Stage.   The child's initial interactions with the world are primarily via the oral cavity. Powerful hunger and thirst drives are satisfied through sucking and needs are expressed through crying. In this early stage, the child is learning a good deal: The world is either responsive or unresponsive to cries for help, the nursing situation is friendly or cold, and pleasure is derived through the intake of food and water. A bit later, the child experiments by putting a host of objects in his or her mouth. Freud assumed that there are qualitative differences with respect to the manner in which oral needs are met. He assumed further that neglect or overindulgence during this stage could have negative consequences for later development. Thus, overindulgence might result in unrealistic optimism, but neglect might result in a pessimistic or angry individual. Freud believed that later adult orientations might be based on fixations at early stages. Such fixations result from failures to meet basic needs during critical periods of development.

Anal Stage.   In the second and third years, the child gradually develops a new awareness of the pleasure associated with the relief of bowel and bladder tension. But this new localization of pleasure is fraught with difficulties because the external world imposes strict rules and regulations concerning the mode and timing of bowel and bladder activities. It is during this stage that there can be dramatic clashes between the adult and child perspectives on elimination. From the child's perspective, elimination is a source of pleasure; the feces are a curiosity and possibly even a part of the self (If my parents love me so much, why are they so anxious to dispose of this part of me?). The adult perspective has been illustrated by DeMause (1974), who quoted Martin Luther's contention that children "befoul the corners." DeMause then noted that "the Latin *merda,* excrement, was the source of the French *merdeux,* little child" (p. 39).

Freud's views on the anal stage are understood most sympathetically in the historical context of toilet training. It is not a pleasant history and it is not an easy history to understand, especially in a

day of disposable diapers, well-ventilated houses, indoor toilets, automatic washing machines, and hot and cold running water. In earlier days, proper toilet training was consequential to a well-ordered house. Children were often forced to sit for long periods on training chairs, were subjected to enemas and purges and were often the victims of whippings and beatings for failures to control bowel or bladder movements (see DeMause, 1974).

Freud was deeply sensitive to the precarious balancing act that confronts the small child. The newly discovered pleasures of elimination and the curiosity about feces must be balanced against the demands of the world for control. Freud believed that excessive punishment during this stage of development had consequences for later personality development. For example, he speculated that later stinginess or later compulsions over rules and regulations might result from harsh controls regarding toilet training. Similarly, he believed that an overly indulgent attitude during the period could have the negative effect of producing what he called an anal-expulsive personality. Such a personality is marked by sloppiness, disorder, attraction to filth, and verbal aggression.

Phallic Stage.   Freud believed that, from ages three to five, the child's interests shift to its sex organs and to the sex organs of the parents. In addition, the child begins to identify with the parent of the opposite sex. This identification involves positive sexual feeling of the boy for his mother and of the girl for her father. At the same time, the parent of the same sex is viewed as a threat and hence evokes hostile and rebellious actions. The affection for the parent of the opposite sex and the hostility toward the parent of the same sex is called the **Oedipus complex.** This terminology comes from Sophocles's (c. 470–399 B.C.) Greek tragedy in which a young man, Oedipus, unknowingly killed his father, Laius, and married his mother, Jocasta. Oedipus had been separated from both parents from birth, so he had no real memories about Laius and Jocasta. Later, when he discovered what had happened, he blinded himself with Jocasta's brooch as an act of repentance.

As noted earlier in the chapter when we discussed the religious experience, the desire for the mother leads to anxiety that is induced by fear of the father. The boy would like to replace his father, but this carries the threat of awesome retaliation; in Freud's theory, such retaliation includes the threat of castration by the father. Thus, the source of pleasure, in this case the genitals, would be eliminated. Because of the fear of retaliatory power of the father, the boy represses his feelings for the mother and gradually identifies with the father. Thus, for the boy, the Oedipal conflict is partially resolved through repression and identification.

The resolution of the Oedipal crisis for the girl, according to Freud, follows an entirely different course and this has proved to be one of the most controversial aspects of his theory (e.g., see Roith, 1987). According to Freud, the girl does not completely repress her striving for the father, nor does she thoroughly identify with her mother. Instead, she gradually transfers her desire for the father to other men and thus the father may become the prototype for the girl's future husband. Freud argued that the girl is envious of the protruding male sex organ and holds her mother responsible for what she considers to be her castrated condition. Freud argued that so-called **penis envy** played an important role in the psychology of women. As with the male, the Oedipal situation (sometimes called the Electra complex for women) may never be completely resolved.

Latency Period.   Freud believed that between the phallic stage and the final genital stage of development there intervenes a period of no new obvious localization of erotic interest. This **latency period,** from about four or five years of age to the beginnings of puberty, is marked by minimal overt symptoms of sexual interest. This is a time of intense physical activity and strong interest in peer groups. Sexual attachments are present but less noticeable than at other periods of development.

Genital Stage.   The **genital stage** of development is associated with the adolescent years. During this stage, the effects of earlier periods are still present, but if development is normal, the individual will develop emotional ties, particularly with members of the opposite sex.

The organization of sexual energy will now be focused on the genitals. During the genital stage, the individual is preoccupied with object choices relating to friends, social institutions, and vocations. The major goal of the genital stage is reproduction and those ancillary activities (work, socialization) critical to the propagation of the species.

Psychoanalysis as a Therapeutic Technique

As noted earlier, psychoanalysis is both a system of psychology and a therapeutic approach to emotional problems. Freud's theory of treatment developed alongside his larger vision of how the human mind works. This theory assumes the operation of specific functional arrangements between conscious and unconscious processes. Freud believed that the unconscious mind is a kind of storehouse containing powerful drives along with repressed materials from earlier periods of our lives. The drives and repressed materials do not show themselves in terms of naked meanings but are expressed instead in symbolic, mediated, or disguised forms. Thus, the conscious mind has only indirect access to the dangerous materials that reside in the unconscious domain. Freud also posited the existence of a **preconscious** area containing materials that are readily available to consciousness. Material that is not now in consciousness, but that can be recalled with relative ease, is stored in the preconscious area. Freud believed that certain dangerous materials (drives, wishes, repressions) in the unconscious are not readily available to consciousness but may, nonetheless, play a crucial role in psychopathology.

We noted earlier that Freud found evidence for unconscious processes in hypnotic phenomena, slips of the tongue, forgotten appointments, and dreams. In each of these areas, however, unconscious content is inevitably disguised. Thus, one who harbors hostility toward another person may forget an appointment with that person. Freud believed that dreams are the most important means for expression of unconscious wishes and drives. He argued that dreams have **manifest content** and **latent content.** The former refers to the dream as described by the dreamer, the symbolic meaning of the dream. The latter refers to the specific way the dream expresses an unconscious wish or drive. The art of dream interpretation is the art of translating manifest content into latent content.

Freud believed that many human emotional problems result from a buildup of repressed material. Excessive pressure in the unconscious may show itself in terms of a host of symptoms such as phobias, skin rashes, obsessive or compulsive behaviors, depression, or anxiety. Since repressed materials in the unconscious were thought to be responsible for many emotional problems, it was important to explore the origins of those materials. Freud assumed that the cautious uncovering of repressions might rob them of their energy. Such energy would no longer be available to feed the troublesome psychological symptoms that brought the patient to analysis in the first place.

In his book *An Outline of Psycho-Analysis,* Freud (1938/1964b) contended that a major goal of therapy is to return back to the ego "its mastery over lost provinces of . . . mental life" (p. 173). In his *New Introductory Lectures on Psycho-Analysis,* Freud (1932/1964a) wrote that the goal of psychoanalysis is "to strengthen the ego, to make it more independent of the super-ego, to widen its field of perception and enlarge its organization, so that it can appropriate fresh portions of the id: "Where id was, there ego shall be" (p. 80). In other words, the broad goal of psychoanalytic therapy is to widen consciousness and to liberate the individual from the control of destructive unconscious forces. How, then, was the goal of psychoanalysis to be carried out?

As noted earlier, Freud believed that dreams provide the most important avenue for the expression of unconscious forces. He also believed there was therapeutic value in simply sharing one's story with another person. In addition, he developed the technique of **free association,** the uninhibited verbal expression of whatever is central in consciousness during the therapeutic session.

Obviously, for the typical patient, free association is no easy task. It requires great trust and a gradual weakening of normal inhibitions and resistances. A deep sense of vulnerability may result from true free association because one's most intimate and private psychic world is laid bare. Most normal daily conversation is guided by in-

hibition, convention, and the influence of a kind of metalevel awareness of what is appropriate to the situation. In free association, such defenses are suspended. Freud assumed that free association, like dreams, might provide a vehicle for the expression of unconscious processes. Thus, patients in psychoanalytic therapy were encouraged to assume a comfortable position, often on a couch, and talk about their dreams and/or free associate.

In time, most patients build trust in the analyst and learn to share the content of their dreams and to free associate. For their part, analysts listen carefully and provide interpretations of dream materials and free associations. Such interpretations are offered with caution and only when patients are judged to be ready to confront the dark side of their mental lives. Freud found that patients often develop emotional attachments to their therapists, and therapists may develop emotional attachments to their patients. He referred to the former as **transference** and the latter as **countertransference.** In successful therapy, the patient gradually works through the transference and develops an independence from the therapist. A major goal of psychoanalytic training is to teach therapists to learn how to cope with the issues of transference and countertransference.

Sometimes the progress of psychoanalytic therapy is slowed or brought to a halt by **resistance.** There are presumably many symptoms of resistance: sustained inability to free associate; failure to talk about a dream because it is judged to be trivial, irrelevant, or simply humorous; out-of-hand rejection of the analysts' interpretations; or broken appointments. Freud found that resistance was weakened as patients gradually gained trust.

In his brief essay entitled "Family Romances," Freud (1908/1959b) remarked that one of the most painful and difficult tasks is to achieve liberation from parents or other significant authority figures. In successful psychoanalytic therapy, the individual is freed not only from the authority of the parents but also from the authority of the analyst. The influences of the id and the superego are also moderated as the ego grows in strength and authority. Ultimately, the goal is that the individual is able to enjoy loving and working and is an effective and contributing member within the human community. The balances necessary for the achievement of such a goal are hard-won because opposing forces from without and from within are powerful and ever-present. Freud's views on the difficulties facing the individual and humankind are set forth in some of his latest works. We turn now to a consideration of his social psychological views.

Freud's Social Psychology

Freud has been accused of neglecting the social dimensions of life, but some of his later works, such as his book *Civilization and Its Discontents* (1930/1961a), did address social issues. One of his most interesting papers is an open exchange of letters with Albert Einstein entitled "Warum Krieg?" ("Why War?"). In the early 1930s, Einstein was deeply sensitive to developments in physics that foreshadowed nuclear weapons. He was distressed that such weapons would soon be available to a species that had been unable to abolish war as a means of solving its difficulties. As a result, Einstein wrote an open letter to Freud who, by that time, had achieved international stature as a leading figure in psychiatry and psychology.

Einstein's letter explored the growing magnitude of the problem of war and proposed a solution. His solution started with the narrow identities of most human beings. Most of us are identified with only a narrow portion of the human group. Einstein saw nationalism as the worst problem of all—a potentially fatal social disease. He believed that human beings could identify on a broader basis, as many have, and set up a world political organization that could settle local disputes. Einstein inquired as to whether Freud agreed with his solution and asked that he share any additional insights on the problem of war.

In a thoughtful reply, Freud agreed on the desirability of a world organization, but reminded Einstein that some of the worst wars in human history have been civil wars. So even centralized political authority is unable to thwart war in every case. Freud agreed on the importance of a broader base of identity, but saw the problem of human aggression as a much deeper problem.

At this late point in his career, Freud had come to believe that there were two broad sets of deeply opposed instincts: those that are erotic in that they seek to preserve and unite, and those that are aggressive because they seek to destroy or kill. Freud viewed both sets of instincts as essential and found that they seldom work in isolation from each other. For example, he argued that "the instinct of self preservation is certainly of an erotic kind, but it must nevertheless have aggressiveness at its disposal if it is to fulfill its purpose" (Freud, 1932/1964a, p. 209). He noted also that erotic love must contain elements of mastery if it is to gain access to its object. Freud believed that motivation is thus always complicated; it is not a simple unidirectional matter. He believed further that events that run counter to the interests of eros may automatically reinforce the operation of its opposite—the destructive instincts.

Unfortunately, civilization itself imposes constraints on eros. The price of civilization is that erotic gratifications must be delayed, drives must be sublimated, and the range of object choices must be restricted. The result is that civilization is at once a valued acquisition but also a source of frustration that may feed the aggressive or destructive instincts. When the erotic instincts are held in check by an especially repressive system, it should come as no surprise that there may be stronger manifestations of destructiveness. Such destructiveness may be directed at the self or at other people. On the other hand, the benefits of civilization are sacrificed in a system that is too permissive.

Freud's final answer to Einstein was complicated. He agreed that an international government is a step in the right direction, but pointed to conflicts of interest both within and between organizations. Freud argued that it is useless to attempt to rid ourselves of aggression because it is a vital part of our biological nature. Accordingly, it is important that social structures be set up so that aggressive and destructive instincts can be diverted and so that erotic instincts can be expressed within reasonable constraints. Freud believed that arbitrary religious and political authority that encroach on freedom of thought work against world peace. In the end, his program called for social structures that are deeply sensitive to the complicated facets of human nature. Such structures will not shut the door completely on any reasonable interest.

Freud also called attention to the importance of finding means to broaden the base of identification by emphasizing common bonds and shared interests. He quoted with approval the golden rule, "Thou shalt love thy neighbor as thyself." In Freud's view, the realization of such an ideal cannot come about simply through a command; rather, the realization is the result of the hard work of reason, education, and emotional and intellectual insight.

Appreciative Overview

There can be little question that psychoanalysis opened new intellectual vistas with far-reaching consequences for psychology and other disciplines. The field of psychology was greatly expanded by the work of Sigmund Freud, and much of the appreciative comment that follows reflects the new scope that Freud gave to the discipline. It is of particular interest that many of the concepts of psychoanalysis have endured and now occupy a respected and undisputed place in standard texts and reference sources. What, then, were some of Freud's major contributions?

1. *Emphasis on development.* Freud was one of the first to recognize the importance of childhood and the special needs associated with the various stages of human development. It makes little difference if his specific stage theory does not hold up. His larger developmental perspective has had a lasting influence.

2. *Unconscious processes.* Though there are those who fail to see the utility of Freud's concept of the unconscious, this concept, along with the concept of repression and the ego defense mechanisms, continues to occupy a central role in mainstream psychology as well as in clinical and counseling psychology.

3. *Focus on motivation.* Though Freud was not the only psychologist to emphasize the importance of motivation, he nevertheless contributed to this content area so that it soon took its place alongside sensation, perception, and learning as a major topic of inquiry.

4. *Psychotherapy.* Though there is much to criticize with respect to the specifics of Freud's therapeutic techniques, he nevertheless contributed

to the idea that many human problems have their origins in everyday life. Proper therapy for such problems is not simply medical but psychological in nature. This idea ran counter to medical thought in Freud's Vienna, so it is little wonder that he was not popular with many of his contemporaries.

5. *Interdisciplinary contributions.* As noted at the outset of the chapter, Freud's thought has had a widespread impact in such diverse fields as history, philosophy, religion, literature, and medicine. Though controversial, his work nevertheless forced psychology to be less insular as a discipline. This in itself is a worthy achievement.

Critical Overview

A system that is as wide ranging as psychoanalysis is bound to be the subject of a great deal of criticism. We outline here some of the better-known criticisms.

1. *Tendency to overgeneralize.* Freud often drew sweeping conclusions based on observations of his patients. The religious experience of the young doctor outlined earlier in the chapter is a case in point. If one wanted to know something about the psychology of conversion, wouldn't it make more sense to study a great many cases? Even then, generalizations should be cautious and couched in language that encourages experimental work. This last point leads to the next criticism.

2. *Empirical verification.* Though there have been experimental studies designed to test psychoanalytic predictions, the system, in general, does not lend itself well to experimental verification. Part of the problem is that many of the terms of the theory (e.g., *libido, eros, primary process,* etc.) are not easily operationalized.

3. *Closedness.* There can be no question that Sigmund Freud had an almost unmatched zeal to discover new truths about the inner workings of the mental world. Furthermore, he sometimes had the ability to back away from a false lead or a blind alley. In time, however, he became increasingly dogmatic about the theoretical structure he was building. People associated with Freud were expected to be disciples dedicated to extending his theory. The range of acceptable ideas was severely truncated and any person who deviated too far from core concepts was viewed as disloyal. Unfortunately, loyalty and orthodoxy became issues as classical psychoanalysis became an increasingly closed system.

4. *Sexual emphasis.* Freud is often accused of advancing a monistic theory of motivation in which all behavior is somehow derived from a single motive—namely, sex. This is a criticism that calls for much greater scholarly scrutiny. Freud did indeed emphasize the role of sexual motivation, but his view of such motivation was much broader than his critics sometimes acknowledge. Further, as we have seen, his later theory emphasized the idea that erotic instincts were opposed by the aggressive or destructive instincts.

5. *Psychoanalytic treatment.* Psychoanalytic treatment has been severely criticized on several grounds. One of the harshest criticisms is that the practitioners are a closed club cut off from the meaningful correctives of truly critical and scholarly scientific research (e.g., see Masson, 1991). Treatment has also been criticized because it is very expensive and time-consuming. Further, despite its cost, there are reasons to question whether it really accomplishes more than other, less expensive therapies.

6. *Theory of female sexuality.* Freud's concept of penis envy and his views on how females resolve the Oedipus conflict have been the subjects of extensive critical comment (e.g., see Horney, 1967; Sprengnether, 1990). Understanding Freud's views on these topics is facilitated by scholarly work that clarifies his context (e.g., see Roith, 1987). Nevertheless, his view that women are "incomplete men" must now be regarded as an error driven more by theory than by sensitivity to the enormous complexity of human sexuality. Freud did welcome the contributions of women in the psychoanalytic movement. Here, as in other institutions, however, they did not enjoy equality (e.g., see Roith, 1987, chapter 3; Wolberg, 1989).

POST-FREUDIAN ANALYTIC PSYCHOLOGIES

As with behaviorism, psychoanalysis quickly turned into a house divided. Many of those who were influenced by Freud disagreed with his emphasis on sexuality. There were deep divisions, however, over a host of other topics, such as the nature of unconscious processes, the autonomy of the ego, the stages of development, and the nature of the therapeutic process. We next examine some alternatives to Freud's theory.

ALFRED ADLER

Alfred Adler (1870–1937) joined Freud's discussion group in 1902, believing there would be a broad intellectual agenda permitting open discussion of a variety of points of view. In time, Adler learned that Freud held strong opinions about a variety of topics and did not tolerate differences of opinion. As a consequence, Adler broke away from Freud in 1911 and worked on an alternative system of thought known as **individual psychology.** Adler was an original thinker and should not be regarded as disloyal nor as a disciple (Ansbacher, 1994).

Adler was born near Vienna on February 7, 1870. His early years were marked by poor health apparently aggravated by a case of rickets. Adler attended the University of Vienna and graduated with an M.D. in 1895. He had a private practice in Vienna, but served in the military in World War I. Following his military tour, Adler opened Vienna's first child-guidance clinic. In 1926, he

Alfred Adler

moved to the United States and served briefly as a visiting professor at Columbia University. Later, he was affiliated with the Long Island College of Medicine. Adler died on May 28, 1937 while on a lecture tour in Scotland.

Some of Adler's better-known books are *The Practice and Theory of Individual Psychology* (1964b), *Understanding Human Nature* (1957), and *Social Interest: A Challenge to Mankind* (1938). An important secondary source by Ansbacher and Ansbacher (1956) is entitled *The Individual Psychology of Alfred Adler.* Scholarly work on Adlerian psychology is published in the periodical *Individual Psychology: The Journal of Adlerian Theory, Research and Practice.* There are other scholarly journals and professional organizations that promote the Adlerian viewpoint. One of the better-known organizations is the North American Society of Adlerian Psychology.

Adler's System of Psychology

In terms of methodology and basic assumptions about human nature, Adler's psychology is a study in contrast with Freud's classic psychoanalytic theory. In a paper devoted to the differences between individual psychology and Freud's psychoanalysis, Adler (1931/1964a) argued that "the Freudian view is that man, by nature [is] bad" (p. 210). Goodness is achieved in a negative way through censorship. By contrast, Adler emphasized **social interest**—a concept that refers to a natural capacity to identify with the goals of society to achieve a common good. Adler also quarreled with Freud's use of pleasure as a regulative principle. According to Adler, happiness is a more important goal than pleasure, but more important yet is a striving for totality, unity, or wholeness. Another important difference between Adler and Freud is that Adler emphasized the centrality of goal setting in human life. His theory is decidedly teleological, whereas Freud's theory emphasized material, efficient, and formal causes. And, unlike Freud, Adler believed that human nature is logical, regardless of however bizarre or psychotic it may seem (Grey, 1998).

On the methodological side, Adler argued for a much broader approach to the study of psycho-

logical phenomena than did Freud. He emphasized the importance of exploring old memories, but balanced this by studying plans or anticipations about the future. Adler also studied body language as manifested in postures and movements. He studied the effects of social structures such as birth order on personality. He studied dreams but did not see dreams as always pointing backward. Adler believed that many dreams are forward-looking.

There are many other ways that Adler's psychology contrasts with Freud's psychology. Adler's (1964a) article "The Differences between Individual Psychology and Psychoanalysis" provides a helpful overview of differences on many substantive issues such as the Oedipus complex, the death wish, dream interpretation, and so on. We turn now to a consideration of some of the key concepts in Adler's system.

Goals and the Style of Life.   In his book, *The Practice and Theory of Individual Psychology,* Adler (1964b) advances the proposition that "every psychic phenomenon, if it is to give us any understanding of a person, can only be grasped and understood if regarded as a preparation for some goal" (p. 4). Adler believed that psychological functions such as feeling and thinking are impossible unless they occur in the context of goals. In one of the more radical stances on the problem of causality, he argued that the psychological world would be marked by a kind of chaos if it resulted only from antecedent causes. In his view, the integration of psychological processes meant that past, present, and future interests are brought together. Without future considerations, ongoing present activities, considered only as results of material and efficient causes, are meaningless.

Adler believed that our experiences and behaviors must be understood in terms of our goals. He used the expression **fictional final goals** to convey his recognition that many goals are not necessarily grounded in realistic considerations. Fictions are nevertheless a major part of the subjective world. For example, an individual may believe she really has the capacity to become a great mathematician, even after struggling through an elementary algebra course. The individual may then start living and behaving in terms of the goal of becoming a great mathematician. Adler used the term **style of life** to refer to all the unique behaviors that characterize personality and that move us in the direction of specific goals. Adler's psychology emphasizes processes, strategies, and movements rather than structures. A style of life includes strategies, plans, short-term and long-term projects, designs, and behaviors that are in the service of life's goals.

Inferiority as a Source of Motivation. In his book *The Science of Living,* Adler (1929) pointed out that "all persons feel inadequate in certain situations" (p. 60). Moreover, as children, we are in fact inadequate or inferior in regard to almost every possible function. We may also have weaknesses with respect to specific organs or functions that set the stage for special difficulties later on. Adler believed that the character and the intensity of feelings of inferiority are keys to understanding personality. He talked about an **inferiority complex** as a symptom of unusually intense or abnormal feelings of inferiority. The inferiority complex may hide a more complicated set of motives. Indeed, Adler (1929, p. 79) pointed out that an inferiority complex may sometimes cover feelings of superiority. In the same manner, those who act superior, or have a *superiority complex,* may be covering deep-seated feelings of inferiority.

Feelings of inferiority are normal and widespread and set the stage for many of our most important goals. Indeed, Adler argued that many of our activities can be understood in terms of the concepts of *compensation* and *overcompensation.* **Compensation** includes normal attempts to overcome specific inferiorities by developing strengths in alternative areas. For example, a crippling disease and life in a wheelchair did not stop the brilliant theoretical physicist Stephen W. Hawking from becoming an innovative thinker in the fields of astrophysics and cosmology. Sometimes there are *compensation ideals* in the form of other people who embody the traits we most desire. Such ideals become models, but extreme identity with such models is a form of pathology. The concept of **overcompensation,** in Adler's view, involves attempts to develop great strength in the very area that is most beset with difficulties. De-

spite a sickly childhood, Theodore Roosevelt became the very embodiment of William James's strenuous life. Likewise, Demosthenes overcame a speech impediment and became one of the greatest orators of antiquity. Finally, actor James Earl Jones conquered a childhood stutter and now has one of the most rich and recognizable voices in the world.

Social Influences. Adler stressed the importance of family constellation as a key influence in personality development. In particular, he believed that birth order influences the way we see our world and the way we respond to our world. A first child may enjoy a favored position in the family constellation for a time, but the arrival of another sibling can have devastating or salutary consequences depending on the way the new arrival is handled and depending on the constitution of the first child. First children can develop a caring attitude or can have great difficulty overcoming the shock of being displaced by the new arrival who can be viewed as a usurper (Adler noted, with some satisfaction, that Sigmund Freud was a first-born child.) A second child may develop a competitive style while attempting to keep up with the older sibling. Adler's contention that birth order has an effect on personality development has had a continuing influence on research (e.g., see Ernst & Angst, 1983; Grey, 1998).

Life's Major Problems. Adler argued that most human problems center around issues of work, interaction with others, and sexual intimacy. He viewed it as a mark of health when we pursue meaningful work-related goals. Adler also argued that most of life's problems must be understood in terms of social context. The prejudices, preferences, and injustices encountered in almost every society have devastating consequences for individual development. Adler thought that all human beings strive for superiority in certain arenas both to overcome their own weaknesses and to overcome social barriers and injustices. He saw the capacity for sexual intimacy as a mark of one's larger relationship with humankind. Sexual intimacy may have a largely selfish and abusive component, or it may reflect social interest in the form of true caring about the happiness and welfare of another person. A primary task of psychology, according to Adler, is to foster the development of social interest (Ansbacher, 1997).

CARL GUSTAV JUNG

Though Carl Gustav Jung (1875–1961) was associated with Freud's psychoanalytic movement from 1907 to 1913, it is a mistake to view Jung as a disciple or as a defector. Many of the ideas that were foundational in Jung's psychology were formulated long before he met Freud. Hence, though there are some similarities in the two psychologies, Jung's system is not merely derivative.

Jung was born in Keswil, Switzerland, on July 26, 1875. Later, the Jung family located near Basel, Switzerland, where Jung received his formal education. In 1895, he enrolled at the University of Basel and received his medical degree five years later (at that time, five years from the date of initial enrollment in the university was normal for attaining the M.D.). After receiving the medical degree, Jung accepted an appointment at a psychiatric hospital in Zurich, where he studied with Eugen Bleuler, one of the premier authorities in psychiatry in that day (Hayman, 2001). After two years with Bleuler, Jung took a brief leave to study with Pierre Janet in Paris.

Upon his return to Zurich, Jung initiated experiments with word association tests. He believed that the speed and content of associations may reveal unconscious materials that are important in the experience of an individual. For example, maybe an immediate association to a stimulus word is hostile, or maybe one cannot immediately respond to a stimulus word. Jung believed that such responses, or failures to respond, may be diagnostic of problems. Jung's work with the word association test was of interest to Freud, and Freud's classic *Interpretation of Dreams* had been of interest to Jung.

In 1907, Jung and Freud met after having exchanged friendly letters. The first meeting is legendary, lasting something like thirteen hours. From the beginning, the collaborative expectations of Freud and Jung were likely on a collision course. Freud was apparently hoping to find a disciple who

Carl Gustav Jung

would help him extend the range and application of his developing system of thought. Like Adler, Jung was an original thinker in his own right and not well suited for any kind of discipleship. Their friendly relationship lasted only about five years. By 1912, strong theoretical differences had surfaced, ideology overshadowed any personal bond, and the relationship was dissolved. Reasons for the separation were published independently by Freud (1914/1957c) and Jung (1961).

In 1909, Jung set up a private practice in a suburb of Zurich where he lived with his wife and children until his death. He traveled extensively to Africa, India, Europe, and the United States to gather information pertinent to his theories. Jung received many honors, including honorary doctorates from leading institutions such as Harvard University, the University of Geneva, and the University of Zurich.

Jung's system of thought, called **analytic psychology,** is now set forth in a twenty-volume collection entitled *The Collected Works of C. G. Jung* (Bollingen Series No. 20, Princeton University, 1953–1979). There are also journals (e.g., the *Journal of Analytic Psychology*) that publish scholarly research, theoretical papers, and book reviews on Jung's psychology. In addition, there are professional organizations and institutes dedicated to the advancement of Jungian thought (Samuels, 1994).

The best-known institute is the C. G. Jung Institute located in Zurich. Helpful secondary sources on Jung include books by Hall and Nordby (1973), Humbert (1988), Mattoon (1981), and Bishop (1999). Jung's later years were particularly productive, even after a heart attack in 1944. He died on June 6, 1961.

Jung's System of Thought

In terms of methodology and content, Jung's approach to science and to psychology was very broad. On the methodological side, he believed that he gained many insights from his patients, but also believed in the value of experimental work. Jung made use of the comparative method in his extensive travels. Specifically, he was interested in cross-cultural comparisons of symbols and their meanings. Jung might best be characterized as a methodological pluralist because he found legitimacy and value in a variety of approaches to knowledge.

Jung was especially suspicious of ideologies and theories that may limit the field of vision. He acknowledged the heuristic value of theories so long as they are used in a proper way. His concern was that human beings can be *used* by theories; the proper approach, in Jung's view, was that theory should be used to enhance vision and that we be ready at any turn to discard a theory. Jung (1910/1954b) once argued that "theories in psychology are the very devil" (p. 7). He was referring to situations where, in his words, "we have not even established the empirical extent of the psyche's phenomenology" (p. 7).

Jung's approach to content was as broad as his approach to methodology. His psychology included many things: the unconscious, an elaborate view of the structure of personality, psychotherapy, and even studies of paranormal phenomena. We turn now to an overview of the key concepts in Jung's psychology.

The Structure of Personality. Jung used the term **psyche** to refer to the totality of human personality. Indeed, for Jung, *psyche* and *personality* are interchangeable terms referring to the compendium of what we are at both conscious and unconscious levels. There are several interacting components in the psyche.

The Ego.   The ego, according to Jung, is the *I* or *me* of the personality and, as such, is the center of consciousness. As in Freud's system, the ego negotiates with the outer world and has the task of forming an accurate picture of the world. The ego is largely associated with conscious processes and is thus only one of many components of the psyche.

Unconscious Processes.   Jung's approach to unconscious processes, markedly different from Freud's approach, is one of the more controversial parts of his system of thought. Jung used the term **personal unconscious** to refer to the storehouse for materials that have been repressed and are thus not available to consciousness and for materials that have been suppressed and thus could be called again to consciousness. The personal unconscious also includes simply unimportant or irrelevant materials. In addition to the personal unconscious, Jung believed in a **collective unconscious,** which includes materials from the biological past in the form of images and response predispositions. The collective unconscious ties us together with other human beings and gives us all something in common.

The collective unconscious, according to Jung, includes **archetypes,** a term that is roughly similar to terms such as *pattern, model, copy,* and *prototype.* Jung believed that archetypes have their origin in the history of the experiences of the race and are present in each of us as potential modes or patterns of thought. For example, the species has had millions of years of experience with darkness, power, death, mothers, fathers, and so forth. It was inconceivable to Jung that collective experience is unrepresented in the life of the individual. It is important to point out that an archetype is not initially a so-called picture in the head; rather, it is a primordial image or a kind of pattern or form that sets us to think or act in somewhat characteristic ways. As we will see, the archetypes in Jung's theory play an important role in the overall structure of the personality.

The Shadow.   The **shadow** is an important component of the psyche that appears antagonistic to consciousness and to the goals of the ego. The shadow is not just the dark or evil side of the personality; it is the antagonist for whatever is publicly dominant in the personality. The shadow includes repressed materials from the personal unconscious and primitive materials from the collective unconscious that may provoke fear, awe, or anger. The shadow forces dialogue in consciousness by challenging conventional niceties and norms. Jung believed that the shadow can be a doorway to reality and wholeness. It is not all evil because a negative quality in the shadow can be transposed into a positive quality in attitude and behavior. Thus, as noted by Mattoon (1981), "Anger can become assertiveness and . . . vulnerability can become sensitivity to the needs of others" (p. 27). Jung believed that we can never achieve wholeness if we deny the positive lessons that are gained by confronting the dark side of life. On the contrary, the failure to allow expression of darker images and motives may show up later in undesirable emotional explosions.

The Persona. Literally, the term **persona** refers to the playactor's mask, but psychologically, the term as used by Jung refers to the public image or the mask that we wear in front of others. Normally, the persona is the socially acceptable counterpart of the shadow. It is what we appear to be—the professional mannerisms, the roles we play, the public profile. The persona is not just conditioned; indeed, it includes powerful unconscious components. Thus, the persona of an individual as a father is tied to the father archetype. The persona may become so dominant in personality that it attempts to murder the ego. In such cases, individuals can no longer discriminate social roles from other dimensions of their true self. When this happens, the persona appropriates and dominates everything and the individual is robbed of wholeness.

The Self. Jung believed that there is a great unifying principle in the psyche, and he referred to this principle as the **self.** Jung believed that self-actualization or self-realization is a major goal of life; those processes that direct us toward wholeness, integration, and assimilation are functions of the self. The self and the ego, in Jung's psychology, perform very different functions but they are interdependent. The ego is the *I* or *me,* the center of consciousness. Its concerns are more obviously immediate and pressing than the concerns of the self. The ego shows up early in personality development, but the self comes along later and seeks to integrate personality into the larger scheme of things. The claims of the ego may need to be subordinated to the claims of the self if wholeness and unity are to be achieved.

The Anima and the Animus. Jung could not accept the idea that male and female sexuality are bipolar opposites. Though there is a male consciousness and a female consciousness, each is complemented by its counterpart. Both males and females come out of a long history marked by both masculine and feminine awareness. Thus, there is a feminine dimension in male consciousness and a male dimension in feminine consciousness. The **anima** is a female archetype in men and the **animus** is a male archetype in women. Again, in his concern for wholeness, Jung saw it as important that the anima find expression in males and that the animus find expression in women. Unfortunately, the persona and social conditioning may work against such awareness and thus lock the individual into a narrow consciousness where sexuality is concerned.

Attitudes and Functions. Jung is perhaps best known for his concepts of extroversion and introversion, which he thought of as **attitudes. Introversion** is marked by inwardness, withdrawal, shyness, and a preference for quiet time alone or with select company. **Extroversion** is marked by an active, outgoing preference for social company and a strong presence in the consciousness of others. Jung believed that both introverts and extroverts have unconscious wishes for the opposite orientation. Hence, the attitude that is manifested has a latent unconscious counterpart. Most of us display both attitudes, but one is usually dominant.

Jung believed in four basic psychological **functions:** thinking, feeling, sensation, and intuition. All functions are prevalent in all people, but there are nevertheless strong preferences so that a given function may be clearly dominant in a given personality. Thus, a *thinking type* prefers rational discourse and problem solving, whereas a *feeling type* tunes quickly to the arousal of positive or negative emotions in every situation. Jung believed that the functions and the attitudes combine in various ways that give insight into the nature of an individual's conscious orientation. For example, an *introverted-thinking* type may seek seclusion and get lost in a world of ideas that are enjoyed in their own right. By contrast, the sensation function combined with extroversion may be illustrated in an individual who relishes company and the polite ceremony of a fine meal served in beautiful surroundings.

Complexes. Another term commonly associated with the work of Jung is the term **complex,** which is illustrated when conscious materials are accompanied by emotional or perceptual distortions. For example, an inferiority complex is typically based on perceptual distortions regarding personal adequacy. Jung identified complexes in his early work with the word association test. Subjects sometimes had difficulties with associations to select words (e.g., *sex, God, father, mother*). A complex, according to Jung, may result when the shadow fails to find expression in awareness. In his view, there is wisdom, knowledge, and dimensionality that comes with awareness of the full spectrum of vantage points, including both the light and the dark side of things.

Causality. Jung believed strongly that teleology, or final causation, complements the important roles played by material, efficient, and formal causation in human life. He stressed the importance of plans, expectations, and meaning orientation and argued that psychology is incomplete without these concepts. Jung stressed causality from several sources, including those from the personal and the collective unconscious, but also argued that there "exist psychic contents which are produced or caused by an antecedent act of the will, and which must therefore be regarded as products of some intentional, purposive and conscious activity" (Jung, 1926/1954a, p. 91). Jung recognized the difficulties attending the problem of free will as he referred to the "popular illusion concerning the 'arbitrariness of psychic processes' " (p. 91). He thus rejected hard-core determinism and pop-

ular notions of free will based on arbitrariness. He was open to a kind of free will born in wholeness and expanded consciousness.

In addition to his beliefs in causality and teleology, Jung embraced the controversial concept of **synchronicity.** This concept was used to explain the simultaneous occurrence of events not explained by the usual principles of causality. There can be little question that there are synchronous events in human experience, but are these anything more than meaningful coincidence? Though Jung did not wish to apply the principle of synchronicity to paranormal phenomena such as clairvoyance or mental telepathy, he was interested in these areas because they are a part of human experience. Although controversial, it is a part of Jung's theory that cannot be dismissed.

Psychotherapy. Jung's approach to psychotherapy is less structured and standardized than Freud's psychoanalytic therapy. Jung relied on standard Freudian approaches, but also analyzed daydreams, used the word association test, asked the client to paint pictures, or just engaged clients in dialogue. Jung varied his approach as a function of the client's personality and problems. No one method could fit all people, thus the therapist must be ready to adjust to the peculiar set of needs and abilities the client brings to the situation. An extroverted-feeling type of client may require a very different form of therapy than an introverted-thinking type.

Evaluation

Jung's concepts of introversion and extroversion have long been a part of mainstream psychology. An examination of the *Psychological Abstracts* will reveal that these concepts are often used as classification variables in research. Jung's early work on the word association test may also be counted as an important contribution with a continuing influence. Jung's approach to therapy also remains as a small but significant part of the work of mental health professionals. His great breadth with respect to content and methodology may also be viewed as a strength. As already noted, there are any number of controversial concepts in Jung's psychology that have been the subjects of severe criticism: the collective unconscious, archetypes, the principle of synchronicity, and the vagueness of most of the terms of the theory. Jung's broad approach to science and his interest in the occult have also been sources of concern. Perhaps the greatest weakness of Jung's psychology has been its failure to generate meaningful experimental studies.

KAREN DANIELSEN HORNEY

Like Adler and Jung, Karen Horney (1885–1952) (*HORN eye*) initially found value in Freud's ideas, but in time became dissatisfied with the traditional assumptions of psychoanalysis. She challenged Freud's ideas about human sexuality, neurosis, and therapy and tried to incorporate a more sociocultural perspective in psychoanalytic thinking.

Karen Clementina Theodora Danielsen was born in Eilbek, Germany, on September 15, 1885. She was the second child of Wackels and Sonni Danielsen. Although close to her mother, she felt alienated from her father, a captain of a steamship, who was often away at sea (Quinn, 1987). At a young age, she declared an interest in medicine and in 1901 became one of the first women to attend the Hamburg Realgymnasium (an accelerated high school) and still later one of the first women in Germany to study medicine. At the University of Freiburg she met Oskar Horney, a student of economics and political science, and the young couple married in 1909 and moved to Berlin. She earned her medical degree in 1915 from the University of Berlin and delivered her first paper on psychoanalysis two years later. She underwent psychoanalysis with the renowned analyst Karl Abraham (1877–1925) who recognized her brilliance and wrote to Freud about her potential (Sayers, 1991). In time, she became the first female professor at the Berlin Psychoanalytic Institute, though her ideas were already at odds with traditional psychoanalysis.

In 1932, Horney immigrated to the United States where she interacted with a diverse mix of scholars including Erich Fromm, Margaret Mead, Harry Stack Sullivan, and Max Wertheimer. In 1939, Karen and Oscar Horney were divorced after years of separation, and the ensuing period marked

Karen Danielsen Horney

a time of great independence in her thinking. That same year, she published a book, *New Ways in Psychoanalysis,* that took a critical stand against Freud's work and made relations difficult with her colleagues in the New York Psychoanalytic Society (Rubins, 1978). She resigned from the Society in 1941 and helped found the Association for the Advancement of Psychoanalysis (Sayers, 1991). She also served as a founder and dean of the American Institute for Psychoanalysis and founder and editor of the *American Journal of Psychoanalysis.* Karen Danielsen Horney died of cancer on December 4, 1952, in New York City.

Horney's System of Thought

Horney was an innovative thinker and prolific critic of Freudian theory, as evidenced in her first book, *The Neurotic Personality of Our Time* (1937). She revised and refined her personality theory in subsequent books including *Self Analysis* (1942), *Our Inner Conflicts* (1945), and *Neurosis and Human Growth* (1950). Following emigration from Europe to the United States, Horney became attuned to sociocultural influences in the development of personality, especially in the shaping of neurosis. She believed that neurotic behavior did not develop from psychic tension between the ego and unconscious forces but instead from conflict in interpersonal and social relationships. Thus, the *neurotic person of our times* was not the victim of sexual instincts, as suggested by traditional psychoanalysis, but rather a product of the sociocultural context of childhood.

Basic Anxiety and Neurosis.   During the course of development, children naturally look to their caregivers for security and satisfaction. This process fosters the development of the **real self,** that "central inner force common to all humans and yet unique in each, which is a deep source of growth" (Horney, 1950, p. 17). Although children are born with a sense of real self, some parents may undermine a child's security through excessive isolation, rejection, indifference, hostility, or ridicule. As a result, the child may experience a sense of **basic anxiety,** a "terrible feeling of being isolated and helpless in a potentially hostile world" (Horney, 1945, p. 39). Such debilitating anxiety is counterproductive to growth because it stifles and distorts a person's view of the real self.

Horney believed that basic anxiety was a universal aspect of childhood and would likely manifest itself in adult neurosis. In time, a person may develop certain **neurotic trends** or irrational strategies of coping against basic anxiety. Horney (1942) believed that her study of neurotic trends set her apart from other scholars in the psychodynamic school.

> Freud believed that the [neurotic] disturbances generate from a conflict between environmental factors and repressed instinctual impulses. Adler, more rationalistic and superficial than Freud, believes that they are created by the ways and means that people use to assert their superiority over others. Jung, more mystical than Freud, believes in collective unconscious fantasies which, though replete with creative possibilities, may work havoc because the unconscious strivings fed by them are the exact opposite of those in the conscious mind. My own answer is that in the center of psychic disturbances are unconscious strivings developed in order to cope with life despite fears, helplessness, and isolation. I have called them "neurotic trends." (p. 40)

During the course of neurotic trends, individuals may develop an insatiable need for affection, ap-

proval, power, perfection, social recognition, or prestige. Likewise, they may feel a need to exploit others, to restrict their life and goals to narrow borders, or to seek a partner who will assume control of their life. Although all people possess such needs to some degree, neurotic people irrationally adopt these trends as absolute needs that dominate their lives and relationships.

In *Our Inner Conflicts* (1945), Horney elaborated on three unconscious *movements* that neurotic individuals rely on to deal with basic anxiety. A **compliant type** of individual is motivated to reduce the anxiety of helplessness by *moving toward* other people in a style of interaction characterized by dependence and unassertiveness. According to Horney (1945), "this type needs to be liked, wanted, desired, loved; to feel accepted, welcomed, approved of, appreciated; to be needed, to be of importance to others, especially to one particular person; to be helped, protected, taken care of, guided" (p. 51). The **hostile type** is likely to use a more aggressive coping style of *moving against* people through exploitation and dominance. For the hostile type, any "situation or relationship is looked at from the standpoint of 'What can I get out of it?'—whether it has to do with money, prestige, contacts, or ideas" (Horney, 1945, p. 65). Finally, the **detached type** employs an interpersonal coping strategy based on withdrawal and detachment from society by *moving away* from people. Horney (1945) believed that this social resignation arises from an

> inner need to put emotional distance between themselves and others. More accurately, it is their conscious and unconscious determination not to get emotionally involved with others in any way, whether in love, fight, co-operation, or competition. They draw around themselves a kind of magic circle which no one may penetrate. (p. 75)

Unfortunately, such neurotic strategies further alienate the person from his or her real self and establish an **idealized self,** a fictitious view of neurotic selfhood that eventually substitutes for the real self. Indeed, Horney noted that her patients often demonstrated a "neurotic search for glory," a powerful need to establish the idealized self even to the point of developing a "neurotic pride" about this false selfhood. To this end, a neurotic person may develop *blind spots* by denying any experiences that are inconsistent with the idealized self. Horney (1945) illustrated this "refusal to see" with a case study:

> A patient, for example, who had all the characteristics of the compliant type and thought of himself as Christlike, told me quite casually that at staff meetings he would often shoot one colleague after another with a little flick of his thumb. True enough, the destructive craving that prompted these figurative killings was at that time unconscious; but the point here is that the shooting, which he dubbed "play," did not in the least disturb his Christlike image. (p. 132)

Blind spots and neurotic pride, together with cynicism, rationalization and other neurotic *solutions,* have potentially destructive effects for healthy personality growth. Horney used the term *self-hatred* to describe the neurotic tendency to despise one's real self. This self-contempt was sometimes mixed with a relentless drive for perfection governed by an unrealistic *tyranny of the should.* For example, a neurotic woman may be driven by rigid and unrealistic expectations about how she *should* be a better student, *should* lose more weight, or *should* be more outgoing. Ultimately, such artificial harmony built around one's idealized self-image will foster neurotic pride and self-hatred but will also push the individual further into neurosis.

Horney provided a compelling alternative to psychoanalysis (Leslie, 1996). She believed that the goal of psychotherapy should be oriented around helping people resolve their inner conflicts by reestablishing the real self over the idealized self. In *Self-Analysis* (1942), she maintained that such *self-realization* decreases conflict and anxiety and helps individuals strive for truth, productivity, and harmony with others and themselves. Near the end of her life, Horney became interested in Zen Buddhism and tried to incorporate it with her ideas about psychoanalysis (DeMartino, 1991).

Feminine Psychology. Between 1923 and 1936, Horney wrote a series of fourteen papers that constituted an aggressive counter to Freud's theory of female sexual development; the posthumous collection of essays appeared in 1967 under the title *Feminine Psychology.* Freud publicly condemned Horney's sociocultural theory but she was undeterred by his criticism (O'Connell, 1990).

She took particular issue with Freud's belief that "anatomy is destiny." Horney concluded that culture, not anatomy, produces differences between women and men and found psychoanalysis to be excessively male oriented and phallocentric in matters of gender development (Gilman, 2001). For example, psychoanalysts discuss *penis envy* but disregard the possibility of *womb envy* despite evidence from several cultures and mythologies that men envy women's ability to bear and nurse children. Indeed, Horney (1967) asserted that the professional accomplishments of men may serve as compensation for an inability to bear children. As her ideas about feminine psychology developed, she placed increasing emphasis on the cultural influences on female personality (Rubins, 1978).

For Horney, personality development and tensions between men and women were largely due to environmental, not biological, conditions. In particular, she believed that women's sense of inferiority is not constitutional but acquired from masculine society and psychology. Horney (1967) challenged society's "dread of women," which results in disparaging and hostile attitudes that define women as emotionally and intellectually inferior to men. To illustrate the prevalence of this patriarchal dread, she surveyed historical examples of female persecution ranging from biblical admonishments to the senseless slaughter of witches. She called for a new understanding of women but realized the discouraging stereotypes of her day.

> Woman's efforts to achieve independence and enlargement of her field of activities are continually met with a skepticism which insists that such efforts should be made only in the face of economic necessity, and that they run counter to her inherent character and natural tendencies. Accordingly, all efforts of this sort are said to be without any vital significance for women, whose every thought should center upon the male or motherhood. (Horney, 1934, p. 605)

Taken as a whole, Horney's work represents an important step in advancing the psychological study of women, a field that gained momentum in the 1960s (Eckardt, 1991; Symonds, 1991). In addition, her ideas about psychotherapy and personality have influenced cognitive and rational-emotive therapy as well as the study of literature (O'Connell, 1990; Paris, 1991).

Unlike Adler and Jung, Karen Horney did not replace psychoanalysis with a new theory of personality but rather revised and restructured the fundamental assumptions of the Freudian model to fit a different time and culture (Wallace, 1993). Her insightful work on cultural influences of personality and feminine psychology opened new frontiers and broadened the scope of psychoanalytic theory (Gilman, 2001; Ingram, 1985).

OTHER DEVELOPMENTS

Fine (1990) observed that psychoanalysis has been beset with "innumerable inner conflicts, so similar in many ways to the inner conflicts that psychoanalysts find in their patients" (p. 3). Psychoanalysts are divided on a great variety of issues, but some of the more important include the autonomy of the ego, female sexuality, and the role of social and cultural influences in experience and behavior.

One of the most important developments in psychoanalytic theory has been the attempt to "mate a new ego and an old id" (Klein, 1983, p. 505). Though he had recognized ego instincts or drives, Freud emphasized the id as the primary source of motivation. A major movement within the psychoanalytic tradition, known as ego psychology, has emphasized ego functions that are autonomous. This movement received much of its impetus from a seminal work by Heinz Hartmann entitled *Ego Psychology and the Problem of Adaptation* (1939). Since the publication of Hartmann's work, there has been a great deal of work (e.g., see Holt, 1967) examining the relation of the ego to Freud's classic drive theory. Such work has led to the claim that there is much more room in Freud's expanded theory for a model of human freedom and rationality (e.g., see Macklin, 1976). The ego psychologists remind classical theorists of Freud's statement in the final chapter of *The Future of an Illusion* that "the voice of the intellect is a soft one, but it does not rest till it has gained

a hearing" (Freud, 1927/1961c, p. 53). The importance of a stronger ego with independent functions is supported by another post-Freudian development that emphasizes the role of social and cultural factors in human experience.

In addition to the neglect of ego functions, there has also been widespread agreement that classical psychoanalytic theory neglected social and cultural influences on personality. Freud's focus was on individual psychological processes and, as noted by Munroe (1955), he "profoundly distrusted environmentalist theories that attempt to explain 'everything' by social and economic causes" (p. 117). He was particularly critical of the Russian communist system, arguing that "the psychological premises on which it is based are an untenable illusion" (see Freud, 1930/1961a, pp. 112–113). Freud's distrust of all-pervasive environmentalist viewpoints may have contributed to his neglect of more moderate approaches. Post-Freudians such as Erich Fromm (1941, 1947), Harry Stack Sullivan (1953), and Erik H. Erikson (1963) have worked to provide the necessary correctives for the neglect of social influences in classic theory.

As noted earlier in the chapter, Freud's views on female sexuality have also been subject to extensive criticism. He was but one of many in his time, joining ranks with such notable figures as Friedrich Nietzsche and Charles Darwin, who, for all their important contributions, were unable to break away from the long history of unfortunate negative stereotypes in which women were regarded as somehow inferior and subordinate to men.

REVIEW QUESTIONS _____

1. The text outlined six general characteristics of Freud's thought. What kind of evidence might Freud have advanced for each characteristic?

2. Compare and contrast Freud and Jung with respect to their views on the structure of personality. Which view seems more adequate? Why?

3. Briefly review the posthypnotic phenomena that impressed Freud and that contributed to his view on the importance of unconscious processes.

4. Contrast Freud and Jung with respect to their positions on the unconscious.

5. Outline the four basic components of instincts according to Freud.

6. Distinguish between the three varieties of anxiety proposed by Freud.

7. Define *repression projection, reaction formation,* and *sublimation.* Why did Freud consider repression to be the most basic?

8. Critically evaluate Freud's stages of psychosexual development.

9. Distinguish between the manifest and latent content of dreams. Also briefly describe Freud's approach to psychotherapy, making sure you cover such topics as transference, free association, and countertransference.

10. Contrast Freud and Einstein with respect to their approaches to the causes of war.

11. Outline some of the new materials you encounter in the work of Freud that are not included in other systems of psychology.

12. Outline major criticisms of Freud's system of thought.

13. Contrast Jung and Freud with respect to their approaches to therapy.

14. Jung believed that the shadow can be a doorway to reality. What did he mean by this? He also believed that encounters with the materials in the shadow can lead to wisdom and wholeness. Do you agree with him? Why?

15. What did Jung mean by the term *archetype*? Give some examples. Briefly argue the pros and cons of the concept of archetypes.

16. Outline the four functions and two attitudes in Jung's psychology.

17. Discuss Jung's general approach to the problem of causality, including his position on teleology and a brief statement regarding his concept of synchronicity.

18. Outline some of the strengths and weaknesses encountered in Jung's system of thought.

19. Contrast Adler and Freud with respect to their approaches to motivation.

20. Contrast compensation and overcompensation in Adler's theory.

21. Briefly outline Adler's approach to the question of causation. Argue the pros and cons of Adler's teleological approach in contrast with an approach that places stronger emphasis on material and efficient causation.

22. Distinguish between the real self and the idealized self. What role does basic anxiety play in isolating the real self?

23. Briefly review Horney's ideas about the compliant, hostile, and detached neurotic types.

24. Compare and contrast Freud and Horney with respect to their position on feminine development.

CHAPTER 17

HUMANISTIC PSYCHOLOGIES

The darkness is habitable.
—Michael Novak (1970)

Nicholas of Cusa (1401–1464), a legal scholar, mathematician, philosopher, and theologian, was remembered among other things for his doctrine of **learned ignorance** (Liddell, 1933). Nicholas applied the doctrine to theology in which it referred to the "discipline of clearly knowing how *not* to talk of God" (Marti, 1983). One way that learned ignorance might be helpful is illustrated in the compulsive behavior of a mental patient who repeatedly made the sign of the cross after she walked every few steps. In the patient's view of the world, the compulsion was a way of appeasing the anger of God and thus averting disaster. This patient desperately needed the wisdom of Nicholas of Cusa, the wisdom of learned ignorance—the discipline of knowing how *not* to talk or think of God.

Those psychologists affiliated with the humanistic school share something in common with Nicholas of Cusa. Such psychologists believe human beings also need the art of knowing how *not* to think about themselves. As Nicholas found wisdom in negative theology, the humanistic psychologists find wisdom in *negative psychology,* which challenges most of the models and metaphors associated with other systems of thought. Specifically, according to the humanistic position, it is misleading and even damaging to regard ourselves as information processors, black boxes, machines, or cultural products. Models such as the computer and the white rat can provide, at best, only partial perspectives; at worst, such models may result in false leads and misinformation.

Humanistic psychologists have been particularly vocal in their criticisms of behaviorism and psychoanalysis (DeCarvalho, 1992). The basic concepts (conditioning and unconscious processes) associated with these two systems are important but, according to humanistic psychologists, these concepts are overextended. The criticism is that behaviorists and psychoanalysts have been so enamored with their core concepts of conditioning and unconscious processes that they have lost sight of the primary subject of interest—human beings.

The criticism of behaviorism does not deny that conditioning plays an important role in human life, but it is argued that humans have the capacity to operate at a metalevel of awareness that makes it possible to overcome or reverse the effects of conditioning. As an example, one might say, I know I have been strongly conditioned all my life to believe that X is bad. Nevertheless, I will read X and I will read positive sources about X and I will make every effort to read in a spirit of openness. The defiant capacity, the ability consciously to neutralize or even transcend conditioning is, according to the humanistic psychologist, a unique feature of a human being.

A similar criticism is leveled at the psychoanalytic school. There may be unconscious forces at work in human beings so that there are unexplained ideas or desires. Some individuals may act blindly on those ideas or desires, but most people are more conscious than unconscious. By overgeneralizing from a small sample of individuals with special kinds of illnesses, psychoanalysts advanced a distorted view of human beings—a view that fails to differentiate between normal human beings and the emotionally disturbed individuals who provided so much of the data for Freud's theories.

The humanistic viewpoint gained momentum in the 1960s at a time when behaviorism and psychoanalysis were dominant forces. The humanistic viewpoint grew rapidly, and was hailed as the "third force" in psychology because it stood in marked contrast to the two dominant systems of thought. Specifically, both behaviorism and psychoanalysis were deterministic, whereas humanistic psychologists emphasized the capacity for free choice (Barton, 1992). Behaviorism and psychoanalysis aped the methods of the other sciences, whereas **third-force psychology** represented a broader epistemology adapted to the unique subject matter of interest. Thus, one might employ scientific, historical, philosophical, literary or even artistic methods in studying human beings. Humanistic psychologists also argued for a broader concept of the subject matter of psychology. Thus, in addition to the traditional study of fear, aggression, learning, habit breaking, and so on, it was argued that psychologists should study topics such as suffering, wisdom, growth, joy, meaning, authenticity, dignity, and peak experiences.

The humanistic psychologists asked nothing less of psychology than that it find ways to come to terms with human life, effectively, cognitively, and volitionally. The youthful discipline of psychology had been too narrow and had carved out too small a domain for itself. As a result, it was losing contact with the fundamental issues of human nature and was in danger of becoming a sterile discipline.

INTELLECTUAL TRADITIONS

The intellectual background of humanistic psychology is encountered in the works of those scholars who emphasized the importance of inner experience, the freedom of human beings to transcend their environmental circumstances, and the intentionality and activity of mind. Contemporary humanistic psychologists would find much to admire in the works of Plato and St. Augustine. In the modern period they admired the work of Leibniz, Reid, Kant, and Herbart. The focus here will be on recent figures and developments that have inspired humanistic psychologists.

William James

There are several reasons why James's psychology and philosophy are important in the intellectual background of humanistic psychology. First, the stream of experience occupied center stage in James's philosophical vision. According to James, an adequate psychology cannot close the door on anything that is experienced. For all his background in physiology, medicine, and chemistry, James realized that experience deserves to be studied in its own right. We may find physiological and biochemical underpinnings and correlates of experience, but experience, as it occurs, is a domain in itself with qualities that cannot be understood simply in terms of other processes.

According to James, psychology ceases to be empirical when it strays too far from experience or attempts to explain away experience as nothing but the product of some more fundamental process. In the Jamesian view, classical behaviorism could not possibly qualify as a truly empirical psychology because it denies the role of experience altogether. Ironically, the behaviorist uses experience to deny its role in psychology. The exclusion of experience as a proper subject matter is based on rational or logical analysis. James would view the behavioristic analysis as faulty and the humanistic psychologists would agree.

There are other reasons for counting James as a forerunner of humanistic psychology. He was a methodological pluralist and was open about what counts as the subject matter of psychology. He hoped that psychology might make a real difference in the world, so he was willing to open many doors. He was interested in the application of psychology to daily life, the problems of education, the world of work, and the problems of those suffering emotional distress. His interest in questions of value and meaning ran deep (Rathunde, 2001) and is illustrated in all of his major works.

The content of James's psychology betrays his humanistic concerns in other ways. For example, one of the richest chapters in his classic two-volume *Principles of Psychology* is the chapter on the self, a topic of central interest in humanistic psychology. Other works by James on topics such as human freedom and the significance of individuals also qualify him as a forerunner of humanistic psychology.

Existentialism

The philosophical ancestry of humanistic psychology is found among those philosophers who devoted themselves to an understanding of the emotional, social, and intellectual issues of life. Such philosophers were not primarily concerned with abstract metaphysical issues but with the daily issues and concerns of humans beings as they live their lives. **Existentialism** is a philosophical orientation marked by such concerns. The focus is on the individual and on the capacity of the individual to exercise freedom to rise above environmental and social constraints. Let us examine some of the teachings of selected philosophers in the existentialist tradition.

Miguel de Unamuno. The Spanish philosopher Miguel de Unamuno was born on September 29, 1864, in the Basque city of Bilbao. He was reared in a strict Catholic tradition and educated at the University of Madrid. In 1884, Unamuno received a doctoral degree and immediately embarked on a course of study to prepare him to take a teaching examination. In 1891, he accepted a position at the University of Salamanca. In that same year, he was married to Concepción Lizarraga. Unamuno worked at the University of Salamanca most of his life, but on several occasions was removed from his professional post for political reasons. From 1924 to 1930, he was deported because of his criticism of Primo de Rivera. Following the fall of Rivera, Unamuno returned to Spain and a post at the university. He died on December 31, 1936.

Unamuno had little interest in the usual abstract metaphysical problems of philosophy; however, he had great interest in what he called "the man of flesh and blood." Indeed, this expression is the title of the first chapter of Unamuno's classic book *The Tragic Sense of Life* (1913/1972). Sounding a theme that would be echoed in the works of the leading humanistic psychologists, Unamuno lamented the failure of science and philosophy to address adequately the issues of human life.

Science and philosophy fail, according to Unamuno, when specialization blocks the larger vision. In characteristic pejorative style, Unamuno reminded his reader that the specialist runs the danger of "murdering his humanity and burying it in the specialty" (Unamuno, 1913/1972, p. 36). Specialization breeds detachment, cold professionalism, and partial perspectives that do violence to human nature.

Science and philosophy also fail, according to Unamuno, when they place too great an emphasis on a purely cognitive intellectual analysis of human beings. He spoke with disdain for those who intellectualize, for "the people who think only with their brain [and] turn into definition-mongers" (Unamuno, 1913/1972, p. 18). For Unamuno, cognition and thinking are not enough; we must also recognize the powerful role of affect in human life. A philosophy or psychology that neglects the affective dimension is too quick to dismiss or reduce some of the most important dimensions of existence. Unamuno pleaded for a perspective that recognizes the role of feeling in human life. The expression "flesh and blood" refers, among other things, to those who think not just with their brains but "with their whole body and soul, with their blood, with the marrow of their bones, with their heart and lungs and viscera, with their whole life" (p. 18).

According to Koestenbaum (1967, p. 183), Unamuno "extols the agony and the importance of the individual [and] the importance of personal integrity." Unamuno called for a new emphasis on emotional and intellectual honesty. Meaning orientation, truthfulness, practicality, and personhood are central themes in the works of Unamuno, just as they are in humanistic psychology.

Søren Aabye Kierkegaard. Søren Kierkegaard (1813–1855) is sometimes called the Danish Socrates and is commonly regarded as one of the founders of existentialism. Kierkegaard was born on May 5, 1813, the youngest of the seven children of Michael Pedersen Kierkegaard. Søren's mother, Anne Sørensdatter Lund, had been a servant in the Kierkegaard home until the death of Michael Pedersen Kierkegaard's first wife. At the time of her marriage to Michael, a year after the death of his first wife, Anne Lund was already five months pregnant with Søren. This was one of many reasons contributing to a cloud of guilt and pessimism that haunted the Kierkegaard home. A sense of guilt and despair also plagued Kierkegaard's father from his youth when he stood on a hill and cursed God. It was an act that was to become a dominating feature in the long life of the elder Kierkegaard.

Though highly successful in business, Kierkegaard's father viewed it as an irony that he prospered financially even though he had cursed God. His own tortured analysis was that God was going to punish him somehow through his wealth. He was also convinced that he suffered the retributive anger of God through the terrible misfortunes of his children. Two died in childhood, another died at age twenty-four, and two of his daughters died in early adulthood while giving birth. Young Kierkegaard grew up in an atmosphere of despair under the stern tutelage of his domineering orthodox Lutheran father who was bent above all on instilling a proper Christian perspective in the child. The mother, according to Lowrie (1970), "counted for little in the household. Whereas the father occupies so large a place in S. K's books and journals, not a single mention is made of his mother" (p. 24).

Søren Kierkegaard, though physically frail, early evinced signs of intellectual brilliance. After attending a private school, he enrolled at the University of Copenhagen. He studied theology, philosophy, history, and language, but had difficulty focusing on any one topic. Indeed, he became something of a professional student and did not take his degree until 1840, two years after his father's death. He inherited a considerable sum of money from his father, making it possible to pursue the career of his choice—writing.

In 1840, the twenty-seven-year-old Kierkegaard was engaged to Regine Olsen, the seventeen-year-old daughter of a highly respected civil servant. The lengthy love story, worthy of a detailed review (see Lowrie, 1970, pp. 191–231), was ended when Kierkegaard came to the conclusion that there was a great chasm between the needs of the young girl and the now middle-aged philosopher so burdened by the dark mysteries of the human mind. Over Olsen's strong and persistent protests, Kierkegaard broke off the engagement. The anguish he experienced as a consequence was to have a profound effect on his thought and the content of the major philosophical works that would subsequently come from his pen.

Following the termination of his relationship with Olsen, Kierkegaard turned to writing. Typically publishing under a pseudonym, he produced the works that occupy such a prominent place in twentieth-century existentialism. Among the many books were *Either/Or: A Fragment on Life* (1843/1987), *Fear and Trembling* (1843/1983), *Philosophical Fragments* (1844/1985), *Stages on Life's Way* (1845/1967), *Concluding Unscientific Postscript* (1846/1941), and *The Sickness Unto Death* (1849/1989).

In Kierkegaard's later years, he launched a bitter attack on the Danish Church, maintaining that church officials were completely neglecting the religion embraced by Jesus. Kierkegaard was more and more embittered and isolated by the counterattacks that followed. He died in 1855, leaving the simple but fitting epitaph, "That Individual."

Kierkegaard was largely ignored or ridiculed in his own time, but his work has enjoyed great prominence in the twentieth century. His philosophical views have had enormous impact in philosophy, religion, psychology, and literature. In a comment on Kierkegaard's influence, Taylor (1987) noted that "the insights of this lonely Dane pervade contemporary thought and shape the way many people now understand their lives" (p. 300).

Kierkegaard is understood partly in terms of his rejection of rationalism. Systematic conceptual schemes, according to Kierkegaard, are inadequate because experience is not yet finished. Furthermore, those truths that are simply grasped by the intellect have little to do with the real issues of life. For the real issues, we must freely and actively appropriate truth. If we fail to do this, we do not achieve real selfhood. Instead, we remain in the mode of the herd, marked by passive, unexamined existence.

In his major works, Kierkegaard examined three modes of existence: the aesthetic, the ethical, and the religious. Each mode has a characteristic dominant goal as well as an ironic element that exposes certain absurdities. The **aesthetic mode of existence** is marked either by sensual goals or by rational-intellectual goals. The sensualist may be in love with love but incapable of real loving commitment to another individual. Instead, other individuals are to be used as means for the sensualist's erotic pleasures. Such an individual has no strong ties to the past or the future; it is only the temporary joy of the passing moment that counts.

In a similar manner, the rational-intellectualist is interested only in abstractions. Concrete individuals get lost in the vague generalizations of the intellect. As noted by Schrag (1982), "Just as for the sensualist every girl is a woman in general, so for the intellectualist all reality is dissolved into general categories. Speculative thought sees only the general movement of history, explained through the mediation of logical categories, but forgets the individuals who [apprehend themselves] within their particular and concrete history" (p. 1296). Both the sensualist and the intellectualist can be insulated from the pain of concrete real-life situations wherein individuals are faced with agonizing and vexing decisions. Both can remain aloof because of all-encompassing definitions and clean logical categories that efficiently and coldly dictate a course of action.

According to Kierkegaard, the aesthetic mode of existence breeds indifference, which may collapse into boredom. Boredom results in a quest for new diversions, but when the excitement of a new diversion has run its course, one is confronted with emptiness, melancholy, and despair.

The **ethical mode of existence,** according to Kierkegaard, is marked by a deep concern for justice, universal good, and genuine moral commitment. Unlike those in the aesthetic mode, those in the ethical mode are reflective and oriented toward a careful evaluation of the future consequences of their actions. The ethical stage is characterized by the growth of individuation and selfhood and a shouldering of responsibility. The ethicist recognizes the critical role of freedom in human life.

Thus, the necessity and anxiety associated with choices have been confronted and accepted as one of the demands placed on a truly integrated self. Clearly, the ethicist is developmentally ahead of the aestheticist in the quest for selfhood.

While aestheticism collapses into emptiness, melancholy, and despair, the ethical mode can lead to a profound sense of irony. The ethicist may become deeply aware of moral complexities, of the difficulties of balancing conflicting claims, and of according proper weights to differing points of view. As a consequence, the ethicist may develop a deep sense of the many faces of irony in human life. Complete justice, balance, equity—the primary goals of the ethical mode—are, in the end, impossible.

The **religious mode of existence,** according to Kierkegaard, is marked by a sensitivity to one's contingency and complete dependence on God. In the religious mode, one is confronted with the crisis of the demands of faith versus human rational demands. Faith may require the impossible and the absurd, and one may collapse in terror at the prospect of faith flying in the face of reason. Authentic selfhood surfaces in the religious mode when one accepts responsibility for adjudicating between the claims of faith and those of reason.

Kierkegaard's modes are not necessarily stage-like or successive and rarely does one live exclusively in one mode. Rather, all of these modes operate in human life, and in the life of most individuals one may see evidence of the operation of all three modes with one more dominant than another at a given time, but another more dominant later.

Kierkegaard had a deep interest in the practical issues of life and in the ways human beings cope with their problems (Watkin, 1998). His work contains a kind of psychological philosophy much different from earlier philosophical systems in which the focus was on more rarefied problems such as the ultimate stuff of the universe, the existence of God, or the nature of truth.

Martin Heidegger.   Martin Heidegger (1889–1976) was one of the most important and original existentialists of the twentieth century. Following the leads of Unamuno and Kierkegaard, he focused extensively on questions that were to have major impact in philosophy, psychology, sociology, religion, and literature.

Heidegger was born on September 26, 1889, in Messkirch, Germany. Reared in a Catholic family, he developed interests in history and theology. For a brief period he was a novitiate in the Jesuit Order, but later pursued the Ph.D. in philosophy at Freiburg. He had had a long-standing interest in the psychology and philosophy of Franz Brentano. After completing his Ph.D. in 1915, he studied with Brentano's student, Edmund Husserl.

During the early 1930s in the initial stages of his academic career, Heidegger, deeply loyal to Germany, supported national socialism. Indeed, for a time, he joined the Nazi party and even supported Hitler in speeches. Later, he changed his views and fell out of favor with the Nazi government. As a consequence, he lost his university position and was forced into common labor. On more than one occasion, Heidegger experienced the difficulty of falling out of favor. Earlier, he had shifted from allegiance to orthodox Catholic theology to a more liberal perspective.

After the defeat of Hitler in World War II, Heidegger was restored to his professorial post at Freiburg, though his position was never secure because of his earlier affiliation with the Nazi movement. Heidegger's masterpiece is the book *Being and Time* (1927/1962). His book stands as one of the major classics in existential metaphysics in twentieth-century philosophy. Heidegger died on May 26, 1976, in the town of his birth, Messkirch, Germany.

Heidegger's first concern was ontology or the nature of being. More specifically, he was concerned with the meaning of individual existence. He was also concerned with the practical questions of *How* are we to exist individually and collectively in this world? What is an authentic mode of being? and How do we get trapped in unauthentic modes of being?

In his *Being and Time,* Heidegger employed the German term **Dasein,** which literally means "being there." He noted that we find ourselves in a world that is not of our own choosing. We simply have being-in-the-world or in a specific environment and we share that world or that environment with others. Three hallmark characteristics of our condition include factuality, existentiality, and fallenness. *Factuality* refers to the bare fact of our being in the world. *Existentiality* surfaces in the broader framework of time. Not only are we in the world but we are inevitably directional creatures, we are going somewhere, there are real possibilities. *Fallenness* refers to breakdowns in existentiality. We simply drift, we fill time with vacuous or meaningless activities. We are propelled by forces outside of ourselves so that there are no projects, no real sense that we appropriate things for our own ends.

An authentic existence depends on successful recognition and confrontation of the facts of our existence and our existentiality. Of paramount importance is the development of a deep sensitivity to our own finitude—the fact that we are going to die. This fact is a source of anxiety and dread and these emotions may work against our achieving an authentic existence.

The challenge for every human being is to exercise freedom and take a stand that is clearly marked by a genuine concern for the future. If we take such a stand, we will be confronted by anxiety, but failure to take such a stand will result in guilt. An authentic existence then is marked by a large awareness and the courage to accept and use whatever freedom we possess.

Heidegger recognized that there are circumstances that make authenticity a more difficult achievement in one situation than in another. He analyzed the world in terms of regions that impose restrictions. For example, one region is the **Umwelt** (the environment). The *Umwelt* for a given individual may be yielding or highly malleable, but another individual may exist in a highly restrictive unyielding situation. Environments are highly variable with respect to their malleability. Another region is the **Mitwelt** (the community) or our life with other people. The *Mitwelt,* like the *Umwelt,* may be yielding and responsive or rigid and constrictive. *Dasein,* or one's being in the world, must be understood in the context of the *Mitwelt* and the *Umwelt.* Appropriation, movement, and authenticity must often be forged in difficult circumstances. Thus, Heidegger recognized the powerful role of causal forces in human life. He used the term

throwness to refer to those conditions—forces or facts that do not easily yield to human effort. But, according to Heidegger, the authentic individual, clearly aware of her or his own *Dasein,* is also a fact and such an individual may produce real effects even when the structures of the *Umwelt* and *Mitwelt* seem almost overwhelming.

Heidegger's work has important implications for psychiatry (Bracken, 1999; Burston, 1998) his method of understanding being-in-the-world is known as *Daseinsanalysis.* He lamented that human beings are so concerned with gadgets and technology that they fail to study the most important thing of all—our being-in-the-world. The most fundamental question of all may be: How will it be with what it is that is?

Phenomenology

The term **phenomenology** has been used in many ways (see Gavin, 1976; Schmitt, 1967), but as used here, it refers to a philosophical movement and to a way of studying or a method of approaching a subject of interest. Literally, the term *phenomenon* means appearance, but it refers, more specifically, to that which is given in experience. The phenomenological method seeks to discover that which is given in experience as opposed to that which is dictated by the presuppositions or the theories of the investigator. It is admittedly difficult to lay aside prejudices, theories, and assumptions that may have guided inquiry in the past, but phenomenological investigations call on the researcher to make such an effort.

The approach is illustrated, in part, by contrasting differences in the approaches of James and Freud to the issue of religious conversion. Both of these pioneers were keenly interested in conversion, but their approaches to the subject were radically different. Freud (1927/1961c) carefully reviewed a case study known to him and then proceeded with an elaborate analysis showing how a conversion was based on a resolution of the Oedipus complex. Following his review of the case, he raised the question of whether "by understanding this case we have thrown any light at all on the psychology of conversion in general" (Freud, 1927/1961c, p. 171).

James, by contrast, in his classic book, *The Varieties of Religious Experience,* provided detailed and careful descriptions of case after case of religious conversion. The primary emphasis was on a presentation of the conversion experience as described by each individual. James's comments always remained close to the data. His approach to the study of religious conversion is much more in keeping with the phenomenological method than the approach of Freud. James's softer methodology was clearly more neutral than Freud's approach. The emphasis was on observation, description, and classification. James's approach was somewhat comparable to the approach set forth by Edmund Husserl, the founder of phenomenology.

Edmund Husserl. The German philosopher Edmund Husserl (1859–1938), commonly regarded as the founder of phenomenology, was born in Prossnitz, Moravia. Though trained initially in mathematics and science, Husserl shifted to philosophy after studying in Vienna with Franz Brentano. He taught at the University of Halle from 1887 to 1901, at Göttingen from 1901 to 1916, and at Freiburg from 1916 to 1929.

Like earlier philosophers such as Bacon and Descartes, Husserl was concerned about sources of error that interfere with knowledge. He argued for a deep epistemic awareness marked by a persistent quest for clarity about any issue that we study. Nothing was to be taken for granted or accepted as truthful without the most careful scrutiny. Husserl believed that our knowledge of the world and our knowledge of ourselves must begin with an examination of human consciousness. Whatever is given, regardless of the nature of the inquiry, is given in consciousness. It is almost a truism that what is given in consciousness may be missed because of the narrowness of an investigation or the prejudices of the observer. The phenomenological method calls for a different approach, one that has been characterized as a kind of "**disciplined naiveté**" (see MacLeod, 1968b, p. 69). Husserl's ideal was to approach the phenomena of consciousness while suspending presuppositions so that such phenomena could be captured in their givenness.

Husserl's phenomenology had many implications for psychology (Mays, 1998; Nissim-Sabat,

1999). First, it opposed any psychology that restricts the range of the field. Psychology, from a phenomenological perspective, should include all of the enormous varieties of materials in consciousness. Another implication is the suspicion that the phenomena of consciousness are not necessarily like anything else. Hence, models (e.g., the computer model or animal models) are, at best, approximations of human life and, at worst, dehumanizing. A third implication is that a phenomenological psychology stands opposed to reductionism. What is given in consciousness (e.g., a fear) is a legitimate subject for investigation in its own right. Nevertheless, phenomenologists may encourage dialogue with those who work with models such as the computer (see Mruk, 1989).

A fourth implication of phenomenology for psychology is methodological. Phenomenology calls for new kinds of *seeing,* a new way of exploring consciousness (see Natsoulas, 1990). The method should not be confused with introspection, as advanced by Titchener. MacLeod (1964, p. 54) noted that "there is no place in introspective analysis for meaning, except insofar as meanings can be reduced to elements and their attributes. For the phenomenologist, meaning is central and inescapable." The phenomenological method, unlike introspection, encourages the subject to report what is naturally there, the content, impressions, meanings, associations, and so on.

The phenomenological approach to psychology had sufficient appeal and generated sufficient research that by 1969 a new journal entitled *Journal of Phenomenological Psychology* was established. Though phenomenology does not represent a major school of thought in psychology, it is influential and, in the words of Mruk (1989), reminds "psychology that it is foremost a human science, and can no more afford the stifling presence of intellectual monopolies than can any other genuinely scientific endeavor" (p. 37).

Franz Brentano. Brentano had a direct influence on Husserl and on phenomenological psychology, but shared additional affinities with humanistic psychologies. Chapter 11 covered that

Brentano embraced numerous adaptations of scientific procedure. He viewed voluntary and involuntary behaviors such as blushing as practical guides to inner processes. Brentano talked about the importance of genetic studies (e.g., studies of the actions of infants) and comparative studies that make use of primitive societies. He spoke often of the importance of applied psychology.

Brentano's emphasis on intentionality and on the unity of consciousness also finds parallels in humanistic psychology. Brentano emphasized the proactive, intentional, or forward-looking aspects of human life. He also emphasized the centripetal and integrative dimensions of the self. Though the root metaphor may not be entirely appropriate, these themes surface again in humanistic psychology and resonate to and extend the vision of Brentano.

THE FORMAL EMERGENCE OF HUMANISTIC PSYCHOLOGIES

In an overview of the history of humanistic psychologies, DeCarvalho (1990) noted that following World War II, many psychologists were unhappy with the pessimistic view of human nature encountered in behaviorism. Such psychologists also advocated a broader methodology and expansion of topics to be studied and a focus on healthy human beings rather than animals or poorly adjusted human beings. Formal support structures for the new orientation were provided by the *Journal of Humanistic Psychology,* founded in 1961, and the American Association of Humanistic Psychology, later retitled the Association of Humanistic Psychology. In the early 1970s, the American Psychological Association established Division 32, the Division of Humanistic Psychology. DeCarvalho (1990, p. 31) noted that "Within the space of a decade, humanistic psychology has earned a small but official place within mainstream psychology." In the 1970s and 1980s, an increasing number of educational programs provided graduate courses and degrees with an emphasis on the humanistic orientation. Subsequently, there have been many additional social support structures for the new orientation, including institutes, correspondence courses, and seminars. We turn now to some of the founders of humanistic psychology.

Abraham Maslow

Abraham H. Maslow was born in Brooklyn, New York, on April 1, 1908. His Ph.D. was granted in 1934 from the University of Wisconsin. Maslow held positions at the University of Wisconsin, Columbia University, Brooklyn College, and Brandeis University. He was president of the American Psychological Association in 1968. He died on June 8, 1970.

Maslow's best-known books include *Motivation and Personality* (1954), *Toward a Psychology of Being* (1962), and *Religion, Values, and Peak Experiences* (1964). Throughout his major works, Maslow criticized the methodological and substantive narrowness of behaviorism and psychoanalysis. He set out to formulate a holistic system of psychology deeply sensitive to the unique features of human experience. A major mark of his system was that it would be *problem-centered* rather than *means-centered*. According to Maslow, a means-centered approach emphasizes methodology, techniques, apparatus, orthodoxy, an overemphasis on premature quantification, and a tendency to work on "safe problems" rather than truly significant problems. For Maslow, problems should be placed in higher priority than methods and psychology should be open to a variety of methods. He accepted the challenge of redrawing and expanding the discipline's boundaries into more humanistic territory without compromising scientific credibility (Nicholson, 2001).

Maslow's goal, as stated in his book *Motivation and Personality,* was to set forth a point of view that was "holistic rather than atomistic, dynamic rather than static, dynamic rather than causal, purposive rather than simple-mechanical" (Maslow, 1954, p. 27). Maslow believed that the fundamental unit in psychology is not a reflex, simple sensation, muscle twitch, or unconscious memory. Rather, the fundamental datum in psychology is something much larger, a whole rather than a part. He insisted that he was not attacking science but an attitude toward science. He believed that science

Abraham Maslow

in the twentieth century can be approached from a holistic-analytic standpoint rather than from a reductive-analytic standpoint. In the holistic-analytic orientation, the scientist studies part of a whole rather than the isolated part itself. The emphasis on the isolated part itself is the reductive-analytic orientation. Maslow did not oppose analysis as such; rather his emphasis was first on a global phenomenon (e.g., blushing, laughter, sense of self-esteem) and then the role of a given part in the organization and dynamics of the whole.

Motivation. Maslow's focus on the dynamic and purposive dimensions of human life emerged early in his well-known hierarchical theory of motivation. His theory of motivation found its way into mainstream psychology and remains the best-known part of his system. He saw his theory as positive and consistent with the established facts of both experimental and clinical psychology. He also saw the theory as consistent with the functionalism of William James and John Dewey, the holism of Gestalt psychology, and some of the dynamic qualities of Freud's and Adler's theories.

Maslow strongly disagreed with monistic theories of motivation that emphasize single or exclusive determinants of behavior. He believed in multiple determinants of behavior and argued for a hierarchical arrangement of motives. Basic physiological needs such as hunger, thirst, and sleep are the starting point in his theory, but he denied the possibility of constructing a meaningful list of such needs. Even at this level, needs are individually tailored by more basic biochemical conditions in the blood (e.g., fat content, acid level, calcium content, etc.). Thus, appetite is based on a great many influences, most of which are unconscious.

The next step in Maslow's hierarchy is the safety needs. According to Maslow (1954), "If the physiological needs are relatively well gratified, there then emerges a new set of needs, which we may categorize roughly as the safety needs" (p. 84). In Maslow's theory, safety needs cannot easily be a dominant force in life until the physiological needs are gratified. A sufficiently hungry or thirsty animal may be forced to forego safety in order to satisfy a physiological need. But once the physiological needs are met, safety may become the dominant organizing feature of life.

Following the gratification of physiological and safety needs, the individual will seek to fulfill needs for love, affection, and belonging. The search for authentic affectional ties with others may now become the dominant force in life. Maslow (1954) contended that the person "may even forget that once, when he was hungry, he sneered at love as unreal or unnecessary or unimportant" (p. 89). Maslow believed that failure to gratify the needs for love and belonging is the most common force in the background of human adjustment problems.

The fourth set of needs in Maslow's hierarchy is the esteem needs. These include feelings of worth, competence, recognition for achievement, and adequacy. Maslow believed that such needs had been recognized by Adler and neglected by Freud. Maslow contended that failure to satisfy these needs diminishes the personality by leading to a sense of weakness, inferiority, and helplessness.

At the top of Maslow's hierarchy is the need for **self-actualization,** a term coined earlier by Kurt Goldstein, and, as we saw in the previous chapter, an idea that occupied a prominent place in Jung's psychology. According to Maslow, *self-actualization* refers to self-fulfillment that comes

about by realizing or accomplishing the potentials with which we were endowed. For one person, self-actualization may come about primarily by achievements in aesthetic activities (e.g., dancing, music, or art), whereas for another it may come about primarily through achievements in cognitive activities (e.g., philosophy or science). Maslow argued that the achievement of self-actualization is typically delayed until the other four sets of needs (i.e., physiological, safety, belonging, and self-esteem) have been satisfied.

Maslow's hierarchical theory of motivation represented a challenge to more monistic theories that emphasize the all-pervasive influence of only one dominant motivational trend (e.g., sex, power, economic motivation). The hierarchical theory has also been the subject of a great variety of criticisms. Shaw and Colimore (1988), for example, argued that the theory is contradictory in that it "contains both democratic and elitist worldviews" (p. 51). They used it as an illustration of how psychological theory is often conditioned by socioeconomic and political context. Such a criticism may be valid but it must also be disciplined. Einstein's physics was, on more than one occasion, accused of being "Jewish." Cognitive work, even if conditioned by political or religious context, may nevertheless be applicable to a larger domain. If self-actualization is an innate need, as Maslow believed, then his theory could have considerable generality.

A related criticism of Maslow's theory is that it is so individualistic that it leads to a kind of self-seeking and to a neglect of emphasis on the common good. Daniels (1988) has noted, in this regard, that "the central issue here is whether self-actualization is a goal to be sought directly or whether it emerges as a 'by-product' of living" (p. 21). The tensions between concepts of self-actualization and deep ecological and social awareness remain a central issue in motivation theory. Maslow found no necessary contradiction between being a truly self-actualized person and one with deep sensitivities to the larger good. Indeed, it is the person who is frustrated with respect to the gratification of lower-level needs who is a problem and a potential danger. This point deserves exploration in more detail.

In his book *Toward a Psychology of Being,* Maslow (1962) contrasted the terms *being* and *deficiency* in relation to a variety of psychological functions such as love, motivation, and cognition. For example, deficiency-love and being-love (expressed by Maslow as D-love and B-love) are markedly different. B-love is nonpossessive, joyful, and less selfish and demanding. It takes pride in the being of another person and it shares happily in the achievements and accomplishments of the other person. D-love, by contrast, is more likely to be selfish, to use the other person merely for one's own need satisfaction. D-love is interested more in its own gratification than in the gratification of the needs of the other person. It is more likely to include jealousy, possessiveness, and unrealistic expectations.

Maslow's application of the D and B concepts to other arenas such as motivation in general and cognition argues against the idea that his theory is overly individualistic. For example, as one grows in B-cognition, one is more likely to be ecologically and socially aware and insightful. By contrast, D-cognition is marked by a more truncated and selective approach to information, such that one is informed by only a single issue or a single system of thought. Under such conditions, information is often used as a means of reducing anxiety rather than as a means for achieving true growth.

The Self-Actualized Person. During the 1930s, Maslow attended Max Wertheimer's lectures at the New School for Social Research and discovered a refreshing alternative to the molecular and mechanistic assumptions of behaviorism and psychoanalysis. Wertheimer promoted Maslow's interest in the role of values in human experience as well as the importance of studying healthy individuals. At about the same time, Maslow noticed that another important mentor in his life, Ruth Fulton Benedict (1887–1948), an eminent cultural anthropologist at Columbia University, shared some remarkable characteristics with Wertheimer. Like Wertheimer, Benedict was a passionate champion of holism over reductionism—both offered Maslow a glimpse into a unique form of personality development. Secretly, Maslow (1971) took notes on Benedict and Wertheimer. He noted that these observations

> started out as the effort of a young intellectual to try to understand two of his teachers whom he loved, adored, and admired and who were very, very wonderful people. It was a kind of high-IQ devotion. I could not be content simply to adore, but sought to understand why these two people were so different from the run-of-the-mill people in the world. (pp. 41–42)

Maslow quickly realized that his training in psychology could not account for the bold and unusual character of his two mentors (Frick, 2000). Maslow hosted a party and was delighted when both Wertheimer and Benedict attended. Following this stimulating evening at his home, he examined their personalities and tried to find a common theme.

> When I tried to understand them, think about them, and write about them in my journal and my notes, I realized in one wonderful moment that their two patterns could be generalized. I was talking about a kind of person, not about two noncomparable individuals. . . . I tried to see whether this pattern could be found elsewhere, and I did find it elsewhere, in one person after another. (Maslow, 1971, pp. 41–42)

Although crude and informal at first, Maslow's observations evolved into a disciplined undertaking that he recorded in a *GHB* (Good Human Being) notebook from 1945 through 1949 (Lowry, 1973). Maslow (1943) believed that his ideas were "in the functionalist tradition of James and Dewey, and is fused with the holism of Wertheimer, Goldstein, and Gestalt psychology, and with the dynamicism of Freud and Adler" (p. 371).

After rejecting terms like *good human being, saintly person, self-fulfilling person,* or the awkward *almost ideally healthy human being,* Maslow seized upon Kurt Goldstein's concept *self-actualization* as a descriptor for his observations. Maslow read biographies and autobiographies of historically eminent women and men, searching for common characteristics of healthy-minded people. In developing his criteria of healthy people, Maslow (1954) was "fairly sure" that he had discovered nine people who seemed to be *self-actualizing* individuals; Benedict and Wertheimer joined Thomas Jefferson and Abraham Lincoln on Maslow's list as well as several anonymous acquaintances of Maslow's. He also identified seven highly probable figures, including Jane Addams, Albert Einstein, Aldous Huxley, William James, Eleanor Roosevelt, Albert Schweitzer, and Baruch Spinoza. Finally, Maslow decided upon thirty-seven potential cases of self-actualized people that included Ralph Waldo Emerson, Johann Wolfgang Goethe, George Washington, and Walt Whitman.

Maslow posited that fifteen positive or favorable characteristics could be identified in self-actualized people, including realistic and problem-centered perception of the world, a refreshing sense of spontaneity and simplicity, and a genuine acceptance of one's self as well as others. He observed that such *good specimens* have a mature, unhostile sense of humor together with a quality of detachment, and a fierce need for privacy and autonomy resulting in deep interpersonal relations with only a few friends. Nonetheless, Maslow believed that self-actualized persons have a great need to identify with humanity, roughly analogous to Alfred Adler's concept of social interest. Additionally, they have a strong ethical sense and belief in democratic values that fosters resistance to the stifling effects of enculturation and obedience. In this context, the Asian schools of Taoism and Zen Buddhism influenced Maslow's investigations of transcendent states of consciousness (Cleary & Shapiro, 1996). For example, the self-actualized person's need for creative expression and continued freshness of appreciation and wonder about the world may manifest itself in periodic mystical or *peak experiences*. Maslow observed many of these traits in Wertheimer, for example, as he would play on the floor with his children or leap onto a desk for emphasis during a lecture (Hoffman, 1988).

Despite the admirable personality characteristics of self-actualized people, Maslow cautioned against the belief that anyone ever achieves perfection. Indeed, there are traits in self-actualized people that may be perceived in a less than favorable way by others. For example, in their quest for truth, such individuals may exhibit periodic absent-

mindedness, unexpected ruthlessness, and *surgical coldness.* They are not free of conflict, occasional self-doubt, mistakes, regrets, and the like. In balance, however, their lives are organized by a realistic, coherent, productive, healthy, and forward-looking perspective.

Other Characteristics of Maslow's Psychology. Maslow believed that there is more to be gained by studying healthy self-actualized people than by studying sick people or nonhuman models. In his view, the study of healthy people will automatically broaden the subject matter of psychology. New topical areas will, for example, include play, love, values, mystical experiences, humor, meanings of freedom, competence, and aesthetic needs. In other words, psychology should focus at least as much on the positive as on the negative dimensions of life. One of the most important topics in Maslow's vision of the discipline is to understand *metalevel awareness.* Such awareness refers to a capacity for meaningful self-appraisal that fosters growth in the direction of meaningful and realistic personal goals. Above all, Maslow advocated a positive psychology as an alternative to the negative emphasis in other systems.

Gordon Allport

In the tradition of William James, Gordon Allport (1897–1967) was deeply concerned that psychology maintain a strong emphasis on individual experience. He was also interested in the development of a psychology that was consistent with the concepts of democracy and freedom, and was deeply opposed to any system that forces us into methodological or substantive straightjackets. Although distinguished in several areas, the psychology of personality became the hallmark of Allport's career (see Nicholson, 1998, for insights about how Allport's work on personality was grounded in the moral and cultural politics of his age).

Allport was born in Montezuma, Indiana, on November 11, 1897. He and his older brother, Floyd H. Allport (1890–1978), were raised in a hardworking midwestern home. While Gordon completed undergraduate studies at Harvard, Floyd

Gordon Allport

took his Ph.D. in 1919 under E. B. Holt and Hugo Münsterberg. Floyd suggested that Gordon consider devoting his dissertation to the study of personality, an unorthodox subject in American psychology at the time (Nicholson, 2000). After completing his doctoral degree at Harvard in 1922, Gordon traveled to Europe, where he had positive encounters with Carl Stumpf, Max Wertheimer, and Wolfgang Köhler among others. (Allport had met Sigmund Freud years before, but came away unimpressed with the man and his depth psychology.) He returned from Europe and accepted a position at Harvard where he worked for most of the next forty years.

During the early 1920s, the Allport brothers worked together on the classification and measurement of personality traits, culminating in their 1928 Ascendance-Submission (A-S) Scale. By 1924, however, their collaboration had soured over theoretical differences as Floyd embraced a more objective behavioral approach and Gordon rejected it (Nicholson, 2000). In time, Gordon became the principal architect of American personality theory and Floyd assumed a significant role in founding social psychology (he wrote an early book in the area and directed America's first doctoral program in social psychology at Syracuse University). Gordon Allport served as president of the American Psychological Association in 1939 and received

the Distinguished Scientific Contribution Award from that organization in 1964. He died at the age of seventy in 1967.

Allport's book, *Personality: A Psychological Interpretation,* published in 1937, ranks as one of the important classics in that field (see Craik, Hogan, & Wolfe, 1993). His better-known works in personality include *Becoming: Basic Considerations for a Psychology of Personality* (1955) and *Pattern and Growth in Personality* (1961). He also published a work with P. E. Vernon and G. Lindzey entitled *A Study of Values* (1951). Among his other works are two standard classics: *The Nature of Prejudice* (1954) and *The Individual and His Religion* (1950).

In his book *Becoming,* Allport distinguished between the **Leibnizian tradition** and the **Lockean tradition** in psychology. The former emphasizes the proactive (purposive or goal-directed) nature of human life and the latter emphasizes the reactive (mechanistic) dimensions of life. Allport said that the Lockean tradition is evident in S-R behavioristic psychologies with their emphasis on animal models, machine theory, conditioning, and determinism. The Leibnizian tradition that he preferred argued for an active intellect, integrative self-actualizing capacities, and the important role of expectation or the forward-looking tendencies in human beings.

Allport also distinguished between **idiographic** and **nomothetic** orientations in psychology. The former places emphasis on individual experience and the latter emphasizes statistical abstractions such as group norms, means, standard deviations, and the like. Allport did not deny the importance of the nomothetic orientation, but was concerned that psychology, in its rush to be scientific, might neglect the most important reality—namely, individual experience in all of its uniqueness and complexity. Allport's insistence on the centrality of individual experience is reminiscent of the position of William James.

Allport was deeply interested in the subject of motivation, and it was in this area that he made some of his most important contributions. He is remembered especially for his principle of **functional autonomy.** Allport believed that biological drives, learned motives, and concepts of homeostasis and maintenance cannot do justice to the dynamic qualities of human motivation. *Functional autonomy,* as the phrase was used by Allport, means that an activity has become independent of its original motivational source and is now motivating in its own right. He gave the example of a person who initially goes to sea to earn a living by fishing or transporting goods. In time, however, going to sea may be motivating in its own right. Thus, one might continue to go to sea even after becoming financially independent. Allport believed that human motivation is not just a matter of maintaining equilibrium nor just a matter of satisfying basic biological urges. On the contrary, it is often oriented toward growth, risk, novelty, and adventure.

Allport saw habit as an important early determiner of activity, but in time human beings begin to make selections and to live in terms of superordinate goals and motives. Thus, we need not be blindly tied to habits. As we mature, we develop traits and these are organizing principles that give stability to personality. In his book *Becoming* (1955) and in his classic contribution to the psychology of religion, *The Individual and His Religion* (1950), Allport discussed the conditions that contribute to radical personality changes. In *Becoming,* Allport (1955) wrote, "It sometimes happens that the very center of organization of personality shifts suddenly and apparently without warning. Some impetus coming perhaps from a bereavement, an illness, or a religious conversion, even from a teacher or a book, may lead to a reorientation" (p. 87). In *The Individual and His Religion,* Allport discussed the effects of battle experiences on such recentering. Allport attempted to advance a broad system of psychology that represented a thoughtful challenge to the behavioristic and psychoanalytic traditions. He was clearly one of the more prominent figures in the founding of third-force or humanistic psychologies.

Carl R. Rogers

The founder of a new approach to therapy (first called nondirective, then client-centered, and finally person-centered), Carl Rogers (1902–1987) was one of the most innovative, almost revolu-

Carl R. Rogers

tionary, figures in the third-force movement. He received world acclaim for a new approach to psychology that influenced psychotherapy, education, and personality theory.

Rogers was born in Chicago on January 8, 1902. He was educated at the University of Wisconsin, at Union Theological Seminary in New York City, and at Columbia University, where he earned a Ph.D. in psychology in 1931. Rogers held positions at the Rochester Guidance Center, Ohio State University, the University of Chicago, and the University of Wisconsin. From 1964 until his death in 1987, he worked in La Jolla, California, at the Center for the Study of the Person, an organization he helped found. In 1947, Rogers served as president of the American Psychological Association and in 1956 was among the first three (along with Wolfgang Köhler and Kenneth Spence) to receive the APA's Distinguished Scientific Contribution Award. Rogers's best-known books are *Client-Centered Therapy* (1951) and *On Becoming a Person* (1961). Rogers died on February 4, 1987.

Gendlin (1988) enumerated Rogers's contributions in terms of the ways he challenged established psychology. The first amounted to an assault on the mystery and secrecy of psychotherapy. Rogers was the first to insist on a wedding of psychotherapy with the objective techniques of experimental psychology. He recorded psychotherapy sessions (with the client's permission) and assessed improvement by employing tests before and after therapy and by comparing his clients to control groups. In the words of Gendlin (1988) it was nothing less than "war against monolithic authority" (p. 127). In the end, however, Rogers's experimental approach prevailed and thereby contributed to substantial changes in the discipline (O'Hara, 1995). Indeed, following Rogers's work, research on the effects of psychotherapy became commonplace. No longer was psychotherapy a mysterious secret reserved for an elite priesthood. Behavior therapists, though theoretically at odds with Rogers, were also major contributors to the new more open approach to psychotherapy (see Suinn & Weigel, 1975, chapter 1).

Another challenge to the profession outlined by Gendlin was Rogers's stance on the role of diagnosis in the treatment of emotional problems. In the usual medical model, diagnosis precedes treatment, but Rogers was concerned about the negative effects of labeling his clients. As a consequence, he rejected diagnosis and proceeded directly to the business of listening to his clients.

Rogers's psychology focused on the **phenomenal field,** or what he referred to as the entire range of experiences that are part of a person's life. The phenomenal field consists of a differentiated and organized region called the *self,* which, according to Rogers, includes all the ways we evaluate ourselves, the ways we evaluate others, and the ways we relate to objects in the environment. The self, in Rogers's view, is constantly valuing the various dimensions of the phenomenal field. He pointed to the possible tensions between the self as it is and the self as one would like it to be, or the **ideal self.** The greater the congruence between the two, for most people, the greater the health. Exceptions occur, however, in cases of severe pathology (Cole, Oetting, & Hinkle, 1967).

The valuing processes of the self develop in social context. Rogers outlined the difference between **unconditional positive regard** and the conditional love to which many children are subjected. Unconditional positive regard conveys a belief in the intrinsic worth of the child. It creates the feeling that the child is loved simply in its very existence. The individual does not have to earn such love; it is a gratuity. Conditional love, by contrast, carries the connotation of I will love you more if . . . (e.g., if you are a better student, conform, dress properly, develop the correct interests, etc., then you will be valued and loved).

After noting that Rogers studied with Alfred Adler from 1927 to 1928, Watts (1998) drew a parallel between the Rogerian ideas of empathy and unconditional positive regard and the Adlerian concept of social interest. Although working from different perspectives, both men were dedicated to facilitating people's health and well-being. Like Adler, Rogers's psychology is highly optimistic about basic human nature and potential. He believed that there is a drive toward self-actualization and that we have the capacity to choose and to appropriate things in such a manner as to contribute to our growth. The task of the therapist is to provide an accepting atmosphere marked by unconditional positive regard. Rogers believed that if the proper relationship could be established between client and therapist, the client would gain insight and freedom and these would produce growth and the ability to assume responsibility for effecting desirable personal changes.

Rogers had an enormous influence on the discipline of psychology, but in later years was increasingly involved in extending his system of thought to other fields such as education and politics. In education, he advocated a student-centered rather than a teacher-centered pedagogy. He hoped also to contribute to the humanization of political systems. He opposed shams and appearances and deeply valued such personal qualities as authenticity, honesty, and openness. He was especially critical of institutional structures that undermine individuality and block the potential for growth.

Viktor Frankl

The Viennese psychiatrist Viktor E. Frankl set forth a system of thought known as **logotherapy.** His views embody some of the clearest expressions of many of the major tenets of third-force thought.

Frankl was born in Vienna, Austria, on March 26, 1905. He received an M.D. and a Ph.D. from the University of Vienna and served as professor of neurology and psychiatry at the University of Vienna Medical School. As a young neurologist, Frankl was not afraid of debating such respected figures as Sigmund Freud and the man who would become his greatest mentor, Alfred Adler (Frankl, 1997). Early in his career, Frankl broke with Adler and founded his own school based on logotherapy. Following the schools of Freud and Adler, Frankl's theory became known as the "Third Viennese School of Psychotherapy" (Barnes, 2000). He enjoyed a prosperous career as a psychiatrist in Vienna. And then came the rise of Adolf Hitler.

Frankl was imprisoned in Nazi war camps from 1942 to 1945. Several members of Frankl's family, also imprisoned by the Nazi regime, did not survive the camps. His experiences in four different camps contributed to the development of his psychological system. Frankl's best-known book, *Man's Search for Meaning* (1985), described his concentration-camp experiences and sketched the system that he developed more fully in subsequent years. His book became an international bestseller. Following the war, Frankl held many positions, most notably as professor of logotherapy at the United States International University (San Diego). He also served as visiting professor at numerous universities, including Harvard and Stanford. Frankl died in September 1997.

In the preface to *Man's Search for Meaning* (1985), Gordon Allport called attention to the fact that Frankl's "father, mother, brother, and his wife died in camps or were sent to the gas ovens" (p. 9). Allport asked how Frankl, in the face of such losses, in the expectation of his own death, and in the midst of barbarous indignities, could go on living. Allport offered the opinion that one who has survived such an ordeal is worthy of our attention.

Frankl called attention to several polls that have asked people to list priorities about what is important in their lives. In each case, the dominant emphasis is on living a purposeful or meaningful existence. The human need for a meaningful existence is therefore a core concept in Frankl's system. It is a need that is easily frustrated and,

unfortunately, is sometimes frustrated by the very systems of psychological and philosophical thought that are designed to alleviate human suffering. Frankl argued that human beings may experience despair and meaninglessness if taught that they are mere products of conditioning or a kind of battleground for a war of unconscious forces.

Frankl did not deny the crucial role of conditioning in human life nor that some human problems may have their origin in the frustration of instinctual drives such as sex. He argued, however, that many human problems have their origin in the failure to find a meaning or purpose in life. Thus, in addition to the psychogenic neuroses (those that result from the frustration of basic drives), there are what Frankl calls **noogenic neuroses.** The Greek *noos* means mind and Frankl employs the term *noogenic* to refer to those neuroses that result from existential distress and from the failure to find a sense of worth in life.

Frankl devised a therapeutic intervention system for treating noogenic neurosis that he called logotherapy. The term *logos* comes from Greek and refers to a reason or a controlling principle. Logotherapy seeks to assist the individual in discovering the *logos* of existence. It assumes that human beings have a unique capacity to work at a kind of metalevel above the ongoing events of life. Unlike the Freudian emphasis on past experiences, logotherapy seeks a balanced solution to human concerns as they exist in the moment (Frankl, 1997). Surely we may get caught up in the monotony of an everyday routine, but we can adopt a positive attitude about our day-to-day lives. Our perspective—be it healthy or unhealthy—can have a powerful effect on the meaning of our daily lives and work. As humans, we have the responsibility and freedom to choose how a situation will affect us (Gerwood, 1998).

Frankl found that, even in concentration camps, certain people could somehow find meaning in their suffering. Indeed, those who found meaning were more likely to be survivors. We often have little choice about the routine of daily life. We may find ourselves, as Frankl did, in overpowering circumstances. Frankl argued, however, that there is an arena in which choice can be real. We can take a stance toward our suffering, we can see it in a larger context, or we can find some possible and meaningful goal that it may serve. As Leslie (1996) observed, Frankl was an unapologetic optimist "in spite of everything."

Frankl believed that humans have a capacity for what he called **paradoxical intention.** The expression refers to the ability to do the very opposite of what we would like most to do. Thus, people who have an irrational fear may consciously do the very thing they fear. Upon several repetitions, the fear may subside. Frankl believed that the capacity for the defiant or even heroic stance lies dormant in all people. It is one of the unique features of being human.

In logotherapy, Frankl works on meaning orientation by helping the client search for alternative perspectives. An illustration is one of his clients who was seemingly unable to overcome the grief associated with the death of his wife. Rejecting the necessity of employing standard psychoanalytic interpretations of sustained grief, Frankl helped the elderly client find meaning in his loss. One day Frankl asked his client to talk about what might have happened had he died first. The man found this to be a horrible thought because now his wife would undoubtedly be suffering much as he now suffered. Then he saw the whole matter in an entirely different light. By outliving his wife, she had been spared the suffering he now endured. Commenting on the case, Frankl (1985) noted that "in some way, suffering ceases to be suffering at the moment it finds a meaning" (p. 135). Much of the purpose of logotherapy is to help clients explore the range of possible meanings relevant to their situation. Given this perspective, researchers have found logotherapy to be effective in many contexts including the treatment of residents in nursing homes (Seeber, 2000).

Frankl rejected the idea that there is one universal meaning orientation relevant to all people. Rather, all individuals must authentically explore the possible meanings in their particular situation. Imitation, secondhand interpretations, rationalizations, and so forth must be rejected in favor of a truly genuine quest.

As noted earlier, Frankl's system is the embodiment of many tenets of existential and third-force psychology. He opposed pandeterminism, reductionism, and all forms of what he called "nothingbutness." He emphasized those things that are uniquely human, including the capacity to take a stance toward the daily events of our lives. The lines by Michael Novak quoted at the beginning of this chapter capture the belief in the defiant human spirit that is so central to the thinking of Viktor Frankl. As one highly trained in neurology and pharmacology, Frankl did not underestimate the importance of the neurochemical basis of life. At the same time, he declared that the error begins when we believe that human beings are "nothing but" neurochemical mechanisms. He thus elevated the role of psychology, mental processes, and values in the overall scheme of things. Frankl's psychology is not pessimistic nor is it naively optimistic (Leslie, 1996); instead, it offers a middle road of hope that, both individually and collectively, human beings can discover meaningful beliefs with survival value.

Joseph F. Rychlak

As we will see later in the chapter, one of the major criticisms of humanistic or third-force psychologies is that they lack the rigor commonly associated with scientific studies. Some members of the third-force movement would not deny the legitimacy of the criticism. They might argue, however, that the theories that have met the test of scientific rigor have largely dealt with trivial phenomena that bear little relation to the lived world. Therefore, their preference is for an approach that has ecological validity in that it speaks to the issues that confront us here and now. Another alternative has been advanced by psychologist Joseph F. Rychlak (1928–   ), who has argued that it is possible to have a psychology that is both rigorous and humanistic.

Rychlak received his Ph.D. in clinical psychology from Ohio State University in 1957. Much of his career has been devoted to the quest for a psychology that is both rigorous and humanistic. His position is set forth in many papers and in major works such as *The Psychology of Rigorous Humanism* (1988) and *Artificial Intelligence and Human Reason: A Teleological Critique* (1991).

Rychlak has argued that traditional psychologies, especially behaviorism, have been built on a model of causality that is too narrow. The emphasis in such psychologies has always been on material and efficient causality (see Chapter 2). According to Rychlak, formal and final causes, as described long ago by Aristotle, cannot be dismissed if we are to have an adequate understanding of events in our world. Even in physical systems, the central role of formal causes is critical. An airplane could be constructed of the proper metals (material cause) and have adequate power (efficient cause), but if some part of the wing or fuselage or tail were not shaped properly (formal cause), the airplane would not function. Rychlak has taken it as axiomatic that human beings live on the basis of their plans, anticipations, and expectations; in short, we are telic creatures. An adequate psychology, according to Rychlak, will embrace a broad concept of causality, emphasizing material, efficient, formal, and final causes. The neglect of any of these, in his view, will result in conceptual blind spots and explanations that are strained and unnatural.

Rychlak has also emphasized the human capacity for oppositional thinking. In his view, like that of William James, relations are as fundamentally real as the things related. Unipolar events are not just joined by mechanical association; instead, relations are often given in the flow and logic of experience itself. Indeed, some unipolarities simply come with their opposites (e.g., the concept *up* implies its opposite *down*). Human beings, in Rychlak's view, are multipolar creatures in that we see alternatives and anticipate their consequences. We then act on the basis of anticipated consequences and are thus telic creatures.

Rychlak has found no reason why these views must be antithetical to science or to scientific understanding, nor do psychologists need to alter the methods they employ as they proceed with their scientific work. What is needed, according to Rychlak, is a radically new orientation regarding the assumptions we make about human behavior in both science and psychotherapy (Rychlak, 2000). In Rychlak's view, psychologists can recognize the capacity for oppositional thinking, teleology (or *telosponsivity* as he calls it) and even some degree of free will without sacrificing their

scientific integrity. He has argued that the so-called hard sciences, such as physics, no longer operate in terms of the Newtonian assumption that every connection in the universe is complete. Psychology, like physics, can proceed with its scientific work, even if there are uncertainties and arenas of random or even chaotic events. According to Rychlak, human research data themselves do not contradict the assumptions of a rigorous humanistic psychology. There is always variance for which the psychologist cannot give an account. Rychlak has also argued that psychologists providing expert testimony in the courtroom need not reject the assumption of the court that human beings have free will (see Rychlak & Rychlak, 1990).

OVERVIEW OF THIRD-FORCE PSYCHOLOGIES: MAJOR POSITIONS AND CRITICISMS

It is clear that third-force psychologies have found a significant niche in the mainstream of the larger discipline. There are journals, professional organizations, institutes, training programs, and a sizable literature supporting the new orientation. Though it was launched in protest against behaviorism and psychoanalysis, it has gradually developed a positive motivation of its own. There are profound disagreements among members of the third-force movement, but nevertheless there are numerous general areas of agreement. A review of these helps place the movement in perspective.

1. *Pluralistic methodology.* Members of the third force believe that psychologists should focus first and foremost on problems. Methods should be adapted to problems rather than vice versa. They might argue that science itself does not consist of a single well-defined method applicable in every situation. In the interest of understanding human beings, humanistic psychologists may also employ methods (e.g., literary or artistic methods) that are not in the scientific tradition.

2. *Opposition to reductionism.* Humanistic psychologists emphasize the uniqueness of human beings and argue against the adequacy of models and analogies. They believe that if we want to know about humans, we should study humans.

3. *Emphasis on experience.* The primary subject matter for humanistic psychologists is not behavior, unconscious processes, a single dominant motive, learning, or the senses; rather, the emphasis is on human experience in all its richness and variety. The humanistic psychologist does not leave anything out of psychology that is a demonstrable part of human experience. A psychology that omits or reduces anything that is experienced is, to that extent, not an empirical psychology. The strong emphasis on experience means that third-force psychologies embrace the mental realm.

4. *Contextualism.* Humanistic psychologists advocate wholistic studies that give due attention to natural context. They are concerned that artificial situations may produce effects that cannot be replicated in the everyday world. Though they would admit that greater rigor can be achieved in artificial situations, they emphasize testing findings in natural context.

5. *Free will.* Humanistic psychologists typically take the experience of free will at face value; however, they do not deny that there are important and limiting biological and social constraints. Given such constraints, or what Heidegger called "throwness," they still argue for the human capacity to take a stance against opposition, misfortune, or constraint. Free will is thus closely tied to attitude or meaning orientation.

6. *Basic human nature.* Humanistic psychologists refuse to accept the pessimistic assumption that basic human nature is nasty, brutish, and self-seeking. Instead, they believe that human beings are naturally growth-oriented and that, in healthy circumstances, they display goodness and altruism.

7. *Emphasis on relevance.* Humanistic psychologists do not accept hard distinctions between basic and applied studies. They seek a discipline that is problem-oriented and that has ecological validity. Thus, their preference is for studies directly connected to real problems or at least having the promise of being connected to real problems. They do not prefer studies of abstractions with no immediately conceivable connection to daily life.

None of the above should lead to the conclusion that third-force psychology is a coherent school. It is not. Indeed, there are many issues and many points of disagreement. For example, De-Carvalho (1990, p. 36) outlined some important distinctions between humanistic psychologists and some dominant trends in European existentialism. The points outlined above, however, do summarize some central themes in third-force psychology. We turn now to some of the criticisms of humanistic psychology.

The third-force critique of the methods, assumptions, and topical areas of behaviorism, psychoanalysis, and other mainstream psychologies of the late 1950s and early 1960s did not go unanswered. Indeed, numerous counterarguments and criticisms quickly surfaced in the literature (e.g., see Child, 1973; Wertheimer, 1978). A summary of some of the typical criticisms follows.

1. *What is humanistic psychology?* In a critique of humanistic psychology, Wertheimer (1978) called attention to contradictions and problems associated with the term *humanistic*. It is a term that has had multiple meanings from the time of the Renaissance. Further, there is sometimes the implication that those in the behavioral or psychoanalytic traditions are not humane or humanistic. That problem was illustrated beautifully when B. F. Skinner was named humanist of the year by the American Humanist Association (see Skinner, 1972). Clearly, there are many psychologists and systems of psychology that could qualify as humanistic.

2. *Views of science.* From its inception, psychology has cast its lot on the side of rigor and science. Psychologists have never denied that there are other approaches (e.g., literary, artistic, philosophical) to the study of human beings. These approaches have existed for centuries, but a truly rigorous scientific approach is novel and recent. Such an approach may not tell the whole story, but deserves a chance, among other approaches, to see what it can accomplish. It is premature to denigrate such an approach or to argue that psychology per se should complement its admittedly privileged perspective with other perspectives.

3. *Attitude toward basic scientific studies.* The history of science provides ample evidence for the value of basic studies and the importance of pursuing knowledge for its own sake. The demand for relevance can have a narrowing effect on the intellectual process and thus interfere with the discovery mission of science. Many studies in the history of science would have failed the test of relevance, yet such studies provided the foundations for later breakthrough studies. The insistence on relevance is, at best, anti-intellectual; at worst, it interferes with discovery.

4. *Antireductionistic position.* Many scientists might agree that the study of part processes, or the use of analogies or models, can never do justice to any global phenomenon of interest. At the same time, they might argue that science cannot neglect part processes. Indeed, it is the very nature of science to begin with simple elements. Any topic of interest, from a mechanical conveyance such as an automobile to a complex biological event such as a disease, must be approached with due emphasis on all the working parts. A scientific approach to human beings is no different. Wertheimer (1978) argued that the holistic approach of the humanistic psychologists is not consistent with the more informed and scientific holism of Gestalt psychology.

5. *Free will.* The celebration of free will may, in fact, impede progress by blinding the psychologist to causes that are real—but subtle. Many traditional psychologists may simply suspend judgment on whether there is or is not free will, but when they function as scientists, they look for causes. Humanistic belief in free will runs the risk of offering overly quick or glib accounts of complex events and, thus, of interfering with scientific analysis.

There are numerous additional criticisms of third-force psychologies. Wertheimer (1978) suggested that their therapeutic procedures are suspect in terms of effecting real change and Child (1973) accused them of neglecting the hard work of systematic observation so essential in scientific work. In a friendly review of humanistic psychology, Smith (1990) commented on strands of this orientation that are affiliated with various counter-cultures and spiritual-mystical groups. There are those who might argue that such affiliations are natural consequences of the general philosophical orientation of this school of thought. In contrast, however, theorists such as Rychlak (1988, 1998) might argue that the best of the humanistic tradition will surface in a fairly rigorous psychology that still does justice to the richness and complexity of human experience and behavior.

REVIEW QUESTIONS

1. In what sense does humanistic psychology follow the doctrine of *learned ignorance* advocated by Nicholas of Cusa?

2. Why was humanistic psychology referred to as a third force? What are some of the distinguishing features of third-force psychology?

3. Describe at least three features in the thought of William James that identify him as an intellectual forerunner of humanistic psychology.

4. What affinities can you find between third-force psychologies and the philosophy of Unamuno?

5. Identify Kierkegaard's three modes of existence and the specific ways that each one can collapse into an undesirable state.

6. Discuss the meaning of Heidegger's term *Dasein* and the significance of that term for psychology.

7. Define Heidegger's terms *throwness, Mitwelt,* and *Umwelt.*

8. Discuss the implications of Husserl's phenomenology for psychology.

9. Why is Franz Brentano included in the intellectual background of third-force psychologies?

10. Outline Maslow's hierarchical theory of motivation and discuss criticisms of the theory that you consider valid.

11. Discuss some of the defining characteristics of a self-actualized person according to Maslow.

12. Define the concept of *functional autonomy* as employed by Allport. How might a behaviorist explain functional autonomy?

13. Some of Carl Rogers's major contributions to psychology were challenges to standard practices. Discuss two such contributions.

14. What did Rogers mean by *unconditional positive regard*?

15. Describe the major focus of Frankl's logotherapy and show how his concept of *paradoxical intention* might play a role in the treatment of a fear.

16. Advance arguments for or against Rychlak's contention that humanistic psychology can be rigorous.

17. Outline five major criticisms of humanistic psychologies.

LATE-TWENTIETH-CENTURY DEVELOPMENTS

Psychology is now characterized by a pluralism of conceptual and methodic posit, and of research interest, so great as to suggest a new humility before the actual complexities of the psychological universe: problems are being addressed, rather than—as in the past—evaded or liquidated by premanufactured explanations.

—Sigmund Koch (1986)

The post–World War II era was an age of dynamic transformation in nearly every facet of Western civilization. Scientific, technological, economical, political, and religious enterprises have all exhibited tremendous change during this period. Far from dormant, psychology has sustained extraordinary growth throughout the last four decades. Membership in professional societies has blossomed and a multitude of innovative instruments, techniques, and ideas have come forward. Major substantive advances have occurred in the content areas of basic experimental psychology and in the various branches of applied psychology.

Regrettably, a comprehensive discussion of psychology's remarkable expansion following World War II is well beyond the scope of this chapter. However, we will explore several dominant recent developments in the discipline.

THE SYSTEMS OF PSYCHOLOGY IN RETROSPECT

The systems of psychology flourished from the time of Wundt until the mid-twentieth century. Subsequently, there were few psychologists who would have identified themselves as members of the functionalist, structuralist, or Gestalt schools. Nonetheless, many trends after 1950 exhibit strong

influences of the early systems. Interestingly, the classic schools of psychoanalysis and neobehaviorism, together with the humanistic psychologies, have flourished and deserve further comment.

Psychoanalysis

Throughout his life, Sigmund Freud encountered both rejection and acceptance of his theories. The political climate in Germany during the 1930s was not conducive to the advancement of psychoanalysis. Jahoda (1969) pointed out, "In October 1933 psychoanalysis was banned from the Congress of Psychology in Leipzig as a 'Jewish science'; soon after that psychoanalytic literature was burned, and the community of practicing psychoanalysts, mostly centered in Berlin, dispersed rapidly to save their lives and livelihoods" (p. 420). This unfortunate trend escalated after Freud's death in 1939. Eissler (1965) stated,

> In his autobiographical sketch, Freud records, with an implicit but justified pride, the fact that the first World War passed without damage to the psychoanalytic movement. Alas, the same cannot be said of World War II, from which psychoanalysis did not emerge without deep injuries. Totally excluded from cultural life in the vast area on the other side of the world, reduced to a precarious existence in the

Catholic countries of the West, it flourishes almost solely in the English-speaking countries, and especially in North America. (p. 2)

Despite a convoluted history, psychoanalysis has achieved marked gains in Western psychology and became the dominant force in psychotherapy during the 1950s (Lazarus, 2000).

A proliferation of journals attests to the growth and strength of psychoanalysis in the West following World War II. In 1909, Sigmund Freud and Eugen Bleuler (1857–1939) established the first psychoanalytic periodical, the *Jahrbuch für Psychoanalytische und Psychopathologische Forschungen.* Later, psychoanalytic journals such as *Imago* (1912) and the *Internationale Zeitschrift für Psychoanalyse* (1913) struggled during Freud's lifetime. Additional psychoanalytic publications have flourished in English, including the *Psychoanalytic Review* (1913), *American Imago* (1944), the *American Psychoanalytic Association Journal* (1952), the *Journal of Analytic Psychology* (1955), *Contemporary Psychoanalysis* (1964), and *Modern Psychoanalysis* (1976). The appeal of these journals is only one index of the health of psychoanalysis. The *Encyclopedia of Associations* (see Burek, Koek, & Novallo, 1989, p. 2989) lists over forty national and international psychoanalytic societies, including the American Psychoanalytic Association, the American Academy of Psychoanalysis, and the International Psycho-Analytic Association.

Despite such accomplishment, some scholars are skeptical about the future of psychoanalysis. Eissler (1965) warned that psychoanalysis was vulnerable to attacks from religion, government, biological and sociological perspectives, and especially medical orthodoxy. Recognizing the validity of such criticism, many psychoanalysts have worked to nullify such dangers (Kirsner, 2001). For example, the American Psychoanalytic Association established criteria during the 1930s that required psychoanalysts to attend medical school. However, in a landmark 1988 out-of-court decision against medical orthodoxy, psychoanalysts began recognizing the right of Ph.D.s to seek psychoanalytic training (Buie, 1988). Prominent psychoanalytic associations agreed to admit more psychologists to membership in professional societies and appointment at training facilities. This bold step should broaden the research base of psychoanalysis and help ensure its future.

The advancement of psychodynamic theory may further lie in its unique contributions to contemporary research (Weinberger, Siegel, & Decamello, 2000). Gilgen (1982) claimed that psychoanalysis has made numerous contributions to the post–World War II study of developmental psychology, motivation, personality, and abnormal psychology. Silverman (1976) reported several psychoanalytic programs that have found scientific evidence for the relationship between psychopathology and unconscious wishes. Furthermore, Baars (1986) claimed that experimental psychologists have too often ignored psychodynamic theory, making it "the single greatest neglected topic in contemporary scientific psychology" (p. 412). Although the American fascination with psychoanalysis has not diminished (Roth, 1998), its influence on psychotherapy has been supplanted, and occasionally superseded, by the growth of humanistic psychology.

Humanistic Psychology

In an overview of the history of humanistic psychologies, DeCarvalho (1990) noted that "some psychologists during the 'golden age' of behaviorism of post World War II, discontented with behaviorism's view of human nature and method, drew on a long tradition linking psychology with humanities and in a rebellious manner instutionally founded humanistic psychology" (pp. 22–23). This rebellious manner informally began with a 1954 mailing list distributed by Abraham Maslow to 125 psychologists who identified with the humanistic rejection of psychoanalysis and neobehaviorism.

As the list of followers grew, plans were made to establish an official humanistic psychology organization (DeCarvalho, 1992). The institutional support structure for the new orientation included the founding of the *Journal of Humanistic Psychology* in 1961 and the founding of the American Association of Humanistic Psychology (AAHP), later retitled the Association of Humanistic Psychology. James F. T. Bugental (1915–) was elected as the first president of the AAHP and the first national meeting, held in Philadelphia in 1963, was attended by over one hundred members. In November 1964, a conference on the so-called new psychology, held in Old Saybrook, Connecticut, was attended by the premiere figures in humanistic psychology; Abraham Maslow, James Bugental, Carl Rogers, Gordon Allport, Jacques Barzun, Charlotte Bühler, George Kelly, Rollo May, Gardner Murphy, and Henry Murray were among the participants (DeCarvalho, 1990). In the early 1970s, a coalition of over three hundred psychologists helped establish Division 32 of the American Psychological Association, entitled the Division of Humanistic Psychology.

Although institutionalized by U.S. psychologists, humanistic psychology has broad appeal in other countries. DeCarvalho (1991) claimed that "outside of the United States, primarily in South America, humanistic psychology has been as popular as behaviorism has been inside the United States" (p. 151). Indeed, the last decade witnessed an ambitious effort to promote humanistic psychology at an international level; in September 1983, 150 North American psychologists visited the former Soviet Union as delegates for the Association of Humanistic Psychology (Hassard, 1990). In the following years, AHP and Soviet exchange conferences were held in Moscow, Leningrad, Tblisi, Vilnius, and Kiev. In 1986, Carl Rogers gave the keynote address to 2,000 North American and Soviet psychologists and educators at the USSR Academy of Pedagogical Science. Such multicultural projects have shared insights into practice and theory, fostered collaboration on mutual problems, and produced international recognition for humanistic psychology.

In the 1970s and 1980s, an increasing number of educational programs provided graduate courses and degrees with a humanistic orientation and there have been many additional social support structures for the new orientation, including institutes, correspondence courses, and seminars. With this growth, humanistic psychologists have considered adopting more rigorous and scientific methods (Cain, 2002; Schneider, Bugental, & Pierson, 2001; Sheldon & Kasser, 2001). In his presidential address to Division 32, M. Brewster Smith (1990) argued that the natural sciences can play a complementary role in the development of humanistic psychology. At present, several prominent humanistic centers, such as the Saybrook Institute, have established research programs that offer challenging new directions for humanistic psychology in the twenty-first century.

Neobehaviorism and the Psychology of Learning

Despite the growth of psychoanalysis and humanistic psychology, neobehaviorism prospered as the dominant school in American psychology in the twentieth century (Mackintosh, 1997). Neobehaviorism attained its apex of popularity under B. F. Skinner, possibly the most celebrated psychologist in the last half of the twentieth century. Gilgen (1982) reported that a random sampling of scholars in the history of psychology and members of the American Psychological Association rated Skinner as both the most important person and most important influence in U.S. psychology during the post–World War II period. During his most productive years, Skinner was regarded as one of America's most visible scientists (see "Visible Scientists," 1975). Although he was never elected president of the American Psychological Association, Skinner's experimental behavior analysis attracted countless researchers and practitioners. Based on careful observation, perseverance, and serendipity, Skinner compiled a corpus of work that revolutionized the study of learning.

Aside from Skinner's ascendancy, other researchers have made substantial contributions to the psychology of learning, many with radically different orientations from that of Skinner. The research of Harry Harlow offers an intriguing alternative to the neobehaviorism of Hull and Skinner.

Harry Frederick Harlow. Born in Fairfeld, Iowa, Harry Harlow (1905–1981) was awarded his Ph.D. in experimental psychology by Stanford University in 1930. That same year, he founded the Primate Laboratory at the University of Wisconsin–Madison, which he directed until 1974, when he became professor emeritus. During his distinguished career, Harlow served as editor of the *Journal of Comparative and Physiological Psychology* from

1951 to 1963 and as president of the American Psychological Association in 1958. He published numerous books and articles on such topics as learning, motivation, and social isolation.

Harlow devised the **Wisconsin General Test Apparatus** to test form discrimination in monkeys (e.g., Harlow, 1949). In this apparatus, a primate is confined in a cage while a variety of stimulus objects are presented on a horizontal tray. The objects are placed over small depressions in the tray, which can contain a desirable food reward. The monkey is trained to select a particular object; if the object shelters a food reward, the animal may eat it. A screen can also be lowered to allow the experimenter to create a new pattern of objects and stimuli. Although the task proved difficult at first, the monkey eventually made fewer errors in new discrimination tasks. According to Harlow, the primate had formed a **learning set;** the monkey's previous experience had facilitated the ability to discriminate among the stimuli.

Harlow's research on learning sets, or learning to learn, was a promising method for the study of learning ability in primates. However, another enduring contribution was the study of attachment. In a seminal line of research, Harlow (1958) studied the impact of cloth and wire surrogate figures on the formation of affectional bonds. Harlow demonstrated that the tactile stimulation afforded by a cloth figure produced greater attachment for baby monkeys than the appetitive features of a wire figure. He also documented the detrimental effects of isolation on social interaction in young rhesus monkeys.

Other Learning Theorists. In the 1960s, Albert Bandura (1925–) advanced a social learning theory focused on observational learning, especially the influence of symbolic models on aggression. As with Skinner, Bandura's ideas have found successful application in the clinical setting. In the last three decades, several enterprising researchers have employed operant and Pavlovian conditioning principles to reveal intriguing new findings about learning. Martin Seligman (1942–) and his colleagues documented that laboratory animals may learn helplessness if the consequences of their behavior appear independent of that behavior. Seligman has vigorously applied his findings on learned helplessness to the study of depression. The research of Robert Rescorla (1940–) on contingencies (learning relations among events) has dramatically expanded the fundamental principles of Pavlovian conditioning. At present, the psychology of learning continues to attract many researchers, and animal research has remained a vital area despite almost prohibitive costs and animal rights activism (Viney, King, & Berndt, 1990).

The research programs of Harlow, Bandura, Seligman, Rescorla, and many other twentieth-century learning theorists do not fit neatly into the system of neobehaviorism; but their work may be viewed as an extension and often a challenge to the behaviorist system.

COGNITIVE PSYCHOLOGY

One of the most conspicuous trends in psychology since the 1950s has been the renewed interest in cognition (Robins, Gosling, & Craik, 1999). The pattern is clearly evident in new research on such topics as memory, pattern recognition, reasoning, child and adult development, and artificial intelligence. According to Neisser (1967), "The term 'cognition' refers to all the processes by which the sensory input is transformed, reduced, elaborated, stored, recovered, and used" (p. 4). **Cognitive psychology** is marked by a breadth of perspective with emphasis on such higher mental operations as sensation and perception, memory, learning, problem solving, and language. Lachman, Lachman, and Butterfield (1979) concluded that the "typical cognitive psychologist is, therefore, a scientist motivated to understand a natural system consisting of the human higher mental processes" (p. 6).

In what follows, we will consider some of the origins, dominant themes, substantive areas, and critiques of cognitive psychology. But first we will consider some of the influences that led to the founding of this orientation.

Intellectual Traditions

While the investigation of mental events dates from the time of the pre-Socratic philosophers, the experimental analysis of cognition is a product of the nineteenth and twentieth centuries, especially a cognitive tradition that can be traced to the 1920s (Greenwood, 1999). The writings of Franz Brentano, William James, Wilhelm Wundt, John Dewey, and Sigmund Freud all exhibit a keen interest in mental events. Although approaching the study of cognition from diverse systems and perspectives, each of these thinkers nurtured ideas that could find a role in contemporary representations of the mind. However, we will confine this discussion to a few specific forces that served to shape cognitive psychology.

Hermann Ebbinghaus.   Hermann Ebbinghaus's seminal research on memory remains a hallmark in the history of cognitive psychology. Like Fechner, Ebbinghaus applied a rigorous experimental method to the study of mental processes. Ebbinghaus's pioneering research contributed to the quantification of memory and inspired future generations of researchers to extend his methodology into new areas (see Eysenck, 1986; Gorfein & Hoffman, 1987). Although criticized for an overemphasis on associationism, artificiality, and reductionism (Kintsch, 1985), Ebbinghaus's research nevertheless contributed to a laboratory analysis of mental operations. Indeed, much of twentieth-century memory research can be traced back to Ebbinghaus's work (Wertheimer, 1986).

Frederick C. Bartlett.   Another important pioneer in the study of cognitive processes was Sir Frederick Charles Bartlett (1886–1969), who stressed the role of abstract representation in cognition. According to Bartlett, memory processes are governed by cognitive themes, or *schemas*. These schemas exert a powerful influence on the retrieval and forgetting of information. Bartlett (1932) tested the role of schemas on story comprehension by such methods as *repeated reproduction* (present the subject with a picture and ask for repeated descriptions of the content) and *serial reproduction* (present the subject with a complex and unfamiliar story such as the Kwakiutl Indian folktale "The War of the Ghosts" and ask additional subjects for verbatim summaries of the story in a serial manner).

Bartlett's primary findings revealed a tendency to replace esoteric terms and abstract concepts with concrete and familiar ideas. He found that as greater intervals of time passed, subjects made more errors in retrieval and substitution. Far removed from associationist interpretations of memory, Bartlett believed his results demonstrated thematic frameworks that modified and organized new information. Consequently, material unfamiliar to the schema would not be fully recalled. Thus, Bartlett claimed that the world is reconstructed in memory based on each person's schematic pattern rather than on the basis of the mechanical laws of association.

Bartlett accepted the objective method of the behaviorists but was highly critical of behaviorist theory, which he likened to a cult (Bartlett, 1923). Because of his mentalistic orientation, Bartlett was largely ignored during the neobehaviorist era of the 1940s and 1950s. However, his ideas have been rediscovered by cognitive researchers interested in schematic and reconstructive processes in memory (Brewer, 2000; Iran-Nejad & Winsler, 2000; Neisser, 1982).

Jean Piaget and Cognitive Development.   Born in Neuchâtel Switzerland, Jean Piaget (1896–1980) quickly became a devoted student of biology and zoology. By 1907, he had published his first article, a brief comment on his observation of an albino sparrow. The paper held a pragmatic purpose: Piaget hoped the publication would win him a job at the Neuchâtel Museum of Natural Sciences (Piaget, 1952). By 1916, the twenty-year-old scholar had produced a significant series of publications, mostly in systematic zoology.

In 1918, Piaget was awarded a doctorate of natural sciences, from the University of Neuchâtel for a thesis on mollusks. In the same year, he authored an essay on "Biology and War," an angry attack on instinctual explanations of war and on individualism, in favor of socialism. His ideas about war were influenced by the Soviet revolution of the Bolsheviks and by Piaget's membership in the liberal Protestant youth movement in Switzerland, an affiliation that would impact his later work as well (Vidal, 1987). Although his formal training was in zoology, Piaget had studied some psychology at the University of Neuchâtel, and after receiving his doctorate, studied experimental psychology and psychopathology at Zurich with Theodore Lipps, Eugen Bleuler, and Carl Jung, and later with Alfred Binet at Paris from 1919 to 1920. Around this time, Piaget studied the writings of Lucien Lévy-Bruhl (1857–1939) on the cognitive abilities of "primitive" people. The young scholar found inspiration in the French sociologist's thesis of "pre-logical mentality" and built it into his studies of children's cognitive abilities (Jahoda, 2000).

Piaget's interest in developmental psychology was evident in his first psychology article, entitled "Relationship between Psychoanalysis and Child Psychology," published in 1920. Two decades later, he had published six major books on such broad developmental topics as language, intelligence, moral judgment, reasoning, causality, and the construction of reality in children. Beginning with his early research on intelligence, Piaget conducted extensive interviews with children rather than administer the tests in a standardized manner. According to Gruber and Vonèche (1977), this unorthodox study of cognition proved to be insightful: "What had been at the outset nothing but a boring and annoying test situation became a real dialogue with suggestions and countersuggestions, an argument developed, a deepening of the child's thought, a new method of interrogating children was born" (p. 53).

Such methods led Piaget to develop a general theory of genetic epistemology that stressed the activation of schemas within serially progressive structural stages (Ferrari, Pinard, & Runions, 2001). Thus, cognition develops in an orderly sequence from sensory-motor coordination to abstract reasoning. In 1940, he continued studying the genesis of human knowledge as professor at the University of Geneva until his appointment as professor emeritus in 1971. As Piaget (1952) remarked in his autobiographical sketch, "Instead of devoting five years to child psychology, as I had anticipated in 1921, I had spent about thirty on it; it was exciting work and I do not in the least regret it" (p. 255).

Although his contributions to developmental psychology are numerous, Piaget should be re-membered primarily as a genetic epistemologist. Whether studying the child's conception of number, physical quantity, space, or time, Piaget's research was guided by the quest for the psychogenesis of cognition. Indeed, one of his final publications was an epistemological account of the history of science (Piaget & Garcia, 1983/1989). Together with physicist and fellow epistemologist John Garcia, Piaget argued for a sequential order in history by investigating the development of science in the context of the psychogenesis of knowledge. This project had been initiated in the 1960s but was not completed until the day before Piaget contracted the illness that would claim his life. In many ways, this book represents an intriguing summary of Piaget's views on epistemology and psychology.

Although widely regarded for his contributions, Piaget was not the first psychologist to advance a cognitive theory of development. As we have seen, Charles Darwin, G. Stanley Hall, and Kurt Koffka also offered insight into the intellectual development of children. However, two names also bear mentioning in this context. More than twenty-five years before Piaget's first publication on cognitive child psychology, James Mark Baldwin (1861–1934) described the processes of *accommodation* and *adaptation* in a three-stage theory of prelogical, logical, and hyperlogical cognition in his book *Mental Development in the Child and the Race* (Baldwin, 1895). In addition, Russian psychologist Lev Semenovich Vygotsky (1896–1934) expanded on Gestalt and Piagetian ideas by placing greater emphasis on the social nature of linguistic and psychological functions (Wertsch, 1985). Although once obscure, Vygotsky's work has been commanding more attention from Western psychologists in recent years (Lloyd & Fernyhough, 1999).

Gestalt Psychology and Edward Tolman. Like Bartlett, the Gestalt psychologists rejected the rigid associationism encountered in behaviorism. Beginning with Max Wertheimer's analysis of the quantitative concept formation of tribal peoples (Wertheimer, 1912/1950), the Gestalt school introduced a dynamic approach to the study of mental

Jean Piaget

events. The research of Wertheimer and Karl Duncker (mentioned in Chapter 15) continues to be cited in the cognitive literature on problem solving. Furthermore, George Katona's (1940) book *Organizing and Memorizing* has a distinctly cognitive orientation. As Baars (1986) noted, even the title of Katona's book sounds like a contemporary cognitive work.

The influences and similarities between Gestalt theory and cognitive psychology have not gone unnoticed. Indeed, Ulric Neisser credited the Gestalt psychologists with providing the early impetus for the study of cognition (see Baars, 1986, p. 274).

Several contemporary research areas exhibit a Gestalt orientation including memory and cognition (German & Defeyter, 2000; Kelley & Nairne, 2001; Murray, 1995), human factors research (Foley & Moray, 1987), visual neuroscience (Westheimer, 1999), evolutionary psychology (Murray & Farahmand, 1998), organizational theories of learning (Baddeley, 1990), artifical intelligence (Guberman & Wojtkowski, 2001), and perception (Chen, 2001; Kellman, 2000).

Although Gestalt psychology did anticipate numerous contemporary trends in cognitive psychology, a word of caution is in order. Clearly, the two approaches seem to converge on some topics but a variety of differences remain between Gestalt psychology and cognitive psychology. Specifically,

the machine metaphor so prevalent in modern cognitive psychology was soundly rejected by the Gestalt school. Current cognitive psychologists may not be wholly cognizant of the Gestalt heritage, although historical research may remedy this misunderstanding (Henle, 1986).

Edward Tolman, also influenced by the Gestalt tradition, was a key figure in the history of cognitive psychology. Tolman forged an uneasy alliance with neobehaviorism but did not acquiesce to the popular explanations of psychology based exclusively on material and efficient causality. His concept of purpose presented a fresh and rich theoretical alternative to much of neobehaviorism (Dewsbury, 2000). Indeed, Tolman's penchant for cognition is evident in such concepts as cognitive maps, sign–gestalt expectancies, and means–end hierarchies (Tolman, 1932). His legacy is still evident in some research in computer science and cognitive neuroscience (Goldman, 1999).

Verbal Learning Theory. Following World War II, developments in information theory, human engineering, linguistics, and computer science created an intellectual climate conducive to a novel study of cognition. Ironically, several followers of neobehaviorism, the dominant force in psychology during the 1950s, provided the greatest impetus to the development of cognitive psychology.

In addition to the topics discussed in Chapter 14, a group of neobehaviorists studied memory under the banner of **verbal learning theory,** an approach that focused on "the acquisition, retention, and transfer of verbal units formed under controlled laboratory situations" (Jung, 1968, p. 3). The subject matter of verbal learning was vast, with a prominent research focus on the retention of verbal units (e.g., words, numbers, and nonsense syllables) and the distribution of errors in recall of those units (such as the serial position effect). Another popular research area centered on interference theory, the idea that forgetting is the product of the negative influence of competing sets of information.

By the 1960s, verbal learning appeared to be at its zenith, culminating in the July 1962 founding of the *Journal of Verbal Learning and Verbal Behavior* (Cofer, 1978). Despite its popularity, several members became disenchanted with the restrictive, overly associationist assumptions of verbal learning theory. Researchers such as George A. Miller (1920–   ) and James J. Jenkins (1923–   ) were considering a more cognitive orientation as the result of new findings that failed to conform to verbal learning explanations (Crowther-Heyck, 1999). Gardner (1985) marveled that "seldom have amateur historians achieved such consensus. There has been nearly unanimous agreement among the surviving principals that cognitive science was officially recognized around 1956. The psychologist George A. Miller has even fixed the date, 11 September 1956" (p. 28). Miller's specific date refers to the Symposium on Information Theory sponsored by the Massachusetts Institute of Technology on September 10–12, 1956. Allen Newell and Herbert Simon delivered their revolutionary results on computer logic, Noam Chomsky laid the foundation for his theory of transformational grammar, and Miller presented his findings on the restricted capacity of short-term memory to roughly seven meaningful units. Other landmark events for cognitive psychology in the 1950s included contributions in the area of concept formation and perception (Bruner, Goodnow, & Austin, 1956) and Chomsky's (1959) critical review of B. F. Skinner's book on verbal behavior.

However, cognitive psychologists faced resistance and criticism from the more established discipline of neobehaviorism. George Miller remembers that during this time " 'cognition' was a dirty word because cognitive psychologists were seen as fuzzy, hand-waving, imprecise people who really never did anything that was testable" (cited in Baars, 1986, p. 254). Nonetheless, the *Zeitgeist* shifted to a more cognitive orientation in American psychology in the next decade. In 1967, Ulric Neisser (1928–   ) wrote *Cognitive Psychology,* an early attempt to present cognitive research in a coherent framework. Shortly thereafter, several scholarly resources were promoting the diverse literature of cognitive psychology. Beginning with the founding of *Cognitive Psychology* in 1969, more than fifteen journals featuring articles on basic and applied cognition were established in the next two decades. By 1985, the *Journal of Verbal Learning and Verbal Behavior* was rechristened the *Journal of Memory and Language,* a subtle victory for the so-called new perspective in psychology. We will consider the broad subject matter of cognitive psychology, but first a brief discussion of some general themes is in order.

Themes and Content Areas of Cognitive Psychology

Cognitive psychology can be distinguished by several dominant themes. The first involves the pervasive influence of the **information-processing metaphor,** the idea that mental events operate in much the same way as a computer (Bower, 2000). More specifically, the organism is conceived as a sophisticated processor of information. For example, memory might entail the processing of information in successive stages or levels (such as sensory memory, short-term memory, and long-term memory) before the execution of a response. For this reason, cognitive psychology has sometimes been referred to as *information-processing psychology.*

The information-processing approach has enjoyed substantial support within the cognitive framework. For example, cognitive psychologists often depict theoretical representations of cognition by using flowcharts, a method borrowed from computer science, which characterize the serial processing of information into various stages. The nomenclature of the cognitivists also exhibited a distinct computer flavor. Thus, the term *stimulus* was occasionally replaced with *cue* or *input,* and *response* was replaced by *output process.* The memory concepts of *encoding, storage,* and *retrieval* also reflect the bond between cognitive psychology and computer science. According to Lachman, Lachman, and Butterfield (1979), this new nomenclature is more than just substitution; the terms "are pointers to a conceptual infrastructure that defines an approach to a subject matter. . . . It implies different beliefs about the behavior's origin, its history, and its explanation" (p. 99). But is the information-processing metaphor a necessary construct?

Long before the invention of the computer, technological innovations provided analogies for understanding the behavior of organisms (recall

Descartes' fascination with hydraulically activated statues described in Chapter 8). Roediger (1980) described numerous metaphors for memory that have been employed from antiquity to modern times, including analogies involving some spatial comparison between memory and an object(s), spatial comparisons without an object, and non-spatial analogies. Most of the cognitive metaphors employ the technology of communication (e.g., a switchboard, tape recorder, or wax tablet). The advantage of such metaphors is that they allow researchers "to exchange cogent ideas regarding cognitive phenomena. The framework is no fixed prescription either for explanation or for research. Rather, it provides us with certain conventions for talking about theoretical or research possibilities" (Bourne, Dominowski, Loftus, & Healy, 1986, pp. 11–12).

A second theme in cognitive psychology concerns the role of the subject in cognitive experimentation. Many neobehaviorists conceptualized the individual as a passive receiver of information in whom associative bonds presumably guide the organization of material in a linear fashion. By contrast, the cognitive psychologists followed the Gestalt psychologists and Tolman by assigning a more dynamic role to the organism. The individual is viewed as an active organizer of information using hierarchical schemas.

Finally, it would be naive to assume that cognitive psychology evolved without some residue of influence from verbal learning and neobehaviorism (Lachman, Lachman, & Butterfield 1979). From these approaches, cognitive psychology inherited a robust empirical approach grounded in laboratory research. In general, cognitive psychology has further adopted from its predecessors a nomothetic or general explanation of cognitive phenomena rather than an idiographic perspective.

From its inception, cognitive psychology has been characterized as one of the most pluralistic and interdisciplinary movements in the history of psychology. Indeed, cognitive research has spilled over so that on occasion the discipline has been called "cognitive science" to reflect its interdisciplinary orientation (Gardner, 1985). Cognitive science is an apt title since scholars in philosophy,

anthropology, engineering, neuroscience, linguistics, and computer science have identified in one way or another with the study of cognitive processes. Research on memory attention, problem solving, concept formation, language, pattern recognition, artificial intelligence, and human development have all emerged as mainstream fields of cognitive science. With advances in methodology and technology, research in behavioral genetics and neuroscience holds great promise for the emerging field of cognitive neuroscience (Kolb, 1999). Likewise, information processing has become almost an addiction among some social psychologists who study social cognition (Schneider, 1991).

Critical Appraisal of Cognitive Psychology

Donald A. Norman (1980) wrote a perceptive article that outlined twelve issues that have been neglected by cognitive scientists. He argued that the science of cognition has neglected but should not ignore belief systems, consciousness, development, emotion, interaction, language, learning, memory, perception, performance, skill, and thought. Norman called for both a reconsideration of some popular research areas (e.g., memory, language, and perception) and a further examination of skill and interaction.

The Computer Metaphor.   As far back as the Victorian era, two British scholars played a critical role in the emergence of cognitive science (Green, 2001b). The Cambridge mathematician Charles Babbage (1792–1871) devoted years and a significant part of his fortune toward the invention of calculating machines. In 1834, he introduced his most ambitious invention, the Analytical Engine, which attracted the attention of Ada B. Lovelace (1815–1852). Although born the daughter of Lord Byron, Lovelace rejected poetry in favor of mathematics and science. In 1843, she wrote a paper about Babbage's Analytical Engine, which became the "first published example of what could be called a computer program—written over a century before the emergence of the technology needed to run it" (Woolley, 1999, pp. 1–2). Employing punched cards and memory elements, Babbage's calculating machine and Lovelace's program proved to be the forerunner to modern computer technology (in 1980, the United States Department of Defense honored Lovelace by using "Ada" as the name for the standard programming language adopted for DOD military systems). As Green (2001b) observed, the work of Babbage and Lovelace also introduced the possibility of a nineteenth-century cognitive science.

During the mid-twentieth century, the computer metaphor of mind liberated the new discipline of cognitive psychology from neobehaviorism. In this context, a computational cognitive science provided a rigorous account of intentionality (Green, 2000) and addressed a growing frustration with the narrow disciplinary vision of neobehaviorism (Crowther-Heyck, 2000). However, cognitive psychology's early reliance on the serial digital computer did not win universal favor. In particular, scholars from the Gestalt tradition have been vocal opponents of the machine metaphor. Heims (1975) claimed that Wolfgang Köhler was skeptical of the machine–organism model's ability to account for field events in perception. From a more contemporary perspective, Wertheimer (1985) argued that computer simulations of cognition are restrictive and unable to account for the role of insight in problem solving. Furthermore, Henle (1985) applauded the computer metaphor for rescuing psychology from associationism, but adamantly called for the abandonment of machine theory in favor of the dynamics of cognition formulated by the Gestalt psychologists.

From a more sympathetic orientation, Gardner (1985) outlined the radical differences between biological and mechanical systems, but saw promise in a synthesis of neurobiology and artificial intelligence. Advocates of the aforementioned connectionism, or PDP approach, might offer their system as a candidate for this interdisciplinary aggregate. Roediger (1980) found value in the computer metaphor, but warned of other erratic trends in the history of psychology:

> The information processing approach has been an important source of models and ideas, but the fate of its predecessors should serve to keep us humble

concerning its eventual success. In 30 years, the computer-based information processing approach that currently reigns may seem as invalid a metaphor to the human mind as the wax-tablet or telephone-switchboard models do today. Unless today's technology has somehow reached its ultimate development, and we can be certain it has not, then we have not reached the ultimate metaphor for the human mind, either. (p. 244)

Succeeding generations of psychologists will doubtless grapple with this important issue and may well abandon the computer metaphor in favor of other models of cognition.

Mentalism. Among a number of critics (Uttal, 2000), B. F. Skinner was a resolute antagonist of the mentalistic foundation of cognitive psychology. Skinner (1963) voiced early concern about cognitive psychology's dependence on a mental rather than behavioral orientation. Troubled by the terminology of the cognitive psychologist, Skinner (1987a) argued against the faddish nature of mentalistic language:

> A curve showing the appearance of the word *cognitive* in the psychological literature would be interesting. A first rise could probably be seen around 1960; the subsequent acceleration would be exponential. Is there any field of psychology today in which something does not seem to be gained by adding that charming adjective to the occasional noun? (p. 783)

He further asserted that science should have a language, but one that is founded upon objectively defined terminology. Skinner (1989) used etymological data to demonstrate that cognitive terms are not novel descriptors but merely reformulations of previous physical and behavioral nomenclature. Thus, words such as *mind, thinking, doing, waiting,* and *sensing* do not warrant inclusion in the psychologist's vocabulary.

Skinner (1977) believed that cognitive psychology is a threatening obstacle in the evolution of a scientific psychology. In his final publication, he found similarity in the tension between cognitive psychology and radical behaviorism and the older dissension between creationist explanations and evolutionary theory. Like Darwin, Skinner (1990) advanced a position that was plagued with opposition:

> After almost a century and a half, evolution is still not widely understood. . . . A creation science has been proposed to be taught in its place. The role of variation and selection in the behavior of the individual suffers from the same opposition. Cognitive science is the creation science of psychology, as it struggles to maintain the position of mind. (p. 1209)

However, Skinner (1989) noted that his condemnation of the cognitive approach

> is sometimes characterized as treating a person as a black box and ignoring the contents. Behavior analysts would study the invention and uses of clocks without asking how clocks are built. But nothing is being ignored. Behavior analysts leave what is inside the black box to those who have the instruments and methods needed to study it properly. (p. 18)

Skinner foresaw the necessary methods to look inside the so-called black box as coming more from physiologists interested in brain science than from the conjectures of cognitive psychologists. Ultimately, he anticipated an interdisciplinary union of ethology, brain science, and behavior analysis. Meanwhile, Skinner (1987c) concluded, "Let us bring behaviorism back from the Devil's Island to which it was transported for a crime it never committed, and let psychology become once again a behavioral science" (p. 111).

Ecological Validity. Although recognized as a founder of cognitive psychology, Ulric Neisser has voiced concern about the artificial nature of this orientation. After numerous discussions with J. J. Gibson (1904–1979), a leader in the field of perception, Neisser revised many early ideas in his landmark text on cognitive psychology. Borrowing from Gibson's approach, Neisser (1976) claimed that **"ecological validity"** is absent in cognitive psychology research. In other words, many cognitive experiments on mental events are artificial; they are hard to generalize to real-world experience. Neisser (1976) declared that "the study of information processing . . . has not yet com-

mitted itself to any conception of human nature that could apply beyond the confines of the laboratory" (p. 6).

Neisser (1982) edited *Memory Observed: Remembering in Natural Contexts,* a volume of ecologically valid research on such topics as flashbulb memories (vivid memories of salient events such as John Kennedy's assassination or the 2001 terrorist attack on the World Trade Center), mnemonics (memory aids that promote efficient retrieval), memorists (people with exceptional memory), and eyewitness testimony. Neisser's plea for ecological soundness provides an intriguing challenge for cognitive psychologists.

Despite such criticism, cognitive psychology has made a substantial contribution to psychology as a whole in the last three decades. Inventive methodologies and designs have been created to explore the impact of cognition in a variety of tasks. Currently, a broad cross section of subject matter is investigated under the guise of cognitive science and, as a result, psychology may be more interdisciplinary than in previous eras. But does cognitive psychology really signify a paradigm shift?

Despite cognitive psychology's relatively short existence, historical treatises on the so-called cognitive revolution have been written (Baars, 1986; Gardner, 1985). But evaluation of such a recent development can only be premature at this stage. An accurate evaluation of cognitive psychology must wait until a later date to be based on an adequate perspective.

DIVERSITY AND PLURALISM IN MODERN PSYCHOLOGY

The expansion of contemporary psychology has produced a kind of *diaspora,* the Greek word for scattering. As we have seen in this chapter, this diaspora is reflected in the pluralistic content of modern psychology in addition to the diversity of its professional organizations. In 1992, the American Psychological Association (APA) listed over 100,000 members and 42 divisions. A close inspection of the APA divisions reveals the growing interest in applied and professional psychology.

Psychologists have been involved in the application of psychology as a profession since the

1870s (Camfield, 1973). A landmark in this evolution was G. Stanley Hall's 1917 founding of the *Journal of Applied Psychology*. However, the enthusiasm of current applied psychologists far outrivals that of previous generations. Gilgen (1982) observed that applied psychology, particularly the expansion of clinical psychology, has rapidly developed since World War II. The proliferation of interest in applied psychology is evident in the growth of APA divisions dedicated to such concerns as health and sport psychology, community psychology, military psychology, consumer psychology, and counseling psychology. Currently the overwhelming majority of APA divisions are of an applied-clinical nature, whereas the minority are academic-research based. The trend toward professionalism is even reflected in some graduate programs. Select academic institutions offer a doctorate of psychology (Psy.D.) degree, which stresses a practice orientation rather than the traditional research-oriented Ph.D. degree. However, the rise of professionalism has produced tension within the discipline. The diversity of psychology is also manifested in the failure of psychologists to agree upon a common core curriculum for doctoral programs (Benjamin, 2001).

Several professional societies have been formed partly in protest against the growing professionalism of psychology. The Psychonomic Society was founded by a group of experimental psychologists in the early 1960s and spawned several outstanding journals, including *Psychonomic Science* (founded in 1964 and changed to the *Bulletin of the Psychonomic Society* in 1973), *Perception and Psychophysics* (1967), *Behavior Research Methods, Instruments and Computers* (1969), and *Memory and Cognition* (1973). Although the Psychonomic Society has a strong legion of followers, some argue that "it represents no more than a supplement to the APA" (Gilgen, 1982, p. 174).

The creation of the American Psychological Society (APS) is another example of the strain between professional and scientific psychology. Following a decade of unsuccessful campaigns to reorganize the APA, the Assembly for Scientific and Applied Psychology formally elected to establish the APS in 1988. This national organization, devoted explicitly to scientific psychology,

grew at a tremendous rate in its first few years. The first APS convention was held in June 1989 in Alexandria, Virginia, and *Psychological Science,* the first APS journal, began publication in January 1990. Nearly 5,000 members and 2,000 student affiliates joined APS during its first year; by 1992, it had more than 13,000 members.

Does such diversity damage or promote a healthy psychology? A growing number of psychologists have expressed concern that a divided psychology undermines its status as a scientific discipline (Staats, 1999). Such concern is undoubtedly fueled partly by the belief that the more mature sciences are unified and coherent disciplines. For example, Staats (1989) has pointed out that "each science undergoes a transition from early disunification to later unification" (p. 143). He noted that this transition has produced considerable consensus regarding theory, methodology and philosophy in the natural sciences while the behavioral sciences are disunited and therefore "relatively backward" (p. 148).

However, in terms of administrative and organizational structures, psychology is as unified in the late twentieth century as any of the sciences and more unified than some. Undergraduate programs especially are typically administered out of a single, usually large department. By contrast, it is not uncommon to encounter twenty or more separate departments in the various branches of the biological sciences, including botany, horticulture, range science, forestry, zoology, anatomy, animal science, microbiology, biophysics, and biochemistry. Perhaps psychologists overestimate the unity of other sciences; if so, such overestimation may result in an unfortunate devaluing of the scientific and professional status of psychology (see Viney, 1996a). In the spirit of William James, we should not dismiss the advantages of disciplinary unity, but we also should explore the advantages that pluralism affords for psychology (e.g., Viney, 1989). With a healthy respect for pluralism, Slife and Williams (1997) have suggested the idea of theoretical consultants trained to educate psychologists about key theoretical issues and themes that influence applied and basic psychology. The idea has merit. A new subdiscipline of theoretical psychology would offset disciplinary fragmentation as well as offer promise for the future of psychology.

Psychology has undergone unprecedented expansion in the decades following World War II. Several of the classic systems such as functionalism and Gestalt psychology have been absorbed into mainstream contemporary psychology, while others such as psychoanalysis, humanistic psychology, and neobehaviorism have exerted varying degrees of influence. The reemergence of research on cognition and a host of statistical methods have broadened the conceptual and methodological foundations of the discipline but concerns continue about the disunited nature of the entire field of psychology.

REVIEW QUESTIONS

1. Outline some of the developments of psychoanalysis in the United States following the Second World War.
2. Identify major events in the institutionalization of humanistic psychology. What attempts have been made to increase the international and scientific appeal of humanistic psychology?
3. What were the main contributions of Harry Harlow's research? How is his work incongruent with the neobehaviorism of B. F. Skinner?
4. Describe specific developments in twentieth-century psychology that contributed to the advance of cognitive psychology.
5. Briefly discuss three major themes in cognitive psychology.
6. What are the main arguments for and against the computer metaphor?
7. In your opinion, does cognitive psychology represent a paradigm shift or revolution? What evidence would you employ in defending your position?
8. How is the diversity of psychology reflected in current psychological organizations? Would you be more likely to support a unified psychology or a pluralistic one?

GLOSSARY

Abelard, Peter (1079–1142) One of the best-known university teachers in the twelfth century. His book *Yes and No* illustrated contradictions in the positions of past authorities. He argued for a stronger role for reason in Christian epistemology.

Academy A facility purchased by Plato by a park named Academeca in Athens. Plato taught students at this facility, which became known as the Academy. The Academy flourished during Plato's life and for hundreds of years after his death.

act psychology A system of psychological thought advanced by Franz Brentano emphasizing the forward-looking, intentional, planful character of experience. Brentano strongly rejected the simplistic characteristics of many of the early systems of psychological thought.

action at a distance Any apparent effect for which one cannot readily identify material and efficient causes.

active mind Refers to intelligent self-organizing properties of mental processes. Contrasts with the "blank slate" hypothesis encountered in empirical philosophies.

Adler, Alfred (1870–1937) Founder of a system of psychological thought known as individual psychology, Adler emphasized the importance of overcoming early feelings of inferiority. He focused on the purposive or goal-directed nature of behavior and on the capacity of the individual to identify with the goals of society at large.

Aesara One of the first Greek philosophers to emphasize the importance of balance to health.

Aesculapius Possibly a historical figure, but the name comes from the Greek mythical God Asclepius, son of Apollo. Asclepius was a great physician who, in Greek mythology, was killed by Zeus because he sinned by raising a man from the dead. Many temples were built in honor of Asclepius.

aesthesiometer A compasslike instrument used to measure tactile sensitivity. Two points can be stimulated simultaneously. The task of subjects is to report whether they feel both points or only one.

aesthetic mode of existence According to Kierkegaard, the emphasis on sensual or intellectual plea-

sure. This mode breeds indifference and boredom and the collapse into melancholy and despair.

aestheticism The belief that the principles of beauty are applicable to other arenas of thought. In epistemology, aestheticism attempts to integrate truth and beauty.

affect (affection) According to Titchener's early theory, affections are the elementary mental processes associated with emotions. Later, he viewed affections primarily as sensations of pleasantness or unpleasantness.

afferent In neurology, the term *afferent* refers to movement inward toward the central nervous system.

Alcmaeon Early Greek physician and son of Pythagoras who worked around 500 B.C. He advocated an empirical, rational, and naturalistic approach to medicine. One of the first to practice dissection.

Alhazen (965–1039) One of the greatest Islamic scientists whose *Book of Optics* is one of the most influential classic works on vision. He made many original contributions on such topics as depth perception, apparent size, and binocular vision.

Allport, Gordon (1897–1967) Well-known personality psychologist interested in the development of a psychology consistent with the principles of freedom and democracy. His individualistic psychology is consistent with many of the main themes of humanistic or third-force psychologies.

anal stage According to Freud, in the second and third years of life, the child develops a deep awareness of the pleasures associated with relief of bowel and bladder tension. The expression of this pleasure may be in conflict with societal norms and thus create special difficulties that must be negotiated with care if the child is to develop normally.

analytic a priori Refers to formal truths in which a predicate completely unpacks a subject. A statement such as *All bachelors are unmarried* is an example.

analytic psychology The name of the system of psychology advanced by Carl Gustav Jung.

Anaximander (610–c. 547 B.C.) Greek scientist and philosopher and one of the first to advance a theory of organic evolution.

Anaximenes (c. 588–c. 524 b.c.)   A cosmologist who taught that air is the primal substance and that this substance is transformed into other things through condensation and rarefaction. Through condensation air becomes clouds, clouds become water, water becomes ice, and so forth. Through rarefaction, heavy windy air becomes light air, and light air becomes fire, and so forth.

Angell, James Rowland (1869–1949)   A powerful advocate of the functionalist viewpoint in U.S. psychology. He argued that psychology should emphasize mental operations rather than the "stuff of experience." His book *Psychology* and his classic article "The Province of Functional Psychology" are important expositions of functionalism.

animal spirits   A concept that has enjoyed wide usage, especially in premodern times. In Galen's pneuma concept of the soul, the expression *animal spirits* was used to account for a vital psychological function, namely, the operation of higher cognitive functions. Animal spirits contrasted with *natural spirits,* which account for vegetative functions. See *vital spirits.*

anima   In Jung's theory, the female archetype in men.

animus   In Jung's theory, the male archetype in women.

anthroponomy   Because of the mentalistic implications of the term *psychology,* Walter Samuel Hunter suggested the term *anthroponomy,* meaning the science of human behavior.

a posteriori   Literally, *from what is latter.* Generally refers to the belief that knowledge is dependent on experience and past learning. Contrast with *a priori.*

apperception   In Wundt's psychology, an apperception is an active set of associations marked by intelligent direction within a larger context. A simple associative combination such as *sky* and *blue* would be counted simply as a perception. Apperception, by contrast, carries far more meaning. Thus, a statement such as "If the weather is clear in the morning, we will go sailing" connotes an intelligent direction within a context, an apperception.

apperceptive mass   A term employed by Johann Friedrich Herbart (1776–1841) to refer to the goal of education to produce not only knowledge of facts but also a higher level of awareness of relationships.

approach-approach conflict   A type of conflict marked by the presence of two attractive but mutually exclusive goals. Thus, the achievement of one goal precludes the possibility of attaining the other.

approach-avoidance conflict   A type of conflict in which a positive goal is associated with some unattractive or undesirable feature.

a priori   Literally, from what is prior. Refers to the presumed capacity to discern truths through intellectual insights with minimal dependence on past experience and past learning. Contrast with a posteriori.

Aquinas, Thomas (1225–1274)   One of the greatest doctors of the church, remembered for his heroic efforts to reconcile faith and reason. He is also remembered for advancing an empirically based system of psychological thought.

archetype   According to Jung, archetypes exist in the collective unconscious. They are patterns or forms that help mold thinking about experiences with topics such as power, death, darkness, mothers, fathers, and so on. Jung assumed that the vast experiences of the entire species with such topics do not go unrepresented in the psychological apparatus of each individual.

Arete   Daughter of Aristippus and head of the school of philosophy at Cyrene following the death of Aristippus.

Aristippus   Student of Socrates who headed the school of Cyrene following the death of Socrates.

Aristotle (384–322 b.c.)   The pupil of Plato and one of the great philosophers who is especially noteworthy for his work in physics, biology, and psychology. Aristotle also founded logic and set forth an original and comprehensive view of causality.

Asch, Solomon (1907–1996)   A second-generation Gestalt psychologist remembered for his work on social psychology, cognition, learning, perception and personality theory.

Asclepiades   A popular Greek physician who practiced in Rome around 124 b.c. He distinguished between delusions and hallucinations and argued that therapy for emotional problems should be pleasant.

associationism   Systematic emphasis on the idea that human knowledge is not innate but grows inevitably out of the gradual buildup of associations from sensory data.

attitudes   According to Jung, an attitude is a pervasive social orientation. Jung identified two attitudes: introversion and extraversion.

attributes of elementary mental processes   According to Titchener, elementary processes such as sensations include four attributes: quality, intensity, clearness, and duration.

attributive pluralism   Emphasizes the varieties of descriptive modes applicable for most phenomena. For example, a sunset may be described in the language of physics, anthropology, psychology, or any of a variety of other disciplinary languages. Events can also be described poetically or musically.

Augustine, Aurelius (354–430)   One of the great doctors of the church who wrote extensively about a number of psychological topics including memory, grief, speech, and dreams.

authority   One of the most common tests of truth. Reference to books, institutions, legal codes, or other people as appropriate and adequate repositories of knowledge.

autonomy   A term employed by Immanuel Kant (1724–1804) that refers to self-government or the ability to act in a moral and responsible manner, not to please an authority but because the individual recognizes the inherent or intrinsic worth of certain actions.

average error, method of   A psychophysical method that permits a subject to manipulate a variable stimulus until it appears to match a standard stimulus.

Averroës (1126–1198)   An Islamic scholar very influential in Europe because of his commentaries on the works of Aristotle. Known also for many substantive scientific discoveries. He discovered that patients once infected with smallpox become immune if they survive the initial infection. He also discovered that the retina is the part of the eye sensitive to light.

Avesta   Holy book of the Zoroastrian religion.

Avicenna (980–1037)   An influential philosopher of the Islamic world who attempted to reconcile the tensions between revelation and reason. Also remembered for his Aristotelian approach to psychological problems.

avoidance-avoidance conflict   A type of conflict marked by the presence of two unattractive or undesirable alternatives.

Bacon, Francis (1561–1626)   Early modern philosopher of science who called for a close examination of the problem of knowledge and increased sensitivity to sources of error. A powerful advocate of a critical empirical-inductive method.

Bacon, Roger (c. 1220–1292)   One of the first to write on the sources of error in human thought. His catalog of errors included such things as being a slave to habit, relying too much on authority, giving in to popular prejudices, conceit about one's own knowledge.

Bain, Alexander (1818–1903)   Founded the journal *Mind,* the first journal devoted extensively to psychological topics. Also the author of some of the first psychological texts.

Bartlett, Frederick C. (1886–1969)   British psychologist who stressed the role of representations or schemas in memory and cognition.

basic anxiety   An overwhelming feeling of helplessness and isolation in a threatening and hostile world.

behaviorism   A system of psychology founded by John B. Watson and marked by a strong commitment to the methods and values of the natural sciences. Watson saw psychology as a branch of the natural sciences and defined the discipline simply as the scientific study of behavior.

Bekhterev, Vladimir Mikailovich (1857–1927)   A contemporary of Ivan Pavlov who advanced an objective psychology in which the reflex served as the fundamental category of inquiry. Bekhterev's system was known as reflexology.

Bell, Charles (1774–1842)   Co-discoverer with François Magendie that spinal nerves are specialized. The ventral root handles motor functions and the dorsal root handles sensory functions.

Bell-Magendie Law   The discovery by Sir Charles Bell in England and by François Magendie in France that motor functions are localized in the ventral root of the spinal cord, whereas sensory functions are localized in the dorsal root.

Bentham, Jeremy (1748–1832)   Founder of utilitarianism. Argued against intuitive approaches to jurisprudence that resulted in punishments that do not fit the crime and argued for a rational system of punishments and rewards and the need to maximize pleasure for the greatest possible number of people.

Berkeley, George (1685–1753)   British philosopher who argued that the real world is not the world of matter but the world of experience. His dictum *esse est percipi* (to be is to be perceived) marks him as one of the most radical of the early empiricists. Advanced an early empirical approach to depth perception, attempting to demonstrate that we learn to see in depth.

Binet, Alfred (1857–1911)   French psychologist and a major figure in the study of intelligence testing.

Boethius (c. 480–524)   Attempted to use reason that he learned from Greek thought as a defense of

Christianity. Some have regarded him as a kind of founder of the intellectual agenda that was to dominate medieval thought.

Brentano, Franz (1838–1917)   Founder of a system of psychological thought known as *act psychology*. Brentano emphasized a developmental and pluralistic methodology and the active, participatory, creative, and intentional characteristics of mental life.

Breuer, Joseph (1842–1925)   German physiologist and colleague of Sigmund Freud. Breuer's treatment of Bertha Pappenheim (*Anna O.*) played a central role in the early development of Freud's psychoanalysis.

Bridgman, Percy W. (1882–1961)   U.S. physicist and mathematician, known for his classic book *The Logic of Modern Physics* and for his emphasis on operationism, or the attempt to tie scientific terms to precise measurements.

Broca, Paul (1824–1880)   A French physician who is remembered, among other things, for his discovery that the anatomical locus for articulate or spoken speech is in a small region of the left frontal lobe—the inferior frontal gyrus, subsequently named *Broca's area*.

Brücke, Ernst (1819–1892)   Famous physiologist who had a powerful influence on Sigmund Freud. Brücke emphasized the importance of a thoroughgoing physical-chemical approach to the study of psychological topics.

Buffon, Comte de (1707–1788)   One of the great French scientists of the eighteenth century remembered, among other things, for an early theory of geological evolution that challenged the strict biblical chronology advanced by Archbishop Ussher. Buffon was also one of the first of the modern scientists to offer a theory of organic evolution.

Cabanis, Pierre Jean Georges (1757–1808)   Argued for a naturalistic approach to psychological processes such as memory, intelligence, and sensation.

Cajal, Santiago Ramón y   See *Ramón y Cajal, Santiago*.

Calkins, Mary Whiton (1863–1930)   First woman president of the American Psychological Association, who argued for a reconciliation of structuralism and functionalism. Advanced a personalistic psychology in which the self is the primary focus of study.

Carr, Harvey A. (1873–1954)   The thirty-fifth president of the American Psychological Association, Carr helped consolidate and amplify the functionalist viewpoint in psychology. At the University of Chicago, he headed a powerful department of psychology that was one of the most prolific in Ph.D. production.

catastrophe theory   A view of evolutionary change advanced by the French scientist Cuvier that earth-wrenching catastrophes may have annihilated entire species and that such catastrophes have produced abrupt changes in populations and their characteristics. Contrast with *uniformitarianism*.

categories of understanding   An expression employed by Kant to refer to inherent ordering principles of the mind that contribute to knowledge. For example, Kant believed that human beings have intuitive understandings of causality and temporal and spatial relationships.

Cattell, James McKeen (1860–1944)   A prominent leader in the U.S. functionalist tradition. Though he published little, he established a laboratory at Columbia University and headed a strong department in that institution. Cattell served as editor of numerous journals and magazines, including *Science, Popular Science Monthly, Psychological Review,* and *School and Society*. Through his efforts, psychology became more visible in the public consciousness and in the scientific community. He also advanced the cause of applied psychology, most notably by founding the Psychological Corporation.

chaos hypothesis   The belief that there is no pattern or direction in history; history has no meaning except that attributed to it by humans.

Charcot, Jean-Martin (1825–1893)   French physician and neurologist who had a strong influence on the development of Freud's thought. Charcot emphasized the psychological basis of some physical symptoms.

Chiarugi, Vincenzo (1759–c. 1820)   Italian humanitarian who instituted reforms in the treatment and care of the mentally disturbed prior to Pinel in France. Chiarugi was one of the first to employ psychodrama as a therapeutic tool.

closure   The tendency psychologically to complete that which is incomplete, to fill in the gaps, or to see wholeness even when it is not present.

cognitive maps   A term employed by Edward Chace Tolman referring to "mental representations" of the environment that make it possible for an animal to grasp relationships and locations.

cognitive psychology   A broad interdisciplinary effort to study the processing of information in memory, problem solving, judgment, and other forms of cognition. Also known as cognitive science or information-processing psychology.

collective unconscious   A controversial concept advanced by Carl Jung. He believed that the human mind includes unconscious memories from the biological past of such topics as darkness, death, and power. Most of what is in the collective unconscious is associated with topics that strongly influence survival.

commonsense philosophy   A term referring to the philosophical orientation of philosophers such as Thomas Reid (1710–1796) and his followers. The expression refers to a deeply held opposition to beliefs that are counterintuitive or that do violence to our experience of the world.

compensation   In Adler's psychology, the normal attempts to overcome specific inferiorities by developing strengths in alternative areas. (e.g., a person who is not athletic may excel in the classroom).

complex   A term employed by Jung to refer to conscious materials that are strongly associated with emotional or perceptual distortions. For example, in Jung's view, an inferiority complex results partly from perceptual distortions regarding personal adequacy.

compliant type   A neurotic attempt to reduce anxiety by *moving toward* people.

Condillac, Etienne Bonnot de (1715–1780)   French radical empiricist who attempted to show specifically how all knowledge could derive from associations that start with simple sensations.

conditioned reflex (CR)   In classical conditioning, a learned reflex elicited by a conditioned stimulus.

conditioned stimulus (CS)   In classical conditioning, any stimulus that is psychologically or biologically neutral prior to conditioning trials. Such a stimulus may be paired repeatedly with an unconditioned stimulus. After repeated pairings, the previously neutral conditioned stimulus will elicit a reflex similar to the unconditioned reflex elicited by the unconditioned stimulus.

Confucius (551–479 B.C.)   Well-known early Chinese philosopher interested primarily in the moral life with a focus on methods that promote personal and interpersonal harmony.

connectionism   A formal term often applied to the theory of learning advanced by Edward Lee Thorndike. Thorndike believed that learning involved the development of connections or bonds between sense impressions and responses. Connectionism is one of the first S-R theories of learning.

constant stimuli, method of   A psychophysical method in which comparison stimuli are judged against a standard stimulus. Various values of the comparison stimuli above and below the standard stimulus are presented on a random basis. The task of the subject is to specify whether each of the comparison stimuli are equal to, greater than, or less than the standard.

context theory of meaning   According to Titchener, meaning depends on context or the association of a stimulus with other relevant surrounding stimuli.

contiguity   Refers to close temporal or spatial conjunction.

Copernicus, Nicolaus (1473–1543)   Polish astronomer, physician, and clergyman remembered as the founder of a scientific revolution marked by the belief that the sun rather than the earth is the center of the solar system.

cosmogony   The study of the origin of the cosmos or the universe.

cosmology   The study of theories of the nature of the universe including the relation of the earth to the rest of the solar system.

countertransference   In Freud's psychology, the emotional attachment of a therapist to a patient.

creative synthesis   The principle advanced by Wundt that psychical combinations are not a mere sum of elements. Rather, a combination of associations includes new attributes not predictable from the sum of the elements.

Cuvier, Dagobert (1769–1832)   French biologist who argued that evolutionary change is often abrupt because it is brought about by great natural catastrophes.

cyclical hypothesis   The belief that history can be understood in terms of repetitive patterns or cycles. For example, it might be argued that freedom is lost, only to be regained and lost again; thus there is endless repetition.

Darwin, Charles (1809–1882)   Modern evolutionary theorist who supported his theory of evolution by a wealth of empirical evidence. Darwin and Alfred Russel Wallace also proposed a mechanism for evolution based on natural selection that was acceptable to a large number of scientists. Darwin was also a pioneer in the study of developmental processes in small children.

Darwin, Erasmus (1731–1802)   Grandfather of Charles Darwin and a member of England's Lunar

Society who argued that natural processes evolve without divine intervention. Erasmus Darwin's theory of evolution was based on the concept of inheritance of acquired characteristics.

Dasein Literally, the term refers to "being-in-the-world." The term was employed by Heidegger to refer to a kind of authentic self-awareness along with a deep awareness of the surrounding environment and one's role in that environment.

deductive argument Any argument in which the conclusion is claimed to follow necessarily from the premises. A deductive argument is valid if, and only if, it is not possible for the premises to be true and the conclusion false. Otherwise, the argument is invalid.

Democritus (c. 460–c. 370 B.C.) Refined the atomic theory set forth earlier by the philosopher Leucippus. Taught that reality was based on atoms and the void. Atoms were thought to be indivisible and invisible. Their basic structures accounted for the nature of the observable material world.

demonology Literally, the study of demons, but the term also refers to belief in demons as causal agents.

Descartes, René (1596–1650) French philosopher who is often regarded as the Father of Modern Philosophy. Descartes made extensive original contributions in a great variety of areas. He helped elaborate early scientific methodology, provided rich and often testable hypotheses about the relationships between behavior and physiology, and is regarded as one of the key figures in modern rationalism.

desire According to Brentano, a way of being conscious of an object marked by attraction or repulsion.

detached type A neurotic attempt to reduce anxiety by *moving away from* people.

determinism The belief in universal causation. Implies that whatever happens is based on antecedents such that, given them, nothing else could happen. Contrast with *free will.*

Dewey, John (1859–1952) U.S. psychologist and philosopher and a key pioneer in the functionalist school of thought. Dewey argued for a process-oriented psychology emphasizing the study of adaptation. He argued against the concept of elements, whether they be units in consciousness or in the reflex.

difference threshold The minimal stimulus difference that is detectable 50 percent of the time.

disciplined naiveté The attempt to approach the phenomena of consciousness while suspending presup-

positions so that such phenomena may be captured in their givenness.

discrimination In classical conditioning, subjects may be conditioned to respond to one stimulus and to ignore or withhold a response to another stimulus. Discrimination is generally established through differential reinforcement.

disinhibition In extinction trials a subject may have stopped responding to a given stimulus. However, a sudden new stimulus may trigger the old conditioned response.

Dix, Dorothea Lynde (1802–1887) American humanitarian reformer who worked for over forty years on behalf of the insane poor. Dix advocated a therapeutic climate for curable patients and humane living conditions for all patients.

double-aspect monism A mind–brain position emphasizing the availability of two languages to describe the same phenomena. In this case, there is the language of physiology versus language that employs mentalistic concepts. The position assumes that both refer to the same underlying reality.

drive A term employed in different ways in different systems of psychology but generally referring to "inner stimulation" that results in action.

dualism The belief that there are two fundamentally different realities. For example, mental processes are considered by the dualist to be largely independent and qualitatively different from brain processes.

Duncker, Karl (1903–1940) Gestalt psychologist remembered for his work on the nature of problem solving and for work on the relativity of perceived movement.

Ebbinghaus forgetting curve A curve demonstrating that forgetting of nonsense material is rapid immediately after learning. After an initial rapid decline, the rate of forgetting slows down.

Ebbinghaus, Hermann (1850–1909) One of the great pioneers in psychology, remembered for developing the nonsense syllable as a means of studying memory experimentally while minimizing past associations. Also developed an early form of a completion test and argued for the legitimacy of pure and applied psychology.

ecological validity The view that psychologists should study real-world, everyday events about the human condition. Cognitive psychology has been criticized for its lack of ecological validity.

efferent   Refers to neurological activity that moves outward from the central nervous system toward the muscles and glands.

efficient cause   According to Aristotle, the force that sets a thing in motion. Thus, domino *A*, impacting domino *B*, is the efficient cause of the fall of *B*.

ego   In Freud's system, the ego is the *I* or *me* of the personality—the center of organization and integration that must adapt to the demands of reality. Jung uses the term to refer to a component of personality that is closely associated with conscious processes.

element   An abstraction referring to a simple irreducible sensation.

emergentism   Two related meanings were discussed in the text. As a mind–brain position, emergentism refers to the idea that mental processes are produced by brain processes. Some emergentists believe that mental processes, though produced by brain processes, are qualitatively different from the physical system from which they emerge. As a theory of psychogeny, emergentism refers to the idea that mental processes develop along with the development of the body.

Empedocles (c. 490–c. 430 B.C.)   Early homeostatic theorist who taught that four basic elements (air, earth, fire, and water) combine with two first principles (love and strife). Love unites and organizes, whereas strife results in disintegration and disorganization.

empiricism   A philosophical position that emphasizes the importance of experience, observation, and learning in the acquisition of knowledge.

Epictetus (A.D. c. 50–c. 135)   A Roman stoic philosopher, popular in his day, who emphasized the stoic virtues of order, discipline, and resignation in those matters beyond our control.

Epicureanism   A philosophy based on the goodness of pleasure and the evil of pain. Epicureanism emphasized moderation and the capacity to forego immediate pleasures for long-term gains.

Epicurus (341–270 B.C.)   An important post-Aristotelian philosopher who founded a school of thought that focused largely on how to live the good life by maximizing pleasure and minimizing pain.

epiphenomenalism   A mind–body position marked by the belief that physical events are causal with respect to mental events. Mental events are viewed as completely dependent on physical functions and, as such, have no independent existence or causal efficacy.

epistemology   A branch of philosophy concerned with problems of knowledge such as What can we know or How can we know?

equipotentiality   A term employed by Karl Lashley referring to the capacity of one part of the cortex to take over the function of another part.

equivalent phase   A Pavlovian term referring to the tendency of a subject to respond in a highly stereotyped fashion to any stimulus. The equivalent phase may follow a biological insult that produces a shock-like reaction. In such circumstances, the subject may respond in the same way to all signals.

essentialism   Belief in the possibility of discerning the fundamental character or intrinsic nature of something.

ethical mode of existence   According to Kierkegaard, the ethical mode of existence is marked by deep concerns for justice, genuine and caring moral concerns, and a capacity to shoulder responsibility. In the face of moral complexities and absurdities, the ethical mode of existence may collapse into a profound sense of irony.

existentialism   A philosophical orientation typically traced to the work of Kierkegaard and Unamuno, marked by an emphasis on the centrality of experience, the role of freedom in human life, the irreducible uniqueness of each person, rejection of reductionism, and the quest for authenticity in the face of all of the absurdities and forces that threaten human dignity.

external history   The consideration of larger social and contextual events that may influence disciplinary histories. See *internal history*.

extinction   A term employed in different ways in the various learning theories but generally referring to the cessation of a response following changes in the circumstances that first supported the response.

extrinsic teleology   The view that design or order in nature reflects the work of a designer.

extroversion   In Jung's psychology, a quality of personality marked by love of other people and social interaction.

eye of the soul   A metaphor employed by Plato to convey the idea that the soul can sometimes apprehend true reality.

Fechner, Gustav Theodor (1801–1887)   His *Elements of Psychophysics,* one of the great original classics in psychology, set forth a systematic approach to psychophysics. He proposed several early psychophysical methods and helped lay the conceptual and methodological foundations for the new discipline of psychology.

Fechner's Law   An integration of Weber's formula expressed as $S = k \log R$, where S is a mental sensation and R is a stimulus magnitude. Thus, according to the law, a mental sensation is a logarithmic function of the stimulus multiplied by a constant.

Feyerabend, Paul K.   Philosopher of science who has argued for an anarchistic epistemology marked by belief that there is no such thing as a single unified and unchanging scientific method.

fictional final goals   According to Adler, fictions play major roles in the subjective world of the individual. Fictional final goals are those things that we wish to achieve. Such wishes are not necessarily grounded in realistic considerations.

field theory   Generally associated with the psychology of Kurt Lewin. Field theory emphasizes the interdependence of the person and the environment. It may be viewed as a corrective to extreme individualistic psychologies that neglect the role of context.

figure–ground   A principle of perception characterized by the tendency of the subject to see some things as standing out and other things as forming background.

final cause   According to Aristotle, the goals or purposes for which an action was intended.

fixation   A strong attachment to a specific stimulus in Freud's theory of instinct. For example, a childhood trauma may result in an oral fixation that might manifest itself in adulthood as a habit of smoking cigars.

Flourens, Pierre Jean Marie (1794–1867)   French physician and neurophysiologist who employed the method of ablation (surgical removal or isolation of specific structures) as a means of establishing the functions performed by various parts of the brain.

formal cause   The form or shape that contributes to a causal sequence. Thus, an airplane could not fly if critical components were not shaped properly.

formal discipline, doctrine of   An early belief that the mind, like certain muscle groups, is developed most effectively by specific exercises such as the study of certain classics (e.g., Latin and geometry).

forms, theory of   According to Plato, there are universal and true principles comprehended through reason. For example, reason reveals the principles of triangularity. The senses reveal only particular triangles. A goal of education is to uncover the true formal properties of things.

Frankl, Viktor (1905–1997)   Viennese psychiatrist and founder of a humanistic orientation known as logotherapy. Frankl emphasized the importance of the quest for meaning and the human capacity to construct alternative meaning orientations.

free association   Therapeutic method developed by Sigmund Freud and marked by the uninhibited sharing of whatever happens to be in the center stage of consciousness at a given time.

free will   The assumption that human beings make choices that are more or less independent of antecedent conditions. Contrast with *determinism*.

Freud, Sigmund (1856–1939)   Founder of psychoanalysis, which is both a major system of psychology and a therapeutic technique.

Fritsch, Gustav Theodor (1838–1927)   German physician and physiologist who, together with Eduard Hitzig, established the field of electrophysiology. Fritsch and Hitzig were pioneers in the use of direct electrical stimulation as a means of establishing brain functions.

function   According to Jung, a function is an expression of the psychic apparatus. He identified four functions: thinking, feeling, sensation, and intuition. He believed that, for many people, specific functions (e.g., thinking) are dominant features of the personality.

functional autonomy   A concept employed by Gordon Allport referring to the possibility that an activity may become independent of its original motivational source and may now become reinforcing in its own right. An example is the person who originally goes to sea to make a living but soon enjoys going to sea in its own right.

functional fixedness   The inability to find productive solutions to new problems. May also refer to the inability to see alternative uses for a particular tool or method.

functionalism   A loose-knit system of psychology having its origin in the work of U.S. scholars such as William James, John Dewey, and G. Stanley Hall. Functionalism emphasized a broad-based methodology applied to basic and applied problems associated with experience and behavior.

Galen (A.D. 129–c. 199)   Rome's greatest physician, remembered for his early anatomical theories and his speculation on a host of medical problems including the problems of emotional illness.

Galileo Galilei (1564–1642)   Italian astronomer and physicist remembered for improving the telescope and using it systematically in the observation of the solar system.

Gall, Franz Joseph (1758–1828)   German anatomist, physician, and pioneer in faculty psychology. Gall believed that faculties of the mind were localized in specific regions of the brain and that well-developed or deficient regions were manifested in protrusions or indentations on the skull. Gall was the founder of phrenology, the attempt to assess character by examining the shape of the head.

Galton, Francis (1822–1911)   Cousin of Charles Darwin and pioneer in the study of individual differences. Galton emphasized the hereditary basis of individual differences.

generalization   Stimuli similar to the original conditioned stimulus may also elicit a conditioned response.

genetic epistemology   The study of ways of knowing and ways of solving problems as a function of developmental level.

genital stage   According to Freud, this stage is associated with the adolescent years and is marked by the development of emotional ties with members of the opposite sex.

geocentric   Literally, earth centered. Generally refers to the ancient view of Ptolemy that the earth is the center of the universe.

Gestalt   There is no exact English equivalent for this German term, but English words such as *whole* and *configuration* are close in meaning.

Gestalt therapy   A form of therapy coming out of the work of Fritz Perls and having little or nothing in common with Gestalt psychology.

Golgi, Camillo (1843–1926)   Italian physician and histologist famous, among other things, for developing a staining technique that made it possible to distinguish fine nervous structures from surrounding tissue. His methods made a singular contribution to the advance of knowledge in neurophysiology.

good continuation   The perceptual tendency toward linearity, continuity, or coherence. Good continuation is manifested when a perceptual pattern is tracked even in the presence of irrelevant or competing cues.

great-person theory   The view that unique individuals play a causal role in history. Contrast with *Zeitgeist* and *Ortgeist*.

group dynamics   In Lewin's psychology, this expression refers broadly to the study of the effects of groups on individuals and the effects of individuals on groups. It also includes the study of group structures and their effect on work, productivity, and achievement of group goals.

Guillotin, Joseph Ignace (1738–1814)   Famous French physician who invented the instrument named after him and used for decapitation.

Guthrie, Edwin Ray (1886–1959)   Well-known U.S. behaviorist and learning theorist remembered for a theory of learning based primarily on the law of contiguity. Guthrie served as the fifty-third president of the American Psychological Association in 1945.

habit strength   A term employed by the learning theorist Clark Hull referring to number of reinforced trials in a situation that have contributed to strength of a connection between a stimulus and a response.

Haeckel, Ernst Heinrich (1834–1919)   German zoologist, one of the first to emphasize the importance of evolutionary theory to psychology.

Hales, Stephen (1677–1761)   One of the first to demonstrate clearly a spinal reflex and the dependence of that reflex on the integrity of the spinal cord.

Hall, Granville Stanley (1844–1924)   Pioneer U.S. psychologist and founder and first president of the American Psychological Association. Hall also founded several journals and served as president of Clark University. One of the first developmental psychologists, Hall was the author of such classic books as *Adolescence* and *Senescence*.

hardening   An early concept that emphasized the beneficial role of self-imposed hardships (e.g., sleeping on an uncomfortable bed, exposure to cold weather) as means of preparing for subsequent tasks. Hardening is not quite the same as conditioning in that it involved practices that were more likely to be damaging.

Harlow, Harry F. (1905–1981)   American psychologist noted for his creative contributions to learning theory and the formation of attachment.

Hartley, David (1705–1757)   Founder of modern associationism and one of the first to establish a classification system of pleasures and pains.

hedonism   See *psychological hedonism*.

Heidegger, Martin (1889–1976)   German philosopher and one of the most important existentialists of the twentieth century. Heidegger's work focused on the theoretical meaning of existence and the practical questions of how we should exist individually and collectively in the world.

heliocentric   Literally, sun centered. Typically refers to the work of Nicolaus Copernicus who taught that the sun is the center of the solar system.

Helmholtz, Hermann Ludwig Ferdinand von (1821–1894)   One of the great scientists of the nineteenth century who, along with Thomas Young, advanced a trichromatic theory of color vision. He also advanced a theory of pitch perception and was the first to measure the speed of conduction of the nervous impulse.

Héloise (c. 1098–1164)   A gifted scholar known primarily for her tragic love affair with Peter Abelard. Her letters illustrated a deep philosophy and psychology of the nature of loving relationships.

Helvétius, Claude-Adrien (1715–1771)   French materialist who argued that human actions can be explained on the basis of rewards and punishments. His views were considered radical in his day and he was forced to recant his position.

Heraclitus   Probably active around 480 B.C., Heraclitus was the first process philosopher. Emphasized that only change is real.

Herbart, Johann Friedrich (1776–1841)   German mathematician, philosopher, and psychologist. Herbart was among the first to attempt to quantify mental functions. He was also interested in the role of unconscious processes in human life and in the application of psychological studies to clinical and educational problems.

Herodotus (c. 484–c. 425 B.C.)   First great Greek historian. Attempted to write history with an emphasis on natural rather than supernatural causes.

heterogony of ends   Wundt's position that an ongoing behavioral sequence must often be understood in terms of an ever-shifting pattern of primary and secondary goals. For example, a cat chasing a mouse may suddenly find it necessary to compete with a partner, overcome an unexpected barrier, or avoid a danger. Ends, goals, and purposes keep changing.

heteronomy   A term employed by Kant to refer to the varieties of forces outside the organism (e.g., rewards, punishments, authority, etc.) that often regulate behavior.

Hippocrates (c. 460–c. 377 B.C.)   Sometimes regarded as the Father of Greek Medicine, Hippocrates advanced a thoroughgoing naturalistic account of all illness, both physical and mental. Advanced the first classification system of mental disorders.

historicism   The commitment to understanding the past for its own sake. Contrast with *presentism.*

historiography   The writing of history along with the study of the methodological and philosophical issues that are pertinent to the work of the historian.

history   The interpretive study of the events of the human past.

Hitzig, Eduard (1838–1907)   German psychiatrist and neurophysiologist who collaborated with Gustav Theodor Fritsch to establish the field of electrophysiology. Fritsch and Hitzig were pioneers in the use of direct electrical stimulation to study brain functions.

Hobbes, Thomas (1588–1679)   One of the first of the modern philosophers to advance a thoroughgoing mechanistic account of human behavior. He also argued that self-interest serves as the primary basis for motivation.

Hollingworth, Leta Stetter (1886–1939)   Psychologist and educator who was one of the first to subject gender differences to rigorous experimental scrutiny. Her work exposed several nineteenth-century myths regarding the intellectual status of women. She is also remembered for pioneering studies on gifted children.

Holt, Edwin Bissell (1873–1946)   Behavioristically oriented psychologist who argued that psychologists should study what organisms do in their environments, but that behavior should be regarded as purposive and goal directed.

hormic   A term employed by McDougall from the Greek *horme* meaning "urge." A hormic psychology emphasizes the role of purpose in living systems.

Horney, Karen Danielsen (1885–1952)   German-American psychoanalyst who enlarged the domain of psychoanalysis with her study of sociocultural factors in neurosis and gender development.

hostile type   A neurotic attempt to reduce anxiety by *moving against* people.

Hsün Tzu (c. 298–c. 212 B.C.)   An early Chinese philosopher who advanced a thoroughgoing naturalistic philosophy. He is sometimes viewed as the Chinese Aristotle.

Huarte, Juan (c. 1530–c. 1592)   One of the first to write on the subjects of individual differences, aptitude, and temperament.

Hull, Clark Leonard (1884–1952)   One of the most famous neobehaviorists, known for a mathematical-deductive approach to animal and human behavior. Hull, a member of the National Academy of Sciences, served as the forty-fourth president of the American Psychological Association in 1935.

Hume, David (1711–1776)   British empiricist who advanced the view that causality is not a property of objects and therefore there are no necessary connections. Causality is thus reduced to a psychological problem and is based on consistent conjunction and our ways of making sense of the successive events in the world.

Hunter, Walter Samuel (1889–1954) Behavioristically oriented psychologist who argued for a variety of methods, including field, clinical and laboratory experimental methods. A member of the National Academy of Sciences, Hunter served as the thirty-ninth president of the American Psychological Association in 1931.

Husserl, Edmund (1859–1938) German philosopher and founder of phenomenology. He emphasized the uniqueness of consciousness, the dangers of reductionism, and an approach to the study of consciousness that attempts to describe what is naturally there in terms of content, impressions, and meanings.

hylomorphism A mind–body position advanced by Aristotle, comes from *hule,* meaning matter and *morphe* meaning form. Aristotle stressed the interdependence of matter and form. Thus, seeing as a mental process cannot be separated from the physical structure of the eye.

hylozoism The view that mind is manifested in all material movement.

Hypatia (c. 370–415) Neo-Platonic philosopher noted for her expertise in astronomy and geometry. Possibly one of the first to recommend music therapy for emotional disorders.

id In Freudian theory, the id is the most primitive component of the personality. It represents powerful biological needs and demands instant expression and immediate gratification.

ideal self According to Rogers, the self as one would like it to be.

idealism A philosophical orientation emphasizing mind or spirit as the preeminent feature of life. Contrast with *materialism.*

idealized self A fictitious view of neurotic selfhood that replaces the real self.

identical elements transfer theory In contrast with the doctrine of formal discipline, the identical elements transfer theory holds that the learning of any new task will be facilitated most by experience with highly comparable previous tasks.

identification In Freudian psychology, a defense mechanism of the ego marked by imitation of another person. The ego attempts to borrow from the success or adequacy of another individual.

identity theory A theory of the origin of psuche that stresses the continuity or identity of the psychically

endowed biological substratum of the organism and the later mature, self-reflective, fully conscious adult.

idiographic According to Gordon Allport, an approach to the study of personality that emphasizes individual experience. This approach makes use of such techniques as case studies, verbal reports, and interviews.

Idols A term employed by Francis Bacon referring to "phantoms of the mind." Idols are sources of error, such as blind reliance on authority, that blind us in our quest for truth.

Idols of the Cave Local prejudices or strongly preferred hypotheses or theories that interfere with objective responses to data.

Idols of the Marketplace The temptation to take words too seriously so that naming is confused with explaining. To guard against the Idols of the Marketplace, one must constantly reexamine definitions and understand the deceptive dimensions of language.

Idols of the Theatre Errors of thought based on the easy acceptance of authority or the naive acceptance of a popular paradigm.

Idols of the Tribe Errors of thought resulting from inherent human limitations such as sensory distortions and the tendency to overgeneralize.

imageless thought Belief that there are objective meanings in experience that are not associated with specific words, symbols, or signs.

incentive Generally refers to the attractive characteristics of reinforcement. For example, for a given subject, a piece of chocolate candy may have a higher incentive value than a dime.

indeterminism The doctrine that it is impossible to apply strict cause and effect explanations to events in the world.

Index of Forbidden Books Generally refers to books forbidden by the Catholic church because they were regarded as dangerous to faith and morality. Though censorship was practiced from the early days of the church, the *Index* started in the sixteenth century and continued until 1966.

individual psychology The name of the system of psychology founded by Alfred Adler.

inductive argument Any argument in which the conclusion is claimed to be more probable than not given the truth of the premises. Inductive arguments are said to be strong or weak, depending on whether the conclusion is or is not made probable depending on the truth of the premises.

indulgences   Refers to various means of raising money practiced by the Catholic church prior to the Reformation. Generally involved payment of money in exchange for a spiritual favor.

inferiority complex   According to Adler, children are inadequate or inferior with respect to most functions. Overcoming inferiority is a task for all people. An inferiority complex is an intense or unusually strong manifestation of feelings that all people experience.

information-processing metaphor   The view that cognition involves the processing of information in a sophisticated manner or sequence. Also known as the computer metaphor.

inheritance of acquired characteristics   Belief held by many early theorists such as Erasmus Darwin and Lamarck that acquisitions of parents are passed on to offspring. This explanation of evolutionary change is rejected in mainstream biology in the twentieth century.

insight   The capacity to see a problem in a large context and perceptually to restructure relationships necessary to the solution of the problem.

instinct   An organized sequence of behaviors characteristic of a given species. It is assumed that instinctive behaviors are not learned.

interactionism   A commonsense belief in the interdependence of the mental and the physical realms. According to this position, mental events may be causal with respect to physical events and vice versa.

internal history   The study of the development of ideas within a discipline such as music, art, or psychology. See *external history*.

intervening variable   An unobserved process that accounts for connections between stimulus events and responses. For example, response rate may slow down under conditions of high effort. According to Clark Hull, response rate is slowed down because of reactive inhibition (I_R), a fatiguelike state. Fatigue, in this case, might be regarded as an intervening variable.

intrinsic teleology   The position that design, order, and purpose are immanent in nature.

introspection   A species of observation, but the subject to be observed is in experience itself. Thus, introspection is a kind of "looking in" to identify elements of experience and the way these elements combine, or the processes and adaptations of experience.

introversion   According to Jung, an attitude marked by preference for inwardness and for minimal or highly selected social contact.

isomorphism   The Gestalt position on the mind–brain problem. Literally, this term refers to similarity of form. Isomorphism, in the context of the mind–brain problem, refers to an assumed functional relationship between experience and underlying brain processes.

Itard, Jean (1775–1838)   A French teacher of the hearing impaired and early pioneer in the training and treatment of mental deficiency.

James, William (1842–1910)   American psychologist and philosopher who emphasized the centrality of experience, individualism, a plurality of methods, and the dangers of reductionism. Some of the intellectual traditions in his work are reflected in the work of humanistic psychologists.

James-Lange theory of emotion   A theory of emotion advanced independently by William James and Carl Lange. The theory emphasizes the somatic substrate of emotional experiences and argues that the experience of emotion is the experience of the activity of the body—thus, the famous statement: We see a bear, we run, and we are afraid. James's later vision of emotion emphasizes constitutional determinants and the impossibility of separating cognition and emotion.

judgment   According to Brentano, consciousness of an object marked by belief or disbelief.

Jung, Carl Gustav (1875–1961)   Founder of a system of psychology known as analytic psychology.

just noticeable difference (jnd)   The smallest detectable difference between a standard stimulus and a comparison stimulus.

Kant, Immanuel (1724–1804)   One of the great German philosophers, remembered among other things for his attempts to reconcile empirical and rational approaches to knowledge. Kant believed that knowledge begins with experience, but in his view, there are meaningful connections given in experience itself. Kant also advanced an early theory of moral development and he was interested in problems associated with nationalism.

Kepler, Johannes (1571–1630)   German astronomer and mathematician who discovered the elliptical or oval-shaped motions of the planets.

Kierkegaard, Søren Aabye (1813–1855)   Danish philosopher commonly regarded as one of the founders of existentialism. Kierkegaard rejected the concern of rationalist philosophy with the abstractions of the intellect and instead called attention to the daily practical issues that individuals encounter and the problems of coping with those issues in an authentic way.

Koffka, Kurt (1886–1941) Pioneering Gestalt psychologist remembered especially for introducing Gestalt psychology to the English-speaking world and for the extension of Gestalt theory into the field of developmental psychology.

Köhler, Wolfgang (1887–1967) Principal spokesman for the Gestalt school. Köhler is remembered for his pioneering work on the role of insight in learning, for his treatment of value theory from a Gestalt perspective, and for his broad systematic approach to science and psychology.

Kornilov, Konstantin Nikolaevich (1879–1957) Founder of a system of psychology in the former Soviet Union known as reactology. Kornilov was seeking a system of psychology completely consistent with Marxist-Leninist political thought. Kornilov's system was rejected by Soviet authorities because it neglected the activity of mind stressed by Lenin.

Kraepelin, Emil (1856–1926) A student of Wundt. He created an influential classification system of psychiatric disorders and made numerous contributions to psychiatry and psychopharmacology.

Kuhn, Thomas S. A philosopher of science who emphasized the importance of understanding science in terms of its community structures and evolutionary processes. His book *The Structure of Scientific Revolutions* is one of the most influential in its field in the twentieth century.

Külpe, Oswald (1862–1915) Student of Wilhelm Wundt and well-known founder of an early psychological laboratory and school of thought at Würzburg. Külpe's experiments on imageless thought challenged the simplistic characteristics of other early systems.

Lamarck, Jean-Baptiste (1744–1829) French biologist remembered for his early original work on the nature of species and for an early theory of organic evolution based on the inheritance of acquired characteristics.

La Mettrie, Julien Offray de (1709–1751) French physician whose famous book *Man a Machine* advanced a deterministic, evolutionary, and mechanistic approach to human mental processes.

Lange, Carl Georg (1834–1900) Danish physiologist remembered for a theory of emotion comparable to one proposed by William James and subsequently known as the James-Lange theory. See *James-Lange theory of emotion.*

Laplace, Pierre Simon Marquis de (1749–1827) French scientist who advanced an early naturalistic account of the solar system known as the *nebular hypothesis.*

Lashley, Karl Spencer (1890–1958) Well-known and highly regarded biologist who collaborated with John B. Watson and who is remembered for classic studies on cerebral correlates of learning.

latency period According to Freud, the period between the phallic stage and the genital stage. In the latency period there is no obvious localization of erotic interest.

latent content of a dream According to Freud, the symbolic way a dream expresses an unconscious wish or drive.

latent learning A term employed by Edward Chace Tolman referring to learning that has occurred but is not observed because environmental conditions have not been favorable to its display. When environmental conditions change appropriately, such learning, heretofore unobservable, may now show itself.

law of effect Refers to Thorndike's early view that connections are strengthened when followed by a satisfying state of affairs and weakened when followed by an annoying state of affairs. Later, Thorndike dropped the second half of the law and argued that satisfiers strengthen associations, but annoyers do not weaken associations.

law of exercise Refers to Thorndike's early belief that connections are strengthened through practice and weakened through disuse. Later, Thorndike denied that exercise alone controls the fate of connections.

learned ignorance A concept coming out of the work of Nicholas of Cusa referring to learning how *not* to think of God. Applied to psychology, the term could refer to the discipline of learning how *not* to think of ourselves.

learning Any change in performance or behavior that is attributable to the effects of practice or experience.

learning set Harlow's finding that previous experience can facilitate a primate's ability to make form discriminiations among stimuli. Harlow also referred to this process as *learning to learn.*

Leibniz, Gottfried Wilhelm (1646–1716) German rational philosopher and mathematician who sought ways to reconcile the legitimate claims of monism and pluralism. Leibniz advocated a universal language and a world united by reason and international government. Leibniz and Isaac Newton independently discovered the differential calculus.

Leibnizian tradition   According to Allport, a tradition that emphasizes the proactive (purposive or goal-directed) nature of human life.

Leonardo da Vinci (1452–1519)   Broad-ranging Renaissance scholar who was an artistic genius, engineer, sculpture, and architect. He is also remembered for his careful studies of human anatomy and his artistic skill in capturing human emotions.

Leucippus   Greek philosopher who lived around 500 B.C. He was the founder of atomic theory later refined by Democritus.

Lewin, Kurt (1890–1947)   Inspired by Wertheimer, Köhler, and Koffka, Lewin attempted to extend the Gestalt vision to other subdisciplinary branches of psychology, including motivation, personality, social psychology, and conflict resolution.

libertarian   In philosophy, one who believes in free will. Contrast with *determinism*.

life space   Key concept in Lewin's psychology referring to all the psychological facts that are influential in the life of an individual at a given point in time.

limits, method of   A psychophysical method whereby a standard stimulus is compared with various values of comparison stimuli presented in both ascending and descending series. The task of the subject is to specify when the standard and the variable appear to be the same. Also called the *method of limits* because it measured the quantitative limits of the variable stimulus values that appear to be greater than, less than, or equal to the standard stimulus.

linear-progressive hypothesis   A view of history marked by belief in the inevitable growth and progress of human knowledge and institutions.

local signs, theory of   A hypothetical sensory representation by means of which one can detect the position or locus of one part of a sensory surface relative to other points on that surface.

Locke, John (1632–1704)   One of the greatest philosophers of English speech who insisted that the mind at birth is like a blank slate devoid of characters or ideas. His emphasis on the centrality of experience and learning elevated the importance of universal education.

Lockean tradition   Allport's expression referring to deterministic and mechanistic approaches to psychology according to which human beings are regarded as primarily reactive or as mere products of social conditioning.

logical positivism   Sometimes called *critical empiricism* or *scientific empiricism,* this school of thought contends that scientific concepts must be explicitly and operationally tied to observable events. Publicly confirmable propositions were to replace "inner experience" in all phases of scientific activity.

logotherapy   Viktor Frankl's approach to psychotherapy emphasizing meaning orientation and the capacity of the individual to appropriate alternative meanings for the events of life.

Lotze, Rudolph Herman (1817–1881)   Wrote the first treatise on physiological psychology. He also advanced an early theory of space perception.

Lucretius (c. 96–c. 55 B.C.)   Roman epicurean philosopher who wrote on a variety of psychological topics, often from the vantage point of the atomic theory of Democritus.

Luther, Martin (1483–1546)   The founder of the Reformation and leader of the Protestant movement. Arguably, Luther contributed to the growth of the empirical spirit by advancing the doctrine of the individual priesthood of the believer, in which people have the right to read and interpret scriptures for themselves.

Lyceum   A school near Athens founded by Aristotle.

Lyell, Charles (1797–1875)   Often regarded as the founder of modern geology. His classic three-volume *Principles of Geology* presented a view of the evolution of the earth marked by the belief that change occurs over vast stretches of time. This view is sometimes called *gradualism* or *uniformitarianism.*

Mach, Ernst (1838–1916)   Nineteenth-century physicist who argued that there are space-form and time-form sensations that are configural in their nature. Mach's analysis served as an inspiration for the early Gestalt psychologists who also argued that there are wholes that are grasped intuitively and that are more than a mere collection of elements.

Machiavelli, Niccolò (1469–1527)   Founder of modern political science and modern military science. One of the first to emphasize the importance of socialization and the techniques for molding public opinion. He advocated the utility of a descriptive social science.

Machiavellianism   Refers to the application of the principles set forth by Niccolò Machiavelli. Sometimes implies amoral, manipulative attitudes, but, strictly speaking, such an implication is a corruption of the teachings of Machiavelli.

Magendie, François (1783–1855) Demonstrated that motor functions are handled by the ventral root of the spinal cord and that sensory functions are handled by the dorsal root. Sir Charles Bell made the same discovery, now referred to as the Bell-Magendie Law.

Maimonides (1135–1204) Influential Jewish philosopher who attempted to reconcile the conflicting claims of reason and revelation. His book *Guide of the Perplexed* was widely read and highly controversial.

Malleus Maleficarum Literally, the *Hammer against Witches*. A book published in 1486 by Dominican friars Heinrich Kramer and Jacob Sprenger that served as a guide for detecting and prosecuting suspected witches during the Inquisition.

Malthus, Thomas Robert (1766–1834) Author of *An Essay on the Principle of Population* that set forth the hypothesis that populations may outgrow their food supply because food supply tends to increase arithmetically while populations increase geometrically.

manifest content of a dream According to Freud, the dream as described by the dreamer; the apparent content of a dream as censored by the ego.

Marcus Aurelius (A.D. 121–180) Roman emperor and stoic philosopher who emphasized the importance of enduring hardships that undoubtedly serve a larger purpose. The expression *stoic resignation* characterizes an important dimension of his thought.

Maslow, Abraham (1908–1970) One of the important founders and leaders of third-force psychology. Maslow is remembered, among other things, for his hierarchical theory of motivation, his studies on self-actualization, and his emphasis on studying healthy people as a means of building an appropriate database for an adequate psychology.

mass action A concept growing out of the work of Karl Lashley referring to the idea that the rate, efficiency, and accuracy of learning depend on the amount of cortex available, and that parts of the brain are interdependent and function as a whole.

material cause Aristotle's contention that things behave as they do partly because of their material structure. For example, a billiard ball could not function properly if it were made of cork or rubber.

material self In James's theory, the material self is the body, friends, and possessions such as clothing, house, automobile, and so on.

materialism A monistic ontology characterized by the belief that all real things are composed exclusively of matter. Implies that all being can be understood in terms of the principles of material structure.

Maxwell, James Clerk (1831–1879) Scottish physicist who demonstrated that he could match any spectral value with various mixtures of red, green, or blue. He thus contributed directly to the Young-Helmholtz theory of color vision.

McDougall, William (1871–1938) Pioneer psychologist with very broad-ranging interests in social psychology, abnormal psychology, and the philosophical problems of psychology. McDougall emphasized the study of purposive behavior and the role of instincts in human life.

Medieval period The historical period from approximately 400 to 1300. Though it was a period marked by reliance on tradition, revelation, and authority, scholars attempted to find an acceptable role for reason and for observational studies.

mental set Predisposition to respond in a given manner or tendency to organize an event in terms of an existing bias.

Mesmer, Franz Anton (1734–1815) French physician who proposed a magnetic therapy that allegedly eliminated sickness by restoring magnetic balance inside the body. Although his career was marked by controversy, he pioneered an early form of hypnosis that became known as "mesmerism."

Meyer, Max Frederick (1873–1967) Early advocate of psychology as the study of behavior. Meyer was also a pioneer in the scientific study of audition and the diagnosis and treatment of the hearing impaired.

Mill, James (1773–1836) British philosopher who advanced an uncompromising mechanistic approach to association. Argued strongly for the education of the masses.

Mill, John Stuart (1806–1873) One of the great philosophers of English speech who envisioned a science of human nature based on probabilistic notions. Also one of the first to deplore the subjugation of women.

Mitwelt Heidegger's term for the community or our life with other people.

molar behavior An expression employed by Tolman to designate the special domain of his psychology. Molar behavior is the behavior of the intact organism engaging in typical day-to-day activities. Molar behavior contrasts with molecular or isolated small units of behavior.

monad   A term employed by Leibniz to refer to a principle of existence. Leibniz believed that the world consisted of many independent monads, but all monads are harmonious with all other monads. Thus, for him, there is a real mental world and that world is completely harmonious with a real physical or physiological world. Hence, mind and body are both real but completely harmonious and independent.

monism   The position that reality is one thing. Thus everything relates to everything else in a completely interconnected world. Contrast with *pluralism.*

Montaigne, Michel de (1533–1592)   Late Renaissance scholar who launched a powerful and influential attack on human knowledge. His skepticism was to have a strong influence on Francis Bacon and René Descartes. Montaigne also speculated on a number of psychological topics such as how to rear children, education, motivation, and emotion.

moral anxiety   According to Freud, anxiety associated with the threat that the irrational demands of the superego might overcome the ego.

Morgan, Conwy Lloyd (1852–1936)   English biologist, philosopher, and psychologist who argued for an extension of Ockham's Razor into the field of comparative psychology. Morgan's argument, sometimes called *Morgan's canon* or the *principle of parsimony,* is that animal actions should not be interpreted as the outcome of higher psychical faculties, if such actions can be adequately explained in terms of the operation of processes that are lower on a psychological scale.

Müller, Georg Elias (1850–1934)   Prominent German psychologist remembered for his work in psychophysics, memory, learning, and vision. Numerous early psychologists studied with Müller at the University of Göttingen.

Müller, Johannes (1801–1858)   Great pioneer in experimental physiology. Remembered, among other things, for his doctrine of specific energies, which argues that each nerve is highly specialized to carry out one kind of function.

Münsterberg, Hugo (1863–1916)   German-American psychologist and a pioneer in applied psychology with his research on forensic, clinical, and industrial psychology.

Myia   Daughter of Pythagoras and Theana. One of the first to give advice on child rearing.

nativism   The position that there are perceptions that are built in or operational from birth and that are informative about the world. For example, the nativist argues that we have an innate capacity to see in depth. Contrast with *empiricism.*

naturalism   The doctrine that scientific procedures and laws are applicable to all phenomena.

natural selection   A concept employed by Darwin to account for survival and extinction. Darwin believed that in any species population, some variants are, by chance, better adapted to certain niches; other variants may, by chance, be less well adapted. Advantages or disadvantages of parents will be passed on genetically to offspring. Thus, there is a natural selection for survival and extinction.

natural spirit   In Galen's pneuma concept of the soul, natural spirit refers to those vital principles responsible for vegetative functions of the body.

nebular hypothesis   In astronomy, the hypothesis that the solar system evolved from bodies of rarefied gases and dust in interstellar space.

neo-Platonism   A school of philosophy founded in the third century that combined selected features of Platonic philosophy with Jewish and Christian mysticism.

neurotic anxiety   According to Freud, this arises when the irrational demands of the id threaten to overwhelm the ego.

neurotic trends   Neurotic needs that form strategies of protection designed to counter basic anxiety.

Nicholas of Cusa (1401–1464)   Early legal scholar, mathematician, and philosopher remembered for his doctrine of learned ignorance, which refers to learning how *not* to think of God.

nomothetic   Allport's term for a research orientation that emphasizes statistical abstractions (e.g., means, standard deviations, etc.).

noogenic neurosis   Frankl's expression referring to the anxiety associated with loss of meaning or a feeling of worthlessness.

normal science   A notion introduced by Thomas Kuhn that refers to conventional ways of solving problems in science at a given time or during the reign of a particular paradigm.

objective anxiety   Objective threats from the world or from other people that threaten to overpower the ego.

objectivity in history   An attitude of the historical researcher marked by an attempt to present fairly all sides of an issue.

Ockham's Razor   The contention of William of Ockham that explanations containing fewer assumptions are to be preferred to those containing more assumptions.

Oedipus complex A young boy's desire for his mother along with feelings of competition with his father. The term is used more generally to refer to strong emotional attachment to the parent of the opposite sex and feelings of competition with the parent of the same sex.

ontogeny recapitulates phylogeny Belief advanced first by Ernst Haeckel that the history of the individual (ontogeny) recapitulates the history of the species (phylogeny).

ontology A branch of philosophy that studies the nature and relations of being. Considers the question "What is real?"

operant conditioning The term *operant* refers to behavior that is emitted. According to Skinner, operant conditioning occurs if reinforcement follows with a response that is emitted in a specific situation.

operationism A programmatic attempt to tie scientific terms to measurements or operations employed in experiments. Thus, abstract terms such as *anxiety* or *intelligence* are defined in terms of the measures or operations employed in research studies.

opthalmoscope An instrument designed by Hermann von Helmholtz for viewing the interior of the eye, especially the retina.

oral stage In Freud's psychology, the first stage of psychosexual development. In this stage, the child's interactions with the world are primarily via the oral cavity and there is primitive learning about the responsiveness of the world to oral activities such as crying and sucking.

Ortgeist The spirit of the place. Contrasts with the great-person theory of history and emphasizes the importance of place and time (*Zeitgeist*) as conditions for the production and acceptance of new ideas.

overcompensation According to Adler, overcompensation involves attempts to develop great strength in the very area that is most beset with difficulties (e.g., a physically handicapped individual who becomes a great athlete).

Paracelsus (1453–1541) Radical Renaissance epistemologist who argued that observational studies should replace old scholastic techniques and blind allegiance to authority.

paradigm According to Thomas Kuhn, the beliefs, attitudes, values, methods, and assumptions that guide the intellectual community at a given time.

paradoxical intention Frankl's expression referring to the capacity to do the very opposite of what one would most like to do. Thus, one who is fearful of flying might prefer to stay home but instead chooses to fly.

paradoxical phase According to Pavlov, a weak stimulus may sometimes produce a strong response and a strong stimulus may produce a weak response. The paradoxical phase sometimes follows shock induced by a biological insult.

Parmenides Early philosopher who did his work shortly after 500 B.C. He was one of the first to attempt to distinguish between appearance and reality. According to Parmenides, the senses reveal only appearances, whereas reason leads to real truths. In contrast with Heraclitus, Parmenides emphasized a philosophy of being as opposed to a philosophy of becoming.

parsimony, principle of Emphasis on simplicity. In comparative psychology, the principle of parsimony holds that simple explanations should be preferred to explanations that glorify "higher mental processes."

Pavlov, Ivan (1849–1936) The most significant figure in the history of Russian psychology and pioneer in research in classical conditioning. His *Lectures on Conditioned Reflexes* is a classic work setting forth a psychology and psychiatry based on the principles of conditioning.

penis envy According to Freud, during the phallic period, the young girl is envious of the protruding sex organ of her father. Freud argued that the young girl holds her mother responsible for her own "castrated condition."

persona Literally, the playactor's mask. In Jung's psychology, the persona is that part of the psychic structure that is most visible socially.

personal unconscious Jung's term for the storehouse of materials based on each individual's experiences that are not immediately available to consciousness.

petites perceptions Leibniz's term referring to small perceptions below the level of awareness. Leibniz believed that small perceptions in concert form the basis of perception. His concept of petites perceptions represents an early concept of unconscious processes.

Petrarch, Francesco (1304–1374) Italian poet, scholar, and moralist who was a founder of Renaissance humanism.

phallic stage In Freud's psychology, that period from ages three to five when the child develops an interest in his or her sex organs and the sex organs of the parent. Freud believed that, at this time, the child begins to identify with the opposite-sexed parent.

phenomenal field An expression employed by Rogers to refer to the entire range of experiences that are part of a person's life.

phenomenology A philosophical orientation and a method for approaching a subject of interest. The method seeks to discover what is given directly in experience itself in contrast to intellectualized content.

phi phenomenon Apparent movement illustrated by successive activation of two stationary lights placed in close spatial conjunction. Phenomenally, what is seen is movement from the first to the second light.

philosophy A term likely coined by Pythagoras from *philo* (meaning love) and *sophia* (meaning knowledge or wisdom). Hence, the love of wisdom.

phrenology Literally *science of the mind.* A theory developed by Franz Joseph Gall and Johann Kaspar Spurzheim that character and personality traits are related to specific regions of the brain. It was also believed that the surface features of the skull (e.g., protrusions and indentations) can be used as a means of assessing character.

Piaget, Jean (1896–1980) French epistemologist and psychologist who advanced a popular developmental theory of serially progressive stages of human cognition

Pinel, Philippe (1745–1826) French physician and humanitarian reformer who advanced an early modern classification system of mental disorders. Pinel is typically remembered for cleaning up living conditions for the mentally ill and advocating therapy instead of custodialism.

Plato (c. 428–c. 347 B.C.) The student of Socrates and the teacher of Aristotle. One of the great philosophers of all time remembered, among other things, for his emphasis on the importance of reason as a means of discerning the formal abstract nature of truth. Advanced an early conflict model of mental illness and speculated on numerous psychological topics such as memory and sensation.

pleasure principle Freud argued that the pleasure principle is the dominant feature of the human mental apparatus. The pleasure principle calls for immediate release of tension and acquisition of those goals that fulfill needs.

Plotinus (A.D. 205–270) Founder of neo-Platonic philosophy and author of a six-volume series entitled *Enneads.* The works of Plotinus are a rich source of psychological thought on such topics as perception, sensation, memory, and thinking.

pluralism A philosophical position that emphasizes the importance of alterative perspectives (methodological pluralism) and the existence of many realities (metaphysical pluralism).

pneuma Refers to the air we draw in as we breathe, but also refers to those vital principles that make life possible.

Popper, Karl Raimond Mathematician and philosopher noted for a hypothetico-deductive approach to science. His book *The Logic of Scientific Discovery* is one of the classics in the philosophy of science.

pragmatism A U.S. philosophical movement associated with the work of Charles S. Pierce and William James. James emphasized the close connections between empiricism, pluralism, and pragmatism. According to pragmatism, concepts must be judged in terms of their cash value or the practical work they do in the world. Thus, truth is judged by utility and the practical consequences achieved by an idea.

Prägnanz, law of The law of Prägnanz, according to Wertheimer, refers to the idea that perceptual organization tends to be as good as possible under prevailing conditions. Thus, perceptual organization is as orderly, coherent, and economical as possible under prevailing conditions.

preconscious A feature of the mental apparatus, according to Freud, containing materials not now in consciousness but readily available to consciousness.

preestablished harmony A concept employed by Leibniz to account for the congruence or harmony of different orders of reality. He believed, for example, that mind and body do not influence each other but they are always congruent. Leibniz believed that God had ordered the world in such a fashion as to permit the simultaneous and harmonious operation of many independent principles of existence.

presentation According to Brentano, consciousness of an object marked by simple awareness of the presence of the object.

presentism An orientation toward history emphasizing the pervasive influence of current prejudices on the interpretation of past events. See *historicism.*

Preyer, William Thierry (1841–1897) Pioneer in child psychology whose classic book *The Mind of the Child* served as a powerful impetus for the study of developmental processes.

primary attention According to Titchener, primary attention is involuntary and typically activated by a sudden or strong stimulus.

primary memory According to William James, primary memory is memory associated with nerve vibrations that have not yet ceased. It is memory associated with the specious present, what is immediately held in consciousness, and somewhat akin to an afterimage.

primary process Freud's term for images and memories of objects that serve to satisfy needs. A dream rich in imagery is an example of primary process material.

primary qualities Qualities such as figure, extension, and solidity that are presumed to inhere in objects.

projection A defense mechanism of the ego manifested when personal faults or weaknesses are externalized or ascribed to objects, events, or other people. Thus, a married person tempted to be unfaithful may ascribe the wish to be unfaithful to the spouse.

Protagoras (c. 485–c. 410 B.C.) A sophist (teacher) who emphasized the doctrine of relativism. Protagoras argued that the world is conditioned by our senses and hence truth is relative.

psuche The Greek term for soul or mind. Includes mental processes such as thought, memory, sensation, perception, and so forth.

psyche According to Jung, the totality of a human personality. See *psuche.*

psychical reflex An early term used briefly in Pavlov's laboratory to describe conditioned responses. See *action at a distance.*

psychoanalysis The system of psychology and/or the treatment procedure set forth by Sigmund Freud. The term also has a broader meaning, referring sometimes to any group of psychologies that share some of the basic concepts associated with Freud's psychology.

psychogeny Literally, the origin of psuche. Theories of the origin of psuche.

psychological hedonism Belief that human beings seek in all things to gain pleasure and avoid pain.

psychophysical parallelism A mind–brain doctrine that assumes the independent existence of mental and physical events. According to parallelism, the

mental and the physical are, by definition, congruent. They do not interact with each other; rather, they are like two clocks that always agree on the time, but are nevertheless independent systems.

psychophysics The formal study of the relationship between the properties of stimuli as measured by a physical scale and the psychological impressions of those stimuli.

Ptolemy (c. 100–c. 165) Egyptian astronomer, geographer, and mathematician known for an early geocentric cosmology that was widely accepted for over 1,400 years.

purposive behaviorism An orientation advanced by Tolman in which behavior is regarded as the proper subject matter of psychology, but behavior is construed as goal directed.

Pyrrho (c. 360–c. 270 B.C.) Founder of a systematic philosophy of skepticism. Also emphasized the importance of finding means to live a calm and untroubled existence.

Pythagoras (c. 580–c. 500 B.C.) An enduring figure in Western intellectual history who did his work around 570 B.C. He is remembered for his emphasis on the importance of quantification and for specific contributions such as the famous Pythagorean theorem. His beliefs in the primacy of reason and the nature of the soul were influential later in the work of Socrates and Plato.

Quételet, Jacques (1796–1874) Early pioneer in statistics who was one of the first to realize that there were quantitative procedures applicable to human behavior. He understood that there are lawful regularities operating in moral and psychological arenas earlier regarded as capricious.

radical empiricism The name William James employed to characterize his larger philosophic vision. Radical empiricism emphasizes the primacy of experience and argues that things genuinely encountered in experience must not be excluded from philosophical and scientific inquiry. Radical empiricism treats various monisms as hypotheses.

Ramón y Cajal, Santiago (1852–1934) Spanish physician, histologist and anatomist who discovered the synapse and developed the modern theory of the neuron.

rationalism A philosophical orientation deriving from the Latin *ratio,* meaning to reason or think. Rationalist philosophers typically emphasize a priori knowledge, deduction, and the concept of an active mind that selectively organizes sensory data.

rationalization   Defense mechanism of the ego marked by the practice of employing false but logical or even plausible explanations designed to excuse weaknesses or errors.

reactology   A system of psychology set forth by Konstantin Kornilov. This system emphasized the importance of physiological and social forces in shaping human and animal behavior.

real self   In Horney's theory, the true source of healthy and positive growth in a human being.

reflexology   A system of psychology set forth by Vladimir Bekhterev, a contemporary of Pavlov. According to this system, molar behavior must be understood in terms of its reflexive origins.

Reformation   A sixteenth-century religious movement founded by Martin Luther and motivated by an attempt to reform the Catholic church. Luther's failure to bring about the changes he desired ultimately led to a major split in the church and the beginnings of Protestantism.

regression   Return or retreat to an earlier stage of development and reinstatement of attitudes or behaviors characteristic of an earlier stage.

Reid, Thomas (1710–1796)   Leader of Scottish common-sense philosophy that sought to reconcile the conflicting claims of empiricism and rationalism.

Reil, Johann Christian (1759–1813)   One of the founders of modern psychotherapy and an early advocate of experimental studies of basic psychological processes.

reinforcement   A term highly subject to theoretical interpretation but generally referring to those objects or events that result, for whatever reason, in an increased probability of responding.

relativism   The doctrine that knowledge is not absolute; rather, it is a product of human mental processes with all their inherent limitations. Thus, according to the position, truths change as a function of time, place, and circumstance.

religious mode of existence   Kierkegaard's expression for an orientation to life marked by a deep sensitivity to one's contingency and dependence on God.

Renaissance   Literally, the term means rebirth. That period in history from approximately 1300 to 1600 marked by the rediscovery of Greek classics, a new interest in mathematics, expanding geographic knowledge, and a wider epistemology.

Renaissance humanism   Refers to a new interest in human affairs. It was manifested in art as the subject shifted from theological figures to human figures and in music as the subject shifted from the sacred to the secular. In science there was a new interest in physiological and anatomical studies and a general new focus on topics of human concern.

repression   An ego defense mechanism in which dangerous thoughts, memories, or perceptions are forced out of consciousness and into the unconscious realm.

resistance   Failure to cooperate with the therapist presumably because of the trauma of dealing with unconscious materials that are about to be brought to the surface.

respondent conditioning   Pavlovian conditioning that investigates correlations between unconditioned and conditioned stimuli.

response compression   In psychophysics, equal intervals on a physical scale may be experienced as a diminishing series. Illustrated in the experience of a diminishing series associated with a three-way light.

Rhazes (c. 854–c. 925)   Physician and author of medical texts. Argued against demonology, superstitous religious beliefs, and the arbitrary use of authority in science. He advocated a rational and empirical approach to the problems of medicine and psychology.

Rogers, Carl R. (1902–1987)   One of the most innovative figures in the tradition of humanistic psychology, remembered for his revolutionary attempts to wed psychotherapy with more traditional experimental psychology. His radical emphasis on the person represented a unique war against the authorities of institutions and systems.

Romanes, George John (1848–1894)   English biologist and Darwinian who helped found a science of comparative psychology. He is often criticized for his anecdotal methods, but he was aware of the problems of anecdotalism and argued for a broad methodology.

Rush, Benjamin (1745–1813)   Early American physician who argued for liberal reforms such as the abolition of slavery and of public whippings. His book *Medical Inquiries and Observations Upon the Diseases of the Mind* advocated humane treatment for the mentally ill. He understood the value of warm baths, meaningful employment, and a supportive psychological environment as part of the treatment program for patients.

Rychlak, Joseph (1928–)   A leader in the humanistic psychology tradition who has argued for a rigorous humanistic psychology. He sees no necessary contradictions between humanistic psychology and modern views of science.

Sabuco, Oliva (1562–1590) Late Renaissance writer who emphasized the wisdom of moderation. Sabuco was among the first to understand the role of emotions in physical and psychological health.

Sanger, Margaret (1883–1966) American reformer deeply concerned about women's health issues. She was instrumental in making accurate information about contraception available to the public. She was a founder of Planned Parenthood Federation of America.

Scaliger, Julius Caesar (1484–1558) A Renaissance scholar remembered for his work on the kinesthetic and muscle senses. One of the first to emphasize the role of the musculature in cognitive and affective processes.

Scott, Walter Dill (1869–1955) American psychologist and a critical early figure in the study of applied and industrial psychology as well as the psychology of advertising.

Scripture, Edward Wheeler (1864–1945) As Wundt's student, Scripture identified four fundamental processes of associations: preparation, influence, expansion, and after-effect. He later had a productive career as a psychologist at Yale University, Clark University, and as a phonetician in Europe.

Sechenov, Ivan (1829–1905) Commonly regarded as the founder of Russian physiology. The author of *Reflexes of the Brain,* Sechenov argued for an objective psychology wedded to physiology and the principles of monistic materialism.

secondary attention According to Titchener, secondary attention is learned and persists under difficult conditions (e.g., staying alert while studying even under noisy circumstances).

secondary memory In James's psychology, secondary memory is memory proper or memory of past events that are not in present consciousness.

secondary process According to Freud, plans and strategies of the ego that provide compromised means for the expression of id impulses.

secondary qualities Powers of objects that contribute to specific sensations such as colors, tastes, and sounds.

Seguin, Edouard (1812–1880) French pioneer in the study and treatment of mentally deficient individuals. Seguin's efforts helped inspire fund raising for training facilities for the mentally deficient. His

work also encouraged the development of scientific studies of basic psychological processes.

self According to Jung, the self is the unifying component of the psychic apparatus. The self is that which seeks optimal development, integration, and wholeness.

self-actualization A term employed by psychologists such as Kurt Goldstein, Carl Gustav Jung, and Abraham Maslow. The term generally refers to fulfillment of positive potentials.

self-esteem A topic explored by William James and discussed in his work as a function of the ratio of success to pretensions.

sensation According to Wundt, an element of consciousness referring to simple awareness of stimulation.

Sextus Empiricus Roman physician and skeptic who criticized dogmatic certainty and argued for the virtues associated with an attitude of suspended judgment.

shadow According to Jung, the dark side of the personality that appears antagonistic to the social goals of the ego. Includes primitive materials from the collective unconscious; these materials may provoke negative emotions such as fear or anger.

Sherrington, Charles (1857–1952) Sherrington was awarded the Nobel prize in 1932 for his monumental work on the integrative action of the nervous system. He laid the foundations for modern work in neurophysiology and coined many of the terms that are common in the field today.

skepticism One of the major systematic approaches to philosophy following the death of Aristotle. The concerns of the skeptics were largely focused on the problems of epistemology and the good life.

Skinner, Burrhus Frederic (1904–1990) One of the foremost behaviorists of the twentieth century, who argued that scientific psychology must concern itself with the analysis of behavior rather than the study of the mind.

social interest The term employed by Adler referring to the capacity of the individual to identify with the larger social good and the altruistic goals of society.

social self In James's view, a dimension of selfhood born in various social contexts. Thus, the self in the presence of a parent may be different in some respects than the self in the presence of a friend.

Socrates (c. 470–c. 399 B.C.) Teacher of Plato and so important in Greek thought that all philosophy before him is called pre-Socratic. He reacted against the relativism of Protagoras and taught that reason is the basis of true knowledge. He emphasized the importance of self-knowledge and is thus an important figure in the history of psychological thought.

solipsism   A subjective philosophical position that makes the claim that the only possible knowledge is self-knowledge.

sophist   A type of teacher in ancient Greece. The sophists often emphasized relativism and how to live successfully. They often offered plausible but fallacious arguments. Hence, terms such as *sophistry* and *sophistic* refer to arguments that appear to be sound, but are later found to be superficial or fallacious.

specific energies of nerves   Early belief that nerves are highly specialized so that they can carry out only one kind of function.

Spencer, Herbert (1820–1903)   English philosopher who attempted to apply evolutionary thought to all branches of human knowledge. Evolution was thus a unifying principle for his philosophy. He is sometimes regarded as a forerunner of American functionalism.

Spinoza, Baruch (Benedict) (1632–1677)   A key figure in the rationalist tradition, Spinoza sought to demonstrate the artificiality of many of the dualisms introduced by Descartes. For Spinoza, there is no gulf between God and the world or mind and body. He believed that most dualities result from problems of language, but different language systems may simply represent different ways of looking at the same reality.

spiritual self   In James's view, the self that is "the home of interest" or that sits in judgment of other selves. The spiritual self, for James, is also the source of effortful striving.

spontaneous recovery   Following extinction trials, a conditioned stimulus may lose its ability to produce a conditioned response. However, following a period of rest, the conditioned stimulus may once again elicit the conditioned response.

Spurzheim, Johann Kaspar (1776–1832)   A student and disciple of Franz Josph Gall, Spurzheim helped develop and popularize the theory of personality and character known as phrenology. Spurzheim developed elaborate charts designed to assess personality via analysis of the shape of the skull.

statistics   Literally refers to characteristics of the state. A branch of mathematics devoted to the study of appropriate means of collecting and interpreting data. A common focus is on establishing the probability of occurrence of a given event.

Stensen, Neils (1638–1682)   Sometimes known as Nicolas Steno. He exposed the anatomical errors of Descartes by demonstrating that animals have pineal glands and that the pineal body is not richly supplied with nerves. He further argued that, contrary to the predictions of Descartes, the pineal gland could not possibly move from side to side. Such findings dealt a severe blow to Descartes's theory of nervous action.

stereoscope   An instrument that produces a three-dimensional effect by simultaneously presenting slightly different two-dimensional views to the left and right eyes.

stimulus intensity dynamism   A term employed by Clark Hull referring to the capacity of a stimulus to energize or direct behavior.

stoicism   A major post-Aristotelian philosophy emphasizing discipline and suppression of desire as means to the greatest happiness and virtue.

stream of thought   A concept advanced by William James that illustrates his view that consciousness is not composed of static elements. According to James, even a strong stimulus, such as a clap of thunder, is not pure; rather, it is "thunder-breaking-upon-silence-and-contrasting-with-it." James regarded consciousness as ever changing; each successive thought, even of the same object, changes by some degree.

structuralism   A system of psychological thought associated primarily with Edward Bradford Titchener, who attempted to model psychology after the more mature sciences, especially chemistry. Structuralism employed the method of introspection to search for the elements of consciousness and the rules by which elements combine.

Stumpf, Carl (1848–1936)   Student of Brentano and pioneer in the psychology of music. His holistic orientation focused on meaningful mental phenomena rather than arbitrary elements of consciousness.

style of life   Adler's term referring to unique personality qualities (including plans, strategies, and projects) designed to accomplish specific goals in life.

sublimation   According to Freud, any of a variety of socially acceptable activities such as work, play, or philanthropic activities that represent a rechanneling of sexual energy into socially acceptable forms. In general, sublimation involves the substitution of a higher, more socially acceptable activity for a less socially acceptable one.

superego   According to Freud, that part of the personality consisting of internalized social norms, values, and ideals. Like the id, the superego is not rational. It serves the goal of perfection and attempts to appropriate ego activities to serve its goal.

Swammerdam, Jan (1637–1680) With a nerve muscle preparation, Swammerdam performed a series of classic experiments demonstrating that a flexed muscle could not possibly grow larger because of the inflow of animal spirits. Swammerdam's demonstrations were contrary to predictions derived from the theory of nervous action advanced by Descartes.

synchronicity A term employed by Jung that describes unlikely simultaneous occurrences or events not easily explained by the usual principles of causality.

synthetic a priori According to Kant, a synthetic a priori truth is known intuitively and is informative about the world. Descartes's statement "I think, therefore I am" may be regarded as a synthetic a priori truth. The truth of the statement is grasped intuitively, but the statement is not a mere tautology; rather, it is informative about the world.

system An organized way of envisioning the world or some aspect of the world.

Taylor, Harriet Wife of John Stuart Mill. Collaborated with Mill and likely influenced his thought on feminism.

teleology Refers to purpose or design. According to Aristotle, design or purpose is an intrinsic part of the natural order. Thus, it is the purpose of a seed to sprout under the proper conditions and grow into a plant. Such a teleology can be thought of as intrinsic and is in contrast with the extrinsic teleology encountered in certain religions. Extrinsic teleology implies that things do what they do because they fulfill purposes imposed by deity.

Thales An early Greek cosmologist active around 600 B.C. Thales was known for his contention that water is the primordial substance. He was also interested in the problem of movement and the nature of motive forces that make movement possible.

Theana An accomplished philosopher and wife of Pythagoras who played a key role in the educational activities of the Pythagorean school.

Theophrastus (c. 372–c. 287 B.C.) Succeeded Aristotle at the Lyceum. Extended many of Aristotle's ideas but emphasized material and efficient causes. He is sometimes regarded as the Father of Botany.

third-force psychology A term commonly employed to refer to humanistic psychology viewed as an alternative to behaviorism and psychoanalysis.

Thorndike, Edward Lee (1874–1949) U.S. psychologist who studied with James at Harvard and Cattell at Columbia. Thorndike was a pioneer in the experimental investigation of animal behavior and advanced one of the earliest and most influential learning theories. His practical work focused on behavior, and he can be considered a forerunner of behaviorism. Nevertheless, he believed that psychology might be best served by a variety of methods and viewpoints.

threshold That stimulus intensity (or change in intensity) that is detected 50 percent of the time.

throwness Heidegger's term referring to those conditions, forces, or facts that do not easily yield to human effort.

Thucydides (c. 460–c. 401 B.C.) Greek historian and author of the *History of the Peloponnesian War.* He worked to achieve accurate naturalistic accounts of historical events.

Titchener, Edward Bradford (1867–1927) One of Wilhelm Wundt's best-known students and founder of a system of psychological thought known as structuralism. Titchener was a dominant force in U.S. psychology from the early 1890s until his death in 1927.

Tolman, Edward Chace (1886–1959) One of the leading behaviorists of the twentieth century, remembered for his attempts to combine features of behaviorism, Gestalt psychology, and McDougall's psychology. Tolman emphasized the purposive nature of behavior. He is properly regarded as one of the precursors of late twentieth-century cognitive psychology.

transference According to Freud, this term refers to emotional attachments that patients may develop for their therapists.

tridimensional theory of feeling According to Wundt, a theory of feeling marked by three fundamental directions: pleasure and pain, strain and relaxation, and excitation and quiescence.

truncated law of effect Thorndike's later theory that reward strengthens associations. In his later work, Thorndike raised doubts that punishment serves to weaken associations.

Tuke, Daniel Hack (1827–1895) For many years, the head of the York Retreat in England and a key figure in promoting scientific studies of mental illness and humanitarian treatment of people who are mentally ill.

Tuke, William (1732–1822) Philanthropist who helped found the York Retreat in England. The York Retreat incorporated the most advanced humanitarian treatment techniques available in its day.

ultramaximal inhibition Sometimes called Protective Transmarginal Inhibition. Refers to the effects of a severe biological or psychological insult. Such insults may produce a shocklike state that Pavlov regarded as protective. Massive inhibition, in this case, may serve a protective function by blocking out further stimulation. In shocklike states, subjects may feel no pain and be incapable of intelligent response.

ultraparadoxical phase Following a severe shock, some subjects display an unusual reversal of values. Thus, a formerly positive or loved stimulus is regarded negatively or hated and a formerly negative or hated stimulus is regarded positively or loved. Such conversions may be relatively permanent.

Umwelt Literally, the world around. Refers to the physical world or the environment.

Unamuno, Miguel de (1864–1936) Spanish philosopher who was deeply concerned about the dangers of specialization and reductionism. Unamuno also stressed the importance of affect and warned against a purely cognitive or intellectual approach to the problems of psychology.

unconditioned positive regard Rogers's term for a belief in the intrinsic worth of another individual. Unconditioned positive regard contrasts with the kind of acceptance or love that comes with conditions.

unconditioned reflex (UCR) Any naturally occurring reflex to a strong stimulus. Examples include salivation when hungry in the presence of food, withdrawal from a painful stimulus, or constriction of the pupil with increasing light.

unconditioned stimulus (UCS) A stimulus that is biologically adequate to produce an unconditioned reflex.

uniformitarianism The belief that evolutionary change is gradual and that most change occurs over vast stretches of time. Contrast with *catastrophe theory*.

Unzer, Johann (1727–1799) First to apply the word *reflex* to simple sensorimotor functions. Also introduced the terms *afferent* and *efferent*.

Upanishads Vedic treatises dealing with philosophical and psychological matters. See *Vedas*.

utilitarianism A philosophy advanced by Jeremy Bentham emphasizing the idea that the moral basis of action should be the greatest good for the greatest number.

valence According to Lewin, the positive or negative characteristics of objects in the life space.

variability hypothesis A commonly held nineteenth-century belief that, in all things physical and mental, men are more variable than women. The research of Leta Stetter Hollingworth effectively dismantled the variability hypothesis.

Vedas Oldest sacred books of India setting forth many early ideas on psychological matters.

verbal learning theory A branch of functionalism and neobehaviorism concerned with associationist explanations of memory and forgetting.

Vesalius, Andreas (1514–1564) Physician and anatomist known for his empirical approach to anatomy based on actual dissections. He revolutionized the study of the human body much as Renaissance explorers such as Columbus and Magellan revolutionized knowledge of geography.

vital spirits In Galen's pneuma concept of the soul, vital spirit refers to activities located in the heart that regulate or control body heat.

Vives, Juan Luis (1492–1540) Spanish humanist who advocated an empirical approach to psychology. His book *De Anima et Vita* is a rich source of Renaissance thought on psychological topics.

Voltaire, François-Marie Arouet de (1694–1778) French philosopher who advanced the cause of new philosophies based on observation and experiment. His sharp attacks on untestable theories and theological dogma continually placed him at risk.

voluntarism Technical term for the system of psychology advanced by Wilhelm Wundt. Voluntary behaviors are those that are varied to meet the demands of varying circumstances.

von Ehrenfels, Christian (1859–1932) One of the first to argue that form qualities are given immediately in experience. Although Ehrenfels believed that the whole is more than the sum of the parts, he still believed that it was derivative and thus acts simply like another part.

von Restorff effect Refers to superiority of recall for isolated items in a list compared to more homogeneous items.

Wallace, Alfred Russel (1823–1913) Simultaneously with Darwin, advanced a theory of organic evolution based on the concept of natural selection.

Washburn, Margaret Floy (1871–1939) First woman to earn a doctorate in psychology and the second female president of the American Psychological Association. Washburn made significant contributions to the study of comparative psychology and was well known for her "motor theory of consciousness."

Watson, John Broadus (1878–1958) Founder of American behaviorism and twenty-fourth president of the American Psychological Association. Watson's system is remembered for its identity with the natural sciences and extreme emphasis on the environment in shaping behavior. With a strong belief in determinism and materialism, Watson argued that complete prediction and control of behavior could be achieved by a truly scientific psychology.

Weber, Ernst Heinrich (1795–1878) Well-known nineteenth-century physiologist who was the first to establish a quantitative relationship between the physical properties of stimuli and the experience of those stimuli. Weber's book, *The Sense of Touch,* launched the field of psychophysics.

Weber's Illusion The perception that two points of a compass appear to move apart when the compass is moved over an insensitive area of the skin. By contrast, the two points appear to move together when the compass is moved over sensitive areas of the skin.

Weber's Law First quantitative law in psychology expressed as $\Delta R/R = K$ where R = the amount of existing stimulation, ΔR = the amount of stimulation that must be added to produce a just noticeable difference, and K = a constant.

Weiss, Albert Paul (1879–1931) The most consistent and thoroughgoing behaviorist, who compared psychology with physics. Weiss believed that psychology, as a science, must reject all mentalistic concepts.

Wernicke, Carl (1848–1905) German neurologist and psychiatrist who discovered the speech comprehension area in the left temporal lobe of the brain.

Wertheimer, Max (1880–1943) Founder of the Gestalt school of thought and author of the influential book, *Productive Thinking.*

Whytt, Robert (1714–1766) First to identify clearly the components of a reflex in terms of the action of a stimulus on nervous tissue, resulting in a response.

William of Ockham (c. 1285–1349) An early philosopher friendly to empirical methods and strongly influenced by Thomas Aquinas. See *Ockham's Razor.*

Wisconsin General Test Apparatus An apparatus designed by Harry Harlow to study form discriminiation in primates.

Witmer, Lightner (1867–1956) One of Wundt's students. Founded the first psychological clinic and coined the expression *clinical psychology.*

Wolff, Christian von (1679–1754) German philosopher and author of early books entitled *Empirical Psychology* (1732) and *Rational Psychology* (1734). Wolff believed in both empirical and rational approaches to psychology, but argued that rational approaches would be more fruitful and lead to the discovery of principles by which the mind operates.

Wollstonecraft, Mary (1759–1797) The most visible early pioneer in the battle for the rights of women. Author of *A Vindication of the Rights of Women.*

Woodworth, Robert Sessions (1869–1962) A pioneer psychologist in the functionalist tradition who greatly extended the domain of experimental psychology. Woodworth was one of the first U.S. psychologists to emphasize the centrality of motivation. His text, *Experimental Psychology,* may be the most important classic in the field.

Wooley, Helen (1874–1947) American psychologist who emphasized practical social problems in her research on educational psychology.

Wundt, Wilhelm Maximilian (1832–1920) The founder of the first psychology laboratory that functioned for a sustained period of time. Wundt also advanced the first systematic vision of psychology known as voluntarism. He is also the first person who, without qualification, can be thought of as a psychologist. His *Principles of Physiological Psychology* is one of the great classics in the discipline. More than any other, he can be viewed as the founder of modern psychology.

Xenophanes (c. 560–c. 478 B.C.) An early Greek philosopher remembered for his epistemological skepticism. He argued that human beings do not have certain knowledge and he scoffed at anthropomorphic concepts of deity.

yang Ancient Chinese concept representing such qualities as force, hardness, masculinity, and heat. Contrasts with but also complements the concept of Yin.

yin Ancient Chinese concept representing such qualities as softness, coldness, passivity, and moistness. Contrasts with but also complements the concept of Yang.

Young, Thomas (1773–1829) English physiologist who formulated the trichromatic (red, green, blue) model of color vision. He speculated that retinal structures must therefore be specialized for color primaries.

Young-Helmholtz trichromatic theory Young's theory that color vision is produced by separate receptor systems on the retina that are responsive to primary colors (red, green, and blue-violet). Maxwell and Helmholtz studied Young's theory in the nineteenth century.

Zarathustra Major prophet of the Zoroastrian religion.

Zeigarnik effect Tendency to remember incompleted tasks better than completed ones.

Zeitgeist The spirit of the time. Contrasts with the great-person theory of history and emphasizes the importance of time and place (*Ortgeist*) as conditions for the production and acceptance of new ideas.

Zend-Avesta See *Avesta*.

Zeno of Cyprus (c. 335–c. 263 B.C.) Founder of the post-Aristotelian school of stoicism, which emphasized self-control, austerity, and suppression as guides to virtue and happiness.

Zeno of Elea Active around 450 B.C., Zeno was a follower of Parmenides. He is remembered for paradoxes that supposedly revealed contradictions between reason and the senses. His paradoxes of motion are particularly noteworthy. For example, an arrow on its way toward a target presents a certain paradox. It must first travel half the distance, but then it must travel half the remaining distance. Because Zeno thought it possible to divide forever, the arrow should never reach its target.

REFERENCES

Adler, A. (1929). *The science of living.* Garden City, NY: Garden City Publishing.

Adler, A. (1938). *Social interest: A challenge to mankind* (J. Linton & R. Vaughan, Trans.). London: Faber and Faber.

Adler, A. (1957). *Understanding human nature* (W. B. Wolfe, Trans). New York: Premier Books, Fawcett World Library.

Adler, A. (1964a). The differences between individual psychology and psychoanalysis. In H. L. Ansbacher & R. R. Ansbacher (Eds.), *Alfred Adler: Superiority and social interest.* Evanston, IL: Northwestern University Press. (Original work published 1931)

Adler, A. (1964b). *The practice and theory of individual psychology* (P. Radin, Trans). London: Routledge & Kegan Paul.

Adler, H. E. (1996). Gustav Theodor Fechner: A German *Gelehrter.* In G. A. Kimble, C. A. Boneau, & M. Wertheimer (Eds.), *Portraits of pioneers in psychology* (Vol. 2, pp. 1–13). Washington, DC: American Psychological Association.

Adler, H. E. (1998). Vicissitudes of Fecherian psychophysics in America. In R. W. Rieber & K. Salzinger (Eds.), *Psychology: Theoretical-historical perspectives* (2nd ed., pp. 3–14). Washington, DC: American Psychological Association.

Afnan, S. M. (1958). *Avicenna, his life and works.* London: G. Allen & Unwin.

Aiton, E. J. (1985). *Leibniz: A biography.* Boston: Adam Hilger.

Alexander, F. G., & Selesnick, S. T. (1966). *The history of psychiatry.* New York: Harper & Row.

Allen, G. (1878a). Nation-making: A theory of national characters. *The Gentleman's Magazine, 245,* 580–591.

Allen, G. (1878b). Hellas and civilization. *The Gentleman's Magazine, 245,* 156–170.

Allen, G. W. (1967). *William James: A biography.* New York: Viking.

Allett, J. (1996). Crowd psychology and the theory of democratic elitism: The contribution of William McDougall. *Political Psychology, 17,* 213–227.

Allport, G. W. (1937). *Personality: A psychological interpretation.* New York: Henry Holt.

Allport, G. W. (1950). *The individual and his religion.* New York: Macmillan.

Allport, G. W. (1954). *The nature of prejudice.* Cambridge, MA: Addison-Wesley.

Allport, G. W. (1955). *Becoming: Basic considerations for a psychology of personality.* New Haven, CT: Yale University Press.

Allport, G. W. (1961). *Pattern and growth in personality.* New York: Holt, Rinehart and Winston.

Allport, G. W. (1985). Preface. In V. E. Frankl (Author), *Man's search for meaning.* New York: Washington Square Press.

Allport, G. W., Vernon, P. E., & Lindzey, G. (1951). *A study of values* (rev. ed.). Boston: Houghton Mifflin.

American Psychological Association distinguished scientific contribution awards: 1957. (1958). *American Psychologist, 13,* 155–158.

Anderson, F. H. (Ed.). (1960). *Francis Bacon: Baron of Verulam, Viscount St. Albans.* New York: Liberal Arts Press.

Andresen, J. (1991). Skinner and Chomsky 30 years later: The return of the repressed. *Behavior Analyst, 14,* 49–60.

Angell, F. (1913). Gustav Theodor Fechner. *Popular Science Monthly, 83,* 40–49.

Angell, F. (1921). Wilhelm Wundt. *American Journal of Psychology, 32,* 161–178.

Angell, J. R. (1909). The influence of Darwin on psychology. *Psychological Review, 16,* 152–169.

Angell, J. R. (1961). James Rowland Angell. In Carl Murchison (Ed.), *A history of psychology in autobiography* (Vol. 3, pp. 1–38). New York: Russell and Russell. (Original work published 1930)

Ansbacher, H. L. (1994). Was Adler a disciple of Freud? A reply. *Journal of Adlerian Theory, Research and Practice, 50,* 496–505.

Ansbacher, H. L., & Ansbacher, R. R. (1956). (Eds.). *The individual psychology of Alfred Adler.* New York: Basic Books.

Ansbacher, R. R. (1997). Alfred Adler, the man, seen by a student and friend. *Individual Psychology: Journal of Adlerian Theory, Research and Practice, 53,* 270–274.

Aristotle. (1908). *Nicomachean ethics*. In W. D. Ross (Ed.), *The works of Aristotle* (Vol. 9). Oxford: Clarendon Press.

Aristotle. (1931a). *De anima*. In W. D. Ross (Ed.), *The works of Aristotle* (Vol. 3). Oxford: Clarendon Press.

Aristotle. (1931b). *On dreams*. In W. D. Ross (Ed.), *The works of Aristotle* (Vol. 3). Oxford: Clarendon Press.

Aristotle. (1931c). *On memory and reminiscence*. In W. D. Ross (Ed.), *The works of Aristotle* (Vol. 3). Oxford: Clarendon Press.

Aristotle. (1931d). *On prophesying by dreams*. In W. D. Ross (Ed.), *The works of Aristotle* (Vol. 3). Oxford: Clarendon Press.

Arnheim, R. (1943). Gestalt and art. *Journal of Aesthetics, 2,* 71–75.

Arnheim, R. (1962). *The genesis of a painting: Picasso's Guernica*. Berkeley and Los Angeles: University of California Press.

Arnheim, R. (1966). *Toward a psychology of art*. Berkeley and Los Angeles: University of California Press.

Arnheim, R. (1974). *Art and visual perception: A psychology of the creative eye*. Berkeley and Los Angeles: University of California Press.

Arnheim, R. (1986). *New essays on the psychology of art*. Berkeley and Los Angeles: University of California Press.

Asch, S. E. (1955). Opinions and social pressure. *Scientific American, 193,* 31–35.

Asch, S. E. (1968). Wolfgang Köhler: 1887–1967. *American Journal of Psychology, 81,* 110–119.

Ash, M. G. (1985). Gestalt psychology: Origins in Germany and reception in the United States. In C. E. Buxton (Ed.), *Points of view in the modern history of psychology* (pp. 295–344). New York: Academic Press.

Ash, M. G. (1995). *Gestalt psychology in German culture, 1890–1967: Holism and the quest for objectivity*. New York: Cambridge University Press.

Ash, M. G., & Woodward, W. R. (1987). (Eds.). *Psychology in twentieth-century thought and society*. New York: Cambridge University Press.

Atherton, M. (1990). *Berkeley's revolution in vision*. Ithaca, NY: Cornell University Press.

Augustine, A. (1955). *Augustine: Confessions and enchiridion* (A. C. Outler, Ed. and Trans.). Philadelphia: Westminster Press.

Austin, C. R. (1989). *Human embryos: The debate on assisted reproduction*. New York: Oxford University Press.

Averill, L. A. (1990). Recollections of Clark's G. Stanley Hall. *Journal of the History of the Behavioral Sciences, 26,* 107–113.

Baars, B. J. (1986). *The cognitive revolution in psychology*. New York: Guilford.

Babkin, B. P. (1949). *Pavlov: A biography*. Chicago: University of Chicago Press.

Bacon, F. (1960). *The New Organon*. New York: Liberal Arts Press. (Original work published 1620)

Baddeley, A. (1990). *Human memory: Theory and practice*. Boston: Allyn & Bacon.

Bakan, D. (1958). *Sigmund Freud and the Jewish mystical tradition*. Princeton, NJ: D. Van Nostrand.

Baldwin, J. M. (1894). The origin of right-handedness. *Popular Science Monthly, 44,* 606–615.

Baldwin, J. M. (1895). *Mental development in the child and the race*. New York: Macmillan.

Baldwin, J. M. (1913). *History of psychology: A sketch and an interpretation* (2 vols.). New York: G. P. Putnam's Sons.

Barnes, J. (Ed.) (1984). *The complete works of Aristotle* (Vol. 1). Princeton, NJ: Princeton University Press.

Barnes, R. C. (2000). Viktor Frankl's logotherapy: Spirituality and meaning in the new millennium. *Texas Counseling Association, 28,* 24–31.

Bartlett, F. C. (1923). *Psychology and primitive culture*. Cambridge: Cambridge University Press.

Bartlett, F. C. (1932). *Remembering: A study in experimental and social psychology*. New York: Macmillan.

Bartol, C. R., & Bartol, A. M. (1999). History of forensic psychology. In A. K. Hess & I. B. Weiner (Eds.), *The handbook of forensic psychology* (pp. 3–23). New York: Wiley.

Barton, A. (1992). Humanistic contributions to the field of psychotherapy: Appreciating the human and liberating the therapist. *Humanistic Psychologist, 20,* 332–348.

Beach, F. A. (1955). The descent of instinct. *Psychological Review, 62,* 401–410.

Beatty, B. (1998). From laws of learning to a science of values: Efficiency and morality in Thorndike's educational psychology. *American Psychologist, 53,* 1145–1152.

Beck, J. (1968). Herman von Helmholtz. In D. L. Sills (Ed.), *International Encyclopedia of the Social Sciences* (Vol. 6, pp. 345–350). New York: Macmillan and Free Press.

Becker, C. L. (1932). *The heavenly city of the eighteenth-century philosophers*. New Haven: Yale University Press.

Behrens, R. R. (1998). On Max Wertheimer and Pablo Picasso: Gestalt theory, cubism and camouflage. *Gestalt Theory, 20,* 111–118.

Benjamin, L. T., Jr. (1974). Prominent psychologists: A selected bibliography of biographical sources. *Journal Supplement Abstract Service. Catalog of Selected Documents in Psychology, 4,* 1 (Ms. No. 535).

Benjamin, L. T., Jr. (1975). The pioneering work of Leta Hollingworth in the psychology of women. *Nebraska History, 56,* 493–505.

Benjamin, L. T., Jr. (1997). *A history of psychology: Original sources and contemporary research.* New York: McGraw-Hill.

Benjamin, L. T., Jr. (2001). American psychology's struggles with its curriculum; should a thousand flowers bloom? *American Psychologist, 56,* 735–742.

Benjamin, L. T., Jr., & Heider, K. L. (1976). History of psychology in biography: A bibliography. *Journal Supplement Abstract Service. Catalog of Selected Documents in Psychology, 6,* 61 (Ms. No. 1276).

Benjamin, L. T., Jr., & Nielsen-Gammon, E. (1999). B. F. Skinner and psychotechnology: The case of the heir conditioner. *Review of General Psychology, 3,* 155–167.

Benjamin, L. T., Jr., Pratt, R., Watlington, D., Aaron, L., Bonar, T., Fitzgerald, S., Franklin, M., Jimenez, B., & Lester, R. (1989). *A history of American psychology in notes and news, 1883–1945: An index to journal sources.* Millwood, NY: Kraus International Publications.

Benn, S. I. (1967). Punishment. In P. Edwards (Ed.), *The encyclopedia of philosophy* (Vol. 7, pp. 29–36). New York: Macmillan and Free Press.

Berenda, C. W. (1965). *World visions and the image of man: Cosmologies as reflections of man.* New York: Vantage Press.

Bergmann, G. (1956). The contribution of John B. Watson. *Psychological Review, 63,* 265–276.

Berkeley, G. (1935). *Three dialogues between Hylas and Philonous.* Chicago: Open Court Publishing. (Original work published 1713)

Berkeley, G. (1948). An essay towards a new theory of vision. In A. A. Luce (Ed.), *The works of George Berkeley, Bishop of Cloyne* (Vol. 1, pp. 141–240). London: Thomas Nelson & Sons. (Original work published 1709)

Berkeley, G. (1957). *Treatise concerning the principles of human knowledge.* Indianapolis: Bobbs Merrill. (Original work published 1710)

Bernard, L. L. (1924). *Instinct: A study in social psychology.* New York: Henry Holt.

Bernard, W. (1972). Spinoza's influence on the rise of scientific psychology: A neglected chapter in the history of psychology. *Journal of the History of the Behavioral Sciences, 8,* 208–215.

Bettmann, O. L. (1974). *The good old days—They were terrible!* New York: Random House.

Bickhard, M. H. (2001). The tragedy of operationalism. *Theory and Psychology, 11,* 35–44.

Biddle, W. (1995). *A field guide to germs.* New York: Henry Holt.

Binet, A., & Féré, C. (1891). *Animal magnetism* (3rd ed.). London: Kegan Paul, Trench, Trubener. (Original work published 1887)

Binger, C. A. (1969). The dreams of Benjamin Rush. *American Journal of Psychiatry, 125,* 1653–1659.

Bishop, P. (1999). *Jung in contexts: A reader.* Florence, KY: Taylor & Francis/Routledge.

Bjork, D. W. (1993). *B. F. Skinner: A life.* New York: Basic Books.

Bloom, H. (Ed.). (1987). *Michel de Montaigne.* New York: Chelsea House.

Blumenthal, A. L. (1975). A reappraisal of Wilhelm Wundt. *American Psychologist, 30,* 1081–1088.

Blumenthal, A. L. (1979). The founding father we never knew. *Contemporary Psychology, 24,* 547–550.

Bochner, S. (1973). Mathematics in cultural history. In P. P. Wiener (Ed.), *Dictionary of the history of ideas.* New York: Charles Scribner's Sons.

Bohan, J. S. (1992a). *Re-placing women in psychology: Readings toward a more inclusive history.* Dubuque, IA: Kendall/Hunt.

Bohan, J. S. (1992b). *Seldom seen, rarely heard: Women's place in psychology.* Boulder: Westview Press.

Boring, E. G. (1927). Edward Bradford Titchener. *American Journal of Psychology, 38,* 489–506.

Boring, E. G. (1942). *Sensation and perception in the history of experimental psychology.* New York: Appleton-Century-Crofts.

Boring, E. G. (1950). *A history of experimental psychology* (2nd ed.). Englewood Cliffs, NJ: Prentice Hall.

Boring, E. G. (1953). John Dewey: 1859–1952. *American Journal of Psychology, 66,* 145–147.

Boring, E. G. (1961). *Psychologist at large.* New York: Basic Books.

Boring, E. G. (1963). *History, psychology, and science: Selected papers.* New York: Wiley.

Bourne, L. E., Dominowski, R. L., Loftus, E. F., & Healy, A. F. (1986). *Cognitive processes.* Englewood Cliffs, NJ: Prentice Hall.

Bower, G. H. (1962). An association model for response and training variables in paired-associate learning. *Psychological Review, 69,* 347–53.

Bower, G. H. (2000). A brief history of memory research. In E. Tulving & F. I. M. Craik (Eds.), *The Oxford handbook of memory* (pp. 3–32). New York: Oxford University Press.

Bozeman, T. W. (1977). *Protestants in an age of science: The Baconian ideal and ante-bellum American religious thought.* Chapel Hill: University of North Carolina Press.

Braaten, E. B., & Viney, W. (2000). Some late nineteenth-century perspectives on sex and emotional expression. *Psychological Reports, 86,* 575–585.

Bracken, P. J. (1999). The importance of Heidegger for psychiatry. *Philosophy, Psychiatry and Psychology, 6,* 83–85.

Brackman, A. C. (1980). *A delicate arrangement: The strange case of Charles Darwin and Alfred Russel Wallace.* New York: Times Books.

Brailsford, H. N. (1963). Mary Wollstonecraft. In E. R. A. Seligman (Ed.), *Encyclopedia of the Social Sciences* (Vol. 15, pp. 436–437). New York: Macmillan.

Brennan, B. P. (1968). *William James.* New York: Twayne Publishers.

Brentano, F. (1973). *Psychology from an empirical standpoint.* (A. C. Rancurello, D. B. Terrell, & L. L. McAlister, Trans.). London: Routledge & Kegan Paul. (Original work published 1874)

Brett, G. S. (1965). *A history of psychology* (2nd rev. ed.). (Edited and abridged by R. S. Peters). Cambridge, MA: MIT Press (Original work published 1912–1921)

Brewer, C. L. (Speaker). (1989). *Some observations on the life and times of John Watson* (cassette recording).

Brewer, W. F. (2000). Bartlett, functionalism, and modern schema theories. *Journal of Mind and Behavior, 21,* 37–44.

Brickhouse, T. C., & Smith, N. D. (1990). What makes Socrates a good man? *Journal of the History of Philosophy, 28,* 169–179.

Bridges, J. H. (1976). *Life and work of Roger Bacon: An introduction to the Opus Majus.* Merrick, NY: Richwood Publishing.

Bridgman, P. W. (1927). *The logic of modern physics.* New York: Macmillan.

Bridgman, P. W. (1954). Remarks on the present state of operationism. *The Scientific Monthly, 79,* 224–226.

Bridgman, P. W. (1955). *Reflections of a physicist.* New York: Philosophical Library.

Bringmann, W. G., Bringmann, N. J., & Balance, W. D. G. (1980). Wilhelm Maximilian Wundt 1832–1874: The formative years. In W. G. Bringmann & R. D. Tweney (Eds.), *Wundt studies: A centennial collection* (pp. 13–32). Toronto: C. J. Hogrefe.

Bringmann, W. G., Bringmann, M. W., & Early, C. E. (1992). G. Stanley Hall and the history of psychology. *American Psychologist, 47,* 281–289.

Bringmann, W. G., Bringmann, N. J., & Ungerer, G. A. (1980). The establishment of Wundt's laboratory: An archival and documentary study. In W. G. Bringmann & R. D. Tweney (Eds.), *Wundt studies: A centennial collection* (pp. 123–157). Toronto: C. J. Hogrefe.

Bromberg, W. (1954). *The mind of man: A history of psychotherapy and psychoanalysis.* New York: Harper Torchbacks.

Bromberg, W. (1975). *From shaman to psychotherapist: A history of the treatment of mental illness.* Chicago, IL: Henry Regnery.

Brown, J. A. C. (1964). *Freud and the post-Freudians.* Baltimore: Penguin.

Brown, L. (1993). *The new shorter Oxford English Dictionary* (2 vols.). New York: Oxford University Press.

Brown-Sequard, C. E. (1890). Have we two brains or one? *Forum, 9,* 627–643.

Brožek, J. (1972). Russian contributions on brain and behavior. In J. Brožek and D. I. Slobin (Eds.), *Psychology in the USSR: An historical perspective.* White Plains, NY: International Arts and Sciences Press. Also published in (1966) *Science, 152,* 930–932.

Bruce, D. (1998). Lashley's rejection of connectionism. *History of Psychology, 1,* 160–164.

Bruner, J. S., Goodnow, J. J., & Austin, G. A. (1956). *A study of thinking.* New York: Wiley.

Brush, S. G. (1974a). The prayer test. *American Scientist, 62,* 561–563.

Brush, S. G. (1974b). Should the history of science be rated x? *Science, 183,* 1164–1172.

Buckley, K. W. (1989). *Mechanical man: John Broadus Watson and the beginnings of behaviorism.* New York: Guilford.

Buckman, S. S. (1895). Babies and monkeys. *Popular Science Monthly, 46,* 371–388.

Buffon, C. de (1977). *Selections from natural history general and particular* (Vol. 1). New York: Arno Press. (Original work published 1780–1785)

Buie, J. (1988, November). Psychoanalysis barriers tumble: Settlement opens doors to non-MDs. *American Psychological Association Monitor, 19*(11), 1, 15.

Buncombe, M. (1995). *The substance of consciousness: An argument for interactionism.* Aldershot, England: Avebury.

Buranelli, V. (1975). *The wizard from Vienna: Franz Anton Mesmer.* New York: Coward, McCann & Geoghean.

Burek, D. M., Koek, K. E., & Novallo, A. (Eds.). (1989). *Encyclopedia of associations* (24th ed.). Detroit: Gale Research.

Burke, R. B. (Trans.) (1962). *The Opus Majus of Roger Bacon* (2 vols.). New York: Russell and Russell.

Burston, D. (1998). Laing and Heidegger on alienation. *Journal of Humanistic Psychology, 38,* 80–93.

Burton, J. H. (1967). *Life and correspondence of David Hume* (Vol. 2). New York: Burt Franklin. (Original work published 1846)

Buss, A. R. (1977). In defense of a critical-presentist historiography: The fact–theory relationship and Marx's epistemology. *Journal of the History of the Behavioral Sciences, 13,* 252–260.

Cadwallader, T. C. (1987). Origins and accomplishments of Joseph Jastrow's 1888—founded Chain of Comparative Psychology at the University of Wisconsin. *Journal of Comparative Psychology, 101,* 231–236.

Cain, D. J. (Ed.). (2002). *Humanistic psychotherapies: Handbook of research and practice.* Washington, DC: American Psychological Association.

Calder, R. (1970). *Leonardo and the age of the eye.* New York: Simon and Schuster.

Calkins, M. W. (1893). Statistics of dreams. *American Journal of Psychology, 5,* 311–343.

Camfield, T. M. (1973). The professionalization of American psychology, 1870–1917. *Journal of the History of the Behavioral Sciences, 9,* 67–68.

Campbell, K. (1967). Materialism. In P. Edwards (Ed.), *The encyclopedia of philosophy* (Vol. 5, pp. 179–188). New York: Macmillan and Free Press.

Cannon, W. B. (1922). What strong emotions do to us. *Harpers Magazine, 145,* 234–241.

Capra, F. (1988). The role of physics in the current change of paradigms. In R. F. Kitchener (Ed.), *The world view of contemporary physics* (pp. 144–155). Albany: State University of New York Press.

Carlson, E. T. (1977). Benjamin Rush and mental health. *Annals of the New York Academy of Sciences, 291,* 95–103.

Carlson, E. T. (1981). The history of multiple personality in the United States: I. The beginnings. *American Journal of Psychiatry, 138,* 666–668.

Carlson, E. T., & Simpson, M. M. (1964). The definition of mental illness: Benjamin Rush (1745– 1813). *American Journal of Psychiatry, 121,* 209–214.

Carlson E. T., Wollock, J. L., & Noel, P. S. (Eds.). (1981). *Benjamin Rush's lectures on the mind.* Philadelphia: American Philosophical Society.

Carr, H. A. (1925). *Psychology: A study of mental activity.* New York: Longmans, Green and Co.

Carr, H. A. (1961). Harvey A. Carr. In C. Murchison (Ed.), *A history of psychology in autobiography* (Vol. 3, pp. 69–82). New York: Russell and Russell. (Original work published 1930)

Cassirer, E. (1981). *Kant's life and thought* (J. Haden, Trans.). New Haven, CT: Yale University Press.

Castiglioni, A. (1941). *A history of medicine* (E. B. Krumbhaar, Ed. and Trans.). New York: Alfred A. Knopf.

Cattell, J. M. (1890). Mental tests and measurements. *Mind, 15,* 373–381.

Cattell, J. M. (1992). Retrospect: Psychology as a profession. *Journal of Consulting and Clinical Psychology, 60,* 7–8. (Original work published 1937)

Chan, W. (1967). Confucius. In P. Edwards (Ed.), *Encyclopedia of philosophy* (Vol. 2, p. 189). New York: Macmillan and Free Press.

Chance, P. (1999). Thorndike's puzzle boxes and the origins of the experimental analysis of behavior. *Journal of the Experimental Analysis of Behavior, 72,* 433–440.

Chen, L. (2001). Perceptual organization: To reverse back the inverted (upside-down) question of feature binding. *Visual Cognition, 8,* 287–303.

Child, I. L. (1973). *Humanistic psychology and the research tradition: Their several virtues.* New York: Wiley.

Chomsky, N. (1959). A review of Skinner's Verbal Behavior. *Language, 35,* 26–58.

Christen, D. (1984). *The genesis of misogynism and woman's subordination within the Christian church.* Unpublished senior honors thesis, Colorado State University Library.

Clanchy, M. T. (1997). *Abelard: A Medieval life.* Malden, MA: Blackwell Publishers.

Clark, E. (1972). Eduard Hitzig. In C. C. Gillispie (Ed.), *Dictionary of Scientific Biography* (Vol. 6, pp. 440–441). New York: Charles Scribner's Sons.

Clark, R. W. (1971). *Einstein: The life and times.* New York: World Publishing.

Clarke, D. M. (1982). *Descartes' philosophy of science.* University Park: University of Pennsylvania Press.

Clarke, E., & O'Malley, C. D. (1968). *The human brain and spinal cord: A historical study illustrated by writings from antiquity to the twentieth century.* Berkeley & Los Angeles: University of California Press.

Cleary, T. S., & Shapiro, S. I. (1996). Abraham Maslow and Asian psychology. *Psychologia: An International Journal of Psychology in the Orient, 39,* 213–222.

Clements, R. D. (1967). Physiological-psychological thought in Juan Luis Vives. *Journal of the History of the Behavioral Sciences, 3,* 219–235.

Cleveland, G. (1905). Would woman suffrage be unwise? *The Ladies Home Journal, 22,* 7–8.

Clodd, E. (1972). *Pioneers of evolution from Thales to Huxley: With an intermediate chapter on the causes of the arrest of the movement.* New York: Books for Libraries Press. (Original work published 1897)

Coe, G. A. (1900). *The spiritual life: Studies in the science of religion.* New York: Eaton & Mains.

Cofer, C. N. (1978). Origins of the Journal of Verbal Learning and Verbal Behavior. *Journal of Verbal Learning and Verbal Behavior, 17,* 113–126.

Cohen, D. (1979). *J. B. Watson: The founder of behaviorism.* London: Routledge & Kegan Paul.

Cole, C. W., Oetting, E. R., & Hinkle, J. E. (1967). Nonlinearity of self-concept discrepancy: The value dimension. *Psychological Reports, 21,* 58–60.

Cole, T. R. (1993). The prophecy of "Senescence": G. Stanley Hall and the reconstruction of old age in twentieth-century America. In K. W. Schaie & W. A. Achenbaum (Eds.), *Societal impact on aging: Historical perspectives* (pp. 165–181). New York: Springer Publishing.

Coleman, S. R. (1981). Historical context and systematic functions of the concept of the operant. *Behaviorism, 9,* 207–226.

Collins, A. F. (1999). The enduring appeal of physiognomy: Physical appearance as a sign of temperament, character, and intelligence. *History of Psychology, 2,* 251–276.

Connors, C. (2000). Freud and the force of history: "The Project for a Scientific Psychology." In M. Rossington & A. Whitehead (Eds.), *Between the psyche and the polis: Refiguring history in literature and theory* (pp. 59–73). Aldershot, England: Ashgate.

Coon, D. J. (1992). Testing the limits of sense and science: American experimental psychologists combat spiritualism, 1880–1920. *American Psychologist, 47,* 143–151.

Coon, D. J. (1993). Standardizing the subject: Experimental psychologists, introspection, and the quest for a technoscientific ideal. *Technology and Culture, 34,* 757–783.

Coon, D. J. (1994). "Not a creature of reason": The alleged impact of Watsonian behaviorism on advertising in the 1920s. In J. T. Todd & E. K. Morris (Eds.), *Modern perspectives on John B. Watson and classical behaviorism* (pp. 37–63). Westport, CT: Greenwood.

Coon, D. J. (1996). "One moment in the world's salvation": Anarchism and the radicalization of William James. *The Journal of American History, 83,* 70–99.

Coplestone, F. (1962). *A history of philosophy Vol. 2 Medieval Philosophy Part II.* New York: Image Books.

Cottingham, J. (1979). Varieties of retribution. *Philosophical Quarterly, 29,* 238–246.

Cottingham, J., Stoothoff, R., & Murdoch, D. (1984–1985). *The philosophical writings of Descartes* (2 vols.). Cambridge: Cambridge University Press.

Craik, K. H., Hogan, R., & Wolfe, R. N. (Eds.). (1993). *Fifty years of personality psychology: Perspectives on individual differences.* New York: Plenum Press.

Cratylus. (1937). *The Dialogues of Plato* (2 vols.) (B. Jowett, Trans.). New York: Random House. (Original work published 1892)

Crews, F. (1996). The verdict on Freud. *Psychological Science, 7,* 63–68.

Crick, F. (1994). *The astonishing hypothesis: The scientific search for the soul.* New York: Charles Scribner's Sons.

Crochetière, K., Vicker, N., Parker, J., King, D. B., & Wertheimer, M. (2001). Gestalt theory and psychopathology: Some early applications of Gestalt theory to clinical psychology and psychopathology. *Gestalt Theory, 23,* 144–154.

Crombie, A. C. (1961). *Augustine to Galileo* (2nd ed.). Cambridge, MA: Harvard University Press.

Crosby, D. A. (1996). Experience as reality: The ecological metaphysics of William James. In D. A. Crosby & C. D. Hardwick (Eds.), *Religious experience and ecological responsibility* (pp. 67–87). New York: Peter Lang.

Crosby, D. A., & Viney, W. (1990, August). *Toward a psychology that is radically empirical.* Paper presented at the annual meeting of the American Psychological Association, Boston.

Crossman, E. K. (1991). Schedules of reinforcement. In W. Ishaq (Ed.), *Human behavior in today's world* (pp. 133–138). New York: Praeger.

Crowther-Heyck, H. (1999). George A. Miller, language, and the computer metaphor and mind. *History of Psychology, 2,* 37–64.

Crowther-Heyck, H. (2000). Mystery and meaning: A reply to Green (2000). *History of Psychology, 3,* 67–70.

Crutchfield, R. S. (1961). Edward Chace Tolman: 1886–1959. *American Journal of Psychology, 74,* 135–141.

Curley, E. (Ed & Trans.). (1985). *The collected works of Spinoza* (Vol. 1). Princeton, NJ: Princeton University Press.

Dain, N. (1964). *Concepts of insanity in the United States, 1789–1865.* New Brunswick, NJ: Rutgers University Press.

Dallenbach, K. M. (1967). Karl M. Dallenbach. In E. G. Boring & G. Lindzey (Eds.). *A history of psychology in autobiography* (Vol. 5, pp. 59–93). New York: Appleton-Century-Crofts.

Daly, M. (1968). *The church and the second sex.* New York: Harper & Row.

Daniels, M. (1988). The myth of self-actualization. *Journal of Humanistic Psychology, 28,* 7–38.

Danziger, K. (1979). The positivist repudiation of Wundt. *Journal of the History of the Behavioral Sciences, 15,* 205–230.

Danziger, K. (2001). Sealing off the discipline: Wilhelm Wundt and the psychology of memory. In C. D. Green & M. Shore (Eds.), *The transformation of psychology: Influences of 19th-century philosophy, technology, and natural science* (pp. 45–62). Washington, DC: American Psychological Association.

Darwin, C. (1877). A biographical sketch of an infant. *Mind, 2,* 285–294.

Darwin, C. (1897). *Journal of researches into the natural history and geology of the countries visited during the voyage of the H.M.S.* Beagle *round the world under the command of Capt. Fitz Roy, R.N.* New York: D. Appleton & Co.

Deason, G. B. (1986). Reformation theology and the mechanistic conception of nature. In D. C. Lindberg & R. L. Numbers (Eds.), *God and nature: Historical essays on the encounter between Christianity and science* (pp. 167–191). Berkeley: University of California Press.

deBeer, G. (1964). *Charles Darwin: Evolution by natural selection.* New York: Doubleday.

DeCarvalho, R. J. (1990). A history of the "third force" in psychology. *Journal of Humanistic Psychology, 30,* 22–44.

DeCarvalho, R. J. (1991). *The founders of humanistic psychology.* New York: Praeger.

DeCarvalho, R. J. (1992). The institutionalization of humanistic psychology. *Humanistic Psychologist, 20,* 124–135.

Delahunty, R. J. (1985). *Spinoza.* Boston: Routledge & Kegan Paul.

Delaunay, P. (1958). Humanism and encyclopedism. In Rene Tafon (Ed.), *History of science: The beginnings of modern science* (A. J. Pomerans, Trans.). New York: Basic Books.

DeMartino, R. J. (1991). Karen Horney, Daisetz T. Suzuki, and Zen Buddhism. *American Journal of Psychoanalysis, 51,* 267–283.

DeMause, L. (Ed.). (1974). *The history of childhood.* New York: Psychohistory Press.

Dennett, D. C. (1991). *Consciousness explained.* Boston: Little, Brown.

Dennis, W. (Ed.). (1948). *Readings in the history of psychology.* New York: Appleton-Century-Crofts.

DeRosa, P. (1988). *Vicars of Christ: The dark side of the papacy.* New York: Crown.

Descartes, R. (1985a). *Discourse and essays* (J. Cottingham, R. Stoothoff, & D. Murdoch, Trans.). *The philosophical writings of Descartes* (Vol. 1, pp. 109–175). Cambridge: Cambridge University Press. (Original work published 1637)

Descartes, R. (1985b). *The passions of the soul* (J. Cottingham, R. Stoothoff, & D. Murdoch, Trans.). *The philosophical writings of Descartes* (Vol. 1, pp. 324–404). Cambridge: Cambridge University Press. (Original work published 1649)

Descartes, R. (1985c). *Treatise on man* (J. Cottingham, R. Stoothoff, & D. Murdoch, Trans.). *The philosophical writings of Descartes* (Vol. 1, pp. 99–108). Cambridge: Cambridge University Press. (Original work published 1664)

Deutsch, M., & Collins, M. E. (1951). *Interracial housing: A psychological evaluation of a social experiment.* Minneapolis: University of Minnesota Press.

Dewey, J. (1896). The reflex arc concept in psychology. *Psychological Review, 3,* 357–370.

Dewsbury, D. A. (Ed.). (1989). *Studying animal behavior: Autobiographies of the founders.* Chicago: University of Chicago Press.

Dewsbury, D. A. (1990). Whither the introductory course in the history of psychology? *Journal of the History of the Behavioral Sciences, 26,* 371–379.

Dewsbury, D. A. (1993). The boys of summer at the end of summer: The Watson-Lashley correspondence of the 1950s. *Psychological Reports, 72,* 263–269.

Dewsbury, D. A. (1998). Celebrating E. L. Thorndike a century after "Animal Intelligence." *American Psychologist, 53,* 1121–1124.

Dewsbury, D. A. (2000). Comparative cognition in the 1930s. *Psychonomic Bulletin and Review, 7,* 267–283.

Diamond, S. (1971). Gestation of the instinct concept. *Journal of the History of the Behavioral Sciences, 7,* 323–336.

Diamond, S. (1974a). Four hundred years of instinct controversy. *Behavior Genetics, 4,* 237–252.

Diamond, S. (Ed.). (1974b). *The roots of psychology: A source book in the history of ideas.* New York: Basic Books.

Diamond, S. (1977). Francis Galton and American psychology. *Annals of the New York Academy of Sciences, 291,* 47–55.

Diamond, S. (1980). Wundt before Leipzig. In R. W. Rieber (Ed.), *Wilhelm Wundt and the making of a scientific psychology* (pp. 3–70). New York: Plenum Press.

Diamond, S., Balvin, R. S., & Diamond, F. R. (1963). *Inhibition and choice.* New York: Harper & Row.

Dix, D. L. (1971). Memorial soliciting a state hospital for the insane submitted to the Legislature of New Jersey. In D. J. Rothman (Ed.), *Poverty U.S.A.: The historical record* (pp. 1–46). New York: Arno Press. (Original work published 1845)

Domenjo, B. A. (2000). Thoughts on the influences of Brentano and Comte on Freud's work. *Psychoanalysis & History, 2,* 110–118.

Donahoe, J. W. (1999). Edward L. Thorndike: The selectionist connectionist. *Journal of the Experimental Analysis of Behavior, 72,* 451–454.

DuBois, P. H. (1970). *A history of psychological testing.* Boston: Allyn & Bacon.

Duncan, C. P. (1980). A note on the 1929 International Congress of Psychology. *Journal of the History of the Behavioral Sciences, 16,* 1–5.

Duncker, K. (1945). On problem solving. *Psychological Monographs, 58,* 1–113.

Duncker, K. (1950). Induced motion. In W. D. Ellis (Ed.), *A source book of Gestalt psychology* (pp. 161–172). New York: Humanities Press. (Original work published 1929)

Durant, W. (1950). *The story of civilization: Part IV, The age of faith.* New York: Simon and Schuster.

Durant, W. (1954). *The story of civilization: Part I, Our Oriental heritage* (p. 259). New York: Simon and Schuster.

Durant, W., & Durant, A. (1961). *The story of civilization: Part VII, The age of reason begins.* New York: Simon and Schuster.

Durant, W., & Durant, A. (1967). *The story of civilization: Part X, Rousseau and revolution.* New York: Simon and Schuster.

Eacker, J. N. (1972). On some elementary philosophical problems in psychology. *American Psychologist, 27,* 553–565.

Eacker, J. N. (1975). *Problems of philosophy and psychology.* Chicago: Nelson-Hall.

Earle, W. J. (1967). William James. In P. Edwards (Ed.), *The encyclopedia of philosophy* (Vol. 4, pp. 240–249). New York: Macmillan and Free Press.

Ebbinghaus, H. (1913). *Memory* (H. A. Ruger & C. E. Bussenius, Trans.). New York: Teachers College, Columbia University. (Original work published 1885)

Eckardt, M. H. (1991). Feminine psychology revisited: A historical perspective. *American Journal of Psychoanalysis, 51,* 235–243.

Edelman, G. (1992). *Bright air, brilliant fire: On the matter of the mind.* New York: Basic Books.

Edwards, D. C. (1999). *Motivation and emotion: Evolutionary, physiological, cognitive, and social influences.* Thousand Oaks, CA: Sage.

Eiseley, L. C. (1957). Charles Darwin. In D. Flanagan (Ed.), *Lives in science.* New York: Simon and Schuster.

Eissler, K. R. (1965). *Medical orthodoxy and the future of psychoanalysis.* New York: International Universities Press.

Elliott, R. M. (1931). Albert Paul Weiss: 1879–1931. *American Journal of Psychology, 43,* 707–709.

Ellis, J. J. (1993). *Passionate sage: The character and legacy of John Adams.* New York: W. W. Norton.

Elmer-DeWitt, P. (1993, November 8). Cloning: Where do we draw the line? *Time,* pp. 64–70.

Emerson, R. W. (1969). *Essays: Second series* (p. 264). Columbus, OH: Charles E. Merrill. (Original work published 1841)

Emerson, R. W. (1981). In D. McQuade (Ed.), *Selected writings of Emerson.* New York: Modern Library. (Original work published 1841)

Engstrom, E. J. (1991). Emil Kraepelin: Psychiatry and public affairs in Wilhelmine Germany. *History of Psychiatry, 2,* 111–132.

Erickson, E. H. (1963). *Childhood and society* (2nd ed.). New York: W. W. Norton.

Ernst, C., & Angst, J. (1983). *Birth order: Its influence on personality.* Berlin: Springer-Verlag.

Esper, E. A. (1964). *A history of psychology.* Philadelphia: W. B. Saunders.

Esper, E. A. (1966). Max Meyer: The making of a scientific isolate. *Journal of the History of the Behavioral Sciences, 2,* 341–356.

Esper, E. A. (1967). Max Meyer in America. *Journal of the History of the Behavioral Sciences, 3,* 107–131.

Estes, W. K. (1950). Toward a statistical theory of learning. *Psychological Review, 57,* 94–107.

Evans, R. B. (1972). E. B. Titchener and his lost system. *Journal of the History of the Behavioral Sciences, 8,* 168–180.

Evans, R. B. (2000). Psychological instruments at the turn of the century. *American Psychologist, 55,* 322–325.

Evans, R. I. (1968). *B. F. Skinner: The man and his ideas.* New York: Dutton.

Evans, R. I. (1975). *Carl Rogers: The man and his ideas.* New York: Dutton.

Eysenck, M. W. (1986). Ebbinghaus: An evaluation. In F. Klix & H. Hagendorf (Eds.), *Human memory and cognitive capacities: Mechanisms and performances.* Amsterdam: Elsevier Science Publishers.

Fagan, T. K. (1992). Compulsory schooling, child study, clinical psychology, and special education: Origins of school psychology. *American Psychologist, 47,* 236–243.

Fagan, T. K. (1996). Witmer's contributions to school psychological services. *American Psychologist, 51,* 241–243.

Fancher, R. E. (1977). Brentano's psychology from an empirical standpoint and Freud's early metapsychology. *Journal of the History of the Behavioral Sciences, 13,* 207–227.

Fancher, R. E. (1996). *Pioneers of psychology* (3rd ed.). New York: W. W. Norton.

Farr, R. (1983). Wilhelm Wundt (1832–1920) and the origins of psychology as an experimental social science. *British Journal of Social Psychology, 22,* 289–301.

Fearing, F. (1970). *Reflex action: A study in the history of physiological psychology.* Cambridge: M.I.T. Press.

Fechner, G. (1966). *Elements of psychophysics* (H. E. Adler, Trans., D. H. Howes & E. G. Boring, Eds.). New York: Holt, Rinehart and Winston. (Original work published 1860)

Fellows, O. E., & Milliken, S. F. (1972). *Buffon.* New York: Twayne Publishers.

Fernberger, S. W. (1935). Fundamental categories as determiners of psychological systems: An excursion into ancient Chinese psychologies. *Psychological Review, 42,* 544–554.

Ferrari, M., Pinard, A., & Runions, K. (2001). Piaget's framework for a scientific study of consciousness. *Human Development, 44,* 195–213.

Ferster, C. S., & Skinner, B. F. (1957). *Schedules of reinforcement.* New York: Appleton-Century-Crofts.

Festinger, L. (1962). *A theory of cognitive dissonance.* Stanford, CA: Stanford University Press.

Feyerabend, P. K. (1975). *Against method.* London: NLB.

Feyerabend, P. K. (1988). *Farewell to reason.* London: Verso.

Feynman, R. P. (1958). The value of science. In E. Hutchings, Jr. (Ed.), *Frontiers in science.* New York: Basic Books.

Fine, R. (1990). *The history of psychoanalysis.* New York: Continuum Publishing.

Fisher, H. A. L. (1936). *A history of Europe.* Toronto: Longmans, Green & Co.

Foley, P., & Moray, N. (1987). Sensation, perception, and systems design. In G. Salvendy (Ed.), *Handbook of human factors.* New York: Wiley.

Ford, J. E. (1990). Systematic pluralism: Introduction to an issue. *The Monist, 73,* 335–349.

Forrest, D. W. (1974). *Francis Galton: The life and work of a Victorian genius.* New York: Taplinger Publishing.

Forrester, J., & Cameron, L. (1999). "A cure with a defect": A previously unpublished letter by Freud concerning "Anna O." *International Journal of Psycho-Analysis, 80,* 929–942.

Frame, D. M. (Trans.). (1960). *The complete essays of Montaigne* (2 vols). Garden City, NY: Anchor Books, Doubleday and Company.

Frankl, V. E. (1985). *Man's search for meaning* (rev. ed.). New York: Washington Square Press.

Frankl, V. E. (1997). *Viktor Frankl recollections: An autobiography.* New York: Insight/Plenum Press.

Fraser, A. C. (Ed.). (1959). *An essay concerning human understanding.* New York: Dover Publications.

Freud, S. (1955). A difficulty in the path of psychoanalysis. In J. Strachey (Ed.), *The standard edition of the complete psychological works of Sigmund Freud* (Vol. 17, pp. 136–144). London: Hogarth Press. (Original work published 1917)

Freud, S. (1957a). Instincts and their vicissitudes. In J. Strachey (Ed.), *The standard edition of the complete psychological works of Sigmund Freud* (Vol. 14, pp. 111–140). London: Hogarth Press. (Original work published 1915)

Freud, S. (1957b). Leonardo da Vinci and a memory of his childhood. In J. Strachey (Ed.), *The standard edition of the complete psychological works of Sigmund Freud* (Vol. 11, pp. 57–137). London: Hogarth Press. (Original work published 1910)

Freud, S. (1957c). On the history of the psycho-analytic movement. In J. Strachey (Ed.), *The standard edition of the complete psychological works of Sigmund Freud* (Vol. 14, pp. 3–66). London: Hogarth Press. (Original work published 1914)

Freud, S. (1959a). An autobiographical study. In J. Strachey (Ed.), *The standard edition of the complete psychological works of Sigmund Freud* (Vol. 20, pp. 7–70). London: Hogarth Press. (Original work published 1924)

Freud, S. (1959b). Family romances. In J. Strachey (Ed.), *The standard edition of the complete psychological works of Sigmund Freud* (Vol. 9, pp. 235–241). London: Hogarth Press. (Original work published 1908)

Freud, S. (1961a). Civilization and its discontents. In J. Strachey (Ed.), *The standard edition of the complete psychological works of Sigmund Freud* (Vol. 21, pp. 55–145). London: Hogarth Press. (Original work published 1930)

Freud, S. (1961b). The ego and the id. In J. Strachey (Ed.), *The standard edition of the complete psychological works of Sigmund Freud* (Vol. 19, pp. 1–66). London: Hogarth Press. (Original work published 1923)

Freud, S. (1961c). The future of an illusion. In J. Strachey (Ed.), *The standard edition of the complete psychological works of Sigmund Freud* (Vol. 21, pp. 3–56). London: Hogarth Press. (Original work published 1927)

Freud, S. (1961d). A religious experience. In J. Strachey (Ed.), *The standard edition of the complete psychological works of Sigmund Freud* (Vol. 21, pp. 167–172). London: Hogarth Press. (Original work published 1927)

Freud, S. (1964a). New introductory lectures on psychoanalysis. In J. Strachey (Ed.), *The standard edition of the complete psychological works of Sigmund Freud* (Vol. 22, pp. 3–182). London: Hogarth Press. (Original work published 1932)

Freud, S. (1964b). An outline of psycho-analysis. In J. Strachey (Ed.), *The standard edition of the complete psychological works of Sigmund Freud* (Vol. 23,

pp. 141–207). London: Hogarth Press. (Original work published 1938)

Frick, P. L. (1928). Behaviorism and its anti-religious implications. *Methodist Review, 111,* 509–521.

Frick, W. B. (2000). Remembering Maslow: Reflections on a 1968 interview. *Journal of Humanistic Psychology, 40,* 128–147.

Frolov, Y. P. (1938). *Pavlov and his school.* London: Kegan Paul, Trench, Trubner.

Fromm, Erich (1941). *Escape from freedom.* New York: Rinehart and Co.

Fromm, Erich (1947). *Man for himself.* New York: Rinehart and Co.

Fromm, Erika (1998). Lost and found half a century later: Letters by Freud and Einstein. *American Psychologist, 53,* 1195–1198.

Fuchs, A. H., & Viney, W. (2002). The course in the history of psychology: Present status and future concerns. *History of Psychology, 5,* 3–15.

Furumoto, L. (1979). Mary Whiton Calkins (1863–1930) fourteenth president of the American Psychological Association. *Journal of the History of the Behavioral Sciences, 15,* 346–356.

Furumoto, L. (1989). The new history of psychology. In I. S. Cohen (Ed.), *The G. Stanley Hall lecture series* (Vol. 9, pp. 9–34). Washington DC: American Psychological Association.

Furumoto, L., & Scarborough, E. (1986). Placing women in the history of psychology: The first American women psychologists. *American Psychologist, 41,* 35–42.

Gale, M. C., & Gale, H. (1902). Children's vocabularies. *Popular Science Monthly, 61,* 45–51.

Galef, B. G., Jr. (1998). Edward Thorndike: Revolutionary psychologist, ambiguous biologist. *American Psychologist, 53,* 1128–1134.

Gallo, D. A., & Finger, S. (2000). The power of a musical instrument: Franklin, the Mozarts, Mesmer, and the glass armonica. *History of Psychology, 3,* 326–343.

Galton, F. (1872). Statistical inquiries into the efficacy of prayer. *Fortnightly Review, 12,* 125–135.

Galton, F. (1907). *Inquiries into human faculty and its development.* New York: E. P. Dutton. (Original work published 1883)

Gantt, W. H. (1928). Ivan P. Pavlov: A biographical sketch. In W. H. Gantt (Ed.), *Lectures on conditioned reflexes* (Vol. 1 by Ivan P. Pavlov). New York: International Publishers.

Gardner, H. (1985). *The mind's new science: A history of the cognitive revolution.* New York: Basic Books.

Garfield, S. L. (1992). Comments on "Retrospect: Psychology as a profession" by J. McKeen Cattell. *Journal of Consulting and Clinical Psychology, 60,* 9–15.

Garforth, F. W. (Ed.). (1964). *John Locke: Some thoughts concerning education.* New York: Baron's Educational Series.

Garraty, J. A., & Carnes, M. C. (1999). *American national biography* (Vol. 19). New York: Oxford University Press.

Gates, A. I. (1968). James McKeen Cattell. In D. L. Sills (Ed.), *International encyclopedia of the social sciences* (Vol. 2, pp. 344–347). New York: Macmillan and Free Press

Gavin, E. A. (1976). What is phenomenological psychology? *Philosophical Psychologist, 10,* 1–4.

Gavin, E. A. (1987). Prominent women in psychology, determined by ratings of distinguished peers. *Psychotherapy in Private Practice, 5,* 53–68.

Gawronski, D. V. (1975). *History, meaning and method* (3rd ed.). Glenview, IL: Scott Foresman.

Gay, P. (1988). *Freud: A life for our time.* New York: W. W. Norton.

Gelfand, T., & Kerr, J. (Eds.). (1992). *Freud and the history of psychoanalysis.* Hillsdale, NJ: Analytic Press.

Gendlin, E. T. (1988). Carl Rogers (1902–1987). *American Psychologist, 43,* 127–128.

George, S. (Executive Producer), & Donner, C. (Director). (1988). *Stealing heaven.* [Film] Los Angeles, CA: Virgin Vision.

Gerard, E. O. (1966). Medieval psychology: Dogmatic Aristotelianism or observational empiricism? *Journal of the History of the Behavioral Sciences, 2,* 315–329.

German, T. P., & Defeyter, M. A. (2000). Immunity to functional fixedness in young children. *Psychonomic Bulletin & Review, 7,* 707–712.

Gerwood, J. B. (1998). The legacy of Viktor Frankl: An appreciation upon his death. *Psychological Reports, 82,* 673–674.

Geuter, U. (1992). *The professionalization of psychology in Nazi Germany* (R. J. Holmes, Trans.). New York: Cambridge. (Original work published 1984)

Gibbons, J. (no date) *I. P. Pavlov: Selected works* (S. Belsky, Trans.). Moscow: Foreign Languages Publishing House.

Gibson, E. J., & Walk, R. D. (1960). The "visual cliff." *Scientific American, 202,* 64–72.

Gilbert, A. R. (1968). Franz Brentano in the perspective of existential psychology. *Journal of the History of the Behavioral Sciences, 4,* 249–253.

Gilbert, F. (1967). Niccoló Machiavelli. In P. Edwards (Ed.), *The encyclopedia of philosophy* (Vol. 5, pp. 119–121). New York: Macmillan and Free Press.

Gilderhus, M. T. (1992). *History and historians: A historiographical introduction.* Englewood Cliffs, NJ: Prentice Hall.

Gilgen, A. R. (1982). *American psychology since World War II: A profile of the discipline.* Westport, CT: Greenwood Press.

Gilman, S. L. (2001). Karen Horney, M. D., 1885–1952. *American Journal of Psychiatry, 158,* 1205.

Gleick, J. (1987). *Chaos: Making a new science.* New York: Viking.

Gleitman, H., Rozin, P., & Sabini, J. (1997). Solomon E. Asch (1907–1996): Obituary. *American Psychologist, 52,* 984–985.

Goldman, M. S. (1999). Expectancy operation: Cognitive-neural models and architectures. In I. Kirsch (Ed.), *How expectancies shape experience* (pp. 41–63). Washington, DC: American Psychological Association.

Gordon, B. L. (1959). *Medieval and Renaissance medicine.* New York: Philosophical Library.

Gorfein, D., & Hoffman, R. R. (Eds.). (1987). *Learning and memory: The Ebbinghaus centennial conference.* Hillsdale, NJ: Erlbaum.

Goshen, C. E. (1967). *Documentary history of psychiatry.* New York: Philosophical Library.

Gotesky, R. (1967). Rudolf Hermann Lotze. In Paul Edwards (Ed.), *Encyclopedia of philosophy.* (Vol 5, pp. 87–89). New York: Macmillan and Free Press.

Goudge, T. A. (1973). Evolutionism. In P. P. Wiener (Ed.), *Dictionary of the history of ideas* (Vol. 2, pp. 174–189). New York: Charles Scribner's Sons.

Gould, S. J. (1981). *The mismeasure of man.* New York: W. W. Norton.

Grace, R. C. (2001). On the failure of operationism. *Theory and Psychology, 11,* 5–33.

Gray, J. (1999). Ivan Petrovich Pavlov and the conditional reflex. *Brain Research Bulletin, 50,* 433.

Green, C. D. (1998). The thoroughly modern Aristotle: Was he really a functionalist? *History of Psychology, 1,* 8–20.

Green, C. D. (2000). Dispelling the "mystery" of computational cognitive science. *History of Psychology, 3,* 62–66.

Green, C. D. (2001a). Operationism again: What did Bridgman say? What did Bridgman need? *Theory and Psychology, 11,* 45–51.

Green, C. D. (2001b). Charles Babbage, the Analytical Engine, and the possibility of a 19th-century cognitive science. In C. D. Green & M. Shore (Eds.), *The transformation of psychology: Influences of 19th-century philosophy, technology, and natural science* (pp. 133–152). Washington, DC: American Psychological Association.

Green, M. (1985). *Descartes.* Minneapolis: University of Minnesota Press.

Greenwood, J. D. (1999). Understanding the "cognitive revolution" in psychology. *Journal of the History of the Behavioral Sciences, 35,* 1–22.

Gregory, R. L. (1974). Choosing a paradigm for perception. In E. C. Carterette & M. P. Friedman (Eds.), *Handbook of perception* (Vol. 1, pp. 255–283). New York: Academic Press.

Grendler, P. F. (1988). Printing and censorship. In C. B. Schmitt (Ed.), *The Cambridge history of Renaissance philosophy* (pp. 25–53). New York: Cambridge University Press.

Grey, L. (1998). *Alfred Adler, the forgotten prophet: A vision for the 21st century.* Westport, CT: Praeger Publishers/Greenwood Publishing.

Grimsley, D. L., & Windholz, G. (2000). The neurophysiological aspects of Pavlov's theory of higher nervous activity: In honor of the 150th anniversary of Pavlov's birth. *Journal of the History of the Neurosciences, 9,* 152–163.

Grmek, M. D. (1974). Francois Magendie. In C. C. Gillispi (Ed.), *Dictionary of scientific biography* (Vol. 9, pp. 7–11). New York: Charles Scribner's Sons.

Groethuysen, B. (1963). Michel de Montaigne. In E. R. A. Seligman & A. Johnson (Eds.), *Encyclopedia of the social sciences* (Vol. 10, pp. 634–635). New York: Macmillan and Free Press.

Gruber, H. E., & Vonèche, J. J. (1977). *The essential Piaget.* New York: Basic Books.

Guberman, S., & Wojtkowski, W. (2001). Reflections on Max Wertheimer's "Productive Thinking": Lessons for AI. *Gestalt Theory, 23,* 132–143.

Guthrie, E. R. (1944). Personality in terms of associative learning. In J. M. Hunt (Ed.), *Personality and the behavioral disorders: A handbook based on experimental and clinical research* (Vol. 1, pp. 49–68). New York: Ronald Press.

Guthrie, R. V. (1998). *Even the rat was white: A historical view of psychology.* Boston: Allyn & Bacon.

Guthrie, W. K. C. (1960). *The Greek philosophers from Thales to Aristotle.* New York: Harper & Row.

Gutmann, J. (Ed.). (1949). *Ethics; preceded by on the improvement of the understanding.* New York: Hafner Publishing Co.

Gutterman, S. S. (1970). *The Machiavellians.* Lincoln: University of Nebraska Press.

Haeckel, E. H. P. K. (1905). *The evolution of man* (5th ed., Vol. 1, J. McCabe, Trans.). New York: Putnam.

Haight, A. L. (1978). *Banned books 387 B.C. to 1987 A.D.* (4th ed.). Updated and enlarged by C. B. Grannis. New York: R. R. Bowker.

Hall, C. S., & Nordby, V. J. (1973). *A primer of Jungian psychology.* New York: Taplinger Publishing.

Hall, G. S. (1890). Children's lies. *American Journal of Psychology, 3,* 59–70.

Hall, G. S. (1891). The contents of children's minds on entering school. *Pedagogical Seminary, 1,* 139–173.

Hall, G. S. (1904). *Adolescence.* New York: D. Appleton and Co.

Hall, G. S. (1910). A children's institute. *Harper's Magazine, 120,* 620–624.

Hall, G. S. (1922). *Senescence: The last half of life.* New York: D. Appleton and Co.

Hall, G. S. (1923). *Life and confessions of a psychologist.* New York: D. Appleton and Co.

Hall, G. S., & Browne, C. E. (1903). Children's ideas of fire, heat, frost and cold. *Pedagogical Seminary, 10,* 27–85.

Hall, G. S., & Smith, T. L. (1903). Showing off and bashfulness as phases of self-consciousness. *Pedagogical Seminary, 10,* 159–199.

Hall, G. S., & Wallin, J. E. W. (1902). How children and youth think and feel about clouds. *Pedagogical Seminary, 9,* 460–506.

Hall, V., Jr. (1950). Life of Julius Caesar Scaliger. *Transaction of the American Philosophical Society, 4,* 85–170.

Hallie, P. P. (1967). Stoicism. In P. Edwards (Ed.), *The encyclopedia of philosophy* (Vol. 8, pp. 19–22). New York: Macmillan.

Harlow, H. F. (1949). The formation of learning sets. *Psychological Review, 56,* 51–65.

Harlow, H. F. (1958). The nature of love. *American Psychologist, 13,* 673–685.

Harms, E. (1967). *Origin of modern psychiatry.* Springfield, IL: Charles C. Thomas.

Harris, B. (1979). Whatever happened to little Albert? *American Psychologist, 34,* 151–160.

Harris, B. (1999a). Otto Klineberg. *American National Biography* (pp. 792–793). New York: Oxford University Press

Harris, B. (1999b). John Broadus Watson. *American National Biography* (pp. 795–797). New York: Oxford University Press

Harris, M. (1974). *Cows, pigs, wars, and witches: The riddles of culture.* New York: Random House.

Harrison, E. (1987). Whigs, prigs, and historians of science. *Nature, 329,* 213–214.

Harrison, P. (2001). Curiosity, forbidden knowledge, and the reformation of natural philosophy in early modern England. *Isis, 92,* 265–290.

Hartley, D. (1966). *Observations on man, his frame, his duty and his expectations.* Demar, NY: Scholars' Facsimiles & Reprints. (Original work published 1749)

Hartmann, H. (1939). *Ego psychology and the problem of adaptation.* New York: International University Press.

Hartshorne, C. (1934). *The philosophy and psychology of sensation.* Port Washington, NY: Kennikat Press.

Hassard, J. (1990). The AHP Soviet exchange project: 1983–1990 and beyond. *Journal of Humanistic Psychology, 30,* 6–51.

Haupt, E. J. (1998). Origins of American psychology in the work of G. E. Müller: Classical psychophysics and serial learning. In R. W. Rieber & K. Salzinger (Eds.), *Psychology: Theoretical-historical perspectives* (2nd ed., pp. 17–75). Washington, DC: American Psychological Association.

Hayman, R. (2001). *A life of Jung.* New York: W. W. Norton.

Healy, D. (1993). One-hundred years of psychopharmacology. *Journal of Psychopharmacology, 7,* 207–214.

Heft, H. (2001). *Ecological psychology in context: James Gibson, Roger Barker, and the legacy of William James's radical empiricism.* Mahwah, NJ: Erlbaum.

Heidbreder, E. (1933). *Seven psychologies.* New York: Appleton-Century-Crofts.

Heidegger, M. (1962). *Being and time* (J. Macquarrie & E. Robinson, Trans.). New York: Harper & Row. (Original work published 1927)

Heims, S. (1975). Encounter of behavioral sciences with new machine-organism analogies in the 1940's. *Journal of the History of the Behavioral Sciences, 11,* 368–373.

Helmholtz, H. L. von (1856). *Handbuch der physiologischen Optik* (2nd ed.). Hamburg und Leipzig: L. Voss.

Helmholtz, H. L. von (1971). The origin and correct interpretation of our sense impressions. In R. Kahl (Ed.), *Selected writings of Hermann Ludwig von Helmholtz* (pp. 501–512). Middletown, CT: Wesleyan University Press. (Original work published 1894)

Helson, H. (1972). What can we learn from the history of psychology? *Journal of the History of the Behavioral Sciences, 8,* 115–119.

Henle, M. (1976). Why study the history of psychology? *Annals of the New York Academy of Sciences, 270,* 14–20.

Henle, M. (1977). The influence of Gestalt psychology in America. *Annals of the New York Academy of Sciences, 291,* 3–12.

Henle, M. (1978a). Gestalt psychology and Gestalt therapy. *Journal of the History of the Behavioral Sciences, 14,* 23–32.

Henle, M. (1978b). One man against the Nazis—Wolfgang Köhler. *American Psychologist, 33,* 939–944.

Henle, M. (1984). Isomorphism: Setting the record straight. *Psychological Research, 46,* 317–327.

Henle, M. (1985). Rediscovering Gestalt psychology. In S. Koch & D. E. Leary (Eds.), *A century of psychology as science* (pp. 100–120). New York: McGraw-Hill.

Henle, M. (1986). The influence of Gestalt psychology in America. In M. Henle, *1879 and all that: Essays in the theory and history of psychology* (pp. 118–137). New York: Columbia University Press. (Original work published 1977)

Henle, M. (1989). Two disciplines, one name? *Contemporary Psychology, 34,* 857–858.

Henle, M. (1993). Man's place in nature in the thinking of Wolfgang Köhler. *Journal of the History of the Behavioral Sciences, 29,* 3–7.

Henle, M., Jaynes, J., & Sullivan, J. J. (Eds.). (1973). *Historical conceptions of psychology.* New York: Springer Publishing.

Herbart, J. F. (1977). *The science of education* (H. M. Felkin & E. Felkin, Trans.). In D. N. Robinson (Ed.), *Significant contributions to the history of psychology* 1750–1920. (Series B, Psychometrics and

Educational Psychology, Vol. 1, pp. 57–268). Washington, DC: University Publications of America (from 1902 edition).

Hergenhahn, B. R. (2001). *An introduction to the history of psychology* (4th ed.). Belmont, CA: Wadsworth.

Herlihy, D. (1997). *The black death and the transformation of the West.* Cambridge, MA: Harvard University Press.

Herrmann, D. J., & Chaffin, R. (Eds.). (1988). *Memory in historical perspective: The literature before Ebbinghaus.* New York: Springer-Verlag.

Herrnstein, R. J., & Boring, E. G. (Eds.). (1966). *A sourcebook in the history of psychology.* Cambridge, MA: Harvard University Press.

Hess, E. H. (1962). Ethology: An approach toward the complete analysis of behavior. In R. Brown, E. Galanter, E. H. Hess, & G. Mandler (Eds.), *New directions in psychology* (pp. 157–266). New York: Holt, Rinehart and Winston.

Hess, M. (1967). Action at a distance and field theory. In P. Edwards (Ed.), *The encyclopedia of philosophy.* (Vol 1, pp. 9–15). New York: Macmillan.

Hildebrand, J. H. (1957). *Science in the making.* New York: Columbia University Press.

Hilgard, E. R. (1996). History of educational psychology. In D. C. Berliner & R. C. Calfee (Eds.), *Handbook of educational psychology* (pp. 990–1004). New York: Macmillan Library Reference.

Hilgard, E. R., & Bower, G. H. (1966). *Theories of learning* (3rd ed.). New York: Appleton-Century-Crofts.

Hirsh, I. J. (1967). Max Frederick Meyer: 1873–1967. *American Journal Psychology, 80,* 644–645.

Hobbes, T. (1962a). *Human nature.* In W. Molesworth (Ed.), *The English works of Thomas Hobbes* (Vol. 4, pp. 1–76). London: Scientia Aalen. (Original work published 1650)

Hobbes, T. (1962b). *Leviathan.* In W. Molesworth (Ed.), *The English works of Thomas Hobbes* (Vol. 3, pp. 1–714). London: Scientia Aalen. (Original work published 1651)

Hodgson, B. (1988). Economic science and ethical neutrality II: The intransigence of evaluative concepts. *Journal of Business, 7,* 321–335.

Hoff, H. E. & Kellaway, P. (1952). The early history of the reflex. *Journal of the History of Medicine and Allied Sciences, 7,* 211–249.

Hoff, P. (1998). Emil Kraepelin and forensic psychiatry. *International Journal of Law and Psychiatry, 21,* 343–353.

Hoffeld, D. R. (1980). Mesmer's failure: Sex, politics, personality and the Zeitgeist. *Journal of the History of the Behavioral Sciences, 16,* 377–386.

Hoffman, E. (1988). *The right to be human: A biography of Abraham Maslow.* Los Angeles: Tarcher.

Hoffman, R. R., & Deffenbacher, K. A. (1992). A brief history of applied cognitive psychology. *Applied Cognitive Psychology, 6,* 1–48.

Hollingworth, L. S. (1914). Functional periodicity: An experimental study of the mental and motor abilities of women during menstruation. *Contributions to Education* (No. 69). New York: Teachers College, Columbia University.

Hollingworth, L. S. (1920). *The psychology of subnormal children.* New York: Macmillan.

Hollingworth, L. S. (1928). *The psychology of the adolescent.* New York: Appleton.

Hollingworth, L. S. (1942). *Children above 180 I.Q.* Yonkers, NY: World Book.

Holt, R. R. (1967). Ego autonomy re-evaluated. *International Journal of Psychiatry, 3,* 481–536.

Horgan, J. (1996, December). Why Freud isn't dead. *Scientific American,* pp. 106–111.

Hornday, W. T. (1883). Mental capacity of the elephant. *Popular Science Monthly, 23,* 497–509.

Horney, K. (1934). The overvaluation of love: A study of a common present-day feminine type. *Psychoanalytic Quarterly, 3,* 605–638.

Horney, K. (1937). *The neurotic personality of our time.* New York: W. W. Norton.

Horney, K. (1939). *New ways in psychoanalysis.* New York: W. W. Norton.

Horney, K. (1942). *Self-analysis.* New York: W. W. Norton.

Horney, K. (1945). *Our inner conflicts.* New York: W. W. Norton.

Horney, K. (1950). *Neurosis and human growth.* New York: W. W. Norton.

Horney, K. (1967). *Feminine psychology.* New York: W. W. Norton.

Hothersall, D. (1995). *History of psychology.* New York: McGraw-Hill.

Huarte, J. (1959). *The examination of men's wits.* (M. Camillo & R. Carew, Trans.). Gainesville, FL: Scholars Facsimiles and Reprints. (Original work published 1594)

Hull, C. L. (1943). *Principles of behavior.* New York: D. Appleton-Century.

Hull, C. L. (1952). Clark L. Hull. In E. G. Boring, H. Werner, R. M. Yerkes, & H. S. Langfeld (Eds.), *A history of psychology in autobiography* (Vol. 4, pp. 143–162). New York: Russell and Russell.

Humbert, E. G. (1988). *C. G. Jung: The fundamentals of theory and practice* (R. G. Jalbert, Trans.). Wilmette, IL: Chiron Publications.

Hume, D. (1978). *A treatise of human nature.* Oxford: Clarendon Press. (Original work published 1739–1740)

Humphrey, T. (1983). *Immanuel Kant—Perpetual peace and other essays on politics, history, and morals.* Indianapolis: Hackett Publishing.

Hunter, W. S. (1928). *Human behavior.* Chicago: University of Chicago Press.

Hunter, W. S. (1952). Walter S. Hunter. In E. G. Boring, H. Werner, R. M. Yerkes, & H. S. Langfeld (Eds.), *A history of psychology in autobiography* (Vol. 4, pp. 163–187). New York: Russell and Russell.

Huxley, T. H. (1898). *Hume with helps to the study of Berkeley.* New York: D. Appleton and Co.

Ingram, D. H. (1985). Karen Horney at 100: Beyond the frontier. *American Journal of Psychoanalysis, 45,* 305–309.

Innis, N. K. (1992). Tolman and Tryon: Early research on the inheritance of the ability to learn. *American Psychologist, 47,* 190–197.

Innis, N. K. (1999). Edward C. Tolman's purposive behaviorism. In W. O'Donohue & R. Kitchener (Eds.), *Handbook of behaviorism* (pp. 97–117). San Diego, CA: Academic Press.

Iran-Nejad, A., & Winsler, A. (2000). Bartlett's schema theory and modern accounts of learning and remembering. *Journal of Mind & Behavior, 21,* 5–35.

Jablensky, A., Hugler, H., von Cranach, M., & Kalinov, K. (1993). Kraepelin revisited: A reassessment and statistical analysis of dementia praecox and manic-depressive insanity in 1908. *Psychological Medicine, 23,* 843–858.

Jackson, P. W. (1998). *John Dewey and the lessons of art.* New Haven, CT: Yale University Press.

Jackson, S. W. (1969). Galen—On mental disorders. *Journal of the History of the Behavioral Sciences, 5,* 365–384.

Jacobi, J. (1985). *Paracelsus: Selected writings.* New York: Pantheon Books.

Jacobs, D. (2001). *Her own woman: The life of Mary Wollstonecraft.* New York: Simon and Schuster.

Jager, M., & VanHoorn, W. (1972). Aristotle's opinion on perception in general. *Journal of the History of the Behavioral Sciences, 8,* 321–327.

Jahoda, G. (2000). Piaget and Lévy-Bruhl. *History of Psychology, 3,* 218–238.

Jahoda, M. (1969). The migration of psychoanalysis. In D. Fleming & B. Bailyn (Eds.), *The intellectual migration: Europe and America, 1930–1960* (pp. 371–419). Cambridge, MA: Harvard University Press.

James, W. (unsigned). (1875). Notice of Wilhelm Wundt's principles of physiological psychology. *North American Review, 121,* 195–201.

James, W. (unsigned). (1876a). Notice of F. von Holtzendorff's psychology of murder. *Nation, 22,* 16.

James, W. (1876b, September 21). The teaching of philosophy in our colleges. *The Nation,* pp. 178–179.

James, W. (1880). Great men, great thoughts and the environment. *Atlantic Monthly, 46,* 441–459.

James, W. (1884a). The dilemma of determinism. *Unitarian Review, 22,* 193–224.

James, W. (1884b). What is an emotion? *Mind, 9,* 188–205.

James, W. (1890). *The principles of psychology* (Vol. 1). New York: Henry Holt.

James, W. (1894). The physical basis of emotion. *Psychological Review, 1,* 516–529.

James, W. (1920). *Letters of William James* (Vol. 1.) Boston: Atlantic Monthly Press.

James, W. (1975a). *The meaning of truth.* Cambridge, MA: Harvard University Press. (Original work published 1909)

James, W. (1975b). *Pragmatism.* Cambridge, MA: Harvard University Press. (Original work published 1907)

James, W. (1976). *Essays in radical empiricism.* Cambridge, MA: Harvard University Press. (Original work published 1912)

James, W. (1977). *A pluralistic universe.* Cambridge, MA: Harvard University Press. (Original work published 1909)

James, W. (1978). Pluralistic mystic. *Essays in philosophy* (pp. 172–190). Cambridge, MA: Harvard University Press. (Original work published 1910)

James, W. (1979a). The dilemma of determinism. In: F. H. Burkhardt (Ed.), *The will to believe* (pp. 114–140). Cambridge, MA: Harvard University Press. (Original work published 1884)

James, W. (1979b). *The will to believe.* Cambridge, MA: Harvard University Press. (Original work published 1897)

James, W. (1980). Letter to John Dewey. In E. Hardwick (Ed.), *The selected letters of William James* (pp. 203–204). Boston: David R. Godine Publisher. (Original letter sent 1903)

James, W. (1981). *Principles of psychology.* Cambridge, MA: Harvard University Press. (Original work published 1890)

James, W. (1983). *The physical basis of emotion.* Essays in psychology (pp. 299–314). Cambridge, MA: Harvard University Press. (Original work published 1894)

James, W. (1985). *The varieties of religious experience.* Cambridge, MA: Harvard University Press. (Original work published 1902)

James, W. (1986a). Letter to Charles William Elliot. In F. J. D. Scott (Ed.), *William James: Selected unpublished correspondence 1885–1910.* Columbus: Ohio State University Press. (Original letter dated February 21, 1897)

James, W. (1986b). Letter to James McKeen Cattell. In F. J. D. Scott (Ed.), William James: *Selected unpublished correspondence 1885–1910.* Columbus: Ohio State University Press. (Original letter dated June 10, 1903)

Jastrow, J. (1903). Helen Keller: A psychological autobiography. *Popular Science Monthly, 63,* 71–83.

Jaynes, J. (1973a). Introduction: The study of the history of psychology. In M. Henle, J. Jaynes, & J. J. Sullivan (Eds.), *Historical conceptions of psychology.* New York: Springer Publishing.

Jaynes, J. (1973b). The problem of animate motion in the seventeenth century. In M. Henle, J. Jaynes, & J. J. Sullivan (Eds.), *Historical conceptions of psychology* (pp. 166–179). New York: Springer Publishing.

Jefferson, T. (1904). Notes on Virginia. In A. A. Lipscomb (Ed.), *The writings of Thomas Jefferson* (Vol. 2). Washington, DC: The Thomas Jefferson Memorial Association. (Original work published 1782)

Jeremias, J. (1975). *Jerusalem in the time of Jesus: An investigation into economic and social conditions during the New Testament period* (F. H. & C. H. Cave, Trans.). Philadelphia: Fortress Press.

Johannsen, D. E. (1971). Early history of perceptual illusions. *Journal of the History of the Behavioral Sciences, 7,* 127–140.

Johnson, D. F. (2000). Cultivating the field of psychology: Psychological journals at the turn of the century. *American Psychologist, 55,* 1144–1147.

Johnson, W. H. (1927). Does the behaviorist have a mind? *Princeton Theological Review, 25,* 40–58.

Jonçich, G. (1968). Edward L. Thorndike. In D. L. Sills (Ed.), *International Encyclopedia of the Social Sciences* (Vol. 16, pp. 8–14). New York: Macmillan and Free Press.

Jonçich, G. (1988). *The sane positivist: A biography of Edward L. Thorndike.* Middletown, CT: Wesleyan University Press.

Jones, E. (1953). *The life and work of Sigmund Freud.* (Vol. 1). New York: Basic Books.

Jones, E. (1955). *The life and work of Sigmund Freud* (Vol. 2). New York: Basic Books.

Jones, M. C. (1924a). The elimination of children's fears. *Journal of Experimental Psychology, 7,* 383–390.

Jones, M. C. (1924b). A laboratory study of fear: The case of Peter. *Pedagogical Seminary, 31,* 308–315.

Joravsky, D. (1989). *Russian psychology: A critical history.* Cambridge, MA: Basil Blackwell.

Juhasz, J. B. (1971). Greek theories of imagination. *Journal of the History of the Behavioral Sciences, 7,* 39–58.

Jung, C. G. (1954a). Analytic psychology and education. In H. Read, M. Fordham, & G. Adler (Eds.), *The collected works of C. G. Jung* (Vol. 17, pp. 63–132). New York: Pantheon Books. (Original work published 1926)

Jung, C. G. (1954b). Psychic conflicts in a child. In H. Read, M. Fordham, & G. Adler (Eds.), *The collected works of C. G. Jung* (Vol. 17, pp. 1–35). New York: Pantheon Books. (Original work published 1910)

Jung, C. G. (1961). *Memories, dreams, reflections* (A. Jaffe, Ed., Richard & Clara Winston, Trans.). New York: Vintage Books.

Jung, J. (1968). *Verbal learning.* New York: Holt, Rinehart and Winston.

Kahl, R. (1967). Hermann von Helmholtz. In P. Edwards (Ed.), *The encyclopedia of philosophy* (Vol. 3, pp. 469–471). New York: Macmillan and Free Press.

Kahl, R. (Ed.). (1971). *Selected writings of Hermann von Helmholtz.* Middletown, CT: Wesleyan University Press.

Kant, I. (1952). *The critique of judgment* (J. C. Meridith, Trans.). Oxford: Oxford University Press. (Original work published 1790)

Kant, I. (1956). *Critique of practical reason* (L. W. Beck, Trans.). Indianapolis: Bobbs-Merrill. (Original work published 1788)

Kant, I. (1960). *Religion within the limits of reason alone* (T. M. Greene & H. H. Hudson, Trans.). New York: Harper. (Original work published 1793)

Kant, I. (1965). *Critique of pure reason* (N. K. Smith, Trans.). New York: St. Martin's Press. (Original work published 1781)

Kastenbaum, R. (1995). "How far can an intellectual effort diminish pain?": William McDougall's journal as a model for facing death. *Omega: Journal of Death and Dying, 32,* 123–164.

Katona, G. (1940). *Organizing and memorizing: Studies in the psychology of learning and teaching.* New York: Columbia University Press.

Keen, S. (1973). *Apology for wonder.* New York: Harper & Row.

Keller, F. S., & Sherman, J. G. (1974). *The Keller plan handbook: Essays on a personalized system of instruction.* Menlo Park, CA: Benjamin.

Keller, M. (1943). The first American medical work on the effects of alcohol: Benjamin Rush's "An inquiry into the effects of ardent spirits upon the human body and mind." *Quarterly Journal of Studies on Alcohol, 4,* 321–341.

Kelley, D. R. (1990). What is happening to the history of ideas? *Journal of the History of Ideas, 51,* 3–35.

Kelley, M. R., & Nairne, J. S. (2001). Von Restorff revisited: Isolation, generation, and memory for order. *Journal of Experimental Psychology: Learning, Memory, and Cognition, 27,* 54–66.

Kellman, P. J. (2000). An update on Gestalt psychology. In B. Landau & J. Sabini (Eds.), *Perception, cognition, and language: Essays in honor of Henry and Lila Gleitman* (pp. 157–190). Cambridge, MA: M.I.T. Press.

Kelly-Gadol, J. (1977). Did women have a Renaissance? In R. Bridenthal & C. Koonz (Eds.), *Becoming visible: Women in European history.* Boston: Houghton Mifflin.

Kenny, A. (Ed. & Trans.) (1970). *Descartes' philosophical letters.* Oxford: Clarendon Press.

Kieckhefer, R. (1976). *European witch trials.* Berkeley: University of California Press.

Kierkegaard, S. (1941). *Concluding unscientific postscript* (D. F. Swenson & W. Lowrie, Trans.). Princeton, NJ: Princeton University Press. (Original work published 1846)

Kierkegaard, S. (1967). *Stages on life's way* (W. Lowrie, Trans.). New York: Schocken Books. (Original work published 1845)

Kierkegaard, S. (1983). *Fear and trembling* (H. V. Hong & E. H. Hong, Eds. & Trans.). Princeton, NJ: Princeton University Press. (Original work published 1843)

Kierkegaard, S. (1985). *Philosophical fragments.* (H. V. Hong & E. H. Hong, Eds. & Trans.). Princeton, NJ: Princeton University Press. (Original work published 1844)

Kierkegaard, S. (1987). *Either/or: A fragment on life* (H. V. Hong & E. H. Hong, Eds. & Trans.). Prince-ton, NJ: Princeton University Press. (Original work published 1843)

Kierkegaard, S. (1989). *The sickness unto death* (A. Hannay, Trans.). London: Penguin Books. (Original work published 1849)

Kimble, G. A. (1996). Ivan Mikhailovich Sechenov: Pioneer in Russian reflexology. In G. A. Kimble, C. A. Boneau, & M. Wertheimer (Eds.), *Portraits of Pioneers in Psychology* (Vol. 2, pp. 33–45). Washington, DC: American Psychological Association.

King, D. B. (1992). Evolution and revision of *The principles of psychology.* In M. E. Donnelly (Ed.), *Reinterpreting the legacy of William James* (pp. 67–75). Washington, DC: American Psychological Association.

King, D. B. (2000). George Croom Robertson and *Mind:* The story of psychology's first editor. In G. A. Kimble & M. Wertheimer (Eds.), *Portraits of pioneers in psychology* (Vol. 4, p. 33–48). Washington, DC: American Psychological Association.

King, D. B., Cox, M., & Wertheimer, M. (1998). Karl Duncker: Productive problems with beautiful solutions. In G. A. Kimble & M. Wertheimer (Eds.), *Portraits of pioneers in psychology* (Vol. 3, pp. 163–178). Washington, DC: American Psychological Association.

King, D. B., & Viney, W. (1992). Modern history of pragmatic and sentimental attitudes toward animals and the selling of comparative psychology. *Journal of Comparative Psychology, 106,* 190–195.

King, D. B., Wertheimer, M., Keller, H., & Crochetière, K. (1994). The legacy of Max Wertheimer and Gestalt psychology. *Social Research, 61,* 907–935.

Kintsch, W. (1985). Reflections on Ebbinghaus. *Journal of Experimental Psychology: Learning, Memory and Cognition, 11,* 461–463.

Kirk, G. S., & Raven, J. E. (1957). *The presocratic philosophers.* Cambridge: Cambridge University Press.

Kirsch, I. (1978). Demonology and the rise of science: An example of the misperception of historical data. *Journal of the History of the Behavioral Sciences, 14,* 149–157.

Kirsner, D. (2001). The future of psychoanalytic institutes. *Psychoanalytic Psychology, 18,* 195–212.

Kitcher, P. (1982). *Abusing science.* Cambridge, MA: MIT Press.

Klein, A. G. (2000). Fitting the school to the child: The mission of Leta Stetter Hollingworth, founder of gifted education. *Roeper Review, 23,* 97–103.

Klein, M. I. (1983). Freud's drive theory and ego psychology: A critical evaluation of the Blancks. *Psychoanalytic Review, 70,* 505–517.

Kline, L. W. (1908). The nature, origin and function of humor. *Popular Science Monthly, 73,* 144–156.

Knapp, T. J. (1995). A natural history of *The Behavior of Organisms.* In J. T. Todd (Ed.), *Modern perspectives on B. F. Skinner and contemporary behaviorism* (pp. 7–23). Westport, CT: Greenwood Press.

Knowles, D. (1967). Anicius Manlius Severinus Boethius. In P. Edwards (Ed.), *The encyclopedia of philosophy* (Vol. 1. pp. 328–330). New York: Macmillan and Free Press.

Knowlton, S. (1867). The silence of women in the churches. *The Congregational Quarterly, 9,* 329–334.

Koch, S. (1969). Psychology cannot be a coherent science. *Psychology Today, 3* (14), 64–68.

Koch, S. (1986). Afterword. In S. Koch & D. E. Leary (Eds.), *A century of psychology as science* (pp. 928–950). New York: McGraw-Hill.

Koestenbaum, P. (1967). Miguel de Unamuno y Jugo. In P. Edwards (Ed.), *Encyclopedia of philosophy* (Vol. 8, pp. 182–185). New York: Macmillan.

Koffka, K. (1922). Perception: An introduction to the Gestalt-Theorie. *Psychological Bulletin, 19,* 531–585.

Koffka, K. (1935). *Principles of Gestalt psychology.* New York: Harcourt.

Koffka, K. (1980). *Growth of the mind.* New Brunswick, NJ: Transaction Books. (Original work published in 1924)

Köhler, W. (1940). *Dynamics in psychology.* New York: Liveright.

Köhler, W. (1947). *Gestalt psychology.* New York: Liveright. (Original work published 1929)

Köhler, W. (1966). *The place of value in a world of facts.* New York: Liveright. (Original work published 1938)

Köhler, W. (1969). *The task of Gestalt psychology.* Princeton, NJ: Princeton University Press.

Köhler, W. (1976) *The mentality of apes.* New York: Liveright. (Original work published 1925)

Köhler, W., & Restorff, H. von (1935). Analyse von Vorgangen in Spurenfeld. *Psychologische Forschung, 13,* 293–364.

Kohn, D. (Ed.). (1985). *The Darwinian heritage.* Princeton, NJ: Princeton University Press.

Kolb, B. (1999). The twentieth century belongs to neuropsychology. *Brain Research Bulletin, 50,* 409–410.

Kovel, J. (1990). Beyond the future of an illusion: Further reflections on Freud and religion. *Psychoanalytic Review, 77,* 69–87.

Kramer, H., & Sprenger, J. (1971). *The malleus maleficarum* (Montague Summers, Trans.). New York: Dover. (Original work published 1486)

Krech, D. (1968). Edward C. Tolman. In D. L. Sills (Ed.), *International encyclopedia of the social sciences* (Vol. 16, pp. 95–98). New York: Macmillan.

Kristeller, P. O. (1967). Petrarch. In P. Edwards (Ed.), *The encyclopedia of philosophy* (Vol. 5, pp. 126–128). New York: Macmillan.

Kruta, V. (1976). Ernst Heinrich Weber. In C. C. Gillispie (Ed.), *Dictionary of scientific biography* (Vol. 14, pp. 199–202). New York: Charles Scribner's Sons.

Kuhn, T. S. (1970). *The structure of scientific revolutions* (2nd. ed.). Chicago: University of Chicago Press.

Kuhse, H., & Singer, P. (1993). Individuals, humans and persons: The issue of moral status. In P. Singer, H. Kuhse, S. Buckle, K. Dawson, & P. Kasimba (Eds.), *Embryo experimentation: Ethical, legal, and social issues* (pp. 65–75). Cambridge, England: Cambridge University Press.

Külpe, O. (1973). *Outlines of psychology* (E. B. Titchener, Trans.). New York: Arno Press. (Original work published 1893)

Kuna, D. P. (1976). The concept of suggestion in the early history of advertising psychology. *Journal of the History of the Behavioral Sciences, 12,* 347–353.

Kuo, Z. Y. (1921). Giving up instincts in psychology. *Journal of Philosophy, 18,* 645–666.

Kuo, Z. Y. (1924). A psychology without heredity. *Psychological Review, 31,* 427–448.

Lachman, R., Lachman, J. L., & Butterfield, E. C. (1979). *Cognitive psychology and information processing: An introduction.* Hillsdale, NJ: Erlbaum.

La Mettrie, J. O. (1912). *Man a machine.* La Salle, IL: Open Court. (Original work published 1747)

Landon, H. C. R. (1990). *The Mozart compendium: A guide to Mozart's life and music.* New York: Schirmer.

Landy, F. J. (1992). Hugo Münsterberg: Victim or visionary? *Journal of Applied Psychology, 77,* 787–802.

Landy, F. J. (1997). Early influences on the development of industrial and organizational psychology. *Journal of Applied Psychology, 82,* 467–477.

Lange, C. G. (1922). *The emotions.* Baltimore: Williams & Wilkins. (Original work published 1885)

Langfeld, H. S. (1937). Carl Stumpf. *American Journal of Psychology, 49,* 316–320.

Langfeld, H. S. (1946). Edwin Bissell Holt: 1873–1946. *Psychological Review, 53,* 251–258.

Lanham, U. (1968). *Origins of modern biology*. New York: Columbia University Press.

Larson, C. A. (1979). Highlights of Dr. John B. Watson's career in advertising. *Journal of Industrial/ Organizational Psychology, 16,* 3.

Lashley, K. (1942). An examination of the "continuity theory" as applied to discriminative learning. *Journal of General Psychology, 26,* 241–265.

Latham, R. E. (1959). Introduction. In R. E. Latham (Trans.), *Lucretius on the nature of the universe*. Baltimore, MD: Penguin.

Latham, R. E. (1967). Lucretius. In P. Edwards (Ed.), *The encyclopedia of philosophy* (Vol. 5, pp. 99–101). New York: Macmillan and Free Press.

Lattal, K. A. (1992). B. F. Skinner and psychology. *American Psychologist, 47,* 1269–1272.

Laver, A. B. (1972). Precursors of psychology in ancient Egypt. *Journal of the History of the Behavioral Sciences, 8,* 181–195.

Lawrence, D. H., & Festinger, L. (1962). *Deterrents and reinforcement. The psychology of insufficient reward*. Stanford, CA. Stanford University Press.

Lazarus, A. A. (2000). Will reason prevail? From classical psychoanalysis to New Age therapy. *American Journal of Psychotherapy, 54,* 152–155.

Lea, H. C. (Ed.). (1957). *Materials toward a history of witchcraft* (Vol. 3). New York: Thomas Yoseloff.

Leahey, T. H. (1981). The mistaken mirror: On Wundt's and Titchener's psychologies. *Journal of the History of the Behavioral Sciences, 17,* 273–282.

Leahey, T. H. (2001). Back to Bridgman? *Theory and Psychology, 11,* 53–58.

Leary, D. E. (1980). The intentions and heritage of Descartes and Locke: Toward a recognition of the moral basis of modern psychology. *Journal of General Psychology, 102,* 283–310.

Lehrer, K. (1989). *Thomas Reid*. New York: Routledge.

Leslie, R. C. (1996). Karen Horney and Viktor Frankl: Optimists in spite of everything. *International Forum for Logotherapy, 19,* 23–28.

Leuba, J. H. (1928). Morality among the animals. *Harper's Magazine, 157,* 97–103.

Levine, H. G. (1978). The discovery of addiction: Changing conceptions of habitual drunkenness in America. *Journal of Studies on Alcohol, 39,* 143–174.

Levine, M., & Wishner, J. (1977). The case records of the Psychological Clinic at the University of Pennsylvania (1896–1961). *Journal of the History of the Behavioral Sciences, 13,* 59–66.

Levy, E. (1986). A Gestalt theory of paranoia. *Gestalt Theory, 8,* 230–255.

Lewin, K. (1931). The conflict between Aristotelian and Galileian modes of thought in contemporary psychology. *Journal of Genetic Psychology, 5,* 141–177.

Lewin, K. (1935). *A dynamic theory of personality: Selected papers* (D. K. Adams & K. E. Zener, Trans.). New York: McGraw-Hill.

Lewin, K. (1937). Carl Stumpf. *Psychological Review, 44,* 189–194.

Lewin, R. (1984). *Hitler's mistakes*. New York: William Morrow.

Liddell, A. F. (1933). Instructed ignorance: The philosophy of Nicholas of Cusa. *Psychological Bulletin, 30,* 606–607.

Lifton, R. J. (1968). *Revolutionary immortality. Mao Tse-Tung and the Chinese Cultural Revolution*. New York: Random House.

Lincoln, A. (1950). Letter to W. H. Herndon. In A. H. Shaw (Ed.), *The Lincoln encyclopedia*. New York: Macmillan. (Original work published 1856)

Lindberg, D. C., & Numbers, R. L. (1986). *God and nature*. Berkeley: University of California Press.

Lindenfeld, D. (1978). Oswald Külpe and the Würzburg School. *Journal of the History of the Behavioral Sciences, 14,* 132–141.

Link, S. W. (1994). Rediscovering the past: Gustav Fechner and signal detection theory. *Psychological Science, 5,* 335–340.

Lippman, T. W. (1995). *Understanding Islam: An introduction to the Muslim world*. New York: Meridian.

Lloyd, P., & Fernyhough, C. (Eds.). (1999). *Lev Vygotsky: Critical assessments: Vygotsky's theory*. Florence, KY: Taylor & Francis/Rutledge.

Locke, J. (1959). *An essay concerning human understanding* (A. C. Fraser, Ed.). New York: Dover Publications. (Original work published 1690)

Locke, J. (1989). *Some thoughts concerning education*. (J. W., & J. S. Yolton, Eds.). Oxford: Clarendon Press. (Original work published 1693)

Logan, F. A. (1968). Clark L. Hull. In D. L. Sills (Ed.), *International encyclopedia of the social sciences* (Vol. 6, pp. 535–539). New York: Macmillan.

Lotze, H. (1973). *Outlines of psychology*. New York: Arno Press. (Original work published 1881)

Lovejoy, A. D. (1922). Paradox of the thinking behaviorist. *Philosophical Review, 31,* 135–147.

Lowrie, W. (1970). *Kierkegaard* (Vol. 1). Gloucester, MA: Peter Smith.

Lowry, R. J. (1973). *A. H. Maslow: An intellectual portrait.* Monterey, CA: Brooks/Cole.

Lucretius. (1959). *On the nature of the universe* (R. E. Latham, Trans.). Baltimore, MD: Penguin.

Luther, M. (1967). Table Talk. In H. T. Lehmann (Ed.), *Luther's works* (Vol. 54, pp. 358–359). Philadelphia: Fortress Press.

MacCormac, E. R. (1990). Metaphor and pluralism. *The Monist, 73,* 411–420.

MacCorquodale, K. C. (1970). On Chomsky's review of Skinner's Verbal Behavior. *Journal of the Experimental Analysis of Behavior, 13,* 83–100.

MacCorquodale, K. C., & Meehl, P. E. (1954). Edward C. Tolman. In W. K. Estes, S. Koch, K. MacCorquodale, P. E. Meehl, C. G. Muller, Jr., W. N. Schoenfeld, & W. S. Verplanck (Eds.), *Modern learning theory.* New York: Appleton-Century-Crofts.

Mach, E. (1959). *The analysis of sensations* (C. M. Williams, Trans. of 5th ed.). New York: Dover Publications. (Original work published 1886; 5th ed. published 1905)

Machiavelli, N. (1977). *The prince* (R. M. Adams, Trans. & Ed.). New York: W. W. Norton. (Original work published 1532)

Mackintosh, N. J. (1997). Has the wheel turned full circle? Fifty years of learning theory, 1946–1996. *Quarterly Journal of Experimental Psychology, 50,* 879–898.

Mackler, B., & Bernstein, E. (1966). Philippe Pinel: The man and his time. *Psychological Reports, 19,* 703–720.

Mackler, B., & Hamilton, K. (1967). Benjamin Rush: A political and historical study of the "Father of American Psychiatry." *Psychological Reports, 20,* 1287–1306.

Macklin, R. (1976). A psychoanalytic model for human freedom and rationality. *Psychoanalytic Quarterly, 45,* 430–454.

MacLeod, R. B. (1964). Phenomenology: A challenge to experimental psychology. In T. W. Wann (Ed.), *Behaviorism and phenomenology: Contrasting bases for modern psychology.* Chicago: University of Chicago Press.

MacLeod, R. B. (1968a). Johannes Müller. In D. L. Sills (Ed.), *International encyclopedia of the social sciences* (Vol. 10. pp. 525–527). New York: Macmillan and Free Press.

MacLeod, R. B. (1968b). Phenomenology. In D. L. Sills (Ed.), *International encyclopedia of the social sciences* (Vol. 12, pp. 68–72). New York: Macmillan and Free Press.

MacLeod, R. B. (Ed.). (1969). *William James: Unfinished business.* Washington, DC: American Psychological Association.

MacLeod, R. B. (1975). *The persistent problems of psychology.* Pittsburgh: Duquesne University Press.

MacMillan, M. (1991). *Freud evaluated: The completed arc.* Amsterdam: North-Holland.

Macnamara, J. (1993). Cognitive psychology and the rejection of Brentano. *Journal for the Theory of Social Behavior, 23,* 117–137.

Madigan, S., & O'Hara, R. (1992). Short-term memory at the turn of the century: Mary Whiton Calkins's memory research. *American Psychologist, 47,* 170–174.

Mahaffy, J. P. (1969). *Descartes.* Freeport, NY: Books for the Libraries Press. (Original work published 1902)

Mahoney, M. J. (1989). Scientific psychology and radical behaviorism: Important distinctions based in scientism and objectivism. *American Psychologist, 44,* 1372–1377.

Mandler, J. M., & Mandler, G. (1969). The diaspora of experimental psychology: The Gestaltists and others. In D. Fleming & B. Bailyn (Eds.), *The intellectual migration: Europe and America, 1930–1960.* Cambridge, MA: Harvard University Press.

Marrow, A. J. (1969). *The practical theorist: The life and work of Lewin.* New York: Basic Books.

Marti, F. (1983). The social and political question of demythologizing. Talk delivered before the Southern Society for Philosophy and Psychology. Atlanta, GA, April 1.

Martinez, J. L., Jr., & Mendoza, R. H. (1984). *Chicano psychology.* New York: Academic Press.

Maslow, A. H. (1943). A theory of human motivation. *Psychological Review, 50,* 370–396.

Maslow, A. H. (1954). *Motivation and personality.* New York: Harper and Brothers.

Maslow, A. H. (1962). *Toward a psychology of being.* Princeton, NJ: D. Van Nostrand.

Maslow, A. H. (1964). *Religion, values, and peak experiences.* New York: Viking Press.

Maslow, A. H. (1971). *The farther reaches of human nature.* New York: Viking.

Masson, J. M. (1991). *Final analysis: The making and unmaking of a psychoanalyst.* Reading, MA: Addison-Wesley.

Mathews, N. (1996). *Francis Bacon: The history of a character assassination.* New Haven, CT: Yale University Press.

Matson, W. I. (1982). De Corpre. In F. N. McGill (Ed.), *World Philosophy, 2,* 851–856.

Mattoon, M. A. (1981). *Jungian psychology in perspective.* New York: Free Press.

Mays, W. (1998). Genetic explanation in Husserl and Piaget. *New Ideas in Psychology, 16,* 1–10.

McCool, G. A. (1990). Why St. Thomas stays alive. *International Philosophical Quarterly, 30,* 275–287.

McCullough, D. (2001). *John Adams.* New York: Simon and Schuster.

McDermott, J. J. (Ed.). (1968). *The writings of William James.* New York: Modern Library.

McDougall, W. (1905). *Physiological psychology.* London: J. M. Dent.

McDougall, W. (1908). *An introduction to social psychology.* Kennebunkport, Maine: Milford House.

McDougall, W. (1923). *Outline of psychology.* Boston: Charles Scribner's Sons.

McDougall, W. (1926a). *An introduction to social psychology.* Boston: Luce.

McDougall, W. (1926b). Men or robots? *Pedagogical Seminary, 33,* 71–102.

McDougall, W. (1942). *The energies of men.* London: Methuen & Co. Ltd.

McDougall, W. (1960). *An introduction to social psychology.* London: Methuen and Co. Ltd. (Original work published 1908).

McGaugh, J. L. (2000). Memory: A century of consolidation. *Science, 287,* 248–251.

McHenry, L. C. (1969). *Garrison's history of neurology.* Springfield, IL: Charles C. Thomas.

McInerny, R. (1990). *A first glance at St. Thomas Aquinas.* Notre Dame, IN: University of Notre Dame Press.

McKeon, R. (Ed.). (1941). *The basic writing of Aristotle.* New York: Random House.

McReynolds, P. (1987). Lightner Witmer: Little known founder of clinical psychology. *American Psychologist, 42,* 849–858.

McReynolds, P. (1996). Lightner Witmer: A centennial tribute. *American Psychologist, 51,* 237–240.

McReynolds, P. (1997). *Lightner Witmer: His life and times.* Washington, DC: American Psychological Association.

McWhirter, P. T., & McWhirter, J. J. (1997). Lightner Witmer: Father and grandfather? *American Psychologist, 52,* 275.

Meade, M. (1979). *Stealing heaven: The love story of Heloise and Abelard.* New York: Soho Press.

Medawar, P. B. (1984). *The limits of science.* New York: Harper & Row.

Meissner, W. W. (1984). *Psychoanalysis and religious experience.* New Haven, CT: Yale University Press.

Melville, H. (1976). *Moby-Dick, or the whale.* New York: W. W. Norton. (Original work published 1851)

Merchant, C. (1979). The vitalism of Anne Conway: Its impact on Leibniz's concept of the monad. *Journal of the History of Philosophy, 17,* 255–269.

Meredith, A. (1986). Later philosophy. In J. Boardman, J. Griffin, & O. Murray (Eds.), *The Oxford history of the classical world* (pp. 708–714). New York: Oxford University Press.

Merlan, P. (1967). Plotinus. In P. Edwards (Ed.), *The encyclopedia of philosophy* (Vol. 6, pp. 351–359). New York: Macmillan and Free Press.

Meyer, M. (1922). *The psychology of the other one* (2nd ed.). Columbia, MO: Missouri Book Company Publishers.

Michell, J. (1999). *Measurement in psychology: A critical history of a methodological concept.* New York: Cambridge University Press.

Michelmore, P. (1962). *Einstein, profile of the man.* New York: Dodd, Mead.

Milar, K. S. (1999). "A course and clumsy tool": Helen Thompson Wooley and the Cincinnati Vocation Bureau. *History of Psychology, 2,* 219–235.

Miles, W. (1949). James Rowland Angell, 1869–1949, Psychologist-educator. *Science, 110,* 1–4.

Mill, J. S. (1969). *Autobiography.* In J. Stillinger (Ed.), Boston: Houghton Mifflin. (Original work published 1873)

Mill, J. S. (1974). *A system of logic.* In J. M. Robson (Ed.), *Collected works of John Stuart Mill* (Vol. 8). Toronto: Routledge & Kegan Paul. (Original work published 1843)

Mill, J. S. (1988). *The subjection of women.* Indianapolis/Cambridge: Hackett Publishing. (Original work published 1869)

Miller, J. (1981). Interpretations of Freud's Jewishness, 1924–1974. *Journal of the History of the Behavioral Sciences, 17,* 357–374.

Mills, J. A. (1988). The genesis of Hull's Principles of Behavior. *Journal of the History of the Behavioral Sciences, 24,* 392–401.

Mills, J. A. (1998). *Control: A history of behavioral psychology.* New York: New York University Press.

Mintz, S. I. (1962). *The hunting of Leviathan.* Cambridge: Cambridge University Press.

Misiak, H. K. & Sexton, V. S. (1966). *History of psychology: An overview.* New York: Grune & Stratton.

Montague, H., & Hollingworth, L. S. (1914). The comparative variability of the sexes at birth. *American Journal of Sociology, 20,* 335–370.

Montaigne, M. (1960). Apology for Raimond Sebond (D. M. Frame, Trans.). *The complete essays of Montaigne, 2,* 112–308. Garden City, NY: Doubleday.

Moody, E. A. (1967). William of Ockham. In P. Edwards (Ed.), *The encyclopedia of philosophy* (Vol. 8, pp. 306–317). New York: Macmillan and Free Press.

Moore, K. G. (1946). Theory of imagination in Plotinus. *Journal of Psychology, 22,* 41–51.

Moore, Y. G. (1956). Some Arab doctrines on imagination: A chapter in the history of psychology. *Journal of Psychology, 41,* 127–133.

Morawski, J. G. (1983). Hugo Münsterberg on the possibilities for psychology and society. *American Psychologist, 38,* 1259–1260.

Morens, D. M. (1999). Death of a president. *New England Journal of Medicine, 341,* 1845–1849.

Morgan, C. L. (1977). *Comparative psychology.* Washington DC: University Publications of America. (Original work published in 1894)

Morgan, C. T. (1968). Karl S. Lashley. In D. L. Sills (Ed.), *International encyclopedia of the social sciences* (Vol. 9, pp. 27–30). New York: Macmillan.

Morris, D. (1967). *The naked ape.* New York: McGraw-Hill.

Morris, E. A., & Todd, J. T. (1999). Watsonian behaviorism. In W. O'Donohue & R. Kitchener (Eds.), *Handbook of behaviorism* (pp. 15–69). San Diego, CA: Academic Press.

Moskowitz, M. J. (1977). Hugo Münsterberg: A study in the history of applied psychology. *American Psychologist, 32,* 824–842.

Mozans (pseudonym for) Zahm, J. A. (1913). *Women in science.* New York: Appleton.

Mruk, C. J. (1989). Phenomenological psychology and the computer revolution: Friend, foe or opportunity? *Journal of Phenomenological Psychology, 20,* 20–39.

Muckle, J. T. (Trans.). (1992). *The story of Abelard's adversities.* Toronto, Canada: Pontifical Institute of Medieval Studies.

Müller, G. E., & Pilzecker, A. (1900). Experimental contributions to the theory of memory. In S. Diamond (Ed.), *The roots of psychology* (pp. 271–273). New York: Basic Books.

Mumford, L. (1934). *Techniques and civilization.* New York: Harcourt, Brace.

Munroe, R. L. (1955). *Schools of psychoanalytic thought.* New York: Holt, Rinehart and Winston.

Münsterberg, H. (1908). *On the witness stand.* New York: Clark Boardman.

Münsterberg, H. (1909). *Psychotherapy.* New York: Moffat, Yard and Company.

Münsterberg, H. (1913). *Psychology and industrial efficiency.* New York: Houghton/Mifflin.

Murphy, G. (1963). Robert Sessions Woodworth, 1869–1962. *American Psychologist, 18,* 131–133.

Murphy, G., & Kovach, J. K. (1972). *Historical introduction to modern psychology* (3rd ed.). New York: Harcourt Brace Jovanovich.

Murray, D. J. (1993). A perspective for viewing the history of psychophysics. *Behavioral and Brain Sciences, 16,* 115–186.

Murray, D. J. (1995). *Gestalt psychology and the cognitive revolution.* New York: Harvester Wheatsheaf.

Murray, D. J., & Farahmand, B. (1998). Gestalt theory and evolutionary psychology. In R. W. Rieber & K. Salzinger (Eds.), *Psychology: Theoretical-historical perspectives* (2nd ed., pp. 255–287). Washington, DC: American Psychological Association.

Myers, G. E. (1986). *William James: His life and thought.* New Haven, CT: Yale University Press.

Natsoulas, T. (1990). Reflective seeing: An exploration in the company of Edmund Husserl and James J. Gibson. *Journal of Phenomenological Psychology, 21,* 1–31.

Neisser, U. (1967). *Cognitive psychology.* New York: Appleton-Century-Crofts.

Neisser, U. (1976). *Cognition and reality.* San Francisco: Freeman.

Neisser, U. (1982). *Memory observed: Remembering in natural contexts.* New York: Freeman.

Newell, A, (1985). Duncker on thinking: An inquiry into progress in cognition. In S. Koch & D. Leary (Eds.), *A century of psychology as science* (pp. 392– 419). New York: McGraw-Hill.

Nicholson, I. A. M. (1998). Gordon Allport, character, and the "culture of personality," 1897–1937. *History of Psychology, 1,* 52–68.

Nicholson, I. A. M. (2000). "A coherent datum of perception": Gordon Allport, Floyd Allport, and the politics of "personality." *Journal of the History of the Behavioral Sciences, 36,* 463–470.

Nicholson, I. A. M. (2001). "Giving up maleness": Abraham Maslow, masculinity, and the boundaries of psychology. *History of Psychology, 4,* 79–91.

Nightmare in Jonestown. (1978, December 4). *Time, 112*(23), pp. 16–21.

Nissim-Sabat, M. (1999). Phenomenology and mental disorders: Heidegger or Husserl? *Philosophy, Psychiatry, & Psychology, 6,* 100–104.

Noel, P. S., & Carlson, E. T. (1970). Origins of the word "phrenology." *American Journal of Psychiatry, 127,* 694–697.

Noel, P. S., & Carlson, E. T. (1973). The faculty psychology of Benjamin Rush. *Journal of the History of the Behavioral Sciences, 9,* 369–377.

Norena, C. G. (1970). *Juan Luis Vives.* The Hague: Nijhoff.

Norena, C. G. (1975). *Studies in Spanish Renaissance thought.* The Hague: Martinus Nijhoff.

Norman, D. A. (1980). Twelve issues for cognitive science. *Cognitive Science, 4,* 1–32.

Novak, M. (1970). *The experience of nothingness.* New York: Harper & Row.

O'Connell, A. N. (1990). Karen Horney (1885–1952). In A. N. O'Connell & N. F. Russo (Eds.), *Women in psychology: A bio-bibliographic sourcebook* (pp. 184–196). New York: Greenwood Press.

O'Connell, A. N., & Russo, N. F. (Eds.). (1983). *Models of achievement: Reflections of eminent women in psychology.* New York: Columbia University Press.

O'Connell, A. N., & Russo, N. F. (Eds.). (1988). *Models of achievement: Reflections of eminent women in psychology,* Vol. 2. Hillsdale, NJ: Erlbaum.

O'Connell, A. N., & Russo, N. F. (Eds.). (1990). *Women in psychology: A bio-bibliograhic sourcebook.* New York: Greenwood Press.

O'Donnell, J. M. (1985). *The origins of behaviorism: American psychology, 1870–1920.* New York: New York University Press.

Ogden, R. M. (1951). Oswald Külpe and the Würzburg school. *American Journal of Psychology, 64,* 4–19.

O'Hara, M. (1995). Carl Rogers: Scientist and mystic. *Journal of Humanistic Psychology, 35,* 40–53.

Okin, S. S. (Ed.). (1988). *The subjection of women.* Indianapolis/Cambridge: Hackett Publishing. (Original work published 1869)

Olds, J. (1954). A neural model for sign-gestalt theory. *Psychological Review, 61,* 59–72.

O'Neil, W. M. (1984). The Wundt's myths. *Australian Journal of Psychology, 36,* 285–289.

O'Neil, W. M. (1995). American behaviorism: A historical and critical analysis. *Theory and Psychology, 5,* 285–305.

Orgel, S. (1990). The future of psychoanalysis. *Psychoanalytic Quarterly, 59,* 1–20.

Pace, E. A. (1921). In memory of Wilhelm Wundt. *Psychological Review, 28,* 159–162.

Palha, A. P., & Esteves, M. F. (1997). The origin of dementia praecox. *Schizophrenia Research, 28,* 99–103.

Papanicolaou, A. C. (1989). *Emotion: A reconsideration of the somatic theory.* New York: Gordon and Breach Science Publishers.

Paris, B. J. (1991). A Horneyan approach to literature. *American Journal of Psychoanalysis, 51,* 319–337.

Pastore, N. (1965). Samuel Bailey's critique of Berkeley's theory of vision. *Journal of the History of the Behavioral Sciences, 1,* 321–337.

Patrick, G. T. W. (1914). The psychology of relaxation. *Popular Science Monthly, 84,* 590–604.

Pauley, P. J. (1986). G. Stanley Hall and his successors: A history of the first half-century of psychology at Johns Hopkins. In S. H. Hulse & B. F. Green, Jr. (Eds.), *One hundred years of psychological research in America* (pp. 21–51). Baltimore: Johns Hopkins University Press.

Pavlov, I. P. (1928). *Lectures on conditioned reflexes* (Vol. 1) (W. H. Gantt, Trans. & Ed.). New York: International Publishers.

Pavlov, I. P. (1941). *Lectures on conditioned reflexes* (Vol. 2.) (W. H. Gantt, Trans. & Ed.). New York: International Publishers.

Pavlov, I. P. (1955). *I. P. Pavlov: Selected works.* (J. Gibbons, Ed.; S. Belsky, Trans.). Moscow: Foreign Languages Publishing House.

Peach, B. (1982). Leviathan. In F. N. MaGill (Ed.), *World philosophy.* (Vol. 2, pp. 839–846). Englewood Cliffs, NJ: Salem Press.

Pearson, K. (1914). *The life, letters, and labors of Francis Galton* (Vol. 1). London: Cambridge University Press.

Perry, R. B. (1954). *The thought and character of William James: Briefer version.* New York: George Braziller.

Petzold, M. (1987). *The social history of Chinese psychology.* In M. G. Ash & W. R. Woodward (Eds.), *Psychology in twentieth-century thought and society* (pp. 213–231). Cambridge: Cambridge University Press.

Phillips, L. (2000). Recontextualizing Kenneth B. Clark: An Afrocentric perspective on the paradoxical legacy of a model psychologist-activist. *History of Psychology, 3,* 142–167.

Piaget, J. (1952). In E. G. Boring (Ed.), *A history of psychology in autobiography* (Vol. 4). New York: Russell and Russell.

Piaget, J., & Garcia, J. (1989). *Psychogenesis and the history of science* (H. Feider, Trans.). New York: Columbia University Press. (Original work published 1983)

Pickenhain, L. (1999). The importance of I. P. Pavlov for the development of neuroscience. *Integrative Physiological & Behavioral Science, 34,* 85–89.

Pickren, W. E., & Dewsbury, D. A. (2002). *Evolving perspectives on the history of psychology.* Washington, DC: American Psychological Association.

Pinel, P. (1977). A treatise on insanity (D. D. Davis, Trans.). In D. N. Robinson (Ed.), *Significant contributions to the history of psychology, 1750–1920.* Series C. Vol. III. Washington, DC: University Publications of America. (Original work published 1806)

Pivnicki, D. (1969). The beginnings of psychotherapy. *Journal of the History of the Behavioral Sciences, 5,* 238–247.

Plaud, J. J. & Montgomery, R. W. (1993). On the influence of Walter S. Hunter in the shaping of modern behaviorism. *Psychological Record, 43,* 361–373.

Plekhanov, G. V. (1967). *Essays in the history of materialism.* New York: H. Fertig.

Plotinus. (1956). *The Enneads* (S. MacKenna, Trans.). London: Faber & Faber.

Plummer, B. L. (1970). Benjamin Rush and the Negro. *American Journal of Psychiatry, 127,* 793–798.

Poffenberger, A. T. (1962). Robert Sessions Woodworth: 1869–1962. *American Journal of Psychology, 75,* 677–689.

Poll finds Americans split on creation ideas. (1982, August 29). *New York Times,* section 1, p. 22.

Popkin, R. H. (1960). *The history of skepticism from Erasmus to Descartes* (rev. ed.). Assen, Netherlands: Koninklijke Van Gorcum & Co.

Popkin, R. H. (1967). Michel Eyquem de Montainge. In P. Edwards (Ed.), *The encyclopedia of philosophy* (Vol. 5, pp. 366–368). New York: Macmillan.

Popkin, R. H. (1979). *The history of skepticism from Erasmus to Spinoza.* Berkeley: University of California Press.

Popper, K. R. (1959). *The logic of scientific discovery.* London: Hutchinson & Co.

Popplestone. J. A. (1995). *Recent variations on a theme by Descartes.* Paper presented at the meeting of the American Psychological Association, New York.

Postman, L. (1973). Hermann Ebbinghaus. In M. Henle, J. Jaynes, & J. J. Sullivan (Eds.), *Historical conceptions of psychology* (pp. 220–229). New York: Springer Publishing. Also published in *American Psychologist, 23* (1968): 149–157.

Pratola, S. (1974). Up with our foremother. *American Psychologist, 29,* 780.

Preyer, W. (1888). The imitative faculty of infants. *Popular Science Monthly, 33,* 249–255.

Pubols, B. H., Jr. (1959). Jan Swammerdam and the history of reflex action. *American Journal of Psychology, 72,* 131–135.

Puglisi, M. (1924). Franz Brentano: A biographical sketch. *American Journal of Psychology, 35,* 414–419.

Quételet, J. A. (1968). *A treatise on man and the development of his faculties.* New York: B. Franklin. (Original work published 1842)

Quinn, S. (1987). *A mind of her own: The life of Karen Horney.* New York: Summit.

Rambo, L. R. (1980). Ethics, evolution, and the psychology of William James. *Journal of the History of the Behavioral Sciences, 16,* 50–57.

Rancurello, A. C. (1968). *A study of Franz Brentano.* New York: Academic Press.

Ranke-Heinemann, U. (1990). *Eunuchs for the kingdom of heaven* (P. Heinegg, Trans.). New York: Penguin.

Rashotte, M. E., & Amsel, A. (1999). Clark L. Hull's behaviorism. In W. O'Donohue & R. Kitchener (Eds.), *Handbook of behaviorism* (pp. 119–158). San Diego, CA: Academic Press.

Rathunde, K. (2001). Toward a psychology of optimal human functioning: What positive psychology can learn from the "experimental turns" of James, Dewey, and Maslow. *Journal of Humanistic Psychology, 41,* 135–153.

Razran, G. (1968). Ivan M. Sechenov. In D. L. Sills (Ed.), *International encyclopedia of the social sciences* (Vol. 14, pp. 129–130). New York: Macmillan and Free Press.

Reck, A. J. (1990). An historical sketch of pluralism. *The Monist, 73,* 367–387.

Reid, T. (1786). *Essays on the intellectual powers of man.* Dublin: L. White.

Reid, T. (1790). *Essays on the active powers of man.* Dublin: P. Byrne and J. Milliken.

Reid, T. (1970). *An inquiry into the human mind* (T. Duggan, Ed.). Chicago: University of Chicago Press. (Original work published 1764)

Reik, M. M. (1977). *The golden lands of Thomas Hobbes.* Detroit: Wayne State University Press.

Reisenzein, R., & Schonpflug, W. (1992). Stumpf's cognitive-evaluative theory of emotion. *American Psychologist, 47,* 34–45.

Richards, R. J. (1980). Wundt's early theories of unconscious inference and cognitive evolution in their relation to Darwinian biopsychology. In W. G. Bringmann & R. D. Tweney (Eds.), *Wundt studies: A centennial collection* (pp. 42–70). Toronto: C. J. Hogrefe.

Richards, R. J. (1987). *Darwin and the emergence of evolutionary theories of mind and behavior.* Chicago: University of Chicago Press.

Richardson, H. S. (1990). Measurement, pleasure, and the practical science in Plato's Protagoras. *Journal of the History of Philosophy, 28,* 7–32.

Richeson, A. W. (1940). Hypatia of Alexandria. *National Mathematics Magazine, 15,* 73–82.

Richter, J. P. (Ed.). (1970). *The literary works of Leonardo da Vinci* (3rd ed.). (2 vols.). London: Phaidon.

Riese, W. (1951). Philippe Pinel (1745–1826): His views on human nature and disease. His medical thought. *Journal of Nervous and Mental Disease, 114,* 313–323.

Rilling, M. (2000a). John Watson's paradoxical struggle to explain Freud. *American Psychologist, 55,* 301–312.

Rilling, M. (2000b). How the challenge of explaining learning influenced the origins and development of John B. Watson's behaviorism. *American Journal of Psychology, 113,* 275–301.

Ringer, F. K. (1969). *The decline of the German mandarins: The German academic community, 1890–1933.* Cambridge, MA: Harvard University Press.

Roback, A. A., & Kiernan, T. (1969). *Pictorial history of psychology and psychiatry.* New York: Philosophical Library.

Robins, R. W., Gosling, S. D., & Craik, K. H. (1999). An empirical analysis of trends in psychology. *American Psychologist, 54,* 117–128.

Robinson, D. N. (1977). *Significant contributions to the history of psychology, 1750–1920.* Series C, Vol. III. Washington, DC: University Publications of America.

Robinson, D. N. (1982). *Toward a science of human nature.* New York: Columbia University Press.

Robinson, D. N. (1989). *Aristotle's psychology.* New York: Columbia University Press.

Rock, I. (Ed.). (1990). *The legacy of Solomon Asch: Essays in cognition and social psychology.* Hillsdale, NJ: Erlbaum.

Rock, I., & Palmer, S. (1990). The legacy of Gestalt psychology. *Scientific American, 263,* 84–90.

Roediger, H. L. (1980). Memory metaphors in cognitive psychology. *Memory and Cognition, 8,* 231–246.

Rogers, A. K. (1912). *A student's history of philosophy.* New York: Macmillan.

Rogers, C. (1959). *Introduction in the examination of men's wits by Juan Huarte.* (M. C. Camilli, Trans., & R. Carew, Trans.). Gainesville, FL: Scholars Facsimiles and Reprints. (Original work published 1594)

Rogers, C. R. (1951). *Client-centered therapy.* Boston: Houghton Mifflin.

Rogers, C. R. (1961). *On being a person: A therapist's view of psychotherapy.* Boston: Houghton Mifflin.

Rogers, E. M. (1960). *Physics for the inquiring mind.* Princeton, NJ: Princeton University Press.

Rogers, T. B. (1989). Operationism in psychology: A discussion of contextual antecedents and an historical interpretation of its longevity. *Journal of the History of the Behavioral Sciences, 25,* 139–153.

Rogow, A. A. (1986). *Thomas Hobbes: Radical in the service of reaction.* New York: W. W. Norton.

Rohles, F. H. (1992). Orbital bar pressing: A historical note on Skinner and the chimpanzees in space. *American Psychologist, 47,* 1531–1533.

Roith, E. (1987). *The riddle of Freud: Jewish influences on his theory of female sexuality* (David Tuckett, Ed.) New Library of Psychoanalysis: 4. New York: Tavistock Publications.

Romanes, G. J. (1881). Intelligence of ants. *Popular Science Monthly, 19,* 495–510, 816–829.

Ronan, C. A. (1982). *Science: Its history and development among the world's cultures.* New York: Facts on File Publications.

Rosenfield, L. C. (1968). *From beast-machine to man-machine: Animal soul in French letters from Descartes to La Mettrie.* New York: Octagon Books.

Rosenzweig, S. (1997). Letters by Freud on experimental psychodynamics. *American Psychologist, 52,* 571.

Ross, D. (1972). *G. Stanley Hall: The psychologist as prophet.* Chicago: University of Chicago Press.

Rotenberg, M., & Diamond, B. L. (1971). The biblical conception of psychopathology: The law of the stubborn and rebellious son. *Journal of the History of the Behavioral Sciences, 7,* 29–38.

Roth, M. S. (1998). *Freud: Conflict and culture.* New York: Alfred A. Knopf.

Rotter, J. B. (1954). *Social learning and clinical psychology.* New York: Prentice-Hall.

Royce, J. (1898). The new psychology and the consulting psychologist. *Forum, 26,* 80–96.

Rozin, P. (2001). Social psychology and science: Some lessons from Solomon Asch. *Personality and Social Psychology Review, 5,* 2–14.

Rubenstein, J., & Slife, B. (1988). *Taking sides: Clashing views on controversial psychological issues* (5th ed.). Guilford, CT: Dushkin Publishing.

Rubins, J. L. (1978). *Karen Horney: Gentle rebel of psychoanalysis.* New York: Dial.

Rush, B. (1806). *Essays, literary, moral, and philosophical* (2nd ed.). Philadelphia: Thomas and William Bradford.

Rush, B. (1818). *Medical inquiries and observations upon the diseases of the mind* (2nd ed.). Philadelphia: John Richardson. (Original work published 1812)

Russell, B. (1959). *Wisdom of the west.* New York: Crescent Books.

Russell, J. B. (1980). *A history of witchcraft.* London: Thames and Hudson.

Rutherford, A. (2000). Radical behaviorism and psychology's public: B. F. Skinner in the popular press, 1934–1990. *History of Psychology, 3,* 371–395.

Rychlak, J. F. (1988). *The psychology of rigorous humanism* (2nd ed.). New York: New York University Press.

Rychlak, J. F. (1991) *Artificial intelligence and human reason: A teleological critique.* New York: Columbia University Press.

Rychlak, J. F. (1994). *Logical learning theory: A human teleology and its empirical support.* Lincoln, NE: University of Nebraska Press.

Rychlak, J. F. (1998). How Boulder biases have limited possible theoretical contributions to psychotherapy. *Clinical Psychology: Science and Practice, 5,* 233–241.

Rychlak, J. F. (2000). A psychotherapist's lessons from the philosophy of science. *American Psychologist, 55,* 1126–1132.

Rychlak, J. F., & Rychlak, R. J. (1990). The insanity defense and the question of human agency. *New Ideas in Psychology, 8,* 3–24.

Sahakian, W. S. (Ed.). (1968). *History of psychology: A sourcebook in systematic psychology.* Itasca, IL: F. E. Peacock.

Sahakian, W. S., & Sahakian, M. L. (1975). *John Locke.* Boston: Twayne Publishers.

Sakuma, A. (1999). Gestalt psychology in Japan. *Japanese Psychological Review, 42,* 326–345.

Salzinger, K. (1994). On Watson. In J. T. Todd & E. K. Morris (Eds.), *Modern perspectives on John B. Watson and classical behaviorism* (pp. 151–158). Westport, CT: Greenwood Press.

Samelson, F. (1985). Organizing for the kingdom of behavior: Academic battles and organizational policies in the twenties. *Journal of the History of Behavioral Sciences, 21,* 33–47.

Samelson, F. (1994). John B. Watson in 1913: Rhetoric and practice. In J. T. Todd & E. K. Morris (Eds.), *Modern perspectives on John B. Watson and classical behaviorism* (pp. 3–18). Westport, CT: Greenwood Press.

Samuels, A. (1994). The professionalization of Carl G. Jung's analytical psychology clubs. *Journal of the History of the Behavioral Sciences, 30,* 138–147.

Sargant, W. (1957). *Battle for the mind.* New York: Harper & Row.

Sarton, G. (1959). *A history of science: Hellenistic science and culture in the last three centuries B.C.* Cambridge: Harvard University Press.

Sartre, J. P. (1965). Reply to Albert Camus. In J. P. Sartre, *Situations* (B. Eisler, Trans.). New York: George Braziller.

Sawyer, T. F. (2000). Francis Cecil Sumner: His views and influence on African American higher education. *History of Psychology, 3,* 122–141.

Sayers, J. (1991). *Mothers of psychoanalysis.* New York: W. W. Norton.

Scarborough, E. (2000). Margaret Floy Washburn. In A. Kazdin (Ed.), *Encyclopedia of psychology* (Vol. 8, pp. 230–232). Washington, DC: American Psychological Association, and New York: Oxford University Press.

Scarborough, E. & Furumoto, L. (1987). *Untold lives: The first generation of American women psychologists.* New York: Columbia University Press.

Scheffield, F. D. (1959). Edwin Ray Guthrie: 1886–1959. *American Journal of Psychology, 72,* 642–650.

Scherez, G. (1976). Niels Stensen also known as Nicolaus Steno. In C. Gillispie (Ed.), *Dictionary of scientific biography* (Vol. 13, pp. 30–35). New York: Charles Scribner's Sons.

Schliemann, H. (1968). *Troy and its remains.* New York: Benjamin Blom. (Original work published 1875)

Schlosberg, H. (1954). Walter S. Hunter: Pioneer objectivist in psychology. *Science, 120,* 441–442.

Schmitt, R. (1967). Phenomenology. In P. Edwards (Ed.), *The encyclopedia of philosophy* (Vol. 6, pp. 135–151). New York: Macmillan and Free Press.

Schneck, J. M. (1978). Benjamin Rush and animal magnetism, 1789 and 1812. *International Journal of Clinical and Experimental Hypnosis, 26,* 9–14.

Schneider, D. J. (1991). Social cognition. *Annual Review of Psychology, 42,* 527–561.

Schneider, K. J., Bugental, J. F. T., & Pierson, J. F. (Eds.). (2001). *The handbook of humanistic psychology: Leading edges in theory, research, and practice.* Thousand Oaks, CA: Sage.

Schneider, W. H. (1992). After Binet: French intelligence testing, 1900–1950. *Journal of the History of the Behavioral Sciences, 28,* 111–132.

Schrag, C. O. (1982). Either/or. In F. N. Magill (Ed.), *World philosophy* (Vol. 3). Englewood Cliffs, NJ: Salem Press.

Schuchhardt, K. (1971). *Schliemann's excavations: An archaeological and historical study* (E. Sellers, Trans.). New York: Benjamin Blom. (Original work published 1891)

Schutz, J. A., & Adair, D. (Eds.). (1966). *The spur of fame: Dialogues of John Adams and Benjamin Rush, 1805–1813.* San Marino, CA: The Huntington Library.

Scobie, A., & Taylor, A. J. W. (1975). Perversions ancient and modern: 1. Agalmatophilia, the statue syndrome. *Journal of the History of the Behavioral Sciences, 11,* 49–54.

Scott, W. D. (1904). The psychology of advertising. *Atlantic Monthly, 93,* 29–36.

Scott, W. D. (1921). In memory of Wilhelm Wundt. *Psychological Review, 28,* 183.

Searle, J. R. (1992). *The rediscovery of the mind.* Cambridge, MA: M.I.T. Press.

Searle, J. R. (1995a, November 2). The mystery of consciousness. *New York Review,* pp. 60–66.

Searle, J. R. (1995b, November 16). The mystery of consciousness: Part II. *New York Review,* pp. 54–61.

Seashore, C. E. (1911). The consulting psychologist. *Popular Science Monthly, 78,* 283–290.

Seeber, J. J. (2000). Meaning in long-term care settings: Viktor Frankl's contribution to gerontology. *Journal of Religious Gerontology, 11,* 141–157.

Seidel, G. E., Jr., & Elsden, R. P. (1989). *Embryo transfer in dairy cattle.* Milwaukee, WI: Hoard & Sons.

Seward, G. H., & Seward, J. P. (1968). Robert S. Woodworth. In D. L. Sills (Ed.), *International encyclopedia of the social sciences* (Vol. 19, pp. 561–564). New York: Macmillan and Free Press.

Sexton, V. S., & Misiak, H. K. (Eds.). (1971). *Historical perspectives in psychology: Readings.* Monterey, CA: Brooks/Cole.

Sexton, V. S., & Misiak, H. K. (Eds.). (1976). *Psychology around the world.* Monterey, CA: Brooks/Cole.

Seymore, M. (2001). *Mary Shelly.* New York: Grove Press.

Shakespeare, W. (1964). *Measure for measure.* In E. Leisi (Ed.), *William Shakespeare: Measure for measure.* New York: Hafner Publishing. (Original work published 1604–1605)

Shaw, R., & Colimore, K. (1988). Humanistic psychology as an ideology: An analysis of Maslow's contradictions. *Journal of Humanistic Psychology, 28,* 51–74.

Shea, W. R. (1986). Galileo and the church. In D. C. Lindberg & R. L. Numbers (Eds.), *God and nature: Historical essays on the encounter between Christianity and science* (pp. 114–135). Berkeley: University of California Press.

Sheffield, F. D. (1959). Edwin Ray Guthrie: 1886–1959. *American Journal of Psychology, 72,* 642–650.

Sheldon, K. M., & Kasser, T. (2001). Goals, congruence, and positive well-being: New empirical support for humanistic theories. *Journal of Humanistic Psychology, 41,* 30–50.

Shereshevskii, A. M. (1994). The mystery of the death of V. M. Bekhterev. *Journal of Russian and East European Psychiatry, 27,* 103–113.

Shields, S. A. (1975). Ms. Pilgrim's progress: The contributions of Leta Stetter Hollingworth to the psychology of women. *American Psychologist, 30,* 852–857.

Shields, S. A. (1991). Leta Stetter Hollingworth: "Literature of opinion" and the study of individual differences. In G. A. Kimble, M. Wertheimer, & C. White (Eds.), *Portraits of pioneers in psychology* (Vol. 1, pp. 243–255). Washington, DC: American Psychological Association.

Shook, J. R. (1995). Wilhelm Wundt's contribution to John Dewey's functional psychology. *Journal of the History of the Behavioral Sciences, 31,* 347–369.

Silverman, L. H. (1976). Psychoanalytic theory: "The reports of my death are greatly exaggerated." *American Psychologist, 31,* 621–637.

Simon, B. (1972). Models of mind and mental illness in ancient Greece: II. The Platonic Model. Section

1. *Journal of the History of the Behavioral Sciences, 8,* 389–404.

Simon, B., & Weiner, H. (1966). Models of mind and mental illness in ancient Greece: The Homeric model of mind. *Journal of the History of the Behavioral Sciences, 2,* 303–314.

Simon, L. (Ed.). (1996). *William James remembered.* Lincoln, NE: University of Nebraska Press.

Sizer, N., & Drayton, H. S. (1892). *Heads and faces and how to study them.* New York: Fowler & Wells.

Skinner, B. F. (1938). *The behavior of organisms: An experimental analysis.* New York: Appleton-Century.

Skinner, B. F. (1948). *Walden two.* New York:- Macmillan.

Skinner, B. F. (1953). *Science and human behavior.* New York: Macmillan.

Skinner, B. F. (1956). A case study in scientific method. *American Psychologist, 11,* 221–233.

Skinner, B. F. (1957). *Verbal behavior.* New York: Appleton-Century-Crofts.

Skinner, B. F. (1958). Teaching machines. *Science, 128,* 969–977.

Skinner, B. F. (1960). Pigeons in a pelican. *American Psychologist, 15,* 28–37.

Skinner, B. F. (1963). Behaviorism at fifty. *Science, 140,* 951–958.

Skinner, B. F. (1967). B. F. Skinner. In E. G. Boring and G. Lindzey (Eds.), *A history of psychology in autobiography* (Vol. 5). New York: Appleton-Century-Crofts.

Skinner, B. F. (1968). *The technology of teaching.* Englewood Cliffs, NJ: Prentice-Hall.

Skinner, B. F. (1971). *Beyond freedom and dignity.* New York: Alfred A. Knopf.

Skinner, B. F. (1972). Humanism and behaviorism. *The Humanist, 32*(4), 18–20.

Skinner, B. F. (1974). *About behaviorism.* New York: Alfred A. Knopf.

Skinner, B. F. (1976). *Particulars of my life.* New York: Alfred A. Knopf.

Skinner, B. F. (1977). Why I am not a cognitive psychologist. *Behaviorism, 5,* 1–10.

Skinner, B. F. (1979). *The shaping of a behaviorist.* New York: Alfred A. Knopf.

Skinner, B. F. (1983a). *A matter of consequences.* New York: Alfred A. Knopf.

Skinner, B. F. (1983b). Origins of a behaviorist. *Psychology Today, 17,* 22–23.

Skinner, B. F. (1984). The shame of American education. *American Psychologist, 39,* 947–954.

Skinner, B. F. (1987a). Whatever happened to psychology as the science of behavior? *American Psychologist, 42,* 780–786.

Skinner, B. F. (1987b). Controversy? In S. Modgil & C. Modgil (Eds.), *B. F. Skinner: Consensus and controversy.* New York: Falmer.

Skinner, B. F. (1987c). *Upon further reflection.* Englewood Cliffs, NJ: Prentice-Hall.

Skinner, B. F. (1989). The origins of cognitive thought. *American Psychologist, 44,* 13–18.

Skinner, B. F. (1990). Can psychology be a science of mind? *American Psychologist, 45,* 1206–1210.

Skinner, B. F., & Vaughn, M. E. (1983). *Enjoy old age: Living fully in your later years.* New York: Warner.

Slife, B. D., & Williams, R. N. (1997). Toward a theoretical psychology: Should a subdiscipline be formally recognized? *American Psychologist, 52,* 117–129.

Slife, B. D., Yanchar, S. C., & Williams, B. (1999). Concepts of determinism in radical behaviorism: A taxonomy. *Behavior & Philosophy, 27,* 75–96.

Smith, C. U. M. (1987). David Hartley's Newtonian neuropsychology. *Journal of the History of the Behavioral Sciences, 23,* 123–136.

Smith, M. B. (1990). Humanistic psychology. *Journal of Humanistic Psychology, 33,* 6–21.

Smith, N. W. (1971). Aristotle's dynamic approach to sensing and some current implications. *Journal of the History of the Behavioral Sciences, 7,* 375–377.

Smith, N. W. (1974). The ancient background to Greek psychology and some implications for today. *Psychological Record, 24,* 309–324.

Sokal, M. M. (1980a). Graduate study with Wundt: Two eyewitness accounts. In W. G. Bringmann & R. D. Tweney (Eds.), *Wundt studies: A centennial collection* (pp. 210–225). Toronto: C. J. Hogrefe.

Sokal, M. M. (1980b). Science and James McKeen Cattell, 1894–1945. *Science, 209* (4 July), 43–52.

Sokal, M. M. (1984). The Gestalt psychologists in behaviorist America. *American Historical Review, 89,* 1240–1263.

Sokal, M. M. (Ed.). (1987). *Psychological testing and American society: 1890–1930.* New Brunswick, NJ: Rutgers University Press.

Sokal, M. M. (1990). G. Stanley Hall and the institutional character of psychology at Clark 1889–1920. *Journal of the History of the Behavioral Sciences, 26,* 114–124.

Sokal, M. M. (1992). Origins and early years of the American Psychological Association. *American Psychologist, 47,* 111–121.

Sokal, M. M. (1995). Stargazing: James McKeen Cattell, "American Men of Science," and the reward structure of the American scientific community, 1906–1944. In F. Kessel (Ed.), *Psychology, science, and human affairs: Essays in honor of William Bevan* (pp. 64–86). Boulder, CO: Westview Press.

Sokal, M. M. (1997). Baldwin, Cattell and the *Psychological Review:* A collaboration and its discontents. *History of the Human Sciences, 10,* 57–89.

Sokal, M. M. (2001). Practical phrenology as psychological counseling in the 19th-century United States. In C. D. Green & M. Shore (Eds.), *The transformation of psychology: Influences of 19th-century philosophy, technology, and natural science* (pp. 21–44). Washington, DC: American Psychological Association.

Sokal, M. M., & Rafail, P. A. (1982). *A guide to manuscript collections in the history of psychology and related areas.* Millwood, NY: Kraus International Publications.

Soles, D. E. (1985). Locke's empiricism and the postulation of unobservables. *Journal of the History of Philosophy, 23,* 339–369.

Soltis, J. F. (1971). John Dewey. In L. C. Deighton (Ed.), *The encyclopedia of education* (Vol. 3, pp. 81–85). New York: Macmillan.

Southall, J. P. C. (Ed.). (1962). *Helmholtz's treatise on physiological optics.* New York: Dover Publications Inc.

Southard, M. M. (1927). *The attitude of Jesus toward women.* New York: George H. Doran.

Spalding, D. A. (1873, February). Instinct. With original observations on young animals. *Macmillan's Magazine, 27,* 282–293.

Spence, K. W. (1952). Clark Leonard Hull: 1884–1952. *American Journal of Psychology, 65,* 639–646.

Spencer, H. (1873). *Study of sociology.* New York: D. Appleton & Co.

Spillmann, J., & Spillmann, L. (1993). The rise and fall of Hugo Münsterberg. *Journal of the History of the Behavioral Sciences, 29,* 322–338.

Sprengnether, M. (1990). *The spectral mother: Freud, feminism, and psychoanalysis.* Ithaca NY: Cornell University Press.

Sprung, H., & Sprung, L. (1996). Carl Stumpf (1848–1936), a general psychologist and methodologist, and a case study of a cross-cultural scientific transition process. In W. Battmann & S. Dutke

(Eds.), *Processes of the molar regulation of behavior* (pp. 327–342). Lengerich, Germany: Pabst Science Publishers.

Staats, A. W. (1989). Unificationism: Philosophy for the modern disunited science of psychology. *Philosophical Psychology, 2,* 143–164.

Staats, A. W. (1999). Unifying psychology requires new infrastructure, theory, method, and a research agenda. *Review of General Psychology, 3,* 3–13.

Stace, W. T. (1962). *A critical history of Greek philosophy.* New York: St. Martin's Press.

Stephen, L. (1993). Mrs. Mary Wollstonecraft Godwin. In L. Stephen and S. Lee (Eds.), *The dictionary of national biography* (Vol. 8, pp. 60–62). New York: Oxford University Press.

Stephen, L., & Lee, S. (Eds.). (1960). *Dictionary of national biography* (Vol. 9). London: Oxford University Press.

Stephens, J. (1975). *Francis Bacon and the style of science.* Chicago: University of Chicago Press.

Stern, C. (1949). *Children discover arithmetic: An introduction to structural arithmetic.* New York: Harper.

Stern, C., & Gould, T. S. (1955). *The early years of childhood: Education through insight.* New York: Harper.

Stern, C., & Gould, T. S. (1968). *Children discover reading: An introduction to structural reading.* Syracuse, NY: Random House/Singer.

Steudel, J. (1974). Johannes Peter Müller. In C. C. Gillispie (Ed.), *Dictionary of scientific biography, 9,* 567–584.

Stevens, G., & Gardner, S. (Eds.). (1982). *The women of psychology: Pioneers and innovators.* Cambridge, MA: Schenkman Publishing.

Stevens, S. S. (1951). Mathematics, measurement, and psychophysics. In S. S. Stevens (Ed.), *Handbook of experimental psychology.* New York: Wiley.

Stewart, D. (1802). *Elements of the philosophy of the human mind.* London: T. Cadell Jun. and W. Davies in the Strand, and W. Creech in Edinburgh. (Original work published 1792)

Stocking, G. W. (1965). On the limits of "presentism" and "historicism" in the historiography of the behavioral sciences [editorial]. *Journal of the History of the Behavioral Sciences, 1,* 211–218.

Strachey, J. (Ed.). (1953–1974). *The standard edition of the complete psychological works of Sigmund Freud.* London: Hogarth Press.

Strandh, S. (1979). *A history of the machine.* New York: A. W. Publishers.

Stromberg, W. H. (1989). Helmholtz and Zoellner: Nineteenth century empiricism, spiritism, and the theory of space perception. *Journal of the History of the Behavioral Sciences, 25,* 371–383.

Strong, E. K. (1955). Walter Dill Scott: 1869–1955. *American Journal of Psychology, 68,* 682–683.

Stumpf, C. (1895). Herman von Helmholtz and the new psychology. *Psychological Review, 2,* 1–12.

Stumpf, C. (1930). Carl Stumpf. In C. Murchison (Ed.), *A history of psychology in autobiography* (Vol. 1, pp. 389–441). Worchester, MA: Clark University Press.

Suinn, R. M., & Weigel, R. G. (1975). *The innovative psychological therapies: Critical and creative contributions.* New York: Harper & Row.

Sukhodolsky, D. G., Tsytsarev, S. V., & Kassinove, H. (1995). Behavior therapy in Russia. *Journal of Behavior Therapy and Experimental Psychiatry, 26,* 83–91.

Sullivan, H. S. (1953). *The interpersonal theory of psychiatry.* New York: W. W. Norton.

Sulloway, F. J. (1979). *Freud, biologist of the mind: Beyond psychoanalytic legend.* New York: Basic Books.

Sully, J. (1886). Development of the moral faculty. *Popular Science Monthly, 29,* 23–33.

Sully, J. (1894, 1895, 1896). Studies of childhood. *Popular Science Monthly, 45,* 323–330, 577–588, 733–742; *46,* 186–197, 348–363, 433–446, 781–792; *47,* 1–11, 340–353, 648–664, 808–817; *48,* 105–113, 166–180, 381–395.

Summers, M. (1965). *The geography of witchcraft.* New York: University Books.

Summers, M. (Trans.). (1971). *The malleus maleficarum of Heinrich Kramer & Jacob Sprenger.* New York: Dover Publications.

Sussman, E. J. (1962). Franz Brentano—Much alive, though dead. *American Psychologist, 17,* 504–506.

Swammerdam, J. (1758). *The book of nature* (T. Flloyd, Trans.). London: C. G. Seyffert.

Swazey, J. P. (1975). Charles Scott Sherrington. In C. C. Gillispi (Ed.), *Dictionary of scientific biography* (Vol. 12, pp. 395–403). New York: Scribner.

Symonds, A. (1991). Gender issues and Horney theory. *American Journal of Psychoanalysis, 51,* 301–312.

Taine, H. A. (1876). Lingual development in babyhood. *Popular Science Monthly, 9,* 129–137.

Taylor, G. R. (1983). *The great evolution mystery.* New York: Harper & Row.

Taylor, M. C. (1987). Søren Kierkegaard. In M. Eliade (Ed.), *The encyclopedia of religion* (Vol. 8, pp. 298–301). New York: Macmillan.

Taylor, R. (1967a). Causation. In P. Edwards (Ed.), *The encyclopedia of philosophy.* New York: Macmillan.

Taylor, R. (1967b). Determinism. In P. Edwards (Ed.), *The encyclopedia of philosophy.* New York: Macmillan.

Teilhard de Chardin. (1961). *The phenomenon of man* (B. Wall, Trans.). New York: Harper & Row.

Thielman, S. B., & Melges, F. T. (1986). Julia Rush's diary: Coping with loss in the early nineteenth century. *American Journal of Psychiatry, 143,* 1144–1148.

Thomas, R. K. (1997). Correcting some Pavloviana regarding "Pavlov's bell" and Pavlov's "mugging." *American Journal of Psychology, 110,* 115–125.

Thorndike, E. L. (1899). Do animals reason? *Popular Science Monthly, 55,* 480–490.

Thorndike, E. L. (1905). Measurements of twins. *Archives of Philosophy, Psychology, and Scientific Method* (No. 1).

Thorndike, E. L. (1920). The psychology of the half-educated man. *Harper's Magazine, 140,* 666–670.

Thorndike, E. L. (1922). The psychology of labor. *Harper's Magazine, 144,* 799–806.

Thorndike, E. L. (1924). Mental discipline in high schools. *Journal of Educational Psychology, 15,* 1–22, 83–98.

Thorndike, E. L. (1936). The psychology of the profit motive. *Harper's Magazine, 173,* 431–437.

Thorndike, E. L., & Woodworth, R. S. (1901). The influence of improvement in one mental function upon the efficiency of other functions. *Psychological Review, 8,* 247–261, 384–395, 553–564.

Thorne, J. O. (Ed.). (1969). *Chambers' biographical dictionary.* New York: St. Martins Press.

Thurston, H. (1994). *Early astronomy.* New York: Springer-Verlag.

Tilman, R., & Knapp, T. (1999). John Dewey's unknown critique of marginal utility doctrine: Instrumentalism, motivation, and values. *Journal of the History of the Behavioral Sciences, 35,* 391–408.

Tinker, M. A. (1980). Wundt's doctorate students and their theses 1875–1920. In W. G. Bringmann & R. D. Tweney (Eds.), *Wundt studies. A centennial collection* (pp. 269–272). Toronto: C. J. Hogrefe.

Titchener, E. B. (1892). The Leipsig school of experimental psychology. *Mind, 1* (new series), 206–234.

Titchener, E. B. (1896). *An outline of psychology.* New York: Macmillan.

Titchener, E. B. (1898). A psychology laboratory. *Mind, 7,* 311–331.

Titchener, E. B. (1910). *A textbook of psychology.* New York: Macmillan.

Titchener, E. B. (1921). Wilhelm Wundt. *American Journal of Psychology, 32,* 61–177.

Tolman, E. C. (1922). A new formula for behaviorism. *Psychological Review, 22,* 44–53.

Tolman, E. C. (1932). *Purposive behavior in animals and men.* New York: Century.

Tolman, E. C. (1952). Edward Chace Tolman. In E. G. Boring, H. Werner, H. S. Langfeld, & R. M. Yerkes (Eds.), *A history of psychology in autobiography* (Vol. 4, pp. 323–339). New York: Russell and Russell.

Tolman, E. C., & Honzik, C. H. (1930). Introduction and removal of reward and maze performance in rats. *University of California Publications in Psychology, 4,* 257–273.

Torrey, C. W. (1867). Women's sphere in the church. *The Congregational Quarterly, 9,* 163–171.

Toulmin, S. (1972). *Human understanding* (Vol. 1). Princeton, NJ: Princeton University Press.

Tsanoff, R. A. (1964). *The great philosophers* (2nd ed.). New York: Harper & Row.

Tuke, D. H. (1892). *A dictionary of psychological medicine.* London: J. & A. Churchill.

Tuke, D. H. (1872). *Illustrations of the influence of the mind upon the body in health and disease.* Philadelphia: Lindsay and Blakiston.

Turner, R. S. (1972). Hermann von Helmholtz. In C. C. Gillispie (Ed.), *Dictionary of scientific biography* (Vol. 6, pp. 241–253). New York: Charles Scribner's Sons.

Turner, R. S. (1977). Hermann von Helmholtz and the empiricist vision. *Journal of the History of the Behavioral Sciences, 13,* 48–58.

Turner, R. S. (1994). *In the eye's mind: Vision and the Helmholtz–Hering controversy.* Princeton, NJ: Princeton University Press.

Tye, M. (1995). *Ten problems of consciousness: A representational theory of the phenomenal mind.* Cambridge, MA: MIT Press.

Tylor, E. B. (1872). Quételet on the science of man. *Popular Science Monthly, 1,* 45–55.

Unamuno, M. (1972). *The tragic sense of life* (A. Kerrigan, Trans.). Princeton, NJ: Princeton University Press. (Original work published 1913)

Uttal, W. R. (2000). *The war between mentalism and behaviorism: On the accessibility of mental processes.* Mahwah, NJ: Erlbaum.

Uytman, J. D. (1967). William McDougall. In P. Edwards (Ed.), *The encyclopedia of philosophy* (Vol. 5, pp. 226–227). New York: Macmillan and Free Press.

Vande Kemp, H. (1992). G. Stanley Hall and the Clark School of Religious Psychology. *American Psychologist, 47,* 290–298.

Vartanian, A. (1967). Julien Offray de La Mettrie. In P. Edwards (Ed.), *The encyclopedia of philosophy* (Vol. 4, pp. 379–382). New York: Macmillan.

Verstegen, I. (2000). Gestalt psychology in Italy. *Journal of History of the Behavioral Sciences, 36,* 31–42.

Vidal, F. (1987). Jean Piaget and the liberal protestant tradition. In M. G. Ash & W. R. Woodward (Eds.), *Psychology in twentieth-century thought and society.* Cambridge: Cambridge University Press.

Viney, D. W. (1984). William James on free will and determinism. *The Journal of Mind and Behavior, 7,* 555–556.

Viney, D. W. (1989). *Questions of value: Readings for basic philosophy.* Needham Heights, MA: Ginn.

Viney, D. W. (1997). William James on free will: The French connection. *History of Philosophy Quarterly, 14,* 29–52.

Viney, W. (1989). The cyclops and the twelve-eyed toad: William James and the unity–disunity problem in psychology. *American Psychologist, 44,* 1261–1265.

Viney, W. (1990). The tempering effect of determinism in the legal system: A response to Rychlak and Rychlak. *New Ideas in Psychology, 8,* 31–42.

Viney, W. (1991). Charles Hartshorne's philosophy and the psychology of sensation. In L. E. Hahn (Ed.), *The philosophy of Charles Hartshorne* (pp. 91–112). *The library of living philosophers* (Vol. 20). LaSalle, IL: Open Court.

Viney, W. (1996a). Disunity in psychology and other sciences: The network or the block universe? *The Journal of Mind and Behavior, 17,* 31–43.

Viney, W. (1996b). Dorothea Dix: An intellectual conscience for psychology. In G. A. Kimble, C. A. Boneau, & M. Wertheimer (Eds.), *Portraits of pioneers in psychology* (Vol. 2, pp. 15–31). Washington, DC: American Psychological Association.

Viney, W. (2001). The radical empiricism of William James and philosophy of history. *History of Psychology, 4,* 211–227.

Viney, W., & Bartsch, K. (1984). Dorothea Lynde Dix: Positive or negative influence on the development of treatment for the mentally ill. *The Social Science Journal, 21,* 71–82.

Viney, W., & Burlingame-Lee, L. (In Press). Margaret Floy Washburn: A quest for the harmonies in the context of a rigorous science. In G. A. Kimble & M. Wertheimer (Eds.), *Portraits of pioneers in psychology* (Vol. 5). Washington, DC: American Psychological Association.

Viney, W., King, D. B., & Berndt, J. (1990). Animal research in psychology: Declining or thriving? *Journal of Comparative Psychology, 104,* 322–325.

Viney, W., King, C. L., & King, D. B. (1992). William James on the advantages of a pluralistic psychology. In M. E. Donnelly (Ed.), *Reinterpreting the legacy of William James* (pp. 91–100). Washington, DC: American Psychological Association.

Viney, W., Wertheimer, M., & Wertheimer, M. L. (1979). *History of psychology: A guide to information sources.* Detroit: Gale Research Co.

Viney, W., & Woody, D. (1995). Psychogeny: A neglected dimension in teaching the mind–brain problem. *Teaching of Psychology, 22,* 173–177.

Viscount, C. (1932). The new patriotism. *Harper's Magazine, 165,* 170–178.

Visible scientists. (1975, May). *Time, 105,* 44.

Vlastos, G. (1967). Zeno of Elea. In P. Edwards (Ed.), *Encyclopedia of philosophy* (Vol. 8, pp. 369–379). New York: Macmillan and Free Press.

Voeks, V. (1950). Formalization and clarification of a theory of learning. *Journal of Psychology, 30,* 341–362.

Voeks, V. (1968). Edwin R. Guthrie. In D. L. Sills (Ed.), *International encyclopedia of the social sciences* (Vol. 6, pp. 296–302). New York: Macmillan.

Voltaire, F. M. (1980). *Letters on England* (L. Tancock, Trans.). Harmondsworth, Middlesex, England: Penguin. (Original work published 1733)

von Mayrhauser, R. T. (1989). Making intelligence functional: Walter Dill Scott and applied psychological testing in World War I. *Journal of the History of the Behavioral Sciences, 25,* 60–72.

Vrooman, J. R. (1970). *René Descartes: A biography.* New York: G. P. Putnam's Sons.

Wade, N. J. (1994). Hermann von Helmholtz (1821–1894). *Perception, 23,* 981–989.

Waithe, M. E. (1987a). Arete, Asclepigenia, Axiothea, Cleobulina, Hipparchia, and Lasthenia. In M. E. Waithe (Ed.), *A history of women philosophers.* Boston: Martinus Nijhoff.

Waithe, M. E. (1987b). Early Pythagoreans: Themistoclea, Theana, Arignote, Myia, and Damo. In M. E. Waithe (Ed.), *A history of women philosophers.* Boston: Martinus Nijhoff.

Waithe, M. E. (1989). Heloise. In M. E. Waithe (Ed.), *A history of women philosophers. Vol. II Medieval, Renaissance and Enlightenment women philosophers A.D. 500–1600* (pp. 67–83). Boston: Kluwer Academic Publishers.

Walker, P. N. (1973). *Punishment: An illustrated history.* New York: Arco.

Wallace, W. A. (1993). *Theories of personality.* Boston: Allyn & Bacon.

Wapner, S. (1990). Introduction [to a series of papers on psychology at Clark University]. *Journal of the History of the Behavioral Sciences, 26,* 107–109.

Ward, J. (1876). An attempt to interpret Fechner's law. *Mind, 1* (old series), 452–466.

Warren, H. (1921). In memory of Wilhelm Wundt. *Psychological Review, 28,* 166–169.

Washburn, D. A. (1997). The MacKay–Skinner debate: A case for "nothing buttery." *Philosophical Psychology, 10,* 473–479.

Washburn, M. F. (1908). *The animal mind: A textbook of comparative psychology.* New York: Macmillan.

Washburn, M. F. (1916). *Movement and mental imagery.* New York: Houghton Mifflin.

Watkin, J. (1998). Søren Kierkegaard's psychology of the self. *Journal of Psychology and Christianity, 17,* 362–373.

Watkins, J. W. N. (1965). *Hobbes's system of ideas.* London: Hutchinson University Library.

Watson, F. (1915). The father of modern psychology. *Psychological Review, 22,* 333–353.

Watson, J. B. (1912, February). Instinctive activity in animals. *Harper's Magazine, 124,* 376–382.

Watson, J. B. (1913). Psychology as the behaviorist views it. *Psychological Review, 20,* 158–177.

Watson, J. B. (1919). *Psychology from the standpoint of a behaviorist.* Philadelphia: Lippincott.

Watson, J. B. (1924a). *Behaviorism.* New York: W. W. Norton.

Watson, J. B. (1924b). The place of kinesthetic, visceral and laryngeal organization in thinking. *Psychological Review, 31,* 339–347.

Watson, J. B. (1924c). The unverbalized in human behavior. *Psychological Review, 31,* 273–280.

Watson, J. B. (1926). What the nursery has to say about instincts. In C. Murchison (Ed.), *Psychologies of*

1925 (pp. 1–34). Worcester, MA: Clark University Press.

Watson, J. B. (1928). *Psychological care of infant and child*. New York: W. W. Norton.

Watson, J. B. (1961). John Broadus Watson. In C. Murchison (Ed.), *A history of psychology in autobiography* (Vol. 3, pp. 271–281). New York: Russell and Russell.

Watson, J. B., & Rayner, R. (1920). Conditioned emotional reactions. *Journal of Experimental Psychology, 3,* 1–14.

Watson, J. D. (1968). *The double helix*. New York: New American Library.

Watson, R. I. (1966). The role and use of history in the psychology curriculum. *Journal of the History of the Behavioral Sciences, 2,* 64–69.

Watson, R. I. (Ed.). (1974/1976). *Eminent contributors to psychology* (2 vols.). New York: Springer Publishing.

Watson, R. I., Sr. (1978). *The history of psychology and the behavioral sciences: A bibliographic guide*. New York: Springer Publishing.

Watson, R. I., & Evans, R. B. (1991). *The great psychologists: A history of psychological thought* (5th ed.). New York: HarperCollins.

Watts, R. E. (1998). The remarkable parallel between Roger's core conditions and Adler's social interest. *Journal of Individual Psychology, 54,* 4–9.

Weber, E. H. (1978). *The sense of touch* (H. E. Ross, Trans.). New York: Academic Press. (Original work published 1834)

Weber, M. M. (1997). Alois Alzheimer, a coworker of Emil Kraepelin. *Journal of Psychiatric Research, 31,* 635–643.

Webster, S., & Coleman, S. R. (1992). Hull and his critics: The reception of Clark L. Hull's behavior theory. *Psychological Reports, 70,* 1063–1071.

Weidman, N. (1994). Mental testing and machine intelligence: The Lashley-Hull debate. *Journal of the History of the Behavioral Sciences, 30,* 162–180.

Weinberger, J., Siegel, P., & Decamello, A. (2000). On integrating psychoanalysis and cognitive science. *Psychoanalysis & Contemporary Thought, 23,* 147–175.

Weiner, D. B. (1992). Philippe Pinel's "memoir on madness" of December 11, 1794: A fundamental text of modern psychiatry. *American Journal of Psychiatry, 149,* 725–732.

Weiss, A. P. (1924a). Behaviorism and behavior I. *Psychological Review, 31,* 32–50.

Weiss, A. P. (1924b). Behaviorism and behavior II. *Psychological Review, 31,* 118–149.

Weiss, A. P. (1928). Behaviorism and ethics. *Journal of Abnormal and Social Psychology, 22,* 388–397.

Weiss, R. (1989). The hedonic calculus in the Protagoras and the Phaedo. *Journal of the History of Philosophy, 27,* 511–529.

Welles, S. (Ed.). (1957). *The world's great religions*. New York: Time.

Wentworth, P. A. (1999). The moral of her story: Exploring the philosophical and religious commitments in Mary Whiton Calkins' self-psychology. *History of Psychology, 2,* 119–131.

Wertheimer, M. (Max) (1912). Experimentelle studien über das Sehen von Bewegung. *Zeitschrift für Psychologie, 61,* 161–265.

Wertheimer, M. (1934). On truth. *Social Research, 1,* 135–146.

Wertheimer, M. (1935). Some problems in the theory of ethics. *Social Research, 2,* 353–367.

Wertheimer, M. (1937). On the concept of democracy. In M. Ascoli & and F. Lehmann (Eds.), *Political and economic democracy* (pp. 271–283). New York: W. W. Norton.

Wertheimer, M. (1940). A story of three days. In R. N. Anshen (Ed.), *Freedom: Its meaning* (pp. 555– 569). New York: Harcourt, Brace.

Wertheimer, M. (1950). Numbers and numerical concepts in primitive peoples. In W. D. Ellis (Ed.), *A source book of Gestalt psychology*. New York: Humanities Press. (Original work published 1912)

Wertheimer, M. (1982). *Productive thinking* (M. Wertheimer, Ed.). Chicago: University of Chicago Press. (Original work published 1945)

Wertheimer, M. (Michael) (1961). Psychomotor coordination of auditory and visual space at birth. *Science, 134,* 1962.

Wertheimer, M. (1972). *Fundamental issues in psychology*. New York: Holt, Rinehart and Winston.

Wertheimer, M. (1978). Humanistic psychology and the humane but tough minded psychologist. *American Psychologist, 33,* 739–745.

Wertheimer, M. (1980a). Historical research—why? In J. Brožek, & L. J. Pongratz (Eds.), *Historiography of modern psychology*. Toronto: C. J. Hogrefe.

Wertheimer, M. (1980b). Max Wertheimer, Gestalt prophet. *Gestalt Theory, 2,* 3–17.

Wertheimer, M. (1983). Gestalt theory, holistic psychologies and Max Wertheimer. *Personale Psychologie, 5,* 32–49.

Wertheimer, M. (1985). A Gestalt perspective on computer simulations of cognitive processes. *Computers in Human Behavior, 1,* 19–33.

Wertheimer, M. (1986). The annals of the house that Ebbinghaus built. In F. Klix & H. Hagendorf (Eds.), *Human memory and cognitive capacities: Mechanisms and performance.* Amsterdam: Elsevier Science Publishers.

Wertheimer, M. (1987). *A brief history of psychology* (3rd ed.). New York: Holt, Rinehart and Winston.

Wertheimer, M. (1991). Personal communication.

Wertsch, J. V. (1985). *Vygotsky and the social formation of mind.* Cambridge, MA: Harvard University Press.

Westheimer, G. (1999). Gestalt theory reconfigured: Max Wertheimer's anticipation of recent developments in visual neuroscience. *Perception, 28,* 5–15.

Westman, R. S. (1986). The Copernicans and the churches. In D. C. Lindberg & R. L. Numbers (Eds.), *God and nature: Historical essays on the encounter between Christianity and science* (pp. 76–113). Berkeley, CA: University of California Press.

Wetterstein, J. R. (1975). The historiography of scientific psychology. A critical study. *Journal of the History of the Behavioral Sciences, 11,* 157–171.

Wheeler, W. M. (1906). The queen ant as a psychological study. *Popular Science Monthly, 68,* 291–299.

White, A. D. (1910). *A history of the warfare of science with theology in Christendom* (2 vols.). New York: D. Appleton and Co. (Original work published 1896)

White, A. D. (1978). *A history of the warfare of science with theology in Christendom* (2 vols.). Gloucester, MA: Peter Smith. (Original work published 1896)

White, S. H. (1992). G. Stanley Hall: From philosophy to developmental psychology. *Developmental Psychology, 28,* 25–34.

Wichler, G. (1961). *Charles Darwin, the founder of the theory of evolution and natural selection.* New York: Pergamon Press.

Wight, R. D. (1993). The Pavlov-Yerkes connection: What was its origin? *Psychological Record, 43,* 351–359.

Williams, H. S. (1899). The century's progress in experimental psychology. *Harper's Magazine, 99,* 512–527.

Wilson, A. N. (1997). *Paul: The mind of the apostle.* New York: W. W. Norton.

Windholz, G. (1984). Pavlov vs. Köhler: Pavlov's little known primate research. *Pavlovian Journal of Biological Science, 19,* 23–31.

Windholz, G. (1990). Pavlov, psychoanalysis, and neurosis. *Pavlovian Journal of Biological Science, 25,* 48–53.

Windholz, G. (1997). Ivan P. Pavlov: An overview of his life and psychological work. *American Psychologist, 52,* 941–946.

Winston, A. S. (1990). Robert Sessions Woodworth and the "Columbia Bible": How the psychological experiment was redefined. *American Journal of Psychology, 103,* 391–401.

Winter, I. J. (1976). *Montaigne's self-portrait and its influence in France, 1580–1630.* Lexington, KY: French Forum, Publishers.

Wisdom, J. O. (1943). Determinism and psychoanalysis. *International Journal of Psychoanalysis, 24,* 140–147.

Wolberg, A. (1989). Pilgrim's process through the psychoanalytic maze. *Psychoanalysis and Psychotherapy, 7,* 18–26.

Wolf, T. H. (1973). *Alfred Binet.* Chicago: University of Chicago Press.

Wollstonecraft, M. (1929). *Mary Wollstonecraft's the rights of women/John Stuart Mill the subjection of women.* New York: E. P. Dutton & Co. (Original work published 1792)

Wolpe, J., & Plaud, J. J. (1997). Pavlov's contributions to behavior therapy: The obvious and the not so obvious. *American Psychologist, 52,* 966–972.

Wood, N. (1968). Niccolò Machiavelli. In D. Sills (Ed.), *International encyclopedia of the social sciences* (Vol. 9, pp. 505–511). New York: Macmillan and Free Press.

Woodward, W. R. (1987). Professionalization, rationality, and political linkages in twentieth-century psychology. In M. G. Ash & W. R. Woodward (Eds.), *Psychology in twentieth-century thought and society* (pp. 295–309). New York: Cambridge University Press.

Woodworth, R. S., & Schlosberg, H. (1954). *Experimental psychology* (rev. ed.). New York: Henry Holt.

Woody, W. D. (2001). Gestalt psychology and William James. In F. Columbus (Ed.), *Advances in psychology research* (Vol. 4, pp. 33–48). Huntington, NY: Nova Science Publishers.

Woolley, B. (1999). *The bride of science: Romance, reason, and Byron's daughter.* New York: McGraw-Hill.

Wundt, W. (1876). Central innervation of consciousness, *Mind, 1* (old series), 161–178.

Wundt, W. (1901). *Ethics* (E. B. Titchener, J. H. Gulliver, & M. F. Washburn, Trans.). New York: Macmillan. (Original work published 1892)

Wundt, W. (1907). *Lectures on human and animal psychology* (J. Creighton & E. B. Titchener, Trans.). New York. Macmillan. (Original work published 1863)

Wundt, W. (1916). *Elements of folk psychology* (E. L. Schaub, Trans.). New York: Macmillan.

Wundt, W. (1969a). *Outlines of psychology.* (C. H. Judd, Trans.). St. Clair Shores, MI: Scholarly Press. (Original work published 1897)

Wundt, W. (1969b). *Principles of physiological psychology* (5th ed., Vol. I). (E. B. Titchener, Trans. New York: Kraus Reprint Co. (Original work published 1873; 5th ed published 1910)

Wundt, W. (1973). *An introduction to psychology.* New York: Arno Press. (Original work published 1912)

Wundt, W. (1977). Lectures on human and animal psychology. In D. N. Robinson (Ed.), *Significant contributions to the history of psychology 1750–1920: Series D: Comparative psychology* (Vol. 1.). Washington, DC: University Publications. (Original work published 1894)

Wyatt, W. J. (2000). Behaviorial science in the crosshairs: The FBI file on B. F. Skinner. *Behavioral and Social Issues, 10,* 101–109.

Yerkes, R. M. (1900). The formation of habits in the turtle. *Popular Science Monthly, 58,* 519–525.

Young, P. T. (1972). An eclectic in psychology. In T. S. Krawiec (Ed.), *The psychologists* (Vol. 1, pp. 325–355). New York: Oxford University Press.

Young, R. M. (1966). Scholarship and the history of the behavioral sciences. In A. C. Crombie & M. A. Hoskin (Eds.), *History of Science* (Vol. 5). Cambridge: W. Heffner & Sons.

Zagorin, P. (1968). Thomas Hobbes. In D. L. Sills (Ed.), *International encyclopedia of the social sciences* (Vol. 6, pp. 481–487). New York: Macmillan.

Zhuravel, V. A. (1995). From the history of the Bekhterev Psychoneurological Institute. *Journal of Russian and East European Psychiatry, 27,* 115–129.

Ziegler, P. (1991). *The black death.* Great Britain: The Bath Press Ltd. (Original work published 1969)

Zilboorg, G. (1941). *A History of medical psychology.* New York: W. W. Norton.

Zilboorg, G. (1961). *Freud and religion.* Westminster, MD: Westminster Press.

Zubov, V. P. (1968). *Leonardo da Vinci* (D. H. Kraus, Trans.). Cambridge, MA: Harvard University Press.

Zusne, L. (1975). *Names in the history of psychology: A biographical sourcebook.* New York: Wiley.

Zusne, L. (1984). *Biographical dictionary of psychology.* Westport, CT. Greenwood Press.

Zweig, A. (1967). Oswald Külpe. In P. Edwards (Ed.), *The encyclopedia of philosophy* (Vol. 4, pp. 367–368). New York: Macmillan and Free Press.